OCP: Oracle Database 11*g* Administrator Certified Professional Study Guide

Sybex®
An Imprint of
 WILEY

OBJECTIVE	CHAPTER
Automating Tasks with the Scheduler	
Create a job, program, and schedule	12
Use a time-based or event-based schedule for executing Scheduler jobs	12
Create lightweight jobs	12
Use job chains to perform a series of related tasks	12
Administering the Scheduler	
Create Windows and Job Classes	12
Use advanced Scheduler concepts to prioritize jobs	12
Globalization	
Customize language-dependent behavior for the database and individual sessions	13
Working with database and NLS character sets	13

Sybex®
An Imprint of
WILEY

Sybex®
An Imprint of
WILEY

Exam objectives are subject to change at any time without prior notice and at Oracle's sole discretion. Please visit Oracle's Training and Certification website (http://www.oracle.com/education/certification/) for the most current exam objectives listing.

Sybex®
An Imprint of
WILEY

OCP

Oracle® Database 11*g* Administrator Certified Professional

Study Guide

OCP
Oracle® Database 11*g*
Administrator Certified
Professional
Study Guide

Robert G. Freeman
Charles A. Pack
Doug Stuns
Tim Buterbaugh

WILEY
Wiley Publishing, Inc.

Acquisitions Editor: Jeff Kellum
Development Editor: Kim Wimpsett
Technical Editors: Arup Nanda and Bob Bryla
Production Editor: Christine O'Connor
Copy Editor: Judy Flynn
Production Manager: Tim Tate
Vice President and Executive Group Publisher: Richard Swadley
Vice President and Publisher: Neil Edde
Assistant Project Manager: Jenny Swisher
Associate Producer: Angie Denny
Quality Assurance: Josh Frank
Book Designer: Judy Fung, Bill Gibson
Compositor: Craig Woods, Happenstance Type-O-Rama
Proofreader: Candace English
Indexer: Nancy Guenther
Project Coordinator, Cover: Lynsey Stanford
Cover Designer: Ryan Sneed

Dear Reader,

Thank you for choosing *OCP: Oracle Database 11g Administrator Certified Professional Study Guide*. This book is part of a family of premium-quality Sybex books, all of which are written by outstanding authors who combine practical experience with a gift for teaching.

Sybex was founded in 1976. More than thirty years later, we're still committed to producing consistently exceptional books. With each of our titles we're working hard to set a new standard for the industry. From the paper we print on, to the authors we work with, our goal is to bring you the best books available.

I hope you see all that reflected in these pages. I'd be very interested to hear your comments and get your feedback on how we're doing. Feel free to let me know what you think about this or any other Sybex book by sending me an email at nedde@wiley.com, or if you think you've found a technical error in this book, please visit http://sybex.custhelp.com. Customer feedback is critical to our efforts at Sybex.

Best regards,

Neil Edde
Vice President and Publisher
Sybex, an Imprint of Wiley

This book is dedicated to my wife, Lisa; my children; and my father.
—Robert G. Freeman

For my wife, Donna, and our daughter, Jenny.
—Charles A. Pack

Acknowledgments

Writing a book is such a vast undertaking that it's hard to know where to start with the acknowledgments. I also hate writing this part because, frankly, someone always gets forgotten. That being said, here we go.

Thanks to my patient wife, Lisa, who sits across from me in our office and typically gets as little sleep as I do. Thanks to my kids who are still managing to grow up into wonderful adults in spite of this crazy world. Thanks to all my great friends at work who support me, who uplift me (imagine working at a job where you can start a meeting with a prayer!), and who are some very smart people. In particular, thanks to David Wright, Bill Johnson, Heber Allen, Jed Brunson, Dan Dredge, and Mandy Cosper. Additional thanks to Dave Prestwich, Mike Bowers, Stephen Shaffer, Brent Moody, and John Harper. Thanks also to my Core team guys Scott Black, Dennis Carlson, Ryan Allen, and Randy Knight. Also thanks to my way cool DBE team members Curt Workman, Bill Francis, Mike Noble, Ben Beishline, and Matthew Newman. You are all awesome. Thanks also to the rest of the EIM team at the church; you are awesome but too numerous to mention in the space I have here. I've worked with more awesome people that I can list in these pages. If I could list all your names here, I would. As it is, just know that I appreciate you and loved working with you over the years.

Writing books is a long, complex, and often frustrating task. Thanks to all the folks at Sybex that participated in the making of this book. Thanks to Jeff Kellum, who was my acquisitions editor, for getting me involved in this project. I'd worked with Jeff before on my very first book, and apparently he didn't remember the pain I caused him well enough, since he asked me to write this book anyway. Thanks to Kim Wimpsett for awesome editing and being the best development editor ever! Thanks to Christine O'Connor for doing a bang-up job with the book and to Judy Flynn, copy editor extraordinaire, the proofreader Candace English, and to Nancy Guenther, indexer.

Finally, a very important thanks goes out to YOU. Thanks for buying this book. Thanks for wanting to become an Oracle Certified Professional. Thanks for any nice comments you might leave on websites here and there. Thanks for trusting us to help you succeed at the test!

—Robert G. Freeman

Thanks to Robert Freeman and Jeff Kellum for the opportunity to write this book. Thanks to David May, Gary Baird, and Greg Sinclair for providing a rock-solid infrastructure, not only in which to practice my art but also to the great benefit of my employer, CSX. Thanks to my capacity management team Chris Roessler, Harry Price, Brian Horan, Jan Shane, Joe Zuleger, and Derryck Zimmerman; my storage team Andy Brackett, Scott Gunter, Joe Fredrickson, Mike Able, John Anderson, Chris Griffith, Rick Ferry, Gene Pate, and Jim Gouvernante. To my coworkers Benny Kronz, Maritza Gonzalez, Chris Wilson, John Kall, Sandra Merwin, Duard Williams, Rich McClain, and Frank Lamon, for building a world-class Oracle database environment at CSX and for making it possible for me to continuously learn, develop, and teach.

This book would not have been written without my wife's permission, of course. Thank you, Donna, for being by my side through these projects, especially during the summer months in Florida. Thank you to my daughter, Jenny, who is 7 and sitting next to me on the sofa writing stories on her MacBook about Chihuahuas and leopard geckos while I write about "the Oracle."

—Charles A. Pack

About the Authors

Robert G. Freeman lives in Salt Lake City, Utah, and is a principle database engineer with the Church of Jesus Christ of Latter-day Saints. Robert has been working with Oracle for some 20 years now. After the latest economic explosion, Robert expects that he will continue to be working for at least another 20 years. He has shelved his pending midlife career-change plans to become a maniacal recluse living in a cabin out in the middle of nowhere due to the economic crisis and current state of his 401(k).

Besides working with Oracle databases (that's his story and he's sticking to it), Robert writes an occasional book (at last count 12 or so), flies airplanes, enjoys karate, and has a family that is awesome. He met Charles Pack, who is a fellow Okie (even if he sometimes roots for the wrong school) years ago and to this day wonders if Charles will ever walk around without wearing sunglasses to hide his eyes and the deep meaning contained in them. Robert is the husband of the patient Lisa and father of five wonderful, if not occasionally misguided, children.

If you liked this book and want to email Robert, you can do so at dbaoracle@aol.com. If you didn't like this book, then make sure you remember that Charles A. Pack wrote it and email him instead.

Charles A. Pack is an Oracle Certified Professional DBA with over 20 years of IT experience. His career has included the roles of PC repairman, network administrator, systems operator, COBOL programmer, backup and storage engineer, DBA, architect, project manager, and people manager. He earned the Bachelor of Science degree from Oklahoma State University, the MBA from the University of Oklahoma, and the Master of Science in Computer Science from Texas A&M University – Corpus Christi. He has taught Oracle DBA classes at Florida Community College Jacksonville and has presented on the subject at universities and to professional organizations. He authored the Oracle Press *Oracle9i Database: OCP 9i Performance Tuning Exam Guide* and collaborated with coauthor Robert Freeman on the *Oracle 8 to 8i Upgrade Exam Cram*. In his current role as technical director of hardware provisioning at CSX Technology in Jacksonville, Florida, he and his teams are responsible for enterprise storage, backups, capacity planning, and performance. He is a true Cowboy at heart, and he loves to barbecue.

Contents at a Glance

Contents

Table of Exercises

Introduction

There is high demand for professionals in the information technology (IT) industry, and Oracle certifications are the hottest credentials in the database world. You have made the right decision to pursue your Oracle certification because it will give you a distinct advantage in this highly competitive market.

Most readers should already be familiar with Oracle and do not need an introduction to the Oracle database world. For those who aren't familiar with the company, here are the basics: Oracle, founded in 1977, sold the first commercial relational database and is now the world's leading database company and largest enterprise software company, with 2008 fiscal year revenues of more than $22 billion.

Oracle databases are the de facto standard for large Internet sites, and Oracle advertisers are boastful but honest when they proclaim, "The Internet Runs on Oracle." Almost all big Internet sites run Oracle databases. Oracle's penetration of the database market runs deep and is not limited to dot-com implementations. Enterprise resource planning (ERP) application suites, data warehouses, and custom applications at many companies rely on Oracle. The demand for DBA resources remains higher than the demand for others during weak economic times.

This book is intended to help you pass the Oracle Database 11g: Administration II exam, which will establish your credentials as an Oracle Certified Professional (OCP). The OCP certification is a prerequisite for obtaining an Oracle Certified Master (OCM) certification. Using this book and a practice database, you can learn the necessary skills to pass the 1Z0-053 Oracle Database 11g: Administration II exam.

Why Become Oracle Certified?

The number-one reason to become an OCP is to gain more visibility and greater access to the industry's most challenging opportunities. Oracle certification is the best way to demonstrate your knowledge and skills in Oracle database systems.

Certification is proof of your knowledge and shows that you have the skills required to support Oracle core products. The Oracle certification program can help a company to identify proven performers who have demonstrated their skills and who can support the company's investment in Oracle technology. It demonstrates that you have a solid understanding of your job role and the Oracle products used in that role.

OCPs are among the best paid in the IT industry. Salary surveys consistently show the OCP certification to yield higher salaries than other certifications, including Microsoft, Novell, and Cisco.

So whether you are beginning your career, changing your career, or looking to secure your position as a DBA, this book is for you!

Oracle Certifications

Oracle certifications follow a track that is oriented toward a job role. These are database administration, application developer, and web application server administrator tracks. Within each track, Oracle has a multitiered certification program.

Within the administration track there are three tiers:

- The first tier is the Oracle 11*g* Certified Associate (OCA). To obtain OCA certification, you must pass the 1Z0-052 Oracle Database 11*g*: Administration I exam.

- The second tier is the Oracle 11*g* Certified Professional (OCP), which builds on and requires OCA certification. To obtain OCP certification, you must attend an approved Oracle University hands-on class and pass the 1Z0-053 Oracle Database 11*g*: Administration II exam.

- The third and highest tier is the Oracle 11*g* Certified Master (OCM), which builds on and requires OCP certification. To obtain OCM certification, you must attend advanced-level classes and take a two-day, hands-on practical exam.

The material in this book addresses only the Administration II exam. Other Wiley books—which can be found at http://www.wiley.com—can help students new to the DBA world prepare for the OCA exam 1Z0-052 Oracle Database 11*g*: Administration I. You can also get information on the Oracle upgrade exam for the Oracle 10*g* OCP, Oracle Database 11*g*: New Features for Administrators (exam 1Z0-050).

> See the Oracle website at http://www.oracle.com/education/
> certification for the latest information on all of Oracle's certification
> paths, along with Oracle's training resources.

Oracle DBA Certification

The role of the DBA has become a key to success in today's highly complex database systems. The best DBAs work behind the scenes but are in the spotlight when critical issues arise. They plan, create, maintain, and ensure that the database is available for the business. They are always watching the database for performance issues and to prevent unscheduled downtime. The DBA's job requires broad understanding of the architecture of Oracle database, and expertise in solving problems.

Because this book focuses on the DBA track, we will take a closer look at the different tiers of the DBA track.

Oracle Database 11*g* Administrator Certified Associate

The Oracle 11*g* Administrator Certified Associate (OCA) certification is a streamlined, entry-level certification for the database-administration track and is required to advance toward the more senior certification tiers. This certification requires you to pass one of the following exams:

- 1Z0-001 Introduction to Oracle: SQL & PL/SQL
- 1Z0-007 Introduction to Oracle9*i* SQL
- 1Z0-047 Oracle Database SQL Expert
- 1Z0-051 Oracle Database 11*g*: SQL Fundamentals I

    And then you must pass the following exam:

- 1Z0-052 Oracle Database 11*g*: Administration I

Oracle Database 11*g* Administrator Certified Professional

The OCP tier of the database-administration track challenges you to demonstrate your enhanced experience and knowledge of Oracle technologies. The Oracle 11*g* Administrator Certified Professional (OCP) certification requires achievement of the OCA certification, completion of one or more approved Oracle University classes, and successful completion of the following exam:

- 1Z0-053 Oracle Database 11*g*: Administration II

    The approved courses for OCP candidates include the following:

- Oracle Database 11*g*: Advanced PL/SQL
- Oracle Database 11*g*: Data Guard Administration
- Oracle Database 11*g*: Performance Tuning
- Oracle Database 11*g*: Administration Workshop I
- Oracle Database 11*g*: Administration Workshop II
- Oracle Database 11*g*: Introduction to SQL
- Oracle Database 11*g*: New Features for Administrators
- Oracle Database 11*g*: Program with PL/SQL
- Oracle Database 11*g*: Develop PL/SQL Program Units
- Oracle Database 11*g*: Implement Streams
- Oracle Database 11*g*: SQL Tuning Workshop
- Oracle Spatial 11*g*: Essentials
- Oracle Database 11*g*: RAC Administration
- Oracle Database 11*g*: SQL Fundamentals 1

    If you already have your OCP in 10*g* or earlier and have elected to take the upgrade path, you are not required to take the Oracle University class to obtain your OCP for Oracle 11*g*.

You should verify the list of approved courses for OCP candidates against the Oracle education website (www.oracle.com/education) because it can change without any notice.

Oracle Database 11g Certified Master

The Oracle Database 11g Administration Certified Master (OCM) is the highest level of certification that Oracle offers. To become a certified master, you must first obtain OCP certification; then complete two advanced-level classes at an Oracle Education facility; pass a hands-on, two-day exam at an Oracle Education facility; and then submit the Hands On Course Requirement form. The classes and practicum exam are offered only at an Oracle Education facility and may require travel.

Details on the required coursework for the OCM exam were not available when this book was written.

Oracle 11g Upgrade Paths

Existing Oracle Professionals can upgrade their certification in several ways:

- An Oracle10g OCP can upgrade to 11g certification by passing the 1Z0-050 Oracle Database 11g: New Features for Administrators exam.

- An Oracle9i OCP can upgrade to 11g certification by passing the 1Z0-055 Oracle Database 11g: New Features for 9i OCPs exam.

- An Oracle8i OCP can upgrade to 10g by passing the 1Z0-045 Oracle Database 10g DBA New Features for Oracle8i OCPs exam, then separately passing the 10g to 11g upgrade exam.

- Oracle 7.3 and Oracle 8 DBAs must first upgrade to an Oracle9i certification with the 1Z0-035 Oracle9i DBA New Features for Oracle 7.3 and Oracle 8 OCPs exam and then upgrade the 9i certification to 11g with the 1Z0-055 Oracle Database 11g: New Features for 9i OCPs exam.

Oracle Exam Requirements

The Oracle Database 11g: Administration II exam covers several core subject areas. As with many typical multiple-choice exams, there are several tips that you can follow to maximize your score on the exam.

Skills Required for the Oracle Database 11*g*: Administration II Exam

To pass the Oracle 11*g* Administration II exam, you need to master the following subject areas in Oracle 11*g*:

Database Architecture and ASM

   Describe Automatic Storage Management (ASM)

   Set up initialization parameter files for ASM and database instances

   Start up and shut down ASM instances

   Administer ASM disk groups

Configuring for Recoverability

   Configure multiple archive log file destinations to increase availability

   Define, apply, and use a retention policy

   Configure the Flash Recovery Area

   Use Flash Recovery Area

Using the RMAN Recovery Catalog

   Identify situations that require RMAN recovery catalog

   Create and configure a recovery catalog

   Synchronize the recovery catalog

   Create and use RMAN stored scripts

   Back up the recovery catalog

   Create and use a virtual private catalog

Configuring Backup Specifications

   Configure backup settings

   Allocate channels to use in backing up

   Configure backup optimization

Using RMAN to Create Backups

   Create image file backups

   Create a whole database backup

   Enable fast incremental backup

   Create duplex backup and back up backup sets

   Create an archival backup for long-term retention

   Create a multisection, compressed and encrypted backup

   Report on and maintain backups

Diagnosing the Database

    Set up Automatic Diagnostic Repository

    Using Support Workbench

    Perform block media recovery

Managing Memory

    Implement Automatic Memory Management

    Manually configure SGA parameters

    Configure automatic PGA memory management

Managing Database Performance

    Use the SQL Tuning Advisor

    Use the SQL Access Advisor to tune a workload

    Understand Database Replay

Space Management

    Manage resumable space allocation

    Describe the concepts of transportable tablespaces and databases

    Reclaim wasted space from tables and indexes by using the segment shrink functionality

Managing Resources

    Understand the database resource manager

    Create and use Database Resource Manager Components

Automating Tasks with the Scheduler

    Create a job, program, and schedule

    Use a time-based or event-based schedule for executing Scheduler jobs

    Create lightweight jobs

    Use job chains to perform a series of related tasks

Administering the Scheduler

    Create Windows and Job Classes

    Use advanced Scheduler concepts to prioritize jobs

Globalization

    Customize language-dependent behavior for the database and individual sessions

    Working with database and NLS character sets

Tips for Taking the Administration II Exam

Use the following tips to help you prepare for and pass the exam:

- The exam contains about 55 to 80 questions to be completed in 90 minutes. Answer the questions you know the answers to first so that you do not run out of time.

- Many questions on the exam have answer choices that at first glance look identical. Read the questions carefully. Do not just jump to conclusions. Make sure you clearly understand exactly what each question asks.

- Some of the questions are scenario-based. Some of the scenarios contain nonessential information and exhibits. You need to be able to identify what's important and what's not important.

- Do not leave any questions unanswered. There is no negative scoring. After selecting an answer, you can mark a difficult question or one that you're unsure of and come back to it later.

- When answering questions that you're not sure about, use a process of elimination to get rid of the obviously incorrect answers first. Doing this greatly improves your odds if you need to make an educated guess.

- If you're not sure of your answer, mark it for review and then look for other questions that may help you eliminate any incorrect answers. At the end of the test, you can go back and review the questions that you marked for review.

> You should be familiar with the exam objectives, which are included in the front of this book as a perforated tear-out card. You can also find them at http://education.oracle.com/pls/web_prod-plq-dad/db_pages .getpage?page_id=41&p_exam_id=1Z0_053.

Where Do You Take the Certification Exam?

The Oracle Database 11*g* certification exams are available at any of the more than 900 Thomson Prometric Authorized Testing Centers around the world. For the location of a testing center near you, call 1-800-891-3926. Outside the United States and Canada, contact your local Thomson Prometric Registration Center.

To register for a proctored Oracle Certified Professional exam:

- Determine the number of the exam you want to take. For the OCP exam, it is 1Z0-053.

- Register with Thomson Prometric online at www.prometric.com or, in North America, by calling 1-800-891-EXAM (1-800-891-3926). At this point, you will be asked to pay in advance for the exam. At the time of this writing, the exams are $125 each and must be taken within one year of payment.

- When you schedule the exam, you'll get instructions regarding all appointment and cancellation procedures, the ID requirements, and information about the testing-center location.

You can schedule exams up to six weeks in advance or as soon as one working day before the day you wish to take it. If something comes up and you need to cancel or reschedule your exam appointment, contact Thomson Prometric at least 24 hours or one business day in advance.

What Does This Book Cover?

This book covers everything you need to pass the Oracle Database11g: Administration II exam. Each chapter begins with a list of exam objectives.

Chapter 1   In this chapter, you'll learn about Automatic Storage Management (ASM). It introduces the ASM architecture and how to create a special type of Oracle instance: an ASM instance. In addition, this chapter describes in detail how to create and manage disk volumes in an ASM environment.

Chapter 2   This chapter introduces oracle user managed backup and recovery. A review of Oracle's architecture with respect to backup and recovery is presented. Management of the Oracle database with respect to backup and recovery is included in the chapter. The chapter covers putting the database in ARCHIVELOG mode. Finally the chapter covers Oracle offline and online backups.

Chapter 3   This chapter introduces the reader to Oracle user managed recoveries. Both complete and incomplete recoveries are covered in this chapter. Backup and recovery of the database control file is included along with the re-creation of the temporary tablespace datafiles. Finally, recovery from the loss of online redo logs and the password files are covered.

Chapter 4   This chapter introduces the reader to RMAN. The chapter discusses configuration of RMAN for backup and recovery operations. Both offline and online backups are discussed in the chapter. The chapter then proceeds to cover backups of an Oracle database by RMAN.

Chapter 5   This chapter provides an introduction to the RMAN recovery catalog. The chapter provides information on when you might want to use a recovery catalog, how to setup a recovery catalog, and register a database with the recovery catalog. We also discuss the use of RMAN's new virtual private catalog.

Chapter 6   This chapter dives into RMAN recoveries. RMAN recoveries in both NOARCHIVELOG and ARCHIVELOG mode are covered. Recoveries using both full backups and incremental backups are discussed. Faster recoveries using image copies are discussed and recoveries using a backup control file are also covered.

Chapter 7   This chapter covers RMAN reporting, monitoring, and tuning. Use of various views to monitor and report on RMAN operations is discussed in this chapter. The RMAN report and list commands are also covered in this chapter. Various RMAN administration commands are covered in the chapter.

Chapter 8   This chapter covers advanced RMAN recovery topics. This includes incomplete recoveries using RMAN. The chapter also discusses using RMAN for database duplication and tablespace point-in-time recoveries. The chapter also includes a discussion on using RMAN in disaster recovery situations.

Chapter 9 In this chapter, you'll learn about flashback technologies, including restoring dropped tables, performing flashback queries, flashback transactions, flashback table operations, flashback database operations, and setting up and using the Flashback Data Archive.

Chapter 10 This chapter discusses database diagnosis and performance management. You will learn about the Automatic Diagnostic Repository, the Support Workbench, performing block media recovery, and using the SQL Tuning Advisor, the SQL Access Advisor, and the Database Replay feature.

Chapter 11 This chapter discusses the management of Oracle resources. You will learn about automatic memory management features, including Automatic Memory Management (AMM), Automatic Shared Memory Management (ASMM), and Automatic PGA Memory Management (APMM) features. You will learn about resumable space allocation, transportable tablespaces, transportable databases, and shrinking segments to recover unused space.

You will learn about the Database Resource Manager (DRM) and how it can be used to manage resources. You will learn to create resource plans, resource consumer groups, and resource plan directives.

Chapter 12 In this chapter, we discuss the Oracle Scheduler. You will learn how the Scheduler can be used to automate repetitive DBA tasks. You will also learn to create the objects necessary to schedule jobs, including job, schedule, program, window, job group, and window group objects.

Chapter 13 This chapter describes Oracle's globalization support features. You will learn about linguistic sorting and searching, datetime datatypes, and how to configure the database to support different language and territorial conventions.

Throughout each chapter, we include Real World Scenario sidebars, which are designed to give a real-life perspective on how certain topics affect our everyday duties as DBAs. Each chapter ends with a list of exam essentials, which give you a highlight of the chapter, with an emphasis on the topics that you need to be extra familiar with for the exam. The chapter concludes with 20 review questions, specifically designed to help you retain the knowledge presented. To really nail down your skills, read and answer each question carefully.

How to Use This Book

This book can provide a solid foundation for the serious effort of preparing for the Oracle 11g: Administration II exam. To best benefit from this book, use the following study method:

1. Take the assessment test immediately following this introduction. (The answers are at the end of the test.) Carefully read over the explanations for any questions you get wrong, and note which chapters the material comes from. This information should help you plan your study strategy.

2. Study each chapter carefully, making sure you fully understand the information and the test objectives listed at the beginning of each chapter. Pay extra close attention to any chapter related to questions you missed in the assessment test.

3. Complete all hands-on exercises in the chapter, referring back to the chapter text so that you understand the reason for each step you take. If you do not have an Oracle database available, be sure to study the examples carefully.

4. Answer the review questions related to each chapter. (The answers appear at the end of each chapter, after the review questions.) Note the questions that confuse or trick you, and study those sections of the book again.

5. Take the two bonus exams that are included on the accompanying CD. This will give you a complete overview of what you can expect to see on the real test.

6. Remember to use the products on the CD included with this book. The electronic flashcards and the Sybex Test Engine exam-preparation software have been specifically designed to help you study for and pass your exam.

To learn all the material covered in this book, you'll need to apply yourself regularly and with discipline. Try to set aside the same time period every day to study, and select a comfortable and quiet place to do so. If you work hard, you will be surprised at how quickly you learn this material. All the best!

What's on the CD?

We have worked hard to provide some really great tools to help you with your certification process. All of the following tools should be loaded on your workstation when you're studying for the test.

The Wiley Test Engine Preparation Software

This test-preparation software prepares you to pass the 1Z0-053 Oracle Database 11*g*: Administration II exam. In this test, you will find all of the questions from the book, plus two additional bonus exams that appear exclusively on the CD. You can take the assessment test, test yourself by chapter, or take the practice exams. The test engine will run on either a Microsoft Windows or Linux platform.

Here is a sample screen from the Wiley Test Engine:

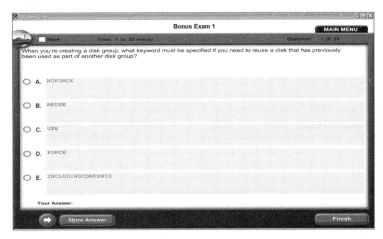

Electronic Flashcards for PC and Palm Devices

After you read the *OCP: Oracle Database 11g Administrator Certified Professional Study Guide*, read the review questions at the end of each chapter and study the practice exams included in the book and on the CD. You can also test yourself with the flashcards included on the CD.

The flashcards are designed to test your understanding of the fundamental concepts covered in the exam. Here is what the Sybex flashcards interface looks like:

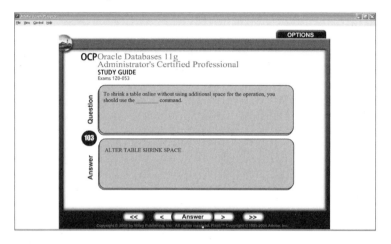

OCP: Oracle 11g Administrator Certified Professional Study Guide in PDF

Many people like the convenience of being able to carry their Study Guide on a CD, which is why we included the book in PDF format. This will be extremely helpful to readers who fly or commute on a bus or train and prefer an e-book, as well as to readers who find it more comfortable reading from their computer. We've also included a copy of Adobe Acrobat Reader on the CD.

Assessment Test

1. ASM supports all but which of the following file types? (Choose all that apply.)

   A. Database files

   B. Spfiles

   C. Redo-log files

   D. Archived log files

   E. RMAN backup sets

   F. Password files

   G. init.ora files

2. After executing the command

   ```
   alter diskgroup disk group2 drop disk dg2a;
   ```

   you issue the following command from the ASM instance:

   ```
   Select group_number, count(*) from v$asm_operation;
   ```

   What is the implication if the query against V$ASM_OPERATION returns zero rows?

   A. The drop disk operation is still proceeding and you cannot yet run the undrop disks operation.

   B. The drop disk operation is complete and you can run the undrop disks command if needed.

   C. The drop disk operation is complete and you cannot run the undrop disk command.

   D. The query will fail since there is not a V$ASM_OPERATION view available in an ASM instance.

   E. None of the above is true.

3. What is the net effect of the following command?

   ```
   alter diskgroup dgroup1 drop disk abc;
   ```

   A. The disk ABC will be dropped from the disk group. Since you did not issue a rebalance command, the data on that disk will be lost.

   B. The command will raise an error indicating that you need to rebalance the disk group to remove the data from that disk prior to dropping the disk.

   C. The disk group will be automatically rebalanced during the drop operation. Once the rebalancing is complete, the disk will be dropped.

   D. This command will fail because you cannot drop a specific disk in an ASM disk group.

   E. The disk drop command will be suspended for a predetermined amount of time, waiting for you to also issue an alter diskgroup rebalance command. Once you have issued the rebalance command, ASM will proceed to rebalance the disk group and then drop the disk.

4. Which of the following is not a configurable attribute for an individual disk group?

A. AU_SIZE

B. COMPATIBLE.RDBMS

C. COMPATIBLE.ASM

D. DISK_REPAIR_TIME

E. DG_DROP_TIME

5. What Oracle process runs when the database is in ARCHIVELOG mode but not when it is in NOARCHIVELOG mode?

A. MMON

B. LGWR

C. ARCH

D. ARWR

E. COPY

6. You are peer reviewing a fellow DBA's backup plan for his NOARCHIVELOG mode database, as shown here:

1. Put the tablespaces in backup mode.

2. Back up the datafiles for all tablespaces.

3. Take the tablespaces out of backup mode.

4. Back up all archived redo logs.

Your colleague asks for you to comment on his plan. Which response would be correct?

A. The plan will work as is.

B. The plan needs to be modified to allow for an archive-log switch after step 3.

C. The plan needs to be modified so that a backup of the archived redo logs occurs before step 1.

D. The plan needs to be adjusted to shut down the database after step 1 and to restart the database after step 2.

E. The plan cannot work as presented.

7. Which of the following statements is true when the database is in ARCHIVELOG mode and tablespaces are in hot backup mode?

A. Archive log generation is suspended until the tablespaces are taken out of hot backup mode.

B. Datafiles are not written to during hot backups.

C. Changes to the database are cached during the backup and not written to the datafiles to ensure that the datafiles are consistent when recovered.

D. The datafile headers are not updated during the backup.

E. The way data is written to the online redo logs is unchanged during the backup.

8. When you create a backup control file, where is the resulting file written to?

   A. The database user dump destination directory

   B. The database diagnostic destination directory

   C. To `$ORACLE_HOME/rdbms`

   D. To `$ORACLE_HOME/admin`

   E. To the directory and filename you specify in the command

9. If a log file becomes corrupted, it may cause the database to stall. How would you correct such a situation?

   A. Recover the online redo log from backup.

   B. Delete and re-create the log file.

   C. Use the `alter database clear logfile` command to clear the log file.

   D. Shut down the database and restart it.

   E. Shut down the database and then mount it. Clear the log file with the `alter database clear logfile` command and then restart the database with `alter database open resetlogs`.

10. You have lost datafiles 1 and 3 from your database, and the database has crashed. In what order should you perform the following steps to recover your database?

   1. Take the datafiles that were lost offline.

   2. `startup mount` the database

   3. Issue the `alter database open` command.

   4. Restore the datafiles that were lost

   5. Recover the datafiles with the `recover datafile` command.

   6. Bring the datafiles back online.

   7. Recover the database with the `recover database` command.

   A. 2, 1, 3, 4, 5, 6

   B. 2, 4, 5, 3

   C. 4, 7, 3

   D. 2, 4, 7, 3

   E. 2, 7, 3

11. Which command is used to open the database after an incomplete recovery?

   A. `alter database open`

   B. `alter database open repairlog`

   C. `alter database open resetlogs`

   D. `alter database open resetlog`

   E. `alter database resetlogs open`

12. Your database has a backup that was taken yesterday (Tuesday) between 13:00 and 15:00 hours. This is the only backup you have. You have lost all the archived redo logs generated since the previous Monday, but you have archived redo logs available from the previous Sunday and earlier. You now need to restore your backup due to database loss. To which point can you restore your database?

    A. 13:00 on Tuesday.

    B. 15:00 on Tuesday.

    C. Up until the last available archived redo log on Sunday.

    D. To any point; all the redo should still be available in the online redo logs.

    E. The database is not recoverable.

13. Which of the following files cannot be backed up by RMAN? (Choose all that apply.)

    A. Database datafiles

    B. Control files

    C. Online redo logs

    D. Database pfiles

    E. Archived redo logs

14. Which of the following RMAN structures can data from a datafile span?

    A. RMAN backup-set pieces spanning backup sets

    B. RMAN backup-set pieces within a given backup set

    C. RMAN backups

    D. RMAN channels

    E. None of the above

15. Which RMAN backup command is used to create the block-change tracking file?

    A. `alter database create block change tracking file`

    B. `alter database enable block change file`

    C. `alter database enable block change tracking using file '/ora01/opt/block_change_tracking.fil'`

    D. `alter system enable block change tracking using file '/ora01/opt/block_change_tracking.fil'`

    E. `alter system block change tracking on`

16. A shoot-out has erupted between your MS development teams using .NET and your Linux development teams using Java. Knowing that your database is in danger, which command would you use to back up your NOARCHIVELOG mode database using RMAN with compression?

    A. `backup database all`

    B. `backup compressed database`

    C. `backup as compressed backupset database;`

    D. `backup as compressed backup database plus archivelog all;`

    E. `backup as compressed backupset database plus compress archivelog all;`

17. What is the purpose of the RMAN recovery catalog? (Choose all that apply.)

    A. Make backups faster

    B. Store RMAN metadata

    C. Store RMAN scripts

    D. Provide the ability to do centralized backup reporting.

    E. Make recovery faster

18. RMAN provides more granular catalog security through which feature?

    A. Virtual private database

    B. Virtual private catalog

    C. RMAN virtual database

    D. RMAN secure catalog

    E. Oracle Database Vault

19. True of false? You can back up the RMAN recovery catalog with RMAN.

    A. True

    B. False

20. What RMAN command must you use before you can back up a database using the recovery catalog?

    A. `create catalog`

    B. `install database`

    C. `catalog database`

    D. `merge Catalog with database`

    E. `register database`

21. You have control-file autobackups enabled. When starting your database from SQL*Plus, you receive the following error message:

```
SQL> startup
ORA-01078: failure in processing system parameters
LRM-00109: could not open parameter file
'C:\ORACLE\PRODUCT\11.1.0\DB_1\DATABASE\INITORCL.ORA'
```

Using RMAN, how would you respond to this error?

    A. Issue the `startup nomount` command and then issue the `restore parameter file` command from the RMAN prompt.

    B. Issue the `startup nomount` command and then issue the `restore spfile` command from the RMAN prompt.

    C. Issue the `startup nomount` command and then issue the `restore spfile from autobackup` command from the RMAN prompt.

    D. Issue the `startup nomount` command and then issue the `restore spfile from backup` command from the RMAN prompt.

    E. Issue the `restore spfile from autobackup` command from the RMAN prompt.

22. While working on a data problem, Curt, Bill, Ben, Mike, and Matt introduced a vast amount of corrupted data into the database. Pablo has discovered this problem and he needs you to recover the database to the point in time prior to the introduction of the corruption. The logical corruption was introduced at 6:30 p.m. on September 6, 2008. Which of the following would be the correct commands to use to restore the database to a point in time before the corruption?

A.
```
restore database until time
'06-SEP-2008 06:30:00');
recover database until time
'06-SEP-2008 06:30:00');

alter database open;
```

B.
```
restore database until time
'06-SEP-2008 06:30:00');
recover database until time
'06-SEP-2008 06:30:00');

alter database open resetlogs;
```

C.
```
restore database until time
'06-SEP-2008 18:29:55');
recover database until time
'06-SEP-2008 18:29:55');
alter database open resetlogs;
```

D.
```
restore database until time '06-SEP-2008 18:29:55');
    alter database open resetlogs;
```

E.
```
restore database until time '06-SEP-2008 18:29:55');
recover database;
alter database open resetlogs;
```

23. What is the purpose of the until change option of the restore command?

A. It allows you to select the SCN that you want to restore to.

B. It allows you to select the log sequence number you want to restore to.

C. It allows you to select the timestamp you want to restore to.

D. It allows you to manually stop the restore at any time as online redo logs are applied.

E. None of the above.

24. What is the purpose of the recover command? (Choose all that apply.)

A. Recover database datafiles from physical disk backup sets.

B. Recover required incremental backups from physical disk backup sets.

C. Recover required archived redo logs from physical disk backup sets.

D. Apply incremental backups to recover the database.

E. Apply archived redo logs to recover the database.

25. What is an obsolete backup set?

  A. A backup set that is missing one or more backup set pieces

  B. A backup that has exceeded the retention criteria and is no longer needed

  C. A backup set that does not include archived redo logs

  D. A backup set that can not be recovered due to corruption

  E. A backup set superceded by a datafile copy

26. What is the purpose of the `list expired backup` command?

  A. Lists all backups impacted by a `resetlogs` command

  B. Lists all backups that are subject to retention criteria

  C. Lists all backups that are missing associated physical backup set pieces

  D. Lists the status of datafile backup failures due to the use of the `duration` command

  E. Lists backups that cannot be used by the restore command because they have been marked as disabled

27. What is the purpose of the `catalog` command?

  A. To review RMAN control file and recovery catalog metadata and ensure that it's correct

  B. To delete RMAN backup-related metadata from the recovery catalog

  C. To create metadata in the control file and the recovery catalog related to backup set pieces

  D. To create a report that lists database backups

  E. To rebuild the recovery catalog

28. Which of the following commands will fail?

  A. `report schema;`

  B. `report need backup;`

  C. `report need backup days 3;`

  D. `report user;`

  E. `report obsolete;`

29. What are the two different types of database duplication? (Choose two.)

  A. Active

  B. Passive

  C. Online

  D. Backup-based

  E. Failure driven

30. When you're performing a tablespace point-in-time recovery, which tablespaces will always be restored to the auxiliary instance? (Choose all that apply.)

   A. The SYSTEM tablespace.

   B. The UNDO tablespace.

   C. All tablespaces with tables.

   D. All tablespaces with indexes.

   E. No tablespaces are automatically restored.

31. Which operation requires that you create an auxiliary instance manually before executing the operation? (Choose all that apply.)

   A. Backup-based database duplication.

   B. Active database duplication.

   C. Tablespace point-in-time recovery.

   D. No operation requires the creation of an auxiliary instance.

32. What RMAN command is used to execute a tablespace point-in-time recovery?

   A. recover

   B. duplicate

   C. restore

   D. copy

   E. None of the above

33. A user performs an update on a table. Shortly after committing the transaction, they realize that they had an error in their WHERE clause causing the wrong rows to be updated. Which Flashback option would allow you to undo this transaction and restore the table to its previous state?

   A. Flashback Drop

   B. Flashback Query

   C. Flashback Versions Query

   D. Flashback Transaction Query

   E. Flashback Table

34. A developer calls and reports that he accidentally dropped an important lookup table from a production database. He needs the table to be recovered. What action would you take?

   A. Initiate an incomplete recovery operation using RMAN.

   B. Copy the table from a development database.

   C. Advise the user to rekey the data.

   D. Perform a Flashback Drop operation.

   E. Perform a Flashback Recovery operation.

35. In a Database Replay workload capture, what client request information is gathered? (Choose all that apply.)

    A. SQL text

    B. Shared server requests (Oracle MTS)

    C. Bind variable values

    D. Information about transactions

    E. Remote `DESCRIBE` and `COMMIT` operations

36. Which of the following are true concerning block media recovery? (Choose all that apply.)

    A. Any gap in archive logs ends the recovery.

    B. If a gap in archive logs is encountered, RMAN will search forward for newer versions of the blocks that are not corrupt.

    C. Uncorrupted blocks from the flashback logs may be used to speed recovery.

    D. The database can be in NOARCHIVELOG mode.

    E. None of the above.

37. The DBA has chosen to manage SGA and PGA memory separately in an OLTP database because of his unique knowledge of the application. Which of these are good starting points to use when configuring the maximum values for SGA and PGA, based on the amount of memory available on the system?

    A. 20% SGA, 80% PGA

    B. 25% SGA, 75% PGA

    C. 50% SGA, 50% PGA

    D. 75% SGA, 25% PGA

    E. 80% SGA, 20% PGA

38. You notice that a long-running transaction is suspended due to a space constraint, and there is no `AFTER SUSPEND` triggered event addressing the issue. You also note that the critical transaction is just about to reach the `RESUMABLE_TIMEOUT` value. Which of these actions is appropriate?

    A. Abort the session, fix the space problem, then resubmit the transaction.

    B. Use the `DBMS_RESUMABLE.SET_SESSION_TIMEOUT` procedure to extend the time-out for the session while you fix the problem.

    C. Do nothing, let the transaction fail, then fix the problem.

    D. Use Segment Shrink to clean up the table.

    E. Use the `DBMS_RESUMABLE.SET_TIMEOUT` procedure to extend the time-out for the session while you fix the problem.

39. Which of the following are not disabled by default?

    A. Jobs

    B. Chains

    C. Windows

    D. Window groups

    E. Schedule

40. You notice that a job in a chain has not completed on a nonconstrained RAC database. Which of these are valid reasons why that might occur?

    A. The job priority is 1 and the resource consumer group CPU emphasis allocation is a low percentage.

    B. The job affinity is to a service and one node in that service is unavailable.

    C. The job affinity is to an instance and that instance is unavailable.

    D. There is no service affinity.

    E. None of the above.

41. The NLS_LANGUAGE parameter specifies the default conventions to be used for which of the following globalization elements?

    A. Languages for server messages

    B. Day and month names and abbreviations

    C. Symbols to represent a.m., p.m., AD, and BC

    D. Affirmative and negative response strings (YES, NO)

    E. None of the above

    F. All of the above

42. The NLS_TERRITORY parameter specifies the default conventions to be used for which of the following globalization elements? (Choose all that apply.)

    A. Date format

    B. Decimal character

    C. Group separator

    D. First day of the month

    E. None of the above

    F. All of the above

Answers to Assessment Test

1. F, G. ASM supports datafiles, log files, control files, archive logs, RMAN backup sets, spfiles, and other Oracle database file types, but not password files or init.ora files. For more information, see Chapter 1, "Using Oracle ASM."

2. C. The V$ASM_OPERATION view will indicate if the drop disk operation is still in progress. If no rows are returned by the view, then the drop disk operation is complete. If the drop disk operation is complete you cannot run the undrop disks command. For more information, see Chapter 1, "Using Oracle ASM."

3. C. The disk group will be automatically rebalanced during a drop (or add) disk operation. Once the rebalancing is complete then the disk is dropped. For more information, see Chapter 1, "Using Oracle ASM."

4. E. DG_DROP_TIME is not a valid configuration attribute for a disk group. For more information, see Chapter 1, "Using Oracle ASM."

5. C. The ARCH process starts up when the database is in ARCHIVELOG mode. It is responsible for moving the online redo logs to the various archived redo log destination directories. For more information, see Chapter 2, "Performing Oracle User-Managed Backups."

6. E. Since the database is in NOARCHIVELOG mode, the entire plan will not work since you can not perform hot backups in NOARCHIVELOG mode. If the database was in ARCHIVELOG mode, then you would choose option B. For more information, see Chapter 2, "Performing Oracle User-Managed Backups."

7. D. When a tablespace is in hot backup mode, the related datafile headers are not updated. The headers will be updated after the tablespaces are taken out of hot backup mode. For more information, see Chapter 2, "Performing Oracle User-Managed Backups."

8. E. When you issue the alter database backup controlfile to 'directory/filename', Oracle will write the backup control file to the directory and filename that you choose. For more information, see Chapter 2, "Performing Oracle User-Managed Backups."

9. C. Use the alter database clear logfile command to clear the log file and free up the database. If the log file has not been archived, you may have to use the alter database clear unarchived logfile command instead. For more information, please see Chapter 3, "Performing Oracle User-Managed Database Recoveries."

10. B. You will have to startup mount the database and then restore the database datafiles that were lost (you could, of course, restore the files first). You then need to recover the datafiles with the recover datafile command. Once the datafiles are recovered, you can then open the database. You may wonder why online recovery is not possible in this case. Datafile 1 is always the SYSTEM tablespace. The database cannot be opened if the SYSTEM tablespace is not available. Also the use of the recover database command is not the best choice in this case. Oracle always wants you to answer the question that is the best choice. In this case, datafile recovery is the better choice. For more information, please see Chapter 3, "Performing Oracle User-Managed Database Recoveries."

11. C. The `alter database open resetlogs` command is used to open an Oracle database after an incomplete recovery. For more information, please see Chapter 3, "Performing Oracle User-Managed Database Recoveries."

12. E. The database is not recoverable. You would need all the archived redo logs generated during the backup on Tuesday, at least, to restore the database after that backup. The online redo logs are very unlikely to have all the redo that would be required. For more information, please see Chapter 3, "Performing Oracle User-Managed Database Recoveries."

13. C, D. RMAN will not back up online redo logs or database parameter files. RMAN will back up database server parameter files (spfiles) however. For more information, see Chapter 4, "Configuring and Backing Up Using RMAN."

14. B. RMAN backup set pieces within the same backup set can contain data from a given datafile. For more information see Chapter 4, "Configuring and Backing Up Using RMAN."

15. C. Use the `alter database enable block change tracking using file` command, followed by the path and filename in single quotes, to create the block change tracking file. For more information, see Chapter 4, "Configuring and Backing Up Using RMAN."

16. C. You would use the `backup as compressed backupset database plus archivelog all` command to back up your database. Of course, the command is so long-winded that the war would be over by the time you finished typing it all in. For more information, see Chapter 4, "Configuring and Backing Up Using RMAN."

17. B, C, D. The RMAN recovery catalog provides a centralized location for all RMAN-related metadata. Thus it makes centralized reporting much easier. Additionally, you can store scripts in the recovery catalog for use across all databases that use RMAN. For more information, see Chapter 5, "Using the RMAN Recovery Catalog."

18. B. The RMAN virtual private catalog provides the ability to allow users granular access to RMAN recovery catalog records based on database name. Thus, specific users can see only records they are allowed to see. For more information, see Chapter 5, "Using the RMAN Recovery Catalog."

19. A. You can back up any database without connecting to the recovery catalog, including the recovery catalog database. In fact, you can back up the recovery catalog database while connected to the recovery catalog. For more information, see Chapter 5, "Using the RMAN Recovery Catalog."

20. E. The `register database` command is used to indicate that the target database should be registered in the recovery catalog. For more information, see Chapter 5, "Using the RMAN Recovery Catalog."

21. C. You would first need to start the database with the `startup nomount` command from the RMAN prompt. Then you restore the spfile using the `restore spfile from autobackup` command. For more information, see Chapter 6, "Recovering Databases with RMAN."

22. C. You would first need to restore the database to the correct point in time with the `restore database` command. You would include the `until time` parameter to indicate what point in time you want to restore to. You then recover the database with the `recover database` command, which will apply the appropriate incremental backups and archived redo logs. Again, you use the `until time` command to indicate the time to recover to. Finally, you would open the database with the `alter database open resetlogs` command. For more information, see Chapter 6, "Recovering Databases with RMAN."

23. A. The `until change` option of the restore command provides the ability to restore the database to a specific SCN. For more information, see Chapter 6, "Recovering Databases with RMAN."

24. B, C, D, E. The recover command will recover the needed incremental backup and archived redo logs from backup sets for recovery purposes. The recover command will then apply the incremental backups and archived redo logs as needed to recover the database. For more information, see Chapter 6, "Recovering Databases with RMAN."

25. B. An obsolete backup set is one that has exceeded the retention criteria. As a result, it is subject to automatic removal in the flash recovery area. For more information, see Chapter 7, "Reporting, Monitoring, and Tuning with RMAN."

26. C. An expired backup is one that is missing one or more physical backup set pieces. The `list expired backup` command lists these types of backups. For more information, see Chapter 7, "Reporting, Monitoring, and Tuning with RMAN."

27. C. The `catalog` command is used to catalog backup set pieces or image copies in both the control file and the recovery catalog so RMAN can use those backup set pieces or image copies. For more information, see Chapter 7, "Reporting, Monitoring, and Tuning with RMAN."

28. D. There is no `report user` command. For more information, see Chapter 7, "Reporting, Monitoring, and Tuning with RMAN."

29. A, D. Active database duplication takes place using network connections between the target database and the auxiliary database instance. Backup-based duplication requires that the RMAN backup set pieces be available on the server where the duplicate database will be created. For more information, see Chapter 8, "Performing Oracle Advanced Recovery."

30. A, B. The SYSTEM and UNDO tablespaces will always be restored during a tablespace point-in-time recovery operation. For more information, see Chapter 8, "Performing Oracle Advanced Recovery."

31. A, B. Database duplication (either backup-based or active) requires that you create the parameter files for the auxiliary database instance and have the auxiliary database instance started in NOMOUNT mode. For more information, see Chapter 8, "Performing Oracle Advanced Recovery."

32. A. You use the recover tablespace command to perform a tablespace point-in-time recovery. For more information, see Chapter 8, "Performing Oracle Advanced Recovery."

33. E. Only the Flashback Table option recovers a table to a previous point in time. The other options allow viewing of past states of the data (B, C, D) or restoration from the Recycle Bin (A), but they do not recover a table to a previous point in time. For more information, see Chapter 9, "Understanding Flashback Technology."

34. D. A Flashback Drop option would allow you to restore the table from the Recycle Bin. Although A, B, and C may all be valid recovery options, they are much less desirable than Flashback Drop. E is an invalid option altogether. For more information, see Chapter 9, "Understanding Flashback Technology."

35. A, C, D. Shared server requests and remote DESCRIBE and COMMIT operations are not captured in a workload. For more information, see Chapter 10, "Diagnosing the Database and Managing Performance."

36. B, C. Option A is incorrect because a gap in archive logs does not automatically end the recovery. RMAN will search forward for uncorrupted newer blocks; if RMAN finds one, it will continue with the restore and recovery operation. RMAN will check the flashback logs for uncorrupted copies of the block before it checks the backups. Option D is incorrect because the database must be in ARCHIVELOG mode. For more information, see Chapter 10, "Diagnosing the Database and Managing Performance."

37. E. A good starting point is to use approximately 20 percent of the available memory for the PGA and approximately 80 percent for the SGA. For more information, see Chapter 11, "Managing Database Resources."

38. B. Since you're running short on time, extend the time-out for the session that's in jeopardy and fix the space problem. Don't put the transaction at risk while you try to find free space and run the commands, and don't kill the transaction—unless you know that the space condition and extended suspend has caused other issues. For more information, see Chapter 11, "Managing Database Resources."

39. E. A schedule is enabled by default. The others are disabled by default. For more information, see Chapter 12, "Using the Scheduler to Automate Tasks."

40. C. Since we've established that the RAC is not performance constrained, option A is not valid—if the resource group were not able to obtain adequate CPU, this might be a valid answer. Option B is not correct because service affinity guarantees that if one instance in the service is available, the Scheduler will attempt to use it to run the job. If there is no service or instance affinity, the Scheduler will attempt to balance the load across surviving nodes. For more information, see Chapter 12, "Using the Scheduler to Automate Tasks."

41. F. The NLS_LANGUAGE parameter specifies the default sorting sequence for character data. For more information, see Chapter 13, "Implementing Globalization Support."

42. A, B, C. The NLS_TERRITORY parameter specifies conventions for local currency symbol, ISO currency symbol, dual currency symbol, credit/debit symbols, ISO week flag, and the list separator. Option D is incorrect because the default first day of the week is specified; the first day of the month is the 1st, not a specific day of the week. For more information, see Chapter 13, "Implementing Globalization Support."

Using Oracle ASM

ORACLE DATABASE 11g: ADMINISTRATION II EXAM OBJECTIVES COVERED IN THIS CHAPTER:

✓ **Database Architecture and ASM**

   ▪ Describe Automatic Storage Management (ASM)

   ▪ Set up initialization parameter files for ASM and database instances

   ▪ Start up and shut down ASM instances

   ▪ Administer ASM diskgroups

Automatic Storage Management (ASM) provides a centralized way to manage Oracle Database disk storage. The Oracle Database 11g OCP exam will test your knowledge of ASM, and thus ASM is the first topic we will tackle in this book.

In this chapter, we will discuss what ASM is, how to configure an ASM instance, how to manage an ASM instance, and finally, how to use ASM from within an Oracle database. As is true in the rest of this book, we will conclude with a review of the chapter, and we will tell you, in the section "Exam Essentials," what you need to know about ASM for the exam. Finally, we will present chapter review questions and answers so you can determine whether you have gained sufficient knowledge of ASM to pass the Oracle Database 11g OCP exam.

On with the show!

Exam objectives are subject to change at any time without prior notice and at Oracle's sole discretion. Please visit Oracle's Training and Certification website (http://www.oracle.com/education/certification/) for the most current exam-objectives listing.

What Is ASM?

ASM is designed to simplify Oracle database storage administration. Database environments have become more and more complex, with large numbers of (and larger) datafiles, storage area networks (SANs), and high-availability requirements. ASM is somewhat like a logical volume manager, allowing you to reduce the management of Oracle files into ASM disk groups. It also provides redundancy configurations, rebalancing operations, and, when installed on top of clusterware, the ability to share database-related files.

ASM stores files in *disk groups*, which are logical entities made up of one or more physical disk drives. ASM is good for more than just storing database datafiles. In an ASM instance, you can store database datafiles, online redo logs, archived redo logs, backup files, and data-pump dumpfiles as well as change-tracking files and control files of one or several Oracle databases, though these databases and the ASM instance must have affinity to a given machine or cluster. ASM also provides the ability to locate the flash recovery area on an ASM disk group, so your backups to disk can be made to ASM.

Here are some features of ASM:

- Automatic software data striping (RAID-0)
- Load balancing across physical disks
- Software RAID-1 data redundancy with double or triple mirrors
- Elimination of fragmentation
- Simplification of file management via support for Oracle Managed Files (OMF)
- Ease of maintenance

ASM fits perfectly into a Real Application Clusters (RAC) environment, but you can use ASM in a non-RAC environment too. In the following sections we will cover these ASM-related topics:

- The ASM instance
- Configuring ASM disks
- Accessing ASM from the database
- Managing ASM
- ASM data dictionary views

You should be aware of a few ASM limitations:

- ASM limits you to 63 disk groups in a given storage system. A disk group is a logical storage entity that is made up of one or more physical disks (we discuss adding ASM disk groups later in this chapter).
- You can have a maximum of 10,000 ASM disks in a given storage system.
- Each ASM disk can be a maximum of 4 petabytes (PB) in size.
- Each ASM instance can manage up to 40 exabytes of storage.
- Each disk group can contain up to one million files.
- Maximum file sizes vary by the type of disk group:
    - External-redundancy disk group: 140PB maximum file size
    - Normal-redundancy disk group: 42PB maximum file size
    - High-redundancy disk group: 15PB maximum file size

Working with the ASM Instance

Driving ASM is the *ASM instance*, which is a separate instance from any database instance. The ASM instance is mounted but never open like an Oracle database. It is, essentially, just a bunch of programs (daemons) running. You will create only one ASM instance per node. You can use the *Oracle Database Configuration Assistant (DBCA)* to create the ASM instance for you, or you can choose to create the ASM instance yourself.

Real World Scenario

Using ASM in the Real World

If you are an Oracle database administrator, ASM will very much be on your mind if you have to deal with Oracle database clustering (RAC). Early on in the architecting process, you will have to decide how to store shared files because RAC depends on sharing of database datafiles among the different nodes of the cluster.

You have several options, including shared raw devices and vendor-supplied products. Another option is ASM sitting on top of Oracle Clusterware. This combination can often provide a less-expensive solution over the vendor-supplied options and is easier to manage than raw disk storage. ASM and Clusterware are very popular options, and it is likely you will encounter them in your Oracle career.

One very positive thing, from a business point of view, is that ASM is included as part of your Oracle database license. This makes Oracle Clusterware/ASM an attractive alternative to products from other vendors that charge extra for their clustering solutions.

At one location we are familiar with, the move to ASM was cautious but direct. Oracle Clusterware was installed and ASM was sitting on top. All new Oracle RAC installs started using ASM instead of shared raw disk partitions. The flash recovery area (FRA) was also moved to ASM. Older RAC databases were moved to ASM over time, and now all clustered databases are using ASM.

We also note that Oracle's future direction calls for the elimination of raw devices for storage of database datafiles. This will make movement to an ASM solution even more attractive.

Creating the ASM Instance

In the following sections, we will review how to create an ASM instance. First we will cover creating the ASM instance with the Oracle Database Configuration Assistant. Then we will cover how to manually create an ASM instance.

Creating the ASM Instance with the DBCA

The DBCA is a Java-based tool that you can use to create or remove Oracle databases. Fortunately for us, it can also be used to create or remove ASM instances. You can create the ASM instance at any time, regardless of whether a database already exists. In Exercise 1.1, you will see how to create an ASM instance.

EXERCISE 1.1

Creating an ASM Instance with the DBCA.

To create the ASM instance with the DBCA, do the following:

1. Start the Oracle DBCA.

2. The DBCA presents a list of options for you to choose from. Select Configure Automatic Storage Management and click Next.

3. The DBCA then prompts you for the SYS password for the new ASM instance to be created. Enter the password for the SYS account.

4. Oracle then creates the ASM instance. A new window appears giving you the option to create new disk groups. You can choose to create disk groups (we will cover that shortly) or you can click Finish to complete the ASM instillation.

5. The name of the resulting instance will be +ASM. You can log into the ASM instance from SQL*Plus, as shown in this example:

```
C:\Documents and Settings\Robert>Set ORACLE_SID=+ASM
C:\Documents and Settings\Robert>Sqlplus sys/Robert as sysasm
SQL*Plus: Release 11.1.0.6.0 - Production on Mon Jul 14 19:55:33 2008
Copyright (c) 1982, 2007, Oracle.  All rights reserved.
Connected to:
Oracle Database 11g Enterprise Edition Release 11.1.0.6.0 - Production
With the Partitioning, OLAP and Data Mining options
SQL> select instance_name from v$instance;
INSTANCE_NAME
----------------
+asm
```

 When we logged into the ASM instance, we did so using the SYSASM role. This role is much like the SYSDBA role when logging into a database and should be used when logging into an ASM instance for administrative purposes.

Creating the ASM Instance Manually

Manual creation of an ASM instance is fairly straightforward. If you have ever manually created a database, then manually creating an ASM instance should be easy for you. To manually create an ASM instance, you would follow these steps:

1. Create directories for the ASM instance.

2. Create the instance parameter file.

3. Perform any Microsoft Windows–specific configuration.

4. Start the ASM instance.

5. Create the ASM server parameter file (spfile).

Let's look at each of these steps in a bit more detail.

Step 1: Creating Directories for the ASM Instance

An ASM instance is almost always called +ASM. An exception exists in RAC environments where the ASM instance will be called +ASM1, +ASM2, and so on. Create the admin directories for the instance using Oracle's OFA standards. In the following examples, we assume that you have defined the ORACLE_BASE parameter.

The following are examples of the commands you might issue:

For Unix

```
mkdir -p $ORACLE_BASE/admin/+ASM/bdump
mkdir -p $ORACLE_BASE/admin/+ASM/cdump
mkdir -p $ORACLE_BASE/admin/+ASM/hdump
mkdir -p $ORACLE_BASE/admin/+ASM/pfile
mkdir -p $ORACLE_BASE/admin/+ASM/udump
```

For Microsoft Windows

```
mkdir %ORACLE_BASE%\admin\+ASM\bdump
mkdir %ORACLE_BASE%\admin\+ASM\cdump
mkdir %ORACLE_BASE%\admin\+ASM\hdump
mkdir %ORACLE_BASE%\admin\+ASM\pfile
mkdir %ORACLE_BASE%\admin\+ASM\udump
```

Of course, you could use a tool such as Windows Explorer to create the directories.

Step 2: Creating the Instance Parameter File

The ASM instance will require a *parameter file*, just as any other Oracle instances does. The number of parameters that you will need to set for an ASM instance is relativity small, so the parameter file typically is smaller than that of a normal Oracle database. You will also find that some parameters that you will set are unique to ASM. Let's look at a sample parameter file, and then we will discuss ASM-specific parameters and what they are for.

First, here is an example ASM parameter file:

```
###############################################
# ASM Parameter File - Unix
# Note, the ASM_DISKGROUPS parameter is commented out for now.
# ASM_DISKGROUPs='DISK GROUP_ROB1'
###############################################
```

```
# Diagnostics and Statistics
###########################################
background_dump_dest=/u01/app/oracle/admin/+ASM/bdump
core_dump_dest=/u01/app/oracle/admin/+ASM/cdump
user_dump_dest=/u01/app/oracle/admin/+ASM/udump
###########################################
# Miscellaneous
# Of course - set compatible to your version of Oracle
###########################################
instance_type=asm
compatible=11.1.0.6.0
remote_login_passwordfile=exclusive
```

Note the following Oracle parameters that are specific to ASM instances:

- INSTANCE_TYPE: Used only with an ASM instance, this parameter indicated to Oracle that this is an ASM instance. The default value is RDBMS, which indicates the instance is an Oracle database instance. This parameter is not dynamic and is the only mandatory parameter in an ASM instance.

- ASM_DISKSTRING: This parameter indicates where Oracle should search for disk devices to be used by ASM. We will discuss this parameter in more detail later in this section. This parameter can be dynamically changed.

- ASM_DISKGROUPS: This parameter lists ASM disk groups that ASM should mount when it is started. You can also use the alter diskgroup all mount command to cause these disk groups to be mounted. This parameter can be dynamically changed.

- ASM_POWER_LIMIT: This parameter controls the rate at which ASM can rebalance disks by increasing or decreasing the degree of parallelism used. Lower values will slow rebalancing but will also result in less of an IO impact by those operations. Higher values may speed up rebalancing by parallelizing the rebalance operation. The default is 1, and this is typically sufficient. This parameter can be set dynamically.

Did you notice that we did not include any of the memory settings (for example, SHARED_POOL_SIZE or DB_CACHE_SIZE) in this parameter file? While ASM does allocate memory, the default settings for the memory parameters are often quite enough.

Step 3: Performing Any Microsoft Windows–Specific Configuration

If you are running in a Windows environment, you will need to create the ASM service with the oradim utility. Here is an example of this operation:

```
C:Oracle\> oradim -new -asmsid +ASM -syspwd my_password
    -pfile C:\oracle\product\11.1.0.6\admin\+ASM\pfile\init.ora -spfile
    -startmode manual -shutmode immediate
```

Note in this example that we made the start mode manual so the service will not start automatically when the system is started. You will want to configure the service startup as required by your system.

Step 4: Starting the ASM Instance

You are now ready to start the Oracle ASM instance. Note that until you have added a disk group, you will get an error when the ASM instance is started. This is expected. In Exercise 1.2, you will see how to start an ASM instance.

EXERCISE 1.2

Starting an ASM Instance

Starting an ASM instance is quite easy, as shown in this exercise.

1. The name of the resulting instance will be +ASM. You can log into the ASM instance from SQL*Plus, as shown in this example:

```
C:\Documents and Settings\Robert>Set ORACLE_SID=+ASM
C:\Documents and Settings\Robert>Sqlplus sys/Robert as sysasm
SQL*Plus: Release 11.1.0.6.0 - Production on Mon Jul 14 19:55:33 2008
Copyright (c) 1982, 2007, Oracle.  All rights reserved.
Connected to:
Oracle Database 11g Enterprise Edition Release 11.1.0.6.0 – Production
With the Partitioning, OLAP and Data Mining options
```

2. Now, start the ASM instance with the startup command:

```
SQL> startup
ASM instance started
Total System Global Area    83886080 bytes
Fixed Size                   1247420 bytes
Variable Size               57472836 bytes
ASM Cache                   25165824 bytes
ORA-15110: no disk groups mounted
```

You will get an ORA-15110 error, but this is no concern at this time. This error is expected because you have not yet created any ASM disk groups. We will cover the creation and management of ASM disk groups later in this chapter.

Step 5: Creating the ASM Spfile

Having started the ASM instance, create the instance spfile from the pfile created in step 2. Here is an example:

```
create spfile from pfile='/u01/opt/oracle/admin/+ASM/pfile/init.ora';
```

Managing the ASM Instance

Management of the ASM instance is typically done from the command-line prompt. In the following sections, we will discuss these topics:

- Starting and stopping the ASM instance
- ASM processes
- ASM disk discovery
- Redundancy, striping, and templates
- Adding an ASM disk group
- Dropping an ASM disk group
- Altering an ASM disk group
- Using the ASMCMD command-line utility

Starting and Stopping the ASM Instance

Starting and stopping the ASM instance is pretty straightforward and much like starting and stopping an Oracle database. Oracle knows that you are starting an ASM instance, so it knows that when you issue the `startup` command, it needs to do something a bit different from what it would with a normal database. Exercise 1.2, shown earlier in this chapter, walks you through starting an ASM instance.

Shutting down the ASM instance is just as easy. A `shutdown immediate`, `shutdown abort`, or just a plain `shutdown` will do fine. If you execute a normal or immediate `shutdown` command on an ASM instance, that shutdown will fail if there is any database using that ASM instance. An error will be returned and the ASM instance will stay up. As a result, before you shut down the ASM instance, you will need to shut down all databases using that ASM instance.

You can perform a `shutdown abort` on the ASM instance. This will cause the ASM instance to shut down immediately and all of the associated databases will be shut down in an inconsistent state. This will require instance recovery when the databases are restarted, which can increase the time it takes to reopen the database. Oracle recommends that you not use the `shutdown abort` command when stopping an ASM instance.

ASM Processes

After you start your ASM instance, you will find that several of the Oracle processes you are acquainted with will be running, such as PMON and DBWR. Additional ASM processes will be started too. These processes include the following:

- The ARB*n* process, used to perform disk group rebalance operations. There may be one or more of these processes running.
- The ASMB process manages ASM storage and provides statistics.
- The GMON process maintains disk membership in ASM disk groups.
- The KATE process performs proxy I/O to ASM metadata files when a disk is offlined.

- The MARK process is responsible for marking ASM allocation units as stale following a missed write to an offline disk.

- The RBAL process runs in both database and ASM instances. RBAL is responsible for performing a global open of ASM disks in normal databases. RBAL coordinates rebalance activity for disk groups in ASM instances.

ASM Disk Discovery

ASM disk discovery is the first step to setting up an ASM disk group. In this section, we will cover configuring the ASM_DISKSTRING parameter, which helps with ASM disk discovery, and then we will discuss the topic of ASM disk discovery in general.

Setting the *ASM_DISKSTRING* Parameter

When you configured the parameter file for your ASM instance, you configured a parameter called ASM_DISKSTRING. This parameter contains the paths that Oracle will use to try to find the various candidate disks available for ASM's use. The process of ASM finding disks in the ASM_DISKSTRING path is known as *discovery*.

You may not need to set ASM_DISKSTRING. ASM_DISKSTRING has a number of different default values depending on the platform you are using. Table 1.1 lists the platform-specific default values (these will be set if ASM_DISKSTRING is set to a NULL value only).

TABLE 1.1   Default ASM Disk String

Platform Name	Default ASM_DISKSTRING Value
AIX	/dev/rhdisk*
HP-UX	/dev/rdsk/*
Linux	/dev/raw/*
Mac OS X	/dev/rdisk*s*s1
Solaris	/dev/rdsk/*
Tru64UNIX	/dev/rdisk/*

You can have multiple locations in the ASM_DISKSTRING parameter (we will provide an example of this in just a moment). If you insert a ? placeholder at the beginning of the string, Oracle will expand that out to represent the location of ORACLE_HOME in the parameter values. The ASM_DISKSTRING can be dynamically altered, which is nice if your friendly system administrator adds some storage to your system that you want Oracle to be able to use. If you happen to change ASM_DISKSTRING dynamically and the new disk path is not present, it will revert to the old disk path. Removing an existing disk path, when that disk path is in use, will result in a failure of the command.

Another thing to consider when determining how to configure the ASM_DISKSTRING parameter is performance. Leaving this parameter set to NULL, and thus taking the Oracle default, will often be sufficient. However, if you set ASM_DISKSTRING using a more restrictive set of parameters, you may find that discovery of disks will be faster. For example, using the default Linux setting of /dev/raw/* will result in ASM scanning the entire /dev/raw file system structure (it does not search subfolders). If you have a large number of devices in this structure, this may take some time. If, however, your disk devices in this structure are all prefixed with the word *raw* (raw1, raw2, raw3, and so on), then setting the ASM_DISKSTRING to /dev/raw/raw* could reduce the time it take ASM to perform discovery and improve performance of the startup of the ASM instance.

Something you will see common to all ASM_DISKSTRING parameters is the use of the asterisk. The asterisk is required when defining the ASM_DISKSTRING parameter. Here are some examples of setting the ASM_DISKSTRING parameter. In this first example, ASM will look for disks in devices when we create disk groups:

```
Alter system set ASM_DISKSTRING='/devices/*';
```

In the next example, we are pointing ASM_DISKSTRING to ORACLE_HOME/disks:

```
Alter system set ASM_DISKSTRING='?/disks/*';
```

In this example, we are pointing ASM_DISKSTRING to two different locations:

```
Alter system set ASM_DISKSTRING='?/disks/d1/*,?/disks/d21/*';
```

We could also use some adjunctive regular expressionish–type extensions and perform the allocation this way:

```
Alter system set ASM_DISKSTRING='?/disks/d[12]/*';
```

ASM Disk Discovery on Instance Start

When the ASM instance is started, it will use the paths listed in the ASM_DISKSTRING parameter and discover the disks that are available. These disks can then be added to ASM disk groups that we will discuss in the next section. Once discovery is complete and the ASM instance is open, you can review the disks discovered by looking at the V$ASM_DISK view, as shown in this example:

```
column path format a20
set lines 132
set pages 50
select path, group_number group_#, disk_number disk_#, mount_status,
header_status, state, total_mb, free_mb
from v$asm_disk
order by group_number;
```

PATH	GROUP_#	DISK_#	MOUNT_S	HEADER_STATU	STATE	TOTAL_MB	FREE_MB
/dev/raw/raw4	0	1	CLOSED	FOREIGN	NORMAL	39	0
/dev/raw/raw5	0	0	CLOSED	FOREIGN	NORMAL	39	0
/dev/raw/raw3	0	2	CLOSED	FOREIGN	NORMAL	39	0
/dev/raw/raw6	0	2	CLOSED	CANIDATE	NORMAL	2048	2048
ORCL:ASM01_004	1	3	CACHED	MEMBER	NORMAL	34212	30436
ORCL:ASM01_005	1	4	CACHED	MEMBER	NORMAL	34212	30408
ORCL:ASM01_006	1	5	CACHED	MEMBER	NORMAL	34212	30420
ORCL:ASM01_007	1	6	CACHED	MEMBER	NORMAL	34212	30297
ORCL:ASM01_008	1	7	CACHED	MEMBER	NORMAL	34212	30507
ORCL:ASM01_009	1	8	CACHED	MEMBER	NORMAL	34212	30404
ORCL:ASM01_010	1	9	CACHED	MEMBER	NORMAL	34212	30509
ORCL:ASM01_011	1	10	CACHED	MEMBER	NORMAL	34212	30449
ORCL:ASM01_012	1	11	CACHED	MEMBER	NORMAL	34212	30340
ORCL:ASM01_013	1	12	CACHED	MEMBER	NORMAL	34212	30357

In this view, you see that there are three disks that are not assigned to any group (those with GROUP_# set to 0). These are unassigned disks that ASM has discovered but that have not been assigned to a disk group. Note the mount status of CLOSED on those three disks, which also indicates that the disk is not being accessed by ASM. The HEADER_STATUS of FOREIGN indicates that these disks contain data already and are owned by some process other than ASM (in this case, these are voting disks for a RAC). If the HEADER_STATUS says CANIDATE, as with /dev/raw/raw6, then we could add this disk to an ASM disk group.

Notice that most of the disks have a MOUNT_STATUS of CACHED and a HEADER_STATUS of MEMBER. This means that the disk is currently part of an ASM disk group (which we will discuss more in the next section).

There are some cases where the V$ASM_DISK view will not report any disks. For example, on our Windows XP system there are no raw disks to discover, so the V$ASM_DISK view will simply be blank. This is not a problem because we can use an existing file system as a location for an ASM disk. We will discuss that in the next section as we show you how to add disk groups to ASM.

Here are some things to be aware of with regard to ASM disk discovery:

- ASM can discover no more than 10,000 disks. If you have more than that, ASM will discover only the first 10,000 disks. This can occur when your ASM disk string is not sufficiently restrictive and the directory that you are searching in has a number of raw devices but many of them are not going to be assigned to ASM.

- ASM will not discover any disk that contains an operating-system partition table.

- ASM may discover disks that already contain Oracle data (as in our previous example with the voting disks).

Redundancy, Striping, and Other ASM Topics

When configuring ASM disk groups, you need to consider recoverability, performance, and other attributes. We will first cover recoverability by discussing the concept of redundancy. We will then discuss striping of ASM disk groups and ASM disk templates. Then we'll discuss ASM disk group attributes, ASM fast disk resync features, and ASM preferred mirror read features. We will end this section with a discussion of ASM Allocation Unit (AU) size and extents in ASM.

Redundancy

When configuring an ASM disk group, you can use one of three different *ASM redundancy* setting options to protect the data in your disk group:

- *Normal*: Typically employs two-way mirroring by default and thus requires allocation of two failure groups.

- *High*: Typically employs three-way mirroring by default and thus requires allocation of three failure groups.

- *External*: Does not employ any mirroring. This setting is typically used when the disk group is being assigned to an external disk that is attached to some device that already employs some disk redundancy.

The Costs of Redundancy

Keep in mind that there is a cost to everything, and this includes redundancy. If you have two 100GB ASM disks that you will be assigning to an ASM disk group, you will be able to effectively use only 100GB of overall space if you use normal redundancy, because each disk will have to go into an individual failure group. If you were to use external redundancy, you would be able to use all 200GB (at a cost, of course, of loss of protection).

Redundancy is supported by one or more *failgroups* (or failure groups) assigned to the ASM disk group when it is created. If you are using external redundancy, you typically would just have one failure group. If you are using the Normal redundancy setting, then the ASM disk group typically will need two failure groups. Each failure group represents a logical allocation of one or more disks to the ASM disk group and provides for mirroring within that disk group. Thus, when you create an ASM disk group, you might have one disk assigned to failure group 1 and one disk assigned to failure group 2. This way your data is protected from failure.

When you're using ASM mirroring, ASM will allocate an extent on a disk that becomes the primary copy (one of the failure groups) and then allocate copies of that extent to the mirrored copies (the other failure groups). When you create a disk group, you can indicate which disk goes in which failure group or you can let Oracle decide for you.

When you define the redundancy setting for a disk group, you are defining things such as what kind of striping occurs and whether the data will be mirrored. These attributes are defined based on which template you have assigned to the ASM disk group. By default, when you create a disk group, Oracle will assign it the default template setting. You can optionally assign another ASM template to a given disk group (We discuss templates later in this chapter).

Table 1.2 gives you some guidance about the redundancy-related settings defined within the default template.

TABLE 1.2   Default-Template Redundancy Settings

Template Name	Striping	Mirroring with Normal Redundancy	Mirroring with High Redundancy	Mirroring with Extended Redundancy
Control file	Fine	Three-way mirroring	Three-way mirroring	No mirroring
Datafile	Coarse	Two-way mirroring	Three-way mirroring	No mirroring
Onlinelog	Fine	Two-way mirroring	Three-way mirroring	No mirroring
Archivelog	Coarse	Two-way mirroring	Three-way mirroring	No mirroring
Tempfile	Coarse	Two-way mirroring	Three-way mirroring	No mirroring
Backupset	Coarse	Two-way mirroring	Three-way mirroring	No mirroring
Parameterfile	Coarse	Two-way mirroring	Three-way mirroring	No mirroring
Dataguardconfig	Coarse	Two-way mirroring	Three-way mirroring	No mirroring
Flashback	Fine	Two-way mirroring	Three-way mirroring	No mirroring
Changetracking	Coarse	Two-way mirroring	Three-way mirroring	No mirroring
Dumpset	Coarse	Two-way mirroring	Three-way mirroring	No mirroring
Xtransport	Coarse	Two-way mirroring	Three-way mirroring	No mirroring
Autobackup	Coarse	Two-way mirroring	Three-way mirroring	No mirroring

Default ASM Template Redundancy Settings

So, if you create a disk group with normal redundancy using the default template and you put datafiles on it, the datafile template would be used by default. In this case, a datafile would use two-way mirroring and coarse striping (see the section "Striping"). This means you would have to allocate at least two disks to an ASM disk group when it was created, one assigned to a different failure group. We will discuss failure groups later in this chapter.

Dealing with ASM Disk Loss

If you lose an ASM disk, then one of two situations will occur. First, ASM will take the lost/damaged disk offline and then automatically drop it. ASM will attempt a rebalance operation to maintain redundancy, using the mirror copies as required. The disk group and its associated data will remain available during this time.

If the disk group cannot be rebalanced, then ASM will take the whole disk group offline and the data in that disk group will not be available until the damaged disk is restored and the disks can be rebalanced.

Striping

Table 1.2 includes a *striping* column. There are two values there, fine and coarse. This refers to the stripe size that ASM applies to the disks that the disk groups are assigned to. If fine striping is selected, the ASM will use a 128KB stripe size. If coarse is selected, then Oracle uses the AU size of the disk group for the stripe size.

Templates

When you create an ASM disk group, Oracle will assign a default *template* to that disk group (see Table 1.2). A template is simply a named collection of attributes. For example, if you create a disk group using the default template and then create datafiles in that disk group, the datafile template will define the redundancy and striping for that data.

There may be cases where you want to define your own template for a disk group. You will need to first create the disk group and then alter it using the add template parameter of the alter diskgroup commands, as shown in this example:

```
CREATE DISKGROUP sp_dgroup2 NORMAL REDUNDANCY
failgroup diskcontrol1 DISK 'c:\oracle\asm_disk\_file_disk3' NAME file_diska1
failgroup diskcontrol2 DISK 'c:\oracle\asm_disk\_file_disk4' NAME file_diskb1;
ALTER DISKGROUP sp_dgroup2 ADD TEMPLATE new_template ATTRIBUTES (mirror);
```

After the mirror template has been added, you can create files in that disk group using the new template. When you add a template to a disk group, the template cannot be retroactively applied to files already in that disk group. As a result, you will need to use RMAN to back up and then restore files that already exist in the disk group in order for them to take on the attributes of the new template.

You can see the templates associated with a given disk group by querying the V$ASM_TEMPLATE view, as shown in this example:

```
SQL> select * from v$asm_template
  2  where group_number=2;
GROUP_NUMBER ENTRY_NUMBER REDUND STRIPE S NAME
------------ ------------ ------ ------ - --------------------
           2            0 MIRROR COARSE Y PARAMETERFILE
           2            1 MIRROR COARSE Y DUMPSET
           2            2 HIGH   FINE   Y CONTROLFILE
           2            3 MIRROR COARSE Y ARCHIVELOG
           2            4 MIRROR FINE   Y ONLINELOG
           2            5 MIRROR COARSE Y DATA FILE
           2            6 MIRROR COARSE Y TEMPFILE
           2            7 MIRROR COARSE Y BACKUPSET
           2            8 MIRROR COARSE Y AUTOBACKUP
           2            9 MIRROR COARSE Y XTRANSPORT
           2           10 MIRROR COARSE Y CHANGETRACKING
           2           11 MIRROR FINE   Y FLASHBACK
           2           12 MIRROR COARSE Y DATAGUARDCONFIG
           2           13 MIRROR COARSE N NEW_TEMPLATE
```

In this output, you can see that our new template (new_template) has been created and is ready for use. You can drop a template with the alter diskgroup command using the drop template parameter, as shown in this example:

```
ALTER DISKGROUP sp_dgroup2
DROP TEMPLATE new_template;
```

And you can alter a user-defined template with the alter template parameter of the alter diskgroup command. Notice in this example that we are actually changing one of the attributes of the default templates. You cannot drop the default templates, but you can modify them, as shown here:

```
ALTER DISKGROUP sp_dgroup2
ALTER TEMPLATE datafile
ATTRIBUTES (coarse);
```

ASM Disk Group Attributes

We have discussed ASM templates that define a set of attributes to the disk group assigned to them. Oracle Database 11g also allows you to define specific *disk group attributes*. Disk group attributes are set using the `attribute` clause of the `create diskgroup` and `alter diskgroup` commands. The following attributes can be set on a specific ASM disk group:

`Au_size`   This is the disk group allocation unit (AU) size. The value defaults to 1MB and can be set only when the disk group is created. You must modify the AU size of the disk group if you want the disk group to be able to hold larger amounts of data. A disk group with the default AU size will be able to grow to 35TB (normal redundancy). Increasing the AU size will significantly increase the maximum size of the disk group. The maximum AU size is 64MB.

`Compatible.rdbms`   Indicates the database version that the disk group is compatible with at a minimum (default is 10.1). This value should be equal to or greater than the compatibility parameter of the database(s) accessing the ASM disk group. This value cannot be rolled back once set.

`Compatible.asm`   Indicates the ASM instance version that the disk group is compatible with at a minimum (default is 10.1). `Compatible.asm` must always be set to a value equal to or greater than `compatible.rdbms`. Once `compatible.asm` is set for a disk group, it can not be rolled back to an earlier value.

`Disk_repair_time`   Indicates the length of time that the disk resync process should maintain change tracking before dropping an offline disk. The default for this parameter is 3.6 hours.

Disk group attributes can be viewed using the V$ASM_ATTRIBUTE view. You can see some examples of setting compatibility here:

```
Create diskgroup robert01 external redundancy
Disk '/oracle/asm/ASM_DISKGROUP_robert01.asm'
Attribute 'ccompatible.asm'='11.1.0';
Alter diskgroup robert01 set attribute 'DISK_REPAIR_TIME'='1200M';
Alter diskgroup robert01 set attribute 'compatible.asm'='11.1.0';
```

ASM Fast Disk Resync

The redundancy features of ASM make it possible for an ASM disk group to survive the loss of a disk associated with that disk group. Disk loss can result from a number of reasons, such as loss of controller cards, cable failures, or power-supply errors. In many cases, the disk itself is still intact. To allow for sufficient time to recover from disk failures that do not involve the actual failure of a disk, ASM provides the ASM *fast disk resync* feature.

By default, when a disk in an ASM disk group fails (including any associated infrastructure pieces), the disk will be taken offline automatically. The disk will be dropped some 3.6 hours later. As a result, you have only 3.6 hours by default to respond to a disk outage. If you correct the problem and the physical disk media is not corrupted, then ASM fast disk resync will quickly resynchronize the disk when it comes back online, correcting the problem very quickly. This type of resynchronization is much faster than rebuilding a newly added disk should the disk media be corrupted.

You can change the amount of time that Oracle will wait to automatically drop the disk by setting the disk_repair_time attribute (see the discussion on attributes earlier, in the section "ASM Disk group Attributes") for the individual disk groups using the alter diskgroup command, as shown in this example, where we set the disk_repair_time attribute to 18 hours:

```
Alter diskgroup dgroup1 set attribute 'disk_repair_time'='18h';
```

ASM Preferred Mirror Read

The ASM *preferred mirror read* feature allows you to define a primary set of disks that are the preferred disks to read from for a given instance. This is most prevalent when using RAC databases. In a RAC configuration, you could have two or more sets of disk arrays. Each disk array might be local to a given RAC instance. ASM preferred mirror read allows you to indicate which disk array is local to a specific RAC instance. As a result, it become the preferred disk set for the instance and thus is likely to be more performant.

The ASM preferred local disk is defined using the optional parameter asm_preferred_read_failure_groups.

ASM AU Size and Extents

ASM files are stored in disk groups. In each disk group, space is allocated in *extents*, and an extent consists of one or more units of space called *allocation units (AUs)*. Allocation units default to a size of 10MB and can be configured from 1 to 64MB at the time the disk group is created. Once the AU size has been determined for a given disk group, it cannot be changed.

To enable support for larger ASM datafiles, to reduce the memory overhead of large databases, and to improve file open and close operations, ASM uses a variable-extent sizing policy. Extents will be initially sized at the size of the AU (for the first 20,000 extents) of the ASM disk group in which the extent is created. The extent size will be increased to 8 times the AU size for the next 20,000 extents and then will increment to 64 times the AU size for subsequent extent allocations.

Adding an ASM Disk Group

We have now talked about discovering disks, and we have talked about templates, redundancy, and striping. Now we need to talk about actually creating a disk group. You use the create diskgroup command to create an ASM disk group. When you issue the command, you will assign the disk group its name, and you will add one or more discovered (unallocated) disks to that disk group. Here is an example of the use of the create diskgroup command:

```
CREATE DISKGROUP dgroup1 NORMAL REDUNDANCY
failgroup diskcontrol1 DISK
'/devices/diska1'
failgroup diskcontrol2 DISK
'/devices/diskb1';
```

In this case, we have created a disk group called dgroup1. It is using normal redundancy and the default template. Two named failure groups are assigned, diskcontrol1 and diskcontrol2. Each failure group represents one physical or logical disk unit, which has been discovered by ASM. Two separate disks and failure groups are required because of the normal redundancy. If we used high redundancy, we would need to add a third disk to the command, as shown here:

```
CREATE DISKGROUP dgroup1 HIGH REDUNDANCY
failgroup diskcontrol1 DISK
'/devices/diska1' NAME diska1
failgroup diskcontrol2 DISK
'/devices/diskb1' NAME diskb1
failgroup diskcontrol3 DISK
'/devices/diskc1' NAME diskc1;
```

You might have noticed the name clause in the create diskgroup command example earlier. You can also name the disks being assigned to the ASM disk group using the name clause of the create diskgroup command. Failure to use the name clause will result in each disk receiving its own system-default assigned name.

When you create an ASM disk group, Oracle will add that disk group to the ASM_DISKGROUPS parameter on the ASM instance only if you are using an spfile. If you are not using an spfile, you will need to manually add the disk group to the ASM_DISKGROUPS parameter. The ASM_DISKGROUPS parameter tells Oracle which disk groups it should mount when the ASM instance is started. You can see the ASM_DISKGROUPS parameter setting by using the show parameter command from SQL*Plus, as shown here:

```
SQL> show parameter ASM_DISKGROUPS
NAME                                 TYPE        VALUE
------------------------------------ ----------- -------------------------
ASM_DISKGROUPS                       string      COOKED_DGROUP1, SP_DGROUP2
```

If you do not add the disk group to the ASM_DISKGROUPS parameter, you will need to manually mount the disk group.

You might have noticed that each time we create a new disk group (and when we add new disks to a disk group), we give the disk a name. For example, here we create a new disk group called DGROUP1:

```
CREATE DISKGROUP dgroup1 EXTERNAL REDUNDANCY
failgroup diskcontrol1 DISK
'/oracle01/oradata/asm/disk group1.dsk' NAME dgroup1_0000;
```

You can reference the disk group and the disk name by joining the V$ASM_DISK and V$ASM_DISKGROUP views, as shown in this query:

```
select adg.name dg_name, ad.name fg_name, path
from v$asm_disk ad
right outer join v$ASM_DISKGROUP adg
on ad.group_number=adg.group_number
where adg.name='DGROUP1';
DG_NAME  FG_NAME         PATH
-------- --------------- ---------------------------------------
DGROUP1  DGROUP1_0000    /oracle01/oradata/asm/disk group1.dsk
```

 Real World Scenario

Why Tiered Storage?

Tiered database storage attempts to reduce the overall costs of disk storage in databases. When you configure ASM, you might want to consider configuring different disk groups for different kinds of tiered storage.

For example, suppose you work at Amalgamated General Consolidated. You have a new database that you are designing. You can choose from fast and expensive solid-state disks that costs $50 a gigabyte. Then there are the Fibre Channel disks that are a bit slower but only $30 a gigabyte. Finally, there are the slow SATA drives at $20 a gigabyte.

You can, of course, architect your 1 terabyte database with all solid-state disks at a cost of $50 million. It will be fast, no doubt, but is this the best choice for Amalgamated?

Amalgamated decides to analyze the needs of the database and determine if it can benefit from a tiered storage approach. If you determined that you need only 100GB of solid-state disk and that you could store the remaining 900GB on your $20 SATA drives, that would be cost savings of $27 million. That's quite a big savings.

This type of architecture requires that you architect physical database objects to sit across these layers using partitioning, creating the more heavily used partitions on better-performing disk; the infrequently used partitions can be moved over time to the cheaper/slower disks. This might take more time and effort, but in the end the dollar savings can be significant! Tiered storage is an idea that is very much taking off!

Dropping an ASM Disk Group

To remove an ASM disk group, you use the drop diskgroup command. By default, if any files exist in the disk group, ASM will not allow you to drop it unless you use the including contents clause. The drop diskgroup statement is synchronous in nature, so once the prompt returns, the deed is done ... no Recycle Bin here. When the drop diskgroup command is executed, ASM will unmount the disk from the ASM instance and write over all the ASM-related information on that disk. The ASM_DISKGROUPS parameter will also be changed if you are using an spfile. Here is an example of removing an ASM disk group with the drop diskgroup command:

```
Drop diskgroup sp_dgroup2;
```

If the ASM disk group has files in it, use this version:

```
Drop diskgroup sp_dgroup2 including contents;
```

Altering an ASM Disk Group

The alter diskgroup command is used to modify ASM disk groups. With the alter diskgroup command, you can do the following:

- Add disks to an ASM disk group
- Remove disks from an ASM disk group
- Add and drop disks from an ASM disk group
- Undrop disks from an ASM disk group
- Resize disks in a disk group
- Manually rebalance a disk group
- Mount and unmount disk groups
- Check the consistency of a disk group
- Create ASM disk group directories
- Manage ASM disk group directories

Adding Disks to an ASM Disk Group

As databases grow, you need to add disk space. The alter diskgroup command allows you to add disks to a given disk group to increase the amount of space available. Adding a disk to an existing disk group is easy with the alter diskgroup command, as shown in this example:

```
alter diskgroup cooked_dgroup1
add disk 'c:\oracle\asm_disk\_file_disk3'
name new_disk;
```

When you add a disk to a disk group, Oracle will start to rebalance the load on that disk group. Also, notice that in the preceding example we did not assign the disk to a specific failure group. As a result, each disk will be assigned to its own failure group when it's created. For example, when we added the disk to the cooked_dgroup1 disk group, a new failure group called cooked_dgroup1_0002 was created, as shown in this output:

```
SQL> select disk_number, group_number, failgroup from v$asm_disk;
DISK_NUMBER GROUP_NUMBER failgroup
----------- ------------ ------------------------------
          1            0
          0            1 DISKCONTROL1
          1            1 DISKCONTROL2
          2            1 COOKED_DGROUP1_0002
```

We can add a disk to an existing failure group by using the failgroup parameter, as shown in this example:

```
alter diskgroup cooked_dgroup1
add failgroup DISKCONTROL1
disk 'c:\oracle\asm_disk\_file_disk4'
name new_disk;
```

Removing Disks from an ASM Disk Group

The alter diskgroup command allows you to remove disks from an ASM disk group using the drop disk parameter. ASM will first rebalance the data on the disks to be dropped, assuming enough space is available. If insufficient space is available to move the data from the disk to be dropped to another disk, then an error will be raised. You can use the force parameter to force ASM to drop the disk, but this can result in data loss. Here is an example of dropping a disk from a disk group:

```
alter diskgroup cooked_dgroup1
drop disk 'c:\oracle\asm_disk\_file_disk4';
```

The alter diskgroup command also gives you the option to drop from a failure group all disks that are assigned to the disk group. Use the in failgroup keyword and then indicate the name of the failure group, as shown in this example:

```
alter diskgroup cooked_dgroup1
drop disks in failgroup diskcontrol1;
```

When you drop a disk from a disk group, the operation is asynchronous. Therefore, when the SQL prompt returns, this does not indicate that the operation has completed. To determine if the operation has completed, you will need to review the V$ASM_DISK view. When the disk drop is complete the column HEADER_STATUS will take on the value of FORMER, as shown in this example:

```
SQL> select disk_number, header_status from v$asm_disk;
DISK_NUMBER HEADER_STATU
----------- ------------
          0 FORMER
          1 FORMER
          1 MEMBER
          2 MEMBER
```

If the drop is not complete (the V$ASM_DISK column STATE will read dropping), you can check the V$ASM_OPERATION view and it will give you an idea of how long the operation is expected to take before it is complete. Here is an example query that will provide you with this information:

```
select group_number, operation, state, power, est_minutes
from v$asm_operation;
```

Adding and Dropping Disks from an ASM Disk Group

The alter diskgroup command will allow you to add and drop a disk from a disk group at the same time. Assuming you want to add a disk /dev/raw/raw6 and drop a disk called d2c, you could issue this command:

```
alter diskgroup mydisk group
add failgroup fg4 disk '/dev/raw/raw6/ name d2d
drop disk d2c;
```

Undropping Disks from an ASM Disk Group

You know you are having a bad day when you accidentally drop a disk from a disk group and you realize your mistake only after the drop operation has completed. Fortunately, this is not one of those mistakes that you cannot recover from. If you have accidentally dropped a disk, simply use the alter diskgroup command with the undrop disks parameter, as shown here:

```
alter diskgroup sp_dgroup2 undrop disks;
```

This will cancel the pending drop of disks from that disk group. You can not use this command to restore disks dropped if you dropped the entire disk group with the drop diskgroup command.

Resizing Disks in an ASM Disk Group

Sometimes when more space is needed, all a disk administrator needs to do is add that additional space to the disk devices that are being presented for ASM to use. If this is the case, you will want to indicate to ASM that it needs to update its metadata to represent the correct size of the disks it's using so you get the benefit of the additional space. This is accomplished using the `alter diskgroup` command with the `resize all` parameter, as shown in this example:

```
alter diskgroup cooked_dgroup1 resize all;
```

This command will query the operating system for the current size of all of the disk devices attached to the disk group and will automatically resize all disks in that disk group accordingly. You can indicate that a specific disk needs to be resized by including the disk name (from the NAME column in V$ASM_DISK), as shown in this example:

```
alter diskgroup cooked_dgroup1 resize disk FILE_DISKB1;
```

You can also resize an entire failure group at one time:

```
alter diskgroup cooked_dgroup1 resize disks in failgroup DISKCONTROL2;
```

Manually Rebalancing Disks Assigned to an ASM Disk Group

Manually rebalancing disks within ASM is typically not required since ASM will perform this operation automatically. However, in cases where you might want to have some more granular control over the disk-rebalance process, you can use the `alter diskgroup` command along with the `rebalance` parameter to manually rebalance ASM disks.

When we discuss rebalancing disks in ASM, we often discuss the power level that is assigned to that rebalance operation. Setting power with regard to a rebalance operation really defines the urgency of that operation with respect to other operations occurring on the system (for example, other databases or applications). When a rebalance operation occurs with a low power (for example, 1, the typical default), then that operation is not given a high priority on the system As a result, the rebalance operation can take some time. When a higher power setting is used (for example, 11, the maximum), the ASM is given higher priority. This can have an impact on other operations on the system. If you use a power of 0, this will have the effect of suspending the rebalance operation. You can set the default power limit for the ASM instance by changing the `asm_power_limit` parameter.

Here is an example of starting a manual rebalance of a disk group:

```
alter diskgroup cooked_dgroup1 rebalance power 5 wait;
```

In this example, you will notice that we used the `wait` parameter. This makes this rebalance operation synchronous for our session. Thus, when the SQL prompt returns, we know that the rebalance operation has completed. The default is nowait, which will cause the operation to be synchronous in nature. You can check the status of the rebalance operation using the V$ASM_OPERATION view during asynchronous rebalance operations. If you use the wait parameter and you want to convert the operation to an asynchronous operation, you can simply press Ctrl+C on most platforms and an error will be returned along with the SQL prompt. The rebalance operation will continue, however.

If you do not use the power parameter during a manual rebalance operation, or if an implicit rebalance operation is occurring (because you are dropping a disk, for example), you can affect the power of that rebalance operation by dynamically changing the ASM_POWER_LIMIT parameter to a higher value with the alter system command.

Finally, you can also use the rebalance parameter along with the power parameter when adding, dropping, or resizing disks within a disk group, as shown in this example:

```
alter diskgroup cooked_dgroup1 resize all rebalance power 5;
```

Manually Mounting and Unmounting an ASM Disk Group

If an ASM disk group is not assigned to the ASM_DISKGROUPS parameter, or if the disk group is unmounted for some other reason, you will need to mount the ASM disk group. You can use the alter diskgroup command with the mount clause to mount the disk group.

Additionally, if you need to dismount an ASM disk group, you can use the alter diskgroup command. Here are some examples:

```
alter diskgroup sp_dgroup2 dismount;
alter diskgroup sp_dgroup2 mount;
```

Note that when you dismount a disk group, that disk group will be automatically removed from the ASM_DISKGROUPS parameter if you are using an spfile. This means that when ASM is restarted, that disk group will not be remounted. If you are using a regular text parameter file, you will need to remove the disk group manually (assuming it's in the parameter file to begin with) or ASM will try to remount the disk group when the system is restarted.

Checking the Consistency of a Disk Group

On occasion you might wonder if there is some problem with an ASM disk group, and you will want to check the consistency of the ASM disk group metadata. This need might arise because of an error that occurs when the ASM instance is started or as the result of an Oracle database error that might be caused by some ASM corruption. To perform this check, simply use the alter diskgroup command with the check all parameter, as shown in this example:

```
alter diskgroup sp_dgroup2 check all;
```

When you execute the alter diskgroup check all command the results are written to the alert log of the instance. ASM will attempt to correct any errors that are detected.

Creating ASM Disk Group Directories

When you create an ASM disk group, it includes a system-generated directory structure for the ASM files that will be stored in that disk group. The system-generated directory structure takes on the following format, where disk_group is the root of the directory hierarchy:

```
+disk_group/database_name/object_type/ASM_file_name
```

The database name will be the name of the database that the data is associated with. The object_type is the type of object being stored (for example, datafile) and the ASM_file_name is the system-generated filename assigned to that ASM file.

ASM allows you to create your own directories within these predefined structures. This allows you to give alias names to the ASM files that you will create. This can make working with ASM files easier.

To create a directory structure, you use the alter diskgroup command with the add directory parameter, as shown in this example:

```
ALTER DISKGROUP cooked_dgroup1
ADD DIRECTORY '+cooked_dgroup1/stuff';
```

Managing ASM Disk Group Directories

The alter diskgroup command is also used to manage ASM disk group directories. If you want to drop an ASM disk group directory, simply use the drop directory clause of the alter diskgroup command, as shown in this example:

```
alter diskgroup cooked_dgroup1
drop directory '+cooked_dgroup1/stuff';
```

You can also rename directories with the alter diskgroup command using the rename directory clause, as shown in this example:

```
alter diskgroup cooked_dgroup1
rename directory '+cooked_dgroup1/stuff' to '+cooked_dgroup1/badstuff';
```

You can see the ASM disk group directories in the V$ASM_ALIAS view, as shown in this example:

```
select a.name "Alias Name", b.name "Disk group"
from v$asm_alias a, v$ASM_DISKGROUPS b
where a.group_number=b.group_number;
Alias Name                                       Disk group
------------------------------------------------ ---------------

badstuff                                         COOKED_DGROUP1
```

Using the ASMCMD Command-Line Utility

The ASMCMD tool is a command-line utility that allows you to manage ASM instances and the disk structures and files within those instances. With ASMCMD, you can do the following:

- List contents of ASM disk groups
- Perform searches (like directory listings)
- Add or remove directories
- Display space availability and utilization

ASMCMD allows you to traverse the ASM disks as you would a directory structure. From the root of the ASM instance, you can move down the various disk structures to find the disks you are interested in. Many of the commands in ASMCMD are Unix-like (in other words, ls, cd) and therefore the ASMCMD is fairly easy to learn how to use.

Starting ASMCMD

To start ASMCMD, simply set your ORACLE_SID to +ASM and then type **asmcmd** from the command line, as shown here:

```
C:\>set ORACLE_SID=+ASM
C:\>asmcmd
```

Or from Unix:

```
/opt/oracle>export ORACLE_SID=+ASM
/opt/oracle>asmcmd
```

 You will need to make sure that perl.exe is in the path before you run ASMCMD. If you have installed more than one ORACLE_HOME, it may take some setup to get the pathing set correctly. Make sure the following is set to the correct ORACLE_HOME:

- ORACLE_HOME
- PATH
- PERL5LIB
- PERLBIN

When ASMCMD starts, you will see the ASMCMD prompt, as shown here:

```
ASMCMD>
```

You can start ASMCMD with the –p option and it will display the current directory level, as shown in this example:

```
C:\oracle\product\11.1.0.6\DB01\BIN>asmcmd -p
ASMCMD [+] >
```

ASMCMD Commands

ASMCMD has a basic set of commands, many of which mimic Unix commands. You can see these commands from the ASMCMD prompt if you type in **help**. The commands are pretty straightforward and easy to use. In the next section, we will introduce each command and provide an example of its use. Table 1.3 lists the different ASMCMD commands and their purposes.

TABLE 1.3 ASMCMD Commands

Command	Purpose	Example
cd	Changes ASM directory.	cd +group1
du	Gets disk use.	du
find	Finds directory or file.	find + rob11g
help	Displays the help screen.	help
ls	Lists files in directory.	ls –l
lsct	Lists all clients using the ASM instance.	lsct
lsdg	Lists information on disk groups in the ASM instance.	lsdg
lsdsk	Lists ASM visible disks. Supported only in Unix.	lsdsk -k -d DATA *
mkalias	Creates an ASM alias for a given ASM filename.	mkalias +cooked_dgroup1/11gDB/ controlfile/Current.258 .613087119 +cooked_dgroup1/ control01.ctl
mkdir	Creates an ASM directory.	mkdir old
md_backup	Backs up ASM metadata.	md_backup –b /tmp/ dgbackup070222 -g dgroup1 -g dgroup2

TABLE 1.3   ASMCMD Commands *(continued)*

Command	Purpose	Example
md_restore	Restores ASM metadata.	md_restore −t full −g dgroup1 −i /tmp/dgbackup070222
pwd	Locates where you are on the ASM directory tree.	pwd
remap	Remaps a range of physical blocks on disk.	remap data data_0003 6000-8000
rm	Removes an ASM directory or file.	rm Current.258.613087119 rm current* rm −r current*
rmalias	Removes an ASM alias.	rmalias +cooked_dgroup1/11gDB/ datafile/alias_tbs_01.dbf

Overview of ASM Data Dictionary Views

You were introduced to Oracle's data dictionary as a part of your OCA studies. Recall that the data dictionary provides views on the operation and performance of the database. The data dictionary also provides a great deal of metadata about database structures. Several data-dictionary views are available for use with ASM. Table 1.4 lists those views and gives descriptions of their use.

You can learn more about the Oracle data dictionary in Chapter 2, "Performing Oracle User-Managed Backups."

TABLE 1.4   ASMCMD Commands

View Name	In ASM Instance	In Database
V$ASM_DISKGROUP	This view will describe a given disk group.	This view contains a single row for each ASM disk group that is mounted by the local ASM instance. Note that discovery will occur each time you query this view. This can have performance impacts.

TABLE 1.4   ASMCMD Commands *(continued)*

View Name	In ASM Instance	In Database
V$ASM_DISK	This view describes each disk that was discovered by the ASM instance. All disks are reported, even those not assigned to disk groups.	This view describes each disk that is assigned to a database. Note that discovery will occur each time you query this view. This can have performance impacts.
V$ASM_DISKGROUP_STAT	This view is equivalent to the V$ASM_DISKGROUP view.	This view contains a single row for each ASM disk group that is mounted by the local ASM instance. No discovery will occur when this view is queried.
V$ASM_FILE	Displays each ASM file contained in the ASM instance.	Not used in a database instance.
V$ASM_DISK_STAT	This view is equivalent to the V$ASM_DISK view.	This view describes each disk that is assigned to a database. No discovery will occur when this view is queried.
V$ASM_TEMPLATE	Displays each ASM template contained in the ASM instance by disk group.	Not used in a database instance.
V$ASM_ALIAS	Displays each alias contained in the ASM instance by disk group.	Not used in a database instance.
V$ASM_OPERATION	Displays each long-running operation occurring on the ASM instance.	Not used in a database instance.
V$ASM_CLIENT	Displays each database that is using at least one disk group managed by the ASM instance.	Not used in a database instance.

Using ASM Storage

We have discussed management of an ASM instance. This section covers how to actually use ASM from an Oracle instance. You can put all sorts of Oracle-related files into an ASM instance, including these:

- Oracle datafiles
- Database tempfiles
- Online redo logs
- Archived redo logs
- Control files
- Spfiles
- RMAN backup sets
- The flash recovery area (FRA)
- Data-pump dump sets

When you create one of these objects, you can decide to create it in an ASM disk group. You can also define default file-creation locations that point to ASM disk groups. Finally, you can mix and match the use of ASM and cooked file systems if you prefer. In the following sections, we will review these topics:

- Defining what ASM files are
- Defining ASM as the default destination for database files
- Creating a tablespace using an ASM disk group as the destination
- Creating a control file in an ASM disk group location
- Creating spfiles or parameter files on an ASM disk group
- Creating online redo logs in an ASM disk group location
- Defining an ASM disk group location as an archived redo-log storage area
- Creating RMAN backup sets on an ASM disk
- Defining an ASM disk group as the location for the FRA

What Are ASM Files?

We have already created ASM disk groups. To actually use the ASM disk groups, we have to populate them with ASM files. In this section, we will discuss what ASM files are and then we will discuss the different kinds of ASM filenames that you might deal with.

ASM Files

ASM files are created in a number of different ways; for example, when you execute the `create tablespace` command and you indicate that the resulting datafile(s) should be stored in an ASM disk group, the result will be the creation of ASM files in that ASM disk group.

A goodly number of Oracle file types can be stored in ASM, including datafiles, control files, redo logs, and archived redo logs. There are some Oracle files that cannot be stored in an ASM group. These are mostly the administrative files like trace files, the alert log, and so on.

ASM Filename Types

When a file is created on an ASM disk, the filename is generated by ASM. There is a number of different kinds of ASM filename types:

- Fully qualified ASM filenames

- Numeric ASM filenames

- Alias ASM filenames

- Alias filenames with templates

- Incomplete filenames

- Incomplete filenames with templates

Let's look at each of these types in a bit more detail.

Fully Qualified ASM Filenames

The full filename is known as the *fully qualified ASM filename*. Here is an example of a fully qualified ASM filename:

```
+sp_dgroup2/mydb/controlfile/Current.56.544956473
```

The naming format for a fully qualified ASM filename is as follows:

- The +group is listed (in our case, +sp_dgroup2). Note that the + indicates the root of the ASM filename.

- The database name (in our case mydb).

- The file type (in our case, this is a control file).

- Next we have the start of the actual ASM file. First we have the file type flag (in our case, Current). This provides additional information on the file type in question. In this case, this is a current control file, as opposed to a control-file backup, which would be listed as backup.

- Finally we have two numbers delineated by a period (56.544956473), which represent the file number and an incarnation number. These two numbers combined guarantee that the ASM filename will be unique from any other ASM filename on the system.

ASM Numeric Filenames

The *ASM numeric filename* is a subset of the fully qualified filename, as you might have noticed. The numeric filename for the fully qualified filename in the preceding section would be

```
+sp_dgroup2.56.544956473
```

Alias ASM Filenames

An *ASM alias filename* takes on the following format:

```
+group_name/your_assigned_alias
```

In this case, if you assign the alias to the file when it's created filenames might look like this:

```
+sp_dgroup2/ctrl_files/control_file_01
+sp_dgroup2/datafile/mydbf_user_data_01
```

Alias ASM Filenames with Templates

You can also reference an alias ASM filename with a template name. Simply include the ASM template name in parentheses next to the alias-name definition, as shown here:

```
+sp_dgroup2/ctrl_files/control_file_01(special)
```

Incomplete ASM Filenames

There are times you will use an *incomplete ASM filename*. An ASM filename is incomplete when the name of the ASM disk group is all that is referenced, as in this case:

```
+Sp_dgroup1
```

So, the incomplete ASM filename really is just a + followed by the disk group name. This is the most commonly used ASM filename type because this type is used when defining default destinations for database files (see more on that in the next section) in parameters, creating tablespaces, or performing RMAN database backups.

Incomplete ASM Filenames with Templates

As with alias filenames, you can also reference a template in an incomplete filename definition, as shown here:

```
+sp_dgroup1(special_template)
```

Adding ASM Filename Aliases to Existing Files

You can add filename aliases to ASM files that have already been created. To add the alias, use the `alter diskgroup` command with the `add alias` parameter. For example, if you wanted to create an alias for ALIAS_TBS.260.613168611, you would issue the following command:

```
Alter diskgroup cooked_dgroup1
add alias '+cooked_dgroup1/alias_dir/alias_tbs_01.dbf'
FOR '+cooked_dgroup1/11GDB/datafile/alias_tbs. 260.613168611';
```

Managing ASM File Alias Names

You can change ASM file alias names with the `rename alias` parameter of the `alter diskgroup` command, as shown in this example:

```
Alter diskgroup cooked_dgroup1
Rename alias '+cooked_dgroup1/alias_dir/alias_tbs_01.dbf'
To '+cooked_dgroup1/datafiles/alias_tbs_01.dbf';
```

You can use the `drop alias` command to drop ASM aliases, as in this example:

```
Drop alias '+cooked_dgroup1/datafiles/alias_tbs_01.dbf';
```

Drop Files from an ASM Disk Group

There may be cases where you will need to drop files from an ASM disk group (for example, the database is removed in an unorderly fashion). To remove ASM files, use the `alter diskgroup` command with the `drop file` clause. Here is an example of removing a file from an ASM disk group (in this case, using an alias name):

```
alter diskgroup cooked_dgroup1
drop file '+cooked_dgroup1/alias_dir/alias_tbs_01.dbf';
```

Defining ASM as the Default Destination for Database Files

If you decide you want to allow Oracle to create all file types as ASM file types, you can set the values of various parameters such that ASM will automatically be employed. One of the big benefits of this feature is the standardization of your database, ensuring that all files get placed where they belong and in the ASM structure to which they belong. You can define default ASM destinations be defining incomplete ASM filenames. The following database parameters take incomplete ASM filenames:

- `DB_CREATE_FILE_DEST`
- `DB_CREATE_ONLINE_LOG_DEST_n`
- `DB_RECOVERY_FILE_DEST`
- `CONTROL_FILES`
- `LOG_ARCHIVE_DEST_n` (`log_archive_dest_format` will be ignored)
- `LOG_ARCHIVE_DEST` (`log_archive_dest_format` will be ignored)
- `STANDBY_ARCHIVE_DEST`

Here is an example of using an incomplete name when setting the `DB_CREATE_FILE_DEST` parameter so that it will use the ASM disk group +sp_dgroup1:

```
alter system set db_create_file_dest='+cooked_dgroup1' scope=both;
```

Creating a Tablespace Using an ASM Disk Group as the Destination

There are different ways to create tablespaces using ASM disks. In this section, we will first look at creating an ASM tablespace, allowing the default ASM disk location to be used (as a result of having set the `DB_CREATE_FILE_DEST` parameter as we did earlier). We will then look at how to create a tablespace datafile by explicitly referencing the ASM disk group that it is supposed to be assigned to.

Creating Tablespaces Using Default ASM Assignments

Now that you have seen how to define a default ASM location, you can use the `create tablespace` command to create a tablespace that will have a file in the ASM disk group by default, as shown in this example:

```
create tablespace test_rgf datafile size 100k;
```

Let's see where Oracle put the datafile now by querying the `DBA_DATA_FILES` view:

```
Select tablespace_name, file_name
from dba_data_files Where tablespace_name='TEST_RGF';

TABLESPACE FILE_NAME
---------- -----------------------------------------------------------
TEST_RGF   +COOKED_DGROUP1/11gDB/datafile/test_rgf.256.613064385
```

Note in this example that Oracle went ahead and filled out the rest of the path, giving us a complete filename in the DBA_DATA_FILES view to work with. We can also see this new file in the ASM instance using the V$ASM_FILES view, as shown here:

```
SQL> select group_number, file_number, type, blocks, bytes from v$asm_file;

GROUP_NUMBER FILE_NUMBER TYPE                     BLOCKS     BYTES
------------ ----------- -------------------- ---------- ----------
           1         256 DATAFILE                     14     114688
```

If you want to drop a tablespace that contains ASM files, you need only issue the drop tablespace command. Oracle will clean up all of the ASM datafiles associated with that tablespace. You can have a mix of ASM datafiles and normal datafiles assigned to a tablespace, as shown in this create table statement:

```
Create tablespace part_asm_tbs
Datafile 'c:\oracle\oradata\11gDB\part_asm_tbs_01.dbf' size 10m,
'+COOKED_DGROUP1' size 100k;
```

Let's look and see where the datafiles were created:

```
Select tablespace_name, file_name
from dba_data_files Where tablespace_name='PART_ASM_TBS';

TABLESPACE_NAME FILE_NAME
--------------- ------------------------------------------------------------
PART_ASM_TBS    C:\ORACLE\ORADATA\11GDB\PART_ASM_TBS_01.DBF
PART_ASM_TBS    +COOKED_DGROUP1/11GDB/datafile/part_asm_tbs.256.613066047
```

Note that in this case, if you drop the PART_ASM_TBS tablespace, only the ASM files related to that tablespace would be removed from the disk when you issue the drop tablespace command. In cases such as these, you need to make sure you include the including contents and datafiles parameter with the drop tablespace command.

Creating Tablespaces Referencing Specific ASM Disk Groups

There are going to be many times when you will not want to define a default ASM disk group to write all tablespaces to. In this case, you will want to reference the specific ASM disk group that you want a datafile created in when you issue the create tablespace command. Here is an example:

```
create tablespace another_test
datafile '+COOKED_DGROUP1' size 100k;
```

Let's see where Oracle put the datafile now by querying the DBA_DATA_FILES view:

```
select tablespace_name, file_name
from dba_data_files Where tablespace_name='ANOTHER_TEST';


TABLESPACE_NAME FILE_NAME
--------------- -----------------------------------------------------------
ANOTHER_TEST    +COOKED_DGROUP1/11GDB/datafile/another_test.256.613065911
```

The create tablespace command comes with a number of different options when you are using cooked file systems, and there is no reason you cannot use those options when you are using ASM file systems. For example, you can create a tablespace with autoextend enabled, as shown here:

```
create tablespace another_test
datafile '+COOKED_DGROUP1' size 100k
autoextend on next 10m maxsize 300m;
```

If you want to create a tablespace using a template other than the default template, this is easy too, as shown in this example:

```
create tablespace different_template
datafile '+COOKED_DGROUP1(alternate_template)';
```

Tablespace Maintenance When Using Tablespaces Referencing Specific ASM Disk Groups

Tablespace maintenance is basically unchanged when using ASM disks. For example, you can add a datafile with the alter tablespace command as you normally would:

```
alter tablespace part_asm_tbs Add datafile '+COOKED_DGROUP1' size 100k;
```

Creating a Database Using ASM Disk Group Locations

You can create a database that completely uses ASM disk group locations. You can do this when creating the database through the DBCA interface or if you are going to manually create the database. In the following sections, we will look at both options.

Creating a Database Using ASM Disks with DBCA

If you are creating the database with the DBCA, you will have the opportunity to indicate that you want to use ASM disks for the database as a part of the DBCA workflow.

After you indicate that you want to use ASM, you will be prompted to create the SYS password to the ASM instance. DBCA will then present to you a list of available disk groups that you can use to create the database.

DBCA will confirm your selection in the next screen. You will then be presented with a screen that asks you where you want the flash recovery area to be assigned. It will prepopulate this screen with one of the disk groups that you selected to use in the previous screen (typically it will be the second disk group in the list).

The DBCA will set all of the different file location parameters to those in the ASM disk groups that you selected (for example, CONTROL_FILES, DB_CREATE_FILE_DEST, DB_RECOVERY_FILE_DEST, and LOG_ARCHIVE_DEST_1). You can edit these choices if you want to use a mix of ASM and cooked file systems for some reason.

You complete the DBCA screens as normal and DBCA will then create a database that is totally (or partially, if you prefer) using ASM.

Creating a Database Manually Using ASM Disks

It can actually be easier to create a database using ASM than to create a database with DBCA, if only because less typing is required! To create an Oracle database with ASM, follow the standard procedures, but when you are creating the parameter file, make sure you assign the following parameters to an ASM disk group:

- DB_CREATE_FILE_DEST
- DB_RECOVERY_FILE_DEST

Once you have done this, issuing the `create database` command requires no parameters at all! Simply issue the command and that's it! Oracle will create the various database files on ASM disk.

Creating a Control File in an ASM Disk Group Location

When you create a database from the DBCA or manually, you can opt to create the database control files in an ASM location by setting the CONTROL_FILES parameter to an ASM disk group. A note about moving control files, or any other database-related files: be very careful. It's dangerous to re-create the control file because it is a rather central part of your database!

If you have an existing database and you want to move the control files to ASM, it gets a bit stickier. You will pretty much have to use the `create controlfile` command to move the database control files to ASM disks. You will need to change the database CONTROL_FILES parameter before you run the create `controlfile` command. Here is an example of this operation:

```
SQL> alter system set control_files='' scope=SPFILE;
SQL> alter system set
DB_CREATE_FILE_DEST='+COOKED_DGROUP1','+COOKED_DGROUP2' scope=spfile;
SQL> shutdown immediate
SQL> startup nomount
SQL>CREATE CONTROLFILE REUSE DATABASE "11GDB"
```

```
NORESETLOGS  NOARCHIVELOG
    MAXLOGFILES 16
    MAXLOGMEMBERS 3
    MAXDATAFILES 100
    MAXINSTANCES 8
    MAXLOGHISTORY 292
LOGFILE
  GROUP 1 'C:\ORACLE\ORADATA\11GDB\REDO01.LOG'  SIZE 50M,
  GROUP 2 'C:\ORACLE\ORADATA\11GDB\REDO02.LOG'  SIZE 50M,
  GROUP 3 'C:\ORACLE\ORADATA\11GDB\REDO03.LOG'  SIZE 50M
-- STANDBY LOGFILE
DATAFILE
  'C:\ORACLE\ORADATA\11GDB\SYSTEM01.DBF',
  'C:\ORACLE\ORADATA\11GDB\UNDOTBS01.DBF',
  'C:\ORACLE\ORADATA\11GDB\SYSAUX01.DBF',
  'C:\ORACLE\ORADATA\11GDB\USERS01.DBF',
  'C:\ORACLE\ORADATA\11GDB\EXAMPLE01.DBF',
  'C:\ORACLE\ORADATA\11GDB\PART_ASM_TBS_01.DBF',
  '+COOKED_DGROUP1/11GDB/datafile/part_asm_tbs.256.613066047',
  '+COOKED_DGROUP1/11GDB/datafile/part_asm_tbs.257.613083267'
CHARACTER SET WE8MSWIN1252;
SQL>RECOVER DATABASE;
SQL>ALTER DATABASE OPEN NORESETLOGS;
```

You can also use RMAN to restore the control file to an ASM disk location, as shown in this example (this assumes you are connected to a recovery catalog):

```
SQL> alter system set control_files='' scope=SPFILE;
SQL> alter system set
DB_CREATE_FILE_DEST='+COOKED_DGROUP1' scope=spfile;
RMAN>shutdown
RMAN>startup nomount
RMAN>restore controlfile;
RMAN>recover database;
RMAN>alter database open resetlogs;
```

If you are using autobackups, then the process is slightly different:

```
SQL> alter system set control_files='' scope=SPFILE;
SQL> alter system set
DB_CREATE_FILE_DEST='+COOKED_DGROUP1' scope=spfile;
```

```
RMAN>shutdown
RMAN>startup nomount
RMAN>restore controlfile from autobackup;
RMAN>recover database;
RMAN>alter database open resetlogs;
```

Note that instead of setting the DB_CREATE_FILE_DEST parameter, you could set the CONTROL_FILES parameter, as shown here:

```
alter system set control_files=
'+COOKED_DGROUP1/11GDB/controlfile/current.259.613088323',
'+COOKED_DGROUP2/11GDB/controlfile/current.257.613088325';
```

If you have restored the control files to a disk group, you may not know what the file-names are in order to set the CONTROL_FILES parameter (the RMAN output does not give you the ASM filenames that are created). In this case, you can query the V$ASM_FILE view from the ASM instance and derive the filename for the newly created control file.

Recall that the format for an ASM filename is file_type_flag.file#.incarnation#. Knowing this, you can derive the control-file names. For example, here is a query against the V$ASM_FILE view in our database after we restored the control files to our ASM instance:

```
SQL> select a.group_number, b.name, a.incarnation, a.file_number, a.type
  2  from v$ASM_DISKGROUPS b, v$asm_file a
  3  where a.group_number= b.group_number
  4  and a.type='CONTROLFILE';
```

```
GROUP_NUMBER NAME                            INCARNATION FILE_NUMBER TYPE
------------ ------------------------------- ----------- ----------- -----------
           1 COOKED_DGROUP1                    613087119         258 CONTROLFILE
           2 COOKED_DGROUP2                    613087131         256 CONTROLFILE
```

From this, we can surmise that our CONTROL_FILES parameter should be set to the following:

```
alter system set control_files=
'+COOKED_DGROUP1/11GDB/controlfile/current.258.613087119',
'+COOKED_DGROUP1/11GDB/controlfile/current.258.613087131'
Scope=spfile;
```

Of course, you can reverse this process and move control files out of ASM and put them into cooked file systems at any time. As should always be standard practice, make sure you back up your database before you begin moving any database-related files around.

Creating Spfiles or Parameter Files on an ASM Disk Group

You can create pfiles or spfiles on an ASM disk group using the `create pfile` or `create spfile` command with the ASM disk group as the location for the parameter file. For example, you could issue this command:

```
create spfile '+COOKED_DGROUP1' from pfile;
```

Creating Online Redo Logs in an ASM Disk Group Location

Creation of redo logs on ASM disks is straightforward. If the database was configured to use ASM from the beginning, then the existing online redo logs will already be on ASM disk groups. Assuming that the parameter `DB_ONLINE_CREATE_LOG_DEST_n` or `DB_CREATE_FILE_DEST` is set, you can simply issue the `alter database add logfile` command and Oracle will add a new redo log group to your database for you, as shown in this example:

```
alter database add logfile size 100m;
```

You can also manually add a redo log file group to a disk group if you prefer using SQL, such as in the following, which will create a new log file group, and multiplex it, between two ASM disk groups:

```
alter database add logfile ('+COOKED_DGROUP1','+COOKED_DGROUP2') size 100m;
```

Defining an ASM Disk Group Location as an Archived Redo Log Storage Area

Once you have created an ASM disk, it's easy to use it as the storage for archived redo logs. Simply set one of the `LOG_ARCHIVE_DEST_n` parameters to point to that ASM disk group, as shown in this example:

```
alter system
set log_archive_dest_1='location=+COOKED_DGROUP2';
```

You can check the ASM instance and see the new archived logs being created, as shown in this example code:

```
SQL> select a.group_number, b.name, a.incarnation, a.file_number, a.type
  2  from v$ASM_DISKGROUPS b, v$asm_file a
  3  where a.group_number=b.group_number
  4  and a.type='ARCHIVELOG';
```

```
GROUP_NUMBER NAME                            INCARNATION FILE_NUMBER TYPE
------------ ------------------------------- ----------- ----------- -----------
           2 COOKED_DGROUP2                    613091705         258 ARCHIVELOG
```

Creating Database Objects Using ASM Filename Aliases

An alias includes the disk group name and then appends a user-defined name to the filename. This makes it possible to reference an ASM file with a name that makes some sense. ASM aliases start with the disk group name, followed by a slash and then the alias name as in this example:

+COOKED_DGROUP1/datafiles/myfile.dbf

Aliases can be created at the time the file is created (such as when you issue the **create tablespace** command), or you can add the alias later. Here is an example of creating a tablespace with an alias filename:

```
create tablespace alias_tbs
Datafile'+COOKED_DGROUP1/myalias.dbf' size 10m;
```

The resulting ASM file would be as follows:

+COOKED_DGROUP1/11GDB/datafile/alias_tbs.256.613066047

You can see this through the following query executed in the ASM instance:

```
SQL> select b.name gname, a.name aname, a.system_created, a.alias_directory,
  2                c.type file_type
  3         from v$asm_alias a, v$ASM_DISKGROUPS b, v$asm_file c
  4         where a.group_number = b.group_number
  5               and a.group_number = c.group_number(+)
  6               and a.file_number = c.file_number(+)
  7               and a.file_incarnation = c.incarnation(+)
  8               and b.name='COOKED_DGROUP1'
  9               and c.type='DATAFILE';
```

```
GNAME                           ANAME                           S A FILE_TYPE
------------------------------- ------------------------------- - - -----------
COOKED_DGROUP1                  ALIAS_TBS.260.613168611         Y N DATAFILE
```

Using RMAN with ASM

You can use RMAN in conjunction with ASM. In the following sections, we will cover the following RMAN-related operations:

- Copying database datafiles to an ASM disk with RMAN
- Creating RMAN backups on ASM

Copying Database Datafiles to an ASM Disk with RMAN

If you want to move your entire database to ASM, you can easily do this with RMAN. First you make an image copy of the database, copying it to an ASM disk group. Then use the RMAN switch database to copy command to switch the database from using the old datafiles to using the new datafiles that were copied onto the ASM drives. Here is an example of moving the database datafiles using the following commands:

```
RMAN>shutdown
RMAN>startup mount
RMAN>backup as copy database format '+COOKED_DGROUP1';
RMAN>switch database to copy;
RMAN>alter database open;
```

Creating RMAN Backups on ASM

RMAN backup sets can be made to ASM disks. This means that the database, archived redo logs, control-file backups, and spfiles can all be backed up to ASM disks. There are two different ways of using ASM for backups. You can send individual backups directly to an ASM disk group, or you can define the flash recovery area to be a disk group and cause backups to be sent to the flash recovery area. Let's look at these two options in a bit more detail.

Backing Up from RMAN to ASM Directly

Backing up to an ASM disk group with RMAN is quite easy. Use the RMAN backup command and add the format parameter indicating the disk group to which you want to back up the database. Here is an example:

```
RMAN>backup as compressed backupset database format '+COOKED_DGROUP1';
```

You can also back up archived redo logs and database control files using RMAN via the same method.

Configuring and Backing Up to an ASM Flash Recovery Area

The flash recovery area is a directory structure that centralizes Oracle backups in one Oracle-defined backup structure (see Chapter 2 for more on the flash recovery area). You define the flash recovery area by setting the DB_ RECOVERY_FILE_DEST and DB_RECOVERY_FILE_DEST_SIZE parameters as required. Here is an example of using the alter system command to point the flash recovery area to an ASM disk group.

```
alter system set db_recovery_file_dest='+COOKED_DGROUP1';
alter system set db_recovery_file_dest_size=4G;
```

Once these parameters have been set, RMAN backups will start using the flash recovery area and ASM since the flash recovery area has been configured to use an ASM disk group.

Summary

In this chapter, we showed you how Automatic Storage Management (ASM) can reduce or eliminate the headaches involved in managing the disk space for all Oracle file types, including online and archived logs, RMAN backup sets, flashback logs, and even initialization parameter files (spfiles).

We reviewed the concepts related to a special type of instance called an ASM instance along with the initialization parameters specific to an ASM instance. In addition, we described the dynamic performance views that allow you to view the components of an ASM disk group as well as to monitor the online rebalancing operations that occur when disks are added to or removed from a disk group. Starting and stopping an ASM instance is similar to starting and stopping a traditional database instance. Of course, other databases that use disk groups within the ASM instance will not be available to users if the ASM instance is not available to service disk group requests.

ASM filenames have a number of different formats and are used differently depending on whether existing ASM files or new ASM files are being referenced. ASM templates are used in conjunction with ASM filenames to ease the administration of ASM files.

Additionally, we reviewed ASM disk group architecture, showing how failure groups can provide redundancy and performance benefits while eliminating the need for a third-party logical volume manager. Dynamic disk group rebalancing automatically tunes I/O performance when a disk is added or deleted from a disk group or a disk in a disk group fails.

Exam Essentials

Enumerate the benefits and characteristics of Automatic Storage Management (ASM).
Understand how ASM can relieve you of manually optimizing I/O across all files in the tablespace by using ASM disk groups. Show how ASM operations can be performed online with minimal impact to ongoing database transactions.

Be able to create an ASM instance and configure its initialization parameters. Understand the initialization parameters INSTANCE_TYPE, ASM_POWER_LIMIT, ASM_DISKSTRING, and ASM_DISKGROUPS. Configure DB_UNIQUE_NAME for an ASM instance. Start up and shut down an ASM instance, noting the dependencies with database instances that are using the ASM instance's disk groups.

Understand the architecture of an ASM instance. Enumerate the different states for an ASM instance. Describe what happens when an ASM instance is shut down normally or is aborted. Understand and describe the differences between an RDBMS instance and an ASM instance.

Understand redundancy and resync. Describe what redundancy is and how it's implemented in ASM. Understand what a failure group is and how it is created. Know what ASM fast disk resync and preferred mirror read are.

Understand how ASM filenames are constructed and used when creating Oracle objects.
Differentiate how different ASM filename formats are used and how files are created depending on whether the file is an existing ASM file, whether a new ASM file is being created, or whether multiple ASM files are being created. Understand the different system templates for creating ASM files with the associated filename and how the characteristics are applied to the ASM files. Show how ASM files are used in SQL commands.

Be able to create, drop, and alter ASM disk groups. Define multiple failure groups for new disk groups and make sure you understand how the number of failure groups is different for two-way and three-way mirroring. Show how disk rebalancing can be controlled or rolled back. Understand the ASM disk group attributes and how they are used.

Identify the steps involved in converting non-ASM files to ASM files using RMAN. Migrate a database to ASM disk groups by shutting down the database, running an RMAN script for each file to be converted, and opening the database with RESETLOGS.

Review Questions

1. What are three benefits of using ASM? (Choose three.)

   A. Ease of disk administration and maintenance

   B. Load balancing across physical disks

   C. Software RAID-1 data redundancy with double or triple mirrors

   D. Automatic recovery of failed disks

2. What components are present in an ASM instance? (Choose three.)

   A. SGA

   B. Database processes

   C. Database datafiles

   D. Control files

   E. Database parameter file or spfile

3. Which of the following is a benefit of ASM fast disk resync?

   A. Failed disks are taken offline immediately but are not dropped.

   B. Disk data is never lost.

   C. By default, the failed disk is not dropped from the disk group ever, protecting you from loss of that disk.

   D. The failed disk is automatically reformatted and then resynchronized to speed up the recovery process.

   E. Hot spare disks are automatically configured and added to the disk group.

4. What is the result of increasing the value of the parameter ASM_POWER_LIMIT during a rebalance operation?

   A. The ASM rebalance operation will likely consume fewer resources and complete in a shorter amount of time.

   B. The ASM rebalance operation will consume fewer resources and complete in a longer amount of time.

   C. The ASM rebalance operation will be parallelized and should complete in a shorter amount of time.

   D. There is no ASM_POWER_LIMIT setting used in ASM.

   E. None of the above.

5. What is the default AU size of an ASM disk group? What is the maximum AU size in an ASM disk group?

    A. 100KB default, 10TB maximum

    B. 256KB default, 1024MB maximum

    C. 10MB default, 126PB maximum

    D. 64KB default, 1EB maximum

    E. 1MB default, 64MB maximum

6. Which initialization parameter in an ASM instance specifies the disk groups to be automatically mounted at instance startup?

    A. ASM_DISKMOUNT

    B. ASM_DISKGROUP

    C. ASM_DISKSTRING

    D. ASM_MOUNTGROUP

7. When an ASM instance receives a SHUTDOWN NORMAL command, what command does it pass on to all database instances that rely on the ASM instance's disk groups?

    A. TRANSACTIONAL

    B. IMMEDIATE

    C. ABORT

    D. NORMAL

    E. None of the above

8. When starting up your ASM instance, you receive the following error:

```
SQL> startup pfile=?/dbs/init+ASM.ora
ASM instance started
Total System Global Area  104611840 bytes
Fixed Size                  1298220 bytes
Variable Size              78147796 bytes
ASM Cache                  25165824 bytes
ORA-15032: not all alterations performed
ORA-15063: ASM discovered an insufficient number of disks for disk group
"DGROUP3"
ORA-15063: ASM discovered an insufficient number of disks for disk group
"DGROUP2"
ORA-15063: ASM discovered an insufficient number of disks for disk group
"DGROUP1"
```

In trying to determine the cause of the problem, you issue this query:

```
SQL> show parameter asm
NAME                                 TYPE        VALUE
------------------------------------ ----------- -------------------------_
asm_allow_only_raw_disks             boolean     FALSE
asm_diskgroups                       string      DGROUP1, DGROUP2, DGROUP3
asm_diskstring                       string
asm_power_limit                      integer     1
asm_preferred_read_failure_groups    string
```

What is the cause of the error?

A. The ASM_DISKGROUPS parameter is configured for three disk groups: DGROUP1, DGROUP2, and DGROUP3. The underlying disks for these disk groups have apparently been lost.

B The format of the ASM_DISKGROUPS parameter is incorrect. It should reference the disk group numbers, not the names of the disk groups.

C. The ASM_POWER_LIMIT parameter is incorrectly set to 1. It should be set to the number of disk groups being attached to the ASM instance.

D. The ASM_DISKSTRING parameter is not set; therefore disk discovery is not possible.

E. There is insufficient information to solve this problem.

9. As DBA for the Rebel Alliance you have decided that you need to facilitate some redundancy in your database. Using ASM, you want to create a disk group that will provide for the greatest amount of redundancy for your ASM data (you do not have advanced SAN mirroring technology available to you, unfortunately). Which of the following commands would create a disk group that would offer the maximum in data redundancy?

A. CREATE DISKGROUP dg_alliance1 NORMAL REDUNDANCY
```
failgroup diskcontrol1 DISK 'c:\oracle\asm_disk\_file_disk3' NAME file_
diska1
failgroup diskcontrol2 DISK 'c:\oracle\asm_disk\_file_disk4' NAME file_
diskb1;
```

B. CREATE DISKGROUP dg_alliance1 EXTERNAL REDUNDANCY
```
failgroup diskcontrol1 DISK 'c:\oracle\asm_disk\_file_disk3' NAME file_
diska1;
```

C. CREATE DISKGROUP dg_alliance1
HIGH REDUNDANCY
```
failgroup diskcontrol1 DISK 'c:\oracle\asm_disk\_file_disk1' NAME file_
disk1
failgroup diskcontrol2 DISK 'c:\oracle\asm_disk\_file_disk2' NAME file_
disk2
failgroup diskcontrol2 DISK 'c:\oracle\asm_disk\_file_disk3' NAME file_
disk3;
```

D. CREATE DISKGROUP dg_alliance1
MAXIMUM REDUNDANCY
failgroup diskcontrol1 DISK 'c:\oracle\asm_disk_file_disk1' NAME file_
disk1
failgroup diskcontrol2 DISK 'c:\oracle\asm_disk_file_disk2' NAME file_
disk2
failgroup diskcontrol2 DISK 'c:\oracle\asm_disk_file_disk3' NAME file_
disk3
failgroup diskcontrol2 DISK 'c:\oracle\asm_disk_file_disk4' NAME file_
disk4;

E. None of the above

10. You want to migrate your database to ASM, so you've done a clean shutdown, made a closed backup of the entire database, noted the location of your control files and online redo log files, and changed your spfile to use OMF. The last step is to run an RMAN script to do the conversion. Using the following steps, what is the correct order in which the following RMAN commands should be executed?

1. STARTUP NOMOUNT

2. ALTER DATABASE OPEN RESETLOGS

3. SQL "ALTER DATABASE RENAME 'logfile1 path' TO '+dgrp4 '"   # plus all
other logfiles

4. SWITCH DATABASE TO COPY

5. BACKUP AS COPY DATABASE FORMAT '+dgrp4'

6. ALTER DATABASE MOUNT

7. RESTORE CONTROLFILE FROM 'controlfile_location'

A. 2, 5, 3, 1, 7, 6, 4

B. 1, 7, 6, 5, 4, 3, 2

C. 5, 1, 2, 7, 4, 6, 3

D. 7, 3, 1, 5, 6, 2, 4

11. How can you reverse the effects of an ALTER DISKGROUP ... DROP DISK command if it has not yet completed?

A. Issue the ALTER DISKGROUP ... ADD DISK command.

B. Issue the ALTER DISKGROUP ... UNDROP DISKS command.

C. Issue the ALTER DISKGROUP ... DROP DISK CANCEL command.

D. Retrieve the disk from the Recycle Bin after the operation completes.

12. To reference existing ASM files, you need to use a fully qualified ASM filename. Your development database has a disk group named DG2A, the database name is DEV19, and the ASM file that you want to reference is a datafile for the USERS02 tablespace. Which of the following is a valid ASM filename for this ASM file?

  A. dev19/+DG2A/datafile/users02.701.2

  B. +DG2A/dev19/datafile/users02.701.2

  C. +DG2A/dev19/users02/datafile.701.2

  D. +DG2A.701.2

  E. +DG2A/datafile/dev19.users.02.701.2

13. Which background process coordinates the rebalance activity for disk groups?

  A. ORBn

  B. OSMB

  C. RBAL

  D. ASMn

14. On the development database rac0, there are six raw devices: /dev/raw/raw1 through /dev/raw/raw6. /dev/raw/raw1 and /dev/raw/raw2 are 8GB each, and the rest are 6GB each. An existing disk group +DATA1, of NORMAL REDUNDANCY, uses /dev/raw/raw1 and /dev/raw/raw2. Which series of the following commands will drop one of the failure groups for +DATA1, create a new disk group +DATA2 using two of the remaining four raw devices, and then cancel the drop operation from +DATA1?

  A. ALTER DISKGROUP DATA1 DROP DISK DATA1_0001;CREATE DISKGROUP DATA2 NORMAL REDUNDANCY FAILGROUP DATA1A DISK '/dev/raw/raw3' FAILGROUP DATA1B DISK '/dev/raw/raw4';ALTER DISKGROUP DATA1 UNDROP DISKS;

  B. ALTER DISKGROUP DATA1 DROP DISK DATA1_0001;CREATE DISKGROUP DATA2 HIGH REDUNDANCY FAILGROUP DATA1A DISK '/dev/raw/raw3' FAILGROUP DATA1B DISK '/dev/raw/raw4';'ALTER DISKGROUP DATA1 UNDROP DISKS;

  C. ALTER DISKGROUP DATA1 DROP DISK DATA1_0001;CREATE DISKGROUP DATA2 NORMAL REDUNDANCY FAILGROUP DATA1A DISK '/dev/raw/raw3' FAILGROUP DATA1B DISK '/dev/raw/raw4';ALTER DISKGROUP DATA1 UNDROP DATA1_0001;

  D. ALTER DISKGROUP DATA1 DROP DISK DATA1_0001 ADD DISK GROUP DATA2 NORMAL REDUNDANCY FAILGROUP DATA1A DISK '/dev/raw/raw3' FAILGROUP DATA1B DISK '/dev/raw/raw4';ALTER DISKGROUP DATA1 UNDROP DISKS;

15. Which type of database file is spread across all disks in a disk group?

  A. All types of files are spread across all disks in the disk group.

  B. Datafiles

  C. Redo log files

  D. Archived redo log files

  E. Control files

16. How can you reverse the effects of an ALTER DISKGROUP … DROP DISK command if it has already completed?

    A. Issue the ALTER DISKGROUP … ADD DISK command.

    B. Issue the ALTER DISKGROUP … UNDROP DISKS command.

    C. Issue the ALTER DISKGROUP … DROP DISK CANCEL command.

    D. Retrieve the disk from the Recycle Bin after the operation completes.

17. Which of the following ALTER DISKGROUP commands does *not* use V$ASM_OPERATION to record the status of the operation?

    A. ADD DIRECTORY

    B. DROP DISK

    C. RESIZE DISK

    D. REBALANCE

    E. ADD FAILGROUP

18. If you use ALTER DISKGROUP … ADD DISK and specify a wildcard for the discovery string, what happens to disks that are already a part of the same or another disk group?

    A. The command fails unless you specify the FORCE option.

    B. The command fails unless you specify the REUSE option.

    C. The command must be reissued with a more specific discovery string.

    D. The other disks, already part of the disk group, are ignored.

19. You are an Oracle DBA responsible for an ASM instance. The disk controller on your system fails. You suspect that the disk itself is okay. You know it will take 24 hours to replace the controller and you don't want to have to rebuild the disks from scratch. What do you do?

    A. Take the whole disk group offline and wait for the controller card to be installed. Once it's installed, bring the disk group online again.

    B. Change the ASM parameter ASM_PREFERRED_READ_FAILURE_GROUPS to indicate that you want to read from the non-failed disk. Once the disk controller is replaced, reset the parameter to its original value.

    C. You have no choice but to rebuild the disk. Drop the disk from the disk group and wait for the controller to be replaced. Once the controller is replaced, add the disk back into the disk group and allow ASM to rebuild it.

    D. If you are using any setting other than REDUNDANCY EXTERNAL for your disk group, you will have to recover any data on that disk from a backup. The database will be unavailable until you can correct the problem and perform recovery.

    E. Change the attribute DISK_REPAIR_TIME on the disk group to a time greater than 24 hours.

20. As the DBA, you run the following query on your ASM instance. What is the implication of the results of the query? (Choose two.)

```
SQL> select group_number, name, state from v$ASM_DISKGROUP;
```

GROUP_NUMBER	NAME	STATE
0	DGROUP1	DISMOUNTED
2	DGROUP2	MOUNTED
3	DGROUP3	MOUNTED

A. The DGROUP1 disk group was unmounted by another DBA.

B. A datafile has been lost, causing the ASM disk group DGROUP1 to go into the DISMOUNTED state.

C. One of the redundant disks (DGROUP1) has been lost in a disk group.

D. This query has no meaning in an ASM instance.

E. A disk associated with a disk group was discovered after the ASM instance initially opened.

Answers to Review Questions

1. A, B, C. Option A is correct because ASM makes administration and maintenance of disks much easier. Option B is correct because ASM provides for load balancing across the physical disks for better performance. Answer C is correct because ASM provides RAID-1 redundancy via double or triple mirrors.

2. A, B, E. Option A is correct because the SGA is allocated when the ASM instance is started. Option B is correct because the Oracle processes are also started when the ASM instance is started. Option E is correct because the ASM instance requires either a parameter file or an spfile.

3. A. When a disk fails, it is taken offline immediately but it is not dropped at that time. By default, you will have 3.6 hours to correct the problem before ASM will automatically drop the disk. You can configure this time by modifying the disk attributes.

4. C. Increasing the value of ASM_POWER_LIMIT will increase the degree of parallelism of the rebalance operation, which may help to increase the performance of that operation.

5. E. The default AU size is 1MB, and 64MB is the maximum AU size for a disk group.

6. B. The initialization parameter ASM_DISKGROUP, valid only in an ASM instance, specifies the disk groups to be automatically mounted when the ASM instance starts. ASM_DISKSTRING is operating system–dependent and restricts the file-system devices that can be used to create disk groups. ASM_DISKMOUNT and ASM_MOUNTGROUP are not valid initialization parameters.

7. E. If you do a normal shutdown of the ASM instance, an error will be returned if any Oracle database is using that ASM instance. Use the shutdown abort command to force the ASM instance to shut down. This will cause all other Oracle databases attached to the ASM instance to be shut down with the equivalent of a shutdown abort command.

8. D. The ASM_DISKSTRING parameter is not set correctly. When the ASM instance is started, it will use the ASM_DISKSTRING to do ASM disk discovery. Correct the ASM_DISKSTRING parameter, and restart the instance to correct the problem.

9. C. High redundancy is the highest redundancy setting available in ASM, or to the Alliance in this case. This will result in a double-mirrored ASM disk group.

10. B. After the RMAN script is run and the database is up and running successfully, you may delete the old database files.

11. B. If the DROP DISK operation has not yet completed, you can cancel and roll back the entire DROP DISK operation by using ALTER DISKGROUP … UNDROP DISKS, with the disk group still being continuously available to all users.

12. B. A fully qualified existing ASM filename has the format *+group/dbname/filetype/tag* *.file.incarnation*. In this case, *filetype* is datafile, and *tag* is the tablespace name to which it belongs, or users02.

13. C. RBAL coordinates rebalance activity for a disk group in an ASM instance.

14. A. Note that the UNDROP operation will cancel a drop operation in progress but cannot reverse a drop operation that has already completed. For HIGH REDUNDANCY, at least three failure groups must be specified. While you can combine a drop and add operation into one command, the command can reference only one disk group.

15. A. All types of database files are spread across all disks in the disk group to ensure redundancy unless the redundancy is set to EXTERNAL.

16. A. If the DROP DISK operation has already completed, you must use ALTER DISKGROUP … ADD DISK to add the disk back to the disk group. In any case, the disk group is continuously available to all users and no data is lost.

17. A. The ADD DIRECTORY command is not likely to use V$ASM_OPERATION to track its progress, because this operation adds only a small amount of metadata—a directory object—to the disk group and takes a minimal amount of time to complete. The V$ASM_OPERATION view provides the status of long-running ASM operations.

18. D. The ALTER DISKGROUP … ADD DISK command adds all disks that match the discovery string but are not already part of the same or another disk group.

19. E. The DISK_REPAIR_TIME attribute will prevent Oracle from automatically dropping the disk in the disk group for a specific period of time. This gives you time to replace the controller indicated in the question.

20. A, E. Apparently, for some reason DGROUP1 was not mounted when the ASM instance was started, or the disk was missing and then reappeared (hardware failure perhaps) after the ASM instance was started. ASM will discover new disks, even after the ASM instance is opened.

Chapter

2

Performing Oracle User-Managed Backups

ORACLE DATABASE 11*g*: ADMINISTRATION II EXAM OBJECTIVES COVERED IN THIS CHAPTER:

✓ **Configuring Backup Specifications**

- ▪ Configure backup settings

✓ **Configuring for Recovery**

- ▪ Configure multiple archive log file destinations to increase availability

✓ **Performing User-Managed Backup and Recovery**

- ▪ Identify the need of backup mode

- ▪ Perform user-managed backups and server-managed backups

- ▪ Back up and recover a control file

With this chapter, you will begin to dive into Oracle backup and recovery. The ability to restore an Oracle database is perhaps one of the DBA's more important jobs. In this chapter, we will do the following:

- Discuss the architecture of the Oracle database with respect to backup and recovery

- Discuss Oracle user-managed backup and recovery

- Show how to configure the database for backup and recovery

- Show how to perform user-managed backups both online and offline

Regarding the objectives listed in this chapter, server-managed backups are covered in Chapter 4, and manually recovering a control file is covered in Chapter 3.

Exam objectives are subject to change at any time without prior notice and at Oracle's sole discretion. Please visit Oracle's Training and Certification website (http://www.oracle.com/education/certification/) for the most current exam-objectives listing.

Understanding the Oracle Database as It Relates to Backup and Recovery

As a DBA, recovering your database should be important to you. Correspondingly, recovery is also important to Oracle, so the database product has been built to be robust with respect to backup and recovery. We'll start this chapter with a quick primer on how Oracle supports backup and recovery. In this section, we'll give you the background you need to understand backup and recovery and to be successful with your OCP exam. In the following sections, we will discuss these topics:

- Oracle processes related to backup and recovery

- Oracle memory structures related to backup and recovery

- The data dictionary

- Oracle datafiles and tablespaces
- Online redo logs
- Control files
- Parameter files
- NOARCHIVELOG and ARCHIVELOG modes
- The Oracle instance and the Oracle database
- Backup and recovery, the big picture

Note this is not the "kitchen sink" when it comes to an Oracle architecture discussion. We assume you are already somewhat familiar with the Oracle database architecture (since to take the OCP exam you must first have passed the OCA exam), so this is just a review of the pieces of it that are involved in backup and recovery in some way.

 There are two different kinds of Oracle recoveries: instance/crash recovery and media recovery. *Instance recovery* is automatically managed by Oracle when you restart the database. Since the OCP exam objectives do not include instance recovery as a topic, we will not be discussing it in any detail. *Media recovery* is a manual process done by the DBA and involves the use of Oracle database backups. In this text and the OCP exam, media recovery will be the principal topic to be discussed.

Oracle Processes Related to Backup and Recovery

The front-line support for Oracle backup and recovery is the Oracle architecture. One part of this architecture is the processes related to the Oracle database. Although the Oracle database has a number of processes, only a few really matter with respect to backup and recovery and will be mentioned in this text. These processes are as follows:

- LGWR
- DBWR
- ARCH
- User processes

Let's discuss each of these processes next so you can better understand how they impact database recovery.

LGWR Process

The *log writer process (LGWR)* is responsible for keeping the online redo logs up-to-date. The job of the LGWR process is to move redo from the volatile (nonpersistent) redo log buffer in the System (sometimes called Shared) Global Area (SGA) to the persistence of the online redo logs. A number of different things cause LGWR to wake up and write the redo data, among them commits and when the redo log buffer fills to a certain point.

DBWR Process

The *database writer process DBWn* is responsible for writing to the database datafiles. This writing occurs during events called *checkpoints*. A database checkpoint may, in reality, happen at just about any time while the database is running. DBWR has very little to do with recovery of the database (other than to support it by writing to the datafiles) because database datafile writes are often delayed and the blocks within the datafiles themselves are not consistent with the current state of the data inside of the SGA.

ARCH Process

The *archiver process ARCn* is responsible for the creation of archived redo logs. In a later section in this chapter on redo logs, we will discuss how redo logs are filled with redo. Once the redo log file fills, a log switch occurs and Oracle will begin to write to the next online redo log. If the database is in ARCHIVELOG mode (see the section "NOARCHIVELOG and ARCHIVELOG Modes"), the ARCH process will be responsible for taking that filled archived redo log and copying it to one or more backup locations.

In Oracle Database 11g, the ARCH process starts automatically. Oracle can also start more than one ARCH process if multiple redo logs need to be archived. For ARCH to work properly, you will need to configure the appropriate archiving locations (see "Configuring the Database for Backup and Recovery" later in this chapter for more). The ARCH process is so vital to backup and recovery of the database that if it cannot copy the archived redo logs to the mandatory archived log destinations, the database will eventually stall until the problem is corrected.

User Processes

At first glance, it might seem that the user processes are not all that important to backup and recovery. As you will see, user processes are actually an integral part of backup and recovery since you have to be able to connect to the database instance to actually do a database backup or recovery.

Oracle Memory Structures Related to Backup and Recovery

The principle SGA memory structure to be aware of when it comes to backup and recovery is the *redo log buffer*. This is typically a small area of memory that is configured for Oracle to store redo in. This is a very transient area of memory and its size can impact the performance of your database. Although the redo log buffer will not have a direct impact on backup and recovery, it's still important to be aware of it in the light of any discussion on backup and recovery.

The Oracle Data Dictionary

The *Oracle data dictionary* is a critical piece of the backup and recovery landscape. In the following sections, we will first introduce you to the data dictionary. We will then give you some information on the basic format of the data dictionary so it will be more familiar to you when you actually use it. Finally, we will provide a list of views that you will find useful during your backup and recovery efforts.

Overview of the Data Dictionary

The data dictionary is a set of views and tables that expose metadata about your Oracle database. For example, if you want to know the name of your database, you can look at the NAME column in a view called V$DATABASE.

The data dictionary is critical because it will give you information on the following critical components of the database:

- Tablespaces
- Datafiles
- Redo logs
- RMAN backup–related information
- Database configuration

This information will be critical when configuring for backups and also when it comes time to recover your database from failure. Throughout this book you will be using the data dictionary, and it behooves you to become comfortable with it.

Forms of the Data Dictionary

The data dictionary views are named using a common naming convention. This convention can be used to identify the source of the data and when a view can be queried. The main types of data dictionary views are as follows:

Static data dictionary views   The *static data dictionary views* are sourced from tables and views created when the database was first created. These tables and views are owned by the SYS schema and are located in the SYSTEM tablespace. The views typically contain structural metadata about the database, including such things as tables, indexes, and other database objects. The names of these views are all prefixed to indicate the scope of the data contained within that view. There are three main prefixes:

DBA_*   The DBA_* views allow those with DBA privileges to see all data contained in the view. For example, if you were a DBA and you wanted to see all tables in the database named MY_DATA, you could query the DBA_TABLES view, as shown here:

```
Select owner, table_name from dba_tables
Where owner='MY_DATA';
```

ALL_*   The scope of the ALL_* views is more reduced than that of the DBA_* views. When you query the ALL_* views, you see only those objects that you have been granted some form of access to. For example, if you wanted to see all instances of a table called MY_DATA that you had access to, you could query the ALL_TABLES view, as shown here:

```
Select owner, table_name from all_tables;
```

USER_* **The** USER_* views are the most restrictive of the data dictionary views. When you query the USER_* views, you see only those objects that are in the schema you are currently logged into. For example, if you wanted to see if there was a table called MY_DATA in your schema, you could query the USER_TABLES view, as shown here:

```
Select table_name from user_tables;
```

Notice in the example query against USER_TABLES that you removed the owner column. It is quite common that the DBA_* and ALL_* views will have an owner column but that the USER_* views will not. This is because the user in the USER_* views is assumed to be the user you are logged in as.

Dynamic performance data dictionary views The *dynamic performance data dictionary views* typically start with a V$ prefix, such as V$DATABASE or V$SESSION. The views are often used for database monitoring and tuning, but there are times when they will be the only database views available to you for recovery purposes.

The data in these views source from either the database control file or C structures that are part of the Oracle database kernel. Typically these views are available when the database instance is mounted (see "Oracle Database Startup and Shutdown" later in this chapter), but some views are available only after the instance has started.

 Real World Scenario

Using Data Dictionary Views

In the real world, DBAs use the data dictionary a great deal. Although Oracle offers a nice graphical database administration tool called OEM that helps reduce the DBAs' need to use the data dictionary, the typical DBA will often find a need to access the data dictionary.

For example, the other day we needed to know which users were on the system and what their OS process IDs were so we could kill a process. We were already in SQL*Plus and it was going to be easier to just query the data dictionary than to open a browser, log into OEM, and surf to the page that would give us the information we wanted.

Our boss thought we were crazy for not using OEM, so we had a race to see who could get the information faster. Want to guess who won? Often DBAs will create their own set of scripts to access the data dictionary views. This makes it even faster to get the information you want without having to switch back and forth to OEM. OEM is a great tool, but sometimes it just pays to know the data dictionary.

Common Data Dictionary and Dynamic Performance Views You Will Use

During your backup and recovery experiences as an Oracle DBA, you will have occasion to use the data dictionary. Table 2.1 provides a list of some data dictionary views that you will want to be aware of and that will be helpful to you on your OCP exam.

TABLE 2.1   Examples of Data Dictionary/Dynamic Performance Views Useful for Recovery

View Name	Description
V$DATABASE	Provides basic database-related information, including the logging mode
V$INSTANCE	Provides basic instance information
V$DATAFILE	Provides database datafile information stored in the control file
V$LOGFILE	Provides information on the individual redo log file members from the control file
V$LOG	Provides information on the redo log groups from the control file
V$ARCHIVED_LOG	Provides archive log information from the control file
V$LOG_HISTORY	Provides information on redo log switches in the database
DBA_DATA_FILES	Provides datafile information from the data dictionary
DBA_TABLESPACES	Provides information on tablespaces in the database

You can find all the data dictionary views available in Oracle by looking at the Oracle reference guide in the Oracle documentation available at http://tahiti.oracle.com.

Oracle Datafiles and Tablespaces

Oracle data is stored in tablespaces, which comprise one or more datafiles. It is very important to understand datafiles and tablespaces and their relationships when it comes to backup and recovery. In the following sections, we will briefly reintroduce you to the important components of the Oracle database.

Oracle Datafiles

The Oracle database *datafiles* are critical database physical files that are used to store all your Oracle data (well, almost all!). The physical datafiles are the structures most likely to be lost and subsequently recovered during a database-recovery operation. You are probably aware that database datafiles are preallocated in size and that they can be configured to grow automatically.

When you perform a physical backup of your database, the database datafiles will be the principle structures you back up. When you restore your database due to a media failure, you will be restoring one or more datafiles. You may also have to restore other database files such as the control file, the online redo logs, and the archived redo logs, which we will discuss later in this section.

Oracle Tablespaces

A *tablespace* is a logical, named, entity in the database that is used to store database objects. For example, your database might have a table called STORES that contains data about stores in your organization. The table STORES will be assigned to a tablespace, perhaps called STORE_DATA.

A tablespace is assigned to one or more database datafiles, and the size of the tablespace is related to the size of the underlying database datafiles. Several recovery options exist with respect to tablespaces, including tablespace point-in-time recovery, which we will discuss in Chapter 8 of this book.

Redo Logs

The redo logs of the database are the principle vehicle for backup and recovery. In the following sections, we will cover two different types of redo logs. First we will discuss the online redo log, and then we will discuss the archived redo log.

Online Redo Logs

Online redo logs are used by Oracle to store all the changes that occur in the database. Think of them as something akin to a videotape recording everything that is going on. Later on, you can rewind that videotape and replay it to see what happened. During recovery, Oracle does just that using the online redo logs.

In this section we will discuss online redo log file basics, redo log file groups, redo log file members, and redo log file sequence numbers.

Redo Log File Basics

Online redo logs are created when the database is created. You must have a minimum of two redo logs in any Oracle database. When the database starts running, it will write to the first redo log. Once that log fills up, it will switch over and begin to write to the next log. Once the second log fills up, the database will clear the first log and begin to write redo into that log. Thus, redo log files are used in a round-robin style.

Redo Log File Groups

Each online redo log file is a member of a specific *redo log file group*. In the case where there are just two online redo logs (the minimum allowed), there will be two groups, likely named group 1 and group 2. You can create new online redo log groups and drop existing groups (until you are down to just two groups) anytime online.

Redo Log File Members

As you might gather, the online redo log files are an important component of the database. If you loose the online log files, you could actually permanently loose data. To protect against this, Oracle provides for multiplexing of online redo logs within each group. Each copy of the online redo log is considered a *redo log file member*, often called just a member.

Multiplexing allows you to indicate to Oracle that it should create and maintain duplicate copies of the online redo log files. When multiplexing online redo logs, it's a good idea to put each member on a different disk for many reasons, even on a SAN.

Redo Log Sequence Numbers

Each time an online redo log group is used, that group is assigned a unique *redo log sequence number* (typically 1 for a new database). As you can see in Figure 2.1, you have two online redo log groups. You start writing to the first online redo log group, which is log sequence 1. Once that log group fills up, you start writing to online group 2, which was assigned sequence number 2. Once that group fills up, you switch back to redo log group one, reusing that redo log group. The sequence number is incremented, though, and the redo associated with that online redo log group will be part of sequence 3. Once that group fills up, Oracle will switch to online log group 3. Once that group fills up, Oracle switches back to redo log group 1, reusing that redo log group.

FIGURE 2.1   Redo log file round-robin writing

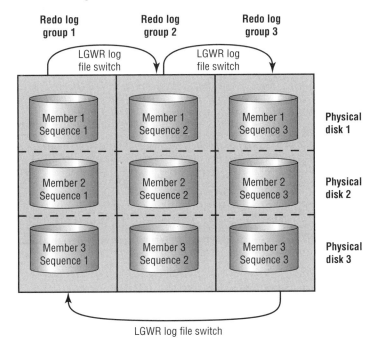

Sequence numbers can be very important when it comes to recovering your database, as you will see in Chapters 3, 6, and 8.

Archived Redo Logs

You may have noticed from the previous discussion on online redo logs that the redo log files get reused over and over. As a result, the records in those log files will be lost forever when the log file is reused. This overwriting of the online redo logs limits the recovery options available for you to use with Oracle.

When the database is put in ARCHIVELOG mode (see the section "NOARCHIVELOG and ARCHIVELOG Modes"), Oracle will make copies of the online redo logs after they have been filled and after Oracle starts to write to the next online redo log group. The copies of the online redo logs are called *archived redo logs*. Archived redo logs are critical to advanced recoveries such as point-in-time recoveries and point-of-failure recoveries.

Control Files

The *control file* of the database is kind of the master control file, if you will. It's a binary file that contains information about physical database structures, redo logs, and archived redo logs, and RMAN information is stored here too. The control file is critical to a good backup and recovery strategy, as you will see in this chapter and other chapters of this book.

Parameter Files

In this section we will address what parameter files and parameters are. We will then discuss the two types of parameter files available in Oracle, the parameter file (pfile) and server parameter file (spfile).

Parameter Files and Parameters

Every Oracle database has a *parameter file*. Inside the parameter file you'll find a variety of parameters that define global settings for that database. Parameter files are stored, by default, in ORACLE_HOME/dbs or ORACLE_HOME/database, depending on the operating system in use.

Each parameter file will contain many different parameters. Parameters are used to configure memory settings, auditing settings, destination directories for log files, and archived redo log files. When configuring a database for backup and recovery, you will configure several parameters, as you will see in the section titled "Configuring the Database for Backup and Recovery."

Parameters come in two flavors, static and dynamic. You must change static parameters and restart the database in order for the parameters to take effect. Dynamic parameters can be changed on the fly, without the need to restart the database.

You can find all the database parameters available in Oracle by looking at the Oracle reference guide in the Oracle documentation available at http://tahiti.oracle.com.

Parameter Files (pfiles)

The pfile parameter file is a text-based parameter file. To modify settings in this file, you simply open the file with your editor and change it. Once your changes are complete, save the file. You will then need to bounce the database to have those settings take effect.

pfiles are kept, by default, in the $ORACLE_HOME/dbs (UNIX) or %ORACLE_HOME%\database (Windows) directory. The default name for a pfile is init<oracle_sid>.ora. So if your Unix database is called ORCL, your pfile will be called initORCL.ora by default. Note that case sensitivity applies here based on the operating system.

Server Parameter Files (spfiles)

The spfile is a parameter file managed by the Oracle server. We will first look closer at the spfile itself, and then we will discuss how to set parameters when using an spfile.

What Is an spfile?

An Oracle spfile differs from a text-based parameter file in that the Oracle server manages it, and you as the DBA should never edit the file directly. The spfile is partly nontext (it has a header and a footer), but the actual parameter settings are in plain text (so you can view the file if you like and see what parameters are set to in the spfile).

spfiles are kept, by default, in the $ORACLE_HOME/dbs (Unix) or %ORACLE_HOME%\database (Windows) directory. The spfile naming convention is sp<oracle_sid>.ora by default. When the DBA starts the Oracle database/instance, Oracle will first look for an spfile using the default filename. If one is not found, it will look for a file called spfile<oracle_sid>.ora in the same default directory. Finally, if no spfile is found, Oracle will look for a regular pfile as described previously. If no parameter file is found, then the database will signal an error and the startup will abort.

Note that if you try to start the database from RMAN without an spfile or pfile available, Oracle will use default parameter settings and actually start the database. This does not happen if you try to start the database from SQL*Plus or OEM. We will discuss RMAN more in Chapter 4.

How Do You Set Parameter Values When Using an spfile?

To modify a parameter when using an spfile, you use the alter system command. For example, if you want to change the parameter DB_RECOVERY_FILE_DEST_SIZE, which is dynamic (so it can be changed on the fly), you would issue the following alter system command:

```
Alter system set db_recovery_file_dest_size=100m;
```

As we said earlier, some parameters are not dynamic. In this case, you have to indicate that you want to change only the parameter file. To do this, use the `alter system` command and include the `scope=spfile` keyword, as shown here:

```
Alter system set memory_max_target=200m scope=spfile;
```

In some cases, you may want to change the parameter in just the current instance of the database, but you will not want that change to persist after the next shutdown. In this case, use the `scope=memory` keyword when issuing the `alter system` command, as shown here:

```
Alter system set db_recovery_file_dest_size=100m scope=memory;
```

NOARCHIVELOG and ARCHIVELOG Modes

The Oracle database runs in two principal modes, NOARCHIVELOG (the default) and ARCHIVELOG. The logging bit has to do with archived redo logs and if they are saved or not, which makes a difference in the kinds of recoveries that you can do. Let's look at each mode in a bit more detail.

NOARCHIVELOG MODE   *NOARCHIVELOG* mode is the default logging mode. In NOARCHIVELOG mode, the online redo logs are overwritten over time and no backups are created. Because of this, you are limited in the way you can back up your database and how you can recover it.

Backups are limited to cold or offline backups. This means that you must shut down your database before you can back it up. As you will see in later sections of this chapter, you will back up all the datafiles of the database plus the online redo logs and the control file(s).

Recovery in NOARCHIVELOG is equally limited. In NOARCHIVELOG mode, you can restore the database only to the point in time that the backup was taken. Thus you will lose any changes to the database that took place after the backup was complete and the database was opened for business. This is typically not an acceptable solution for production databases.

We will discuss how to back up your database in NOARCHIVELOG mode later in this chapter. In Chapter 3 we will discuss recovering your database with backups taken in NOARCHIVELOG mode. In Chapter 4 we will discuss using RMAN to perform offline backups, and in Chapter 6 we will discuss using RMAN to restore these backups.

ARCHIVELOG MODE   *ARCHIVELOG* mode is a much more flexible method of operating your database. In this mode, you can back up your database while it's up and running, allowing users to work at the same time that the backups are running.

When the database is in ARCHIVELOG mode, changes are recorded in the online redo logs as usual. What is different is that the archived redo logs are copied to a backup directory once they have filled up. These copies of the redo log files are called *archived redo logs* and the Oracle database process that copies them is called the *ARCH process*. In Oracle Database 11*g*, the ARC*n* process starts automatically when the database is in ARCHIVELOG mode.

The archived redo logs may be copied to one or a number of different destinations. We will discuss configuring where Oracle should copy these archived redo logs to in the section "Configuring the Database for Backup and Recovery."

We will discuss how to back up your database in ARCHIVELOG mode later in this chapter. In Chapter 3 we will discuss recovering your database with backups taken in ARCHIVELOG mode. In Chapter 4 we will discuss using RMAN to perform online backups, and in Chapter 6 we will discuss using RMAN to restore these backups. Finally, in Chapter 8 we will discuss more-advanced recoveries with backups taken in ARCHIVELOG mode.

The Oracle Instance and the Oracle Database

In the following sections, we will first review knowledge you should already have on the basics of the Oracle instances and the Oracle database. Then we will discuss the startup and shutdown of the Oracle instance and the Oracle database.

Oracle Instances and Oracle Databases: A Review

With respect to backup and recovery of Oracle databases, it is important to understand that there is a difference between an Oracle instance and an Oracle database. This is because certain backup and recovery operations must occur while the Oracle instance is running and the database is not. Other operations will require that the database be open (which presumes the instance is already running).

No doubt you are already somewhat familiar with the notion of the instance from your OCA experience as well as your actual database experience. To review, an Oracle *instance* is the collection of shared memory (SGA) and processes (LGWR, DBWR, and so on). When these are all up and running, the instance is said to be started (see the next section for more details on starting and stopping a database).

The Oracle *database* is essentially the collection of database datafiles. When the instance is running, Oracle will attach to the database and open it for business. Once the database is open, users can begin to do their work, assuming there are no problems during the database open process that prevents it from opening.

 Sybex's *OCA: Oracle Database 11*g *Administrator Certified Associate Study Guide* provides complete coverage on the Oracle database memory and processes. In this text, we assume you have already taken and passed the OCA exam and that you understand the body of knowledge consanguineous to that exam.

Oracle Database Startup and Shutdown

It is important to understand the startup and shutdown process of an Oracle database. In this section we will first discuss the different stages of the Oracle database startup and shutdown processes. We will then discuss the mechanics of actually starting and stopping the database in its different phases. We will quickly discuss restricted-mode database operations, and finally we will discuss the different stages the database must be in for specific types of backup and recovery operations to occur.

Exploring the Stages of Database Startup and Shutdown

When an Oracle database is started, it goes through four different and distinct stages:

Shutdown   When the database and instance are shut down, they are at rest. There are no processes present, no memory allocated, nothing is going on. It is important to note that even though the database/instance may be shut down and closed, other Oracle processes (like the listener or OEM agents) maybe still running.

Nomount   When the database is in nomount mode, the instance has been started. Thus, processes have been started and memory allocated.

Mount   When the database is in mount mode (or mounted), the instance is started and the database has opened the control file. The control file is read, but is contents are not validated.

Open   When the database is opened, the control-file contents have been validated against the physical database. The datafiles are all confirmed to be present, and they are opened. Oracle will then analyze the datafiles to determine if the database is in a consistent state. If the database is not in a consistent state, some form of recovery will be required.

Typically, the form of recovery required, *crash or instance recovery*, does not require any DBA involvement. If instance recovery is not possible, then *media recovery* is required. Media recovery requires the application of backups and recovery operations to bring the database current to the point of failure (if this is possible). The principal determining factors for media recovery is the presence of the needed datafiles and the availability in the online redo logs of the redo needed to bring those files current. If either of these conditions does not exist, then media recovery is required.

Database shutdowns occur in much the same way as startups, except in reverse. There are two different kinds of shutdowns, however: consistent and inconsistent.

Consistent shutdowns   If your database shutdown is a *consistent shutdown*, then the database datafiles and the database control file will be synchronized upon shutdown. The dirty buffers in the database buffer cache will be flushed out to the database datafiles, making them consistent. A consistent shutdown is a nice, tidy shutdown.

Inconsistent shutdowns   An *inconsistent shutdown* is another term for a mess. When your database is shut down in an inconsistent manner, it is in a indeterminate state and will require some form of recovery (typically instance recovery, which requires no DBA intervention) when it is restarted. Inconsistent shutdowns, however bad they might sound, often are the only way to shut down a database in a timely manner.

Sybex's OCA preparation guide for Oracle Database 11g *(OCA: Oracle Database 11g Administrator Certified Associate Study Guide*, 2009) provides complete coverage on starting the Oracle database and the different stages of opening the Oracle database, so this is just a quick review.

Starting and Stopping the Database

During backup and recovery operations, you will need to know how to start up and shut down your database correctly. To start up the database in any of the modes described in the previous section, you will use the `startup` command or the `alter database` command, as required. To stop the database, you will use the `shutdown` command. Typically, database startup operations are performed from SQL*Plus or Oracle Enterprise Manager.

The `startup` command   This command is used to start the instance and/or database when the database is in a shutdown state only. The `startup` command can be used to completely open the database, as shown in this code snippet:

```
SQL> startup
```

The `startup` command also has options that you can use to indicate that you want Oracle to start the startup operation at a certain point. For example, you can indicate that you want the instance to be started only by using the `startup nomount` command:

```
SQL> startup nomount
```

Or perhaps you want to start the instance and mount the database. In this case, the command would be as follows:

```
SQL> startup mount
```

Sometimes you want to shut down the database and start it up in one command. You can use the `startup force` command to perform this action. Note that the `startup force` command will shut down your database in an inconsistent manner (which we discussed earlier in this chapter), and some operations (such as putting the database in ARCHIVELOG mode) will not complete successfully if the database was shut down in an inconsistent manner. Here is an example of the `startup force` command:

```
SQL> startup force
```

The `shutdown` command   The `shutdown` command does what it says; it shuts down the database. As with the `startup` command, it comes with a few options. First there is the plain-Jane `shutdown` command, which will shut down the database if absolutely nothing is going on and if absolutely no one is logged in. You can guess how often those conditions happen in reality! Until its conditions are met, the `shutdown` command will just sit there, waiting for its opportunity to shut down the database.

Here is an example of the `shutdown` command:

```
SQL> shutdown
```

If waiting is not your forte, then you may want to try the `shutdown immediate` command. The `shutdown immediate` command will prevent new logons, roll back any uncommitted transactions, and then bring the database down. It's a consistent-shutdown, no-waiting approach to stopping the database and lots of DBAs like it. Here is an example:

```
SQL> shutdown immediate
```

The cousin of `shutdown immediate` is `shutdown transactional` (we are not sure if it's a first cousin or second cousin; Oracle has not defined this within the body of the Oracle documentation yet). The main difference here is that the `shutdown transactional` command will wait for active transactions to complete (commit) before shutting down those sessions. As a result, the `shutdown transactional` command can take a while longer to complete its task, but on the positive side, users might be a little bit happier (if they are actually able to be happy anytime the database comes down). Here is an example of the `shutdown transactional` command:

```
SQL> shutdown transactional
```

The bad boy of database shutdowns is the `shutdown abort` command. If you want your database to come down without debate, this is the way to do it. This is like pulling the power cord on your database; it is a crash of the database, shutting it down in an inconsistent manner. Here is an example of the `shutdown abort` command:

```
SQL>shutdown abort
```

The *shutdown abort* Command: The Truth Is Out There

As long as the shutdown abort command has been around it has been surrounded in controversy. It is believed by some that the Seven-Day War was actually started as the result of a disagreement between DBAs over the shutdown abort command (they conveniently ignore the fact that Oracle didn't even exist then). The truth is that the shutdown abort command is the fastest way to shut down your database. Because the database will be shut down in an inconsistent manner, it may result in a delayed database startup because of the recovery process that Oracle must go through internally. Often, though, shutdown abort may well be the way to get your database shut down and started back up in the shortest amount of time possible.

The `alter database` command   The `alter database` command is used to move the instance/database from one state to another. For example, if the instance was started with the `startup nomount` command, you may want to mount the database. To do so, you would use the `alter database mount` command, as shown here:

```
SQL>alter database mount;
```

If the database is already mounted and you want to open it, then the `alter database mount` command would be appropriate, as shown in this example:

```
SQL>alter database open;
```

Performing Database Restricted-Mode Operations

Sometimes it's nice to have the house to yourself, isn't it? Oracle allows you the equivalent of having the house to yourself when you put the database in restricted mode. When the database is in restricted mode, only those with the restricted session privilege can access it. Since DBA accounts have restricted session privileges, this means you can log into the database and do your work, feeling secure that other users won't get in and cause problems. You may find that during certain recovery operations restricted session will help when you need to get into the database to perform some DBA-related activities but you don't want other users to log in yet.

To open the database in restricted mode you will issue the `startup restrict` command. If your database is already open, you can put it in restricted mode with the `alter database enable restricted session` command. To disable restricted session and allow users to connect to the database, use the `alter database disable restricted session` command.

Performing Backup and Recovery Operations and Getting Database Status

So, what kind of operations would you do given the different open or closed combinations of the database and instance? Here are some examples:

Operations while the instance is down and the database is not open:

- Copy the spfile to a pfile.
- Copy the pfile to a spfile.
- Perform manual cold backups.

Operations while the instance is open and the database is not open:

- Create a database.
- Create a database control file.
- Restore the database control file or spfile from RMAN.

Operations while the instance is mounted and the database is not open:

- Cold backup with RMAN
- Recovery of critical datafiles (SYSTEM, UNDO tablespaces).
- Offline recovery of entire database.

Operations while the instance is mounted and the database is open:

- Online datafile or tablespace recovery of noncritical tablespaces.
- Online backups of the database.

Configuring the Database for Backup and Recovery

The ARCHIVELOG and NOARCHIVELOG modes of the database really boil down to what your backup and recovery needs and requirements are. If your recovery needs are simple, you just want to restore to the point of your last backup; then you can leave your database in NOARCHIVELOG mode and do offline backups. If your database uptime requirements provide time to shut down the database for your backup, then NOARCHIVELOG mode will work fine for you.

If you are going to do offline backups of your database in NOARCHIVELOG mode, then you can pretty much ignore this section. All you will need to do there (as we will cover in the next section) is determine the location of the files you need to back up and the location to which you want to back them up, shut down the database, and back it up.

When you want to perform online backups, or if you want to be able to recover offline backups beyond the time of the backup, then the database needs to be in ARCHIVELOG mode. Putting the database in ARCHIVELOG mode requires some configuration, which we will discuss first. Once you have configured the database, you will then actually put it in ARCHIVELOG mode, which we will cover next.

In the following sections we will discuss configuring the database for ARCHIVELOG mode operations (no additional configuration for NOARCHIVELOG mode operations is required unless you want to configure the flash recovery area for RMAN, which is covered in Chapter 4), and then we will discuss actually putting the database in ARCHIVELOG mode. Finally we will discuss some database views that will be useful when managing a database in ARCHIVELOG mode.

 **Real World Scenario**

Mixing NOARCHIVELOG and ARCHIVELOG Modes

In the real world, you might find that some of your databases are running in NOARCHIVELOG mode and some of your databases are running in ARCHIVELOG mode. For example, your development and test databases may be able to be shut down at night for backups. Additionally, they might not have a need for point-in-time or point-of-failure recovery. Thus, NOARCHIVELOG mode is just fine for them.

You may find that your production databases have different requirements. First, it may be that shutting down your production systems for backups at any time is not acceptable to your customer. Further, you probably will also find that people prefer not to lose data in production and that they would prefer to be able to restore the database and then recover all work that occurred after the last backup. You will have to put your database in ARCHIVELOG mode to satisfy those requirements.

Configuring for ARCHIVELOG Mode

The first step to putting the database in ARCHIVELOG mode is to set the database parameters. You need to set the database parameters so that the ARCH process will work correctly when it needs to archive the online redo logs, creating archived redo logs.

You will want to consider setting several parameters when you are going to put the database in ARCHIVELOG mode. A number of parameters are directly associated with user-managed backup and recovery in ARCHIVELOG mode. Table 2.2 describes these parameters.

Perhaps you are asking yourself, "What about this flash recovery area thing I've been hearing about?" We will discuss the flash recovery area (FRA) in more detail in Chapter 4. As a result, the parameters related to the RMAN and the FRA are not included in Table 2.2.

TABLE 2.2   Oracle Parameters Associated with User-Managed Backup and Recovery

Parameter Name	Description
LOG_ARCHIVE_DEST	Indicates the destination to copy archived redo logs to. Typically this parameter is not set and the LOG_ARCHIVE_DEST_N parameter is set instead.
LOG_ARCHIVE_DEST_n	Indicates one of up to 10 destinations to copy archived redo logs to. The first destination starts with 1 (LOG_ARCHIVE_DEST_01).
LOG_ARCHIVE_DEST_STATE_n	Indicates the state of LOG_ARCHIVE_DEST_N (ENABLED, DEFERRED, or ALTERNATE).]
LOG_ARCHIVE_FORMAT	Indicates the format of the archived redo log filenames.

Assume that you have a database called orcl and you have decided that you want Oracle to back up your archived redo logs to a directory called c:\oracle\archivelog\orcl (in Unix, perhaps it's called /oracle/archivelog/orcl). You would first have to create the file-system directory structures and then you would need to set the appropriate parameters. In this case, you would use the alter system command to set the LOG_ARCHIVE_DEST_1 parameter to point to c:\oracle\archivelog\mydb, as shown in this code example:

```
Alter system set log_archive_dest_1='location=c:\oracle\archivelog\orcl';
```

You can also clear this parameter setting by just using blank quotes, as shown in this example:

```
Alter system set log_archive_dest_1='';
```

With the `LOG_ARCHIVE_DEST_n` parameter, you can configure up to 10 different archive-log destination directories. This feature can be used to provide redundant backup locations for your archive logs to protect them in the event of a failure of one or more of those locations. For example, you could archive to a local disk, and you could archive to an NFS-mounted disk. In that case, you would have two `LOG_ARCHIVE_DEST` parameters set like this:

```
-- Local mount on C: drive
Alter system set log_archive_dest_1='location=c:\oracle\archivelog\orcl';
-- NFS Mount on Z: drive
Alter system set log_archive_dest_2='location=Z:\oracle\archivelog\orcl';
```

Oracle will archive to both destinations, in parallel. This type of configuration is also used in more advanced database setups such as standby databases.

> Archive-log destination directories can take on different states, such as ENABLED, DEFERRED, or ALTERNATE (I tried to get the folks at Oracle to add a state of EXAUSTION or FRUSTRATION; they said no, but they did seem to like the suggestion of a state of CONFUSION). They can also be defined as MANDATORY or OPTIONAL. You will not need to be aware of these advanced settings for your OCP exam, but you might need to use these options as a part of your normal duties. You can find more information on these different attributes in the Oracle documentation.

You may also want to control how Oracle names the archived redo logs. This is done with the `LOG_ARCHIVE_FORMAT` parameter. For example, you may want to put the database name in the name of the archive logs being created, but you also want them to be numbered in such a way that the name will always be unique. You can set the `LOG_ARCHIVE_FORMAT` string to a value of `orcl_%s_%t_%r.arc`, as shown in this example:

```
Alter system set log_archive_format='orcl_%s_%t_%r_%d.arc';
```

You may wonder what the %s, %t, %r, and %d represent. These are variables that represent values for particular components of the archived redo log. The %s represents the sequence number, which is always unique for a given database (until a `resetlogs` command occurs, which we will discuss in Chapter 3). The %t is the thread number that represents an individual node on a cluster when your database is running on Oracle's Real Application Clusters (RAC). The %r represents the resetlogs number (see Chapter 3). Finally, the %d represents the DBID that should be unique for each database. Together, this string of variables will make the archive log filenames unique for every database on your system.

Every database in Oracle has a DBID, which is a unique identifier for the database (see the DBID column in V$DATABASE to see your DBID). Be careful, though! It is possible to have databases on two different boxes with the same name and even with the same DBID. If you will be sharing an ARCHIVELOG mount point between boxes (say, via NFS), you will need to make sure you do not accidentally overwrite archived redo logs originating from databases with the same name and/or DBID! You won't need to know about the DBID for your OCP exam, but we thought we'd tell you anyway!

Putting the Database in ARCHIVELOG Mode

Putting the database in ARCHIVELOG mode is as easy as following these steps:

1. Configure archiving-related parameters as shown in the previous section.

2. Shut down the database in a consistent state using the shutdown, shutdown immediate, or shutdown transactional command.

3. Mount the database with the startup mount command.

4. Put the database in ARCHIVELOG mode with the alter database archivelog command.

5. Open the database with the alter database open command.

One thing to be aware of when the database is in ARCHIVELOG mode is that if you have not configured archiving correctly, you could find yourself with a database that just stops running. If Oracle cannot archive the online redo logs, it will suspend all database operations once it cycles through all the online redo log groups. So, for example, if your database does log switches every 10 minutes and has three redo log groups, your database will mysteriously freeze after 30 minutes. Lack of configuration is not as big of a problem in Oracle Database 11g as it was in earlier versions since Oracle defaults to using the flash recovery area (discussed in Chapter 4).

Similar problems can occur if the archive-log destination directory runs out of space or if the permissions are not set correctly. If Oracle starts to have problems of this sort, it will log an error in the alert log of the database. Here is an example of an error you might see in the alert log:

```
All online logs needed archiving
ARCH: Archival stopped, error occurred. Will continue retrying
ORA-16014: log 2 sequence# 29 not archived, no available destinations
ORA-00312: online log 2 thread 1: 'C:\ORACLE\ORADATA\ORCL\REDO02.LOG'
```

Also, users logging into the database will find their logins just hanging until the archive-log problems are solved.

We've covered the parameters needed to put the database in ARCHIVELOG mode and the basic steps involved in the process. Let's look at an example of actually putting the database in ARCHIVELOG mode. Exercise 2.1 provides an example of doing just that.

 Real World Scenario

Online Redo Logs Stop Being Archived

We can't tell you how many times this has happened to us as DBAs. You are busy designing some cool model and the operations guys call. "Hey," they say, "we are getting calls. The database isn't working anymore."

"What?" you respond, "What do you mean it's not working?"

"The user sessions are just stalled, sitting there not doing anything. It's like the database has gone out to lunch or something," the operations guy says.

Immediately you are pretty sure you know what's wrong. So you ask the operations guy, "So, the mount point for the archived redo logs. Are you possibly getting an alert that it's full?"

The operations guy fumbles around to look at the alerts. Sure enough, the archived redo log destination is filled up. "Oh, yeah...I was going to call you about that but I forgot."

So, you proceed to back up the archived redo logs and then remove them from the system to free up space. You also follow up to make sure some additional disk space is added to the file system.

This kind of situation happens a lot if you do not have enough space available for your archived redo logs or if your backups stop working. I've seen this happen a lot in shops where the database was originally designed for a certain amount of use and that usage has increased significantly.

EXERCISE 2.1

Putting a Database in ARCHIVELOG Mode

In this exercise you will take a database that is in NOARCHIVELOG mode and put it in ARCHIVELOG mode.

1. First, validate that the database is in NOARCHIVELOG mode using the V$DATABASE column LOG_MODE:

```
SQL> Select log_mode from v$database;
LOG_MODE
```

```
------------
NOARCHIVELOG
```

2. Next, look at the settings for the parameters LOG_ARCHIVE_DEST_1 and LOG_ARCHIVE_
    FORMAT:

```
SQL> show parameter log_archive_dest_1
NAME                                   TYPE          VALUE
------------------------------------  ------------  ------------
log_archive_dest_1                     string
log_archive_dest_10                    string
SQL> show parameter log_archive_format
NAME                                   TYPE          VALUE
------------------------------------  ------------  ------------
log_archive_format                     string        ARC%S_%R.%T
```

3. Create the archive log directory c:\oracle\arch\orcl:

```
SQL> host mkdir c:\oracle\arch\orcl
```

4. You want to modify LOG_ARCHIVE_DEST_1 and LOG_ARCHIVE_FORMAT so that they are
    set correctly. LOG_ARCHIVE_DEST_1 should be set to c:\oracle\arch\orcl and LOG_
    ARCHIVE_FORMAT should be orcl_%r_%t_%s.arc. You will use the alter system com-
    mand to set these parameters. You will then check to make sure they are set correctly.

```
Alter system set log_archive_dest_1='location=c:\oracle\arch\orcl';
-- Note that we have to use the scope=spfile on this next parameter.
-- This is because it's not dynamic!
Alter system set log_archive_format='orcl_%r_%t_%s.arc' scope=spfile;
```

5. Next, shut down the database in a consistent manner with the shutdown immediate
    command:

```
SQL> shutdown immediate
Database closed.
Database dismounted.
ORACLE instance shut down.
```

6. Now nomount the database with the startup nomount command:

```
SQL> startup nomount;
ORACLE instance started.
Total System Global Area   418484224 bytes
Fixed Size                   1333592 bytes
Variable Size              348128936 bytes
```

```
Database Buffers           62914560 bytes
Redo Buffers                6107136 bytes
Database Mounted.
```

7. Put the database in ARCHIVELOG mode with the alter database archivelog command:

```
SQL> alter database archivelog;
Database altered.
```

8. Open the database for operations:

```
SQL> alter database open;
Database altered.
```

9. Make sure the database is in ARCHIVELOG mode:

```
SQL> Select log_mode from v$database;
LOG_MODE
------------
ARCHIVELOG
```

10. It is a good idea to make sure that everything is configured correctly and that the archived redo logs are getting generated in the place you expect them to be getting generated in. So, first you will force an archive-log switch with the alter system switch logfile command. This will cause a log switch to the next redo log group and ARCH will need to copy the redo log to an archived redo log.

```
SQL> alter system switch logfile;
System altered.
```

11. Look in the c:\oracle\arch\orcl directory. You should see a file in that directory.

```
SQL> host dir c:\oracle\arch\orcl
 Volume in drive C has no label.
 Volume Serial Number is 08DE-E1AB
 Directory of c:\oracle\arch\orcl
08/02/2008  12:44 PM    <DIR>          .
08/02/2008  12:44 PM    <DIR>          ..
08/02/2008  12:44 PM        41,032,192 ORCL_658485967_1_2.ARC
               1 File(s)     41,032,192 bytes
               2 Dir(s)  17,065,476,096 bytes free
```

The ORCL_659495967_1_2.ARC file is your archive-log file, so ARCH is copying the log file to the correct location. Excellent job!

What If the Archived Redo Logs Are Not Getting Created?

So, what if you don't see an archived redo log in the directory where you think it's supposed to be? Double-check the log_archive_dest_1 parameter and make sure it's set correctly. This is usually the problem. You can issue the command show parameter log_archive_dest_1 from SQL*Plus to do this. Make sure the directory exists, check the security permissions on the directory, and make sure you have enough space available on the file system.

If the archive logs are not getting created correctly, you will need to quickly figure out why. If Oracle switches through all of the available online redo logs and tries to switch into one that has previously been used and is waiting to be archived, all database activity will be suspended until the archived redo log can be completely written out.

Using ARCHIVELOG Mode Data Dictionary Views

Oracle provides several data dictionary views that can be used to monitor and manage the online and archived redo logs. Table 2.3 describes those views.

TABLE 2.3 Oracle dynamic Performance Views Associated with User-Managed Backup and Recovery

View Name	Description
V$ARCHIVE	The V$ARCHIVE view provides information on redo logs that are in need of being archived.
V$ARCHIVE_DEST	The V$ARCHIVE_DEST view provides information on each individual archive-log destination. Typically this view is used for Oracle Data Guard.
V$ARCHIVE_DEST_STATE	The V$ARCHIVE_DEST_STATE view provides status information on each of the individual archive-log destination directories.
V$ARCHIVE_PROCESSES	The V$ARCHIVE_PROCESSES view provides information on the different ARCH processes running on your system.
V$ARCHIVED_LOG	The V$ARCHIVED_LOG view provides information on individual archived redo logs.
V$LOG	The V$LOG view provides information on the online redo log groups.
V$LOGFILE	The V$LOGFILE view provides information on specific online redo logs.
V$LOG_HISTORY	The V$LOG_HISTORY view provides historical information on all online/archived redo logs.

Using the V$ views is easy to do, and they can tell you a lot about the status of both online and archived redo logs, as shown in Exercise 2.2.

EXERCISE 2.2

Putting the V$ Views to Work

The V$ views are very useful when want to find out something about your database related to backup or recovery. In this exercise we will look at some V$ views related to the database online redo logs.

1. Let's look at the current redo logs that have been archived:

```
SQL> select name, thread#, sequence# from v$archived_log;
NAME                                                 THREAD#   SEQUENCE#
---------------------------------------------------- --------- ---------
C:\ORACLE\ARCH\ORCL\ORCL_658485967_1_2.ARC               1         2
C:\ORACLE\ARCH\ORCL\ORCL_658485967_1_3.ARC               1         3
C:\ORACLE\ARCH\ORCL\ORCL_658485967_1_4.ARC               1         4
C:\ORACLE\ARCH\ORCL\ORCL_658485967_1_5.ARC               1         5
```

In the output you will find the name of the archived redo log. You also display the thread number (in case you are running RAC) and the log sequence number. Note that since you have put the database in ARCHIVELOG mode, you have generated four archived redo logs.

2. You can see where your online redo logs are by using the V$LOGFILE view, as shown in this example:

```
SQL> select group#, status, member from v$logfile;
    GROUP# STATUS  MEMBER
---------- ------- -----------------------------------
         3         C:\ORACLE\ORADATA\ORCL\REDO03A.LOG
         2         C:\ORACLE\ORADATA\ORCL\REDO02.LOG
         1         C:\ORACLE\ORADATA\ORCL\REDO01.LOG
         3         C:\ORACLE\ORADATA\ORCL\REDO03B.LOG
```

In this output, you can see you have three online redo log groups. It is interesting to note that group 3 actually has two members, whereas groups 1 and 2 have one member each.

3. You can see which is the current online redo log group by querying the V$LOG view, as shown here:

```
SQL> select group#, sequence#,  status from v$log;
    GROUP#  SEQUENCE# STATUS
```

```
---------- ---------- ----------------
        1         13 CURRENT
        2         11 ACTIVE
        3         12 ACTIVE
```

In this example, log group 1 is (marked with a CURRENT status) is the group that Oracle is currently writing to. Note that sequences 11 and 12 are marked active. This implies that they have not been archived yet or that they are being archived. They will be marked inactive once ARCH has finished archiving them.

Performing Oracle Offline Backups

We have been talking a lot about ARCHIVELOG mode and preparing for online backups, but we first need to talk about how to do offline backups in Oracle. Offline backups are actually quite easy to do, as you will see in the Exercise 2.3, where you will be backing up a database with an offline backup.

Executing an Offline Backup

In this exercise you will be executing an offline backup of your database. Follow these steps to back up a database with an offline backup:

1. First you need to determine which files to back up. You will need to know the location of the datafiles, the control file, and the online redo logs. You use the FILE_NAME column of the DBA_DATA_FILES view to find the datafiles first.

    ```
    SQL> Select file_name from dba_data_files;
    FILE_NAME
    -------------------------------------------
    C:\ORACLE\ORADATA\ORCL\USERS01.DBF
    C:\ORACLE\ORADATA\ORCL\UNDOTBS01.DBF
    C:\ORACLE\ORADATA\ORCL\SYSAUX01.DBF
    C:\ORACLE\ORADATA\ORCL\SYSTEM01.DBF
    C:\ORACLE\ORADATA\ORCL\REVEAL_DATA_01.DBF
    C:\ORACLE\ORADATA\ORCL\REVEAL_INDEX_01.DBF
    C:\ORACLE\ORADATA\ORCL\USERS02.DBF
    7 rows selected.
    ```

2. You use the MEMBER column in the V$LOGFILE view to find the location of all the online redo logs:

    ```
    SQL> select member from v$logfile;
    MEMBER
    ----------------------------------
    C:\ORACLE\ORADATA\ORCL\REDO03A.LOG
    C:\ORACLE\ORADATA\ORCL\REDO02.LOG
    C:\ORACLE\ORADATA\ORCL\REDO01.LOG
    C:\ORACLE\ORADATA\ORCL\REDO03B.LOG
    ```

3. You use the NAME column in V$CONTROLFILE to find the control files:

    ```
    SQL> select name from v$controlfile;
    NAME
    ------------------------------------
    C:\ORACLE\ORADATA\ORCL\CONTROL01.CTL
    C:\ORACLE\ORADATA\ORCL\CONTROL02.CTL
    C:\ORACLE\ORADATA\ORCL\CONTROL03.CTL
    C:\ORACLE\ORADATA\ORCL\CONTROL04.CTL
    ```

4. Having found all the files you will need for your backup, create a directory to back up all your files to. Of course, you might back your files up to tape or a thumb drive or some such thing. In this case, you will just copy the files to a directory that you will create called c:\backup\orcl\backup1.

    ```
    SQL> host mkdir c:\backup\orcl\backup1
    ```

5. Having created your backup directory, you need to shut down the database with the shutdown immediate command before you start your backup.

    ```
    SQL> shutdown immediate
    Database closed.
    Database dismounted.
    ORACLE instance shut down.
    ```

6. Now copy the files that you found in steps 1, 2, and 3 to the backup directory created in step 4. Notice that all the files in this example reside in one directory, c:\oracle\oradata\orcl, so the copy command is quite easy. Backups can take a while, so be patient. It's probably a good time to go grab a cool refreshment from the vending machine!

    ```
    C:\>copy c:\oracle\oradata\orcl\*.* c:\backup\orcl\backup1
    c:\oracle\oradata\orcl\CONTROL01.CTL
    ```

```
c:\oracle\oradata\orcl\CONTROL02.CTL
c:\oracle\oradata\orcl\CONTROL03.CTL
c:\oracle\oradata\orcl\CONTROL04.CTL
c:\oracle\oradata\orcl\REDO01.LOG
c:\oracle\oradata\orcl\REDO02.LOG
c:\oracle\oradata\orcl\REDO03A.LOG
c:\oracle\oradata\orcl\REDO03B.LOG
c:\oracle\oradata\orcl\REVEAL_DATA_01.DBF
c:\oracle\oradata\orcl\REVEAL_INDEX_01.DBF
c:\oracle\oradata\orcl\SYSAUX01.DBF
c:\oracle\oradata\orcl\SYSTEM01.DBF
c:\oracle\oradata\orcl\TEMP01.DBF
c:\oracle\oradata\orcl\UNDOTBS01.DBF
c:\oracle\oradata\orcl\USERS01.DBF
c:\oracle\oradata\orcl\USERS02.DBF
        16 file(s) copied.
```

7. Once the copy is complete, verify that the backup is where you expect it to be:

```
C:\>dir c:\backup\orcl\backup1
 Volume in drive C has no label.
 Volume Serial Number is 08DE-E1AB
 Directory of c:\backup\orcl\backup1
08/02/2008  02:16 PM    <DIR>          .
08/02/2008  02:16 PM    <DIR>          ..
08/02/2008  02:02 PM        10,174,464 CONTROL01.CTL
08/02/2008  02:02 PM        10,174,464 CONTROL02.CTL
08/02/2008  02:02 PM        10,174,464 CONTROL03.CTL
08/02/2008  02:02 PM        10,174,464 CONTROL04.CTL
08/02/2008  02:02 PM        52,429,312 REDO01.LOG
08/02/2008  02:02 PM        52,429,312 REDO02.LOG
08/02/2008  02:02 PM       104,858,112 REDO03A.LOG
08/02/2008  02:02 PM       104,858,112 REDO03B.LOG
08/02/2008  02:02 PM        15,736,832 REVEAL_DATA_01.DBF
08/02/2008  02:02 PM        15,736,832 REVEAL_INDEX_01.DBF
08/02/2008  02:02 PM       851,386,368 SYSAUX01.DBF
08/02/2008  02:02 PM       754,982,912 SYSTEM01.DBF
08/02/2008  02:02 PM        50,339,840 TEMP01.DBF
08/02/2008  02:02 PM       519,053,312 UNDOTBS01.DBF
```

EXERCISE 2.3 *(continued)*

```
08/02/2008  02:02 PM         581,246,976 USERS01.DBF
08/02/2008  02:02 PM          10,493,952 USERS02.DBF
              16 File(s)  3,154,249,728 bytes
               2 Dir(s)  13,330,685,952 bytes free
```

8. Start the database. Your backup is complete!

```
SQL> startup
ORACLE instance started.
Total System Global Area  418484224 bytes
Fixed Size                  1333592 bytes
Variable Size             348128936 bytes
Database Buffers           62914560 bytes
Redo Buffers                6107136 bytes
Database mounted.
Database opened.
```

 You could always decide to compress the backup files with a utility like PKZIP to save space if you wanted. By the way, RMAN can do this for you!

That's all there is to an offline database backup. In the next chapter, you will see that recovering the database using this backup is just as easy!

Temporary Tablespaces and Backups

Temporary tablespaces created with the create temporary tablespace command do not need to be backed up. The tempfiles associated with temporary tablespaces can be re-created on the fly as needed. This is true with both online backups and offline backups. If you are using the old-style temporary tablespaces that are not using tempfiles, you will still need to back up those datafiles.

To re-create tempfiles, simply use the alter tablespace command with the add tempfile keyword, as shown here:

```
Alter tablespace my_temp
Add tempfile '/u01/db01/mytempfile01.dbf' size 100m;
```

Performing Oracle Online Backups

Oracle online backups are not difficult to do; they just require a few additional steps. In this section, we will introduce you to Oracle online backups. First we will discuss online backups and generally how to do them. We will then present an example of actually performing an online backup.

The Mechanics of Online Backups

To do Oracle online backups, your database must be in ARCHIVELOG mode. You can back up the entire database or you can choose to back up a specific tablespace or set of tablespaces. If you choose to back up only specific tablespaces, you will not be able to recover your database until you have at least a base backup of all of its tablespaces. That said, you can back up the tablespaces at different times if you prefer (though this is not common practice). For example, you could back up the SYSTEM tablespace on Monday, the USERS tablespace on Tuesday, and so on. As long as you have a complete cumulative backup of the database (taken at different times), you can recover it.

To start an online backup, you will need to put each tablespace in hot backup mode. This can be done by using the `alter database begin backup` command, or you can individually put tablespaces in hot backup mode with the `alter tablespace begin backup` command. After you have put the tablespaces in hot backup mode, you back up the underlying datafiles of that tablespace. If you need to know where the datafiles related to that tablespace reside, you can use the DBA_DATA_FILES view.

When a Tablespace Is in Hot Backup Mode

When you put a tablespace in hot backup mode, Oracle will start writing block-sized records to the redo logs. These records are much bigger than the normal-sized records, so this can cause performance problems.

One odd misconception we hear from time to time is that Oracle will stop writing to the database datafiles during a hot backup. In fact Oracle will continue to write changes to the datafiles; however, it will not update the datafile headers until the backup is complete.

When you put a tablespace in hot backup mode, you are really putting the underlying datafiles of the that tablespace in hot backup mode. You can determine if a datafile is in hot backup mode by querying the V$BACKUP view. The STATUS column will indicate ACTIVE if the given datafile is in hot backup mode. Here is an example of such a query where our users tablespace is in hot backup mode, as indicated by the ACTIVE status.

```
SQL>  select a.tablespace_name, b.status
   2    from dba_data_files a, v$backup b
```

```
 3   where a.file_id=b.file#
 4   order by tablespace_name;
TABLESPACE_NAME                      STATUS
------------------------------       -----------
REVEAL_DATA                          NOT ACTIVE
REVEAL_INDEX                         NOT ACTIVE
SYSAUX                               NOT ACTIVE
SYSTEM                               NOT ACTIVE
UNDOTBS1                             NOT ACTIVE
USERS                                ACTIVE
USERS                                ACTIVE
```

Another thing to be aware of is what happens if the database is shut down while datafiles are in hot backup mode. First, Oracle will not allow you to shut down a database with most shutdown commands (shutdown, shutdown immediate, shutdown transactional, or startup force) while a tablespace is in hot backup mode. Instead it will generate an error, as shown here:

```
ORA-01149: cannot shutdown - file 4 has online backup set
ORA-01110: data file 4: 'C:\ORACLE\ORADATA\ORCL\USERS01.DBF'
```

This error identifies the datafile that is in hot backup mode. You would need to determine which tablespace the datafile is assigned to by looking at the DBA_DATA_FILES view. You would then issue the alter tablespace end backup command to take it out of hot backup mode.

If you issue a shutdown abort or if the database crashes for some reason or the server shuts down without shutting down the database in a natural fashion, Oracle will not restart with a datafile in hot backup mode. You will see the following error when you try to restart the database:

```
ORA-10873: file 4 needs end backup before opening a database
ORA-01110: data file 4: 'C:\ORACLE\ORADATA\ORCL\USERS01.DBF'
```

You simply issue the command alter database end backup to take the datafiles out of hot backup mode and then alter database open to open the database.

Once the backup is complete, you will take the tablespaces out of hot backup mode with the alter database end backup command, or you can individually take each tablespace out of hot backup mode by issuing the alter tablespace end backup command.

Once you complete the online backup, one more very important step is to back up the archived redo logs that were generated during the backup. You will need each log that was generated from the time you issued the alter database begin backup command until you issued the alter database end backup command. After the backup, use the alter system switch logfile command to force a log switch to cause the current online redo log (which contains redo generated during the backup) to be archived after you have completed the backup. You will need the redo in this log file, and any other archived redo logs that might have been generated during the backup, in order to recover the database from the backup you just completed.

In addition to regular online backups, you will want to schedule regular backups of your archived redo logs to protect them as much as possible. For example, if the online backup in the exercise ended at 4 p.m., you would be able to restore the database up to 4 p.m. with the archived redo logs you backed up. Archived redo logs will continue to be generated, though, and if you want to be able to recover your database to a point beyond 5 p.m., you will need to have those later-generated archived redo logs available (more on recovery in the next chapter). Thus it is a good idea to have regular backups of your archived redo logs!

In Exercise 2.4, we walk you through the process of doing an online backup.

EXERCISE 2.4

Executing an Online Backup

In this exercise we will be performing an online database backup. As mentioned in the text, your database will need to be in ARCHIVELOG mode to successfully execute this backup.

1. We assume your database is already running in ARCHIVELOG mode. If it's not, return to Exercise 2.1 and put your database in ARCHIVELOG mode.

2. As with the previous offline/cold backup, you need to know what datafiles need to be backed up.

   ```
   SQL> Select file_name from dba_data_files;
   FILE_NAME
   --------------------------------------------
   C:\ORACLE\ORADATA\ORCL\USERS01.DBF
   C:\ORACLE\ORADATA\ORCL\UNDOTBS01.DBF
   C:\ORACLE\ORADATA\ORCL\SYSAUX01.DBF
   C:\ORACLE\ORADATA\ORCL\SYSTEM01.DBF
   C:\ORACLE\ORADATA\ORCL\REVEAL_DATA_01.DBF
   C:\ORACLE\ORADATA\ORCL\REVEAL_INDEX_01.DBF
   C:\ORACLE\ORADATA\ORCL\USERS02.DBF
   7 rows selected.
   ```

3. Having determined which datafiles need to be backed up, you need to know where the archived redo logs are being copied to.

   ```
   SQL> show parameter log_archive_dest_1
   NAME                      TYPE         VALUE
   ------------------------- -----------  -----------------------------
   log_archive_dest_1        string       location=c:\oracle\arch\orcl
   ```

4. You should note the current online redo log sequence number at this point. You will need this, plus all log sequences generated during the backup, in order to be able to perform your recovery. You can get this number from the v$log view:

```
SQL> select group#, sequence#, status from v$log;
    GROUP#  SEQUENCE# STATUS
    ---------- ---------- ----------------
         1         13 INACTIVE
         2         14 CURRENT
         3         12 INACTIVE
```

In this case, you see that you will need all log files from sequence number 14 on in order to restore the backup you are preparing to use.

5. You now need to put the database in hot backup mode. Oracle Database 11*g* provides the command alter database begin backup for this purpose. You can also back up specific tablespaces with the alter tablespace begin backup command.

```
SQL> alter database begin backup;
Database altered.
-- ALTERNATE - Run this for each tablespace to be backed up.
-- alter tablespace users begin backup;
```

6. The database datafiles are now ready to be backed up. You will copy the files to a directory that you will create called c:\backup\orcl\backup2.

```
SQL> host mkdir c:\backup\orcl\backup2
```

7. Now copy all the database datafiles to this directory. In this case, all the files are in the directory c:\oracle\oradata\orcl, and the filenames all end with an extension of .DBF, so the command to copy them is pretty easy. Once you have started the datafile copy, go get something to eat. It might take a while.

```
SQL> host copy c:\oracle\oradata\orcl\*.dbf c:\backup\orcl\backup2
c:\oracle\oradata\orcl\REVEAL_DATA_01.DBF
c:\oracle\oradata\orcl\REVEAL_INDEX_01.DBF
c:\oracle\oradata\orcl\SYSAUX01.DBF
c:\oracle\oradata\orcl\SYSTEM01.DBF
c:\oracle\oradata\orcl\TEMP01.DBF
c:\oracle\oradata\orcl\UNDOTBS01.DBF
c:\oracle\oradata\orcl\USERS01.DBF
c:\oracle\oradata\orcl\USERS02.DBF
        8 file(s) copied.
```

8. Having patiently waited for the backup to complete, you now need to take the database out of hot backup mode. Oracle Database 11*g* provides the command `alter database end backup` for this purpose. You can also back up specific tablespaces with the `alter tablespace end backup` command.

```
SQL> alter database end backup;
Database altered.
-- ALTERNATE - Run this for each tablespace to be backed up.
-- alter tablespace users end backup;
```

9. Next you need to determine the current log file sequence number. You will need the earlier log file that you identified and all log files generated during the backup up to the current log file in order to be able to restore this backup. The query is the same against V$LOG that you saw earlier:

```
SQL> select group#, sequence#, status from v$log;
    GROUP#   SEQUENCE# STATUS
---------- ---------- ----------------
        1         13 INACTIVE
        2         14 ACTIVE
        3         15 CURRENT
```

In this example, you can see that during the backup you had a log file switch, from sequence number 14 to sequence number 15. You see that log sequence 15 is the current sequence number. You know now that you will need to back up the logs with sequence numbers 14 and 15 in order to be able to restore this backup.

10. You now need to force a log switch so the log with sequence number 15 (the current online redo log sequence number) will be archived. To do this, you issue the `alter system switch logfile` command. This will cause Oracle to switch to the next log file (sequence 16), and the current archive log (Sequence 15) will be copied to the archive-log directory by the ARCn processes.

```
SQL> Alter system switch logfile;
System altered.
```

11. Having switched log files, you need to wait for ARCH to complete copying the last log file to the archive-log directory. You can check for this completion by looking at the V$ARCHIVED_LOG view.

```
SQL> Select sequence#, archived, status from v$archived_log
  2  Where sequence# between 14 and 15;
 SEQUENCE# ARC S
---------- --- -
```

```
14 YES A
15 YES A
```

Here you see that the logs with sequence numbers 14 and 15 (already identified as critical to restoring this backup) have been archived successfully. The ARCHIVED column indicates this with the use of the YES value.

12. Now back up all archived redo logs, ensuring that all logs with numbers between sequence *x and sequence y* are backed up. You will simply copy all archived redo logs from the directory identified in step 3 (c:\oracle\arch\orcl) to your backup directory.

```
SQL> Host copy c:\oracle\arch\orcl\*.* c:\backup\orcl\backup2
c:\oracle\arch\orcl\ORCL_658485967_1_10.ARC
c:\oracle\arch\orcl\ORCL_658485967_1_11.ARC
c:\oracle\arch\orcl\ORCL_658485967_1_12.ARC
c:\oracle\arch\orcl\ORCL_658485967_1_13.ARC
c:\oracle\arch\orcl\ORCL_658485967_1_14.ARC ← Log sequence 14
c:\oracle\arch\orcl\ORCL_658485967_1_15.ARC ← Log sequence 15
c:\oracle\arch\orcl\ORCL_658485967_1_2.ARC
c:\oracle\arch\orcl\ORCL_658485967_1_3.ARC
c:\oracle\arch\orcl\ORCL_658485967_1_4.ARC
c:\oracle\arch\orcl\ORCL_658485967_1_5.ARC
c:\oracle\arch\orcl\ORCL_658485967_1_6.ARC
c:\oracle\arch\orcl\ORCL_658485967_1_7.ARC
c:\oracle\arch\orcl\ORCL_658485967_1_8.ARC
c:\oracle\arch\orcl\ORCL_658485967_1_9.ARC
      14 file(s) copied.
```

You can tell that the logs with sequence numbers 14 and 15 were backed up since you know that the log sequence number is part of the filename (it's the number right before the extension). We also marked them for you in the output just because we are nice guys. After copying the archived redo logs to the backup location, you can delete the source location if you want to save space. Once the backup of the archived redo logs is complete, your database backup is done.

We hope you also realize that you will need to back up files like the database parameter file, any other Oracle-related configuration files (like for networking), and the Oracle database software itself. Backing up these structures (except for the spfile, which is a special RMAN case we cover in Chapter 4) is beyond the scope of the OCP exam.

Backing Up the Control File

Finally, we need to talk about control-file backups. We introduced you to the control file in Chapter 1. In Oracle there are three ways to manually back up a control file (again, RMAN methods will be covered in Chapter 4):

- Backing up the original control file during a cold backup
- Creating a backup control file
- Creating a trace file with the `create control file` command in it

We have really already covered the first method in this chapter. Let's look at the remaining two methods in some more detail. We will address recovering from a lost control file in Chapter 3.

Creating a Backup Control File

The backup control file is almost the same as a regular control file. It has some areas in it that are marked such that Oracle recognizes that it's a backup control file. When a backup control file is used, some form of recovery will be required (typically just involving the use of the archived and online redo logs if the database is otherwise intact).

To create the backup control file simply issue the `alter database backup controlfile to` command, indicating at the end of the command where you want the control file to be created.

For example, if you wanted to create a backup control file after the online backup you performed in Exercise 2.4, you would simply need to issue the following command:

```
SQL> alter database backup controlfile to
'c:\backup\orcl\backup2\backup_control.ctl';
Database altered.
```

The result is the creation of a backup control file called `backup_control.ctl` found in the `c:\backup\orcl\backup2` directory, as you can see here:

```
SQL> host dir c:\backup\orcl\backup2\backup_control.ctl
 Volume in drive C has no label.
 Volume Serial Number is 08DE-E1AB
 Directory of c:\backup\orcl\backup2
08/02/2008  03:24 PM        10,174,464 BACKUP_CONTROL.CTL
               1 File(s)     10,174,464 bytes
               0 Dir(s)   9,930,571,776 bytes free
```

We will cover recovering from control-file loss using a backup control file in Chapter 3.

Creating a Trace File with the *Create Control File* Command in It

If all else fails and you do not have a backup control file, don't worry; you have another option, the `create controlfile` command. Normally, manually executing the command can be challenging because you need to know a lot of information about your database (like the names and locations of all the database datafiles). However, you can prepare for the possibility of having to use the `create controlfile` command by creating one in advance. The `alter database backup controlfile to trace` command will create a trace file with the `create controlfile` command in it for you. The trace file is stored in the new diagnostic directory structure in Oracle Database 11g.

The diagnostic directory structure is a new standard introduced in Oracle Database 11g that defines where Oracle stores files related to database troubleshooting and diagnostics. The base directory of this structure is defined by the parameter DIAGNOSTIC_DEST. Here is an example of the setting of DIAGNOSTIC_DEST on an Oracle database:

```
SQL> show parameter diag
NAME                                 TYPE        VALUE
------------------------------------ ----------- ---------
diagnostic_dest                      string      C:\ORACLE
```

A whole book could be written on the new 11g diagnostic capabilities, but what we are interested in is where user-generated trace files get created, because when we issue the `alter database backup controlfile to trace` command, the resulting file will be a user-generated trace file.

In this case, the trace file will be created in $DIAGNOSTIC_BASE\diag\rdbms\orcl\orcl\trace as shown in this code example:

```
SQL> alter database backup controlfile to trace;
Database altered.
C:\oracle\diag\rdbms\orcl\orcl\trace>dir
 Volume in drive C has no label.
 Volume Serial Number is 08DE-E1AB
 Directory of C:\oracle\diag\rdbms\orcl\orcl\trace
08/02/2008  03:38 PM    <DIR>          .
08/02/2008  03:38 PM    <DIR>          ..
08/02/2008  03:38 PM         1,027,520 alert_orcl.log
08/02/2008  03:38 PM             9,572 orcl_ora_12120.trc
08/02/2008  03:38 PM                91 orcl_ora_12120.trm
               4 File(s)      1,037,183 bytes
               4 Dir(s)   9,964,507,136 bytes free
```

The trace file is called `orcl_ora_12120.trc` (it's easy to tell since there are no other trace files in the directory). Another option with the `alter database backup controlfile to trace` command is to define an alternate location for the trace file. The syntax for this command is as follows:

```
alter database backup controlfile to trace as '/tmp/my_control_trace.trc';
```

If you look in the file, you will find a trace-file header in it first. Later down the trace file you will find two different versions of the `create controlfile` command. Here is an example of the `create control file` command that you might find in this file:

```
CREATE CONTROLFILE REUSE DATABASE "ORCL" NORESETLOGS  ARCHIVELOG
    MAXLOGFILES 16
    MAXLOGMEMBERS 3
    MAXDATAFILES 100
    MAXINSTANCES 8
    MAXLOGHISTORY 292
LOGFILE
  GROUP 1 'C:\ORACLE\ORADATA\ORCL\REDO01.LOG'  SIZE 50M,
  GROUP 2 'C:\ORACLE\ORADATA\ORCL\REDO02.LOG'  SIZE 50M,
  GROUP 3 (
    'C:\ORACLE\ORADATA\ORCL\REDO03A.LOG',
    'C:\ORACLE\ORADATA\ORCL\REDO03B.LOG'
  ) SIZE 100M
-- STANDBY LOGFILE
DATAFILE
  'C:\ORACLE\ORADATA\ORCL\SYSTEM01.DBF',
  'C:\ORACLE\ORADATA\ORCL\SYSAUX01.DBF',
  'C:\ORACLE\ORADATA\ORCL\UNDOTBS01.DBF',
  'C:\ORACLE\ORADATA\ORCL\USERS01.DBF',
  'C:\ORACLE\ORADATA\ORCL\REVEAL_DATA_01.DBF',
  'C:\ORACLE\ORADATA\ORCL\REVEAL_INDEX_01.DBF',
  'C:\ORACLE\ORADATA\ORCL\USERS02.DBF'
CHARACTER SET WE8MSWIN1252;
```

You will notice that this output includes the datafile names, the location and names of the online redo logs, and other information needed by the `create controlfile` command. The trace file contains other output that will be required to complete the recovery process, so you should back up the trace file as it is. In Chapter 3 we will address the process of recovering from a control-file loss using the output contained in the trace files.

Summary

In this chapter, we covered all aspects of user-managed Oracle database backups. We started with a quick review of the Oracle architecture related to backup and recovery so you could have a good foundation on which to build your knowledge. In that review, we discussed processes and memory in Oracle. We discussed ARCHIVELOG and NOARCHIVELOG mode. We also discussed startup and shutdown of the database, the different modes the database is in while starting up or shutting down, and why those modes are important during a recovery exercise.

We then reviewed configuring your database for backup and recovery, which mostly pertained to backups in ARCHIVELOG mode. We talked about archive logs, and the archive-log destination parameters. We talked about how an archive log is named when its created. We provided you with a list of parameters that are commonly used when configuring Oracle online backups, and we also provided you with a list of data dictionary views you might need to use to manage archived redo logs.

We then moved on to the topic of offline (cold) backups. We demonstrated how you could do an offline backup of your database. We proceeded to the topic of online backups, demonstrating that they are almost as simple as offline backups. Finally, we discussed backup control files and how they could be created.

Exam Essentials

Be able to configure a database of user-initiated online backups.   Understand the different parameters that need to be configured when you are going to back up a database with user-based online backups. You will need to understand parameters such as LOG_ARCHIVE_ DEST_1 and how to configure them. You will need to understand what happens if you have two archive-log destination directories defined.

Be able to back up your database with an offline backup.   Understand the steps that need to be performed to do an offline backup. Understand the difference between an offline backup and an online backup and how these differences can be used to decide the optimal backup strategy.

Be able to back up your database with an online backup.   Know how to configure your database for an online backup. Understand how to put the database in ARCHIVELOG mode so you can do online backups. Understand how to determine which archived redo logs you will need to back up when doing an online backup.

Be able to back up your database control file.   Understand why it is important to back up your control file. Understand the different methods of backing up your control file. Understand what a backup control file is.

Review Questions

1. Your database is in NOARCHIVELOG mode. You start to do a backup, but your users complain that they don't want you to shut down the database to perform the backup. What options are available to you?

    A. Put the database in hot backup mode and perform an online backup, including backing up the archived redo logs.

    B. Just back up the database datafiles without shutting down the database.

    C. You will have to wait until you can shut down the database to perform the backup.

    D. Mark each datafile as backup in progress, back them up individually, and then mark them as backup not in progress. No archived redo logs will need to be backed up.

    E. Only back up the datafiles that the user will not be touching. Once the user has finished what they were doing, you can shut down the database and back up the datafiles the user changed during the course of the remaining backup.

2. When performing an online backup, what is the proper order of the following steps?

    a. Issue the `alter database end backup` command.

    b. Back up the archived redo logs.

    c. Issue the `alter database begin backup` command.

    d. Back up the database files.

    e. Determine the beginning log sequence number.

    f. Determine the ending log sequence number.

    g. Force a log switch with the `alter system switch logfile` command.

    A. a, b, c, d, e, f, g

    B. c, d, a, b, e, g, f

    C. f, d, b, g, a, c, e

    D. e, c, d, a, g, f, b

    E. a, f, b, g, e, c, d

3. You want to put a specific tablespace called MY_DATA in hot backup mode so you can back it up. What command would you use?

    A. `alter tablespace MY_DATA begin backup;`

    B. `alter tablespace MY_DATA start backup;`

    C. `alter tablespace MY_DATA backup begin;`

    D. `alter MY_DATA begin backup;`

    E. You cannot back up individual tablespaces.

4. You backed up the database at 8 a.m. today using an online backup. Accounting made a large change to the underlying data between 10 a.m. and noon. Which of the following actions would ensure that the changes could be recovered using the 8 a.m. backup?

    A. Create a manual incremental online database backup.

    B. Back up all the archived redo logs generated since the 8 a.m. backup.

    C. Create a brand-new backup after all the changes have been applied.

    D. There is no way to make the changes recoverable based on the 8 a.m. backup.

    E. Perform an online backup of the tablespace(s) that contained changed data.

5. What are the different logging modes available in Oracle Database 11g? (Choose two.)

    A. NOLOG mode

    B. NOARCHIVELOG mode

    C. LOGGING mode

    D. HOTDATABASE mode

    E. ARCHIVELOG mode

6. Which is the correct command to put the database in ARCHIVELOG mode?

    A. `alter database archivelog`

    B. `alter system enable archivelog mode`

    C. `alter database enable archive`

    D. `alter database archivelog enable`

    E. None of the above

7. What is the correct order of steps to perform an online database backup?

    a. `alter database begin backup;`

    b. `alter database end backup;`

    c. Back up the database datafiles.

    d. Back up the archive log files.

    e. `alter system switch logfile;`

    A. a, b, c, d, e

    B. e, d, a, b, c

    C. a, c, b, d, e

    D. d, b, c, a, e

    E. a, c, b, e, d

8. Which command will result in a trace file being created with the `create controlfile` command contained in it?

   A. `alter database backup controlfile;`

   B. `alter database backup controlfile to trace;`

   C. `alter database controlfile backup;`

   D. `alter database controlfile backup to '/ora01/oracle/ctrl_backup.ctl';`

   E. `alter database begin controlfile backup;`

9. Which of the following is a valid way of putting a tablespace named DAVE_TBS into hot backup mode?

   A. `alter tablespace DAVE_TBS backup mode;`

   B. `alter tablespace DAVE_TBS start backup;`

   C. `alter tablespace DAVE_TBS begin backup;`

   D. `alter tablespace DAVE_TBS backup begin;`

   E. `alter tablespace DAVE_TBS backup;`

10. Every Sunday the Unix system administrator has a job that executes a full backup of the entire Unix system your database is on. Is this backup usable for backup and recovery of your database?

   A. Yes, if the database is in ARCHIVELOG mode.

   B. Yes, if the database is in NOARCHIVELOG mode.

   C. No, the backup is not usable in any way.

   D. Only if the ENABLE_ONLINE_BACKUP parameter is set to TRUE.

11. Which is not a valid way of backing up a control file?

   A. Backing up the control file to trace

   B. Copying the existing control file of the database to the backup location during a hot backup

   C. Copying the existing control file of the database to the backup location during a cold backup

   D. Creating a backup control file

   E. Using the `create controlfile` command

12. Which of the following parameters defines the location where Oracle should create archived redo logs?

   A. `LOG_ARCHIVE_1`

   B. `LOG_DESTINATION_1`

   C. `LOG_ARCHIVED_DESTINATION_1`

   D. `LOG_ARCHIVE_DEST_1`

   E. `LOG_ARCHIVE_SOURCE_1`

13. True or false? Archived redo logs can be copied to more than one destination by Oracle.

   A. True

   B. False

14. What will be the result of the following configuration?

```
Log_archive_dest_1='location=c:\oracle\arch\mydb'
Log_archive_dest_2='location=z:\oracle\arch\mydb'
```

   A. An error will occur during database startup because the second parameter is not valid.

   B. An error will occur during database startup since you are trying to create archived redo logs in two different locations.

   C. Archived redo logs will be created in two different locations by the ARCH process.

   D. Archived redo logs will be created in two different locations by the LGWR process.

   E. Neither parameter setting is valid, so the database will not start up.

15. Which view provides information on the backup status of the datafiles in the database?

   A. V$BACKUP

   B. V$BACKUP_STATUS

   C. V$BACKUP_DATAFILE

   D. V$DATAFILE_BACKUP

   E. V$TABLESPCE_BACKUP

16. Another DBA issues a `shutdown abort` command on a database on which you were running an online backup. What will happen when you try to restart the database?

   A. Oracle will automatically take the datafile out of hot backup mode, generate a warning message, and then open the database.

   B. Oracle will automatically take the datafile out of hot backup mode and then open the database.

   C. Oracle will generate an error when trying to open the database, indicating that a datafile is in hot backup mode. You will need to correct this error before you can open the database.

   D. The database will open with the file in hot backup mode. You can restart the backup at any time.

   E. The datafile in hot backup mode will be corrupted and you will have to recover it.

17. What is the proper command to shut down the database in a consistent manner?

   A. Shutdown abort

   B. Shutdown kill

   C. Shutdown nowait

   D. shutdown immediate

   E. shutdown halt

18. If you issue the command `shutdown abort` prior to trying to put the database in ARCHIVELOG mode, what will be the result when you issue the command `alter database archivelog`?

   A. The `alter database archivelog` command will fail.

   B. The `alter database archivelog inconsistent` command must be used to put the database in ARCHIVELOG mode.

   C. The `alter database archivelog` command will succeed.

   D. The `alter database archivelog` command will ask if you want to make the database consistent first.

   E. There is no `alter database archivelog` command. The correct command is `alter database alterlogging`.

19. Your archive-log destination directory runs out of space. What is the impact of this on the database?

   A. None. The database will switch over to the stand-by archive-log destination directory.

   B. A warning message will be written to the alert log of the database, but no adverse impacts to the database will be experienced.

   C. The database will shut down, and will not restart until you correct the out-of-space situation.

   D. The database will continue to try to write to the archive-log destination directory for one hour. After one hour, the database will shut down normally.

   E. Once Oracle has cycled through all online redo logs, it will stop processing any DML or DDL until the out-of-space condition is corrected.

20. How many individual archive-log destination directories are supported by Oracle Database 11*g*?

   A. 7

   B. 1

   C. 10

   D. 11

   E. 21

Answers to Review Questions

1.   C. You will have to wait until you can shut down the database since it's in NOARCHIVELOG mode. No other option will give you a backup that is recoverable.

2.   D. The correct answer is D. First you determine the beginning log sequence number, then you issue the `alter database begin backup` command, then you back up the database files, and then you issue the `alter database end backup` command. Next you force a log switch with the `alter system switch logfile` command, and then you determine the ending log sequence number. Finally, you back up the archived redo logs.

3.   A. The correct answer is A. The `alter tablespace` command is followed by the name of the tablespace and then the `begin backup` keyword.

4.   B. The most correct answer is B. This is because the question asked you what would be done using the 8 a.m. backup.

5.   B, E. B and E are the correct answers because ARCHIVELOG and NOARCHIVELOG are the two logging modes available in Oracle Database 11g.

6.   A. The `alter database archivelog` will put the database in ARCHIVELOG mode.

7.   E. The correct answer is E. You first put the database in ARCHIVELOG mode with the `alter database begin backup` command. You then back up the database datafiles. Then take the database out of backup mode with the `alter database end backup` command. Issue the `alter system switch logfile` command and then back up the archived redo logs.

8.   B. The `alter database backup controlfile to trace` command will create a trace file in the `DIAGNOSTIC_DEST` directory structure that contains your control file.

9.   C. The correct command would be `alter tablespace DAVE_TBS begin backup;`.

10.   C. The correct answer is C. Regardless of the logging mode, the backup would not be usable since the tablespaces were not put in hot backup mode.

11.   B. The correct answer is B. You would never back up the actual control file during an online database backup.

12.   D. The correct answer is D. The `LOG_ARCHIVE_DEST_1` parameter is a parameter that would be used to define the location where Oracle would create your archived redo logs.

13.   A. Oracle can be configured to copy archived redo logs to up to 10 different locations.

14.   C. The archived redo logs will be created in two different locations. The ARCH process is responsible for the creation of the archived redo logs.

15.   A. The `V$BACKUP` view provides information on the online backup status for datafiles in the database.

16. C. Oracle will generate an error indicating that a datafile is in hot backup mode. You will need to issue the `alter database end backup` command to make sure all datafiles in hot backup mode are no longer in hot backup mode. You can then use the `alter database open` command to open the database.

17. D. The `shutdown immediate` command is used to shut down the database in a consistent manner.

18. A. The `alter database archivelog` command will fail. You will need to open the database and then shut it down in a consistent manner.

19. E. Oracle will cycle through all of the online redo logs, trying to archive them after they have been filled. After cycling through the last online redo log, Oracle will suspend all database operations until the out-of-space condition is corrected.

20. C. Oracle provides support for up to 10 different archive-log destination directories.

Chapter

3

Performing Oracle User-Managed Database Recoveries

ORACLE DATABASE 11*g*: ADMINISTRATION II EXAM OBJECTIVES COVERED IN THIS CHAPTER:

✓ **Performing User-Managed Backup and Recovery**

- Perform user-managed complete database recovery

- Perform user-managed incomplete database recovery

- Backup and recover a control file

- Recover from a lost TEMP file

- Recover from a lost redo log group

- Recover from the loss of a password file

In Chapter 2 we showed you how to perform user-based database backups. Of course, those backups are of little good if you don't know how to use them to restore your database. In this chapter, we will show you how to restore your database with user-based backups. First we will show you how to use the offline backup you took in NOARCHIVELOG mode and use it to restore your database. We will then address online backups taken in ARCHIVELOG mode and show you how to restore them. We will then talk about different kinds of user-based incomplete recoveries, also called *point-in-time* recoveries.

Finally, we will cover other recovery processes, such as recovering from a lost control file and a lost temporary tablespace tempfile, recovering from the loss of an online redo log group, and how to recover from loss of a password file. So, buckle in, keep your hands and arms inside the vehicle at all times, and enjoy the ride!

Exam objectives are subject to change at any time without prior notice and at Oracle's sole discretion. Please visit Oracle's Training and Certification website (http://www.oracle.com/education/certification/) for the most current exam-objectives listing.

Performing a Recovery in NOARCHIVELOG Mode

Recovering a database that was backed up in NOARCHIVELOG mode is perhaps the easiest recovery task to do. The thing to keep in mind is that there are no archived redo logs to apply. You simply will be restoring your database to the point in time of the backup you took. It does not matter if you lost one datafile or the entire enchilada; you have to restore all the files you backed up to recover the database.

The process is simple. You copy all the files you backed up during your offline backup (datafiles, control files, redo logs) and then start the database. You simply must copy all of these files; you can't pick and choose what to recover. Exercise 3.1 provides an example of such a recovery operation.

EXERCISE 3.1

Restoring a Database Using a Cold Backup

In this exercise you will be restoring the database with a cold backup. It is assumed the database is in NOARCHIVELOG mode.

1. Make sure the database is shut down.

2. Copy the files on the backup media to the original location. You would copy the following files:

   - Database datafiles

   - Database control files

   - Database online redo logs

   If the original location of the database files is not available, copy them to an alternate location. Having copied the files to an alternate location, you will likely need to execute an optional step 3 for the control files and optional step 4 for all database files and/or online redo logs. Here is an example of the copy command:

   ```
   C:\Documents and Settings\Robert>copy c:\oracle\oradata\orcl\cold\*.*
   c:\backup\orcl\backup1
   ```

3. (Optional) If you copied the database control files to a location other than their original location, you will need to modify the database parameter CONTROL_FILES to point to the control files in their new location.

   If you are using a text-based parameter file (pfile), simply edit the file and change the CONTROL_FILES parameter value contained within that file.

   If you are using a server-based parameter file (spfile), then you will need to start the database in NOMOUNT mode and change the SPFILE entry for the CONTROL_FILES parameter using the alter system command. We will have to use the scope=spfile keyword when issuing the alter system command since changing the CONTROL_FILE parameter is not supported as a dynamic change.

   After you have changed the parameter file (manually or using the alter system command), use the shutdown command to shut down the database (the parameter file will be reread when you open it again in the next steps). Here is an example:

   ```
   SQL> startup nomount
   ORACLE instance started.
   Total System Global Area  397557760 bytes
   Fixed Size                  1333452 bytes
   Variable Size             289408820 bytes
   Database Buffers          100663296 bytes
   ```

```
Redo Buffers                  6152192 bytes
SQL> alter system set control_files='C:\ORACLE\ORADATA\ORCL\CONTROL01.CTL',
'C:\ORACLE\ORADATA\ORCL\CONTROL02.CTL',
'C:\ORACLE\ORADATA\ORCL\CONTROL03.CTL' scope=spfile;
System altered.
SQL> shutdown immediate
ORA-01507: database not mounted
ORACLE instance shut down.
```

4. (Optional) If you copied the database online redo logs or the database datafiles to a different location, you will need to indicate to Oracle that you have done so. This is so Oracle will know where the files are now so it can open them. This is known as a rename operation. (Don't be fooled, though. It renames only the files inside of Oracle; it does not rename them on the operating system).

To rename the database files (redo log and datafiles) you must have the database mounted first. Once the database is mounted, you will issue the alter database rename file command for each database file that needs to be changed.

Here is an example where we have moved the online redo logs and database data-files from c:\oracle\oradata\orcl to c:\oracle\oradata\orclnew. You need to indicate to Oracle that you have made this change by using the alter database rename file command. This will change the pointers to the database files inside the control file so Oracle will be looking for the files in the correct location.

Note that for the rest of this exercise we will assume that the files were moved to their original locations. In this example, you rename the online redo logs and then you rename the database datafiles:

```
SQL> startup mount
ORACLE instance started.
Total System Global Area  397557760 bytes
Fixed Size                   1333452 bytes
Variable Size              272631604 bytes
Database Buffers           117440512 bytes
Redo Buffers                 6152192 bytes
Database mounted.
SQL>alter database rename file 'c:\oracle\oradata\orcl\REDO01.LOG' to
 'c:\oracle\oradata\orclnew\REDO01.LOG';
SQL>alter database rename file 'c:\oracle\oradata\orcl\REDO02.LOG' to
 'c:\oracle\oradata\orclnew\REDO02.LOG';
```

EXERCISE 3.1 *(continued)*

```
SQL>alter database rename file 'c:\oracle\oradata\orcl\REDO03.LOG' to
 'c:\oracle\oradata\orclnew\REDO03.LOG';
SQL>alter database rename file 'c:\oracle\oradata\orcl\SYSAUX01.DBF' to
 'c:\oracle\oradata\orclnew\SYSAUX01.DBF';
SQL>alter database rename file 'c:\oracle\oradata\orcl\SYSTEM01.DBF' to
 'c:\oracle\oradata\orclnew\SYSTEM01.DBF';
SQL>alter database rename file 'c:\oracle\oradata\orcl\TEMP01.DBF' to
 'c:\oracle\oradata\orclnew\TEMP01.DBF';
SQL>alter database rename file 'c:\oracle\oradata\orcl\UNDOTBS01.DBF' to
 'c:\oracle\oradata\orclnew\UNDOTBS01.DBF';
SQL>alter database rename file 'c:\oracle\oradata\orcl\USERS01.DBF' to
 'c:\oracle\oradata\orclnew\USERS01.DBF';
```

5. Now that the files are copied into place, you can start up the database:

```
SQL> startup
ORACLE instance started.
Total System Global Area  418484224 bytes
Fixed Size                  1333592 bytes
Variable Size             348128936 bytes
Database Buffers           62914560 bytes
Redo Buffers                6107136 bytes
Database mounted.
Database opened.
```

That's it. You have recovered your database! Query to your heart's delight!

 Real World Scenario

Recovering in NOARCHIVELOG Mode

Because of its limitations, you might ask yourself whether anyone really uses a database in NOARCHIVELOG mode. The answer is yes.

The main benefit to running in NOARCHIVELOG mode is that you are not generating archived redo logs. Archived redo logs require more space (sometimes a lot more space). Often development or test databases do not require online backups or point-in-time recovery, so running them in NOARCHIVELOG mode might make sense. Most bigger shops will run all databases in ARCHIVELOG mode because of the added flexibility it gives you.

Performing a Full Database Recovery in ARCHIVELOG Mode

You might think there's something slightly mystical about database recoveries in ARCHIVELOG mode the first few times you do them. You take a backup that may be days or even weeks old, apply some magic in the form of application of the archived redo logs, and *voila* (Robert's wife, the French expert, will appreciate that word), your database is up-to-date and ready to roll.

It's true that some DBAs (and managers) actually don't believe that you can back up a database while it's up and running and be able to restore it fully without losing any data. Well, we're here to tell you that you can, that it works, and it's not magic but just some good programming. It's reliable too. We've been working with Oracle for a very long time. We've yet to see an online backup that's not recoverable unless someone did something wrong, and it's pretty hard to do something wrong unless you are just not paying attention.

In the following sections, we will talk about user-based recovery of your database when it's in ARCHIVELOG mode. We will talk about preparing for the recovery and then we will talk about the actual recovery process. Note that we are discussing a full database recovery to the point of failure of the database and not a point-in-time recovery. We assume that the online redo logs are intact since full point-of-failure recovery requires this.

The OCP exam may ask you about conditions where the online redo logs have been lost, you have to use a backup control file, or all the files associated with the database are lost. See the sections "Performing Incomplete Recoveries" and "Performing Other Types of Recoveries" for more details on these special types of database recoveries.

Loss of Online Redo Logs or Control Files

Remember, if you have lost your online redo logs, then recovery becomes more complex (and the OCP exam is likely to ask you questions about these kinds of losses). We will discuss these kinds of losses later in this chapter.

Preparing for the Recovery

When preparing for recovery, you have to consider what kind of datafile loss you have experienced. There are three types you might experience:

- Loss of all datafiles
- Loss of one or more non-SYSTEM or -UNDO tablespace datafiles.
- Loss of the SYSTEM or UNDO tablespace datafile

The recovery for each of these types of datafile losses is similar. Some recoveries can be done online (with the database up and running) and other recoveries will require that the database be shut down (though in these cases it's likely going to have crashed anyway). We will cover each of these types of loss in the following sections.

Restoring Datafiles After the Loss of All Datafiles

If you have lost all of your database datafiles, then you will need to perform a database recovery with the database down. It is most likely in these cases that the database will have already crashed anyway (or refused to restart); Oracle does not do well if all of the database datafiles go missing.

The procedure in this case is simple. Restore the datafile backups from your backup media. You can restore these datafiles to their original locations or to new locations depending on your needs. Once you have restored the datafiles, you are ready to recover the entire database. We discuss full database recovery in the section "Recovering the Database" (an original title, we know).

Restoring Datafiles After the Loss of the *SYSTEM or UNDO* Tablespace Datafile

If you have lost only datafiles related to the SYSTEM or UNDO tablespace, then you should restore only those datafiles. You will still need to do an offline recovery, but the recovery will be much quicker since all you will need to do is recover those database datafiles. Once you have recovered the datafiles from your backup media, perform a tablespace- or datafile-level recovery, which is covered in the section "Recovering the Database."

Specific Recovery Actions

The OCP exam expects you to answer a question with the best answer. For example, in the case of the loss of a single, non-SYSTEM or -UNDO tablespace datafile, the best answer is to restore just that datafile and not all database datafiles. Sure you can restore all the datafiles, but that would not be the best course of action.

Restoring Datafiles After the Loss of One or More Non-*SYSTEM or -UNDO* Tablespace Datafiles

If you lose a datafile related to a tablespace other than the SYSTEM or UNDO tablespace, then you can actually perform online recovery of the database. In these cases, it is unlikely that the database will crash, and if the database is started up, it will seem to start up normally. To perform this kind of recovery, you will need to first indicate to the database that the file is in an offline state. You do this by using the `alter database` command, as shown here:

```
alter database datafile 4 offline;
alter database datafile 'C:\ORACLE\ORADATA\ORCL\USERS01.DBF' offline;
```

Now you will find that the STATUS column for this datafile in V$DATAFILE will show that the file has a RECOVER status as seen here:

```
SQL> select file#, status from v$datafile;
     FILE# STATUS
---------- -------
         1 SYSTEM
         2 ONLINE
         3 ONLINE
         4 RECOVER
```

You should also note that the status of the datafile in the DBA_DATA_FILES view does not change when you offline a file. It will still show as AVAILABLE. A row will also appear for the datafile you have taken offline in the V$RECOVER_FILE view.

Datafile IDs

Did you notice in the alter system command where we used a number instead of the location of the datafile? This is the datafile ID, and you can use the datafile ID in lieu of the entire path many times. You can find the datafile ID in the V$DATAFILE and DBA_DATA_FILES views as shown here:

```
SQL> select file_id, file_name from dba_data_files;
   FILE_ID FILE_NAME
---------- ---------------------------------------
         4 C:\ORACLE\ORADATA\ORCL\USERS01.DBF
         3 C:\ORACLE\ORADATA\ORCL\UNDOTBS01.DBF
         2 C:\ORACLE\ORADATA\ORCL\SYSAUX01.DBF
         1 C:\ORACLE\ORADATA\ORCL\SYSTEM01.DBF
```

Recovering the Database

If you restore the database files to different locations, you will need to modify the database parameter file and/or the database control file with the new file locations using the alter system command as demonstrated in optional steps 3 and 4 of Exercise 3.1.

Recovering the database depends, again, on the type of datafile outage you have experienced. In the next sections, we will cover the recover database command first. Then we'll cover restoring the database after loss of all datafiles, loss of SYSTEM or UNDO tablespace datafiles, and loss of non-SYSTEM or -UNDO tablespace datafiles.

Renaming Database files

Sometimes during a recovery you will need to restore database files to different locations. If this is the case, you will need to indicate to Oracle where the new location is. The types of files you are likely to move are control files, online redo logs, and database datafiles.

If you are restoring control files to a different location, then simply change the CONTROL_ FILES parameter.

If the relocation involves the online redo logs or the database datafiles, then you will need to use the alter database rename file command. This command works only when the database is mounted, and in some cases when it's open (like when datafiles to be renamed are offline).

To rename a file, restore the files to the new location and issue the alter database rename file command, as shown here:

```
alter database rename file '/ora01/oracle/oradata/orcl/system01.dbf'
To '/ora02/oracle/oradata/orcl/system01.dbf';
```

This will rename the file in the control file. Note that it has no impact on the actual physical file.

Using the *recover database* Command

The recover database command is used in Oracle to recover the database from the SQL prompt. When you issue the recover database command without any parameters, Oracle will assume a *point-of-failure recovery* or *complete recovery*. That is, it will try to recover the database up to the last redo-log entry. This results in a complete recovery of your database down to the last transaction. During recovery operations, Oracle will inspect the datafile headers and the control file and determine where datafile recovery needs to begin for each datafile. To do this, Oracle will inspect the SCN contained in each database datafile. It will use the SCN to determine where it needs to start recovering the datafile.

What is the SCN? The System Change Number (SCN) is a counter, and its job is to keep track of everything going on inside the database and assign it a temporal identity. This serves to keep transactions that occurred in a particular order in the same order later down the road (such as during recovery). We need to preserve the order of transactions because of dependencies that occur between transactions. For example, if you have a parent and child table, you want to make sure that during recovery all inserts into the parent table occur before inserts into the child table. This is because of the foreign key constraint that exists between the two tables to ensure the integrity of that parent/child relationship. The SCN helps Oracle to track the temporal flow of those changes, and thus the parent table insert will have a lower SCN than the child table insert. As a result, in the end, all is right with the world.

SCNs are loosely coupled with time. Thus, 12:30pm local time would be associated with a specific SCN in a given individual database. The thing to remember is that 12:30pm local time will most likely be associated with a different SCN in each database, so the coupling is very loose. The concept of the SCN is very important because there may be times when you will want to restore your database back to a specific SCN. This is supported during recovery operations. Also, Oracle's Flashback features support the use of the SCN when flashing back the database. See Chapter 9 for more information on the vast number of features available with Oracle Flashback Database.

When you issue the `recover database` command from the SQL prompt, you have a number of options. You can recover the entire database with `recover database`, you can recover a specific tablespace with `recover tablespace`, and you can recover a datafile with `recover datafile`. As you progress through this chapter, you will see several examples of the use of the `recover database` command, including the use of the database SCN to recover your database.

After you have issued the `recover database` command, you will be prompted for the archived redo log it thinks it needs to apply. You can simply press the Enter key and Oracle will apply the redo in that archived redo log. Once the redo has been applied, the `recover database` command will prompt you for the next redo log in the sequence, and you press Enter again.

As you can imagine, this can get a little long-winded if you have to apply a number of archived redo logs. Another thing you can do at the prompt is type in `auto`. This will cause the `recover database` command to automatically start applying archived redo-log files without prompting you for the name or location of those files. This is much easier!

Recovering the Database After the Loss of All Datafiles

You can use the `recover database` command to recover the entire database all at once. Having restored all the database datafiles from the backup media, you would follow these steps:

1. Log into the database as SYS.

2. Mount the database with the `startup mount` command.

3. Issue the `recover database` command from the SQL prompt.

4. The `recover database` command will recommend to you the correct archived redo log to apply. At the prompt, type **AUTO**; the `recover database` command automatically starts applying all redo until the database is recovered.

5. Once database recovery is complete, the `recover database` command will return you to the SQL prompt. You can then issue the `alter database open` command to open the database for business.

Note that in this case you have performed a full recovery. Your database should have been completely restored without any data loss. There is no need to perform a special backup after this recovery (other than your regularly scheduled backups). In Exercise 3.2, you'll be doing a full recovery of your database after it has lost all datafiles.

EXERCISE 3.2

Recovering the Database from the Loss of All Datafiles

In this exercise, you will perform a full (complete) database recovery, restoring all datafiles. It is important to note that this recovery presupposes that the online redo logs and control files of the database are intact.

1. Back up the database. Details on how to do a full online database backup are found in Chapter 2.

2. In summary, follow these steps:

   - First put the database in hot backup mode.

   - Copy all database datafiles to a backup location.

   - Take the database out of hot backup mode.

   - Force a log switch. Back up the archived redo logs.

   Here is an example of a backup:

   ```
   [oracle@localhost orcl]$ sqlplus "/ as sysdba"
   SQL*Plus: Release 11.1.0.6.0 - Production on Sun Aug 17 15:35:48 2008
   Copyright (c) 1982, 2007, Oracle.  All rights reserved.
   Connected to:
   Oracle Database 11g Enterprise Edition Release 11.1.0.6.0 - Production
   With the Partitioning, OLAP, Data Mining and Real Application Testing options
   SQL> alter database begin backup;
   Database altered.
   SQL> host cp /oracle01/oradata/orcl/*.dbf /oracle01/backup/orcl
   SQL> alter database end backup;
   Database altered.
   SQL> alter system switch logfile;
   System altered.
   SQL> host cp /oracle01/backup/arch/* /oracle01/backup/orcl/*
   SQL> alter database backup controlfile to trace;
   Database altered.
   SQL> alter database backup controlfile to '/oracle01/oradata/orcl/control1.bak';
   Database altered.
   ```

3. Now remove all datafiles from the database. On some operating-system platforms (Linux, for example), you can do this with the database up and running, and on others (Windows) you will have to shut down the database.

   ```
   SQL> quit
   Disconnected from Oracle Database 11g Enterprise Edition Release
   ```

```
11.1.0.6.0 - Production
With the Partitioning, OLAP, Data Mining and Real Application Testing options
[oracle@localhost orcl]$ pwd
/oracle01/oradata/orcl
[oracle@localhost orcl]$ ls -al *.dbf
-rw-r-----  1 oracle oinstall  104865792 Aug 17 15:49 example01.dbf
-rw-r-----  1 oracle oinstall  104865792 Aug 17 15:49
my_second_secure_tbs_01.dbf
-rw-r-----  1 oracle oinstall  104865792 Aug 17 15:49 my_secure_tbs_01.dbf
-rw-r-----  1 oracle oinstall  104865792 Aug 17 15:49 retention_archives_01.
dbf
-rw-r-----  1 oracle oinstall  778051584 Aug 17 15:49 sysaux01.dbf
-rw-r-----  1 oracle oinstall  744497152 Aug 17 15:49 system01.dbf
-rw-r-----  1 oracle oinstall  182525952 Aug 17 14:03 temp01.dbf
-rw-r-----  1 oracle oinstall 1121984512 Aug 17 15:49 undotbs01.dbf
-rw-r-----  1 oracle oinstall  159326208 Aug 17 15:49 users01.dbf
[oracle@localhost orcl]$ rm *.dbf
```

4. Connect to the database and shut down the database. It may be possible that you
    will not be able to connect to the database, and yet the database will still be running.
    In this case you will have to manually kill the Oracle processes if you are running in
    Unix or shut down the database service in Windows. In our case, we are not able to
    log into the database, so we kill the LGWR process.

```
[oracle@localhost trace]$ sqlplus "/ as sysdba"
SQL*Plus: Release 11.1.0.6.0 - Production on Sun Aug 17 15:58:16 2008
Copyright (c) 1982, 2007, Oracle.  All rights reserved.
ERROR:
ORA-01075: you are currently logged on
Enter user-name:
ERROR:
ORA-01017: invalid username/password; logon denied
Enter user-name:
ERROR:
ORA-01017: invalid username/password; logon denied
SP2-0157: unable to CONNECT to ORACLE after 3 attempts, exiting SQL*Plus
[oracle@localhost trace]$ ps -ef|grep orcl|grep lgwr
oracle   23118     1  0 15:48 ?        00:00:01 ora_lgwr_orcl
[oracle@localhost trace]$ kill -9 23118
```

EXERCISE 3.2 *(continued)*

5. Once you are sure the database is down, restore the database datafiles from their backup location to the location where the database files belong.

```
[oracle@localhost orcl]$ pwd
/oracle01/backup/orcl
[oracle@localhost orcl]$ cp *.dbf /oracle01/oradata/orcl/*
```

6. Now connect to the database and issue the startup mount command.

```
[oracle@localhost orcl]$ sqlplus / as sysdba
SQL*Plus: Release 11.1.0.6.0 - Production on Sun Aug 17 16:26:56 2008
Copyright (c) 1982, 2007, Oracle.  All rights reserved.
Connected to an idle instance.
SQL> startup mount
ORACLE instance started.
Total System Global Area  167395328 bytes
Fixed Size                  1298612 bytes
Variable Size             142610252 bytes
Database Buffers           20971520 bytes
Redo Buffers                2514944 bytes
Database mounted.
SQL>
```

7. To recover the database, issue the recover database command. The command may return a response that says "media recovery complete," as shown here:

```
SQL> recover database
Media recovery complete.
```

You may also be prompted to apply archived redo logs. Simply enter **AUTO** at the prompt.

```
SQL> recover database
ORA-00279: change 5071334 generated at 08/17/2008 15:35:51 needed for thread 1
ORA-00289: suggestion :
/oracle01/flash_recovery_area/ORCL/archivelog
/2008_08_17/o1_mf_1_5_4bk6onh8_.arcORA-00280:
change 5071334 for thread 1 is in sequence #5
Specify log: {<RET>=suggested | filename | AUTO | CANCEL}
auto
ORA-00279: change 5071583 generated at 08/17/2008
15:40:04 needed for thread 1
```

```
ORA-00289: suggestion :
/oracle01/flash_recovery_area/ORCL/archivelog
/2008_08_17/o1_mf_1_6_4bk76kwk_.arcORA-00280:
change 5071583 for thread 1 is in sequence #6
ORA-00279: change 5091960 generated at 08/17/2008
15:49:05 needed for thread 1
ORA-00289: suggestion :
/oracle01/flash_recovery_area/ORCL/archivelog
/2008_08_17/o1_mf_1_7_4bk9ksb4_.arcORA-00280:
change 5091960 for thread 1 is in sequence #7
ORA-00279: change 5112317 generated at 08/17/2008
16:29:13 needed for thread 1
ORA-00289: suggestion :
/oracle01/flash_recovery_area/ORCL/archivelog
/2008_08_17/o1_mf_1_8_4bk9p236_.arcORA-00280:
change 5112317 for thread 1 is in sequence #8
ORA-00279: change 5112647 generated at 08/17/2008
16:31:29 needed for thread 1
ORA-00289: suggestion :
/oracle01/flash_recovery_area/ORCL/archivelog
/2008_08_17/o1_mf_1_9_4bk9p2mz_.arcORA-00280:
change 5112647 for thread 1 is in sequence #9
Log applied.
Media recovery complete.
```

8. Oracle will apply the needed redo and then return you to the SQL prompt. Assuming no errors occur, you can now open the database with the alter database open command as shown here:

```
SQL> alter database open;
Database altered.
```

Recovering the Database After the Loss of the *SYSTEM or UNDO* Tablespace Datafile

In this case, we will just restore the tablespaces or datafiles that were lost. Of course, because these are critical tablespace objects, the database itself is down. After restoring the datafiles that were lost (do not restore any datafiles that are intact), recover the database following these steps:

1. Log into the database as SYS.

2. Mount the database with the `startup mount` command.

3. For recovery, you have two options. You can use the `recover tablespace` or the `recover datafile` command to recover the datafiles that were lost. It's kind of up to you which one you want to use (we like the `recover tablespace` command in this situation more).

4. The `recover database` command will recommend to you the correct archived redo log to apply. At the prompt, type **AUTO**; the `recover database` command automatically starts applying all redo until the database is recovered.

5. Once database recovery is complete, the `recover database` command will return you to the SQL prompt. You can then issue the `alter database open` command to open the database for business.

Recovery of the *UNDO* Tablespace

There are cases where the UNDO tablespace can be recovered online. If the database was shut down in a consistent manner before the UNDO tablespace was lost, it may be that all you will need to do is take the UNDO tablespace datafiles offline (you won't be able to take the tablespace itself offline) and then open the database.

Oracle has a default SYSTEM tablespace that would be used in this case, when the database initially comes up. You could then just create a new UNDO tablespace and drop the old one. This might be a quicker recovery method in some cases.

Recovering the Database After the Loss of One or More Non-*SYSTEM* or -*UNDO* Tablespace Datafiles

If the tablespace/datafile you lost is not associated with the SYSTEM or UNDO tablespaces, then you are in luck. You don't even need to shut down the database to recover! All you need to do is take the datafiles offline, restore the impacted datafiles, recover the datafiles (or the tablespace), and bring them back online.

The nice thing about this is if your users are not using the tablespace, they will never know there was a problem. If the users are using the tablespace, they will be impacted only if they try to use the datafiles that are offline (which is one good reason in some cases to take just datafiles offline rather than the whole tablespace).

The first question is, How do you know which datafiles are missing? There are a couple of things that will give you a clue. First of all, your users will start getting these messages:

```
SQL> select * from scott.emp;
select * from scott.emp
              *
```

```
ERROR at line 1:
ORA-00376: file 4 cannot be read at this time
ORA-01110: data file 4: 'C:\ORACLE\ORADATA\ORCL\USERS01.DBF'
```

You can also look at the V$RECOVER_FILE view for more information on datafiles that need recovery. Here is an example of such a query:

```
SQL> select * from v$recover_file;
     FILE# ONLINE  ONLINE_ ERROR                          CHANGE# TIME
---------- ------- ------- -------------------- ---------- ---------
         4 ONLINE   ONLINE FILE NOT FOUND                        0
```

Missing Datafiles

Don't expect that these errors indicating datafiles are missing will always show up in the alert log. Sometimes they will (for example, on database startup), but often they won't (for example, when a query fails because a datafile is offline). If you want to monitor for this problem reliably, then the V$RECOVER_FILE view is the way to go.

So, here is the general recovery process from such an error. In this case we assume the database is up and running:

1. Take the datafile offline using the `alter database datafile offline` command as shown here:

   ```
   alter database datafile 'C:\ORACLE\ORADATA\ORCL\USERS01.DBF' offline;
   ```

   As an alternative, you can use FILE_ID as shown in this example:

   ```
   alter database datafile 4 offline;
   ```

   FILE_ID will appear in the error message, or you can use the FILE_ID column of DBA_DATA_FILES or the FILE# column in the V$DATAFILE view.

2. Restore the missing datafiles.

3. Restore all archived redo logs that will be needed for recovery. This would be all archived redo logs generated from the beginning of the backup image you restored in step 2.

When you are restoring backup files, never restore backed-up online redo logs over the existing online redo logs. This is so important, in fact, that when we talked about hot backups in Chapter 2, we did not even back up the online redo logs. Restoring old online redo logs over your existing ones will lead to data loss. Fair warning!

4. Recover the missing datafiles with the `recover datafile` or `recover tablespace` command.

5. Bring the datafiles or the tablespace online with the `alter database` or `alter tablespace` command.

So, what do you do if your database was down and you discover the files are lost when you start it up? That's simple too.

1. Log in as SYS and start up the database. If a datafile is missing, you will get an error message that looks something like this:

```
SQL> startup
ORACLE instance started.
Total System Global Area  397557760 bytes
Fixed Size                  1333452 bytes
Variable Size             289408820 bytes
Database Buffers          100663296 bytes
Redo Buffers                6152192 bytes
Database mounted.
ORA-01157: cannot identify/lock data file 4 - see DBWR trace file
ORA-01110: data file 4: 'C:\ORACLE\ORADATA\ORCL\USERS01.DBF'
```

2. It may be that you are missing more than datafile 4, since Oracle will alert you to only the first datafile that it finds missing. Use the V$RECOVER_FILE, V$DATAFILE, and V$TABLESPACE views to determine exactly which datafiles are missing and which tablespaces they are associated with, as shown in this example:

```
SQL> l
  1  select b.name ts_name, a.error, c.name datafile
  2  from v$recover_file a, v$tablespace b, v$datafile c
  3  where a.file#=c.file#
  4* and b.ts#=c.ts#
SQL> /
```

```
TS_NAME    ERROR               DATAFILE
---------  ------------------- -------------------------------------
USERS      FILE NOT FOUND      C:\ORACLE\ORADATA\ORCL\USERS01.DBF

select
```

3. Review the results of the query. As long as the missing datafiles are not part of the SYSTEM or UNDO tablespace, you can simply take those datafiles offline and open the database. The intent will be to recover those tablespaces/datafiles with the database open. First use the alter database datafile offline command to take the tablespaces offline:

```
SQL> alter database
datafile 'C:\ORACLE\ORADATA\ORCL\USERS01.DBF' offline;
Database altered.
```

4. Next, open the database with the alter database open command:

```
alter database open
```

5. Now restore the database backup datafiles from your hot backup media.

6. Restore all archived redo logs that will be needed for recovery. You will need to restore all archived redo logs generated from the beginning of the backup image you restored in step 2.

Figuring Out Which Archived Redo Logs You Need

If you need to figure out exactly which archived redo logs you need to restore your backup (so, perhaps, you can restore those files off of backup media), you can use the V$RECOVER_FILE and the V$LOG_HISTORY views. The V$RECOVER_FILE view provides the last change number (in the CHANGE# column) present in the file(s) needing recovery. The V$LOG_HISTORY view will tell you which archived redo logs the changes are in. Here is an example:

```
ORA-01157: cannot identify/lock data file 4 - see DBWR trace file
ORA-01110: data file 4: 'C:\ORACLE\ORADATA\ORCL\USERS01.DBF'
SQL> host copy users01.dbf.backup users01.dbf
        1 file(s) copied.
SQL> Select a.file#, a.change#, b.first_change#, b.next_change#, b.sequence#
  2  From v$recover_file a, v$log_history b
```

```
  3  Where a.change#<=b.next_change#;
      FILE#     CHANGE# FIRST_CHANGE# NEXT_CHANGE#  SEQUENCE#
---------- ---------- ------------- ------------ ----------
         4    1418889       1417349      1438925         20
```

You could also find the name of the actual archived redo logs needed for recovery by que-rying the V$ARCHIVED_LOG view. In some cases, the log sequence number will not show up here if the associated online redo log file has not yet been archived.

```
SQL> Select a.file#, a.change#, b.first_change#, b.next_change#,
  2  b.sequence#, b.name
  3  From v$recover_file a, v$archived_log b
  4  Where a.change#<=b.next_change#;
      FILE#     CHANGE# FIRST_CHANGE# NEXT_CHANGE#  SEQUENCE#
---------- ---------- ------------- ------------ ----------
NAME
------------------------------------------------
         4    1418889       1417349      1438925         20
C:\ORACLE\ARCH\ORCL\ARC00020_0662757171.001
```

7. Recover the datafiles or tablespaces using the `recover datafile` or `recover tablespace` command.

```
SQL> recover datafile 4;
```

8. Bring the datafiles or tablespaces online using the `alter database datafile online` or `alter tablespace online` command. Once you have done this, you have recovered the missing tablespace datafiles and your database is back to normal.

```
SQL>Alter database datafile 4 online;
```

Backing Up After the Recovery

There really is no requirement to do a special backup after a datafile or tablespace recovery. All your backup files are still usable, and Oracle will keep generating archived redo logs just like before.

Real World Scenario

Performing Database Recoveries in the Real World

In this book, we are providing you with some of the most common recovery situations that you might face and that appear on the OCP exam. The reality is that in the real world, recovery can quickly become very complex and overwhelming. You have people looking over your shoulder, 200 opinions on how to fix the problem (all of them different, of course), and you face an issue that does not quite neatly fit into the backup and recovery case studies that you have experienced in your training.

The key to figuring out what to do is to sit back and think about what the problem is and why it is happening. Another key is if you feel that you might be getting in over your head, get Oracle support on the line. Sometimes it takes a while to get them geared up to really help you, and the sooner you get them engaged, the better you will be in the end.

Finally, when you are troubleshooting, don't shotgun solutions. If you are not sure about your solution, think it out very carefully. Talk to other DBAs around you and get their opinions. Nothing makes a bad day worse like having a database failure and then realizing that you just made it a bigger problem by screwing up the recovery process.

Performing Incomplete Recoveries

Incomplete recovery (also called *point-in-time recovery*) is the process of recovering the database to a different point in time than the most current point in time. Why would one do such a thing, you ask? There may be a number of reasons:

- Loss of one of the online redo log groups making full recovery impossible
- User error requiring a recovery of the database to a different point in time
- Creation of a duplicate database to a point in time other than that of the source database.

In the following sections, we will cover the basics of incomplete recovery. First we will discuss the requirements for and mechanics of incomplete recovery, and then we will cover preparation for incomplete recovery. Finally, we will walk through the process of an actual incomplete recovery.

Requirements for and Mechanics of an Incomplete Recovery

The requirements for incomplete recovery are much like those of a complete recovery from an online backup. First, the database must be in ARCHIVELOG mode. Second, you have to have a backup of the database (online or offline) and all of the archived redo logs required to get your database to the point in time that you are interested in.

Preparing for an Incomplete Recovery

The first step in performing an incomplete recovery is to restore the database from a backup that was taken before the point in time to which you want to restore the database.

Notice that you have to restore the entire database. This can sometimes confuse less-experienced DBAs. With incomplete recovery, you must restore the entire database, and it must be restored to a point in time before the point in time that you wish to recover to.

For example, suppose it's 2 p.m. and you wish to recover just the USERS tablespace objects to 1 p.m. because someone messed something up. To do so, it's not just as simple as restoring the USERS tablespace datafiles to 1 p.m. You have to restore the entire database to 1 p.m.

Tablespace Point-in-Time Recovery

There is a concept of tablespace point-in-time recovery that allows you to restore just a tablespace to a point in time different from that of the database. We will discuss tablespace point-in-time recovery using RMAN in Chapter 8. The OCP exam does not require that you know how to do tablespace point-in-time recovery manually, so we are not covering that topic in this book.

Oracle is persnickety about datafile consistency. Recall the concept of the SCN, which is Oracle's internal counter for all operations. When you do an insert, it is assigned an SCN. When you then commit that insert, it is assigned a different, higher SCN. This way, Oracle knows the insert came first and the commit came second.

When you start the Oracle database, it's a demanding bit of software. It requires that the SCN in each datafile be the same before it will open the database (there is an exception to this with read-only tablespaces). Also, there are SCNs stored in the control file that have to jibe with the SCNs in the datafiles. If the SCNs don't jibe, then some form of recovery is required.

So, if the entire database is at SCN 12345 (see Figure 3.1) and you restore the USERS tablespace to SCN 1234, that will be a problem. Oracle will detect the different SCNs and require a complete recovery. Not quite what we hoped for.

So, when you want to perform an incomplete database recovery, you have to restore all the datafiles to a point in time at or before the point in time that you actually want to recover to. In Figure 3.2, you can see that all the datafiles are recovered to SCN 1230 or less, so you can now begin an incomplete recovery to SCN 1234 as you wish.

Note that you do not need to restore the control file to a previous version for incomplete recovery to work. Once you have finished the incomplete-recovery process, Oracle will reset the control file so that it will correctly reflect the current state of the database.

FIGURE 3.1 Database with datafiles restored incorrectly for incomplete recovery

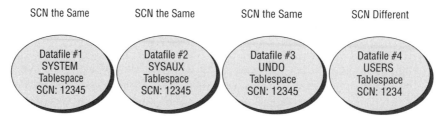

You want to recover to SCN 1234. Datafiles 1, 2, and 3 are at SCN 12345, which is after SCN 1234. Incomplete recovery to SCN 1234 is not possible because recovery rolls forward SCNs, not backward.

FIGURE 3.2 Database with datafiles restored correctly for incomplete recovery

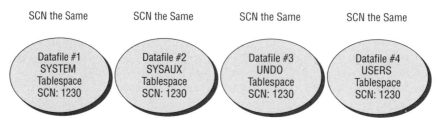

You want to recover to SCN 1234. All datafiles are at SCN 1230. It's now easy to recover them all to SCN 1234.

You will also need to restore all archived redo logs that were generated from the time of the backup image until the point that you want to restore to. You can determine which archived redo log sequence numbers you want to restore by looking at the V$ARCHIVED_LOG view (we provided a query using the V$ARCHIVED_LOG view in a note earlier in this chapter). Keep in mind that you may also need redo contained in an online redo log that has not been archived yet. Since you will not be restoring any online redo logs, this won't be a problem.

Now that you have restored all the database datafiles and the needed archived redo logs, you are ready to execute your incomplete database recovery.

Performing an Incomplete Recovery

Having restored the database datafiles, recovery is pretty easy. First you determine the type of recovery that you want to do, and then you perform the recovery using the recover database command. Finally, you open the database. Let's look at these steps in some more detail next.

Determining the Type of Point-in-Time Recovery

There are three types of point-in-time recovery that you can perform:

Time-based recovery   *Time-based recovery* is based on the time that you want to recover your database to. Time-based recovery is granular to the nearest second.

Log sequence–based recovery   *Log sequence–based recovery* is based on defining the log sequence number you wish the database to be recovered to. You will need to determine the correct log sequence number. The V$ARCHIVED_LOG and V$LOG views may be helpful in making this determination.

Change-based recovery   *Change-based recovery* is based on the SCN that you wish to restore your database to. You can determine what the current SCN of the database is by querying the CURRENT_SCN column of the V$DATABASE view. You can also associate a given time to an approximate SCN by using the TIMESTAMP_TO_SCN, SCN_TO_TIMESTAMP, or SMON_SCN_TIME view.

Perform Your Point-in-Time Recovery

Regardless of which of the three point-in-time recoveries you choose to perform, the overall process is very similar. You will use the `recover database` command for your recovery. Each recovery type will take a different keyword, as shown here:

Time-based recovery   To perform time-based recovery use the `recover database until time` command. The format of the time in the command is `'yyyy-mm-dd:hh24:mi:ss'`, which is consistent in each Oracle database (so it is not dependent on parameters such as NLS_DATE_FORMAT). Here is an example of the use of the `recover database until time` command:

```
Recover database until time '2008-10-23:13:00:00'
```

In this example, the database will be recovered up to October 23, 2008 at 1 p.m. Any transaction that are committed after that point will be rolled back.

Log sequence–based recovery   To perform log sequence–based recovery, use the `recover database until sequence` command. This example recovers to log sequence 34:

```
Recover database until sequence 34;
```

Change-based recovery   To perform change-based recovery, use the `recover database until change` command followed by the SCN you wish to recover to. In this example, we recover to SCN 226250:

```
Recover database until change 226250;
```

Once the recovery begins, you will be prompted for the appropriate archived redo logs to apply just as with a complete database recovery. The main difference is that the application of archived redo logs (and possibly online redo logs) will automatically cease once the point in time, change, or SCN has been reached. Once the redo has been applied, the database is ready to be opened.

Opening the Database

Having recovered the database, you will want to open it. A point-in-time recovery will result in a new incarnation of the database. A new incarnation is a new logical version of the database. The data remains the same, of course, but the redo stream essentially starts over. The log sequence number is reset to 1 (the SCN is not reset) and a new life begins for the database.

To indicate to Oracle that you are doing an incomplete recovery, you will open the database in a slightly different way. You will still use the alter database open command, but you will also include the keyword resetlogs. The resetlogs command indicates to Oracle that it should reset the control file and the redo log sequence number and open the database as a brand-new incarnation. The entire command looks like this:

```
alter database open resetlogs;
```

Through Oracle Database 10g, Oracle recommended that you back up the database anytime you issue a resetlogs operation. This was because Oracle did not support recovering a database through a resetlogs operation. In Oracle Database 11g, Oracle has been modified to allow for a recovery through resetlogs. This is supported through the new %r format string available in the LOG_ARCHIVE_FORMAT parameter (see Chapter 2 for more on this parameter). This format string will include a resetlogs number in the naming of each archived redo log. This will help Oracle keep the redo-log stream straight.

If you should need to do a recovery after a resetlogs operation, simply restore the same backup that you used to do the point-in-time recovery and recover using that backup. You can do full recovery or point-in-time recovery using the redo associated with the new incarnation. In Exercise 3.3, you'll perform a point-in-time recovery.

EXERCISE 3.3

Performing a Point-in-Time Recovery

In this exercise, you will do a point-in-time recovery by restoring the database to a previous SCN.

1. Back up the database. Details on how to do a full online database backup are found in Chapter 2. In summary, follow these steps:

    ▪   First put the database in hot backup mode.

    ▪   Copy all database datafiles to a backup location.

    ▪   Take the database out of hot backup mode.

    ▪   Force a log switch. Back up the archived redo logs.

EXERCISE 3.3 *(continued)*

Here is an example of a backup:

```
[oracle@localhost orcl]$ sqlplus "/ as sysdba"
SQL*Plus: Release 11.1.0.6.0 - Production on Sun Aug 17 15:35:48 2008
Copyright (c) 1982, 2007, Oracle.  All rights reserved.
Connected to:
Oracle Database 11g Enterprise Edition Release 11.1.0.6.0 - Production
With the Partitioning, OLAP, Data Mining and Real Application Testing options
SQL> alter database begin backup;
Database altered.
SQL> host cp /oracle01/oradata/orcl/*.dbf /oracle01/backup/orcl
SQL> alter database end backup;
Database altered.
SQL> alter system switch logfile;
System altered.
SQL> host cp /oracle01/backup/arch/* /oracle01/backup/orcl/*
SQL> alter database backup controlfile to trace;
Database altered.
SQL> alter database backup controlfile to '/oracle01/oradata/orcl/control1.bak';
Database altered.
```

2. Next, log into the database as scott/tiger and create a new table. Insert two records into the new table and commit the insert.

```
SQL> connect scott/tiger
Connected.
SQL> create table test_table (id number);
Table created.
SQL> insert into test_table values (1);
1 row created.
SQL> insert into test_table values (2);
1 row created.
SQL> commit;
Commit complete.
```

3. Now log in as SYS and determine the current SCN by using the CURRENT_SCN column of the V$DATABASE table. Your SCN will be different from that in the example.

```
SQL> connect sys as sysdba
Enter password:
```

EXERCISE 3.3 *(continued)*

```
Connected.
SQL> select current_scn from v$database;
CURRENT_SCN
-----------
   5135413
```

4. Log back in as scott/tiger and add two more records. Commit the inserts.

```
SQL> connect scott/tiger
Connected.
SQL> insert into test_table values (3);
1 row created.
SQL> insert into test_table values (4);
1 row created.
SQL> commit;
Commit complete.
```

5. Log in as SYS again and query the current SCN by using the CURRENT_SCN column of the V$DATABASE table. Notice that the SCN has changed.

```
SQL> connect sys as sysdba
Enter password:
Connected.
SQL> select current_scn from v$database;
CURRENT_SCN
-----------
   5135522
```

6. Shut down the database.

```
SQL> shutdown immediate
Database closed.
Database dismounted.
ORACLE instance shut down.
```

7. Once you are sure the database is down, restore the database datafiles from their backup location to the location where the database files belong.

```
[oracle@localhost orcl]$ pwd
/oracle01/backup/orcl
[oracle@localhost orcl]$ cp *.dbf /oracle01/oradata/orcl/*
```

8. Mount the database.

```
[oracle@localhost orcl]$ sqlplus "/ as sysdba"
SQL*Plus: Release 11.1.0.6.0 - Production on Sun Aug 17 17:53:14 2008
Copyright (c) 1982, 2007, Oracle.  All rights reserved.
Connected to an idle instance.
SQL> startup mount
ORACLE instance started.
Total System Global Area  167395328 bytes
Fixed Size                  1298612 bytes
Variable Size             142610252 bytes
Database Buffers           20971520 bytes
Redo Buffers                2514944 bytes
Database mounted.
```

9. Recover the database using the recover database until change command. You will use the SCN you queried in step 3 as the SCN to recover to. Enter **AUTO** when prompted for an archived redo log to apply.

```
SQL> Recover database until change 5135413;
ORA-00279: change 5071334 generated at 08/17/2008 15:35:51 needed for thread 1
ORA-00289: suggestion :
/oracle01/flash_recovery_area/ORCL/archivelog/2008_08_17
/o1_mf_1_5_4bk6onh8_.arc
ORA-00280: change 5071334 for thread 1 is in sequence #5
Specify log: {<RET>=suggested | filename | AUTO | CANCEL}
auto
ORA-00279: change 5071583 generated at 08/17/2008 15:40:04 needed for thread 1
ORA-00289: suggestion :
/oracle01/flash_recovery_area/ORCL/archivelog/2008_08_17
/o1_mf_1_6_4bk76kwk_.arc
ORA-00280: change 5071583 for thread 1 is in sequence #6
ORA-00279: change 5091960 generated at 08/17/2008 15:49:05 needed for thread 1
ORA-00289: suggestion :
/oracle01/flash_recovery_area/ORCL/archivelog/2008_08_17
/o1_mf_1_7_4bk9ksb4_.arc
ORA-00280: change 5091960 for thread 1 is in sequence #7
ORA-00279: change 5112317 generated at 08/17/2008 16:29:13 needed for thread 1
ORA-00289: suggestion :
/oracle01/flash_recovery_area/ORCL/archivelog/2008_08_17
/o1_mf_1_8_4bk9p236_.arc
```

```
ORA-00280: change 5112317 for thread 1 is in sequence #8
ORA-00279: change 5112647 generated at 08/17/2008 16:31:29 needed for thread 1
ORA-00289: suggestion :
/oracle01/flash_recovery_area/ORCL/archivelog/2008_08_17
/o1_mf_1_9_4bk9p2mz_.arc
ORA-00280: change 5112647 for thread 1 is in sequence #9
ORA-00279: change 5112649 generated at 08/17/2008 16:31:30 needed for thread 1
ORA-00289: suggestion :
/oracle01/flash_recovery_area/ORCL/archivelog/2008_08_17
/o1_mf_1_10_4bk9p3gz_.arc
ORA-00280: change 5112649 for thread 1 is in sequence #10
Log applied.
Media recovery complete.
```

10. Open the database with the alter database open resetlogs command. Note that once you have done this you will not be able to recover any data that was entered after the point of the recovery.

    ```
    SQL> alter database open resetlogs;
    Database altered.
    ```

11. Log into the scott schema. Do a select * from test_table. You should have only two records in the table.

    ```
    SQL> Connect scott/tiger
    Connected.
    SQL> Select * from test_table;
            ID
    ----------
             1
             2
    ```

Performing Other Types of Recoveries

You will need to be prepared for other types of user-managed recoveries when taking your OCP exam or just in the course of managing your Oracle database. In the following sections, we will talk about the following types of user-managed recoveries:

- Loss of a tempfile
- Loss of an online redo log group

- Loss of the control file
- Loss of the password file
- Loss of everything

Recovering from the Loss of a Tempfile

Tempfiles are used with temporary tablespaces. As discussed in Chapter 2, you do not need to back up a tempfile. Because of its temporary nature, the contents of a tempfile are not needed during a recovery. You will need to re-create the tempfile after any recovery that includes the temporary tablespace. This is done by using the `alter tablespace add tempfile` command as shown in this example, where we add a tempfile to the TEMP tablespace:

```
ALTER TABLESPACE TEMP ADD TEMPFILE '/oracle01/oradata/orcl/temp01.dbf'
SIZE 200m  REUSE AUTOEXTEND ON;
```

Recovering from the Loss of an Online Redo Log Group

Loss of the online redo logs comes in four different flavors:

- Loss of a redo log file group member
- Loss of an inactive online redo log group
- Loss of an active but not current online redo log group
- Loss of the current online redo log group

Any loss of an entire online redo log group makes for a very bad day. Loss of the last two categories (loss of an active or current online redo log) is often a disaster.

Recall that the redo logs are written to as soon as there is a commit (and other events can cause writes too). Remember also that the database datafiles are written to later, sometimes much later. Thus, the database datafiles are often way out of synchronization with the actual current state of the database. If the database crashes, then often the database datafiles are not up-to-date and this forces Oracle to apply redo to get them current when you start up the database. Normally, Oracle will do this automatically in a process called *instance recovery*.

As a result of the fact that the database datafiles are often out of synch with the actual state of the database, loss of an active or the current online redo log group can be disastrous. Loss of an *active online redo log* can result in loss of data. Loss of the current online redo log will likely result in data loss, but this is not always the case. As a result, redo logs are quite important. You may wonder what the difference between the current, active, and inactive redo logs is:

- Current: Current online redo log group.

- Active: Not currently in use but the dirty blocks associated with the redo in the log file still need to be written to the datafiles by DBWR. Also, the group may still need to be archived.

- Inactive: Not currently in use and dirty blocks associated with the redo in the log file have been written to datafiles by DBWR.

You can see the status of an online redo log group by querying the STATUS column of the V$LOG view. Let's look at what to do when it comes to recovering from loss of redo log groups.

Dealing with the Loss of an Inactive Online Redo Log Group Member

If you have lost one or more members of an online redo log group (but not the entire group) then the response is pretty easy. You can simply re-create the member using the `alter database add logfile member` command. For example, you might see this error in the alert log:

```
ORA-00313: open failed for members of log group 2 of thread 1
ORA-00312: online log 2 thread 1: 'C:\ORACLE\ORADATA\ORCL\REDO02.LOG'
```

If the database has not shut down, you should immediately attempt to checkpoint the database using the `alter system checkpoint` command. The `alter system checkpoint` command forces the database to write any dirty blocks from the database buffer cache to the database datafiles in an urgent manner. This will be helpful in the event the database crashes because of this missing online redo log.

Once the checkpoint has completed, you would issue the `alter database add logfile` command to re-create the redo log group member redo02.log:

```
SQL>alter database add logfile 'C:\ORACLE\ORADATA\ORCL\REDO02.LOG' reuse to
group 2;
```

If the database happened to crash before you could add the log file, you would mount the database and then issue the `alter database add logfile` command. You should then be able to open the database.

Another option is to shut down the database in a consistent manner (`shutdown`, `shutdown transactional`, `shutdown normal`) and then copy another member of the redo log group to the location of the missing member. You can then restart the database normally.

Dealing with the Loss of an Inactive Online Redo Log Group

Loss of an inactive online redo log group is not a terribly big deal in and of itself and is quite easy to recover from. There are two different situations you will need to be prepared for. First is loss of an inactive online redo log group during database startup. Second is loss of an inactive online redo log group during database operations. Let's look at these two situations in more detail.

Dealing with the Loss of an Inactive Online Redo Log Group on Startup

First, if you start up the database and the inactive online redo log group can not be opened, you will get the following error message:

```
ORA-00313: open failed for members of log group 2 of thread 1
ORA-00312: online log 2 thread 1: 'C:\ORACLE\ORADATA\ORCL\REDO02.LOG'
```

The response to this condition is to drop the log-file group using the `alter database` command as shown here:

```
SQL> alter database drop logfile group 2;
```

You can then re-create the online redo log group using the `alter database add logfile` command:

```
SQL> alter database add logfile
2   group 2 'c:\oracle\oradata\orcl\redo02.log' size 50m;
SQL> alter database add logfile
2   group 2 'c:\oracle\oradata\orcl\redo02.log' size 50m;
```

Dealing with the Loss of an Inactive Online Redo Log Group When the Database Is Running

If you lose an inactive online redo log group (or it becomes corrupted) while the database is running, the database will sometimes keep operating. It will sometimes skip the online redo log group that went missing and continue to operate normally. In this case, you can issue an `alter system checkpoint` command and then clear the log-file group with the `alter database clear logfile group` command as shown here:

```
SQL>alter system checkpoint;
SQL>alter database clear logfile group 1;
```

It may be that when you try to clear the log file you will receive an error that indicates that the log file needs to be archived:

```
SQL> alter database clear logfile group 1;
alter database clear logfile group 1
*
ERROR at line 1:
ORA-00350: log 1 of instance orcl (thread 1) needs to be archived
ORA-00312: online log 1 thread 1: '/oracle01/oradata/orcl/redo01.log'
```

Since the log file is not there, it cannot be archived. You can use the `alter database clear unarchived logfile` command to clear the unarchived log file, and rebuild the log file in its current location as shown here:

```
SQL> alter database clear
2 unarchived logfile '/oracle01/oradata/orcl/redo01.log';
```

You will need to back up your database in this case, since an archived redo log will have been lost.

Sometimes the database will not crash but will freeze. In this case, you will open another SQL*Plus session and issue the `alter database checkpoint` command followed by either the `alter database clear logfile` or the `alter database clear unarchived logfile` command, depending on the type of recovery required. After issuing these commands, the database should operate as usual.

Back Up the Database After Clearing Unarchived Log Files

Sometimes the database will crash as a result of the loss of the online redo log group. In this case, you will need to follow this procedure:

- From the SQL*Plus, log in as SYS using SYSDBA privileges.

- Mount the database using the `startup mount` command.

- Issue the `alter database clear logfile` group SQL command.

- Open the database with the `alter database open` command.

Dealing with the Loss of an Active but Not Current Online Redo Log Group

Loss of an ACTIVE (as shown in V$LOG column status) online redo log group requires the use of the `alter database clear unarchived logfile` command as shown in the previous section. This is because the active online redo log will not have been archived and you need to indicate to Oracle that this is okay. This command will rebuild the online redo log and allow Oracle to proceed with normal operations. You should always back up the database after this operation.

Dealing with the Loss of the Current Online Redo Log Group

Losing the current online redo log group is, perhaps, the worst disaster your Oracle database could encounter. This is because there is a significant risk of loss of data in such cases. When you lose the current online redo log group, you can expect that the database will shut down.

If the database has not yet shut down, you should immediately attempt to checkpoint the database using the `alter system checkpoint` command and then shut down the database afterward as soon as practical. The `alter system checkpoint` command forces the database to write any dirty blocks from the database buffer cache to the database datafiles in an urgent manner.

It may be that you can open the database without any recovery being required. This is the best-case situation. To try to restart the database do the following:

- Issue the `startup mount` command

- Issue the `alter database clear unarchived logfile` for the redo log group that was lost. Examples of this command can be seen in earlier sections of this chapter.

- Issue the `alter database open` command.

If the database opens successfully, you are in luck. If the database fails to open, you are in a bad way. You will need to perform incomplete recovery of the database as discussed in the section "Performing an Incomplete Recovery." You can see an example of recovering the database as a result of the loss of the current online redo log group in Exercise 3.1.

Recovering from the Loss of a Control File

Recovery from loss of a control file depends on the nature of the loss. There are two different situations you might encounter. You might lose one or more but not all control files. You might also lose all control files. Let's look at what to do in these cases.

Dealing with the Loss of One or More Control Files but Not All

If you have but one control file left, recovery is quite simple. Follow these steps:

- Shut down the database normally.

- Copy one of the remaining control files to the location of the lost control files and give it the same name as the lost control file.

- Restart the database.

Recovering from Loss of All Control Files

If you lose your control files, Oracle is not shy about telling you. If you are trying to start up your database and your control files are missing, you will see an error like this:

```
SQL> startup
ORACLE instance started.
Total System Global Area  171581440 bytes
Fixed Size                  1298640 bytes
Variable Size             146804528 bytes
Database Buffers           20971520 bytes
Redo Buffers                2506752 bytes
ORA-00205: error in identifying control file, check alert log for more info
```

This error will occur on startup if any of your control files are missing. If your database is running, loss of some of your control files will not cause it to stop operating. As a result, you can plan to shut down your database and then simply copy a surviving copy of the control file to the location of the lost control file. If the location is no longer available, you can modify the CONTROL_FILES parameter so that it points to the location of the new control file.

If you lose your control files while the database is running, it is quite likely that the database will crash in short order. There are some cases where it might stay up for a little while, but it will eventually come down on you.

Loss of all control files will require that you use a backup control file or issue the create control file command from the SQL prompt. We discussed the creation of a backup control file in Chapter 2. We also discussed how to create a trace file with the create control file command in it in Chapter 2. Let's look at each of these recoveries in a bit more detail.

Recovering Lost Control Files with a Backup Control File

If you have a backup control file, follow these steps to recover from the loss of all your control files:

1. Copy the backup control file to the location of each control file defined by the parameter CONTROL_FILES. Modify the CONTROL_FILES parameter if required.

2. Mount the database with the startup mount command.

3. Recover the database using the recover database using backup controlfile command. At the prompt, type in **AUTO** to apply all archived redo logs.

4. Recovery will end, likely with an error. This is because the final redo log sequence number you need to apply is not in an archived redo log but is in one of the online redo logs. Issue the recover database using backup controlfile command again. This time, when prompted for the archived redo log to apply, enter one of your online redo log names (for example, redo01.log). Continue to attempt to apply each online redo log group until you find the correct log sequence number.

5. Once the final online redo log is applied, recovery will complete automatically and without error.

6. You can now open the database using the alter database open resetlogs command.

Recovering Lost Control Files Using the *create control file* Command

In Chapter 2, we introduced the alter database backup controlfile to trace command. This created a trace file that you can use to re-create your control file. If you lose your control files, a backup control file is the easiest way to manually recover. However, if you do not have a backup control file, you have two options:

- Use the contents of the script created as a result of the alter database backup controlfile to trace command.

- Manually issue the create control file command.

As already discussed in Chapter 2, the `alter database backup controlfile to trace` command creates a script that you can use to recover your control file. The script will need to be modified before it can be used.

The script contains the following sections:

- Trace-file header
- List of parameters related to archiving
- NORESETLOGS case for re-creating the control file
- RESETLOGS case for re-creating the control file

As you can see, the script has two different versions of the `create controlfile` command. One is for recoveries where the online redo logs are intact. You will want to edit the script so that the correct type of recovery is done. Each version of the script also contains code to register archived redo logs, recover the database, and then open the database automatically.

Let's look at the following code, which is an example of using the NORESETLOGS case. The script is designed to do it all without any DBA interference. First it starts the database instance. It then proceeds to issue the `create control file` command. The script records some archived redo log records in the control file that will be needed for recovery. The database is then recovered and opened. Finally, the temporary tablespace tempfile is re-created.

```
STARTUP NOMOUNT
CREATE CONTROLFILE REUSE DATABASE "ORCL" NORESETLOGS  ARCHIVELOG
    MAXLOGFILES 16
    MAXLOGMEMBERS 3
    MAXDATAFILES 100
    MAXINSTANCES 8
    MAXLOGHISTORY 292
LOGFILE
  GROUP 1 (
    '/oracle01/oradata/orcl/redo01.log',
    '/oracle01/oradata/orcl/redo01a.log'
  ) SIZE 100M,
  GROUP 2 (
    '/oracle01/oradata/orcl/redo02.log',
    '/oracle01/oradata/orcl/redo02a.log'
  ) SIZE 50M,
  GROUP 3 (
    '/oracle01/oradata/orcl/redo03.log',
    '/oracle01/oradata/orcl/redo03a.log'
  ) SIZE 50M
-- STANDBY LOGFILE
DATAFILE
  '/oracle01/oradata/orcl/system01.dbf',
```

```
    '/oracle01/oradata/orcl/sysaux01.dbf',
    '/oracle01/oradata/orcl/undotbs01.dbf',
    '/oracle01/oradata/orcl/users01.dbf',
    '/oracle01/oradata/orcl/example01.dbf',
    '/oracle01/oradata/orcl/retention_archives_01.dbf',
    '/oracle01/oradata/orcl/my_secure_tbs_01.dbf',
    '/oracle01/oradata/orcl/my_second_secure_tbs_01.dbf'
CHARACTER SET WE8MSWIN1252
;
-- Configure RMAN configuration record 1
VARIABLE RECNO NUMBER;
EXECUTE :RECNO :=
SYS.DBMS_BACKUP_RESTORE.SETCONFIG('COMPRESSION ALGORITHM','''BZIP2''');
-- Configure RMAN configuration record 2
VARIABLE RECNO NUMBER;
EXECUTE :RECNO := SYS.DBMS_BACKUP_RESTORE.SETCONFIG('CONTROLFILE
AUTOBACKUP','ON');
-- Commands to re-create incarnation table
-- Below log names MUST be changed to existing filenames on
-- disk. Any one log file from each branch can be used to
-- re-create incarnation records.
-- ALTER DATABASE REGISTER LOGFILE
'/oracle01/flash_recovery_area/ORCL/archivelog/2008_08_16/o1_mf_1_1_%u_.arc';
-- ALTER DATABASE REGISTER LOGFILE
 '/oracle01/flash_recovery_area/ORCL/archivelog/2008_08_16/o1_mf_1_1_%u_.arc';
-- ALTER DATABASE REGISTER LOGFILE
 '/oracle01/flash_recovery_area/ORCL/archivelog/2008_08_16/o1_mf_1_1_%u_.arc';
-- Recovery is required if any of the datafiles are restored backups,
-- or if the last shutdown was not normal or immediate.
RECOVER DATABASE
-- Set Database Guard and/or Supplemental Logging
ALTER DATABASE ADD SUPPLEMENTAL LOG DATA (PRIMARY KEY) COLUMNS;
-- All logs need archiving and a log switch is needed.
ALTER SYSTEM ARCHIVE LOG ALL;
-- Database can now be opened normally.
ALTER DATABASE OPEN;
-- Commands to add tempfiles to temporary tablespaces.
-- Online tempfiles have complete space information.
-- Other tempfiles may require adjustment.
ALTER TABLESPACE TEMP ADD TEMPFILE '/oracle01/oradata/orcl/temp01.dbf'
     SIZE 182517760  REUSE AUTOEXTEND ON NEXT 655360  MAXSIZE 32767M;
```

Recovering from the Loss of the Password File

If you lose the database password file, it is simple to recover. First, if you have backed up the password file and it has not changed since the backup, you can simply restore it. If you did not have a backup of the password file, all you need to do is rerun the orapwd command to re-create the password file. The orapwd command is used to create password files. It's executed from the command line as shown in this example:

```
[oracle@localhost dbs]$ cd $ORACLE_HOME/dbs
[oracle@localhost dbs]$ orapwd file=orapwtest entries=20 password=Robert
```

In this example, we first changed to the $ORACLE_HOME/dbs directory where password files are stored. Next we ran the orapwd command to create the password file. We passed the name of the password file using the file= parameter. Password files always start with orapw followed by the name of the database (test in this case). The entries parameter indicates the number of SYSADM entries that are allowed for, and password indicated the password associated with the SYS account.

Recovering from the Loss of Everything

Loss of everything might rightly be called the "full-meal deal." It's the worst possible case of data loss. If you have lost everything, you will need the following to recover your database when running in ARCHIVELOG mode:

- Oracle software
- Oracle networking–related parameter files
- Oracle database parameter file
- Oracle database datafiles
- Backup control file or create controlfile command ready to run

The procedure to fully restore your database is as follows:

1. Create any new directories required.
2. Restore the Oracle software.
3. Restore or re-create the Oracle networking parameter files.
4. Restore the Oracle parameter file.
5. Rebuild the Oracle password file if required.
6. Restore the Oracle database datafiles.
7. Start up the database.
8. Recover the database using the procedure outlined in the section titled "Recovering from Loss of All Control Files."

Summary

As you can see, backup and recovery in Oracle can be a big deal. There are a number of different situations you will find yourself in. Sometimes these situations take some deep thinking to get out of. Often, understanding how Oracle actually works will help guide you through the problem and find a solution.

The Oracle 11*g* OCP exam contains a number of recovery-related questions, so you will want to know this stuff well. You should also work through the different exercises so that you understand what to do in different situations. In this chapter, we discussed a number of recovery cases:

- NOARCHIVELOG recovery

- ARCHIVELOG recovery

- Point-in-time recoveries

- Special recovery cases

It is probably clear to you that recovery in Oracle can be quite complex. It becomes even harder when you are actually doing it under the gun, when people are breathing down your neck to get that database up.

Exam Essentials

Restore and recover your database in NOARCHIVELOG mode.   Understand how to restore and recover your database in NOARCHIVELOG mode. Understand that you have to shut down the database and that you have to restore all the datafiles, the control files, and the online redo logs from your backup.

Restore and recover your database to the point of failure in ARCHIVELOG mode.
Understand how to restore and recover your database in ARCHIVELOG mode. Understand that you can recover the entire database or just a given tablespace or datafile. Understand what recoveries can be done with the database up and which require that the database be shut down.

Restore and recover your database to a different point in time.   Understand how to perform point-in-time recovery with your database. Understand how to restore the datafiles. Understand the types of recovery that are available (time-based, change-based, and SCN-based). Understand how to use the `recover database` command to perform point-in-time recovery and how to open the database after recovery has been completed.

Recover your database in the event of a lost online redo log.   Understand how to recover your database if you lose an inactive or current online redo log file. Understand the benefit of using the `alter database checkpoint` command if you have lost an online redo log group and the database is still running. Understand how to use the `alter database clear` command to clear unarchived redo log files and to re-create lost online redo log files. Understand the impacts of losing the current or an active online redo log file.

Recover your database in the event of a lost control file.   Understand how to recover your database if you lose one or more control files. Learn how to recover a lost control file by using a backup control file. Learn how to recover a lost control file by using the `create controlfile` command contained in the trace file resulting from the `alter database backup controlfile to trace` command.

Review Questions

1. Your database has experienced a loss of datafile users_01.dbf, which is associated with a tablespace called USERS. The database is still running. Which answer properly describes the order of the steps that you would use to recover from this error?

    a. Shut down the database.

    b. Take the users_01.dbf datafile offline with the alter database command.

    c. Restore the users_01.dbf datafile from backup media with the required archived redo logs.

    d. Restore all users tablespace-related datafiles from backup media.

    e. Issue the recover tablespace users command.

    f. Issue the recover datafile users_01.dbf command.

    g. Start up the database.

    h. Bring the users_01.dbf datafile online with the alter database command.

    A. a, c, f, g

    B. b, c, f, h

    C. a, b, c, f, g

    D. a, b, c, f, g, h

    E. b, c, f, e, g

2. As soon as you discover that you have lost an online redo log, if the database is still functioning, what should be your first action?

    A. Shut down the database.

    B. Clear the online redo log.

    C. Back up the database.

    D. Checkpoint the database.

    E. Call Oracle support.

3. You have lost all your SYSTEM tablespace datafiles (system_01.dbf and system_02.dbf) and the database has crashed. What would be the appropriate order of operations to correct the situation?

    a. Mount the database with the startup mount command.

    b. Take the SYSTEM datafile offline with the alter database command.

    c. Restore the SYSTEM_01.dbf datafile from backup media with the required archived redo logs.

    d. Restore all SYSTEM tablespace–related datafiles from backup media.

    e. Issue the recover tablespace SYSTEM command.

    f. Issue the recover datafile SYSTEM_01.dbf command.

g. Open the database with the `alter database open` command.

h. Open the database with the `alter database open resetlogs` command.

A. a, c, f, g

B. b, d, e, h

C. a, b, c, f, g

D. d, a, e, g

E. b, c, f, e, g

4. You have discovered that one of three control files has been lost. What steps would you follow to recover that control file?

a. Shut down the database.

b. Restore a control-file copy from backup media.

c. Use the `create control file` command to create a new control file.

d. Copy the backup control file into place.

e. Create a new copy of the control file from one of the surviving control files.

f. Recover the database using the `recover database using backup controlfile` command.

g. Start up the database.

A. a, b, f, g

B. c, f, g

C. a, d, f, g

D. a, f, g

E. a, e, g

5. Which files will you need to perform a full recovery of a database backed up in NOARCHIVELOG mode? (Choose all that apply.)

A. Database datafiles

B. Control files

C. Archived redo logs

D. Online redo logs

E. Flashback logs

6. Which are the correct steps, in order, to deal with the loss of an online redo log if the database has not yet crashed?

a. Issue a checkpoint.

b. Shut down the database.

c. Issue an `alter database open` command to open the database.

d. `Startup mount` the database.

e. Issue an `alter database clear logfile` command.

f. Recover all database datafiles.

A. a, b, c, d

B. b, d, e, c

C. a, b, d, e, c

D. b, f, d, f, c

E. b, d, a, c

7. What methods of point-in-time recovery are available? (Choose all that apply.)

A. Change-based

B. Cancel-based

C. Time-based

D. Sequence number-based

E. Transaction number-based

8. Which files are required for a full recovery of the database in ARCHIVELOG mode? (Choose three.)

A. Database datafiles

B. Online redo logs

C. Archived redo logs

D. Backup control file

E. Control file from a backup

9. What is the proper procedure to recover a lost tempfile?

A. Restore the backup copy of the tempfile from the backup media.

B. Re-create the tempfile with the `create tempfile` command.

C. Copy an existing tempfile from another database.

D. Re-create the tempfile with the `create tablespace` command.

E. Re-create the tempfile with the `alter tablespace` command.

10. Upon starting your database, you receive the following error:

```
SQL> startup
ORACLE instance started.
Total System Global Area  171581440 bytes
Fixed Size                  1298640 bytes
Variable Size             146804528 bytes
Database Buffers           20971520 bytes
Redo Buffers                2506752 bytes
Database mounted.
ORA-00313: open failed for members of log group 1 of thread 1
ORA-00312: online log 1 thread 1: '/oracle01/oradata/orcl/redo01.log'
ORA-00312: online log 1 thread 1: '/oracle01/oradata/orcl/redo01a.log'
```

You can choose from the following steps:

a. Restore the database datafiles.

b. Issue the `alter database clear unarchived logfile group 1` command.

c. Issue the `alter database open` command.

d. Issue the `alter database open resetlogs` command.

e. Recover the database using point-in-time recovery.

f. Issue the `Startup Mount` command to mount the database.

g. Back up the database.

Which is the correct order of these steps in this case?

A. a, f, e, d, g

B. f, e, d

C. f, b, c, g

D. a, f, c

E. The database cannot be recovered.

11. A user sends you an email with the following error message:
```
create table idtable(id number)
    *
ERROR at line 1:
ORA-01116: error in opening database file 4
ORA-01110: data file 4: '/oracle01/oradata/orcl/users01.dbf'
ORA-27041: unable to open file
Linux Error: 2: No such file or directory
Additional information: 3
```

You can choose from the following steps:

a. Restore the missing database datafiles.

b. Take the missing datafile offline.

c. Shut down the database.

d. Issue the `recover tablespace USERS` command.

e. Issue the `Startup Mount` command to mount the database.

f. Bring the USERS tablespace online.

g. Issue the `alter database open` command.

Which is the correct order of these steps in this case?

A. b, a, d, f

B. c, a, e, b, d, f, g

C. c, e, d, g

D. b, d, f

E. e, d, g

12. You have lost all your database control files. To recover them, you are going to use the results of the `alter database backup controlfile to trace` command. Your datafiles and your online redo logs are all intact. Which of the following is true regarding your recovery?

   A. You will need to open the database with the `resetlogs` command.

   B. All you need to do is execute the trace file from SQL*Plus and it will perform the recovery for you.

   C. You will use the `resetlogs` version of the `create controlfile` command.

   D. You will use the `noresetlogs` version of the `create controlfile` command.

   E. You will use the trace file to create a backup control file, and then you will recover the database with the `recover database using backup controlfile` command.

13. Your developers have asked you to restore the development database, which is in NOARCHIVELOG mode, back to last Tuesday the 20th. Your last backup is from Monday the 19th. What do you do?

   A. Restore the 19th's backup, restore all archived redo logs, recover the database to the 20th, and open the database.

   B. Tell them that their request cannot be met with the current backup strategy.

   C. Restore the 19th's backup, apply the online redo logs, and open the database.

   D. Switch the database into ARCHIVELOG mode, restore the 19th's backup, restore all archived redo logs, and recover the database to the 20th.

   E. Use the `recover database` command to roll back the database from today to the 19th of the month.

14. What methods are available to recover lost control files? (Choose all that apply.)

   A. Backup control file.

   B. Emergency control file.

   C. The `create controlfile` command.

   D. The `restore controlfile` SQL*Plus command.

   E. No backup is required. The database will re-create the control file when it is discovered to be lost.

15. Your ARCHIVELOG-mode database has lost three datafiles and shut down. One is assigned to the SYSTEM tablespace and two are assigned to the USERS tablespace. You can choose from the following steps to recover your database:

   a. Restore the three database datafiles that were lost.

   b. Issue the `Startup Mount` command to mount the database.

   c. Issue the `alter database open` command.

   d. Issue the `alter database open resetlogs` command.

   e. Recover the database using the `recover database` command.

   f. Recover the datafiles with the `recover datafile` command.

   g. Take the datafiles offline.

Which is the correct order of these steps in this case?

A. a, b, e, c

B. b, e, d

C. a, b, d, c

D. b, g, c, f

E. a, b, d, f

16. You have lost all your online redo logs. As a result, your database has crashed. You have tried to restart the database and clear the online redo log files, but when you try to open the database you get the following error.

```
SQL> startup
ORACLE instance started.
Total System Global Area  167395328 bytes
Fixed Size                  1298612 bytes
Variable Size             142610252 bytes
Database Buffers           20971520 bytes
Redo Buffers                2514944 bytes
Database mounted.
ORA-00313: open failed for members of log group 2 of thread 1
ORA-00312: online log 2 thread 1: '/oracle01/oradata/orcl/redo02a.log'
ORA-27037: unable to obtain file status
Linux Error: 2: No such file or directory
Additional information: 3
ORA-00312: online log 2 thread 1: '/oracle01/oradata/orcl/redo02.log'
ORA-27037: unable to obtain file status
Linux Error: 2: No such file or directory
Additional information: 3
SQL> alter database clear logfile group 2;
alter database clear logfile group 2
*
ERROR at line 1:
ORA-01624: log 2 needed for crash recovery of instance orcl (thread 1)
ORA-00312: online log 2 thread 1: '/oracle01/oradata/orcl/redo02.log'
ORA-00312: online log 2 thread 1: '/oracle01/oradata/orcl/redo02a.log'
```

What steps must you take to resolve the error?

a. Issue the `recover database redo logs` command.

b. Issue the `Startup Mount` command to mount the database.

c. Restore the last full database backup.

d. Perform a point-in-time recovery, applying all archived redo logs that are available.

    e. Restore all archived redo logs generated during and after the last full database backup.

    f. Open the database using the `alter database open resetlogs` command.

    g. Issue the `alter database open` command.

    A. b, a, f

    B. e, b, a, f

    C. e, b, a, g

    D. b, a, g

    E. c, e, b, d, f

17. What does the SCN represent?

    A. The system change number, which is a point in time relative to transactions within a given database.

    B. A number that represents time. Thus, at 1300 hours, the SCN is the same on all databases.

    C. The security change number, which represents the security code that is needed to access any database structure.

    D. A conversion factor that converts internal database time to external clock time.

    E. UTC time in the database, providing a standardized way of tracking time in Oracle.

18. You have lost datafile 4 from your database. Which is typically the fastest way to restore your database?

    A. Restore and recover the datafile.

    B. Restore and recover the tablespace.

    C. Restore and recover the database.

    D. Restore and recover the control file.

    E. Restore and recover the parameter file.

19. You are trying to recover your database. During the recovery process, you receive the following error:

```
ORA-00279: change 5033391 generated at 08/17/2008 06:37:40
needed for thread 1
ORA-00289: suggestion :
/oracle01/flash_recovery_area/ORCL/archivelog/2008_08_17
/o1_mf_1_11_%u_.arc
ORA-00280: change 5033391 for thread 1 is in sequence #11
ORA-00278: log file
'/oracle01/flash_recovery_area/ORCL/archivelog/2008_08_17
/o1_mf_1_10_4bj6wnqm_.arc' no longer needed for this recovery
Specify log: {<RET>=suggested | filename | AUTO | CANCEL}
ORA-00308: cannot open archived log
```

```
'/oracle01/flash_recovery_area/ORCL/archivelog/2008_08_17
/o1_mf_1_11_%u_.arc'
ORA-27037: unable to obtain file status
Linux Error: 2: No such file or directory
Additional information: 3
```

How do you respond to this error? (Choose two.)

A. Restore the archived redo log that is missing and attempt recovery again.

B. Recovery is complete and you can open the database.

C. Recovery needs redo that is not available in any archived redo log. Attempt to apply an online redo log if available.

D. Recover the entire database and apply all archived redo logs again.

E. Recovery is not possible because an archived redo log has been lost.

20. During recovery, you need to know if log sequence 11 is in the online redo logs, and if so, you need to know the names of the online redo logs so you can apply them during recovery. Which view or views would you use to determine this information? (Choose all that apply.)

A. V$LOGFILE

B. V$RECOVER_LOG

C. V$RECOVER_DATABASE

D. V$LOG_RECOVER

E. V$LOG

Answers to Review Questions

1. B. First you would take the `users_01.dbf` datafile offline. You would then restore the `users_01.dbf` datafile from the most current backup. Once you have restored the datafile, recover the datafile with the `recover datafile` command. Finally, bring the datafile online with the `alter database` command.

2. D. When you discover that you have lost an online redo log, and if the database is still up, the first action should be to checkpoint the database. This can serve to reduce the overall risk of data loss. After you checkpoint the database, you can then attempt to clear the online redo log. A backup afterward is highly recommended.

3. D. First you would restore the missing datafiles. Notice in the question that there are two datafiles that were lost. Next you would mount the database and then you would recover the SYSTEM tablespace. Since it is the SYSTEM tablespace, you would not be able to open the database first. Then you open the database with the `alter database open` command.

4. E. If you lose one or more control files but at least one remains, you should shut down the database. Then use any remaining control file as the source to create new control-file copies for the control files that were lost. Then restart the database. No recovery is required in this situation.

5. A, B, D. You will need the database datafiles, the control files, and the online redo logs all in place to be able to restore the database when it's in NOARCHIVELOG mode.

6. C. If the database has not shut down yet, you have an opportunity to preserve your data changes. Issue a checkpoint, which will flush dirty buffers to disk. Then shut down the database normally, if possible (`shutdown`, `shutdown immediate`). You then should mount the database with the `startup mount` command followed by clearing and rebuilding the log file with the `alter database clear logfile` command. Finally, attempt to open the database with the `alter database open` command.

7. A, B, C, D. Change-based application allows you to recover the database to a specific SCN. Cancel-based recovery provides the ability for you to cancel recovery after each archived redo log application. Time-based recovery provides the ability to recover the database up to a specific point in time. Sequence number–based recovery allows you to recover the database up to a specific log sequence number.

8. A, C, D. To perform a full recovery of the database that is in ARCHIVELOG, you would need the database datafiles, the archived redo logs, and a backup control file.

9. E. You use the `alter tablespace add tempfile` command to re-create a missing tempfile or add a new tempfile to a temporary tablespace.

10. C. You should first start the database in mount mode using the `startup mount` command. You then issue the `alter database clear unarchived logfile` command. This will clear the log file if it needs to be archived and re-create the online redo log group. If that command is successful, then you issue the `alter database open` command. The last step, backing up the database, is very important since your previous backup will not be able to recover the database beyond the point of the cleared redo log sequence number. This is because you have skipped a redo log in the redo log stream.

11. A. You would first take the missing datafile offline with the `alter database datafile 4 offline` command. You should then restore the datafiles that have been lost. Then issue the `recover tablespace USERS` command to recover the USERS tablespace. Use the `alter database datafile 4 online` command to bring the USERS tablespace online.

12. D. Since the online redo logs are intact, you will be able to use the `noresetlogs` version of the `create controlfile` command.

13. B. Since the database is in NOARCHIVELOG mode, their request cannot be met because point-in-time recovery is supported only in ARCHIVELOG mode.

14. A, C. You can create a backup control file with the `alter database backup controlfile` command. You can create a trace file that contains the `create controlfile` command.

15. A. First you would want to restore the three datafiles that were lost. Then you would want to issue the `startup mount` command to mount the database to prepare for recovery. You would then recover the database (you could opt to recover just the datafiles if you wished). Finally, open the database with the `alter database open` command.

16. E. In this situation, you have gotten yourself in real trouble and you will have data loss. First you will need to restore the last full database backup and also all archived redo logs that were generated during the backup and since the backup was completed. You will then issue the `startup mount` command to mount the database, and then issue the `recover database until cancel` command. Apply all the archived redo logs you can. Then cancel the recovery and open the database using the `alter database open resetlogs` command.

17. A. The SCN is a number that represents a point in time in the database relative to transactions within a given database.

18. A. If you have only lost a datafile, you should just restore and then recover the datafile.

19. A, C. This error will appear if an archived redo log is not available. In this case you need sequence 11. First you would try to restore archived redo log sequence 11. If log sequence 11 is not available as an archived redo log, you might find that it is available in one of the online redo logs.

20. A, E. The `V$LOGFILE` view will give you the name of the online redo logs associated with each group. The `V$LOG` view will provide the current sequence number assigned to each group.

Chapter

4

Configuring and Backing Up Using RMAN

ORACLE DATABASE 11g: ADMINISTRATION II EXAM OBJECTIVES COVERED IN THIS CHAPTER:

✓ **Configuring Backup Specifications**

- Allocate channels to use in backing up
- Configure backup optimization

✓ **Configuring for Recovery**

- Define, apply and use a retention policy
- Configure the Flash Recovery Area
- Use Flash Recovery Area

✓ **Using RMAN to Create Backups**

- Create image file backups
- Create a whole database backup
- Enable fast incremental backup
- Create duplex backup and back up backup sets
- Create an archival backup for long-term retention
- Create a multi-section compressed and encrypted backup

Backup and recovery is one of the central themes in the Oracle Database 11g OCP exam. In Chapters 2 and 3 we talked about user-managed backup and recovery in Oracle, and now we will move on to what is termed *server-managed* backups, which are managed by RMAN. RMAN is like SQL*Plus in some ways. RMAN is a client. It connects to the Oracle database and issues a few commands to the server, and the server actually does the work (hence the term *server-based backups*). The server reports the results to RMAN and RMAN reports those results to you.

In this chapter we will introduce you to RMAN. We will discuss the features and configuration of RMAN, including configuration of the flash recovery area (FRA). We will also discuss using RMAN to back up your Oracle database. In Chapter 5 we will continue with a discussion of using RMAN to restore and recover your Oracle database.

Exam objectives are subject to change at any time without prior notice and at Oracle's sole discretion. Please visit Oracle's Training and Certification website (http://www.oracle.com/education/certification/) for the most current exam-objectives listing.

Why Use RMAN?

RMAN has many capabilities to facilitate the backup and recovery process. It comes in both web-based GUI and command-line versions. In general, RMAN performs and standardizes the backup and recovery process, which can reduce mistakes made during this process. The following are just a few of the exciting RMAN features:

- It's free with the Oracle license.
- You can perform full and incremental backups of the entire database, specific tablespaces, and datafiles. You can also back up control files and archive logs.
- RMAN offers persistent parameter configuration for easy backup and recovery.
- RMAN offers automated backups of control files and spfiles.
- You can validate your database backups without actually recovering your database.
- RMAN offers actual compression of backup images through various means.
- RMAN offers actual encryption of database backups.
- RMAN provides various backup reporting capabilities.

- RMAN provides scripting capabilities when you are using a recovery catalog.
- With the Media Management Library (MML) you can integrate easily with third-party tape media software.
- RMAN provides for parallel processing of backups and restores.
- With RMAN, you can create duplicate databases.
- RMAN helps you migrate datafiles across operating-system platforms.
- With RMAN, you can perform tablespace point-in-time recovery (TSPITR).
- RMAN allows you to recover datafiles that aren't backed up.
- RMAN will automatically recover tempfiles during a database recovery.

Exploring the RMAN Architecture

As you can see, RMAN has a rich feature set, and with each version of Oracle, the feature set becomes even richer. Oracle Database 11*g* offers a very full-featured backup and recovery tool in the form of RMAN.

RMAN is based on a robust architecture consisting of the following main components:

- The RMAN client interface
- The database server
- The database control file
- The optional recovery catalog
- Database pfile or spfile
- Backup media and the Media Management Library (MML)
- Backup sets and backup set pieces
- RMAN channels
- Snapshot control file

Let's look at each component in a bit more detail:

RMAN client interface   The *RMAN command-line interface (RCLI)* provides access to Recovery Manager. This process spawns off-server sessions that connect to the *target database*, which is the database that will be backed up. From the RMAN client interface you will issue RMAN commands to execute RMAN backup, recovery, and restore operations.

 Previous versions of this text (and OCP exams) contained significant coverage of Oracle Enterprise Manager (OEM). The Oracle Database 11*g* OCP exam contains no coverage specific to OEM, and much more coverage on user-based backup and recovery. As a result, there is little coverage of OEM within this text.

Database server   The database server is the principal mechanism used to back up the database. Built into the core of the Oracle kernel code are stored packages used by RMAN to back up, restore, and recover the database. RMAN cannot execute back up, restore, or recover operations without having first attached to the database server. Depending on the operation, the database will need to be opened in NOMOUNT, MOUNT, or OPEN mode.

Control file   The *database control file* is used to store RMAN-related information for each database. The control file is the principal storage mechanism for all RMAN-related records. All records with respect to database backups, archive-log backups, and control-file backups are stored in the control file. Control files have limitations with respect to how many RMAN records they can hold, and as a result, certain retention requirements may call for the use of a recovery catalog to augment a control file. RMAN provides an automated means of backing up the control file and restoring it when a control file is not readily available. This method is called a control-file autobackup.

Recovery catalog   The *recovery catalog* is an optional component that stores RMAN-related information inside an Oracle database. This is similar to the RMAN repository stored in the control file, but the recovery catalog provides some additional features and longer-term storage of RMAN records. The recovery catalog is a special schema that contains backup-related information in a set of tables. During normal database operations, RMAN will synchronize the database control file with the recovery catalog, ensuring that the recovery-catalog schema is in synchronization with the database control file.

Database pfile or spfile   You should already be familiar with the *database parameter file (pfile)* and the *server parameter file (spfile)*. These files are critical to RMAN operations because they contain parameters that impact RMAN operations. RMAN can be used to back up and recover an spfile using an option called autobackups. Pfiles can not be backed up with RMAN.

Backup media and the Media Management Library   Obviously, if RMAN is going to back up your database, it needs to back it up somewhere. RMAN, out of the box, allows you to back up your database to disk. This can be the local disk, or a network-attached disk (in other words, NFS) can be used. RMAN also offers the *Media Management Library (MML)*. The MML is an API set that media vendors (for example, tape-drive vendors) can write to and that allows RMAN to communicate directly with their products.

Backup sets and backup set pieces   Backup sets are logical entities that consist of one or more backup set pieces. Backup set pieces are physical files that actually store the RMAN backup data.

RMAN channels   *Channels* are used in RMAN to indicate the device to back up to. They are also used to partition a backup operation, essentially parallelizing the operation. For example, if you had two tape units, you could create two different RMAN channels and stream your backup to the two different tape devices in parallel. This can reduce backup and recovery times significantly.

RMAN offers *automated channel failover* for both backup and recovery operations. With automated channel failover, if a channel in a multichannel backup fails, the other channels will continue to back up the remainder of the database. This can be helpful when, for example, a tape device fails. In addition, Oracle will retry to back up the data that was on the failed channel across the remaining channels.

Snapshot control file   When RMAN does its business, it bases its knowledge of the database on information in the database control file. That's fine and well, but if the control file changes during an RMAN operation, what is RMAN to do, use the old information or the new information? The answer to this dilemma is the snapshot control file.

When RMAN performs any operation that requires a consistent view of the control file (such as a backup), it will first create a copy of the control file. This copy is called the *snapshot control file*. The snapshot control file will be used for the duration of that operation and will be overwritten by any subsequent operation. Even related operations (say, during a backup database plus archive-log operation that does an archive log backup, a database backup, and then another archive log backup) will use newly created snapshot control files, one for each operation.

Connecting to RMAN

Connecting to the RMAN client is quite simple. RMAN is a command-line tool, so you would want to open a command-line window for your operating system. Once you have done that you will set your ORACLE_HOME environment to the database that you want to connect to. Now you can start RMAN and connect to the target database (or the database that you want to backup and recover). Here is an example of connecting to a database with the RMAN client:

```
C:\oracle\admin\ORCL\wallet>set oracle_sid=orcl
C:\oracle\admin\ORCL\wallet>rman target=/
Recovery Manager: Release 11.1.0.6.0 - Production on Thu Sep 11 18:28:24 2008
Copyright (c) 1982, 2007, Oracle.  All rights reserved.
connected to target database: ORCL (DBID=1190537904)
```

Sometimes you may need to connect to your target database using Oracle Net connection strings. If you are using a recovery catalog or an auxiliary database you will normally connect to those using Oracle Net connection strings, as seen in these examples:

```
C:\oracle\admin\ORCL\wallet>rman target=sys/robert@orcl
C:\oracle\admin\ORCL\wallet>rman target=sys/robert@orcl
catalog=rcat_user/robert@rcat
```

The RMAN command line contains a number of different command-line parameters. You will see many of these in use throughout these next few chapters. Table 4.1 provides an overview of the most commonly used command-line parameters you might use:

 Real World Scenario

Putting Files in *ORACLE_HOME* Is Not a Best Practice

You might have noticed that RMAN puts the snapshot control file in an ORACLE_HOME location by default. This is not unusual; Oracle does this for other types of files (for example, the FRA defaults to ORACLE_HOME) by default.

In the real world, defaults like this are never acceptable, and we never allow ORACLE_HOME to be the destination for any type of file other than those associated with the Oracle install and certain configuration files (thus its size is fairly static). This is because you do not want the disk space in ORACLE_HOME to unexpectedly become exhausted because Oracle databases are writing files into it. This becomes even more important as you add more databases to your server and those databases are using the same ORACLE_HOME concurrently. Allowing those databases to write to ORACLE_HOME can cause problems for all databases on the server.

RMAN snapshot control files, files and directories associated with the Automatic Diagnostic Repository (ADR), database datafiles, and most other database-related files should be created in directories specific to each database other than ORACLE_HOME. (See Chapter 10 for more on ADR.)

The real-world solution generally involves the creation of different mount points for database-specific data. These mount points might be shared among different databases, or there might be a unique mount point for each database (or perhaps several mount points for one or more databases). For example, if your database is ORCL, you might have the following mount points/directories created:

- /oracle01/oracle/product/11.1.0/db_1: ORACLE_HOME

- /oracle02/oracle/oradata/orcl (for Oracle Database datafiles)

- /oracle03/oracle/oradata/orcl (for Oracle Database datafiles)

- /oracle04/oracle/diag (for the ADR)

For more information, you may want to review Oracle's OFA recommendations. OFA is outside the scope of the OCP exam and this book, but it provides some guidance from Oracle on directory naming and placement for Oracle-related files.

TABLE 4.1 RMAN Command-Line Parameters

Parameter Name	Description
Target	Connection string for the target database
Catalog	Connection string for the recovery catalog database
Nocatalog	Indicates no recovery catalog is to be used. Default.
Cmdfile	Name of command file to run.
Log	Name of log file to log RMAN output.
Trace	Name of file for debugging messages.
Append	Append to log file rather than overwrite.
Auxiliary	The connection string for the auxiliary database.

Configuring RMAN for Use

RMAN will work out of the box without any configuration. Unfortunately, this is generally not a good idea. RMAN tends to throw things into ORACLE_HOME if you have not configured the database and RMAN correctly. In this section, we will address configuring RMAN correctly.

In the following sections, we will introduce you to the flash recovery area (FRA) in RMAN. We will then address RMAN persistent configuration settings to allow for streamlined backups followed by using nonpersistent settings when required. Finally, we will cover configuring RMAN for its first use.

The Flash Recovery Area

The Oracle *flash recovery area (FRA)* was introduced in Oracle Database 10g as the central repository for all files related to Oracle backup and recovery. In this section, we will discuss the flash recovery area. First we will have a quick overview of what the FRA is generally used for. Then you'll learn about configuring the FRA for your Oracle database.

Introducing the FRA

The FRA is the principal store for all Oracle database backup–related files. The FRA can be stored on disk or within an ASM instance. It cannot be stored on tape, but files backed up in the FRA can be backed up to tape via the RMAN `backup recovery area` command.

The FRA stores the following types of Oracle database files:

- Backup set pieces
- Archive log backups
- Database archive logs
- Control-file autobackups
- Image copies
- Database online redo logs
- Database control files
- Flashback logs

The FRA supports RMAN's backup and retention policies by automatically removing files when they are no longer needed and when FRA space is required (obsolete RMAN backups to non-FRA locations will not be removed by RMAN automatically).

Configuring the FRA

Configuring the FRA is easy. First you create the base directory of the FRA from the OS, and then you set the following parameters in any database that will use the FRA:

- `DB_RECOVERY_FILE_DEST`
- `DB_RECOVERY_FILE_DEST_SIZE`

The `DB_RECOVERY_FILE_DEST` parameter defines the FRA base directory location. This is the only directory you will need to create when configuring the FRA. You will need to make sure that this directory is owned by the owner of the Oracle executable so that Oracle can create other subdirectories beneath it.

The `DB_RECOVERY_FILE_DEST_SIZE` parameter defines the total amount of space for this database instance is allowed to consume in the FRA. This is a logical limit, which can be greater than or less than the actual physical limit of space on that device. For example, you may have a file system with 500GB of space available on it. However, you may want to indicate that your database can consume only up to 100GB of space within the FRA while assigning the FRA to the 500GB file system.

You use the `alter system` command to configure the FRA. Note that `DB_RECOVERY_FILE_DEST` is not dynamic, while `DB_RECOVERY_FILE_DEST_SIZE` is dynamic. To configure the FRA, do the following:

1. Create the base FRA directory:

```
/u01>mkdir /oracle01/fra
```

2. Log into SQL*Plus:

```
C:\oracle\orabackup\orcl>sqlplus sys as sysdba
SQL*Plus: Release 11.1.0.6.0 - Production on Thu Aug 14 18:57:13 2008
Copyright (c) 1982, 2007, Oracle.  All rights reserved.
Enter password:
Connected to:
Oracle Database 11g Enterprise Edition Release 11.1.0.6.0 - Production
With the Partitioning, OLAP, Data Mining and Real Application
Testing options
SQL>
```

3. Now use the `alter system` command to set the parameter DB_RECOVERY_FILE_DEST to /oracle01/fra and DB_RECOVERY_FILE_DEST_SIZE to 2GB.

```
sql>alter system set db_recovery_file_dest_size=2GB;
sql>alter system set db_recovery_file_dest='/oracle01/fra' scope=spfile;
```

4. Now shut down and restart the database. Once the database has been restarted, the FRA will become operational.

```
SQL> shutdown immediate
Database closed.
Database dismounted.
ORACLE instance shut down.
SQL> startup
ORACLE instance started.
Total System Global Area  397557760 bytes
Fixed Size                  1333452 bytes
Variable Size             268437300 bytes
Database Buffers          121634816 bytes
Redo Buffers                6152192 bytes
Database mounted.
Database opened.
```

Managing the FRA

Management of the FRA is done principally by Oracle based on backup retention settings for RMAN (see the section "Retention Policies" later in this chapter). Thus, as backups become obsolete and as FRA space is exhausted by an instance, Oracle will remove those obsolete backups automatically. As a result, over time FRA space tends to reach an equilibrium, assuming that the database datafiles do not grow at a great rate.

Real World Scenario

Really Using the FRA

In the real world, it's hard to get things right the first time. Using the FRA is no exception. One of us had a client that had a few problems when they first switched to using the FRA. The databases were not set up correctly, so the FRA would fill up.

Over time, the FRA became more stable as we understood the load profile and its relationship to the creation of archived redo logs and backups. We eventually found the sweet spot with respect to how much disk space we needed to allocate to the FRA. This is actually a good thing because it forced them to realize that understanding the disk-usage profile of their databases was important.

Monitoring of the FRA is another real-world issue to be aware of. Many companies that are using the FRA are investing some time in scripts to monitor FRA disk-space usage. OEM can be used for this too.

The FRA does require some care and feeding by the DBA, however, particularly at first. Sometimes it's hard to properly estimate the correct setting for the DB_RECOVERY_FILE_DEST_SIZE and you will find the FRA filling up. Archived redo logs are stored in the FRA, so if the FRA fills up, archived redo logs will no longer be able to be written.

If this occurs, Oracle will first try to free space in the FRA by removing obsolete backups. If Oracle cannot free up enough space, then eventually the inability to archive will cause the database to freeze until the out-of-space condition can be rectified. In this case, you can free up space by changing DB_RECOVERY_FILE_DEST_SIZE to a higher value. This parameter is dynamic, so the change can be made immediately.

You can use the V$DB_RECOVERY_FILE_DEST view to determine the state of the FRA. In the following example, we find that the FRA is sized to 2GB and that we have used 251MB in total. We also see that 41MB of that space is reclaimable. In short, this FRA looks pretty good at this point.

```
SQL> select name, space_limit, space_used, space_reclaimable
2 from v$recovery_file_dest;
NAME                            SPACE_LIMIT    SPACE_USED SPACE_RECLAIMABLE
------------------------------ -------------- ------------ ------------------
c:\oracle\flash_recovery_area   2,147,483,648  251,173,376         41,127,424
```

 If you manually remove files from the FRA, you will have to let Oracle know that you have done so. By default Oracle will not detect that the files have been removed. Oracle can detect the file removals by using the RMAN crosscheck and delete expired commands. See Chapter 7 for more information on using these commands.

RMAN Persistent Configuration Settings

When RMAN first came out in Oracle version 8.0, you had to manually indicate in each backup where the backup destination was to be, any limits related to the backup (such as the maximum size of backup set pieces), and so on. This required a lot of work and made RMAN a bit more archaic-looking and difficult to use.

Oracle Database version *9i* introduced the concept of persistent configuration in RMAN. *RMAN persistent configuration settings* are settings that are configured through the RMAN interface, stored in the control file, and automatically used during each backup unless they are overridden.

Oracle Database 11*g* provides for a number of persistent settings, including the following:

- Backup (database and archive log) retention criteria
- Backup optimization
- Default channel/device configuration
- Control-file autobackup configuration
- Datafile and archive log backup-copy configuration
- Default encryption settings
- Default compression settings
- Default location for the snapshot control file

You can see the current settings for all persistent parameters in RMAN by using the RMAN show all command, as shown here:

```
RMAN> show all;
using target database control file instead of recovery catalog
RMAN configuration parameters for database with db_unique_name ORCL are:
CONFIGURE RETENTION POLICY TO REDUNDANCY 1; # default
CONFIGURE BACKUP OPTIMIZATION OFF; # default
CONFIGURE DEFAULT DEVICE TYPE TO DISK; # default
CONFIGURE CONTROLFILE AUTOBACKUP OFF; # default
CONFIGURE CONTROLFILE AUTOBACKUP FORMAT FOR DEVICE TYPE DISK TO '%F'; #default
CONFIGURE DEVICE TYPE DISK PARALLELISM 1 BACKUP TYPE TO BACKUPSET; # default
CONFIGURE DATAFILE BACKUP COPIES FOR DEVICE TYPE DISK TO 1; # default
CONFIGURE ARCHIVELOG BACKUP COPIES FOR DEVICE TYPE DISK TO 1; # default
CONFIGURE CHANNEL DEVICE TYPE DISK MAXPIECESIZE 100 M;
CONFIGURE MAXSETSIZE TO UNLIMITED; # default
CONFIGURE ENCRYPTION FOR DATABASE OFF; # default
CONFIGURE ENCRYPTION ALGORITHM 'AES128'; # default
CONFIGURE COMPRESSION ALGORITHM 'BZIP2'; # default
```

```
CONFIGURE ARCHIVELOG DELETION POLICY TO NONE; # default
CONFIGURE SNAPSHOT CONTROLFILE NAME TO
 'C:\ORACLE\PRODUCT\11.1.0\DB_1\DATABASE\SNCFORCL.ORA'; # default
```

You can also look at an individual setting by using the show command followed by the setting you are interested in. In this example, we are interested in the retention policy:

```
RMAN> show retention policy;
RMAN configuration parameters for database with db_unique_name ORCL are:
CONFIGURE RETENTION POLICY TO REDUNDANCY 1; # default
```

You can clear configuration settings using the configure clear command, as shown in this example:

```
RMAN>configure device type disk clear;
```

Unique RMAN Configuration Settings

Sometimes you need to do something different. Perhaps you have configured your default channels to go to tape but you want a particular backup to go to disk one time. You can configure unique one-time-only settings in RMAN through the use of a combination of the set command, a *run block*, and individual keywords available in specific commands. Here is an example of using a run block to override channel defaults. We also use the allocate channel command to manually allocate channels:

```
run {
allocate channel c1 device type disk format 'c:\oracle\oraback1\orcl\%U';
allocate channel c2 device type disk format 'c:\oracle\oraback2\orcl\%U';
backup database plus archivelog;
};
```

You can also use options within the backup command to override default settings. For example, by default RMAN will write backups to the FRA, so the backup command (which we will discuss later in this chapter) is as simple as backup database plus archivelog. If you want to write to a directory other than the FRA for a single backup, you would include the format keyword to override the default setting, as in this example:

```
backup database format 'c:\oracle\backup\backup\%U.bak' plus archivelog
format 'c:\oracle\backup\arch\%U.bak';
```

The RMAN Backup and Recovery Manuals

Oracle provides some great sources of information within the Oracle documentation set. We strongly recommend you acquaint yourself with the Oracle documentation and especially the Oracle RMAN documentation. The place to go for the online Oracle documentation is http://tahiti.oracle.com. For RMAN backup and recovery, look at the following books while you are preparing for your OCP exam:

- Backup and Recovery Reference - Part Number B28273-02

- Backup and Recovery Users Guide - Part Number B27270-02

And finally, if we may pat our own backs a little bit, a great book on getting to know RMAN is *Oracle Database 10g* RMAN Backup *&* Recovery by Robert G. Freeman and Matthew Hart (Oracle Press/McGraw-Hill, 2007). It's a comprehensive guide to all things RMAN. The Oracle Database 11g version should be available sometime in 2009.

Preparing RMAN for Use

Before you use RMAN, you will want to customize it to use your preferences. This makes the backup process easy and repeatable with a minimum of effort. In this section, we will discuss a number of configurable features of RMAN:

- Setting the control_file_record_keep_time parameter
- Backup retention policies
- Backup compression
- Backup encryption
- Specific channel configurations
- Control-file autobackups
- Backup optimization
- Setting the location of the snapshot control file

    Let's look at each of these in some more detail.

Setting the *control_file_record_keep_time* Parameter

When using RMAN without a recovery catalog (which we discuss in Chapter 5), you will need to make sure that you have set the CONTROL_FILE_RECORD_KEEP_TIME parameter correctly. This parameter is used to determine how long RMAN-related control-file records are maintained in the control file. Make sure this parameter is set high enough so that it will not interfere with your retention-policy requirements (see the next section for more on retention policies).

You can set the CONTROL_FILE_RECORD_KEEP_TIME (defined in days) parameter using the alter system command, as shown here:

```
-- Set control_file_record_keep_time to 14 days.
SQL> alter system set control_file_record_keep_time=14;
```

The parameter is a dynamic parameter; therefore, you can change it without having to shut down the database.

Retention Policies

RMAN *retention policies* are used to manage how long Oracle will maintain backups. When you're using the FRA, retention policies are used for automated cleanup of unneeded backup sets, which eliminates the need to manually manage space usage. When you're not using the FRA, retention policies can be used to manually manage space usage. In the following sections, you'll learn about the two different kinds of retention policies and how to configure them.

Types of Retention Policies

These are the different types of retention policies that you can set in RMAN:

- None
- Redundancy (the default)
- Recovery window

Let's look at the redundancy and recovery window retention criteria in a bit more detail. Then we will cover how to override the retention criteria with the keep operand.

REDUNDANCY RETENTION POLICY

The redundancy retention policy ensures that there will be a certain number of backups available for recovery. Once a backup is no longer needed, Oracle will mark it as obsolete, making it eligible for removal. For example, if the retention criterion is set to redundancy 2, then the following happens as you back up your database:

- Backup 1 occurs; when successful, it is considered current.
- Backup 2 occurs. Backups 1 and 2 are considered current.
- Backup 3 occurs. Backup 1 is marked as obsolete and backups 2 and 3 are considered current.

The default retention setting in RMAN is a redundancy retention policy of 1 copy.

If an FRA is configured, the backup will be removed when space is needed. If an FRA is not used, you will need to use the RMAN command delete obsolete (discussed in Chapter 8) to remove the backup metadata and physical files.

RECOVERY WINDOW RETENTION POLICY

The recovery retention policy provides the ability to define a recovery window to be applied to your backups in a period of days. For example, if you want to be sure you can restore your database to 14 days ago, you would establish a recovery retention policy of 14 days and earlier. Note that this setting does not impact the lifetime of a specific backup based on when the backup occurred but rather ensures that all backups that are retained can be restored based on the retention policy. This means that backups taken 15, 16, or 30 days ago may remain valid backups as demonstrated here and in Figure 4.1:

- Your database retention policy is 14 days.

- You perform database backup #1 on day 1; it is of course valid.

- Archive log backups are taken on days 1 through 14. Backup #1 is now 15 days old. It remains valid because it is needed to restore the database to days 0 through 14.

- Database backup #2 is taken on day 16. Database backup #1 is still valid. Why? Because we need database backup #1 to restore the database to day 10, or day 9, since database backup #2 is valid for only day 16 and beyond.

- Archive log backups are taken on days 17 through 29, which is the 14th day since backup #2.

- On day 29, backup #1 and all the associated archived redo logs are finally eligible for removal.

FIGURE 4.1   Recovery-window retention-policy example: 14 days

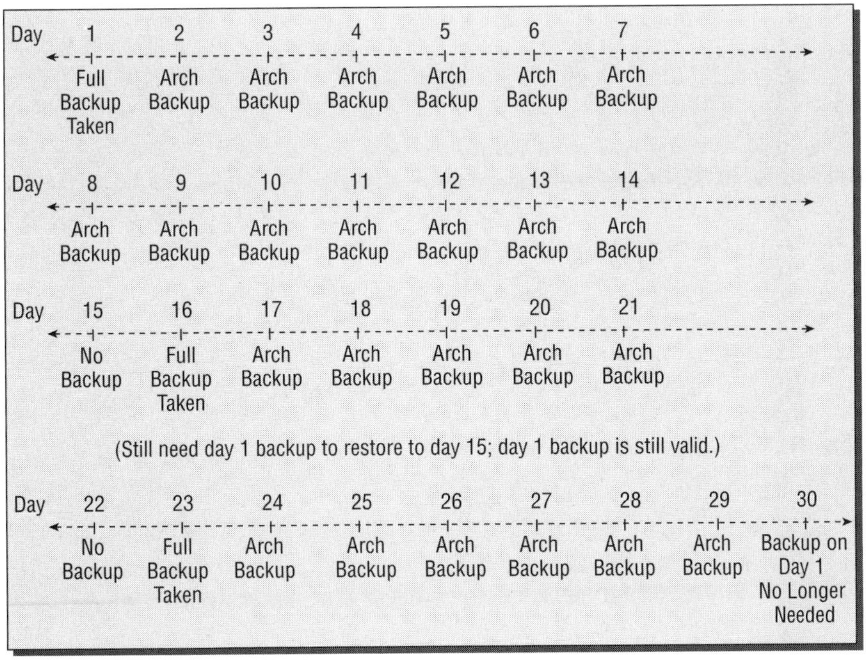

When the backup is marked obsolete, it is eligible for removal. If it exists in the FRA, then Oracle will remove it automatically. If it is not in the FRA, you can use the `list obsolete`

command to list those backups subject to removal based on the retention policy and then use the delete obsolete command to remove those backups. Here is an example:

```
RMAN> report obsolete;
RMAN retention policy will be applied to the command
RMAN retention policy is set to redundancy 2
Report of obsolete backups and copies
Type                    Key   Completion Time  Filename/Handle
------------------- ----- --------------- --------------------
Backup Set              19    05-SEP-08
  Backup Piece          36    05-SEP-08       C:\ORACLE\BACKUP\0MJPS3LL_3_1.ORCL
Backup Set              19    05-SEP-08
  Backup Piece          35    05-SEP-08       C:\ORACLE\BACKUP\0MJPS3LL_2_1.ORCL
Backup Set              19    05-SEP-08
  Backup Piece          34    05-SEP-08       C:\ORACLE\BACKUP\0MJPS3LL_1_1.ORCL
Backup Set              20    05-SEP-08
  Backup Piece          37    05-SEP-08       C:\ORACLE\BACKUP\0NJPS3VG_1_1.ORCL
Backup Set              21    05-SEP-08
  Backup Piece          38    05-SEP-08       C:\ORACLE\BACKUP\0OJPS402_1_1.ORCL
Backup Set              22    07-SEP-08
  Backup Piece          39    07-SEP-08       C:\ORACLE\FLASH_RECOVERY_AREA\ORCL
\BACKUPSET\2008_09_07\O1_MF_ANNNN_TAG20080907T170612_4D8QMNYR_.BKP
RMAN> delete noprompt obsolete;
RMAN retention policy will be applied to the command
RMAN retention policy is set to redundancy 2
using channel ORA_DISK_1
Deleting the following obsolete backups and copies:
Type                    Key   Completion Time  Filename/Handle
------------------- ----- --------------- --------------------
Backup Set              19    05-SEP-08
  Backup Piece          36    05-SEP-08       C:\ORACLE\BACKUP\0MJPS3LL_3_1.ORCL
Backup Set              19    05-SEP-08
  Backup Piece          35    05-SEP-08       C:\ORACLE\BACKUP\0MJPS3LL_2_1.ORCL
Backup Set              19    05-SEP-08
  Backup Piece          34    05-SEP-08       C:\ORACLE\BACKUP\0MJPS3LL_1_1.ORCL
Backup Set              20    05-SEP-08
  Backup Piece          37    05-SEP-08       C:\ORACLE\BACKUP\0NJPS3VG_1_1.ORCL
Backup Set              21    05-SEP-08
  Backup Piece          38    05-SEP-08       C:\ORACLE\BACKUP\0OJPS402_1_1.ORCL
Backup Set              22    07-SEP-08
```

```
  Backup Piece      39    07-SEP-08         C:\ORACLE\FLASH_RECOVERY_AREA\ORCL
\BACKUPSET\2008_09_07\O1_MF_ANNNN_TAG20080907T170612_4D8QMNYR_.BKP
deleted backup piece
backup piece handle=C:\ORACLE\BACKUP\0MJPS3LL_3_1.ORCL RECID=36
STAMP=664670185
deleted backup piece
backup piece handle=C:\ORACLE\BACKUP\0MJPS3LL_2_1.ORCL RECID=35
STAMP=664670069
deleted backup piece
backup piece handle=C:\ORACLE\BACKUP\0MJPS3LL_1_1.ORCL RECID=34
STAMP=664669886
deleted backup piece
backup piece handle=C:\ORACLE\BACKUP\0NJPS3VG_1_1.ORCL RECID=37
STAMP=664670208
deleted backup piece
backup piece handle=C:\ORACLE\BACKUP\0OJPS402_1_1.ORCL RECID=38
STAMP=664670216
deleted backup piece
backup piece handle=C:\ORACLE\FLASH_RECOVERY_AREA\ORCL
\BACKUPSET\2008_09_07\O1_MF_ANNNN_TAG20080907T170612_4D8QMNYR_.BKP RECID=39
STAMP=664823188
Deleted 6 objects
```

USING THE *KEEP* OPTION

If you have a defined retention policy, you may well want to override it for specific backups. Perhaps you have a policy that says at the end of the year you will make a backup of the database and keep it forever, or perhaps you have a "gold" copy backup that you want to keep for a longer period of time than the default retention policy allows. The keep option provides the ability to override the default retention policy. You can define a different retention policy for the specific backup (for example, remove it in 180 days) or you can choose to keep the backup until you decide to obsolete it manually with the unkeep command.

For example, if you wanted to create a backup with a retention criterion of 365 days, you would issue the following command:

```
RMAN> backup database plus archivelog delete input
keep until time 'sysdate + 365';
```

Using the keep forever option, you could keep the backup indefinitely, as shown here:

```
RMAN> backup database plus archivelog tag=gold_copy
delete input keep forever;
```

Note that the use of the keep option does not require that you back up archived redo logs at the same time. Issuing the keep command will cause RMAN to back up the archived redo logs needed to restore the backup you are indicating you want to keep. So you could avoid the plus archivelog option if you wanted, as shown here:

```
RMAN> backup database format 'c:\oracle\backup\%U'
keep until time "sysdate+300" tag='DavidW_HeberA_BillJ_JedB_DanD_MandyC';
```

The keep forever option requires that you use a recovery catalog. The keep until time option does not require the use of a recovery catalog.

You can use the change command to subsequently decide to keep a backup or to change the setting on a backup so that the status of the backup is no longer set to keep. For example, you can take a backup with a tag of gold_backup that was backed up with the keep command and start to enforce the retention criteria on that backup by using the change nokeep command, as shown here:

```
RMAN>backup database plus archivelog tag=gold_copy delete input format
'c:\oracle\backup\%U' keep until time "sysdate+300";
RMAN>change backupset tag gold_backup nokeep;
```

You cannot create backups on which you've used the keep option in the FRA. If you want to create backups that have nonstandard retention criteria, you will have to use a non-FRA location to create them. This often requires the use of the format parameter, as shown in this example:

```
backup database format 'c:\oracle\backup\%U' keep until time
"sysdate+300" ;
```

Configuring Retention Policies

Retention policies are configured in RMAN using the configure command. When configuring a redundancy configuration policy, you will use the configure command with the retention policy to redundancy keywords, as shown here:

```
RMAN> configure retention policy to redundancy 1 ;
```

To configure a recovery-window retention policy, you use the configure command with the retention policy to recovery window of days keywords, as shown here:

```
RMAN> configure retention policy to recovery window of 2 days;
```

To disable the retention policy, use the configure command with the retention policy to none keywords, as shown here:

```
RMAN> configure retention policy to none;
```

Compression

RMAN has long offered *white-space compression*. Essentially, this means that blocks in a datafile that are not used do not get backed up. White-space compression is quite helpful for a database that is sized quite large but contains little data. It is less helpful for well-packed databases.

In these cases, you will want to take advantage of actual *backup set compression*. This is compression not unlike that available with operating system programs like pkzip, gzip, and compress. Oracle Database 11*g* offers two flavors of compression, zlib and bzip2 (the default). Zlib is designed to compress with a minimum of CPU impact. The result is often a slightly bigger backup image than you get with the bzip2 compression format.

You can configure compression as a default value with the `configure compression algorithm` command followed by the compression format name, as shown in this example:

```
RMAN> configure compression algorithm 'zlib';
```

To actually perform a backup with compression, you will need to configure the default device type to use compression, or you will have to use the `as compressed` keyword when issuing the backup command. Here is an example of configuring the default device type to use compression:

```
RMAN> configure device type disk backup type to compressed backupset;
```

And here is an example of using the `as compressed` keyword when creating a backup:

```
backup as compressed backupset database plus archivelog;
```

 Real World Scenario

The Hidden Talents of Compression

Sometimes there's a product feature that has hidden benefits. Compression is one of these. While compression can help reduce the size of your backup sets, there is another potential feature that we look at in the real world, and that is an overall reduction in I/O. With compression enabled, we often see a reduction in backup and recovery times since there is less disk I/O associated with the backup. This can result in reduced backup times, and the backups may have less impact on the overall system.

Everything comes with a price, though, and in this case it's CPU. Compression comes with a high CPU cost. On systems where there was plenty of CPU to go around, we have seen compression significantly reduce backup times and I/O impacts.

Encryption

You can choose to encrypt your backups in Oracle Database 11g. Several encryption options are available to you, and they can be found by querying the V$RMAN_ENCRYPTION_ALGORITHMS view. You can use the `configure` command to define the default level of encryption that you want to use. You then use the `configure` command to enable encryption for the entire database or for specific tablespaces.

For example, if you wanted to configure encryption for the entire database, you would use the following commands:

```
RMAN> configure encryption algorithm "AES128";
RMAN> configure encryption for database on;
```

Encryption options for a given tablespace will take precedence over the database global settings. Thus, you can enable global encryption for the database and disable it for a specific tablespace.

There are three different modes of encryption (as opposed to the algorithm used). These are transparent mode, password-based encryption, and dual-mode encryption, which encompasses both modes of encryption. For transparent encryption, you will need to create a wallet, and it must be open. Transparent encryption will then occur automatically after you have issued the `configure encryption for database on` or `configure encryption for tablespace on` command.

For password authentication, you will need to use the `set encryption identified by` command first to enable password-based authentication. If you are restoring you will have to use the `set decryption identified by` command to set the password to decrypt a backup. You can also use the `set` command to change the type of encryption for a specific backup or to turn off encryption. Here is an example of the use of the `set encryption` command:

```
RMAN> set encryption identified by my_pass only on for all tablespaces;
```

Channel Configuration

When you initiate an RMAN backup, RMAN will create one or more channels that connect the database to a backup device. By default, RMAN will create a single channel to back up or recover to or from the FRA. You can override the defaults using the `configure` command. Along with backup locations, the `configure` command allows you to define other settings for your backup channels, including parallelism and backup-set and piece-set sizing. In the following sections, you'll learn about using the `configure` command to define default backup locations, about configuring parallelism, and then about using the `configure` command to set other channel-related parameters.

Configuring Backup Locations

The configure default device command is used to configure a backup location other than the default location. If, for example, you wanted to back up to a directory called /oracle01/backup/orcl, you would issue the following command:

```
RMAN> configure channel device type disk format '/oracle01/backup/orcl/%U';
```

RMAN will use this path for future backups. You can configure multiple channels with the configure command by specifying each individual channel, as shown here where we have indicated different default backup locations for each channel:

```
RMAN> configure channel 1 device type disk format '/oracle01/backup/orcl/%U';
RMAN> configure channel 2 device type disk FORMAT '/oracle02/backup/orcl/%U';
```

You might have wondered about the %U in the backup location format. The %U is an *RMAN backup format specification*. There are a number of different format specifications. %U is the most common because it ensures a unique filename for each backup set piece created by RMAN. Table 4.2 provides a list of the most common format specifications.

TABLE 4.2   Format Options

Option	Description
%a	Specifies the activation ID of the database
%c	Specifies the copy number of the backup piece within a set of duplexed backup pieces
%d	Specifies the name of the database
%D	Specifies the current day of the month from the Gregorian calendar
%e	Specifies the archived log sequence number
%f	Specifies the absolute file number
%F	Combines the database ID (DBID), day, month, year, and sequence into a unique and repeatable generated name
%h	Specifies the archived redo log thread number
%I	Specifies the DBID
%M	Specifies the month in the Gregorian calendar in *MM* format

TABLE 4.2   Format Options *(continued)*

Option	Description
%N	Specifies the tablespace name.
%n	Specifies the name of the database, padded on the right with *n* characters to a total length of eight characters.
%p	Specifies the piece number within the backup set.
%s	Specifies the backup-set number.
%t	Specifies the backup-set timestamp.
%T	Specifies the year, month, and day in the Gregorian calendar.
%u	Specifies an eight-character name constituted by compressed representations of the backup-set or image-copy number.
%U	Specifies a system-generated unique filename (this is the default setting).

Configuring Parallelism

Now that you can configure multiple channels, you might want to use them! To do so, you use the `configure` command along with the `parallelism` keyword, as shown here:

```
RMAN> configure device type disk parallelism 2;
```

This will cause any `backup database` command to use two channels, performing the backup in parallel.

Other Channel Configuration Options

You have already seen how to configure channels for alternate backup locations and parallelism, but there are other things you might want to configure for a given channel. In this section we will discuss the following channel-configuration options, which you will want to be aware of:

- SBT channel configuration
- `Maxsetsize` and `Maxpiecesize` configuration

SBT CHANNEL CONFIGURATION

First, most of our examples in this chapter have identified disk-based locations for backups. You may well want to have your backup go to tape instead. To do so, you will need to install the vendor's interface into RMAN's MML API, following the vendor's instructions. Once you have done so, you would then allocate a channel (or more if you want parallel backups) to a device called SBT to send it to the tape device. Here is an example where we use the configure command to make the SBT device the default device:

```
configure device type sbt parallelism 2;
```

Or you could configure individual channels like this:

```
RMAN> configure channel 1 device type sbt;
RMAN> configure channel 2 device type sbt;
```

During the backup, you could manually allocate channels to SBT also within a run block:

```
run {
allocate channel c1 device type sbt;
allocate channel c2 device type sbt;
backup database plus archivelog;
};
```

MAXSETSIZE AND *MAXPIECESIZE* CONFIGURATION

You may find that you need to limit the size of your backups. For example, you may find that the OS that you are working on has a maximum file-size limit of 2GB. Thus, you need to make sure your backup set pieces are no larger than 2GB. This is facilitated through the use of the maxsetsize and maxpiecesize operators.

The maxsetsize operator will limit the size of any backup set. The maxpiecesize operator will limit the size of any individual backup set piece. Here is an example of configuring a default channel with a maxpiecesize setting:

```
RMAN> configure channel 1 device type disk maxpiecesize 2g;
```

The main use of the maxpiecesize parameter is to ensure that your backup set pieces do not grow bigger than some OS, file system, or storage device limit. For example, if each of your tapes can hold only 200GB of data, then you would want to limit the size of each backup set piece to 200GB.

Maxsetsize has essentially the same purpose, to limit the overall size of one backup set. The downside to using maxsetsize is that if you end up with a datafile that is larger than maxsetsize, it will never get backed up since each datafile must be backed up within the scope of one backup set.

Control-File Autobackups

When enabled, RMAN will perform automatic control-file autobackups after each backup. Additionally, RMAN/Oracle will automatically create a backup of the control file to disk anytime a database change occurs that impacts the control file and the database physical structure, such as adding a tablespace or datafile.

To enable control-file autobackups through RMAN, use the `configure` command with the `controlfile autobackup on` keyword, as shown here:

```
RMAN> configure controlfile autobackup on;
```

Control-file autobackups are stored in the FRA if one is configured. You can also use the `configure` command to configure RMAN to create the control-file autobackup in a different location, as shown in this example:

```
configure controlfile autobackup format for device type disk to
'/oracle01/oracle/controlfilebackup/%F';
```

In this example, notice the use of the %F format specifier. %F is required when defining the location of the backup control file. This will ensure that the backup control file name is unique each time the backup is created.

Backup Optimization

Sometimes things don't change, like some of our T-shirts (they are older than we are!) and read-only datafiles. When this happens, you don't need to back them up if they have already been backed up. *Backup optimization* provides the ability to tell RMAN that you don't want to back up a database datafile if that backup is not needed. This saves time and effort on the part of RMAN. RMAN still follows all the rules of retention, backup files are expired when they are set to expire, and if the retention policy calls for two copies of a datafile, then the datafile will be backed up two times. However, on the third backup of the database, the read-only datafile will not be backed up, because the two identical copies are sufficient for recovery.

To configure backup optimization, use the `configure` command with the `backup optimization on` keyword, as shown here:

```
RMAN> configure backup optimization on;
```

Snapshot Control-File Location

As we mentioned earlier, Oracle places the snapshot control file in the `ORACLE_HOME/dbs` directory. As a part of the setup of RMAN, you should change the location of the snapshot control file by using the `configure` command, as shown here:

```
configure snapshot controlfile name to '/oracle01/backup/sncf/sncforcl.ora';
```

Backup Tags

When you create backups, you can optionally tag them. If you do not tag a backup, RMAN will tag it for you. A *tag* is a name that you assign to the backup, such as, for example, Gold Copy (perhaps you re-create your database every day with the backup tagged Gold Copy). You can easily restore and recover the database using the tag as the key for the recovery. We will discuss using tags to recover your database in Chapter 6. Here is an example of performing a backup with a tag included:

```
RMAN> backup database tag 'DPrestwich' plus archivelog
tag='ARCH_GOLD' delete input;
```

Duplexing Backups

You may want to create duplicate copies of backup sets when they are created. This is called *duplexing*. Duplexing of backup sets can be configured as a default setting by using the `configure` command, as shown here:

```
RMAN>configure datafile backup copies for device type disk to 2;
```

You can also configure duplexing for archive log backups, as shown here:

```
RMAN>configure archivelog backup copies for device type disk to 2;
```

Note that you can duplex across similar devices only. So you can duplex across tape devices or across disk devices but not both.

If you want to duplex an individual backup rather than set a persistent configuration setting, you would use the `set backup copies` command within a RUN block, as in this example:

```
RMAN> run
2> {
3> allocate channel d1 device type disk format 'c:\oracle\backup\%U';
4> set backup copies 2;
5> backup incremental level 0 database plus archivelog delete input;
6> }
```

In Exercise 4.1, you'll configure some RMAN settings.

EXERCISE 4.1

Configuring RMAN

1. Start RMAN from the command line:

   ```
   C:\oracle\admin\ORCL\wallet>rman target=/
   Recovery Manager: Release 11.1.0.6.0 - Production
   ```

on Thu Sep 11 18:28:24 2008

Copyright (c) 1982, 2007, Oracle. All rights reserved.

connected to target database: ORCL (DBID=1190537904)

2. Display your RMAN configuration (yours may look different than our output—that's okay):

```
RMAN> show all;
RMAN configuration parameters for database with db_unique_name ORCL are:
CONFIGURE RETENTION POLICY TO REDUNDANCY 1;
CONFIGURE BACKUP OPTIMIZATION ON;
CONFIGURE DEFAULT DEVICE TYPE TO DISK; # default
CONFIGURE CONTROLFILE AUTOBACKUP OFF;
CONFIGURE CONTROLFILE AUTOBACKUP FORMAT FOR DEVICE
TYPE DISK TO '%F'; # default
CONFIGURE DEVICE TYPE DISK PARALLELISM 1 BACKUP
TYPE TO BACKUPSET; # default
CONFIGURE DATAFILE BACKUP COPIES FOR DEVICE TYPE DISK TO 1; # default
CONFIGURE ARCHIVELOG BACKUP COPIES FOR DEVICE TYPE DISK TO 1; # default
CONFIGURE MAXSETSIZE TO UNLIMITED; # default
CONFIGURE ENCRYPTION FOR DATABASE OFF;
CONFIGURE ENCRYPTION ALGORITHM 'AES128';
CONFIGURE COMPRESSION ALGORITHM 'zlib';
CONFIGURE ARCHIVELOG DELETION POLICY TO NONE; # default
CONFIGURE SNAPSHOT CONTROLFILE NAME TO 'C:\ORACLE\PRODUCT\11.1.0\DB_1\
DATABASE\SNCFORCL.ORA'; # default
```

3. Configure the retention policy to redundancy of 2:

```
RMAN> CONFIGURE RETENTION POLICY TO REDUNDANCY 2;
old RMAN configuration parameters:
CONFIGURE RETENTION POLICY TO REDUNDANCY 1;
new RMAN configuration parameters:
CONFIGURE RETENTION POLICY TO REDUNDANCY 2;
new RMAN configuration parameters are successfully stored
```

4. Configure control-file autobackups on:

```
RMAN> CONFIGURE CONTROLFILE AUTOBACKUP on;
old RMAN configuration parameters:
CONFIGURE CONTROLFILE AUTOBACKUP OFF;
new RMAN configuration parameters:
```

EXERCISE 4.1 *(continued)*

```
CONFIGURE CONTROLFILE AUTOBACKUP ON;
new RMAN configuration parameters are successfully stored
```

5. Configure for compressed backup sets:

```
RMAN> CONFIGURE DEVICE TYPE DISK PARALLELISM 1 BACKUP
TYPE TO COMPRESSED BACKUPSET;
new RMAN configuration parameters:
CONFIGURE DEVICE TYPE DISK PARALLELISM 1 BACKUP TYPE
TO COMPRESSED BACKUPSET;
new RMAN configuration parameters are successfully stored
```

6. Create a directory to hold the snapshot control file (you will want to use your own directory paths, of course):

```
RMAN> host "mkdir \oracle01";
host command complete
RMAN> host "mkdir \oracle01\snapshot";
host command complete
```

7. Configure RMAN so the snapshot control file will be created in the new directory:

```
RMAN> CONFIGURE SNAPSHOT CONTROLFILE NAME TO 'c:\oracle01\snapshot';
new RMAN configuration parameters:
CONFIGURE SNAPSHOT CONTROLFILE NAME TO 'c:\oracle01\snapshot';
new RMAN configuration parameters are successfully stored
```

8. Exit RMAN:

```
RMAN> exit
Recovery Manager complete.
```

Backing Up Your Database with RMAN

We will discuss backups of your database using RMAN in the following sections. We will first talk about the different types of backups that you can make with RMAN. Then we will discuss what you can back up using RMAN, such as the database, archived redo logs, and so forth.

Using the RMAN Command Line

Like SQL and SQL*Plus, RMAN has its own unique command set. You use these commands to do a number of things:

- Configure RMAN
- Back up database structures (tablespaces, datafiles, control files, and so on)
- Restore and recover your database
- Produce various reports and lists that contain backup-related information.
- Create duplicate databases
- Restore specific tablespaces

This is just a partial list of all the things RMAN can do for you. Table 4.3 describes the RMAN commands you will need to be aware of for the OCP exam.

TABLE 4.3   RMAN Commands

RMAN Command	Description
@	Run a command file.
@@	Run a command file in the same directory as another command file that is currently running. The @@ command differs from the @ command only when run from within a command file.
ALLOCATE CHANNEL	Establish a channel, which is a connection between RMAN and a database instance.
ALLOCATE CHANNEL FOR MAINTENANCE	Allocate a channel in preparation for issuing maintenance commands such as DELETE.
allocOperandList	A subclause that specifies channel control options such as PARMS and FORMAT.
ALTER DATABASE	Mount or open a database.
archivelogRecordSpecifier	Specify a range of archived redo-log files.
BACKUP	Back up database files, copies of database files, archived logs, or backup sets.
BLOCKRECOVER	Recover an individual data block or set of data blocks within one or more datafiles.
CATALOG	Add information about a datafile copy, archived redo log, or control file copy to the repository.

TABLE 4.3 RMAN Commands *(continued)*

RMAN Command	Description
CHANGE	Mark a backup piece, image copy, or archived redo log as having the status UNAVAILABLE or AVAILABLE; remove the repository record for a backup or copy; override the retention policy for a backup or copy.
completedTimeSpec	Specify a time range during which the backup or copy completed.
CONFIGURE	Configure persistent RMAN settings. These settings apply to all RMAN sessions until explicitly changed or disabled.
CONNECT	Establish a connection between RMAN and a target, auxiliary, or recovery catalog database.
connectStringSpec	Specify the username, password, and net service name for connecting to a target, recovery catalog, or auxiliary database. The connection is necessary to authenticate the user and identify the database.
CONVERT	Convert datafile formats for transporting tablespaces across platforms.
CREATE CATALOG	Create the schema for the recovery catalog.
CREATE SCRIPT	Create a stored script and store it in the recovery catalog.
CROSSCHECK	Determine whether files managed by RMAN, such as archived logs, datafile copies, and backup pieces, still exist on disk or tape.
datafileSpec	Specify a datafile by filename or absolute file number.
DELETE	Delete backups and copies, remove references to them from the recovery catalog, and update their control-file records to status DELETED.
DELETE SCRIPT	Delete a stored script from the recovery catalog.
deviceSpecifier	Specify the type of storage device for a backup or copy.
DROP CATALOG	Remove the schema from the recovery catalog.
DROP DATABASE	Delete the target database from disk and unregister it.

TABLE 4.3 RMAN Commands *(continued)*

RMAN Command	Description
DUPLICATE	Use backups of the target database to create a duplicate database that you can use for testing purposes or to create a standby database.
EXECUTE SCRIPT	Run an RMAN stored script.
EXIT	Quit the RMAN executable.
fileNameConversionSpec	Specify patterns to transform source to target filenames during BACKUP AS COPY, CONVERT, and DUPLICATE.
FLASHBACK	Return the database to a previous state as defined by a previous time or system change number (SCN).
formatSpec	Specify a filename format for a backup or copy.
HOST	Invoke an operating-system command-line subshell from within RMAN or run a specific operating-system command.
keepOption	Specify that a backup or copy should or should not be exempt from the current retention policy.
LIST	Produce a detailed listing of backup sets or copies.
listObjList	A subclause used to specify which items will be displayed by the LIST command.
maintQualifier	A subclause used to specify additional options for maintenance commands such as DELETE and CHANGE.
maintSpec	A subclause used to specify the files operated on by maintenance commands such as CHANGE, CROSSCHECK, and DELETE.
obsOperandList	A subclause used to determine which backups and copies are obsolete.
PRINT SCRIPT	Display a stored script.
QUIT	Exit the RMAN executable.
recordSpec	A subclause used to specify the objects on which the maintenance commands should operate.

TABLE 4.2   RMAN Commands Description *(continued)*

RMAN Command	Description
RECOVER	Apply redo logs and incremental backups to datafiles restored from backup or datafile copies in order to update them to a specified time.
REGISTER	Register the target database in the recovery catalog.
RELEASE CHANNEL	Release a channel that was allocated with an ALLOCATE CHANNEL command.
releaseForMaint	Release a channel that was allocated with an ALLOCATE CHANNEL FOR MAINTENANCE command.
REPLACE SCRIPT	Replace an existing script stored in the recovery catalog. If the script does not exist, then REPLACE SCRIPT creates it.
REPORT	Perform detailed analyses of the content of the recovery catalog.
RESET DATABASE	Inform RMAN that the SQL statement ALTER DATABASE OPEN RESETLOGS has been executed and that a new incarnation of the target database has been created, or reset the target database to a prior incarnation.
RESTORE	Restore files from backup sets or from disk copies to the default or to a new location.
RESYNC	Perform a full resynchronization, which creates a snapshot control file and then copies any new or changed information from that snapshot control file to the recovery catalog.
RUN	Execute a sequence of one or more RMAN commands, which are one or more statements executed within the braces of a RUN block.
SEND	Send a vendor-specific quoted string to one or more specific channels.
SET	Set the value of various attributes that affect RMAN behavior for the duration of a RUN block or a session.
SHOW	Display the current CONFIGURE settings.
SHUTDOWN	Shut down the target database. This command is equivalent to the SQL*Plus SHUTDOWN command.

TABLE 4.2 RMAN Commands Description *(continued)*

RMAN Command	Description
SPOOL	Write RMAN output to a log file.
SQL	Execute a SQL statement from within RMAN.
STARTUP	Start up the target database. This command is equivalent to the SQL*Plus STARTUP command.
SWITCH	Specify that a datafile copy is now the current datafile; that is, the datafile pointed to by the control file. This command is equivalent to the SQL statement ALTER DATABASE RENAME FILE as it applies to datafiles.
UNREGISTER DATABASE	Unregister a database from the recovery catalog.
untilClause	A subclause specifying an upper limit by time, SCN, or log sequence number. This clause is usually used to specify the desired point in time for an incomplete recovery.
UPGRADE CATALOG	Upgrade the recovery-catalog schema from an older version to the version required by the RMAN executable.
VALIDATE	Examine a backup set and report whether its data is intact. RMAN scans all of the backup pieces in the specified backup sets and looks at the checksums to verify that the contents can be successfully restored.

Types of RMAN Backups

There are two principle types of RMAN backups. The first type is called backup sets. *Backup sets* are a very flexible way of backing up your Oracle database. The downside is that backup sets are not direct copies of Oracle database datafiles. As a result, you need RMAN to put the backup sets back together to restore your database.

Oracle also supports *image copies*. Image copies are direct copies of database datafiles. Image copies offer faster recovery options but typically take up a great deal more space. In the following sections, we will address these two types of RMAN backups in more detail.

RMAN Backup Sets

By default, when you create a backup in RMAN, it writes the backups to physical files. These physical files are called *backup set pieces* (RMAN can also create backups called image copies, which we will discuss later in this section). A given backup may create more than one backup set piece. A collection of related backup set pieces is called a *backup set*. A backup set is a logical entity that is used to maintain the association of independent backup set pieces.

In addition to multiple backup set pieces, you may have more than one backup set. This occurs when you parallelize a backup. Each channel will represent one backup set, each with its own backup set pieces. New backup sets will also be created on a channel if a backup set exceeds the backup set size limitations.

Note that a given datafile can span backup set pieces but cannot span backup sets. The ability of a given datafile to span backup set pieces is known as *multiplexing*. Multiplexing is another form of parallelization, as it allows RMAN to read from multiple datafiles in parallel and write them to a single backup set piece. Thus a given backup set piece may have data from many datafiles in it.

In the default RMAN configuration, a given tablespace/datafile backup may find itself in more than one backup set piece. However, each individual tablespace/datafile backup can be associated with only a single RMAN backup set and thus will be backed up by only one channel.

Oracle Database 11g has a new feature called multisection backups. *Multisection backups* allow you to parallelize the backup of large datafiles (bigfile tablespaces or normal tablespaces). You may well find questions on multisection backups on your OCP exam.

Figure 4.2 demonstrates the relationship between backups, backup sets, and backup set pieces.

FIGURE 4.2 Relationship between RMAN backups, backup sets, and backup set pieces

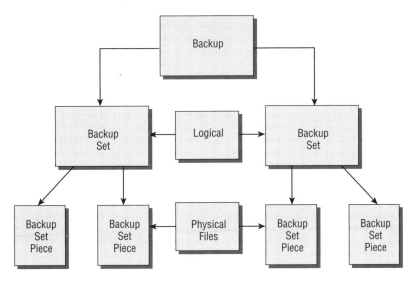

RMAN Image Copies

RMAN image copies are one-to-one copies of database datafiles. When you do an image-copy backup of your database, you will receive no benefits of compression, so the disk-space requirement is a one-to-one requirement. Image copies must be made to disk. Figure 4.3 shows the difference between image and regular backups.

FIGURE 4.3 Image vs. regular backups

Original Datafile   Regular RMAN backupset   Image Copy

The upside to an image copy is that it can be much faster to restore. RMAN will always choose to restore image copies over backup sets if an image copy is available. In fact, using the switch to copy command makes it even faster, as RMAN will simply switch to the image copy on disk and start using that copy (applying redo as required). To make an image copy, use the backup as copy command, as shown in this example:

```
RMAN> Backup as copy database;
```

You can also make image copies of datafiles or tablespaces, as shown in these examples:

```
RMAN>backup as copy datafile 4;
RMAN>Backup as copy tablespace users;
```

If you prefer to always use image copies rather than backup sets, you can configure RMAN to do so by default with the configure command, as seen here:

```
configure device type disk backup type to copy;
```

RMAN can use a mixture of image copies, incremental backups, and archived redo logs when performing recovery (which we will discuss in more detail in Chapter 5). This can make total recovery of your database, a tablespace, or a datafile much quicker.

RMAN Offline Backups

We discussed manual offline backups in Chapter 2. Offline backups in RMAN are not much different except that you use the RMAN interface to actually do the backup rather than an OS file-copy utility. You will still need to close the database, but your backup will be done with the database in mount mode rather than completely shut down.

No parameter-file adjustments are required for an RMAN offline backup. We recommend that you configure and use the FRA (discussed earlier in this chapter) even if you are doing offline backups. This makes for a standardized backup location and also allows the Oracle database to manage the overall backup space utilization more efficiently.

To perform an offline backup of your database with RMAN, follow these steps:

1. Start the RMAN client.

2. Shut down the database from the RMAN client, SQL*Plus, or OEM. The shutdown should be a consistent shutdown, so use the `shutdown`, `shutdown immediate`, or `shutdown transactional` command.

3. Start up the database in mount mode using the `startup mount` command.

4. Back up the database with the RMAN `backup` command:

    ```
    RMAN>backup database;
    ```

5. When the backup is complete, open the database with the `alter database open` command.

RMAN Online Backups

For online backups in RMAN, the database must be configured in ARCHIVELOG mode (see Chapter 2 for more on configuring the database for ARCHIVELOG-mode operations). Once the database is configured properly, and RMAN is configured properly (as discussed earlier in this chapter), you can do online backups.

Online backups with RMAN are easy. You need to make sure the database and the archived redo logs are backed up; thus you issue the command `backup database plus archivelog`. That's it. That command will create a recoverable backup of the database. This is known as a *whole database backup*.

If you want to delete the archived redo logs after the backup, you would append the `delete input` clause to the command. Other options are available depending on your needs.

In the following example we perform an online backup of our database using the `backup as compressed backupset database plus archivelog delete input` command. This will create a compressed backup of the database, backing up the archived redo logs and then deleting those backed-up archived redo logs after the backup is complete. Also note that we have configured control-file autobackups.

```
RMAN> backup as compressed backupset database plus archivelog delete input;
Starting backup at 05-SEP-08
current log archived
allocated channel: ORA_DISK_1
channel ORA_DISK_1: SID=131 device type=DISK
channel ORA_DISK_1: starting compressed archived log backup set
channel ORA_DISK_1: specifying archived log(s) in backup set
input archived log thread=1 sequence=41 RECID=40 STAMP=664583178
input archived log thread=1 sequence=42 RECID=41 STAMP=664621168
```

```
input archived log thread=1 sequence=43 RECID=42 STAMP=664650496
input archived log thread=1 sequence=44 RECID=43 STAMP=664655636
channel ORA_DISK_1: starting piece 1 at 05-SEP-08
channel ORA_DISK_1: finished piece 1 at 05-SEP-08
piece handle=C:\ORACLE\FLASH_RECOVERY_AREA\ORCL\BACKUPSET\2008_09_05\
01_MF_ANNNN_TAG20080905T183357_4D3N085C_.BKP tag=TAG20080905T183357
comment=NONE
channel ORA_DISK_1: backup set complete, elapsed time: 00:00:15
channel ORA_DISK_1: deleting archived log(s)
archived log file name=C:\ORACLE\ARCH\ORCL\ARC00041_0662757171.001
RECID=40 STAMP=664583178
archived log file name=C:\ORACLE\ARCH\ORCL\ARC00042_0662757171.001
RECID=41 STAMP=664621168
archived log file name=C:\ORACLE\ARCH\ORCL\ARC00043_0662757171.001
RECID=42 STAMP=664650496
archived log file name=C:\ORACLE\ARCH\ORCL\ARC00044_0662757171.001
RECID=43 STAMP=664655636
Finished backup at 05-SEP-08
Starting backup at 05-SEP-08
using channel ORA_DISK_1
channel ORA_DISK_1: starting compressed full datafile backup set
channel ORA_DISK_1: specifying datafile(s) in backup set
input datafile file number=00002 name=C:\ORACLE\ORADATA\ORCL\SYSAUX01.DBF
input datafile file number=00001 name=C:\ORACLE\ORADATA\ORCL\SYSTEM01.DBF
input datafile file number=00005 name=C:\ORACLE\ORADATA\ORCL\UNDOTBS02.DBF
input datafile file number=00004 name=C:\ORACLE\ORADATA\ORCL\USERS01.DBF
channel ORA_DISK_1: starting piece 1 at 05-SEP-08
channel ORA_DISK_1: finished piece 1 at 05-SEP-08
piece handle=C:\ORACLE\FLASH_RECOVERY_AREA\ORCL\BACKUPSET\2008_09_05\
01_MF_NNNDF_TAG20080905T183432_4D3N0Z0Z_.BKP tag=TAG20080905T183432
comment=NONE
channel ORA_DISK_1: starting piece 2 at 05-SEP-08
channel ORA_DISK_1: finished piece 2 at 05-SEP-08
piece handle=C:\ORACLE\FLASH_RECOVERY_AREA\ORCL\BACKUPSET\2008_09_05
\01_MF_NNNDF_TAG20080905T183432_4D3N63Y8_.BKP tag=TAG20080905T183432
comment=NONE
channel ORA_DISK_1: starting piece 3 at 05-SEP-08
channel ORA_DISK_1: finished piece 3 at 05-SEP-08
```

```
piece handle=C:\ORACLE\FLASH_RECOVERY_AREA\ORCL\BACKUPSET\2008_09_05\
O1_MF_NNNDF_TAG20080905T183432_4D3N9PY8_.BKP tag=TAG20080905T183432
comment=NONE
channel ORA_DISK_1: backup set complete, elapsed time: 00:04:48
channel ORA_DISK_1: starting compressed full datafile backup set
channel ORA_DISK_1: specifying datafile(s) in backup set
including current control file in backup set
including current SPFILE in backup set
channel ORA_DISK_1: starting piece 1 at 05-SEP-08
channel ORA_DISK_1: finished piece 1 at 05-SEP-08
piece handle=C:\ORACLE\FLASH_RECOVERY_AREA\ORCL\BACKUPSET\2008_09_05\
O1_MF_NCSNF_TAG20080905T183432_4D3NBHXS_.BKP tag=TAG20080905T183432
comment=NONE
channel ORA_DISK_1: backup set complete, elapsed time: 00:00:02
Finished backup at 05-SEP-08
Starting backup at 05-SEP-08
current log archived
using channel ORA_DISK_1
channel ORA_DISK_1: starting compressed archived log backup set
channel ORA_DISK_1: specifying archived log(s) in backup set
input archived log thread=1 sequence=45 RECID=44 STAMP=664655986
channel ORA_DISK_1: starting piece 1 at 05-SEP-08
channel ORA_DISK_1: finished piece 1 at 05-SEP-08
piece handle=C:\ORACLE\FLASH_RECOVERY_AREA\ORCL\BACKUPSET\2008_09_05\
O1_MF_ANNNN_TAG20080905T183946_4D3NBS89_.BKP tag=TAG20080905T183946
comment=NONE
channel ORA_DISK_1: backup set complete, elapsed time: 00:00:01
channel ORA_DISK_1: deleting archived log(s)
archived log file name=C:\ORACLE\ARCH\ORCL\ARC00045_0662757171.001
RECID=44 STAMP=664655986
Finished backup at 05-SEP-08
```

You can also do backups of tablespaces and datafiles using the backup command, as shown in these examples:

```
RMAN>Backup tablespace users;
RMAN>Backup datafile 3;
```

In Exercise 4.2, you'll execute an online backup using RMAN.

EXERCISE 4.2

Executing an Online Backup

In this exercise you will perform an online backup of your ARCHIVELOG mode database. Your database should already be in ARCHIVELOG mode (see Exercise 2.1). Once the database is in ARCHIVELOG mode you can do this exercise.

1. Log into the database using SQL*Plus:

```
C:\oracle\admin\ORCL\wallet>set oracle_sid=orcl
C:\oracle\admin\ORCL\wallet>sqlplus "/ as sysdba"
SQL*Plus: Release 11.1.0.6.0 - Production on Thu Sep 11 18:56:27 2008
Copyright (c) 1982, 2007, Oracle.  All rights reserved.
Connected to:
Oracle Database 11g Enterprise Edition Release 11.1.0.6.0 - Production
With the Partitioning, OLAP, Data Mining and Real Application
Testing options
SQL>
```

2. Query the LOG_MODE column of the V$DATABASE view to confirm that the database is in ARCHIVELOG mode. If the database is not in ARCHIVELOG mode, refer to Chapter 2 for information on how to put the database in ARCHIVELOG mode.

```
SQL> Select log_mode from v$database;
LOG_MODE
------------
ARCHIVELOG
```

3. Exit SQL*Plus and start RMAN:

```
SQL> exit
Disconnected from Oracle Database 11g Enterprise Edition
Release 11.1.0.6.0 - Production
With the Partitioning, OLAP, Data Mining and Real Application
Testing options
C:\oracle\admin\ORCL\wallet>rman target=/
Recovery Manager: Release 11.1.0.6.0 - Production on
Thu Sep 11 18:58:55 2008
Copyright (c) 1982, 2007, Oracle.  All rights reserved.
connected to target database: ORCL (DBID=1190537904)
```

4. Execute the RMAN backup using the backup database command. Back up the archived redo logs at the same time with the plus archivelog option. Remove the archived redo logs after they are backed up using the delete input option.

```
RMAN> Backup database plus archivelog delete input;
```

5. Review the output, and make sure the backup was successful. Here is an example of our output. We bolded the messages that indicate a successful backup.

```
RMAN> Backup database plus archivelog delete input;
Starting backup at 11-SEP-08
current log archived
using target database control file instead of recovery catalog
allocated channel: ORA_DISK_1
channel ORA_DISK_1: SID=128 device type=DISK
channel ORA_DISK_1: starting compressed archived log backup set
channel ORA_DISK_1: specifying archived log(s) in backup set
input archived log thread=1 sequence=87 RECID=86 STAMP=665092065
input archived log thread=1 sequence=88 RECID=87 STAMP=665138962
input archived log thread=1 sequence=89 RECID=88 STAMP=665172239
input archived log thread=1 sequence=90 RECID=89 STAMP=665172313
input archived log thread=1 sequence=91 RECID=90 STAMP=665172466
input archived log thread=1 sequence=92 RECID=91 STAMP=665175694
channel ORA_DISK_1: starting piece 1 at 11-SEP-08
channel ORA_DISK_1: finished piece 1 at 11-SEP-08
piece handle=C:\ORACLE\FLASH_RECOVERY_AREA\ORCL
\BACKUPSET\2008_09_11\O1_MF_ANNNN_TAG20080911T190135_4DMHVZFK_.BKP
tag=TAG20080911T190135 comment=NONE
```
channel ORA_DISK_1: backup set complete, elapsed time: 00:00:07
```
channel ORA_DISK_1: deleting archived log(s)
archived log file name=C:\ORACLE\ARCH\ORCL\
ARC00087_0662757171.001 RECID=86 STAMP=665092065
archived log file name=C:\ORACLE\ARCH\ORCL\
ARC00088_0662757171.001 RECID=87 STAMP=665138962
archived log file name=C:\ORACLE\ARCH\ORCL\
ARC00089_0662757171.001 RECID=88 STAMP=665172239
archived log file name=C:\ORACLE\ARCH\ORCL\
ARC00090_0662757171.001 RECID=89 STAMP=665172313
archived log file name=C:\ORACLE\ARCH\ORCL\
ARC00091_0662757171.001 RECID=90 STAMP=665172466
archived log file name=C:\ORACLE\ARCH\ORCL\
ARC00092_0662757171.001 RECID=91 STAMP=665175694
```
Finished backup at 11-SEP-08
```
Starting backup at 11-SEP-08
using channel ORA_DISK_1
```

```
channel ORA_DISK_1: starting compressed full datafile backup set
channel ORA_DISK_1: specifying datafile(s) in backup set
input datafile file number=00002
name=C:\ORACLE\ORADATA\ORCL\SYSAUX01.DBF
input datafile file number=00001
name=C:\ORACLE\ORADATA\ORCL\SYSTEM01.DBF
input datafile file number=00005
name=C:\ORACLE\ORADATA\ORCL\UNDOTBS02.DBF
input datafile file number=00004
name=C:\ORACLE\ORADATA\ORCL\USERS01.DBF
channel ORA_DISK_1: starting piece 1 at 11-SEP-08
channel ORA_DISK_1: finished piece 1 at 11-SEP-08
piece handle=C:\ORACLE\FLASH_RECOVERY_AREA\ORCL
\BACKUPSET\2008_09_11\O1_MF_NNNDF_TAG20080911T190200_4DMHWM1T_.BKP
tag=TAG20080911T190200 comment=NONE
```
channel ORA_DISK_1: backup set complete, elapsed time: 00:05:36
```
Finished backup at 11-SEP-08
Starting backup at 11-SEP-08
current log archived
using channel ORA_DISK_1
channel ORA_DISK_1: starting compressed archived log backup set
channel ORA_DISK_1: specifying archived log(s) in backup set
input archived log thread=1 sequence=93 RECID=92 STAMP=665176062
channel ORA_DISK_1: starting piece 1 at 11-SEP-08
channel ORA_DISK_1: finished piece 1 at 11-SEP-08
piece handle=C:\ORACLE\FLASH_RECOVERY_AREA\ORCL
\BACKUPSET\2008_09_11\O1_MF_ANNNN_TAG20080911T190742_4DMJ7H29_.BKP
tag=TAG20080911T190742 comment=NONE
```
channel ORA_DISK_1: backup set complete, elapsed time: 00:00:01
```
channel ORA_DISK_1: deleting archived log(s)
archived log file name=C:\ORACLE\ARCH\ORCL
\ARC00093_0662757171.001 RECID=92 STAMP=665176062
```
Finished backup at 11-SEP-08
```
Starting Control File and SPFILE Autobackup at 11-SEP-08
piece handle=C:\ORACLE\FLASH_RECOVERY_AREA\ORCL
\AUTOBACKUP\2008_09_11\O1_MF_S_665176080_4DMJ7SOT_.BKP comment=NONE
```
Finished Control File and SPFILE Autobackup at 11-SEP-08

RMAN Incremental Backups

Incremental database backups are a way to quickly back up your database. In the following sections, we will discuss incremental backups. First you'll learn about configuring for incremental backups, next we will look at the two different kinds of incremental backups that are available, and then you'll learn how to actually do incremental backups.

Configuring for Incremental Backups

Technically, you don't have to configure anything to do an incremental backup. RMAN will perform an incremental backup when you issue the appropriate backup command. However, without any configuration, RMAN must inspect each block and determine whether it has indeed changed since the last backup and if it must go into the backup image.

Optionally you can create a *block-change tracking file* that will keep track of blocks that have changed since the last full or incremental backup. This can significantly reduce the time it takes to perform an incremental backup of your database, because it removes the need for Oracle to inspect each data block to determine if it's been changed since the last backup. Figure 4.4 demonstrates the block-change tracking file.

FIGURE 4.4   The block-change tracking file

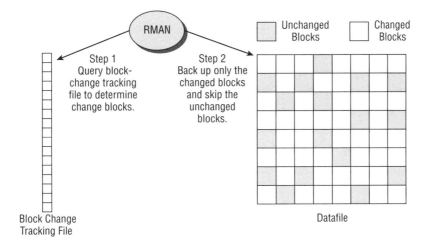

The block-change tracking file can track only a maximum of seven different incremental level-1 backups. After the seventh backup, the initial level-0 backup records will be overwritten in the block-change tracking file. This will result in RMAN having to scan all database blocks on subsequent incremental backups. As a result, limit incremental backups without an intervening level 0 to a maximum of seven.

To create the block-tracking file, use the `alter database enable block change tracking` command. By default, Oracle will create the block-change tracking file in the location defined by the `DB_CREATE_FILE_DEST` parameter. If that parameter is not set, Oracle will require that you provide a destination and filename for the block-change tracking file. Here is an example of the creation of a block-change tracking file:

```
SQL> alter database enable block change tracking using file
'c:\oracle\block_change_tracking\orcl_block_change.fil';
```

You can find the location of the current block-change tracking file by looking at the `FILENAME` column of the `V$BLOCK_CHANGE_TRACKING` view. You can use the `STATUS` column of the `V$BLOCK_CHANGE_TRACKING` view to determine if block-change tracking is enabled.

You should perform a level 0 incremental backup after creating the block-change tracking file. This is because the parent level-0 backup bitmap must be in the block-change tracking file.

Types of Incremental Backups

Two types of incremental backups are available for you to choose from:

- Level-0 incremental backup
- Level-1 incremental backup

The level-0 backup is like a full backup (sometimes it's called a base backup), except that incremental backups can be based on it (they can not be based on a regular full backup).

The level-1 backup is the incremental backup that backs up changed blocks. There are two different kinds of level-1 backups:

- Differential incremental backup
- Cumulative incremental backup

The *differential incremental backup* will back up all changed blocks since the last level-1 backup. These images are typically smaller. The *cumulative incremental backup* is one where the data backed up is the data that changed since the last level-0 full backup. Thus it is a cumulative backup of all changed blocks since the last level-0 backup. This makes for faster recoveries since you don't have to apply several incremental backups during the database restore. Figure 4.5 provides a visual example of the differences between these types of backups.

Performing Incremental Backups

Performing incremental backups is almost exactly like performing regular backups except that you include the `incremental level` option in the backup command. For example, to create a base, level-0 backup, you would issue this command:

```
RMAN> Backup as compressed backupset incremental level 0 database plus archivelog
delete input;
```

When you are ready to run your first incremental backup you would use the backup command with the incremental level-1 option, as shown here:

```
RMAN> Backup as compressed backupset incremental level 1 database plus
archivelog delete input;
```

FIGURE 4.5   Differential vs. cumulative incremental backups

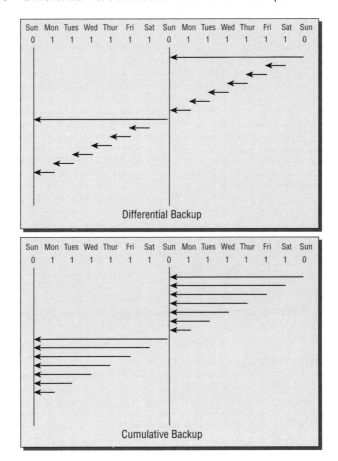

Differential backups are the default type of incremental backup in Oracle. If you want to perform a cumulative backup, you will need to include the cumulative keyword, as shown here:

```
RMAN> Backup as compressed backupset incremental level 1 cumulative database
plus archivelog delete input;
```

Note that if you try to do a level-1 backup and a level-0 does not exist, RMAN will not generate an error. It will simply perform a level-0 backup for you instead.

RMAN Incrementally Updated Backups

Incrementally updated backups involve a combination of a full image backup of the database and then subsequent level-1 incremental backups of the database, which are applied to the image-copy backup. An incrementally updated backup makes for a quicker restore but for a bigger backup image.

To create an incrementally updated backup, all you need do is run the following script:

```
RUN { # the recover copy command does not really recover anything.
      # it simply tells RMAN that the incremental to be executed should
      # be applied to the database copy we made above.
      Recover copy of database with tag 'Jacob_Jared_Lizzie';
      Backup incremental level 1
      for recover of copy with tag 'Jacob_Jared_Lizzie' Database; }
```

On the first execution of this script, RMAN will detect that no backup copy exists. Warnings will be generated, but no errors. RMAN will proceed to create the initial copy of the database. No incremental copy will be created.

On subsequent executions, RMAN will detect that an image copy does exist, and it will then apply the previous level-1 incremental-and then execute another level-1 incremental backup. Note that on the second run, RMAN will detect that no incremental backup exists to apply to the datafile copy and a warning will be raised because of this. That is normal.

This method limits the recovery window for your database to one day. For example, if you executed this script on day 1, day 2, and day 3, after day 3's execution you would not be able to restore your database to any point before day 3's backup.

You could provide for longer recovery windows by including the until time clause. In this example, we allow for a recovery window of five days:

```
run {
  recover copy of database with tag 'lisa' until time 'sysdate - 5';
  backup  incremental level 1 for recover of copy with tag 'lisa' database;
}
```

RMAN Multisection Backups

Prior to Oracle Database 11g, you could not parallelize the backup of a given database datafile. Since datafiles had to be contained wholly within a single backup set, this meant that the backup of that datafile was serialized. This can be a bit of a problem if your database consists of one or two huge datafiles and several smaller datafiles. Also, if you are using bigfile tablespaces, the lack of inner-file backup parallelization could be a big issue.

Oracle Database 11*g* provides a new feature called *multisection backups* that provides the ability to parallelize the backup of a single datafile. This feature is supported by the section size clause in the backup command followed by the desired section size. Here is an example:

```
RMAN> backup section size 40m database;
```

In this example, RMAN will chunk up each datafile into 40MB chunks, and each allocated channel can process those individual 40MB chunks. Note that if you allocate only one channel, only one chunk at a time will get backed up! Also note that the size parameter does not indicate the size of the resulting backup set piece. Rather, it is the equivalent amount of data within the datafile that each RMAN channel will process. The resulting pieces can vary wildly in size.

RMAN Backup of Archived Redo Logs

Backing up archived redo logs is an important task since it serves to protect the database's principal recovery mechanism, which is redo. Backing up archived redo logs is done via the `backup archivelog` command. This command requires that you include keywords from the `archivelog specifier` clause, which is used to indicate the archived redo logs that you want to back up. Common keywords that you might use include the following:

- `All`: Backs up all archived redo logs currently on disk

- `Sequence between n and o`: Backs up all archived redo logs available on disk between sequence number n and sequence number o

- `Time between t1 and t2`: Backs up all archived redo logs available on disk between time t1 (the earlier time) and time t2 (the later time)

Here is an example of backing up all archived redo logs, still on disk, that were generated in the last 24 hours:

```
RMAN> backup archivelog time between "sysdate-1" and "sysdate";
Starting backup at 05-SEP-08
using channel ORA_DISK_1
channel ORA_DISK_1: starting archived log backup set
channel ORA_DISK_1: specifying archived log(s) in backup set
input archived log thread=1 sequence=46 RECID=45 STAMP=664657241
channel ORA_DISK_1: starting piece 1 at 05-SEP-08
channel ORA_DISK_1: finished piece 1 at 05-SEP-08
piece handle=C:\ORACLE\FLASH_RECOVERY_AREA\ORCL\BACKUPSET\2008_09_05\
01_MF_ANNNN_TAG20080905T190103_4D3OLO2G_.BKP tag=TAG20080905T190103
comment=NONE
channel ORA_DISK_1: backup set complete, elapsed time: 00:00:01
Finished backup at 05-SEP-08.
```

Be Careful What You Ask For...You Might Just Get It (Or Not)

Look at the example where we backed up the archived redo logs for the last 24 hours. The command was as follows:

```
backup archivelog time between "sysdate-1" and "sysdate";
```

But guess what happens if you change this command just slightly:

```
RMAN> backup archivelog time between "sysdate" and "sysdate-1";
Starting backup at 05-SEP-08
using channel ORA_DISK_1
RMAN-00571: ===========================================================
RMAN-00569: =============== ERROR MESSAGE STACK FOLLOWS ===============
RMAN-00571: ===========================================================
RMAN-03002: failure of backup command at 09/05/2008 19:02:56
RMAN-20242: specification does not match any archived log in the
recovery catalog
```

If you didn't know any better, you might just think that there are no archived redo logs to back up and assume the backup archivelog command worked fine and dandy. In fact, the command failed because you had the from/to dates in the wrong order. This highlights how important it is to make sure you carefully review the syntax of the command you are getting ready to execute and then review the output of RMAN commands and make sure RMAN did what you thought you told it to do.

RMAN Backup of the Spfile and Control Files

We have already discussed control-file autobackups in this chapter. You may find that on occasion you want to do an individual backup of the control file or the spfile.

You have two options in RMAN for control-file backups, using the backup current controlfile command or the backup controlfilecopy command.

The backup as copy command will cause the current control file to be backed up. This is a copy of the control file, so it's like a backup control file. Thus, you could just copy the file into place and treat it as a backup control file. By default the backup will be created in the FRA as would happen in this example:

```
RMAN> backup as copy current controlfile;
```

Or you can choose to define the location of the output control file, as shown in this example:

```
RMAN>backup as copy current controlfile format
'c:\oracle\controlfilebackup\contrf_backup.ctl';
```

The `backup controlfilecopy` command will back up a control-file copy (created with the `alter database backup controlfile to` command or the `backup as copy current controlfile` command). Here is an example of the use of the `backup controlfilecopy` command:

```
SQL>Alter database backup controlfile to
'c:\oracle\controlfilebackup\contrf_backup.ctl';
RMAN>backup controlfilecopy 'c:\oracle\controlfilebackup\contrf_backup.ctl';
```

You can also back up spfiles with RMAN using the `backup spfile` command, as shown in this example:

```
RMAN>Backup spfile;
```

Backing Up RMAN Backup Sets

Often database backups will be initially made to disk, and then later those backups will be backed up to tape. The reason for this is that backing up to disk is generally much faster than backing up to tape. Yet you want to back up to tape so you can offsite the media and because tape tends to be less expensive for longer-term storage (though this is quickly becoming less true).

To back up a backup set, you use the `backup backupset` command, as shown here:

```
RMAN> backup device type sbt backupset all;
```

Summary

In this chapter, we introduced you to RMAN, Oracle's backup and recovery tool of choice. We discussed the many features that make RMAN truly a power backup and recovery tool. We discussed the architecture of RMAN, including backup set pieces, which are the critical component of any RMAN backup.

We then talked about how to configure RMAN so that it is easy to use. Persistent configuration parameters are the key to RMAN's ease of use, and understanding what they are and what they do is key to understanding how RMAN works. There is a number of different configuration options to consider, including parallelism, compression, and encryption, and the OCP exam is poised to ask you about all of them.

Finally, we talked about actually backing up your database with RMAN. We talked about the various kinds of backups available to you, from complete database backups to incremental backups. We covered backing up tablespaces and datafiles and backing up archived redo logs. We even talked about backing up the backups themselves if we were not already talking you into circles enough.

In the following chapters, we will be covering the RMAN recovery catalog, recovering your database with RMAN, reporting from RMAN, and finally, advanced RMAN recovery topics. So there is plenty of fun yet to go. Hang tight—it's going to be a fun ride!

Exam Essentials

Be able to describe the basic RMAN architecture.   Understand what backup sets and backup set pieces are. Understand that backup set pieces are physical files that contain the data that has actually been backed up. Understand what the flash recovery area is, what its benefits are, and what parameters are required to configure it.

Be able to configure RMAN.   Understand what the RMAN `configure` command does and how to use it. Understand how to use the `show` command to display persistent configuration settings. Understand the use of the different persistent configuration settings, such as compression, encryption, and devices. Know the difference between a disk device and the SBT device (tape). Explain how RMAN retention policies work and how to configure them. Explain what backup optimization is and how it works. Understand how to configure for duplexed backups.

Know how to back up your database with RMAN.   Understand the different kinds of backups available in RMAN. Know what a whole database backup is and how to perform it both with configured settings and using a run block. Know how to use the `keep` command to override retention policies. Know what an incremental database backup is and how to perform it. Understand the different kinds of incremental database backups and how to create a block-change tracking file. Know what multiselection backups are and how to create them. Know what image copies are and how to create them. Know how to back up archived redo logs, control files, and spfiles. Know how to back up backup sets.

Review Questions

1. How is block-change tracking enabled?

   A. With `alter database enable block change tracking`

   B. With `alter system enable block change tracking`

   C. With an `init.ora` parameter change

   D. With an spfile parameter change

2. What type of backup is stored in a proprietary RMAN format?

   A. Backup set

   B. Image copy

   C. Backup section

   D. Backup group

3. Consider the following command:

   `Backup database plus archivelog delete input;`

   How many backup sets would be created by this command if the following were true:

   - Control-file auto backups were enabled.

   - The size of backup sets was not restricted.

   - One channel was allocated.

   A. 1

   B. 2

   C. 3

   D. 4

   E. 5

4. Which command creates an image copy?

   A. `backup as copy`

   B. `backup copy`

   C. `copy as backup`

   D. `copy back`

5. Compressed backups work with which of the following commands?

    A. `copy as backup`

    B. `backup as copy`

    C. `backup`

    D. `copy`

6. Which is the correct command to back up the database, back up the archived redo logs, and then remove the backed-up archived redo logs?

    A. `backup database`

    B. `backup database and archivelogs`

    C. `backup database plus archivelogs`

    D `backup database plus archivelog delete input`

    E. `backup database and archivelog delete input`

7. Which of the following best describes a full backup?

    A. All datafiles of a database

    B. All datafiles, archive logs, and control files

    C. All datafiles and control files

    D. All the used blocks in a datafile

8. Which type of backup backs up only data blocks modified since the most recent backup at the same level or lower?

    A. Differential incremental backup

    B. Different incremental backup

    C. Cumulative backup

    D. Cumulative incremental backup

9. Which type of backup must be performed first with an incremental backup?

    A. Level 1

    B. Level 0

    C. Level 2

    D. Level 3

10. Which backup option defines a user-defined name for a backup?

    A. FORMAT

    B. NAME

    C. TAG

    D. FORMAT U%

11. Given the following steps, which would be the correct order to create a backup of an Oracle database in NOARCHIVELOG mode?

a. `shutdown immediate` from RMAN

b. Log into RMAN

c. `startup mount` from RMAN

d. `backup database`

e. `alter database open`

f. `backup database plus archivelog delete input`

A. b, c ,a, d, e

B. b, a, c, f, e

C. a, c, e, d

D. b, a, c, e, f

E. b, a, c, d, e

12. Which of the following most closely represents an image copy?

A. Unix cp command of a file

B. Bit-by-bit copy of a file

C. Windows COPY command of a file

D. All of the above

13. Which dynamic view displays the status of block-change tracking?

A. V$BLOCK_CHANGE

B. V$BLOCK_CHANGE_TRACKING

C. V$BLOCKCHANGE

D. V$BLOCK_TRACKING

14. What feature comes into play to help ensure the completion of the backup should one of three backup devices fail during a backup that is using three different channels?

A. Channel failover

B. Restartable backups

C. Rescheduable backups

D. Automatic backup recovery

E. Channel recovery

15. What command would you use to set a persistent setting in RMAN so that backups are all written to a tape device?

A. CONFIGURE DEFAULT DEVICE TYPE TO TAPE MEDIA

B. CONFIGURE DEFAULT DEVICE TYPE TO TAPE

C. CONFIGURE DEFAULT DEVICE TYPE TO SBT

D. CONFIGURE DEFAULT DEVICE TYPE TO SBT_TAPE

16. The CONTROL_FILE_RECORD_KEEP_TIME initialization parameter should be set to what value? (Choose all that apply.)

A. The initialization parameter should be set to 0 when the RMAN repository is being used.

B. The initialization parameter should be set to greater than 0 with the RMAN repository utilizing the recovery catalog only.

C. The initialization parameter should be set to greater than 0 with the RMAN repository utilizing the control file or the recovery catalog.

D. The initialization parameter should be set to 0 with the RMAN repository utilizing the control file or the recovery catalog.

E. The initialization parameter should never be set to 0 if you are using RMAN.

17. Given the following steps, which would be the correct order to create a backup of an Oracle database in ARCHIVELOG mode with control-file autobackups enabled?

a. backup archivelog all;

b. backup database all;

c. backup controlfile;

d. backup archivelog, database, controlfile delete input;

e. backup database plus archivelog delete input

A. e

B. a, b, a, c

C. d

D. b, a, c

E. b, a, c, d, e

18. Which of the following statements are true about the BACKUP command? (Choose all that apply.)

A. The BACKUP command can not be used to make image copies of a datafile.

B. The BACKUP command can improve performance by multiplexing backup files.

C. The BACKUP can take advantage of the block-change tracking capability.

D. The BACKUP command cannot store data in incremental backups.

E. The BACKUP command can store data in cumulative incremental backups only.

19. Which command is used to configure RMAN to perform a compressed backup for every backup executed?

A. BACKUP AS COMPRESSED BACKUPSET DATABASE

B. BACKUP AS COMPRESSED COPY OF DATABASE

C. CONFIGURE DEVICE TYPE DISK BACKUP TYPE TO COMPRESSED BACKUPSET

D. CONFIGURE DEVICE TYPE DISK BACKUP TYPE COMPRESS

E. BACKUP DATABASE COMPRESS

20. You issue the following command:

```
RMAN>CONFIGURE BACKUP OPTIMIZATION ON;
```

What is the result of this command on your backups?

A. An incremental backup strategy will be used automatically.

B. Read-only datafiles will not be backed up as long as backups of those files already exist and those backups meet established retention criteria.

C. RMAN will configure itself for maximum performance at the cost of CPU.

D. RMAN will configure itself for minimal OS/CPU impact at the cost of time to back up the database.

E. RMAN will automatically compress backups.

Answers to Review Questions

1. A. Block-change tracking must be enabled with `alter database enable block change tracking`. The physical location and name of the block-change tracking file must be supplied.

2. A. The backup set is stored in a proprietary RMAN format, where only used blocks are backed up.

3. D. The following backup sets would be created:

- One for an archive log backup before the main backup.
- One for the main backup. Since we are using a single channel with no backup-set size restriction, RMAN would create a single backup set.
- One for an archive log backup after the main backup.
- One for the control-file autobackup.

4. A. The `backup as copy` command is used to create an image-copy backup.

5. C. Compressed backups work only with backup sets, not image copies. Thus, compressed backups will work only with the `backup` command.

6. D. The correct answer is to use the `backup database plus archivelog delete input` command.

7. D. A full backup is best described by backing up all the used blocks in a datafile or any database file. A full backup can be taken on one database file.

8. A. A differential incremental backup backs up only blocks that have been modified since a backup at the same level or lower.

9. B. A level-0 backup is the first backup that is performed when implementing an incremental backup strategy. A level-0 backup copies all the used blocks as a baseline.

10. C. The TAG option is used to name a backup with a user-defined character string.

11. E. The correct order of operations is to log into RMAN and then shut down the database with the `shutdown immediate` command. You then mount the database with the `startup mount` command. Once the database is mounted, you back up the database with the `backup database` command. Finally, after the backup is complete, you open the database.

12. D. Image copies are similar to operating-system copy commands. These equate to bit-by-bit copies of a file.

13. B. The V$BLOCK_CHANGE_TRACKING dynamic view shows the filename, status, and size of the block-change tracking file.

14. A. Channel failover is the RMAN feature that provides the ability for other channels to take over the work of a failed channel during backup and recovery operations. Obviously, channel failover requires the allocation of more than one channel.

15. C. The command that sets the persistent setting that directs RMAN to back up to tape is `CONFIGURE DEFAULT DEVICE TYPE TO SBT`.

16. C, E. The `CONTROL_FILE_RECORD_KEEP_TIME` initialization parameter should never be set to 0 if you are using RMAN. If this value is set to 0, there is a potential to lose backup records.

17. A. Backing up in ARCHIVELOG mode is as easy as issuing the `backup database plus archivelog delete input` command.

18. B, C. The `BACKUP` command can take advantage of multiplexing datafiles to the same backup set. The `BACKUP` command can also use the block-change tracking capability.

19. C. Use the `CONFIGURE DEVICE TYPE DISK BACKUP TYPE TO COMPRESSED BACKUPSET` command to configure RMAN to always create a compressed backup by default.

20. B. Backup optimization is a feature whereby Oracle will not back up a read-only tablespace as long as that tablespace has been backed up such that it meets the backup retention criteria.

Chapter

5

Using the RMAN Recovery Catalog

ORACLE DATABASE 11g: ADMINISTRATION II EXAM OBJECTIVES COVERED IN THIS CHAPTER:

✓ **Using the RMAN Recovery Catalog**

- Identify situations that require RMAN recovery catalog

- Create and configure a recovery catalog

- Synchronize the recovery catalog

- Create and use RMAN stored scripts

- Back up the recovery catalog

- Create and use a virtual private catalog

The RMAN recovery catalog is an optional component that you can use with RMAN. In this chapter, we will review the recovery catalog so you will be prepared to answer recovery-catalog OCP exam questions. This chapter will contain the following information on the recovery catalog:

- Introducing the recovery catalog
- Creating the recovery catalog
- Using the recovery catalog
- Recovery-catalog RMAN scripting
- Recovery-catalog maintenance
- Virtual private catalog

So, let's get on with learning about the recovery catalog!

Introducing the Recovery Catalog

The *RMAN recovery catalog* is a schema that sits in an Oracle database. This schema is designed to store RMAN-related information. The information stored in the recovery catalog is in large part just like that stored in the control file. Since most RMAN information is stored in the control file of a database, the recovery catalog serves as a backup repository for RMAN information.

Using the recovery catalog has some clear benefits that need to be carefully considered. The first is that it acts as a single location to store all your RMAN backup-related information. The views of the recovery catalog are well documented, and as a result you can build reports off of those views that will help you to understand the current status of your database backups.

The second benefit is that the recovery catalog also makes global scripting of RMAN operations much easier. You simply store the scripts in the recovery catalog and call them as needed.

Another benefit is that the recovery catalog enables a few RMAN operations not available without a recovery catalog, like using the keep forever option (discussed in Chapter 4) or keeping RMAN-related records for a period of time greater than a year.

As you can see, the recovery catalog adds to the overall RMAN architecture nicely. It provides redundancy and additional features that make it very useful. Not all environments will need a recovery catalog. If you have just one or two databases, then a recovery catalog may be more trouble than it's worth. If you have a large environment though, the recovery catalog can make managing that environment much easier.

Database duplication can cause the recovery catalog all sorts of problems if you are not careful. This is because each database in the recovery catalog is uniquely identified by its database ID, or DBID. If you duplicate a database manually, you must change the DBID of the newly created duplicate database with the Oracle NID utility. If you do not do this and you register the new database in the recovery catalog, RMAN will get confused as to who the individual catalog records belong to. This can put your ability to recover your database with RMAN at risk. Note that when you do an RMAN database duplication, it will change the DBID for you automatically when the duplication is complete.

The recovery catalog provides a number of views (called *recovery catalog views*) into the metadata contained therein. The OCP exam will likely not expect you to memorize these views, but it's still best to be aware of them. All the recovery catalog views start with an RC_ prefix and then end with a descriptive name of the data contained in the view. The following are some more popular recovery catalog views:

- RC_DATABASE
- RC_BACKUP_PIECE
- RC_PIECE_DETAILS
- RC_ARCHIVED_LOG
- RC_BACKUP_ARCHIVELOG_SUMMARY
- RC_BACKUP_SET
- RC_BACKUP_SET_DETAILS
- RC_BACKUP_SPFILE

Creating the Recovery Catalog User and Schema Objects

As we mentioned, the recovery catalog is a schema in an existing Oracle database. This schema typically will have its own tablespace, where the RMAN recovery-catalog schema data will be stored. Creating the recovery catalog user and schema is fairly easy. You use the create user command to create the database user first. You will then need to create the tablespace that will store the recovery catalog data.

 Real World Scenario

To Use the Recovery Catalog or Not to Use the Recovery Catalog; That Is the Question

Adding components to any system has the potential to inject problems into that system. The same is true with the recovery catalog. One database shop implemented the Oracle recovery catalog at the same time they started using RMAN (this was using Oracle Database 10*g*).

Initially things worked great, but over time backup performance became slower and slower. These performance problems were not seen when the recovery catalog was not in use. In the end, after lots of troubleshooting, it was discovered that a couple of queries being issued against the recovery-catalog schema were not tuned well and that these queries would slow down a great deal as the catalog schema got larger. They opened a service request with Oracle and after some time Oracle found the problem and made a patch available.

The moral of this story, in our minds, is to use the KISS (keep it simple, stupid) principle when deciding if you need a recovery catalog or not. If you can justify the additional component because it will provide significant benefit, then by all means use it. Just understand that it's something else that may well break, and things always break at the most inopportune times.

In Exercise 5.1, you'll create a recovery-catalog schema.

 How much space you will need for the recovery-catalog schema is a function of how often you back up the database and how long you retain the RMAN backup database in the recovery catalog. Oracle indicates that for one database with one backup per day and one archive-log backup per day, you can estimate metadata storage requirements of between 15MB and 120MB per year, per database, depending on how many backups (database, archive log, and so on) you do per day. The Oracle documentation provides more guidelines. You will not need to be familiar with these sizing guidelines when taking your OCP exam.

EXERCISE 5.1

Creating a Recovery-Catalog Schema

Here are the steps to follow when creating the recovery-catalog schema:

1. Open a command-line window. For this example, you will use a database called RCAT. You need to set the ORACLE_SID to RCAT as shown here:

    ```
    C:\Documents and Settings\dstuns>set ORACLE_SID=RCAT
    ```

2. Sign into the database using SQL*Plus:

    ```
    C:\Documents and Settings\Robert>sqlplus sys/robert as sysdba
    SQL*Plus: Release 11.1.0.6.0 - Production on Mon Sep 15 21:48:06 2008
    Copyright (c) 1982, 2007, Oracle.  All rights reserved.
    Connected to:
    Oracle Database 11g Enterprise Edition Release 11.1.0.6.0 - Production
    With the Partitioning, OLAP, Data Mining and Real Application Testing
    options
    SQL>
    ```

3. Create a tablespace called RCAT_DATA. This tablespace will be used to store the recovery-catalog schema data:

    ```
    SQL> create tablespace rcat_data
      2  datafile 'c:\oracle\oradata\rcat\rcat_data_01.dbf' size 60m
      3  autoextend on next 10m maxsize 200m;
    Tablespace created.
    ```

4. Create the user that will store the catalog. Use the name RMAN with the password RMAN. Make RCAT_DATA the default tablespace (we assume you have a default temporary tablespace already defined). Also, you will grant an unlimited quota on RCAT_DATA to RCAT_USER:

    ```
    SQL> create user rcat_user identified by rcat_user
      2  default tablespace rcat_data
      3  quota unlimited on rcat_data;
    User created.
    ```

5. The recovery catalog–owning user requires only a grant to the RECOVERY_CATALOG_OWNER role using the grant command:

    ```
    SQL> grant recovery_catalog_owner to rcat_user;
    Grant succeeded.
    ```

EXERCISE 5.1 *(continued)*

6. Test to see whether you can connect to the recovery-catalog schema that you have just created:

   ```
   SQL> connect rcat_user/rcat_user
   Connected.
   ```

7. Now you need to create the recovery-catalog schema. To do this, use the create catalog command as shown in this example:

   ```
   C:\Documents and Settings\Robert>Rman catalog=rcat_user/rcat_user@rcat
   Recovery Manager: Release 11.1.0.6.0 - Production on
   Mon Sep 15 23:10:13 2008
   Copyright (c) 1982, 2007, Oracle.  All rights reserved.
   connected to recovery catalog database
   RMAN> create catalog
   recovery catalog created
   ```

Some texts may show you granting connect or resource roles to the recovery catalog–schema owner. This is not required in Oracle Database 11*g* and may represent a security risk.

Using a Recovery Catalog

Using a recovery catalog is pretty straightforward with RMAN. You simply indicate that you want to connect to the recovery catalog when you start RMAN. You will also have to register the database before your first RMAN operation when connected to the recovery catalog. Most RMAN operations when connected to the recovery catalog are pretty much the same; it's just that RMAN metadata will now be stored in both the control file and the recovery catalog. In the following sections, we will discuss these topics:

- Connecting to the recovery catalog from RMAN
- Registering the database with the recovery catalog
- Unregistering a database from the recovery catalog

Connecting to the Recovery Catalog from RMAN

When you start RMAN, you will need to indicate that you want to connect to a recovery catalog if you want the session to use the recovery catalog. There are a couple of ways of connecting to the recovery catalog. The first is to use the `catalog` RMAN command-line parameter, as shown in this example:

```
C:\Documents and Settings\Robert>Set oracle_sid=orcl
C:\Documents and Settings\Robert>Rman target=sys/Robert
catalog=rcat_user/rcat_user@rcat
Recovery Manager: Release 11.1.0.6.0 - Production on Mon Sep 15 22:17:11 2008
Copyright (c) 1982, 2007, Oracle.  All rights reserved.
connected to target database (not started)
connected to recovery catalog database
RMAN>
```

Note the use of the terms `target` and `catalog`. As we first mentioned in Chapter 4, the database you are intending to back up is called the *target database*. In the previous example, you connected directly to the target database with RMAN. At the same time, you connected to the catalog database through Oracle Net. If you desired, you could connect directly to the catalog database and connect to the target database via Oracle Net, or you could connect to both databases via Oracle Net. Since the server itself does the backup work via locally allocated channels, connecting to the server or the recovery catalog through Oracle Net should not impose any undue performance constraints on the performance of your backups.

Another way of connecting to the recovery catalog is to do so from the RMAN command-line prompt using the `connect` command, as shown in this example:

```
C:\Documents and Settings\Robert>Rman target=sys/Robert
Recovery Manager: Release 11.1.0.6.0 - Production on Mon Sep 15 22:18:05 2008
Copyright (c) 1982, 2007, Oracle.  All rights reserved.
connected to target database (not started)
RMAN> Connect catalog rcat_user/rcat_user@rcat
connected to recovery catalog database
```

Registering the Target Database with the Recovery Catalog

Once you have connected to the recovery catalog, you will have to register the database with the `register database` command. To be registered, the database must be mounted or open. In this example, you connect to the target database and the recovery catalog and then register the database with the recovery catalog:

```
C:\Documents and Settings\Robert>Rman target=sys/Robert
catalog=rcat_user/rcat_user@rcat
```

```
Recovery Manager: Release 11.1.0.6.0 - Production on Mon Sep 15 23:12:51 2008
Copyright (c) 1982, 2007, Oracle.  All rights reserved.
connected to target database: ORCL (DBID=1190537904, not open)
connected to recovery catalog database
RMAN> register database;
database registered in recovery catalog
starting full resync of recovery catalog
full resync complete
```

Unregistering a Database

If you are preparing to remove a database, you will want to remove its metadata from the recovery catalog. This is done with the unregister command, as shown in this example:

```
C:\Documents and Settings\Robert>Rman target=sys/Robert
catalog=rcat_user/rcat_user@rcat
Recovery Manager: Release 11.1.0.6.0 - Production on Mon Sep 15 23:13:45 2008
Copyright (c) 1982, 2007, Oracle.  All rights reserved.
connected to target database: ORCL (DBID=1190537904, not open)
connected to recovery catalog database
RMAN> unregister database;
database name is "ORCL" and DBID is 1190537904
Do you really want to unregister the database (enter YES or NO)? yes
database unregistered from the recovery catalog
```

Unregistering a database from the recovery catalog will cause all recovery catalog–related records to be removed from the recovery catalog. Control-file records for that database will be retained, of course. You might have had older backup records stored in the recovery catalog, though. When you unregister a database, those old records will be lost if the age of the backups exceeds the setting of the CONTROL_FILE_RECORD_KEEP_TIME parameter. Also, any scripts related to the database in the recovery catalog will be lost (we will talk more about scripting later in this chapter).

Using Scripts in the RMAN Recovery Catalog

One benefit of the recovery catalog is the ability to store RMAN scripts. In the following sections, these topics will be addressed:

- Executing external scripts
- Creating stored scripts

- Replacing stored scripts
- Removing stored scripts
- Executing stored scripts
- Printing stored scripts
- Using script-substitution variables

Executing External Scripts

RMAN provides the ability to execute external scripts. You can do so from the RMAN command line using the `cmdfile` option, as shown here:

```
Rman target=/ cmdfile=run_me.rman
```

You can also run an external script from within RMAN using the @ command, as shown here:

```
RMAN> @run_me.rman
```

Creating Stored Scripts

Recovery catalog stored scripts provide the ability to centrally manage your backup and recovery scripts. Using global stored scripts allows you to use common scripts across the entire enterprise.

Use the `create script` RMAN command to store scripts in the recovery catalog. You will assign a name to the stored script when you create it. Stored scripts can be created to do many RMAN operations, including backups, recoveries, and database-maintenance operations. As mentioned earlier, you must be connected to the recovery catalog to be able to create a script.

Here is an example of using the `create script` command to create a script. This script does a backup of the database and the archived redo logs:

```
create script db_backup_script
{ backup database plus archivelog delete input;}
```

Note that if you are using virtual private catalogs (see more on these later in this chapter), you will need to create the script as a global script as shown here:

```
create global script db_delete_obsolete
{ delete obsolete;}
```

Replacing Stored Scripts

The `replace script` command is used to replace stored RMAN scripts. The following example demonstrates the use of the `replace script` command:

```
Replace script db_delete_obsolete
{ delete noprompt obsolete;}
```

Removing Stored Scripts

If you need to remove a stored script permanently, you can use the `delete script` command as shown here:

```
Delete script db_delete_obsolete;
```

Executing Stored Scripts

Once you have created the script, it might be nice to actually run it! To run the script, you will use the `execute script` command. This command must be run within the confines of an RMAN run block, as shown in this example:

```
Run {execute script db_delete_obsolete;}
```

Printing Stored Scripts

The `print script` command will print your script to the standard output device, allowing you to cut and paste its contents. Here is an example of the `print script` command:

```
RMAN> Print script db_delete_obsolete;
printing stored script: db_delete_obsolete
{ delete obsolete;}
```

Using Script Substitution Variables

Oracle Database 11g provides for the use of *substitution variables* in RMAN scripts or command files. You define the substitution variables using the ampersand (&) character followed by a number, as shown in this example:

```
Restore database from tag &1;
```

The RMAN executable includes the `using` command-line parameter that allows you to define the value of the substitution variable. For example, if the previous `restore` command were in a file called `restore.cmd` and you wanted to restore a backup with the tag `MINE`, you would call RMAN in this manner:

```
Rman target=/ @restore.cmd using MINE
```

You can also use substitution variables with stored scripts. For example, you can create a script to back up your database and use a tag as shown here:

```
RMAN> create script db_backup_script
2> { backup database tag  '&1' plus archivelog delete input;}
Enter value for 1: test
created script db_backup_script
```

You can then execute the script, setting the variable with the `using` command, as shown here:

```
RMAN> Run {execute script db_backup_script using 'TEST';}
```

Maintaining the Recovery Catalog

If you are running the recovery catalog, you will need to know how to synchronize it with the control file of the database. Additionally, you will need to back up the recovery catalog. We briefly cover these two topics next.

Synchronizing the Recovery Catalog

Typically during an RMAN operation, the recovery catalog will be synchronized with the control file. New records will be updated or added during this synchronization process. There may be times you will want to synchronize the recovery catalog yourself manually. You can use the `resync catalog` command to perform manual catalog synchronization. Here is an example of using the `resync` command:

```
RMAN> resync catalog;
starting full resync of recovery catalog
full resync complete
```

Backing Up the Recovery Catalog

You can actually back up the recovery catalog using RMAN. You would simply use the control file of the recovery catalog to store the backup-related information. You can do online or offline backups and complete or point-in-time restores as your needs dictate.

You can also use Oracle's flashback features (see Chapter 9 for more on Oracle Flashback Database) on the recovery catalog.

 Real World Scenario

Why Resync the Catalog?

You might be asking yourself, "If RMAN resynchronizes the catalog automatically after a backup, why would I ever need to use the resync catalog command?" That's a fair question.

One place where one of us was employed had a large number of databases and used RMAN and the recovery catalog. As more and more records were added to the recovery catalog, we found our backups were taking longer. This ended up being because of a bug in RMAN. To work around the problem until Oracle could give us a fix, we did our backups without connecting to the recovery catalog. These made the backups perform much faster. We would then connect to the recovery catalog in a different operation and resync the control file to the recovery catalog.

This corrected the performance problem while still allowing us to use the recovery catalog to store our database backup metadata.

Using the RMAN Virtual Private Catalog

You might have noticed that the catalog-schema owner has access to all data in the recovery catalog. You may want to allow other users access to the recovery catalog, but you may want them to see information on only specific databases. Oracle provides the RMAN virtual private catalog for just such cases. In the following sections, we will discuss how to create a virtual catalog and how to grant users access to databases contained within it. We will discuss how to create the RMAN virtual private catalog first, and then we will discuss administration of the virtual private catalog.

Creating the RMAN Virtual Private Catalog

If you want to use the *RMAN virtual private catalog (RVPC)*, you start with a regular recovery catalog. The recovery-catalog schema should have been created and the databases registered (you can, of course, register databases later), and it can be brand-new or already have been in use.

Now that you have a recovery catalog, let's assume you have registered two databases in the recovery catalog; one is called orcl and one is called secret. Let's assume you have a DBA named Ed who you don't quite trust (he's a seedy-looking guy with tattoos of the Smurfs all over his arms). Because you don't trust him, you want him to be able to access only the orcl database RMAN records. The secret database records will remain a mystery to him (you assume, of course, that he does not have SYS access to your recovery catalog, or all is lost!).

To create the RVPC account for Ed, you would execute the following steps:

Step 1: Create the RVPC database account.   First you create the RVPC database account log in the recovery-catalog database as a privileged user (for example, SYS) and issue the create user command. You will also need to grant the recovery_catalog_owner privilege to the new user.

Step 2: Create the RVPC.   Once the RVPC user has been created, you need to create the virtual catalog. To do this, you log into RMAN and use the create virtual catalog command, as shown here:

```
Create virtual catalog;
```

Step 3: Grant the RVPC access to the appropriate catalog databases.   Now that you have created the RVPC account, you need to indicate to the recovery-catalog database which databases this account will have access to. You will use the RMAN command to perform this operation as shown here, where we grant access to the ORCL database catalog metadata:

```
grant catalog for database orcl to rcat_001;
```

Administering the RMAN Virtual Private Catalog

Once you have set up RVPC, there are other administrative activities you can perform. For example, you can grant the register database privilege to RVPC owners using the RMAN grant command as shown here:

```
RMAN> grant register database to rcat_002;
Grant succeeded.
```

The revoke RMAN command is used to revoke privileges to databases in the RVPC or other privileges, such as the register database privilege, as shown here:

```
RMAN>Revoke catalog for database abcs;
RMAN>Revoke register database from rcat_002;
```

Finally, you can drop the RVPC with the `drop catalog` command as shown in this example:

```
RMAN>connect catalog rcat_002/rcat002@rcat;
RMAN> drop catalog;
```

After using the `drop catalog` command, it's safe to drop the RVPC catalog user with the drop user SQL command:

```
SQL> drop user rcat_001;
```

Summary

The recovery catalog is an optional but very powerful tool in your RMAN arsenal. It can make your life as a DBA easier by providing a centralized repository for all your RMAN-related data. The recovery catalog is easy to create and maintain. Oracle's new virtual private catalog features make the recovery catalog even more powerful, increasing the security within the catalog.

Exam Essentials

Identify situations that will require the RMAN recovery catalog.   Understand that the recovery catalog is largely optional. A recovery catalog will be needed for storing scripts, and it will be required if you want to store backup records longer than one year or beyond the setting of `CONTROL_FILE_RECORD_KEEP_TIME`.

Create and configure an RMAN recovery catalog.   Understand the process required to create the RMAN recovery catalog. Know how to create the recovery-catalog user and what privileges are required. Understand how to register and unregister databases with the recovery catalog and how to create a virtual private catalog and configure users to use it.

Maintain the RMAN recovery catalog.   Understand how to back up the recovery catalog. Know how to synchronize the target database with the recovery catalog.

Review Questions

1. What is the purpose of the RMAN recovery catalog? (Choose all that apply.)

    A. It must be used because all RMAN-related backup and recovery metadata information is contained in it.

    B. It provides a convenient, optional, repository of backup- and recovery-related metadata.

    C. It provides the ability to store RMAN scripts for global use by any database that has access to the repository.

    D. It provides a means of storing all RMAN backup sets physically in an Oracle database server.

    E. It provides the ability to store backup records for more than a year.

2. What privileges must be granted to allow an account to create the recovery catalog? (Choose all that apply.)

    A. RECOVERY_CATALOG_OWNER

    B. DBA

    C. RESOURCE

    D. SELECT ANY DICTIONARY

    E. CONNECT

3. Which command do you use to create a recovery-catalog schema?

    A. create recovery catalog

    B. create catalog

    C. build catalog

    D. catalog create

    E. mount catalog

4. If you back up a database without connecting to the recovery catalog, which operations will cause the recovery catalog to be updated? (Choose all that apply.)

    A. The next time you back up the database when you are also connected to the recovery catalog and the target database

    B. The next time you are connected to the target database and the recovery catalog database and issue the resync command

    C. The next time you connect RMAN to just the recovery catalog

    D. The next time you connect to the recovery catalog and the target database with RMAN

    E. Connecting to the recovery catalog and issuing the resync all databases command

5. You have created a script in the recovery catalog called `backup_database`. Which of the following commands would successfully execute that script?

A.

```
run {
      open script backup_database;
      run script backup_database
      }
```

B.

```
run {
      engage script backup_database;
      }
```

C.

```
run {
      run script backup_database;
      }
```

D.

```
Run {
      execute script backup_database;
      }
```

E. The name `backup_database` is an invalid name for an RMAN script. Trying to run it from RMAN would result in an error.

6. In what order would you execute the following steps to create a recovery catalog?

a. Issue the `create catalog` command.

b. Create the recovery-catalog database.

c. Create the recovery-catalog user.

d. Grant the `recovery_catalog_owner` privilege to the recovery-catalog user.

e. Issue the `register database` command from the target database.

A. a, b, c, d, e

B. b, a, d, c, e

C. b, c, d, a, e

D. b, c, d, e, a

E. b, d, c, a, e

7. How would you grant the RVPC user access to specific RMAN database records in the RMAN virtual private catalog?

   A. Issue the `grant` command from the SYS user (or equivalent) of the target database.

   B. Issue the `grant` command from the SYS user (or equivalent) of the recovery-catalog database.

   C. Issue the `grant` command from the recovery catalog–owning schema user account in the recovery catalog.

   D. Issue the `grant` command from RMAN when connected to the recovery catalog–owning schema.

   E. Issue the `grant` command from RMAN when connected to the target database.

8. The RVPC user can do which of the following? (Choose all that apply.)

   A. Register databases if granted the `register database` privilege

   B. See all databases in the recovery-catalog schema

   C. See all database-related metadata in the recovery catalog if they are granted access to that database

   D. Unregister databases from the RVPC catalog that were not granted to the RVPC catalog owner with the `grant` command

   E. Not be connected to with the RMAN command-line catalog parameter for backup or recovery purposes

9. Given the script

   ```
   create script db_backup_datafile_script
   {backup datafile &1, &2 plus archivelog delete input;}
   ```

   what is the result of running this command?

   ```
   Run {execute script db_backup_datafile_script using 2;}
   ```

   A. The script will fail since you instructed RMAN to back up only one datafile rather than two.

   B. The script will successfully back up datafile 3 without error.

   C. The script will fail since it uses a substitution variable which is not supported.

   D. The `execute script` command will prompt for the value of &2 since it's not included in the command.

   E. The script will fail because you cannot use the `plus archivelog` command when backing up database datafiles.

10. Which is the correct way to connect to both the target database and the recovery catalog from the RMAN command line? Assume that the target database is called ORCL and that the recovery catalog database is called RCAT. Also assume that the recovery-catalog owner is called RCAT_OWN. Assume the environment is configured for the ORCL database. (Choose all that apply.)

A.   `rman target=/ catalog=/@rcat`

B.   `rman target=/ catalog=rcat_own/rcat_own`

C.   `rman target=/ catalog=rcat_own/rcat_own@RCAT`

D.   `rman target=sys/robert@orcl catalog=rcat_own/rcat_own@RCAT`

E.   You cannot connect to the target database and the recovery catalog at the same time.

Answers to Review Questions

1. B, C, E. The recovery catalog provides a means of storing metadata related to a database's RMAN backup and recovery operations. Additionally, it provides the ability to store scripts that can be used by any database connecting to the repository via RMAN. Finally, the recovery catalog provides the means to store backup records for longer than a year.

2. A, C. The RECOVERY_CATALOG_OWNER and RESOURCE privileges are required to create the recovery catalog. The DBA privilege includes RESOURCE and CONNECT and will work, but this role has many additional privileges that are unneeded. SELECT ANY DICTIONARY is not required.

3. B. Use the create catalog command to create the recovery-catalog schema.

4. A, B. Anytime you execute an RMAN backup operation when connected to the recovery catalog, RMAN will automatically resynchronize the recovery-catalog metadata with the database control file. The resync command is used to manually resynchronize the recovery catalog with the database.

5. D. You would use the execute script RMAN command, contained within a run block, to execute the backup_database script.

6. C. You would first create the recovery catalog database. Then you create the recovery catalog user, granting that user the RECOVERY_CATALOG_OWNER role. You then issue the create catalog command from RMAN, which will create the recovery-catalog schema. Finally, you connect to the target database and register the database with the register database command.

7. D. To give the RVPC user rights to specific databases, you must connect to the recovery catalog with RMAN. You then grant those rights to that user from the RMAN prompt using the grant command.

8. A, C. The RVPC user can **register database** if they are granted the register database privilege. They can also see all recovery-catalog database metadata to which they are granted access.

9. D. The script will prompt for the missing substitution variable. The script will return an error if you do not put in a value for the second substitution variable.

10. C, D. Options C and D show the correct format for the RMAN command line. Option C connects to the database locally, while option D connects through Oracle Net. Both methods are completely legal.

Chapter

6

Recovering Databases with RMAN

ORACLE DATABASE 11*g*: ADMINISTRATION II EXAM OBJECTIVES COVERED IN THIS CHAPTER:

✓ **Using RMAN to Perform Recovery**

- Perform complete recovery from a critical or non-critical data file loss using RMAN

- Perform incomplete recovery using RMAN

- Recover using incrementally updated backups

- Switch to image copies for fast recovery

- Recover using a backup control file

Database recovery ought to be easy in our minds. You have enough problems when your database has unexpectedly left the building, and those problems should not be made worse by a bad piece of database-backup-and recovery software. RMAN makes recovery of your database easy as long as you have crafted a solid backup and recovery strategy (discussed in previous chapters). Additionally, the old adage that practice makes perfect very much applies to database recoveries. So take some time and practice a recovery or two before you have to deal with the real thing. All too often, people wait for disaster to strike rather than learning what to do beforehand.

This chapter is about what to do when disaster strikes and you are under the gun to get your backup restored. In this chapter, we will discuss the following topics:

- RMAN database-recovery basics
- Recovering a database in NOARCHIVELOG mode
- Recovering a database in ARCHIVELOG mode
- Recovering datafiles or tablespaces in ARCHIVELOG mode
- Recovering a database using incomplete recovery
- Using image copies to recover your database
- Other recovery topics

The best way to really learn about backup and recovery is to do it. A lot. The exercises in this chapter along with the examples of the various forms of recovery will certainly get you on your way.

Exam objectives are subject to change at any time without prior notice and at Oracle's sole discretion. Please visit Oracle's Training and Certification website (http://www.oracle.com/education/certification/) for the most current exam-objectives listing.

In this chapter and in Chapter 8 we have opted not to use a recovery catalog in our examples. The functionality demonstrated is the same with or without a recovery catalog. Where there are exceptions to this rule, we will note them or provide additional examples.

RMAN Database-Recovery Basics

There is a common theme or pattern when recovering databases in RMAN that you will want to be familiar with. This pattern for recovery is as follows:

Step 1: Put the database in the proper mode.   Putting the database in the proper mode is the first step to recovering it. The proper mode is dependent on the type of recovery you want to be able to make. For example, in NOARCHIVELOG mode your database must always be in MOUNT mode to perform a recovery. We will cover the modes the database should be in for individual recovery in the later sections of this chapter.

RMAN provides commands that you can use to put the database in the mode you want it to be in (you'll find a summary of the RMAN commands in Chapter 4). If you want the database mounted, then you can use the RMAN `startup mount` command, for example. RMAN recoveries will occur in almost any mode, NOMOUNT for control-file or spfile recoveries, MOUNT for offline database recoveries or OPEN for ARCHIVELOG noncritical datafile or tablespace recoveries. For the OCP exam, it will be a very good idea if you learn which modes are required for which recovery types.

> The RMAN client is full-featured. There should be few times when any recovery operation will require you to use anything other than RMAN. If you do have to use something else, it probably means you have made a mistake, you are having a really bad day, or you have run into a bug (which in and of itself means you are having a really bad day).

Putting the database in the proper mode may also require restoring files required to put it in that mode. For example, if the spfile is missing, you may need to restore it. Perhaps the control file will need to be restored. You will find more information on these kinds of recoveries later in this chapter.

Step 2: Restore the database datafiles.   After the database has been put in the correct mode for the recovery chosen, you will use the RMAN `restore` command to begin the database recovery. The `restore` command will determine which backup set pieces or image copies need to be used to recover the database to the point in time that you direct. By default, RMAN will restore the database to the point of failure if you are running in ARCHIVELOG mode. If you are in NOARCHIVELOG mode, the restore will be to the point of the last backup. Once the datafiles have been restored, you will be returned to the RMAN prompt so you can issue the `recover database` command.

The `restore` command comes in different flavors, allowing you to restore the entire database, datafiles, or tablespaces. We understand that a future version will also allow you to restore your broken heart, but that's still in beta.

Step 3: Recover the database.   One the database datafiles are restored, the RMAN `recover` command is used to start the actual recovery process. During the execution of the `recover` command, RMAN will extract the needed archived redo logs (if running in ARCHIVELOG mode) and apply them as needed. Obviously during a NOARCHIVELOG-mode recovery no redo will be applied (and in fact, you will indicate this when you do the recovery, as you will see later in this chapter). Once the `recover` command has completed its job, you will be returned to the RMAN prompt so you can complete the recovery process by opening the database or bringing the tablespace or datafile online.

As with the `restore` command, the `recover` command has a number of different variations, such as `recover database`, `recover tablespace`, and `recover datafile`. You will see these demonstrated throughout the rest of this chapter.

Step 4: Complete the recovery.   If your restore and recovery required the database to be in MOUNT mode, then all you need to do is open the database for business and you are the hero of the day. To do so, issue the `alter database open` command from the RMAN prompt. If you did everything correctly, your database should open and your users will erect a statue in your honor. At one time we had upward of 15 statues erected in our honor, only to be toppled by DBAs who succeeded us. Statues are, in the end, highly overrated.

Of course, if you didn't get your backup strategy right, your users may well throw another party in your honor—the going-away party, if your boss even allows that. So, you'll want to make sure you get it right the first time and even test it a few times before the real deal comes to town.

If your restore and recovery permitted the database to be open, then you probably had a tablespace or a datafile offline. In this case, you will use the RMAN `sql` command, embedding the `alter tablespace online` or `alter datafile online` command within the confines of that command. With the successful completion of those commands, your recovery will be complete and you can celebrate!

Now that we have showed you the basic pattern for recovering from a downed database, let's talk in some more specifics about the different kinds of database recoveries you will encounter.

Recovering a Database in NOARCHIVELOG Mode

Recovering your NOARCHIVELOG-mode database is perhaps the easiest thing you could do. There is no application of redo to worry about; only restoring the database datafiles and getting the database up and running. One important thing to understand is that your best recovery situation is from a database backup that is consistent. Fortunately RMAN will force you to do consistent database backups when the database is in NOARCHIVELOG mode, so this isn't a problem. We discussed this situation in detail in Chapter 3, so please make sure you reference that chapter and understand this important concept in backup and recovery. Oftentimes knowing how something works and why will help you answer an OCP exam question that you otherwise don't really know the answer to.

So, how easy is recovery of your database in NOARCHIVELOG mode? Here are the steps in summary form. We will give you more detail as this chapter progresses:

1. If you have lost your control file or spfile (or database parameter file), you will need to reference the section on recovering your control file or spfile with RMAN, which appears later in this chapter. To start any RMAN recovery, you must have a control file and an spfile (or database parameter file).

2. If you are not already logged into RMAN (for example, if you had to restore your control file), then log into RMAN now. You will see lots of examples of this later in this chapter.

3. Mount your database with the `startup mount` command.

4. Issue the RMAN `restore database` command.

5. Issue the RMAN `recover database` command. Because this is a NOARCHIVELOG-mode database recovery, you will need to include the `noredo` keyword to indicate that there is no redo to be applied.

6. Open the database with the `alter database open` command.

Here is an example of an RMAN restore of a database in NOARCHIVELOG mode:

```
RMAN> connect target /
RMAN> shutdown abort
using target database control file instead of recovery catalog
Oracle instance shut down
RMAN> startup mount
connected to target database (not started)
Oracle instance started
database mounted
Total System Global Area      397557760 bytes
Fixed Size                      1333452 bytes
Variable Size                 339740468 bytes
Database Buffers               50331648 bytes
Redo Buffers                    6152192 bytes
RMAN> restore database;
Starting restore at 28-SEP-08
allocated channel: ORA_DISK_1
channel ORA_DISK_1: SID=154 device type=DISK
channel ORA_DISK_1: starting datafile backup set restore
channel ORA_DISK_1: specifying datafile(s) to restore from backup set
channel ORA_DISK_1: restoring datafile 00002 to
C:\ORACLE\ORADATA\ORCL\SYSAUX01.DBF
```

```
channel ORA_DISK_1: reading from backup piece
 C:\ORACLE\FLASH_RECOVERY_AREA\ORCL\BACKUPSET\2008_09_22
\O1_MF_NNNDF_TAG20080922T182631_4FJFXXVT_.BKP
channel ORA_DISK_1: piece
handle=C:\ORACLE\FLASH_RECOVERY_AREA\ORCL\BACKUPSET\2008_09_22
\O1_MF_NNNDF_TAG20080922T182631_4FJFXXVT_.BKP tag=TAG20080922T182631
channel ORA_DISK_1: restored backup piece 1
channel ORA_DISK_1: restore complete, elapsed time: 00:02:25
channel ORA_DISK_1: starting datafile backup set restore
channel ORA_DISK_1: specifying datafile(s) to restore from backup set
channel ORA_DISK_1: restoring datafile 00001 to
C:\ORACLE\ORADATA\ORCL\SYSTEM01.DBF
channel ORA_DISK_1: restoring datafile 00004 to
C:\ORACLE\ORADATA\ORCL\USERS01.DBF
channel ORA_DISK_1: restoring datafile 00005 to
C:\ORACLE\ORADATA\ORCL\UNDOTBS02.DBF
channel ORA_DISK_1: reading from backup piece
C:\ORACLE\FLASH_RECOVERY_AREA\ORCL\BACKUPSET\2008_09_28\
O1_MF_NNNDF_TAG20080928T165801_4G02ZZC7_.BKP
channel ORA_DISK_1: piece
 handle=C:\ORACLE\FLASH_RECOVERY_AREA\ORCL\BACKUPSET\2008_09_28
\O1_MF_NNNDF_TAG20080928T165801_4G02ZZC7_.BKP tag=TAG20080928T165801
channel ORA_DISK_1: restored backup piece 1
channel ORA_DISK_1: restore complete, elapsed time: 00:02:55
Finished restore at 28-SEP-08
RMAN> recover database noredo;
Starting recover at 28-SEP-08
using channel ORA_DISK_1
Finished recover at 28-SEP-08
RMAN> alter database open;
database opened
```

Recovering a Database in ARCHIVELOG Mode

If your database is in ARCHIVELOG mode, then your recovery options might include a complete database recovery or an online datafile or tablespace recovery. Another option is point-in-time recovery, which we discuss later in this chapter. Other more advanced options, including tablespace point-in-time recovery, are also available. These are covered in Chapter 8 of this book.

Complete recovery is called for when all or most of the datafiles of the database have been lost. Tablespace or datafile recovery is a better solution if you have lost only a few datafiles or perhaps all datafiles of one or two tablespaces. Let's look at each of these recovery methods in more detail next.

Complete Database Recovery in ARCHIVELOG Mode

A *complete* database recovery in ARCHIVELOG mode is required when most or all of the database datafiles have been lost. In this mode, the database is shut down (if it has not already done so itself because of the loss of datafiles). It is then mounted and recovered. Here are the steps to follow for a complete database recovery in ARCHIVELOG mode:

1. Shut down the database if it is not already down.

2. If you have lost your control file or spfile, you will need to reference the section, "Other Basic Recovery Topics" which appears later in this chapter. To start any RMAN recovery, you must have a control file and an spfile or parameter file.

3. If you are not already logged into RMAN (for example, if you had to restore your control file), then log into RMAN now.

4. Mount your database with the `startup mount` command.

5. Issue the RMAN `restore database` command.

6. Issue the RMAN `recover database` command. The command will restore the needed incremental backups and archived redo logs, recovering the database to the point of failure.

7. Open the database with the `alter database open` command. If you restored your control file, you will need to use the `alter database open resetlogs` command.

Here is an example of a recovery in ARCHIVELOG mode:

```
RMAN> shutdown abort
using target database control file instead of recovery catalog
Oracle instance shut down
RMAN> startup mount
connected to target database (not started)
Oracle instance started
database mounted
Total System Global Area     397557760 bytes
Fixed Size                     1333452 bytes
Variable Size                339740468 bytes
Database Buffers              50331648 bytes
Redo Buffers                   6152192 bytes
RMAN> restore database;
```

```
Starting restore at 28-SEP-08
allocated channel: ORA_DISK_1
channel ORA_DISK_1: SID=154 device type=DISK
channel ORA_DISK_1: starting datafile backup set restore
channel ORA_DISK_1: specifying datafile(s) to restore from backup set
channel ORA_DISK_1: restoring datafile 00002 to
C:\ORACLE\ORADATA\ORCL\SYSAUX01.DBF
channel ORA_DISK_1: reading from backup piece
 C:\ORACLE\FLASH_RECOVERY_AREA\ORCL\BACKUPSET\2008_09_22
\O1_MF_NNNDF_TAG20080922T182631_4FJFXXVT_.BKP
channel ORA_DISK_1: piece
handle=C:\ORACLE\FLASH_RECOVERY_AREA\ORCL\BACKUPSET\2008_09_22
\O1_MF_NNNDF_TAG20080922T182631_4FJFXXVT_.BKP tag=TAG20080922T182631
channel ORA_DISK_1: restored backup piece 1
channel ORA_DISK_1: restore complete, elapsed time: 00:02:35
channel ORA_DISK_1: starting datafile backup set restore
channel ORA_DISK_1: specifying datafile(s) to restore from backup set
channel ORA_DISK_1: restoring datafile 00001 to
 C:\ORACLE\ORADATA\ORCL\SYSTEM01.DBF
channel ORA_DISK_1: restoring datafile 00004 to
 C:\ORACLE\ORADATA\ORCL\USERS01.DBF
channel ORA_DISK_1: restoring datafile 00005 to
 C:\ORACLE\ORADATA\ORCL\UNDOTBS02.DBF
channel ORA_DISK_1: reading from backup piece
C:\ORACLE\FLASH_RECOVERY_AREA\ORCL\BACKUPSET\2008_09_28
\O1_MF_NNNDF_TAG20080928T172015_4G049OQX_.BKP
channel ORA_DISK_1: piece
handle=C:\ORACLE\FLASH_RECOVERY_AREA\ORCL\BACKUPSET\2008_09_28
\O1_MF_NNNDF_TAG20080928T172015_4G049OQX_.BKP tag=TAG20080928T172015
channel ORA_DISK_1: restored backup piece 1
channel ORA_DISK_1: restore complete, elapsed time: 00:02:45
Finished restore at 28-SEP-08
RMAN> recover database;
Starting recover at 28-SEP-08
using channel ORA_DISK_1
starting media recovery
media recovery complete, elapsed time: 00:00:03
Finished recover at 28-SEP-08
RMAN> Alter database open;
database opened
```

> **NOTE** If you added a datafile or a tablespace to the database after your last RMAN backup, RMAN will add that tablespace or datafile for you automatically during a restore. Additionally, RMAN will re-create any tempfiles needed during a restore process automatically.

In Exercise 6.1, you'll restore your ARCHIVELOG-mode database with RMAN.

EXERCISE 6.1

Restoring Your ARCHIVELOG-Mode Database with RMAN

This activity builds on the backup done in Exercise 4.2 from Chapter 4. You should have completed Exercise 4.2 prior to executing this activity. Please note that the output you experience from this exercise will probably differ from the output shown in this exercise.

1. Complete Exercise 4.2.

2. Log into the database as SYS using SQL*Plus:

```
C:\oracle>set oracle_sid=orcl
C:\oracle>sqlplus sys as sysdba
SQL*Plus: Release 11.1.0.6.0 - Production on Fri Oct 3 00:31:07 2008
Copyright (c) 1982, 2007, Oracle.  All rights reserved.
Enter password:
Connected to:
Oracle Database 11g Enterprise Edition Release 11.1.0.6.0 - Production
With the Partitioning, OLAP, Data Mining and
Real Application Testing options
SQL>
```

3. Determine the location of the database datafiles by issuing the `select file_name from dba_data_files;` query:

```
SQL> select file_name from dba_data_files;
FILE_NAME
----------------------------------------------------------------
C:\ORACLE\FLASH_RECOVERY_AREA\ORCL\DATAFILE\O1_MF_USERS_4G2Q1YTC_.DBF
C:\ORACLE\ORADATA\ORCL\UNDOTBS01.DBF
C:\ORACLE\ORADATA\ORCL\SYSAUX01.DBF
C:\ORACLE\ORADATA\ORCL\SYSTEM01.DBF
```

4. Shut down the database:

```
SQL> shutdown abort
ORACLE instance shut down.
```

5. Exit SQL*Plus:

```
SQL> quit
Disconnected from Oracle Database 11g Enterprise Edition
Release 11.1.0.6.0 - Production
With the Partitioning, OLAP, Data Mining and
Real Application Testing options
C:\oracle>
```

6. From the operating system prompt, delete all the database datafiles listed in step 3. Be careful not to do a wildcard delete because you might delete files in that directory that you do not want to remove, such as the online redo logs or the database control files.

```
C:\oracle>Del C:\ORACLE\FLASH_RECOVERY_AREA\ORCL\DATAFILE\O1_MF_
USERS_4G2Q1YTC_.DBF
C:\oracle>Del C:\ORACLE\ORADATA\ORCL\UNDOTBS01.DBF
C:\oracle>Del C:\ORACLE\ORADATA\ORCL\SYSAUX01.DBF
C:\oracle>Del C:\ORACLE\ORADATA\ORCL\SYSTEM01.DBF
```

7. Log into the database as SYS using SQL*Plus:

```
C:\oracle>sqlplus sys as sysdba
SQL*Plus: Release 11.1.0.6.0 - Production on Fri Oct 3 00:35:25 2008
Copyright (c) 1982, 2007, Oracle.  All rights reserved.
Enter password:
Connected to an idle instance.
```

8. Start the database. Notice the error that you receive:

```
SQL> startup
ORACLE instance started.
Total System Global Area  364081152 bytes
Fixed Size                  1333228 bytes
Variable Size             264243220 bytes
Database Buffers           92274688 bytes
Redo Buffers                6230016 bytes
Database mounted.
ORA-01157: cannot identify/lock data file 1 - see DBWR trace file
ORA-01110: data file 1: 'C:\ORACLE\ORADATA\ORCL\SYSTEM01.DBF'
```

9. Shut down the database:

```
SQL> shutdown abort
ORACLE instance shut down.
```

EXERCISE 6.1 *(continued)*

10. Exit SQL*Plus:

```
SQL> quit
Disconnected from Oracle Database 11g Enterprise Edition
Release 11.1.0.6.0 - Production
With the Partitioning, OLAP, Data Mining and
Real Application Testing options
C:\oracle>
```

11. Start RMAN. We will assume you are not using a recovery catalog during this exercise.

```
C:\oracle>rman target=/
Recovery Manager: Release 11.1.0.6.0 -
Production on Fri Oct 3 00:37:44 2008
Copyright (c) 1982, 2007, Oracle.  All rights reserved.
connected to target database (not started)
```

12. Start up the database with the Startup mount command from RMAN:

```
RMAN> startup mount
Oracle instance started
database mounted
Total System Global Area     364081152 bytes
Fixed Size                     1333228 bytes
Variable Size                264243220 bytes
Database Buffers              92274688 bytes
Redo Buffers                   6230016 bytes
```

13. Restore the database files with the restore database command:

```
RMAN> restore database;
Starting restore at 10/03/2008 00:38:55
using target database control file instead of recovery catalog
allocated channel: ORA_DISK_1
channel ORA_DISK_1: SID=155 device type=DISK
channel ORA_DISK_1: starting datafile backup set restore
channel ORA_DISK_1: specifying datafile(s) to restore from backup set
channel ORA_DISK_1: restoring datafile 00001 to
C:\ORACLE\ORADATA\ORCL\SYSTEM01.DBF
channel ORA_DISK_1: restoring datafile 00002 to
C:\ORACLE\ORADATA\ORCL\SYSAUX01.DBF
channel ORA_DISK_1: restoring datafile 00003 to
```

```
C:\ORACLE\ORADATA\ORCL\UNDOTBS01.DBF
channel ORA_DISK_1: restoring datafile 00004 to
C:\ORACLE\FLASH_RECOVERY_AREA\ORCL\DATAFILE\O1_MF_USERS_4G2Q1YTC_.DBF
channel ORA_DISK_1: reading from backup piece
C:\ORACLE\FLASH_RECOVERY_AREA\ORCL\BACKUPSET\2008_10_03
\O1_MF_NNNDF_TAG20081003T001928_4GCGCQQ4_.BKP
channel ORA_DISK_1: piece
handle=C:\ORACLE\FLASH_RECOVERY_AREA\ORCL\BACKUPSET\2008_10_03
\O1_MF_NNNDF_TAG20081003T001928_4GCGCQQ4_.BKP tag=TAG20081003T001928
channel ORA_DISK_1: restored backup piece 1
channel ORA_DISK_1: restore complete, elapsed time: 00:04:05
Finished restore at 10/03/2008 00:43:02
RMAN>
```

14. Recover the database with the recover database command:

```
RMAN> recover database;
Starting recover at 10/03/2008 01:43:59
using channel ORA_DISK_1
starting media recovery
media recovery complete, elapsed time: 00:00:04
Finished recover at 10/03/2008 01:44:05
RMAN>
```

15. Open the database with the alter database open command:

```
RMAN> alter database open;
database opened
```

The database is open.

Datafile or Tablespace Recovery in ARCHIVELOG Mode

If you have lost one or a few database datafiles, or perhaps all the datafiles lost are part of a tablespace, you can perform recovery actions specific to those few lost datafiles rather than to the database as a whole. *Datafile recoveries* and *tablespace recoveries* can be far faster than recovering the entire database with a complete recovery.

Some datafile and tablespace recoveries require that the database be in MOUNT mode. If you have lost the SYSTEM tablespace or the active UNDO tablespace (or an inactive tablespace that contained transactions when the database was shut down), then your recovery will have to be done with the database mounted.

The best recoveries (if there is really any kind of recovery that is even considered good) are those that your users know nothing about. If the datafile or tablespace that was lost was not the SYSTEM or active UNDO tablespace, then you can recover that datafile or tablespace while the rest of the database is still online. Thus, unless the users need access to the tablespace that is being restored, they will never know that you were in the throes of some form of recovery.

In the following sections, we will address these two kinds of datafile and tablespace recoveries. First we will address recovery of a datafile or tablespace when the SYSTEM or active UNDO tablespace is down and the database is not open. We will then address datafile and tablespace recoveries when the database is open and running.

Recovering Critical Database Datafiles and/or Tablespaces with the Database Down

If the SYSTEM or the active UNDO tablespace, or datafiles associated with those tablespaces, are lost, then you will have to recover with the database shut down. In fact, if datafiles associated with these tablespaces are lost, it's likely that the database will have crashed anyway. You can use the `restore datafile` or `restore tablespace` RMAN command to restore the lost datafiles or tablespaces quickly, in turn getting the database recovered as quickly as possible.

To restore a database datafile or tablespace with the database shut down, follow these steps.

1. If the database is not already shut down, try to force a checkpoint and then shut down the database as normally as possible. It is possible that when you force the checkpoint, the database will crash.

2. If you have lost your control file or spfile, you will need to reference the section, "Other Basic Recovery Topics" which appears later in this chapter. To start any RMAN recovery, you must have a control file and an spfile or parameter file.

3. Mount your database with the `startup mount` command.

4. You will use the RMAN `restore` command to restore the datafiles or tablespaces. If you have lost all or most of the datafiles related to a given tablespace, then issue the RMAN `restore tablespace` command. If you have lost one or just a few datafiles, use the `restore datafile` command. Once the restore is complete, you will be returned to the RMAN prompt.

5. You now need to recover the database with the RMAN `recover` command. This will apply any incremental backups and any archived redo logs to the datafiles being restored. If you used the `restore tablespace` command, recover the tablespace with the `recover tablespace` command. If you used the `restore datafile` command, use the `recover datafile` command to start recovery. Once recovery is complete, you will be returned to the RMAN prompt.

6. Open the database with the `alter database open` command. If you restored your control file, you will need to use the `alter database open resetlogs` command.

In this example, we will try to start up our database from the RMAN prompt only to find that the SYSTEM tablespace datafile is missing for some odd reason:

```
RMAN> startup
Oracle instance started
database mounted
RMAN-00571: ============================================================
RMAN-00569: =============== ERROR MESSAGE STACK FOLLOWS ===============
RMAN-00571: ============================================================
RMAN-03002: failure of startup command at 09/28/2008 17:37:53
ORA-01157: cannot identify/lock data file 1 - see DBWR trace file
ORA-01110: data file 1: 'C:\ORACLE\ORADATA\ORCL\SYSTEM01.DBF'
```

We could, of course, restore the entire database, but the size of the SYSTEM tablespace/datafile is a very small part of the overall size of the database. So we will just restore and recover the SYSTEM tablespace. Note that the SYSTEM tablespace is a critical tablespace; thus, this recovery cannot be done online:

```
RMAN> startup
Oracle instance started
database mounted
RMAN-00571: ============================================================
RMAN-00569: =============== ERROR MESSAGE STACK FOLLOWS ===============
RMAN-00571: ============================================================
RMAN-03002: failure of startup command at 09/28/2008 17:37:53
ORA-01157: cannot identify/lock data file 1 - see DBWR trace file
ORA-01110: data file 1: 'C:\ORACLE\ORADATA\ORCL\SYSTEM01.DBF'
RMAN> restore tablespace system;
Starting restore at 28-SEP-08
using target database control file instead of recovery catalog
allocated channel: ORA_DISK_1
channel ORA_DISK_1: SID=153 device type=DISK
channel ORA_DISK_1: starting datafile backup set restore
channel ORA_DISK_1: specifying datafile(s) to restore from backup set
channel ORA_DISK_1: restoring datafile 00001 to
C:\ORACLE\ORADATA\ORCL\SYSTEM01.DBF
channel ORA_DISK_1: reading from backup piece
C:\ORACLE\FLASH_RECOVERY_AREA\ORCL\BACKUPSET\2008_09_28
\O1_MF_NNNDF_TAG20080928T172015_4G049OQX_.BKP
channel ORA_DISK_1: piece
handle=C:\ORACLE\FLASH_RECOVERY_AREA\ORCL\BACKUPSET\2008_09_28
```

```
\O1_MF_NNNDF_TAG20080928T172015_4G049OQX_.BKP tag=TAG20080928T172015
channel ORA_DISK_1: restored backup piece 1
channel ORA_DISK_1: restore complete, elapsed time: 00:03:35
Finished restore at 28-SEP-08
RMAN> recover tablespace system;
Starting recover at 28-SEP-08
using channel ORA_DISK_1
starting media recovery
media recovery complete, elapsed time: 00:00:03
Finished recover at 28-SEP-08
RMAN> alter database open;
database opened
```

Restoring Datafiles to Different Locations

If during a recovery you need to restore datafiles to a different location, you will need to use the RMAN set newname command to reset the location of each datafile that is to be relocated. For example, if you wanted to relocate the USERS01.DBF datafile from c:\ oracle\oradata\orcl to d:\oracle\oradata\orcl during an RMAN recovery, you would issue this command:

```
set newname for 'c:\oracle\oradata\orcl\users01.dbf' to
'd:\oracle\oradata\orcl\users01.dbf';
```

Note that if you use the set newname command, you will have to include it and all restore-and-recovery-related commands within a run block, as shown here:

```
run { set newname for datafile 'c:\oracle\oradata\orcl\users01.dbf' to
'c:\oracle\oradata\orcltwo\users01.dbf';
restore database;
recover database; }
```

Recovering Noncritical Database Datafile and/or Tablespaces with the Database Open

When you have lost a datafile or a few datafiles or all the datafiles of one or several tablespaces, RMAN provides the ability to restore those datafiles online without having to shut down the database. This is known as an *online datafile recovery* or *online tablespace recovery*. Online recoveries allow users to access unaffected tablespaces/datafiles of the database without knowing that other parts of the database are unavailable. To be sure, anyone who tries to use the parts of the database that are being recovered will know that something is not right, but something is better than nothing, right?

The SYSTEM and active UNDO tablespaces are considered critical tablespaces and thus are the only tablespaces that will require recovery of the database with the database down (see the previous section for a discussion on recovery of these critical tablespaces). Any other tablespace can be restored with the database running. Let's look at online database recoveries with datafiles and then tablespaces in the next sections.

 You never need to restore temporary files that are associated with temporary tablespaces. First, RMAN will never back up the temporary tablespace, because it does not need to. All RMAN needs to know is that the temporary tablespace exists, and it knows this by virtue of reading the control file of the database. Knowing what temporary tablespace and what tempfiles are needed, RMAN will simply add the tempfiles to the temporary tablespace after a complete or point-in-time database restore. No datafile restore needed!

Preparing to Restore Datafiles or Tablespaces Online

It may be that your database is already shut down and will not start because of the missing datafiles. It may or may not make sense to open the database before starting the restore so users can access unaffected data. To open the database when noncritical datafiles are missing, follow these steps:

1. From the RMAN prompt, issue the startup command. An error will appear indicating the datafile that is missing. This will report on just a single missing datafile. You can use the report schema command to report on any other missing datafiles. Any datafile with a size of 0 will be a missing datafile and will likely need to be restored. Here is an example of the output from the list schema command that indicates the USERS01.DBF datafile is missing. Note the 0 value in the Size(MB) column:

```
RMAN> report schema;
Report of database schema for database with db_unique_name ORCL
List of Permanent Datafiles
===========================
File Size(MB) Tablespace           RB segs Datafile Name
---- -------- -------------------- ------- ------------------------
1    700      SYSTEM               ***
C:\ORACLE\ORADATA\ORCL\SYSTEM01.DBF
2    716      SYSAUX               ***
C:\ORACLE\ORADATA\ORCL\SYSAUX01.DBF
4    0        USERS                ***
C:\ORACLE\ORADATA\ORCL\USERS01.DBF
5    30       UNDOTBS2             ***
C:\ORACLE\ORADATA\ORCL\UNDOTBS02.DBF
```

2. From the RMAN prompt, take all the datafiles or tablespaces to be recovered offline. You do this by using the RMAN `sql` command followed by the appropriate `alter database datafile offline` command or the `alter tablespace offline` command.

3. From the RMAN prompt, issue the `alter database open` command. The database should open without complaining about any missing datafiles.

Here is a case where we have tried to start our database and the USERS01.DBF datafile is not available. We will make sure that this is the only datafile that needs to be restored. We then take the datafile offline and open the database:

```
RMAN> startup
Oracle instance started
database mounted
RMAN-00571: ===========================================================
RMAN-00569: =============== ERROR MESSAGE STACK FOLLOWS ===============
RMAN-00571: ===========================================================
RMAN-03002: failure of startup command at 09/28/2008 17:50:49
ORA-01157: cannot identify/lock data file 3 - see DBWR trace file
ORA-01110: data file 3: 'C:\ORACLE\ORADATA\ORCL\USERS01.DBF'
RMAN> report schema;
Report of database schema for database with db_unique_name ORCL
List of Permanent Datafiles
===========================
File Size(MB) Tablespace        RB segs Datafile Name
---- -------- ----------------- ------- -----------------------
1    700      SYSTEM            ***     C:\ORACLE\ORADATA\ORCL\SYSTEM01.DBF
2    716      SYSAUX            ***     C:\ORACLE\ORADATA\ORCL\SYSAUX01.DBF
3    0        USERS             ***     C:\ORACLE\ORADATA\ORCL\USERS01.DBF
5    30       UNDOTBS2          ***     C:\ORACLE\ORADATA\ORCL\UNDOTBS02.DBF

List of Temporary Files
=======================
File Size(MB) Tablespace        Maxsize(MB) Tempfile Name
---- -------- ----------------- ----------- --------------------
1    20       TEMP              32767       C:\ORACLE\ORADATA\ORCL\TEMP01.DBF
RMAN> sql 'alter database datafile 3 offline';
sql statement: alter database datafile 3 offline
RMAN> alter database open;
database opened
```

Restoring Database Datafiles Online

Once the database is up and running or if the database was already running, follow these steps to restore one or more missing datafiles:

1. From the RMAN prompt, take the datafile or datafiles offline using the RMAN `sql` command calling the `alter database datafile offline` command. Do this for each datafile that you need to take offline.

2. From the RMAN prompt, restore the datafiles using the `restore datafile` command. You can restore one or multiple datafiles in one shot. You will be returned to the RMAN prompt once the restore is complete.

3. Having restored the datafiles, use the `recover datafile` command to recover each specific datafile. This will apply any incremental backups and archived redo logs to the restored datafile. You will be returned to the RMAN prompt once the recovery is complete.

4. Bring the datafile(s) back online using the RMAN `sql` command to issue the `alter database datafile online` SQL command. This will bring each datafile online, completing the recovery process.

In this example, the USERS01.DBF datafile is already offline (we offlined the datafile in the earlier example). We will restore that datafile (referring to it by its datafile number) and then recover it. Finally, we will bring the datafile online so that the database may access it:

```
RMAN> restore datafile 3;
Starting restore at 28-SEP-08
allocated channel: ORA_DISK_1
channel ORA_DISK_1: SID=136 device type=DISK
channel ORA_DISK_1: starting datafile backup set restore
channel ORA_DISK_1: specifying datafile(s) to restore from backup set
channel ORA_DISK_1: restoring datafile 00003 to
C:\ORACLE\ORADATA\ORCL\USERS01.DBF
channel ORA_DISK_1: reading from backup piece
C:\ORACLE\FLASH_RECOVERY_AREA\ORCL\BACKUPSET\2008_09_28
\O1_MF_NNNDF_TAG20080928T185206_4GO9OW7B_.BKP
channel ORA_DISK_1: piece
handle=C:\ORACLE\FLASH_RECOVERY_AREA\ORCL\BACKUPSET\2008_09_28
\O1_MF_NNNDF_TAG20080928T185206_4GO9OW7B_.BKP tag=TAG20080928T185206
channel ORA_DISK_1: restored backup piece 1
channel ORA_DISK_1: restore complete, elapsed time: 00:00:15
Finished restore at 28-SEP-08
RMAN> recover datafile 3;
Starting recover at 28-SEP-08
using channel ORA_DISK_1
```

```
starting media recovery
media recovery complete, elapsed time: 00:00:02
Finished recover at 28-SEP-08
RMAN> sql 'alter database datafile 3 online';
sql statement: alter database datafile 3 online
```

Restoring Database Tablespaces Online

If you have lost most or all datafiles related to one or more tablespaces, it might be easier to recover the entire tablespace rather than individual datafiles. Of course, a tablespace recovery really is a datafile recovery; it just makes RMAN do the extra legwork to figure out which datafiles need to be restored. Once the database is up and running or if the database was already running, follow these steps to restore one or more tablespaces:

1. From the RMAN prompt, take the tablespace(s) offline using the RMAN `sql` command calling the `alter tablespace offline` command. Do this for each tablespace that you need to take offline.

2. From the RMAN prompt, restore the tablespace using the `restore tablespace` command. You can restore one or multiple tablespaces in one shot. You will be returned to the RMAN prompt once the restore is complete.

3. Having restored the tablespace datafiles, use the `recover tablespace` command to recover the tablespace and its associated datafiles. This will apply any incremental backups and archived redo logs to the restored tablespace. You will be returned to the RMAN prompt once the recovery is complete.

4. Bring the datafile(s) back online using the RMAN `sql` command to issue the `alter database datafile online` SQL command. This will bring each datafile online, completing the recovery process.

Here is an example of a recovery of the USERS tablespace from RMAN (note that if the database was running, we could use the `alter tablespace offline` command to take the tablespace offline):

```
RMAN> startup
Oracle instance started
database mounted
RMAN-00571: ===========================================================
RMAN-00569: =============== ERROR MESSAGE STACK FOLLOWS ===============
RMAN-00571: ===========================================================
RMAN-03002: failure of startup command at 09/28/2008 20:01:30
ORA-01157: cannot identify/lock data file 3 - see DBWR trace file
ORA-01110: data file 3: 'C:\ORACLE\ORADATA\ORCL\USERS01.DBF'
RMAN> sql 'alter tablespace users datafile offline';
sql statement: alter tablespace users datafile offline
```

```
RMAN> alter database open;
database opened
RMAN> restore tablespace users;
Starting restore at 28-SEP-08
using target database control file instead of recovery catalog
allocated channel: ORA_DISK_1
channel ORA_DISK_1: SID=153 device type=DISK
channel ORA_DISK_1: starting datafile backup set restore
channel ORA_DISK_1: specifying datafile(s) to restore from backup set
channel ORA_DISK_1: restoring datafile 00003 to
C:\ORACLE\ORADATA\ORCL\USERS01.DBF
channel ORA_DISK_1: reading from backup piece
C:\ORACLE\FLASH_RECOVERY_AREA\ORCL\BACKUPSET\2008_09_28
\O1_MF_NNNDF_TAG20080928T185206_4G09OW7B_.BKP
channel ORA_DISK_1: piece
handle=C:\ORACLE\FLASH_RECOVERY_AREA\ORCL\BACKUPSET\2008_09_28
\O1_MF_NNNDF_TAG20080928T185206_4G09OW7B_.BKP tag=TAG20080928T185206
channel ORA_DISK_1: restored backup piece 1
channel ORA_DISK_1: restore complete, elapsed time: 00:00:15
Finished restore at 28-SEP-08
RMAN> recover tablespace users;
Starting recover at 28-SEP-08
using channel ORA_DISK_1
starting media recovery
media recovery complete, elapsed time: 00:00:02
Finished recover at 28-SEP-08
RMAN> sql 'alter tablespace users online';
sql statement: alter tablespace users online
```

Recovering a Database Using Incomplete Recovery

We discussed *incomplete recovery* or *point-in-time recovery* back in Chapter 3. It is, essentially, restoring the database to some point in time that is not the current point in time. If you are not familiar with what incomplete recovery is, please review Chapter 3 for more details. In the following sections we will discuss point-in-time recoveries. First we will discuss the types of recoveries that are available and then we will discuss the mechanics of such recoveries.

Real World Scenario

What Happens If the Control File Has Lost the Backup Records

Most RMAN restores are easy and require only the use of the RMAN client. However, we've seen cases where the RMAN client was not enough. In one case, the database site had lost its recovery catalog, and the CONTROL_FILE_RECORD_KEEP_TIME parameter was set to 7 days. Guess what happened to all the RMAN metadata after 7 days when the recovery catalog was lost.

At the same time, we had a need to restore a database to a point in time of perhaps 30 days before to check on the state of some data. Of course, the metadata for the restore was not available. This was clearly a bad day.

There are several ways to address this problem. The Oracle Database 11g *RMAN* catalog command provides the ability to catalog backup set pieces in the database (this was not available prior to Oracle Database 10g). In the case of the loss listed earlier, we opted to write some PL/SQL and use the PL/SQL packages that RMAN uses itself to restore the backups from tape. RMAN uses a PL/SQL package called *dbms_backup_restore* to perform most backup and restore operations. Using this package (documented pretty well on Oracle's support site at metalink.oracle.com), we were able to restore a database from an older backup.

The bottom line is that as long as you have the backup set pieces, any RMAN backup can be restored. It just might take some time and effort and perhaps a bit of help from Oracle support.

Remember that point-in-time backups must be consistent. That means you have to restore the whole database to the specific point in time you are aiming for. Oracle offers the ability to do tablespace point-in-time recoveries, which we will discuss in Chapter 8.

Types of Point-in-Time Recovery

RMAN supports point-in-time recovery using the until clause of the restore and recover commands as seen in this example, where we will be restoring to 9/30/2008 at 18:00 hours:

```
Restore database until time '09/30/2008:18:00:00';
Recover database until time '09/30/2008:18:00:00';
```

When using a run block, you will use the set command to set the recovery window for RMAN, as shown in this example:

```
Run {
Set until time until time '09/30/2008:18:00:00';
Restore database;
Recover database;
}
```

You can do point-in-time recovery using the following:

Time   The *Time-based point-in-time recovery* method is based on the timestamps in the online redo logs. RMAN will restore the database to the closest possible timestamp listed in the command. You can find the timestamp ranges contained in specific online redo logs by querying the FIRST_TIME column of the V$LOG_HISTORY view for each redo log. In this example, RMAN will restore the database to 9/29/2008 at 15:00:00:

```
restore database until time '09/29/2008:15:00:00';
recover database until time '09/29/2008:15:00:00';
alter database open resetlogs;
```

SCN   The *SCN-based point-in-time recovery* method is based on recovery to a specific SCN in the database. You can determine the current SCN of the database from the CURRENT_SCN column of the V$DATABASE view. You can determine the SCN range contained within a given redo log by querying the FIRST_CHANGE# and NEXT_CHANGE# columns of the V$LOG_HISTORY view. Here is an example of an SCN-based point-in-time recovery:

```
restore database until SCN 12345;
recover database until SCN 12345;
alter database open resetlogs;
```

Log sequence number   The *log sequence number point-in-time recovery* method is based on recovery up to, and including, a specific log sequence number. Log sequence numbers for individual redo logs can be found in the V$LOG_HISTORY and V$LOG views. Here is an example of a point-in-time recovery based on a log sequence number:

```
restore database until sequence 12345;
recover database until sequence 12345;
alter database open resetlogs;
```

In Exercise 6.2, you'll perform a point-in-time recovery with RMAN.

EXERCISE 6.2

Perform a Point-in-Time Recovery with RMAN

This activity builds on the backup done in Exercise 4.2 in Chapter 4. You should have completed Exercise 4.2 prior to executing this activity. Please note that the output you experience from this exercise will probably differ from the output shown in this exercise.

1. Complete Exercise 4.2.

2. Set the NLS_DATE_FORMAT environment variable from the operating system.

   In Unix (may vary based on the shell you are using):

   export NLS_DATE_FORMAT='mm/dd/yyyy hh24:mi:ss'

   In DOS:

   set NLS_DATE_FORMAT=mm/dd/yyyy hh24:mi:ss

3. Start RMAN. We will assume you are not using a recovery catalog during this exercise.

   ```
   C:\oracle>rman target=/
   Recovery Manager: Release 11.1.0.6.0 -
   Production on Fri Oct 3 00:37:44 2008
   Copyright (c) 1982, 2007, Oracle.  All rights reserved.
   connected to target database (not started)
   ```

4. Start up the database with the startup force mount command from RMAN.

   ```
   RMAN> startup force mount
   Oracle instance started
   database mounted
   Total System Global Area     364081152 bytes
   Fixed Size                     1333228 bytes
   Variable Size                264243220 bytes
   Database Buffers              92274688 bytes
   Redo Buffers                   6230016 bytes
   ```

5. Determine the current backups that are available for restore with the list backup of database summary command (to be discussed in Chapter 7):

   ```
   RMAN> list backup of database summary;
   List of Backups
   ===============
   ```

Key	TY	LV	S	Device Type	Completion Time	#Pieces	#Copies	Compressed	Tag
6	B	F	A	DISK	09/29/2008 14:07:23	1	1	NO	
SILVER_COPY									
11	B	F	A	DISK	10/02/2008 00:46:25	1	1	YES	

EXERCISE 6.2 *(continued)*

```
GOLD_COPY
17      B  F  A DISK          10/03/2008 00:25:19 1        1         YES
TAG20081003T001928
```

6. From the output generated in step 5, choose the date and time of the most current backup (in our case, it's 10/03/2008 at 00:25:19). We will restore the database to 10 minutes after this date and time (in our case, 10/03/2008 at 00:35:19).

7. Issue the `restore database until time` command to restore the database to the date and time selected. In our case, the command will be `restore database until time '10/03/2008:00:35:19'`; your command will have a different date and time (unless you have reset the clock so precisely that you got the same date!).

```
RMAN> restore database until time '10/03/2008:00:35:19';
Starting restore at 10/03/2008 01:57:31
allocated channel: ORA_DISK_1
channel ORA_DISK_1: SID=155 device type=DISK
channel ORA_DISK_1: starting datafile backup set restore
channel ORA_DISK_1: specifying datafile(s) to restore from backup set
channel ORA_DISK_1: restoring datafile 00001 to
C:\ORACLE\ORADATA\ORCL\SYSTEM01.DBF
channel ORA_DISK_1: restoring datafile 00002 to
C:\ORACLE\ORADATA\ORCL\SYSAUX01.DBF
channel ORA_DISK_1: restoring datafile 00003 to
C:\ORACLE\ORADATA\ORCL\UNDOTBS01.DBF
channel ORA_DISK_1: restoring datafile 00004 to
C:\ORACLE\FLASH_RECOVERY_AREA\ORCL\DATAFILE\O1_MF_USERS_4G2Q1YTC_.DBF
channel ORA_DISK_1: reading from backup piece
C:\ORACLE\FLASH_RECOVERY_AREA\ORCL\BACKUPSET\2008_10_03
\O1_MF_NNNDF_TAG20081003T001928_4GCGCQQ4_.BKP
channel ORA_DISK_1: piece
handle=C:\ORACLE\FLASH_RECOVERY_AREA\ORCL\BACKUPSET\2008_10_03
\O1_MF_NNNDF_TAG20081003T001928_4GCGCQQ4_.BKP tag=TAG20081003T001928
channel ORA_DISK_1: restored backup piece 1
channel ORA_DISK_1: restore complete, elapsed time: 00:07:15
Finished restore at 10/03/2008 02:04:47
```

8. Recover the database with the `recover database until time` command. Our command would be `recover database until time '10/03/2008:00:35:19'`; your command will have a different date and time.

```
RMAN> recover database until time '10/03/2008:00:35:19';
Starting recover at 10/03/2008 02:06:01
```

```
using channel ORA_DISK_1
starting media recovery
media recovery complete, elapsed time: 00:00:03
Finished recover at 10/03/2008 02:06:05
```

9. Open the database with the `alter database open resetlogs` command:

```
RMAN> alter database open resetlogs;
database opened
```

The database is open.

What Can I Recover To?

You may want to make sure you can actually recover to the point in time that you are interested in before you haul off and try the recovery. Nothing makes for a worse day than trying to do a point-in-time restore, after having removed the existing datafiles, than finding out that you can't do the restore.

The `restore validate` command can come in handy here. You can use this command to make sure that all of the backup set pieces you will need to restore your database are available. This includes backup sets for datafile backups and archived redo logs as well as any datafile image copies. Here is an example of the `restore validate` command for a point-in-time database recovery:

```
RMAN> restore database until time 'sysdate -1/24' validate;
Starting restore at 28-SEP-08
using channel ORA_DISK_1
channel ORA_DISK_1: starting validation of datafile backup set
channel ORA_DISK_1: reading from backup piece
C:\ORACLE\FLASH_RECOVERY_AREA\ORCL\BACKUPSET\2008_09_28
\O1_MF_NNNDF_TAG20080928T185206_4G09OW7B_.BKP
channel ORA_DISK_1: piece
handle=C:\ORACLE\FLASH_RECOVERY_AREA\ORCL\BACKUPSET\2008_09_28
\O1_MF_NNNDF_TAG20080928T185206_4G09OW7B_.BKP tag=TAG20080928T185206
channel ORA_DISK_1: restored backup piece 1
channel ORA_DISK_1: validation complete, elapsed time: 00:00:25
Finished restore at 28-SEP-08
```

Point-in-Time Recovery Mechanics

Regardless of the type of point-in-time recovery you are going to do, the mechanics are the same. During a point-in-time recovery, the database must be in MOUNT mode. There is no online point-in-time recovery for an entire Oracle database (though RMAN does offer tablespace point-in-time recovery, which can be done online).

Once the point-in-time recovery is complete, you will open the database with the `alter database open resetlogs` command. This will reset (or re-create if need be) the online redo logs of the database and open it for business. The end result is a new incarnation of the database (see Chapter 3 for more on database incarnations), which can impact future backups. Oracle Database 11g and RMAN will be able to use the same backup to restore the database (as well as any old and new archived redo logs). Still, it's probably a good idea to perform another backup of your database, as it just makes things cleaner and easier.

Here is a list of the RMAN commands needed to perform a time-based point-in-time recovery to September 29, 2008, at 15:00 hours:

```
shutdown abort
startup mount
restore database until time '09/29/2008:15:00:00';
recover database until time '09/29/2008:15:00:00';
alter database open resetlogs;
```

And here is the result of the execution of those commands:

```
C:\Documents and Settings\Robert>rman target=/
Recovery Manager: Release 11.1.0.6.0 - Production on Wed Oct 1 22:30:48 2008
Copyright (c) 1982, 2007, Oracle.  All rights reserved.
connected to target database: ORCL (DBID=1194488809)
RMAN> shutdown abort
Oracle instance shut down
RMAN> startup mount
connected to target database (not started)
Oracle instance started
database mounted
Total System Global Area    364081152 bytes
Fixed Size                    1333228 bytes
Variable Size               239077396 bytes
Database Buffers            117440512 bytes
Redo Buffers                  6230016 bytes
RMAN> restore database until time '09/29/2008:15:00:00';
Starting restore at 10/01/2008 22:32:44
allocated channel: ORA_DISK_1
channel ORA_DISK_1: SID=151 device type=DISK
```

```
channel ORA_DISK_1: starting datafile backup set restore
channel ORA_DISK_1: specifying datafile(s) to restore from backup set
channel ORA_DISK_1: restoring datafile 00001 to
C:\ORACLE\ORADATA\ORCL\SYSTEM01.DBF
channel ORA_DISK_1: restoring datafile 00002 to
C:\ORACLE\ORADATA\ORCL\SYSAUX01.DBF
channel ORA_DISK_1: restoring datafile 00003 to
C:\ORACLE\ORADATA\ORCL\UNDOTBS01.DBF
channel ORA_DISK_1: restoring datafile 00004 to
C:\ORACLE\FLASH_RECOVERY_AREA\ORCL
\DATAFILE\O1_MF_USERS_4G2Q1YTC_.DBF
channel ORA_DISK_1: reading from backup piece
C:\ORACLE\FLASH_RECOVERY_AREA\ORCL
\BACKUPSET\2008_09_29\O1_MF_NNNDF_SILVER_COPY_4G2DQT1Y_.BKP
RMAN> recover database until time '09/29/2008:15:00:00';
Starting recover at 10/02/2008 00:09:47
using channel ORA_DISK_1
starting media recovery
archived log for thread 1 with sequence 5 is already on disk as file
C:\ORACLE\PRODUCT\11.1.0\DB_1\RDBMS\ARC00005_0666708076.001
archived log for thread 1 with sequence 6 is already on disk as file
C:\ORACLE\FLASH_RECOVERY_AREA\ORCL\ARCHIVELOG\2008_09_30
\O1_MF_1_6_4G4QPYYR_.ARC
archived log file name=
C:\ORACLE\PRODUCT\11.1.0\DB_1\RDBMS\ARC00005_0666708076.001
thread=1 sequence=5
media recovery complete, elapsed time: 00:00:14
Finished recover at 10/02/2008 00:10:03
RMAN> alter database open resetlogs;
database opened
```

You could also have executed this restore using the following commands:

```
shutown abort
startup mount
run {
set until time '09/30/2008:18:00:00';
restore database;
recover database;
}
sql 'alter database open resetlogs';
```

One time that you might need to perform point-in-time recovery is during a database recovery after a complete loss of the online redo logs of the database. This might include cases where just the online redo logs were lost or cases when the entire database was lost, including the online redo logs. While it is possible to save your database data in the event of such a loss (see Chapter 3 for more information on such a case), it is likely that you will have to perform a point-in-time recovery to get your database operational again. This will, of course, result in some data loss.

You can also restore databases using tags. A tag allows you to choose a specific backup image that you want to use for the restore. You can also use a tag during a recovery to indicate specific incremental backups that you want to use for a restore. When you use tags, Oracle will still do a complete recovery unless you use the `until time` parameter to indicate that you want to recover to a specific point in time.

Here is an example where we are restoring the database using the tag `gold_copy`:

```
shutdown immediate
startup mount
restore database from tag 'gold_copy';
recover database from tag 'gold_copy';
alter database open;
```

We discussed database incarnations in Chapter 3. Sometimes for specific types of RMAN recoveries you will need to reset the database incarnation. We will cover this in more detail in Chapter 8.

Using Image Copies to Recover Your Database

Recall that an *image copy* is an exact copy of a given database datafile. You can use image copies to restore your database. This can provide for quick database recovery, though the image copies will require much more storage than a compressed backup set piece.

Oracle provides the `switch` command to use in place of the `restore` command. This will essentially change the control file so it will point to the datafile copy(ies). You then would call the `recover` command to apply any incremental backups and archived redo logs to restore the datafile(s) or tablespace(s). You can switch the entire database, tablespaces, or specific datafiles depending on your needs. Here is an example where we are restoring datafile 4:

```
Sql 'alter database datafile 4 offline';
Switch datafile 4 to copy '/oracle/backup/users_01.dbf';
Recover datafile 4;
Sql 'alter database datafile 4 online';
```

Note that if you are making image copies and backup-set copies, RMAN will determine which to use during a normal restore operation. This includes image copies that are updated with incremental backups (discussed in Chapter 4). So, with image copies you have two options for restore and recovery really:

- Use the `restore` command to have RMAN copy the image copies to the original location of the database datafiles. This will not result in any changes to datafile locations in the database control file.

- Use the `switch` command to cause RMAN to instantly start using the image copy of the datafile in its current location. This will cause the database control file to be changed with locations of the new database datafiles.

Other Basic Recovery Topics

There are other recovery-related topics you will need to be aware of. In the following sections, we will cover some of those, and in Chapter 8 we will cover other, more advanced recovery topics. In this section we will discuss block media recovery and recovering from lost control files and lost spfiles with RMAN.

Block Media Recovery

Sometimes one or a few blocks will become corrupt. It's rare, but it happens. RMAN provides the ability to do online block media recovery. With *block media recovery*, RMAN will recover the corrupted blocks online. The only user impact will be to those users who want to access the corrupt blocks, and they will have been impacted anyway.

In Oracle Database 11*g* you use the `recover` command with the `datafile…block` option to perform block media recovery. To use the `recover block` command the following requirements must be met:

- The database must be in ARCHIVELOG mode.
- The database must be mounted or open.
- There must be a current database control file in place.
- All redo logs must be accessible.
- Only blocks marked as MEDIA_CORRUPT can be recovered.

For example, sometimes you will issue a DML or DDL statement and get an error such as the one found here:

```
ORA-01578: ORACLE data block corrupted (file # 6, block # 55)
ORA-01110: data file 6: '/oracle/oradata/trgt/users01.dbf'
```

In this case, you could issue the `recover datafile` command using the block parameter as seen in this example:

Recover datafile 6 block 55;

In some cases, you may want to repair a range of blocks, as shown here:

Recover datafile 6 block 55 to 105;

You can also recover a range of blocks and several datafiles at one time:

Recover datafile 6 block 55 to 105 datafile 7 block 27 to 44;

You can also run the `backup database validate` command to determine if any blocks are media corrupt. Any blocks that are corrupt will be listed in the `V$DATABASE_BLOCK_ CORRUPTION` view. The column `CORRUPTION_TYPE` will indicate if they are media corrupt.

You can attempt to recover all corrupted blocks listed in the `V$DATABASE_BLOCK_ CORRUPTION` view by using the `recover` command with the `corruption list` parameter from RMAN, as seen in this example:

```
RMAN> recover corruption list;
Starting recover at 28-OCT-08
using target database control file instead of recovery catalog
allocated channel: ORA_DISK_1
channel ORA_DISK_1: SID=153 device type=DISK
starting media recovery
media recovery complete, elapsed time: 00:00:01
Finished recover at 28-OCT-08
```

Recovering the Control File

One recovery that you need to be prepared for is the recovery of a lost control file. There are two different situations that come into play here. The first is recovering the control file from a control-file autobackup; the second is recovering a control file if you are not using control-file autobackups. Let's look at each of these methods in more detail.

Recovering Control Files with Control-File Autobackups

We talked about RMAN *control-file autobackups* in Chapter 4. They are a way of automating the backup of database control files. Recovering the control file is quite easy if you are using control-file autobackups. There are two different situations that you will deal with when using control-file autobackups: one when you are using the flash recovery area (FRA) and the other when you are not using the FRA. Let's look at these in a bit more detail.

Control-File Backups Using the FRA

If you are using the FRA and have enabled control-file autobackups, then restoring the current control file is easy. Simply do the following:

- Start the database instance with the `startup nomount` command.

- Issue the `restore controlfile from autobackup` command. RMAN will proceed to restore the control file from the latest automated control-file backup on disk.

- Mount the database after the restore is complete.

- Recover the database with the RMAN `recover` command.

- Open it using the `alter database open resetlogs` command.

Here is an example of the RMAN code:

```
RMAN> Startup nomount;
connected to target database (not started)
Oracle instance started
Total System Global Area     535662592 bytes
Fixed Size                     1334380 bytes
Variable Size                369099668 bytes
Database Buffers             159383552 bytes
Redo Buffers                   5844992 bytes
RMAN> Restore controlfile from autobackup;
Starting restore at 28-SEP-08
allocated channel: ORA_DISK_1
channel ORA_DISK_1: SID=153 device type=DISK
channel ORA_DISK_1: looking for AUTOBACKUP on day: 20080928
channel ORA_DISK_1: AUTOBACKUP found:
c:\oracle\controlfilebackup\c-437680418-20080928-00
channel ORA_DISK_1: restoring control file from AUTOBACKUP
 c:\oracle\controlfilebackup\c-437680418-20080928-00
channel ORA_DISK_1: control file restore from AUTOBACKUP complete
output file name=C:\ORACLE\ORADATA\RCAT\CONTROL01.CTL
output file name=C:\ORACLE\ORADATA\RCAT\CONTROL02.CTL
output file name=C:\ORACLE\ORADATA\RCAT\CONTROL03.CTL
Finished restore at 28-SEP-08
RMAN> alter database mount;
database mounted
released channel: ORA_DISK_1
RMAN> recover database;
Starting recover at 28-SEP-08
allocated channel: ORA_DISK_1
```

```
channel ORA_DISK_1: SID=153 device type=DISK
starting media recovery
archived log for thread 1 with sequence 13 is already on disk as file
C:\ORACLE\ORADATA\RCAT\REDO01.LOG
archived log for thread 1 with sequence 14 is already on disk as file
C:\ORACLE\ORADATA\RCAT\REDO02.LOG
archived log file name=C:\ORACLE\ORADATA\RCAT\REDO01.LOG thread=1 sequence=13
archived log file name=C:\ORACLE\ORADATA\RCAT\REDO02.LOG thread=1 sequence=14
media recovery complete, elapsed time: 00:00:01
Finished recover at 28-SEP-08
RMAN> alter database open resetlogs;
Database opened
```

When you use the `restore controlfile from autobackup` command, Oracle will start searching for the most current control-file autobackup by default. If you have used the `set until` command to perform a point-in-time recovery, RMAN will start searching for the most current control file starting with that day/time and moving backwards.

The `restore controlfile` command also comes with the `maxseq` and `maxdays` parameters to further control how much effort is used to search for a backup control file.

The `maxseq` parameter   Each control-file backup on a given day is assigned a sequence number. That number increments by one for each additional control-file autobackup, until the next day when the sequence resets itself. The maximum sequence number is 256 and the minimum number is 0. RMAN will always search for the highest sequence number (or the most current file) first. The `maxseq` parameter indicates to RMAN which sequence number it should start with when looking for the correct control-file autobackup. This allows you to skip certain sequence numbers if you know you do not want to use them. Here is an example of using `maxseq`:

```
Restore controlfile from autobackup maxseq 200;
```

The `maxdays` parameter   By default RMAN will look back 7 days (from the current date or the `set until` date) to find the correct control-file autobackup. If you want to change this default setting, use the `maxdays` parameter when calling the `restore controlfile from autobackup` command. You can search from 0 until 366 days for the current control-file autobackup. Here is an example of using `maxdays` where we will go back 30 days to find the correct control-file autobackup.

```
Restore controlfile from autobackup maxdays 30;
```

The maxdays and maxseq parameters also apply to spfile autobackup restore operations.

Control-File Backups Not Using the FRA

If you are not using the FRA but have enabled control-file autobackups, you will need to determine the database ID (DBID) of the database. Each database has a DBID, which uniquely identifies it. You should maintain a list of DBIDs for each of your databases if you are not using the FRA but want to use control-file autobackups. You can find the DBID in the DBID column of the V$DATABASE view as seen in this query:

```
SQL> select dbid from v$database;
     DBID
----------
437680418
```

 The database DBID is included in the filename of the control-file auto-backup backup set pieces (if you're not using the FRA). Thus, in a worst-case situation, you can determine the DBID for your database by looking at these files and determining the DBID from the filenames. If you are not using the FRA, this is one very good reason to have control-file autobackups be put in different directories for different databases!

Now that you have the DBID, you are ready to restore the database control file. To do so, follow these steps:

1. Start up the database in NOMOUNT mode. This will start the database and load the database parameter file. The FRA parameters will be set at this point.

2. Issue the set dbid command to set the database DBID that RMAN will look for.

3. Set the control-file autobackup location with the set controlfile autobackup format command.

4. Restore the control file with the restore command.

5. Mount the database for recovery.

6. Issue the recover database command.

7. Open the database using the alter database open resetlogs command.

Here is an example of recovering a control file when the FRA is not in use:

```
RMAN> startup force nomount;
Oracle instance started
Total System Global Area     535662592 bytes
Fixed Size                     1334380 bytes
Variable Size                369099668 bytes
Database Buffers             159383552 bytes
Redo Buffers                   5844992 bytes
RMAN> Set dbid 437680418;
```

```
executing command: SET DBID
RMAN> set controlfile autobackup format for device type
disk to 'c:\oracle\controlfilebackup\%F';
executing command: SET CONTROLFILE AUTOBACKUP FORMAT
RMAN> Restore controlfile from autobackup;
Starting restore at 28-SEP-08
using channel ORA_DISK_1
channel ORA_DISK_1: looking for AUTOBACKUP on day: 20080928
channel ORA_DISK_1: AUTOBACKUP found:
c:\oracle\controlfilebackup\c-437680418-20080928-04
channel ORA_DISK_1: restoring control file from AUTOBACKUP
c:\oracle\controlfilebackup\c-437680418-20080928-04
channel ORA_DISK_1: control file restore from AUTOBACKUP complete
output file name=C:\ORACLE\ORADATA\RCAT\CONTROL01.CTL
output file name=C:\ORACLE\ORADATA\RCAT\CONTROL02.CTL
output file name=C:\ORACLE\ORADATA\RCAT\CONTROL03.CTL
Finished restore at 28-SEP-08
RMAN> Alter database mount;
database mounted
released channel: ORA_DISK_1
RMAN> Recover database;
Starting recover at 28-SEP-08
allocated channel: ORA_DISK_1
channel ORA_DISK_1: SID=153 device type=DISK
starting media recovery
archived log for thread 1 with sequence 1 is already on disk as file
C:\ORACLE\ORADATA\RCAT\REDO01.LOG
archived log for thread 1 with sequence 2 is already on disk as file
C:\ORACLE\ORADATA\RCAT\REDO02.LOG
archived log file name=C:\ORACLE\ORADATA\RCAT\REDO01.LOG thread=1 sequence=1
archived log file name=C:\ORACLE\ORADATA\RCAT\REDO02.LOG thread=1 sequence=2
media recovery complete, elapsed time: 00:00:02
Finished recover at 28-SEP-08
RMAN> alter database open resetlogs;
database opened
```

You can also use the `restore controlfile` command to restore a control file to a different location and filename using the to keyword as seen in this example:

```
Restore controlfile to '/tmp/orcl.ctl' from autobackup;
```

Recovering Control Files When Not Using Control-File Autobackups

If you have not enabled control-file autobackups you need to use the recovery catalog to restore a control file (there are other ways—see the sidebar "Emergency Control-File Recoveries"). Simply follow these steps:

1. Start RMAN and connect to the recovery catalog.

2. Use the `startup force nomount` command to start the database instance.

3. Issue the `restore controlfile` command and RMAN will restore the control file.

4. Mount the database with the `alter database mount` command.

5. Issue a `recover database` command

6. Open the database with the `alter database open resetlogs` command.

Here is an example of the commands you would use to perform a control-file restore using the recovery catalog:

```
Startup force nomount
restore controlfile;
alter database mount;
recover database;
Alter database open resetlogs;
```

You can also use the `restore controlfile` command to restore a control file to a different location and filename using the to keyword, as seen in this example:

```
Restore controlfile to '/tmp/orcl.ctl';
```

Emergency Control-File Recoveries

If you are not using control-file autobackups and you are not using a recovery catalog, what are you to do when you lose your control file? You can always re-create the control file with the `create controlfile` command (see Chapter 2 for more on this command). You can then use the `catalog` command to catalog the backup set pieces. One complication may be if you are backing up to tape. In this case, you may have to restore your backups from tape to local disk before you can run the `catalog` command.

It is not a fun exercise to have to create your own `create controlfile` command from scratch and we strongly recommend that you configure control-file autobackups instead.

Recovering the Spfile

If you have enabled control-file autobackups, then RMAN will back up the current spfile each time a control-file autobackup occurs. To restore your spfile, you will first need to start the database from RMAN without a parameter file of any sort. Just simply type in **startup nomount** and the database will start using default parameter settings. This positions the database to be able to restore the spfile from the autobackup. RMAN will display a message when it's using default parameter settings as seen in this output:

```
RMAN> startup nomount
connected to target database (not started)
startup failed: ORA-01078: failure in processing system parameters
LRM-00109: could not open parameter file
'C:\ORACLE\PRODUCT\11.1.0\DB_1\DATABASE\INITORCL.ORA'
starting Oracle instance without parameter file for retrieval of spfile
Oracle instance started
Total System Global Area       159019008 bytes
Fixed Size                       1331852 bytes
Variable Size                   67112308 bytes
Database Buffers                83886080 bytes
Redo Buffers                     6688768 bytes
```

The restore process for an spfile differs a bit depending on if you have been using the FRA or not using the FRA. We will look into these two different options in the next sections.

Restoring the spfile When Using the FRA

Restoring the spfile when using the FRA is a bit more complex than restoring the control file. First you will need to start the database instance, as demonstrated previously. Then you will need to configure the FRA location. Because the FRA parameter DB_RECOVERY_FILE_DEST is not dynamic, you need to create a temporary pfile based on the current memory settings and then update it with the correct FRA location.

First, you create the temporary pfile from the in-memory settings using the SQL command create pfile from memory. This command will create a database parameter file that you will edit. The parameter settings in this file will be based on the default, in-memory settings used when RMAN started the database. Here is an example of the creation of the pfile from memory:

```
RMAN> sql 'create pfile from memory';
using target database control file instead of recovery catalog
sql statement: create pfile from memory
```

Note that you must create a pfile and not an spfile. This is because you cannot restore over an existing spfile that is in use. Using your editor of choice, edit the pfile you just created. The pfile will typically be created in ORACLE_HOME/database in Win and $ORACLE_HOME/dbs in linux.

You will want to set the DB_RECOVERY_FILE_DEST parameter to the location of the FRA and DB_RECOVERY_FILE_DEST_SIZE to the size of the FRA. When setting the DB_RECOVERY_FILE_DEST_SIZE parameter, don't worry about how big you need to size it because this is just a temporary parameter setting for the spfile restore. The real value of the parameter will be set after the spfile has been restored. Here is an example of what those parameters would look like in a pfile:

```
db_recovery_file_dest='c:\oracle\flash_recovery_area'
db_recovery_file_dest_size=10g
```

Once the parameter has been set correctly, save the file and restart the database using the temporary pfile, as shown here:

```
C:\Documents and Settings\Robert>rman target=/
Recovery Manager: Release 11.1.0.6.0 - Production on Sun Sep 28 14:56:38 2008
Copyright (c) 1982, 2007, Oracle.  All rights reserved.
connected to target database (not started)
RMAN> startup force nomount pfile=?/database/initorcl.ora
Oracle instance started
Total System Global Area     163213312 bytes
Fixed Size                     1331852 bytes
Variable Size                 71306612 bytes
Database Buffers              79691776 bytes
Redo Buffers                  10883072 bytes
```

You can now restore the spfile backed up in the last control-file autobackup using the restore spfile from autobackup command, as shown here:

```
RMAN> restore spfile from autobackup;
Starting restore at 28-SEP-08
using target database control file instead of recovery catalog
allocated channel: ORA_DISK_1
channel ORA_DISK_1: SID=98 device type=DISK
recovery area destination: c:\oracle\flash_recovery_area
database name (or database unique name) used for search: ORCL
channel ORA_DISK_1: AUTOBACKUP
C:\ORACLE\FLASH_RECOVERY_AREA\ORCL\AUTOBACKUP\2008_09_28
\O1_MF_S_666628278_4FZTDYVC_.BKP found in the recovery area
AUTOBACKUP search with format "%F" not attempted because DBID was not set
```

```
channel ORA_DISK_1: restoring spfile from AUTOBACKUP
C:\ORACLE\FLASH_RECOVERY_AREA\ORCL\AUTOBACKUP\2008_09_28
\O1_MF_S_666628278_4FZTDYVC_.BKP
channel ORA_DISK_1: SPFILE restore from AUTOBACKUP complete
Finished restore at 28-SEP-08
```

Now all you need to do is shut down and start up the database (assuming further restore and/or recovery operations are not required) or use the startup force command, as shown here:

```
RMAN> startup force
Oracle instance started
database mounted
database opened
Total System Global Area     397557760 bytes
Fixed Size                     1333452 bytes
Variable Size                335546164 bytes
Database Buffers              54525952 bytes
Redo Buffers                   6152192 bytes
```

Just to summarize the steps needed to perform this recovery, here they are:

1. startup nomount the database from RMAN.

2. Issue the create pfile from memory command from SQL*Plus or using the SQL RMAN command.

3. Edit the pfile so that it contains the correct setting for the parameter DB_RECOVERY_FILE_DEST and the parameter DB_RECOVERY_FILE_DEST_SIZE.

4. Shut down and restart the database instance using the newly created pfile.

5. Use the restore spfile from autobackup command to restore the spfile.

6. Restart the database using the startup force command.

Restoring the Spfile When Not Using the FRA

If you are not using the FRA, the procedure to restore the spfile from an autobackup is actually slightly easier. First, you have already started the database instance. You will have to set two RMAN parameters. The first parameter identifies the DBID of the database (discussed earlier in this chapter). You use the set dbid command to do this, as shown here:

```
RMAN> Set dbid= 437680418
executing command: SET DBID
```

Now you need to use the `set controlfile autobackup format` parameter to indicate where the control-file autobackups can be found, as shown here:

```
RMAN> SET CONTROLFILE AUTOBACKUP FORMAT FOR DEVICE TYPE DISK TO
2> 'c:\oracle\controlfilebackup\%F';
executing command: SET CONTROLFILE AUTOBACKUP FORMAT
using target database control file instead of recovery catalog
```

All that remains is the restore of the spfile:

```
RMAN> Restore spfile from autobackup;
Starting restore at 28-SEP-08
allocated channel: ORA_DISK_1
channel ORA_DISK_1: SID=98 device type=DISK
channel ORA_DISK_1: looking for AUTOBACKUP on day: 20080928
channel ORA_DISK_1: AUTOBACKUP found:
c:\oracle\controlfilebackup\c-437680418-20080928-00
channel ORA_DISK_1: restoring spfile from AUTOBACKUP
c:\oracle\controlfilebackup\c-437680418-20080928-00
channel ORA_DISK_1: SPFILE restore from AUTOBACKUP complete
Finished restore at 28-SEP-08
```

You can also include the `set` commands within the confines of a run block, as shown here:

```
RUN
{
  SET CONTROLFILE AUTOBACKUP FORMAT FOR DEVICE TYPE DISK TO
   'c:\oracle\controlfilebackup\%F';
  RESTORE CONTROLFILE FROM AUTOBACKUP MAXSEQ 100;
}
```

You can now open the database with the `startup force` command, as shown here:

```
RMAN> startup force
Oracle instance started
database mounted
database opened
Total System Global Area       535662592 bytes
Fixed Size                       1334380 bytes
Variable Size                  369099668 bytes
Database Buffers               159383552 bytes
Redo Buffers                     5844992 bytes
```

To summarize the steps for this recovery, here they are:

1. Start up the database in NOMOUNT mode.

2. Set the database DBID.

3. Use the `set` command to set the RMAN parameter `controlfile autobackup format` to point to the correct control-file autobackup location.

4. Restore the spfile with the `restore spfile from autobackup` command.

5. Recycle the database to reread the newly recovered spfile parameter file.

Summary

As you can see, there are several ways to recover a database with RMAN. From database recoveries to tablespace recoveries to datafile recoveries and beyond, there is a lot that can go wrong—and a number of different ways to fix what may go wrong.

For your OCP exam, you will want to be familiar with the different kinds of database restores and recoveries that are possible. In this chapter we have provided you with the information you need to successfully answer the RMAN-recovery-oriented questions.

We strongly recommend that you practice these recovery techniques before you take the test. This is particularly important if you have not have any experience with RMAN restore and recovery operations. You might attempt to follow the exercises in this chapter to give you more experience with recovery of your database and to better prepare you for the exam.

Backup and recovery is the lifeblood of being a DBA. Truly there is nothing more important than knowing not only how to recover your database but also how to craft an overall backup and recovery strategy for your database.

Exam Essentials

Describe the basic process used when performing an RMAN database restore and recovery. Understand the essentials behind RMAN backup and recovery. Know what might be required to prepare for an RMAN recovery. Understand the basic steps of a typical RMAN recovery and what they are for.

Know how to use the `restore` command. Understand the use of the `restore` command. Know the different options of the `restore` command, such as `restore database`, `restore tablespace`, and `restore datafile`. Understand what happens when you call the `restore` command.

Know how to use the recover command.   Understand and be able to successfully use the recover command. Know the different options of the recover command, such as recover database, recover tablespace, and recover datafile. Understand what happens when you call the recover command.

Understand point-in-time recovery.   Understand and be able to perform point-in-time recovery with RMAN. Know how to use the until time parameter of the recover and restore commands to perform a point-in-time recovery. Know how to use the set until time command to perform a point-in-time recovery.

Understand how to perform other recoveries.   Understand how to recover from loss of a control file. Understand how to recover from loss of an spfile.

Review Questions

1. What command would you issue to enable automated backups of control files?

   A. `alter database controlfile autobackup on`

   B. `alter system controlfile autobackup on`

   C. `configure controlfile autobackup on`

   D. `enable controlfile autobackup`

2. Given the following RMAN commands, choose the option that reflects the order required to restore your currently operational ARCHIVELOG-mode database.

   a. `restore database;`

   b. `recover database;`

   c. `shutdown immediate`

   d. `startup`

   e. `restore archivelog all;`

   f. `alter database open`

   A. a, b, c, d, e, f

   B. c, b, a, d, e, f

   C. c, b, a, d, f

   D. c, a, b, d

   E. c, a, e, b, d, f

3. Which commands are used for RMAN database recovery? (Choose all that apply.)

   A. `restore`

   B. `repair`

   C. `copy`

   D. `recover`

   E. `replace`

4. Given a complete loss of your database, in what order would you need to perform the following RMAN operations to restore it?

   a. `restore controlfile`

   b. `restore database`

   c. `restore spfile`

   d. `recover database`

   e. `alter database open`

   f. `alter database open resetlogs`

A. b, a, c, d, e

B. a, c, b, d, f

C. c, a, b, d, e

D. c, a, b, d, f

E. e, a, b, d, c

5. If you lost your entire database, including the database spfile, control files, online redo logs, and database datafiles, what kind of recovery would be required with RMAN?

   A. Complete database recovery.

   B. Incomplete database recovery.

   C. Approximate database recovery.

   D. Archived database recovery.

   E. The database could not be recovered with RMAN.

6. Which command will restore all datafiles to the date 9/30/2008 at 18:00 hours?

   A. `restore datafiles until time '09/28/2008:21:03:11';`

   B. `restore database files until time '09/28/2008:18:00:00';`

   C. `restore database until time '09/28/2008:18:00:00';`

   D. `recover database until time '09/28/2008:18:00:00';`

   E. `recover database until timestamp '09/28/2008:18:00:00';`

7. What is the end result of these commands if they are successful?
   ```
   RMAN> show retention policy;
   RMAN configuration parameters for database with db_unique_name ORCL are:
   CONFIGURE RETENTION POLICY TO REDUNDANCY 1; # default
   Backup database tag='gold_copy' plus archivelog
   tag='gold_copy' delete input;
   Backup database tag='silver_copy' plus archivelog
   tag='silver_copy' delete input;
   ```

   A. Attempting to restore `silver_copy` will fail.

   B. Attempting to restore `gold_copy` will fail.

   C. Both backups will be available for restore without question.

   D. Attempting to restore `gold_copy` may or may not succeed.

   E. You will not be able to restore either `gold_copy` or `silver_copy`.

8. You are using RMAN to backup your ARCHIVELOG mode database. You have enabled control-file autobackups. Which files are not backed up during the RMAN backup?

   A. Database Datafiles

   B. Database Control Files

   C. Online redo logs

   D. Archived redo logs

   E. The database SPFILE

   F. None of the above, all these files are backed up.

9. True or false: RMAN offers the equivalent of the SQL command `alter database backup controlfile to trace`.

   A. True

   B. False

10. You need to restore your database back to 9/30/2008 at 18:00. In what order would you run the following commands to compete this task?

   a. `restore controlfile until time`
   `'09/30/2008:18:00:00';`

   b. `restore database until time`
   `'09/30/2008:18:00:00';`

   c. `restore spfile until time`
   `'09/30/2008:18:00:00';;`

   d. `recover database until time`
   `'09/30/2008:18:00:00';`

   e. `alter database open resetlogs;`

   f. `alter database open;`

   A. b, d, e

   B. b, d, f

   C. c, a, b, d, e

   D. c, a, b, d, f

   E. a, b, d, e

11. What is the correct order of the following commands if you wanted to restore datafile 4, which was accidentally removed from the file system?

   a. `sql 'alter database datafile 4 online';`

   b. `restore datafile 4;`

   c. `recover datafile 4;`

   d. `sql 'alter database datafile 4 offline';`

   e. `startup`

   f. `shutdown`

A. a, c, b, d

B. d, b, c, a

C. f, d, b, c, a, e

D. c, a, b, d, f

E. a, b, d, e

12. Your database is up and running and one of your three control files is accidentally erased. You start RMAN and run the following command:

```
RESTORE CONTROLFILE FROM AUTOBACKUP;
```

Which of the following statements is true? (Choose all that apply.)

A. The command restores only the missing control file.

B. The command restores all the control files.

C. The command fails because the database is running.

D. This is the correct way to address this problem.

E. This is not the correct way to address this problem.

13. Which of the following are valid `until` command options when attempting point-in-time recovery in RMAN? (Choose all that apply.)

A. `until time`

B. `until change`

C. `until sequence`

D. `until SCN`

E. `until commit`

14. Which of the following does the `recover` command not do?

A. Restore archived redo logs.

B. Apply archived redo logs.

C. Restore incremental backups.

D. Apply incremental backups.

E. Restore datafile images.

15. You have a database with the following tablespaces: SYSTEM, SYSAUX, UNDO, USERS, TEMP. You want to "roll back" the data in the USERS tablespace to the way it looked yesterday. Which tablespaces do you need to perform a point-in-time restore operation on in order to complete this task? (Choose all that apply.)

A. SYSTEM

B. SYSAUX

C. UNDO

D. USERS

E. TEMP

F. This restore is not possible.

16. You have backed up your database using image copies. You have lost the SYSTEM tablespace and need to restart your database as quickly as possible. What is the correct solution?

    A. Restore the SYSTEM tablespace from the last backup set and then recover the database.

    B. Restore the SYSTEM tablespace image copy using the `restore` command and then restore the database.

    C. Use the `switch datafile` command to instantly switch to the datafile copy, recover the tablespace, and open the database.

    D. The database is not recoverable in this situation with image copies.

    E. Manually copy the datafile image copy to the correct location and then manually restore the database from SQL*Plus.

17. If you find errors in the view V$DATABASE_BLOCK_CORRUPTION with a status of MEDIA_CORRUPT, what RMAN command would you run to correct the problem?

    A. `recover lost blocks;`

    B. `recover corrupt blocks;`

    C. `recover media corrupt blocks from list;`

    D. `recover corrupt blocks from list;`

    E. `recover corruption list;`

18. What will be the end result of this set of RMAN commands?

```
shutdown abort
startup mount
restore datafile 4 until time '09/30/2008:15:00:00';
recover datafile 4 until time '09/29/2008:15:00:00';
alter database open resetlogs;
```

    A. Datafile 4 will be recovered until 9/30/2008 at 15:00 and the database will open.

    B. The `restore` command will fail.

    C. The `recover` command will fail.

    D. The `alter database open resetlogs` command will fail.

    E. All these commands will fail because they must be in the confines of a run block.

19. Which of the following represents the correct way to perform an online recovery of datafile 4, which is assigned to a tablespace called USERS?

A. `shutdown`
`restore datafile 4;`
`recover datafile 4;`
`alter database open;`

B. `Sql 'alter database datafile 4 offline';`
`restore datafile 4;`
`recover datafile 4;`
`alter database open;`

C. `Sql 'alter database datafile 4 offline';`
`restore datafile 4;`
`Sql 'alter database datafile 4 online';`

D. `Sql 'alter database datafile 4 offline';`
`restore database datafile 4;`
`recover database datafile 4;`
`Sql 'alter database datafile 4 online';`

E. `Sql 'alter database datafile 4 offline';`
`restore datafile 4;`
`recover datafile 4;`
`Sql 'alter database datafile 4 online';`

20. David managed to accidentally delete the datafiles for database called DSL. He called Heber and Heber tried to help but he managed to delete the control files of the database. Heber called Bill and Bill saved the day. They are using a recovery catalog for this database. What steps did Bill perform to recover the database and in what order?

a. Restored the control file with the RMAN `restore controlfile` command.

b. Mounted the DSL instance with the `alter database mount` command.

c. Restored the datafiles for the DSL database with the RMAN `restore` command.

d. Opened the DSL database with the `alter database open resetlogs` command.

e. Recovered the datafiles for the DSL database with the RMAN `recover` command.

f. Started the DSL instance.

g. Connected to the recovery catalog with RMAN.

A. a, b, c, d, e, f, g

B. b, c, d, g, f, e, a

C. g, f, a, b, c, e, d

D. c, a, d, b, f, e, g

E. g, f, a, b, e, c, d

Answers to Review Questions

1. C. Enable control-file autobackups by executing the command `configure controlfile autobackup on`.

2. D. You would shut down the database with the `shutdown immediate` command before the recovery. You would then issue the `restore database` command followed by the `recover database` command. After you have recovered the database, you will want to open it with the `startup` command.

3. A, D. The `restore` command is used to restore datafiles during a database recovery. The `recover` command is used to apply incremental backups and archived redo logs to recover the database to the needed point in time.

4. D. In the event of complete loss of your database, you will need to first restore the database spfile. Once you have restored the database spfile, you will need to restore the database control file. Having restored the database control file, you would restore the database and then recover the database. Finally, since this would be an incomplete recovery (because you lost the entire database, the online redo logs are gone too), you would need to open the database using the `alter database open resetlogs` command.

5. B. A loss of the entire database will result in a requirement for an incomplete database recovery. This is because the online redo logs would not be available to perform a complete recovery.

6. C. The `restore database` command is used to restore database datafiles. The `until time` parameter is used to indicate the point in time to which you want to restore the database datafiles.

7. D. Since the retention policy is set to redundancy of 1, the `gold_copy` backup is not required to meet the retention criteria. Since the backup was not made in a way that will exclude or alter the retention criteria, then the `gold_copy` backup is no longer needed and may be removed at any time. It is possible that it will still be available for restore purposes, however.

8. C. The online redo logs are never backed up by Oracle no mater what kind of backup you are performing.

9. B. There is no equivalent RMAN command that creates a trace file with the `create controlfile` statement in it.

10. A. In this case you would first issue the `restore database` command using the `until time` option. You would then use the `recover database` command using the same `until time` option. Finally, since this is an incomplete recovery, you would need to open your database with the `alter database open` resetlogs command.

11. B. To perform the restore of datafile 4, you would first need to take the datafile offline with the `alter database` command. Once the datafile is offline, use the `restore datafile` and `recover datafile` commands to restore and recover the datafile in question. After the restore and recover, you will need to bring the datafile back online.

12. C, E. This is not the correct way to address this problem. The command will fail because the database is running. Additionally, this is not the correct way to approach the loss of one of several control files. The better way to approach this loss is to shut down the database and simply copy one of the surviving control files over to where the missing control file existed.

13. A, C, D. The `until time` clause provides the ability to restore to a specific point in time. The `until sequence` clause provides the ability to restore to a specific redo log sequence number, and `until SCN` provides the ability to restore to a specific database SCN number.

14. E. The recover command does not restore datafile images. It does restore and apply archived redo logs and incremental backup images during the recovery process.

15. A, B, C, D, E. You will need to restore the datafiles associated with each tablespace in the database in order to successfully complete the point-in-time database restore operation.

16. C. You would use the `switch datafile` command (for example, `switch datafile 1 to copy`) to instantly switch to the image copy. Issue the `restore` command and then start up the database.

17. E. You would run the RMAN command `recover corruption list` to recover the corrupted blocks using block media recovery.

18. D. The commands will run without error until you attempt to open the database. At that time, the `alter database open resetlogs` command will fail. This will be because datafile 4 and the rest of the database will be inconsistent with each other and Oracle does not allow this. If you are going to restore and recover an Oracle database using point-in-time recovery, you must do so with the entire database.

19. E. For this recovery, you would use the RMAN `sql` command to issue an `alter database datafile offline` command. You would then use the RMAN `restore` and `recover` commands to recover the lost datafile. Finally, you would use the RMAN `sql` command to issue the `alter database datafile online` command.

20. C. To restore the database, in this case they needed to connect to the recovery catalog with RMAN. They then started the DSL instance with the `startup nomount` command and restored the control file with the `restore controlfile` command. After restoring the control file, they mounted the database with the `alter database mount` command and then restored the database with the `restore database` command. After restoring the database, they recovered it with the `recover database` command and then opened it with the `alter database open` resetlogs command.

Chapter 7

Reporting, Monitoring, and Tuning with RMAN

ORACLE DATABASE 11g: ADMINISTRATION II EXAM OBJECTIVES COVERED IN THIS CHAPTER:

✓ **Monitoring and Tuning RMAN**

- Monitoring RMAN sessions and jobs
- Tuning RMAN
- Configure RMAN for Asynchronous I/O

✓ **Using RMAN to Create Backups**

- Report on and maintain backups

Overview of the RMAN Report and List Commands

RMAN provides a wealth of reporting with respect to backups, the database, and other various RMAN-related information. In the following sections, we will discuss the RMAN report command and the RMAN list command. You will need to be familiar with both commands.

Exam objectives are subject to change at any time without prior notice and at Oracle's sole discretion. Please visit Oracle's Training and Certification website (http://www.oracle.com/education/certification/) for the most current exam-objectives listing.

Using the RMAN *report* Command

First we will cover the RMAN report command. We will describe the purpose of the report command in RMAN, and then we will provide several examples of its use.

Introducing the RMAN *report* Command

The RMAN report command provides information on records within the database control file or the RMAN recovery catalog. The report command provides the following information:

- Database, tablespace, or datafiles that need to be backed up.

- Obsolete backups. These are backups that meet the retention criteria and can be removed with the delete obsolete commands.

- Objects in the database that need to be backed up because of unrecoverable SQL operations.

- Information on the database schema.

Let's look at some examples of how to use the report command.

Seeing the RMAN *report* Command in Action

Now we will show a number of examples of the use of the RMAN report command. First we will show the report backup command, and we will then show the report schema command.

Example of the *report need backup* Command

For example, if you wanted to know which datafiles need to be backed up in your database based on the retention criteria, you could use the report need backup command:

```
RMAN> report need backup;
RMAN retention policy will be applied to the command
RMAN retention policy is set to redundancy 1
Report of files with less than 1 redundant backups
File #bkps Name
---- ----- ----------------------------------------
5    0     C:\ORACLE\ORADATA\ORCL\MY_DATA_01.DBF
```

In this example you see that datafile 5 is in need of backup with respect to the retention policy. You also see that it has 0 backups (in the #bkps column). In this case, this is a new datafile that has never been backed up.

You can use various options with the report need backup command to customize the report. For example, you could say that you want to see a report of all files that have not been backed up in the last three days. The report would look like this:

```
RMAN> report need backup days 3;
Report of files whose recovery needs more than 3 days of archived logs
File Days  Name
---- ----- ----------------------------------------------------
1    6     C:\ORACLE\ORADATA\ORCL\SYSTEM01.DBF
2    6     C:\ORACLE\ORADATA\ORCL\SYSAUX01.DBF
3    6     C:\ORACLE\ORADATA\ORCL\UNDOTBS01.DBF
4    6     C:\ORACLE\ORADATA\ORCL\USERS01.DBF
```

There are other reporting options besides days:

Incremental   Maximum number of incrementals to apply.

Recovery window of   Indicates the recovery-window criteria to apply. This can be handy when trying to determine the impacts of changing the recovery-window retention policy.

Redundancy   Indicates the level of backup redundancy for datafiles. This can be handy when trying to determine the impacts of changing the redundancy retention policy.

Example of the *report obsolete* Command

The report obsolete command is used to list backup sets that are marked as obsolete in the control file or the recovery catalog. Depending on your configuration, you might look at the `report obsolete` command output and ensure that the backups listed in that command are supposed to be deleted. If so, you could remove them with the `delete obsolete` command (discussed later in this chapter).

In this example, you can see that several backup set pieces are obsolete and no longer needed. If these were present in a flash recovery area (FRA), then Oracle would automatically delete the backup set pieces when space was needed or when you ran the `delete obsolete` command. If you were not using the FRA, you would need to run the `delete obsolete` command to remove those pieces.

```
RMAN> report obsolete;
RMAN retention policy will be applied to the command
RMAN retention policy is set to redundancy 1
Report of obsolete backups and copies
Type                 Key    Completion Time    Filename/Handle
-------------------- ------ ------------------ --------------------
Backup Set           424    11-OCT-08
  Backup Piece       432    11-OCT-08
C:\ORACLE\FLASH_RECOVERY_AREA\ORCL\BACKUPSET\
2008_10_11\01_MF_ANNNN_TAG20081011T142547_4H22YY00_.BKP
Backup Set           426    11-OCT-08
  Backup Piece       434    11-OCT-08
C:\ORACLE\FLASH_RECOVERY_AREA\ORCL\BACKUPSET\
2008_10_11\01_MF_NCSNF_TAG20081011T142622_4H23CVNJ_.BKP
Backup Set           429    11-OCT-08
  Backup Piece       437    11-OCT-08
C:\ORACLE\FLASH_RECOVERY_AREA\ORCL\AUTOBACKUP\
2008_10_11\01_MF_S_667838162_4H23KXWB_.BKP
Backup Set           430    12-OCT-08
  Backup Piece       438    12-OCT-08
C:\ORACLE\FLASH_RECOVERY_AREA\ORCL\AUTOBACKUP\
2008_10_12\01_MF_S_667915771_4H4HCM7L_.BKP
```

Example of the *report schema* Command

The `report schema` command provides information on the tablespaces and related datafiles (and tempfiles) in the database. Displayed by the `report schema` command is the datafile ID, the size of the datafile, and the tablespace that the datafile is associated with. An example of the use of the `report schema` command is shown next:

```
RMAN> report schema;
using target database control file instead of recovery catalog
Report of database schema for database with db_unique_name ORCL
```

```
List of Permanent Datafiles
===========================
File Size(MB) Tablespace          RB segs Datafile Name
---- -------- ------------------  ------- ------------------------
1    680      SYSTEM              ***     C:\ORACLE\ORADATA\ORCL\SYSTEM01.DBF
2    612      SYSAUX              ***     C:\ORACLE\ORADATA\ORCL\SYSAUX01.DBF
3    25       UNDOTBS1            ***     C:\ORACLE\ORADATA\ORCL\UNDOTBS01.DBF
4    5        USERS               ***     C:\ORACLE\ORADATA\ORCL\USERS01.DBF
5    50       MY_DATA             ***     C:\ORACLE\ORADATA\ORCL\MY_DATA_01.DBF
List of Temporary Files
=======================
File Size(MB) Tablespace          Maxsize(MB) Tempfile Name
---- -------- ------------------- ----------- --------------------
1    20       TEMP                32767       C:\ORACLE\ORADATA\ORCL\TEMP01.DBF
```

Note the report in its header indicates that the control file is being used instead of the recovery catalog.

Example of the *report unrecoverable* Command

Certain types of SQL operations can make an object unrecoverable. This is because these operations do not produce redo, in an effort to make the process more performant. Since there is no redo, there is no recovering the object, and what you end up with after a recovery is a shell of an object with no data in it. Here is an example.

First, you log into RMAN and issue the command `report unrecoverable database`:

```
RMAN> report unrecoverable database;
starting full resync of recovery catalog
full resync complete
Report of files that need backup due to unrecoverable operations
File Type of Backup Required Name
---- ----------------------- -----------------------------------
```

Next, you create an object in the SCOTT schema and load it with data:

```
SQL> create table unrecover_table (id number);
SQL> begin
 2  for dd in 1..50
 3  loop
 4  insert into unrecover_table values (dd);
 5  end loop;
 6* end;
SQL>commit;
```

Now you will crate a table based on the UNRECOVER_TABLE. You will make the operation an unrecoverable operation:

```
SQL> Create table test_norecover nologging as select * from unrecover_table;
```

Now you see that the RMAN report unrecoverable command indicates that your USERS tablespace needs a backup:

```
C:\>rman target=/ catalog=rcat_user/rcat_user@rcat
Recovery Manager: Release 11.1.0.6.0 - Production on Sat Oct 18 01:15:17 2008
Copyright (c) 1982, 2007, Oracle.  All rights reserved.
connected to target database: ORCL (DBID=1195614221)
connected to recovery catalog database
RMAN> report unrecoverable database;
Report of files that need backup due to unrecoverable operations
File Type of Backup Required Name
---- --------------------- -----------------------------------
4    full or incremental    C:\ORACLE\ORADATA\ORCL\USERS01.DBF
```

To fix this problem, you back up the USERS tablespace, as shown here:

```
RMAN> backup tablespace users;
Starting backup at 18-OCT-08
allocated channel: ORA_DISK_1
channel ORA_DISK_1: SID=134 device type=DISK
channel ORA_DISK_1: starting datafile copy
input datafile file number=00004 name=C:\ORACLE\ORADATA\ORCL\USERS01.DBF
output file name=C:\ORACLE\FLASH_RECOVERY_AREA\ORCL\DATAFILE\
01_MF_USERS_4HM3CGQX_.DBF tag=TAG20081018T011646 RECID=1
STAMP=668395023
channel ORA_DISK_1: datafile copy complete, elapsed time: 00:00:03
Finished backup at 18-OCT-08
Starting Control File and SPFILE Autobackup at 18-OCT-08
piece handle=C:\ORACLE\FLASH_RECOVERY_AREA\ORCL\AUTOBACKUP\2008_10_18\
01_MF_S_668395027_4HM3CWNZ_.BKP comment=NONE
Finished Control File and SPFILE Autobackup at 18-OCT-08
RMAN> report unrecoverable database;
Report of files that need backup due to unrecoverable operations
File Type of Backup Required Name
---- --------------------- -----------------------------------
```

In Exercise 7.1, you will get to experiment with the report command.

EXERCISE 7.1

Using the *report* Command

1. Log into RMAN, connecting to your recovery catalog.

```
C:\>rman target=/ catalog=rcat_user/rcat_user@rcat
Recovery Manager: Release 11.1.0.6.0 -
Production on Sun Oct 19 14:51:06 2008
Copyright (c) 1982, 2007, Oracle.  All rights reserved.
connected to target database: ORCL (DBID=1195614221)
connected to recovery catalog database
```

2. Just type in the command **report;**. Review the output. Notice how RMAN prompts you for the syntax it is expecting. For example, in this case it's expecting something akin to report device, report need, report obsolete, and so on.

```
RMAN> report;
RMAN-00571: ===========================================================
RMAN-00569: =============== ERROR MESSAGE STACK FOLLOWS ===============
RMAN-00571: ===========================================================
RMAN-00558: error encountered while parsing input commands
RMAN-01009: syntax error: found ";": expecting one of:
"device, need, obsolete, schema, unrecoverable"
RMAN-01007: at line 1 column 7 file: standard input
```

3. See what datafiles and tempfiles are in the database by using the report schema command:

```
RMAN> report schema;
Report of database schema for database with db_unique_name ORCL
List of Permanent Datafiles
===========================
File Size(MB) Tablespace        RB segs Datafile Name
---- -------- ----------------  ------- ------------------------
1    680      SYSTEM            YES     C:\ORACLE\ORADATA\ORCL\SYSTEM01.DBF
2    631      SYSAUX            NO      C:\ORACLE\ORADATA\ORCL\SYSAUX01.DBF
3    25       UNDOTBS1          YES     C:\ORACLE\ORADATA\ORCL\UNDOTBS01.DBF
4    5        USERS             NO      C:\ORACLE\ORADATA\ORCL\USERS01.DBF
5    50       MY_DATA           NO      C:\ORACLE\ORADATA\ORCL\MY_DATA_01.DBF
List of Temporary Files
=======================
File Size(MB) Tablespace        Maxsize(MB) Tempfile Name
---- -------- ----------------  ----------- --------------------
1    20       TEMP              32767       C:\ORACLE\ORADATA\ORCL\TEMP01.DBF
```

EXERCISE 7.1 *(continued)*

4. See what backups in the database have become obsolete because they do not meet the retention criteria. To do so, you will use the report obsolete command:

```
RMAN> report obsolete;
RMAN retention policy will be applied to the command
RMAN retention policy is set to redundancy 1
Report of obsolete backups and copies
Type                 Key    Completion Time    Filename/Handle
-------------------- ------ ------------------ --------------------
Archive Log          926    18-OCT-08
C:\ORACLE\PRODUCT\11.1.0\DB_1\RDBMS\ARC00022_0667833490.001
Backup Set           978    18-OCT-08
  Backup Piece       980    18-OCT-08
C:\ORACLE\FLASH_RECOVERY_AREA\ORCL\AUTOBACKUP\2008_10_18
\O1_MF_S_668446569_4HNOPMRF_.BKP
Backup Set           1252   18-OCT-08
  Backup Piece       1260   18-OCT-08             C:\ORACLE\FLASH_RECOVERY_AREA\
ORCL\BACKUPSET\2008_10_18
\O1_MF_ANNNN_TAG20081018T153543_4HNOP6OH_.BKP.OLD
Backup Set           1253   18-OCT-08
  Backup Piece       1261   18-OCT-08             C:\ORACLE\FLASH_RECOVERY_AREA\
ORCL\BACKUPSET\2008_10_18\
O1_MF_NNNDF_TAG20081018T152908_4HNO9DX9_.BKP.OLD
```

5. Log out of RMAN and log into the database with SQL*Plus:

```
RMAN> quit
Recovery Manager complete.
C:\Documents and Settings\Robert>sqlplus "/ as sysdba"
SQL*Plus: Release 11.1.0.6.0 - Production on Sun Oct 19 15:37:03 2008
Copyright (c) 1982, 2007, Oracle.  All rights reserved.
Connected to:
Oracle Database 11g Enterprise Edition Release 11.1.0.6.0 - Production
With the Partitioning, OLAP, Data Mining
and Real Application Testing options
SQL>
```

6. Add a tablespace to the database, and then log out of SQL*Plus. You may want to put your tablespace in a different location; this is fine.

```
SQL> create tablespace testtbs
  2  datafile 'c:\oracle\oradata\orcl\testtbs.dbf' size 20m;
```

```
Tablespace created.
SQL> exit
Disconnected from Oracle Database 11g Enterprise Edition
Release 11.1.0.6.0 - Production
With the Partitioning, OLAP, Data Mining and
Real Application Testing options
```

7.   Log into RMAN, connecting to your recovery catalog:

```
C:\>rman target=/ catalog=rcat_user/rcat_user@rcat
Recovery Manager: Release 11.1.0.6.0 -
Production on Sun Oct 19 14:51:06 2008
Copyright (c) 1982, 2007, Oracle.  All rights reserved.
connected to target database: ORCL (DBID=1195614221)
connected to recovery catalog database
```

8.   Now generate a report of datafiles that need to be backed up with the report need
     backup command. You will see that the new datafile shows up as needing a backup.
     Note that as long as you have the archived redo logs that were generated since the
     datafile was created, you can still recover this datafile and any data in it.

```
RMAN> report need backup;
RMAN retention policy will be applied to the command
RMAN retention policy is set to redundancy 1
Report of files with less than 1 redundant backups
File #bkps Name
---- ----- ----------------------------------------
6    0     C:\ORACLE\ORADATA\ORCL\TESTTBS.DBF
```

Using the RMAN *list* Command

The RMAN list command provides information on backups in your Oracle database. The
list command has the following functionality:

- Listing expired backups
- Listing the database incarnation
- Listing database restore points
- Listing scripts
- Listing information on database backups and image copies

Additionally, information can often be listed in two formats, detail and summary, as you will see in the following sections.

Seeing the *list expired backup* Command in Action

When you run the crosscheck command (discussed later in this chapter), any missing backup files will be marked as EXPIRED, meaning that they are no longer on the media where they are expected to be. The list expired command will show you the backups that are expired. You can review this list and then use the delete command to mark the backup files as deleted in the control file and the recovery catalog. Here is an example of the list expired backup command in use:

```
RMAN> list expired backup of database;
List of Backup Sets
===================

BS Key  Type LV Size        Device Type Elapsed Time Completion Time
------- ---- -- ---------- ----------- ------------ ---------------
425     Full    176.72M     DISK        00:06:02     11-OCT-08
BP Key: 433    Status: EXPIRED  Compressed: YES  Tag: TAG20081011T142622
Piece Name: C:\ORACLE\FLASH_RECOVERY_AREA\ORCL\BACKUPSET\2008_10_11\
01_MF_NNNDF_TAG20081011T142622_4H22ZOMK_.BKP
  List of Datafiles in backup set 425
  File LV Type Ckp SCN    Ckp Time  Name
  ---- -- ---- ---------- --------- ----
  1       Full 903859     11-OCT-08 C:\ORACLE\ORADATA\ORCL\SYSTEM01.DBF
  2       Full 903859     11-OCT-08 C:\ORACLE\ORADATA\ORCL\SYSAUX01.DBF
  3       Full 903859     11-OCT-08 C:\ORACLE\ORADATA\ORCL\UNDOTBS01.DBF
  4       Full 903859     11-OCT-08 C:\ORACLE\ORADATA\ORCL\USERS01.DBF
```

In this case, you have one backup set that is expired. Each backup set has its own unique backup-set key that you will find in many reports. In this report, the backup-set key 425 is missing. This backup includes backups of four datafiles. Since it's expired, this essentially means it's missing from the database. Expired backups will not show up on this report until the crosscheck command detects they are missing. You can find more information on the crosscheck command later in this chapter. If you want to mark these as deleted in the recovery catalog, you can use the delete expired command. You can find more information on the delete expired command later in this chapter.

Seeing the *list incarnation* Command in Action

In previous chapters, we gave you a little bit of a preview of the list incarnation command. The list incarnation command provides information related to database incarnation from the control file or the recovery catalog. You can use this command to guide you in situations in which you need to reset the database incarnation for certain types of database recoveries (see Chapter 6 for more on this topic).

The `list incarnation` command output is slightly different depending on whether you are connected to a recovery catalog or the database control file. For example, here is some sample output from the `list incarnation` command when we were connected to the control file of the database:

```
RMAN> list incarnation;
List of Database Incarnations
DB Key  Inc Key DB Name  DB ID            STATUS  Reset SCN  Reset Time
------- ------- -------- ---------------- --- ---------- ----------

1       1       ORCL     1195614221       PARENT  1          15-OCT-07
2       2       ORCL     1195614221       CURRENT 886308     11-OCT-08
```

Note that there are two records here, and the DBID for each record is the same. When you execute the same command from the recovery catalog, you may get different results, as shown here:

```
RMAN> list incarnation;
List of Database Incarnations
DB Key  Inc Key DB Name  DB ID            STATUS  Reset SCN  Reset Time
------- ------- -------- ---------------- --- ---------- ----------

1       15      ORCL     1194488809       PARENT  1          15-OCT-07
1       16      ORCL     1194488809       PARENT  886308     29-SEP-08
1       17      ORCL     1194488809       ORPHAN  907851     02-OCT-08
1       2       ORCL     1194488809       PARENT  953055     02-OCT-08
1       270     ORCL     1194488809       CURRENT 988211     02-OCT-08
321     335     ORCL     1195614221       PARENT  1          15-OCT-07
321     322     ORCL     1195614221       CURRENT 886308     11-OCT-08
```

This is a case where we have two databases called ORCL in our recovery catalog. Notice that each of those databases has a different DBID. Oracle will be able to separate the databases based on this unique ID, but both databases show up in the report because the report is generated based on the database name, not the DBID.

Seeing the *list restore point* Command in Action

Database restore points are a function of Oracle Flashback Database technologies (see Chapter 9 for more information on Oracle Flashback Database). You can set restore points from the SQL prompt with the `create restore point` command. In this example, we use the `list restore point all` command to list all restore points:

```
RMAN> list restore point all;
SCN              RSP Time  Type       Time      Name
---------------- --------- ---------- --------- ----
1219891                               18-OCT-08 ROBERT
```

You could also list a specific restore point as in this example:

```
RMAN> list restore point robert;
SCN              RSP Time  Type       Time      Name
---------------- --------- ---------- --------- ----
1219891                               18-OCT-08 ROBERT


RMAN> list restore point davep;
SCN              RSP Time  Type       Time      Name
---------------- --------- ---------- --------- ----
```

Seeing the *list all script names* Command in Action

The `list all script names` command generates a report with the names of all scripts in the recovery catalog. This command is available for use only when you are connected to the recovery catalog. Here is an example of the `list all script names` command where you find you have one script in the recovery catalog called db_backup_script:

```
RMAN> list all script names;
List of Stored Scripts in Recovery Catalog
    Scripts of Target Database ORCL
        Script Name
        Description
        -----------------------------------
        db_backup_script
```

Examples of Listing Backup-Related Information

DBAs will, from time to time, want to know what backups have been made on their database. The `list` command provides all sorts of information on database backups. For example, if you want to see what full backups of your database are available, then you can run the `list backup of database` command:

```
RMAN> list backup of database;
List of Backup Sets
```

```
====================
BS Key  Type LV Size        Device Type Elapsed Time Completion Time
------- ---- -- ---------- ----------- ------------ ---------------
2       Full   176.72M    DISK          00:06:02    11-OCT-08
        BP Key: 2   Status: EXPIRED  Compressed: YES  Tag: TAG20081011T142622
        Piece Name: C:\ORACLE\FLASH_RECOVERY_AREA\ORCL\BACKUPSET\2008_10_11\
01_MF_NNNDF_TAG20081011T142622_4H22ZOMK_.BKP
  List of Datafiles in backup set 2
  File LV Type Ckp SCN   Ckp Time  Name
  ---- -- ---- ---------- --------- ----
  1      Full 903859      11-OCT-08 C:\ORACLE\ORADATA\ORCL\SYSTEM01.DBF
  2      Full 903859      11-OCT-08 C:\ORACLE\ORADATA\ORCL\SYSAUX01.DBF
  3      Full 903859      11-OCT-08 C:\ORACLE\ORADATA\ORCL\UNDOTBS01.DBF
  4      Full 903859      11-OCT-08 C:\ORACLE\ORADATA\ORCL\USERS01.DBF

BS Key  Type LV Size        Device Type Elapsed Time Completion Time
------- ---- -- ---------- ----------- ------------ ---------------
11      Full   186.89M    DISK          00:04:43    18-OCT-08
        BP Key: 11   Status: AVAILABLE  Compressed: YES  Tag: TAG20081018T032019
        Piece Name: C:\ORACLE\FLASH_RECOVERY_AREA\ORCL\BACKUPSET\2008_10_18\
01_MF_NNNDF_TAG20081018T032019_4HMBLT5V_.BKP
  List of Datafiles in backup set 11
  File LV Type Ckp SCN   Ckp Time  Name
  ---- -- ---- ---------- --------- ----
  1      Full 1195239     18-OCT-08 C:\ORACLE\ORADATA\ORCL\SYSTEM01.DBF
  2      Full 1195239     18-OCT-08 C:\ORACLE\ORADATA\ORCL\SYSAUX01.DBF
  3      Full 1195239     18-OCT-08 C:\ORACLE\ORADATA\ORCL\UNDOTBS01.DBF
  4      Full 1195239     18-OCT-08 C:\ORACLE\ORADATA\ORCL\USERS01.DBF
  5      Full 1195239     18-OCT-08 C:\ORACLE\ORADATA\ORCL\MY_DATA_01.DBF

BS Key  Type LV Size        Device Type Elapsed Time Completion Time
------- ---- -- ---------- ----------- ------------ ---------------
15      Full   187.63M    DISK          00:05:37    18-OCT-08
        BP Key: 15   Status: AVAILABLE  Compressed: YES  Tag: TAG20081018T134250
        Piece Name: C:\ORACLE\FLASH_RECOVERY_AREA\ORCL\BACKUPSET\2008_10_18\
01_MF_NNNDF_TAG20081018T134250_4HNH25TC_.BKP
  List of Datafiles in backup set 15
  File LV Type Ckp SCN   Ckp Time  Name
  ---- -- ---- ---------- --------- ----
  1      Full 1218699     18-OCT-08 C:\ORACLE\ORADATA\ORCL\SYSTEM01.DBF
  2      Full 1218699     18-OCT-08 C:\ORACLE\ORADATA\ORCL\SYSAUX01.DBF
  3      Full 1218699     18-OCT-08 C:\ORACLE\ORADATA\ORCL\UNDOTBS01.DBF
```

```
4       Full 1218699    18-OCT-08 C:\ORACLE\ORADATA\ORCL\USERS01.DBF
5       Full 1218699    18-OCT-08 C:\ORACLE\ORADATA\ORCL\MY_DATA_01.DBF
```

Of course, when you read the output of the previous example, you probably said to yourself, "Wow! That's a lot more output than I needed!" You can use the summary keyword to produce summary output that is often all you need, as shown in this example:

```
RMAN> list backup of database summary;
List of Backups
===============
Key     TY LV S Device Type Completion Time #Pieces #Copies Compressed Tag
------- -- -- - ----------- --------------- ------- ------- ---------- ---
2       B  F  X DISK        11-OCT-08       1       1       YES
TAG20081011T142622
11      B  F  A DISK        18-OCT-08       1       1       YES
TAG20081018T032019
15      B  F  A DISK        18-OCT-08       1       1       YES
TAG20081018T134250
```

Now that's a lot easier to read! Here you see that there are three backups of the database, when they were taken, the type, and other interesting information on the backups.

You can get the following details on the various types of backups that you might be taking with RMAN:

- Lists of all backups
- Lists of backup-set backups
- Lists of archive-log backups
- Lists of image copies
- Lists of control-file backups
- Backups of specific tablespaces or datafiles

For example, here is a list of the backup of all archive logs. Note that the list backup of archivelog command provides the ability to list specific archive logs based on numerous criteria, such as a log-sequence number range, time range, and SCN range, or you can just list them all as we do in this example:

```
RMAN> list backup of archivelog all summary;
List of Backups
===============
Key     TY LV S Device Type Completion Time #Pieces #Copies Compressed Tag
------- -- -- - ----------- --------------- ------- ------- ---------- ---
1       B  A  A DISK        11-OCT-08       1       1       YES
TAG20081011T142547
```

4	B	A	A DISK	11-OCT-08	1	1	YES
TAG20081011T143308							
5	B	A	A DISK	11-OCT-08	1	1	NO
TAG20081011T143528							
10	B	A	A DISK	18-OCT-08	1	1	YES
TAG20081018T031922							
12	B	A	A DISK	18-OCT-08	1	1	YES
TAG20081018T032513							
14	B	A	A DISK	18-OCT-08	1	1	YES
TAG20081018T134136							
16	B	A	A DISK	18-OCT-08	1	1	YES
TAG20081018T134839							

In Exercise 7.2, you will get to experiment with the list command.

EXERCISE 7.2

Using the *list* Command

1. Log into RMAN, connecting to your recovery catalog:

```
C:\>rman target=/ catalog=rcat_user/rcat_user@rcat
Recovery Manager: Release 11.1.0.6.0 -
Production on Sun Oct 19 14:51:06 2008
Copyright (c) 1982, 2007, Oracle.  All rights reserved.
connected to target database: ORCL (DBID=1195614221)
connected to recovery catalog database
```

2. You can see what backups are available by calling the list backup of database summary command:

```
RMAN> list backup of database summary;
List of Backups
===============
```

Key	TY	LV	S	Device Type	Completion Time	#Pieces	#Copies	Compressed	Tag
1253	B	F	A	DISK	18-OCT-08	1	1	YES	
TAG20081018T152908									
1342	B	F	A	DISK	18-OCT-08	1	1	YES	
TAG20081018T163034									

3. To look at one of these backups in more detail, call the list backup command:

```
RMAN> list backup of database;
List of Backup Sets
```

```
===================
BS Key   Type LV Size        Device Type Elapsed Time Completion Time
-------  ---- -- ----------  ----------- ------------ ---------------
1253     Full    187.77M     DISK           00:00:00    18-OCT-08
         BP Key: 1261    Status: AVAILABLE  Compressed: YES
Tag: TAG20081018T152908
    Piece Name: C:\ORACLE\FLASH_RECOVERY_AREA\ORCL\BACKUPSET\2008_10_18
\01_MF_NNNDF_TAG20081018T152908_4HNO9DX9_.BKP.OLD
List of Datafiles in backup set 1253
File LV Type Ckp SCN    Ckp Time  Name
---- -- ---- ---------- --------- ----
1       Full 1222465    18-OCT-08 C:\ORACLE\ORADATA\ORCL\SYSTEM01.DBF
2       Full 1222465    18-OCT-08 C:\ORACLE\ORADATA\ORCL\SYSAUX01.DBF
3       Full 1222465    18-OCT-08 C:\ORACLE\ORADATA\ORCL\UNDOTBS01.DBF
4       Full 1222465    18-OCT-08 C:\ORACLE\ORADATA\ORCL\USERS01.DBF
5       Full 1222465    18-OCT-08 C:\ORACLE\ORADATA\ORCL\MY_DATA_01.DBF


BS Key   Type LV Size        Device Type Elapsed Time Completion Time
-------  ---- -- ----------  ----------- ------------ ---------------
1342     Full    187.87M     DISK           00:56:47    18-OCT-08
         BP Key: 1348    Status: AVAILABLE  Compressed: YES
Tag: TAG20081018T163034
    Piece Name: C:\ORACLE\FLASH_RECOVERY_AREA\ORCL\BACKUPSET\2008_10_18
\01_MF_NNNDF_TAG20081018T163034_4HNRWKVC_.BKP
List of Datafiles in backup set 1342
File LV Type Ckp SCN    Ckp Time  Name
---- -- ---- ---------- --------- ----
1       Full 1224452    18-OCT-08 C:\ORACLE\ORADATA\ORCL\SYSTEM01.DBF
2       Full 1224452    18-OCT-08 C:\ORACLE\ORADATA\ORCL\SYSAUX01.DBF
3       Full 1224452    18-OCT-08 C:\ORACLE\ORADATA\ORCL\UNDOTBS01.DBF
4       Full 1224452    18-OCT-08 C:\ORACLE\ORADATA\ORCL\USERS01.DBF
5       Full 1224452    18-OCT-08 C:\ORACLE\ORADATA\ORCL\MY_DATA_01.DBF
```

4. Next, simulate the loss of a backup set piece by using the host command and delet-
    ing the backup set piece. In this case, you will remove the backup set piece called
    01_MF_NNNDF_TAG20081018T163034_4HNRWKVC_.BKP, which showed up in the report
    in step 3. Your backup set piece will probably be named differently.

    RMAN> Host 'del C:\ORACLE\FLASH_RECOVERY_AREA\ORCL\BACKUPSET\2008_10_18
    \01_MF_NNNDF_TAG20081018T163034_4HNRWKVC_.BKP';

5. Now you need to use the crosscheck command so RMAN will detect that you have deleted the backup set piece. Note that the backup set piece you removed is now marked as expired.

```
RMAN> crosscheck backup;
allocated channel: ORA_DISK_1
channel ORA_DISK_1: SID=122 device type=DISK
crosschecked backup piece: found to be 'AVAILABLE'
backup piece handle=C:\ORACLE\FLASH_RECOVERY_AREA\ORCL\AUTOBACKUP\
2008_10_18\O1_MF_S_668446569_4HNOPMRF_.BKP RECID=29 STAMP=668446579
crosschecked backup piece: found to be 'AVAILABLE'
backup piece handle=C:\ORACLE\FLASH_RECOVERY_AREA\ORCL\BACKUPSET\
2008_10_18\O1_MF_ANNNN_TAG20081018T153543_4HNOP6OH_.BKP.OLD RECID=31
STAMP=668449007
crosschecked backup piece: found to be 'AVAILABLE'
backup piece handle=C:\ORACLE\FLASH_RECOVERY_AREA\ORCL\BACKUPSET\
2008_10_18\O1_MF_NNNDF_TAG20081018T152908_4HNO9DX9_.BKP.OLD RECID=32
STAMP=668449009
crosschecked backup piece: found to be 'EXPIRED'
backup piece handle=C:\ORACLE\FLASH_RECOVERY_AREA\ORCL\BACKUPSET\
2008_10_18\O1_MF_NNNDF_TAG20081018T163034_4HNRWKVC_.BKP RECID=33
STAMP=668449841
crosschecked backup piece: found to be 'AVAILABLE'
backup piece handle=C:\ORACLE\FLASH_RECOVERY_AREA\ORCL\AUTOBACKUP\
2008_10_18\O1_MF_S_668453268_4HNW82VT_.BKP RECID=34
STAMP=668453282
crosschecked backup piece: found to be 'AVAILABLE'
backup piece handle=C:\ORACLE\FLASH_RECOVERY_AREA\ORCL\AUTOBACKUP\
2008_10_19\O1_MF_S_668533219_4HQBBXCQ_.BKP RECID=35 STAMP=668533245
Crosschecked 6 objects
```

6. Now issue the list expired backup command to get a report of expired RMAN backup set pieces:

```
RMAN> list expired backup;
List of Backup Sets
===================

BS Key  Type LV Size       Device Type Elapsed Time Completion Time
------- ---- -- ---------- ----------- ------------ ---------------
1342    Full    187.87M    DISK        00:56:47     18-OCT-08
```

```
BP Key: 1348   Status: EXPIRED  Compressed: YES Tag: TAG20081018T163034
        Piece Name: C:\ORACLE\FLASH_RECOVERY_AREA\ORCL\BACKUPSET\2008_10_18
\01_MF_NNNDF_TAG20081018T163034_4HNRWKVC_.BKP
  List of Datafiles in backup set 1342
  File LV Type Ckp SCN  Ckp Time   Name
  ---- -- ---- -------- ---------- ----
    1      Full 1224452  18-OCT-08 C:\ORACLE\ORADATA\ORCL\SYSTEM01.DBF
    2      Full 1224452  18-OCT-08 C:\ORACLE\ORADATA\ORCL\SYSAUX01.DBF
    3      Full 1224452  18-OCT-08 C:\ORACLE\ORADATA\ORCL\UNDOTBS01.DBF
    4      Full 1224452  18-OCT-08 C:\ORACLE\ORADATA\ORCL\USERS01.DBF
    5      Full 1224452  18-OCT-08 C:\ORACLE\ORADATA\ORCL\MY_DATA_01.DBF
```

7. Now, mark the backup set piece as deleted by using the delete expired backup command. You will need to respond when prompted to verify that you want to delete the backup set piece:

```
RMAN> delete expired backup;
using channel ORA_DISK_1
List of Backup Pieces
BP Key  BS Key  Pc# Cp# Status      Device Type Piece Name
-------  -------  --- --- ----------- ----------- ----------
1348    1342    1   1   EXPIRED     DISK        C:\ORACLE\FLASH_RECOVERY_AREA\
ORCL\BACKUPSET\2008_10_18
\01_MF_NNNDF_TAG20081018T163034_4HNRWKVC_.BKP
Do you really want to delete the above objects (enter YES or NO)? yes
deleted backup piece
backup piece handle=C:\ORACLE\FLASH_RECOVERY_AREA\ORCL\BACKUPSET\
2008_10_18\01_MF_NNNDF_TAG20081018T163034_4HNRWKVC_.BKP RECID=33
STAMP=668449841
Deleted 1 EXPIRED objects
```

Monitoring, Administering, and Tuning RMAN

For the OCP exam, you will be expected to know a little bit about how to monitor RMAN operations. The exam will also test your knowledge of RMAN administration and tuning options. In the following sections, we will address all of these items.

Monitoring RMAN Operations

More often than not, RMAN works just fine. However, there are times when you will want to be able to monitor RMAN operations. In the next sections, we will discuss RMAN tuning, including enabling asynchronous I/O and monitoring RMAN operations with data dictionary views.

Configuring for Asynchronous I/O

In most cases, your operating system (OS) will already support asynchronous I/O operations natively. In these cases, no special configuration is required.

If your OS does not support native asynchronous I/O operations, then you may want to consider configuring your database, and RMAN, to simulate asynchronous I/O. Oracle provides Oracle slave I/O processes, which are individual processes that Oracle starts that are used to simulate asynchronous I/O.

You can enable these asynchronous I/O processes by configuring the parameter dbwr_io_slaves. This parameter indicates to Oracle how many I/O slaves should be started when the database is started. When this parameter is zero, simulated asynchronous I/O is disabled. When the parameter is greater than zero, Oracle will automatically start four backup I/O slaves.

When using IO slaves to simulate asynchronous I/O, you will also want to configure the large pool using the large_pool_size parameter. RMAN will use the large pool, if configured, instead of the shared pool. If the large pool is allocated when you're using I/O slaves but insufficient memory exists, then RMAN will generate an error and will not use asynchronous I/O. If the large pool is not allocated and IO slaves are enabled, RMAN will use the shared pool and try to simulate asynchronous I/O operations. If the large pool is not allocated and there is not enough shared-pool memory, then Oracle will use the PGA. In this case, simulated asynchronous I/O operations will not occur.

Using the *V$SESSION_LONGOPS* View to Monitor RMAN

Oracle provides the V$SESSION_LONGOPS view as a means to monitor long-running processes within the Oracle database. Since RMAN uses internal database calls, records for long-running RMAN operations will appear in V$SESSION_LONGOPS. This view can be useful when you're trying to determine just how long a database backup or restore is likely to take. In this example, you first start an RMAN backup in one session. And as the backup is running, you will query the V$SESSION_LONGOPS view with this query:

```
SQL> Select sid, serial#, opname, time_remaining
  2  From v$session_longops
  3  Where sid in (select sid from v$session
  4                           Where program like '%rman%')
  5  And time_remaining > 0;
     SID    SERIAL# OPNAME                          TIME_REMAINING
```

```
---------- ---------- ------------------------------------ --------------
   129        415 RMAN: aggregate input                      188
   121        269 RMAN: full datafile backup                 161
```

In the output from this example, it appears that the overall time for the RMAN backup in question is about 188 seconds (the aggregate input figure is the one to use here). Keep in mind that these figures are just for the individual backup operation that is currently running. The output is not cumulative for the entire backup command.

For example, if you executed a backup using a command like backup as compressed backup database plus archivelog delete input, the output displayed would be only for the database backup or the archived redo-log backup. Keep in mind that the backup database plus archivelog command can show a series of backups. These would include two individual archive-log backups, the database backup, and then the control-file autobackup. Each of these operations will appear in the V$SESSION_LONGOPS view differently. Notice in the previous example that OPNAME is displayed as full datafile backup. The value for OPNAME would be different for different stages in the RMAN backup operation.

 Real World Scenario

Tuning RMAN: It's the Little Things That Count

In the real world, tuning RMAN can make a huge difference. RMAN works fine as it is out of the box, but very often there is a lot you can do to make things run faster. Sometimes even the smallest things can make a huge difference. One place where one of us worked had limited tape drives for performing backups.

The problem was that individual DBAs were scheduling their backups for each of their individual databases and there wasn't a lot of coordination of schedules going on. We started getting complaints because backups were taking a long time.

It turned out that everyone was hitting the tape drives all at the same time. The tape drives would be working a specific backup, and all the other backups would sit and wait for a tape device to become available. Once we worked out a reasonable schedule, the backups started working better and everyone was much happier!

Using the *V$SESSION* and *V$SESSION_WAIT_HISTORY* Views to Troubleshoot RMAN Problems

Trouble. We hate trouble. Sometimes you get into problems with RMAN and are not sure what the trouble is. The V$SESSION and V$SESSION_WAIT views can be a big help in your troubleshooting efforts. These views can help identify the cause of RMAN processes that are not running as fast as you would like. In this example, we have an RMAN backup running, rather slowly at that. We query the V$SESSION view to determine the total number of waits that the session has experienced and the wait event that the session is currently experiencing:

```
SQL> Select sid, serial#, event, seconds_in_wait
  2  From v$session
  3  Where sid in (select sid from v$session
  4                Where program like '%rman%');
     SID    SERIAL# EVENT                           SECONDS_IN_WAIT
---------- ---------- ------------------------------ ---------------
     121        269 RMAN backup & recovery I/O                    2
     129        415 SQL*Net message from client                  63
     130        270 SQL*Net message from client                   8
```

Here you see that the backup-and-recovery I/O on SID 121 appears to be a problem. It's been waiting 2 seconds, which is a long time for an I/O request. Note that the two other wait events are considered idle waits and are likely not a problem. Later we might run the query again and see something like this:

```
     SID    SERIAL# EVENT                           SECONDS_IN_WAIT
---------- ---------- ------------------------------ ---------------
     121        269 control file sequential read                  3
     129        415 SQL*Net message from client                   3
     130        270 SQL*Net message from client                   3
```

The control-file sequential read is now the main wait.

The V$SESSION view lists waits that are occurring at that moment. We could query V$SESSION_WAIT_HISTORY and find out all waits for the session since it started, as shown here:

```
SQL> Select sid, event, wait_time
  2  From v$session_wait_history
  3  Where sid in (select sid from v$session
  4                Where program like '%rman%')
  5 And wait_time>0;
     SID EVENT                            WAIT_TIME
---------- ------------------------------ ----------
     121 RMAN backup & recovery I/O              11
     129 SQL*Net message from client              1
     129 SQL*Net message from client              2
     129 SQL*Net message from client              2
     130 SQL*Net message from client            400
     130 SQL*Net message from client            200
     130 SQL*Net message from client            100
     130 SQL*Net message from client            766
```

This gives us the cumulative wait times for a given session. You might wait for a few moments and run the query again. Perhaps you would get these results:

```
    SID EVENT                                WAIT_TIME
---------- ------------------------------   ----------
    121 RMAN backup & recovery I/O               85
    121 RMAN backup & recovery I/O               47
    129 SQL*Net message from client               1
    129 SQL*Net message from client               2
    129 SQL*Net message from client               2
    130 SQL*Net message from client            1000
    130 SQL*Net message from client            1000
    130 SQL*Net message from client            1000
    130 SQL*Net message from client            1000
    130 SQL*Net message from client            1000
```

The difference in session 121's wait titled RMAN backup & recovery I/O might indicate a problem with the disk subsystem that we are backing up to (which is quite correct in this situation, as we ran this on a slow computer).

Administering RMAN Operations

For the OCP exam, you will be expected to know how to administer RMAN. The principal commands used to administer RMAN are the `delete` command, the `crosscheck` command, the `catalog` command, and finally, the `resync` command.

Using the *delete* Command

The `delete` command is used to mark backup set pieces, image copies, or archived redo logs as deleted if they have been previously marked as expired (missing) or obsolete (retention criteria–related). Previously in this chapter you saw the `list expired` command used to indicate which backup set pieces were expired. After running the `list expired` command, we would use the `delete expired backup` command to mark those as permanently deleted from the control file and the recovery catalog.

When the delete expired command is executed, all records for those backup set pieces in the control file and/or the recovery catalog are marked as deleted. When the delete obsolete command is executed, that command will mark the records for the backupset pieces as deleted in the control file and recovery catalog. The delete obsolete command will also remove any physical-backup set pieces present on the backup media.

Here is an example where we list the expired (missing) backup set pieces and then delete them:

```
RMAN> list expired backup;
List of Backup Sets
```

```
====================
BS Key  Type LV Size       Device Type Elapsed Time Completion Time
------- ---- -- ---------- ----------- ------------ ---------------
425     Full    176.72M    DISK        00:06:02     11-OCT-08
        BP Key: 433   Status: EXPIRED  Compressed: YES  Tag: TAG20081011T142622
        Piece Name: C:\ORACLE\FLASH_RECOVERY_AREA\ORCL\BACKUPSET\2008_10_11
\01_MF_NNNDF_TAG20081011T142622_4H22ZOMK_.BKP
  List of Datafiles in backup set 425
  File LV Type Ckp SCN    Ckp Time  Name
  ---- -- ---- ---------- --------- ----
  1       Full 903859     11-OCT-08 C:\ORACLE\ORADATA\ORCL\SYSTEM01.DBF
  2       Full 903859     11-OCT-08 C:\ORACLE\ORADATA\ORCL\SYSAUX01.DBF
  3       Full 903859     11-OCT-08 C:\ORACLE\ORADATA\ORCL\UNDOTBS01.DBF
  4       Full 903859     11-OCT-08 C:\ORACLE\ORADATA\ORCL\USERS01.DBF
RMAN> delete expired backup;
using channel ORA_DISK_1
List of Backup Pieces
BP Key  BS Key  Pc# Cp# Status      Device Type Piece Name
------- ------- --- --- ----------- ----------- ----------
433     425     1   1   EXPIRED     DISK
C:\ORACLE\FLASH_RECOVERY_AREA\ORCL\BACKUPSET\2008_10_11
\01_MF_NNNDF_TAG20081011T142622_4H22ZOMK_.BKP
Do you really want to delete the above objects (enter YES or NO)? yes
deleted backup piece
backup piece handle=C:\ORACLE\FLASH_RECOVERY_AREA\ORCL\BACKUPSET\2008_10_11\
01_MF_NNNDF_TAG20081011T142622_4H22ZOMK_.BKP RECID=2 STAMP=667837589
Deleted 1 EXPIRED objects
```

One important thing to note is that once you have marked a backup set with a DELETED status, that status cannot be changed. Thus, if you ever needed to restore that backup set piece, you would have to use the catalog command to reimport it into the database control file and recovery catalog (assuming it was still available).

Using the *crosscheck* Command

The crosscheck command is used to validate RMAN records in the database control file and the recovery catalog against what is physically on the backup media. The crosscheck command can be used on both disk backups and tape backups. In this example, we are using it to validate that all the backups set pieces recorded in the control file of our database are actually on the media where they are supposed to be:

```
RMAN> crosscheck backup of database;
using channel ORA_DISK_1
crosschecked backup piece: found to be 'EXPIRED'
```

```
backup piece handle=C:\ORACLE\FLASH_RECOVERY_AREA\ORCL\BACKUPSET\2008_10_18
\O1_MF_NNNDF_TAG20081018T152908_4HNO9DX9_.BKP RECID=27 STAMP=668446156
Crosschecked 1 objects
```

In this case, we had some bad news because one of our backup set pieces is marked EXPIRED, or missing. If we know that it's permanently gone, we can use the delete expired command (discussed earlier in this chapter) to mark it as deleted. Sometimes the backup set piece is expired just because the backup media is offline (for example, a bad disk cable). Once the backup media is back online, you would rerun the crosscheck command and the backup set piece would be marked as AVAILABLE once it is again accessible by RMAN.

As with other administration commands, you can cross-check the gambit of backups. From database backups and archive-log backups to image copies, the crosscheck command covers them all.

Using the *catalog* Command

The catalog command is used to import one or more backup set pieces, image copies, control-file copies, or archived redo logs into the recovery catalog. For example, say we had executed a crosscheck of our database backups and then deleted the expired backup set pieces with the delete expired command. That would mark the expired backup set piece as deleted in our control file and recovery catalog. This is okay until the missing backup set piece reappears (say we restore it from a tape backup). In this case, you will have to use the catalog command to reregister the backup set piece in the control file and recovery catalog. Here is an example of the use of the catalog command:

```
RMAN> crosscheck backup of database;
using channel ORA_DISK_1
crosschecked backup piece: found to be 'EXPIRED'
backup piece handle=C:\ORACLE\FLASH_RECOVERY_AREA\ORCL\BACKUPSET\2008_10_18
\O1_MF_NNNDF_TAG20081018T152908_4HNO9DX9_.BKP RECID=27 STAMP=668446156
Crosschecked 1 objects
RMAN> catalog backuppiece
'C:\ORACLE\FLASH_RECOVERY_AREA\ORCL\BACKUPSET\2008_10_18
\O1_MF_NNNDF_TAG20081018T152908_4HNO9DX9_.BKP';
cataloged backup piece
backup piece handle=C:\ORACLE\FLASH_RECOVERY_AREA\ORCL\BACKUPSET\2008_10_18
\O1_MF_NNNDF_TAG20081018T152908_4HNO9DX9_.BKP RECID=30 STAMP=668447953
```

The crosscheck command can also import complete directories, as shown in this example:

```
RMAN> catalog start with
'C:\ORACLE\FLASH_RECOVERY_AREA\ORCL\BACKUPSET\2008_10_18\';
```

```
searching for all files that match the pattern
C:\ORACLE\FLASH_RECOVERY_AREA\ORCL\BACKUPSET\2008_10_18\
List of Files Unknown to the Database
=====================================
File Name: C:\ORACLE\FLASH_RECOVERY_AREA\ORCL\BACKUPSET\2008_10_18\
01_MF_ANNNN_TAG20081018T153543_4HNOP6OH_.BKP.old
File Name: C:\ORACLE\FLASH_RECOVERY_AREA\ORCL\BACKUPSET\2008_10_18\
01_MF_NNNDF_TAG20081018T152908_4HNO9DX9_.BKP.old
Do you really want to catalog the above files (enter YES or NO)? yes
cataloging files...
cataloging done
List of Cataloged Files
=======================
File Name: C:\ORACLE\FLASH_RECOVERY_AREA\ORCL\BACKUPSET\2008_10_18\
01_MF_ANNNN_TAG20081018T153543_4HNOP6OH_.BKP.old
File Name: C:\ORACLE\FLASH_RECOVERY_AREA\ORCL\BACKUPSET\2008_10_18\
01_MF_NNNDF_TAG20081018T152908_4HNO9DX9_.BKP.old
RMAN> list backup of database summary;
List of Backups
===============

Key     TY LV S Device Type Completion Time #Pieces #Copies Compressed Tag
------- -- -- - ----------- --------------- ------- ------- ---------- ---
1253    B  F  A DISK        18-OCT-08       1       1       YES
TAG20081018T152908
```

The `catalog` command can come in quite handy during disaster-recovery exercises when all you have are backup set pieces and an Oracle database instance. You can create the instance, catalog the backup set pieces (including control-file autobackups), and then restore your database. The `catalog` command works only with disk devices, so in disaster-recovery cases you might first have to restore datafiles from tape before you can catalog them.

Using the *resync* Command

The `resync` command is used to synchronize the recovery catalog with the control file. RMAN will often perform automatic resync operations, but there may be times when you will want to perform a manual resync operation. Simply issue the `resync catalog` command and the catalog will be synchronized with the recovery catalog, as shown in this example:

```
RMAN> resync catalog;
starting full resync of recovery catalog
full resync complete
```

Tuning RMAN Operations

The final topic in this chapter is how to tune RMAN operations. Of course, standard Oracle tuning methodologies apply here; use enough backup devices to get good I/O performance. Allocate enough memory to the database, and make sure your CPUs can handle the load.

Another method of tuning your RMAN operations is through parallel channel operations. Recall that using channels is the method that RMAN uses to write backup-related information from the database to the backup device. If you can create multiple channels to different backup devices (say two channels to two different disk drives or tape devices), then you can speed up the performance of your backups in many cases.

Oracle also provides the duration parameter associated with the backup command, which allows you to indicate to Oracle how much overall impact it should allow the backup to have on the database as a whole. When using the duration parameter, you indicate the overall duration that you want the backup to run. If it runs over that (say 5 hours), then RMAN will terminate the backup. The datafiles already backed up will still be valid, but there may be datafiles that are not backed up. RMAN will prioritize any missed datafile backups on the subsequent backup operation.

Note that if a backup does not complete after the amount of time identified in the duration parameter, then the whole backup will be considered to have failed. Other backup operations within a run block will not be executed as a result. You can use the partial keyword to indicate to RMAN that it should consider the backup to have been successful and not return an error. This will allow subsequent commands (like archive-log backups) to execute. Here is an example of the use of the partial keyword:

```
RMAN> Backup as compressed backupset duration 1:00
partial minimize load database ;
```

If you use the duration minimize load parameter when performing a backup, then you will be indicating to Oracle that you want it to reduce the load that the backup has on the database as a whole. When minimize load is used, Oracle will try to spread the backup over the entire time identified in the duration parameter. This will result in slower backup times but improved overall database performance. Here is an example of the use of the duration parameter in the backup command:

```
RMAN> Backup as compressed backupset duration 1:00 minimize load database;
```

Summary

In some ways, this is the most important chapter when it comes to RMAN overall. In previous chapters we have shown you that typical backup and recovery is not a very complex task most of the time in RMAN. When things go wrong, however, RMAN can become a bit trickier. Of course, things tend to go wrong just when the stress is the highest and the need to get your database up and running is the highest.

To help you with these difficult moments and prepare you for the OCP exam, we covered RMAN reporting, tuning, and monitoring. Reporting is quite important because you need to be able to see what backups are available (for example, to determine what types of incomplete recovery are actually available).

Tuning is important because we want our backups and our recoveries to go as fast as possible. Everyone wants the backups to go fast, and the longer they take the more impact they have on the system. Of course, everyone wants restores to go fast. That's where strategies like parallelism come in handy.

Monitoring is important too because we need to be able to look at backup or restore operations as they are happening and answer the question, Does this look normal? Monitoring gives us that ability. It's important to know what is normal for your backups and your recoveries so that when the time comes, you will be able to understand just what is not normal and how deviant a statistic actually is from the norm. Then you can address the problem.

This is the last chapter on RMAN in this book. Questions on RMAN will be a significant portion of your OCP exam. Study it hard, and practice backup and recovery a lot before you take your test (both RMAN and user-managed). If you do so, we suspect you will do well on your exam.

Exam Essentials

Be able to use the `list` and `report` commands.   Understanding the `list` and `report` commands is very important to RMAN operations and to being successful on your OCP exam. They allow you to review metadata contained within the database control file and recovery catalog, understand backups that have been taken, and take corrective action when certain conditions arise.

Be able to administer the RMAN environment.   Understanding how to administer RMAN is quite important. Knowing how to use commands like `catalog`, `delete`, and `crosscheck` is critical to properly administering the RMAN environment. These commands will come in especially handy after disaster recovery when you need to get your database up and running quickly.

Be able to performance-tune your RMAN operations.   Understanding how parallelism can make your database backups and restores perform faster is critical to making RMAN performant. Understand how to control the duration of a backup and how to reduce the overall I/O load with the `duration` command.

Review Questions

1. Which command would you use to determine what database backups are currently available for restore?

   A. `list database backup;`

   B. `report database backup;`

   C. `list backup of database;`

   D. `list summary backup;`

   E. `report backup of database;`

2. What command would you use to ensure that backup records in the control file are pointing to actual physical files on the backup media?

   A. `crosscheck`

   B. `list backup`

   C. `confirm`

   D. `resync`

   E. `backup validate`

3. You have backed up your database twice without connecting to the recovery catalog. What command do you issue to transfer the control-file metadata to the recovery catalog?

   A. `synch catalog`

   B. `resync catalog`

   C. `replicate catalog`

   D. `update catalog`

   E. `restore catalog`

4. You want to make sure that your database backup does not exceed 10 hours in length. What command would you issue that would meet this condition?

   A. `backup database plus archivelog;`

   B. `backup database plus archivlog until time '10:00';`

   C. `backup database plus archivelog timeout '10:00';`

   D. `backup database plus archivelog duration 10:00;`

   E. `backup database plus archivelog timeout 10:00;`

5. You have lost all your RMAN backup set pieces due to a disk failure. Unfortunately, you have an automated cross-check script that also does a `delete expired backupset` command. You have restored all the backup set pieces from tape. What command would you use to get those backup set pieces registered in the recovery catalog and the control file of the database again?

A. `register database`

B. `recover catalog`

C. `load backupset`

D. `synch metadata`

E. `catalog start with`

6. You run the following commands:

```
RMAN> list expired backup;
RMAN> delete expired backup;
```

What will happen to the backup set pieces associated with the backups that appear in the `list expired backup` command?

A. They will be renamed.

B. Nothing will happen to them. The backup set pieces do not exist.

C. They will be deleted immediately since they are not in the flash recovery area.

D. You will need to manually remove the physical files listed in the output of the commands.

E. They will become hidden files and removed 10 days later.

7. Why would you run the `delete obsolete` command? (Choose all that apply.)

A. To remove missing backup set pieces physically from disk

B. To remove metadata related to backup set pieces in the control file and the recovery catalog

C. To mark as deleted records in the control file and the recovery catalog associated with obsolete backup sets

D. To delete backup set pieces associated with backups that are no longer needed due to retention criteria

E. To remove old versions of RMAN backups

8. What does it mean if a backup is expired?

A. The backup set has exceeded the retention criteria set in RMAN and is eligible for removal.

B. The backup set has one or more invalid blocks in it and is not usable for recovery.

C. The backup set contains one or more tablespaces no longer in the database.

D. The backup set contains one or more missing backup set pieces.

E. The backup set is from a previous version of RMAN and was not upgraded.

9. If a backup set is expired, what can you do to correct the problem?

A. Change the retention criteria.

B. Make the lost backup set pieces available to RMAN again.

C. Run the `crosscheck` command to correct the location for the backup set piece contained in the metadata.

D. Nothing. The backup set piece is lost forever.

E. Call Oracle support. Their assistance is required.

10. How long will this backup be allowed to run?

`Backup as compressed backupset duration 2:00 minimize load database ;`

A. 2 minutes

B. 2 hours

C. 2 days

D. The command will generate an error.

E. This backup is not constrained by any time limitation.

11. What is the impact of the following backup if it exceeds the duration allowance? (Choose all that apply.)

`Backup as compressed backupset duration 2:00 partial minimize load database ;`

A. The entire backup will fail. It will not be usable for recovery.

B. The entire backup will fail, but any datafile successfully backed up will be usable for recovery.

C. If this backup fails, subsequent backups will prioritize datafiles not backed up.

D. If this backup fails, an error will be raised and any other commands will not be executed.

E. If this backup fails, no error will be raised and any other commands will be executed.

12. In what view are you likely to see the following output?

SID	SERIAL#	EVENT	SECONDS_IN_WAIT
121	269	RMAN backup & recovery I/O	2
129	415	SQL*Net message from client	63
130	270	SQL*Net message from client	8

A. V$SESSION_EVENT

B. V$SESSION

C. V$WAITS

D. V$WAITSTAT

E. V$SYSSTAT

13. What view might you use to try to determine how long a particular backup will take?

   A. V$SESSION_EVENT

   B. V$SESSION

   C. V$WAITS

   D. V$WAITSTAT

   E. V$SESSION_LONGOPS

14. What is the impact of the results of the output of the following command?

```
RMAN> report unrecoverable database;
Report of files that need backup due to unrecoverable operations
File Type of Backup Required Name
---- ---------------------- -----------------------------------
4    full or incremental    C:\ORACLE\ORADATA\ORCL\USERS01.DBF
```

   A. There are no backup sets with any backups of the users01.dbf datafile.

   B. The users01.dbf datafile has had unrecoverable operations occur in it. It will need to be backed up or some data loss is possible during a recovery.

   C. The users01.dbf datafile is corrupted.

   D. The users01.dbf datafile backup exceeds the retention criteria.

   E. The last backup of the users01.dbf datafile failed and must be rerun.

15. What does the output on this report indicate?

```
RMAN> report need backup;
RMAN retention policy will be applied to the command
RMAN retention policy is set to redundancy 1
Report of files with less than 1 redundant backups
File #bkps Name
---- ----- ------------------------------------------
5    0     C:\ORACLE\ORADATA\ORCL\MY_DATA_01.DBF
```

   A. The my_data_01.dbf datafile is corrupted and needs to be restored.

   B. The my_data_01.dbf datafile has not yet been backed up. This report does not imply that the data in the datafile can not be recovered.

   C. The my_data_01.dbf datafile has not yet been backed up. This report implies that the data in the datafile can not be recovered.

   D. The my_data_01.dbf datafile no longer meets the retention criteria for backups.

   E. Datafile 5 is missing.

16. What does the `minimize load database` parameter mean when backing up a database?

A. RMAN will attempt to make the backup run as fast as possible without any IO limitations.

B. RMAN will automatically restrict the number of channels in use to one.

C. RMAN will spread the backup IO over the total duration stated in the `backup` command.

D. RMAN will skip any datafile that currently is involved in an IO operation. RMAN will retry backing up the datafile later and an error will be raised at the end of the backup if the datafile cannot be backed up.

E. Datafiles will be backed up; those having the lowest current number of IO operations will be backed up first.

17. What is the result of this command?

RMAN> Report need backup days 3;

A. Lists all datafiles created in the last three days that are not backed up.

B. Lists all datafiles not recoverable based on the current retention criteria.

C. Lists all datafiles not backed up in the last three days. The datafile is not recoverable.

D. Lists all datafiles that need to be backed up due to unrecoverable operations.

E. Lists all datafiles not backed up in the last three days. It does not imply that the datafile is not recoverable.

18. Why would you execute the `report obsolete` command?

A. To list all backups that were no longer available for restore operations

B. To list all backups that had aged beyond the RMAN retention criteria

C. To list all backup set pieces listed in control-file or recovery-catalog metadata that are not on the backup media

D. To list all datafiles that are no longer part of the database and thus do not need to be backed up

E. To list all archived redo logs that are no longer needed for any database recovery

19. What information does the `report schema` command not provide? (Choose all that apply.)

A. Size of the datafiles

B. Size of the tempfiles

C. Date of last backup for datafiles and tempfiles

D. Filenames for each datafile

E. Checkpoint SCN associated with the last RMAN backup

20. If a backup is expired, which of the following is true?

A. It can never be used for a restore/recover operation.

B. Oracle will remove the backup set pieces from the flash recovery area.

C. The backup has been used at least once to restore and recover the database.

D. The backup is no longer valid because of a `resetlogs` operation.

E. The physical backup set pieces are missing from the media.

Answers to Review Questions

1. C. The `list backup of database` command provides information on all database backups that are available for restore via RMAN.

2. A. The `crosscheck` command is used to validate all RMAN-related metadata with associated physical backups on backup media.

3. B. The `resync catalog` command is used to synchronize the recovery catalog with the database control file.

4. D. The `duration` command is used to limit the overall time of a database backup.

5. E. The `catalog` command is used to load backup set pieces that do not already exist into the recovery catalog or the control file.

6. B. Expired backup set pieces are those backup set pieces that do not exist. They are discovered via the `crosscheck` command and marked as expired. The `list expired` command reports backup set records that are marked as expired. The `delete expired backup` command marks the backup metadata in the control file and recovery catalog with a status of DELETED.

7. C, D. The `delete obsolete` command will mark the related metadata records for the backups as DELETED in the control file and the recovery catalog.

8. D. If a backup is expired, it means that a `crosscheck` command has detected that one or more backup set pieces associated with that backup are missing.

9. B. You would make the lost backup set available again by running the `crosscheck` command once the backup set piece becomes available on the backup media.

10. B. The backup will be allowed to run for 2 hours.

11. B, C, E. The backup will fail after the duration period expires, but the datafiles that were backed up successfully will be able to be used in any restore operation. RMAN will prioritize any datafiles not backed up in subsequent backups. Also, the backup will not return an error when the duration expires and other commands will be executed.

12. B. This output would be from the V$SESSION view. It contains the current wait event for each session as well as how long the wait has been occurring.

13. E. The V$SESSION_LONGOPS view is used to estimate how long a given running operation has until it is complete.

14. B. The users01.dbf database datafile has had an unrecoverable operation occur. Because an unrecoverable operation does not generate redo records, the data involved in that operation will be lost in the event of a recovery. The datafile should be backed up.

15. B. The #bkps columns shows zero, which indicates that the datafile has not been backed up. The datafile may yet still be recoverable as long as the archived redo logs are available.

16. C. RMAN will attempt to spread the overall IO over the total stated duration of the backup listed in the `duration` parameter. This will have the effect of limiting the overall load on the database and reducing the performance impacts of the backup.

17. E. This command lists all database datafiles that would require that more than three days of archived redo logs be applied in order to be restored.

18. B. The `report obsolete` command will list all RMAN backups that have aged beyond the RMAN retention criteria and are eligible for removal.

19. C, E. The `report schema` command does not contain the date of the last backup of the datafiles and tempfiles. Also, the `report schema` command does not report the checkpoint SCNs associated with each RMAN backup.

20. E. If a backup is expired, then the physical backup set pieces are missing from the backup media. This backup cannot be restored unless the physical backup set pieces are found, and either re-cataloged or re-crosschecked.

Chapter

8

Performing Oracle Advanced Recovery

ORACLE DATABASE 11*g*: ADMINISTRATION II EXAM OBJECTIVES COVERED IN THIS CHAPTER:

✓ **Using RMAN to Perform Recovery**

- Restore a database onto a new host

- Perform disaster recovery

✓ **Using RMAN to Duplicate a Database**

- Creating a duplicate database

- Using a duplicate database

✓ **Performing Tablespace Point-in-Time Recovery**

- Identify the situations that require TSPITR

- Perform automated TSPITR

We have already discussed the basics of recovering your Oracle database. You now know how to use the `restore` and `recover` commands to recover your database to the point of failure. In this chapter, we will cover more advanced recovery topics. First we will cover RMAN incarnations, and then we will introduce you to RMAN database duplication. After that we will discuss tablespace point-in-time recovery, and we will close the chapter with some discussion of disaster recovery of your Oracle database.

Switching Between RMAN Incarnations

We introduced you to the idea of RMAN incarnations in Chapter 2 and have talked about incarnations in several other chapters. A *database incarnation* is the measure of the logical lifetime of an Oracle database. A database's first incarnation begins when it is created and ends whenever the `resetlogs` option is used to open the database. The next incarnation starts at the point of the `resetlogs` operation and ends at the point of the next `resetlogs` operations and so on. When a new incarnation is started, the log sequence numbers are reset, the online redo logs are flushed, and the database literally has a new future.

Sometimes when performing RMAN operations it is necessary to reset to a previous database incarnation. This is pretty rare and is typically done in cases where you have restored your database using point-in-time recovery. After such cases, if you need to perform another restore and that restore needs to be to an SCN that is before the current reset-log SCN, then you will have to reset the database incarnation.

For example, look at this output of this `list incarnation` command:

```
RMAN> list incarnation;
using target database control file instead of recovery catalog
List of Database Incarnations
DB Key  Inc Key DB Name  DB ID        STATUS   Reset SCN  Reset Time
------- ------- -------- ----------- ------   ---------- ----------
1       1       ORCL     1194923408   PARENT   1          10/15/2007 10:08:59
2       2       ORCL     1194923408   PARENT   886308     10/03/2008 13:24:36
3       3       ORCL     1194923408   CURRENT  904361     10/03/2008 14:05:15
```

If you wanted to restore the database to a point in time before 10/03/2008 at 14:05:15 (or SCN 904361), you would need to reset the database to one of the previous incarnations. If, however, you wanted to restore the database to the resetlog time/SCN or after that time, then you would not need to reset the database incarnation.

To reset the database incarnation, you would need to mount the database first. Then use the `reset database to incarnation` command. You include the incarnation number that you want to switch to in the command. This number comes from the `Inc Key` column displayed in the `list incarnation` command output. Here is an example of switching the database to incarnation number 2:

```
RMAN> shutdown immediate
database closed
database dismounted
Oracle instance shut down
RMAN> startup mount
connected to target database (not started)
Oracle instance started
database mounted
Total System Global Area      364081152 bytes
Fixed Size                      1333228 bytes
Variable Size                 239077396 bytes
Database Buffers              117440512 bytes
Redo Buffers                    6230016 bytes
RMAN> Reset database to incarnation 2;
database reset to incarnation 2
```

Figure 8.1 provides a graphic example of database incarnations. In this graphic, the database crashes at SCN 40000 (shown in point A in the figure). We restore the database from a backup taken at SCN 10000 (shown in point B in the figure) and recover it to SCN 25000 (shown in point C). Perhaps we have lost the redo logs needed to restore the database beyond SCN 25000, and so we open the database at SCN 25000 with the `alter database open resetlogs` command. This creates a new incarnation of the database. Note that the SCNs are greater than 40000 (because the SCN does not change), but notice that there is a new timeline with which the changes are being recorded (the tangent line heading to the northeast in the figure). This is the new incarnation of the database (demonstrated in point D). It's a completely new life for the database, and everything that happened in the database in the previous life after the previous SCN 25000 is as if it had never happened. There will now actually be two SCN 25000s in the redo stream.

FIGURE 8.1 Example of an Oracle incarnation

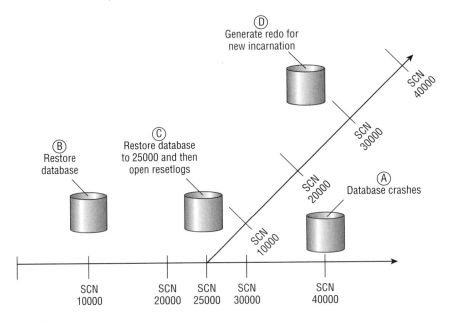

Overview of RMAN Database Duplication

One frequent use of RMAN is to duplicate an existing database. *Database duplication* can be used for a number of different purposes, such as creating development and test databases from production databases or creating a database to test upgrades. In the following sections, we will discuss RMAN duplication basics. Then we will cover how to use the RMAN duplicate database command to duplicate a database. We will fist look at how to prepare to duplicate the database. We will then walk you through actually duplicating the database, and finally we will discuss things to do after.

RMAN Database Duplication Basics

The host from which the database is being duplicated is the *source host*. The host to which the database is being duplicated is called the *destination host*. The source host and destination host can be the same computer or a different computer, depending on your needs. One requirement is that the source and destination host must be on the same platform. The target or source database is the database that you will be duplicating from. You will be duplicating to a database instance that will be associated with the new database. This instance is called the *auxiliary instance*.

Two types of database duplication exist:

Active database duplication   Active database duplication duplicates the live target database to the auxiliary instance over the network. As a result, no backup of the target database is required and the destination host need not have access to the RMAN backup set pieces.

Backup-based database duplication   Backup-based database duplication requires that a backup of the database being duplicated be available. This backup can be an RMAN backup set or image copy. The target host must have access to these backup sets in order to complete the database duplication.

Database duplication takes place over what is called the auxiliary channel. This channel is created during the duplication process and is a server process associated with the auxiliary instance.

When you connect to RMAN to start a database duplication, you will connect to both the target database and the auxiliary instance. This implies that network connectivity to the auxiliary instance is available, and as you will see, getting the auxiliary instance up and running is one prerequisite to starting a database-duplication operation.

Performing an RMAN Database Duplication

Duplicating a database is an operation that many DBAs find themselves doing. RMAN provides the `duplicate database` command to help ease the database-duplication process.

Preparing to Duplicate Your Database

Preparing to duplicate your database requires a few steps:

1. Backing up the target database (backup-based database duplication only)

2. Making backup images available to the destination host (backup-based database duplication only)

3. Deciding where to put the duplicate-database-related files

4. Preparing the auxiliary instance for the duplication

Let's look at each of these steps in more detail next.

Backing up the target database is not required if you are using active database duplication. If you are doing backup-based duplication, you will need a complete backup of the target database. Follow the steps outlined in Chapter 3 to perform an RMAN backup of your database. The database can be in NOARCHIVELOG or ARCHIVELOG mode.

Making backup images available to the destination host is not required if you are using active database duplication. If you are doing backup-based duplication, you will need to make the backup set pieces associated with the backup of the target database, and all associated archived redo logs, available to the destination host. This is so they can be read by RMAN during the duplication process. You can make everything available to the destination host by putting the backup set pieces on shared devices (such as Network File System, or NFS) or some other shared disk environment. You could also manually copy the needed files to the destination host via Secure File Transfer Protocol (SFTP) or some equivalent file-copy protocol.

You will need to decide where you want to put the database files that will be associated with the newly duplicated database. Files like the control files, the online redo logs, and the database datafiles need a home, and you have to know where that will be before you start the duplication process. In the next step, you will use this information to configure the auxiliary instance for duplication.

Before you can begin the duplication process, you must configure the auxiliary instance so that it will start. To do so, follow these steps:

Step 1: Configure any OS-specific requirements.   Different operating systems require that certain prerequisites be completed before you can start a database instance. For example, in Windows you must create the Windows service, and in most Unix flavors you will need to configure shared memory. You will need to make sure that these preconfiguration steps are complete before you can start the auxiliary instance and begin the duplication process.

Step 2: Configure the database password file for the auxiliary instance.   The auxiliary instance will require a password file. Use the `orapwd` command (see Chapter 3 for more on `orapwd`) to create the password file. If you prefer, you can instruct Oracle to copy the password file from the target database to the duplicated database when you issue the duplication command.

Step 3: Configure Oracle networking for the auxiliary instance.   If you will be executing the `duplicate` command from a host other than the destination host, or if you are going to use active database duplication, you will have to configure Oracle networking so that you can connect to the auxiliary instance via Oracle Net. You can use the Oracle Net Configuration Assistant to configure both the database listener and the `tnsnames.ora` file for naming resolution.

Step 4: Configure the database parameter file for the auxiliary instance.   Configuring the database parameter file correctly can make for successful database duplication. Incorrectly configuring the parameter file can make for a frustrating exercise in futility. The parameter file must be configured to be able to start the auxiliary instance. The parameters listed in Table 8.1 are available for use during the database-duplication process. You may not need to use all of the parameters listed in Table 8.1 when duplicating databases. In some cases these parameters can also be defined on the RMAN command line as parameters of the duplication command.

Step 5: Start the auxiliary instance.   The auxiliary instance should be ready to start at this time. To start it, simply connect to the auxiliary instance from SQL*Plus and issue the `startup nomount` command. Once you have been able to get the auxiliary instance started, you are ready to duplicate to it.

TABLE 8.1 Auxiliary Database Parameters Related to Database Duplication

Parameter Name	Purpose
DB_NAME	The name of the duplicated database. This same name will be used in the RMAN duplicate command. This name should be unique for databases on a given host. This parameter is a required parameter for any database duplication.
CONTROL_FILES	Identifies the location of the control files for the auxiliary instance. This parameter is required unless you are using OMF.
DB_BLOCK_SIZE	Block size of the database to be created. This parameter is required if the same parameter has been defined on the source database.
DB_FILE_NAME_CONVERT	Contains pairs of strings that indicate the conversion path for database files from the source database to the target database. For example, if the parameter were set to '/ora01/oracle/oradata','/ora02/oracle/oradata', all files contained in /ora01/oracle/oradata would be re-created on the duplicate database in /ora02/oracle/oradata. This parameter can also be defined as part of the call to the RMAN duplicate command.
LOG_FILE_NAME_CONVERT	Contains pairs of strings that indicate the conversion path for database redo-log files from the source database to the target database. For example, if the parameter were set to '/ora01/oracle/oradata','/ora02/oracle/oradata', all online redo-log files contained in /ora01/oracle/oradata would be re-created on the duplicate database in /ora02/oracle/oradata.

This parameter can also be defined as part of the call to the RMAN duplicate command.

Duplicating Your Database

As mentioned previously, there are two different modes of database duplication. They are active database duplication and backup-based database duplication. Both duplication methods are achieved via the use of the duplicate database command. Let's look at the duplicate database command in more detail. Following that we will look at both database-duplication modes in more detail.

Connecting to RMAN for a Database Duplication

Before starting database duplication, you will need to start RMAN and connect to the correct databases. When starting RMAN, you will need to connect to the following:

- The target database
- The auxiliary database

Typically you will connect to the target database locally and connect to the auxiliary database via Oracle Net, but this is not a requirement. Here is an example of connecting to RMAN to perform a database duplication. In this example, we are connecting to a local target database called orcl. We use the auxiliary command-line parameter to indicate that we are connecting to an auxiliary database. In this case, it is the database pointed to by the net service name of mydb.

```
set oracle_sid=orcl
rman target=/ auxiliary=sys/password@mydb
```

You could also use these variations to connect with RMAN for a database duplication:

```
rman target=sys/robert auxiliary=sys/password@mydb
rman target=sys/robert@orcl auxiliary=sys/password@mydb
```

 You might have noticed that we don't use SYSDBA when connecting to RMAN. That is because all connections from RMAN to any database are always with SYSDBA privileges.

The RMAN *duplicate database* Command

The RMAN duplicate database command is used when performing either mode of database duplication. The command comes with a number of different options that give you ability to complete the following operations:

- Copy the source spfile to the auxiliary instance.
- Change specific parameters when copying a source spfile to the auxiliary instance.
- Indicate the location that the duplicated files should be copied to using the database filename conversion options DB_FILE_NAME_CONVERT and LOG_FILE_NAME_CONVERT.
- Create a stand-by database environment on the auxiliary instance.
- Open the duplicated database in a restricted session.
- Use the password file from the target database to create the password file on the auxiliary instance (active database duplication only).
- Skip read-only tablespaces.
- Include or exclude specific tablespaces.
- Restore to a specific restore point or use the until clause to restore to a specific time, SCN, or log sequence number (backup-based database duplication only).

During the duplication process, RMAN will automatically create the needed tempfiles for any temporary tablespaces. Here is an example of the RMAN duplication command:

```
Duplicate target database to neworcl nofilenamecheck spfile;
```

The duplicate command comes with a number of options, including the ability to exclude tablespaces, as shown here:

```
Duplicate target database to neworcl nofilenamecheck spfile skip tablespace users;
```

You can also define a restore point, as seen in this example:

```
Duplicate target database to neworcl nofilenamecheck spfile skip
tablespace users to restore point 'Test';
```

You can have Oracle open the duplicated database in restricted mode by adding the **open restricted** parameter, as shown here:

```
Duplicate target database to neworcl nofilenamecheck spfile open restricted;
```

 As with pretty much everything else Oracle, the duplicate command is well documented. We strongly recommend that you review the Oracle Database Backup and Recovery Reference (Oracle part number B28273-02) for more information on all RMAN-related commands.

Active Database Duplication

Active database duplication is started by issuing the RMAN duplicate database command and including the from active database parameter. Active database duplication is not the default.

When you perform active database duplication, Oracle will create the auxiliary channel to the auxiliary database. An additional target-database RMAN channel will also be required. If you have configured automated channels, this should be sufficient. If not, you will need to allocate a channel manually with the allocate channel command.

Finally, the until and to restore point clauses are not valid when doing an active database duplication. Here is an example of the RMAN duplicate command performing an active database duplication:

```
duplicate target database to neworcl from active database nofilenamecheck
spfile set control_files 'c:\oracle\oradata\neworcl\control01.ctl',
'c:\oracle\oradata\neworcl\control02.ctl'
set db_file_name_convert 'c:\oracle\oradata\orcl','c:\oracle\oradata\neworcl'
set log_file_name_convert
'c:\oracle\oradata\orcl','c:\oracle\oradata\neworcl';
```

Backup-Based Database Duplication

Using the duplicate database command without the from active database parameter starts backup-based database duplication. The auxiliary channel will be allocated automatically. No additional channel is required with backup-based database duplication.

When executing a backup-based database duplication, RMAN will determine the last archived redo log available. RMAN will then restore the duplicate database to the point of that last available archived redo log by default. You can use the `until` or `to restore point` parameter to change this behavior. Here is an example of the RMAN `duplicate` command performing a backup-based database duplication:

```
duplicate target database to neworcl
spfile
set control_files 'c:\oracle\oradata\neworcl\control01.ctl',
'c:\oracle\oradata\neworcl\control02.ctl'
set db_file_name_convert 'c:\oracle\oradata\orcl','c:\oracle\oradata\neworcl'
set log_file_name_convert 'c:\oracle\oradata\orcl',
'c:\oracle\oradata\neworcl';
```

After the Duplication

Once the database duplication is complete, the duplicated database will be opened and operational. You can use the `restricted session` parameter of the `duplicate` command to indicate that RMAN should open the database in a restricted session only. You should, of course, consider backing up the newly created database on a regular basis.

In Exercise 8.1, you'll be duplicating a database using backup-based database duplication.

EXERCISE 8.1

Duplicating a Database Using Backup-Based Duplication

In this exercise, you will use backup-based duplication to create a database on the same system that the target database resides on. For this exercise, your database should be running in ARCHIVELOG mode and all networking to the target database should be already configured.

1. Back up your database as shown in Exercise 4.2.

2. Start RMAN and confirm that you have a valid backup with the `list backup of database summary` command and with the `restore database validate` command. Note that your output will likely look very different from ours.

    ```
    C:\Documents and Settings\Robert>rman target=/
    Recovery Manager: Release 11.1.0.6.0 -
    Production on Sat Oct 4 22:56:10 2008
    Copyright (c) 1982, 2007, Oracle. All rights reserved.
    connected to target database: ORCL (DBID=1194923408)
    RMAN> list backup of database summary;
    ```

EXERCISE 8.1 *(continued)*

```
using target database control file instead of recovery catalog
List of Backups
===============
Key     TY LV S Device Type Completion Time #Pieces #Copies Compressed
------- -- -- - ----------- --------------- ------- ------- ----------
Tag
---
2       B  F  A DISK        03-OCT-08         1       1       YES
TAG20081003T135426
RMAN> restore database validate;
Starting restore at 04-OCT-08
allocated channel: ORA_DISK_1
channel ORA_DISK_1: SID=127 device type=DISK
channel ORA_DISK_1: starting validation of datafile backup set
channel ORA_DISK_1: reading from backup piece C:\ORACLE\FLASH_RECOVERY_AREA\
ORCL\BACKUPSET\2008_10_03
\01_MF_NNNDF_TAG20081003T135426_4GDY3S9H_.BKP
channel ORA_DISK_1: piece handle=C:\ORACLE\FLASH_RECOVERY_AREA\ORCL\
BACKUPSET\2008_10_03
\01_MF_NNNDF_TAG20081003T135426_4GDY3S9H_.BKP tag=TAG20081003T135426
channel ORA_DISK_1: restored backup piece 1
channel ORA_DISK_1: validation complete, elapsed time: 00:01:36
Finished restore at 04-OCT-08
C:\Documents and Settings\Robert>set oracle_sid=orcl
```

3. If you are running in Windows, create the service for the new database with oradim. In this example, you are creating a new database instance called neworcl:

```
C:\>oradim -new -sid neworcl
Instance created.
```

If there are any other OS-specific operations required to create a database instance, complete them now.

4. Create the password file for the neworcl instance:

```
C:\>orapwd file=c:\oracle\product\11.1.0\db_1\database\pwdneworcl.ora
Enter password for SYS:
```

5. Create a temporary pfile for the neworcl auxiliary instance using your editor of choice. The pfile should be contained in the ORACLE_HOME\database directory of the auxiliary instance and should be named initneworcl.ora. The pfile should have these parameters in it:

```
db_name=neworcl
memory_target=300m
control_files='c:\oracle\oradata\neworcl\control01.ctl',
'c:\oracle\oradata\neworcl\control02.ctl'
```

We will do the actual file-location conversions during the duplication.

6. Create the directory c:\oracle\oradata\neworcl:

```
mkdir c:\oracle\oradata\neworcl
```

7. Start up the auxiliary instance:

```
C:\oracle\product\11.1.0\db_1\database>set oracle_sid=neworcl
C:\oracle\product\11.1.0\db_1\database>sqlplus "/ as sysdba"
SQL*Plus: Release 11.1.0.6.0 - Production on Sat Oct 4 23:09:52 2008
Copyright (c) 1982, 2007, Oracle.  All rights reserved.
Connected to an idle instance.
SQL> startup nomount
ORACLE instance started.
Total System Global Area  313860096 bytes
Fixed Size                  1332892 bytes
Variable Size             192940388 bytes
Database Buffers          113246208 bytes
Redo Buffers                6340608 bytes
```

8. Configure service name resolution for your new auxiliary database. The method of this configuration will vary based on your site. In our case, we created an entry in the tnsnames.ora file on our server that looked like this:

```
NEWORCL =
  (DESCRIPTION =
    (ADDRESS = (PROTOCOL = TCP)(HOST = 192.168.2.2)(PORT = 1521))
    (CONNECT_DATA =
      (SERVER = DEDICATED)
      (SERVICE_NAME = neworcl)
    )  )
```

9. Now you will need to hard-code the instance name into the `listener.ora` file until the duplication of the database has been completed. You will get network errors if you do not hard-code the auxiliary instance in the `listener.ora` file. An example of the entry in our `listener.ora` is as follows:

```
SID_LIST_LISTENER =
  (SID_LIST =
    (SID_DESC =
        (ORACLE_HOME=C:\oracle\product\11.1.0\db_1\NETWORK\ADMIN)
        (SID_NAME=neworcl)
    )  )
LISTENER =
  (DESCRIPTION_LIST =
    (DESCRIPTION =
      (ADDRESS = (PROTOCOL = TCP)(HOST = 192.168.2.2)(PORT = 1521))
      (ADDRESS = (PROTOCOL = IPC)(KEY = EXTPROC1521))
    )  )
```

10. Test the network connectivity to the auxiliary instance:

```
C:\>sqlplus sys/robert@neworcl as sysdba
SQL*Plus: Release 11.1.0.6.0 - Production on Sat Oct 4 23:17:50 2008
Copyright (c) 1982, 2007, Oracle.  All rights reserved.
Connected to:
Oracle Database 11g Enterprise Edition Release 11.1.0.6.0 - Production
With the Partitioning, OLAP, Data Mining and
Real Application Testing options
SQL> select instance_name from v$instance;
INSTANCE_NAME
----------------
neworcl
```

If the connection fails, review the network configuration and ensure that the new auxiliary instance is running.

11. Start RMAN, connecting to the target and the auxiliary databases:

```
C:\oracle\product\11.1.0\db_1\database>Set oracle_sid=orcl
C:\oracle\product\11.1.0\db_1\database>Rman target=/ auxiliary=sys/Robert@
neworcl
```

EXERCISE 8.1 *(continued)*

```
Recovery Manager: Release 11.1.0.6.0 -
Production on Sat Oct 4 23:19:55 2008
Copyright (c) 1982, 2007, Oracle.  All rights reserved.
connected to target database: ORCL (DBID=1194923408)
connected to auxiliary database: NEWORCL (not mounted)
```

12. You are now ready to start the database duplication. Issue the duplicate database command, as shown here:

```
duplicate target database to neworcl nofilenamecheck
spfile set control_files=
'c:\oracle\oradata\neworcl\control01.ctl',
'c:\oracle\oradata\neworcl\control02.ctl'
set db_file_name_convert 'c:\oracle\oradata\orcl',
'c:\oracle\oradata\neworcl'
set log_file_name_convert 'c:\oracle\oradata\orcl',
'c:\oracle\oradata\neworcl';
```

This command does the following:

- It starts the duplication process.

- The spfile parameter will result in the target database spfile being copied over to the duplicate database. The duplicate database will use this spfile.

- The set commands (set control_files, set db_file_name_convert, and set log_file_name_convert) modify or add parameters to the spfile being copied to the duplicate database.

This duplicate command will result in a great deal of output, which we have decided not to include here as it seems a great waste of a perfectly good tree. Here is the output that you hopefully will see at the end of the database duplication:

```
database opened
Finished Duplicate Db at 04-OCT-08
```

13. Connect to the duplicated database to verify it is open:

```
C:\oracle\product\11.1.0\db_1\database>set oracle_sid=neworcl
C:\oracle\product\11.1.0\db_1\database>sqlplus sys/Robert as sysdba
SQL*Plus: Release 11.1.0.6.0 - Production on Sun Oct 5 00:04:02 2008
```

```
Copyright (c) 1982, 2007, Oracle.  All rights reserved.
Connected to:
Oracle Database 11g Enterprise Edition Release 11.1.0.6.0 - Production
With the Partitioning, OLAP, Data Mining and
Real Application Testing options
SQL> select name, open_mode from v$database;
NAME      OPEN_MODE
--------- ----------
AUXDB     READ WRITE
```

If you want to run this exercise again after the first successful run, you will need to perform these steps:

1. Shut down the auxiliary instance (now it's a new database!).

2. Remove the spfile assigned to the auxiliary instance.

3. Startup nomount the auxiliary instance.

4. Run this exercise again starting at step 11.

Performing an RMAN Tablespace Point-in-Time Recovery

As you may recall, when you do a point-in-time recovery of an Oracle database, you
have to restore the entire database to the point in time selected. There are times when
you may want to restore a specific tablespace to a specific point in time. DBAs have
been doing this type of recovery manually for a long time. Simply, they restore a backup
to another database on the same or a different server to the point in time they want to
restore the tablespace to. They then export the objects they want to restore (or use transportable tablespaces) to the original database.

Of course, this is a lot of manual work. RMAN automates *tablespace point-in-time
recovery (TSPITR)* for you, making recovery much easier to perform. In this section we
will address TSPITR. We will first look at the TSPITR-related prerequisites and considerations and then look at the aftereffects of a TSPITR. We will then look into setting up for
and executing a TSPITR.

For the `until time` commands shown in this chapter, we set NLS_DATE_
FORMAT at the Windows OS level to a value of mm/dd/yyyy hh24:mi:ss as
seen in this example:

`Set nls_date_format=mm/dd/yyyy hh24:mi:ss`

How you set the NLS_DATE_FORMAT OS level parameter will vary by platform.

If you are using a date format other than ours, you will need to reformat
the date/time in the commands to meet that format. You can also use the
to_date function to format the date as seen in this example:

```
recover tablespace users
until time "to_date('10/06/2008:22:42:00','mm/dd/yyyy:hh24:mi:ss')"
auxiliary destination 'c:\oracle\auxiliary';
```

TSPITR Overview

RMAN provides the ability to do a full TSPITR on a given tablespace or set of tablespaces
with minimal user interaction. This is known as fully automated TSPITR. You may want
to exercise more granular control over TSPITR, in which case you might want to choose to
perform customized RMAN TSPITR where you have more control over the creation of the
auxillary instance and other aspects of the operation. For the purposes of this book, we will
be concerned with only fully automated TSPITR.

Before starting TSPITR   Since TSPITR creates an auxiliary-instance database, it needs to
know where you want to put the files associated with that database. For automated TSPITR,
you are going to use the `auxiliary destination` parameter of the `recover tablespace`
command (discussed shortly); then you will need to create the directory associated with the
auxiliary destination before executing the TSPITR.

Starting TSPITR   You will start TSPITR using the RMAN command `recover tablespace`.
Special syntax (which we will cover shortly) that you will include in the body of the command
will indicate to RMAN that this is a tablespace TSPITR rather than a normal tablespace
recovery. Here is an example of the use of the `recover tablespace` command to start a
TSPITR recovery:

```
recover tablespace users
until time '10/06/2008:22:42:00'
auxiliary destination 'c:\oracle\auxiliary';
```

In this case, we are executing a TSPITR of the USERS tablespace. We want to recover the
entire USERS tablespace to 10/6/2008 at 22:42:00 hours. The `auxiliary destination`
clause, discussed earlier, indicates where we want RMAN to create the auxiliary instance
database files—in this case, the directory c:\oracle\auxiliary.

Now that we have executed the `recover tablespace` command, what happens next?

The TSPITR auxiliary instance   TSPITR requires the use of an auxiliary instance just as
database duplication does. The *auxiliary instance* (in RMAN output, it's called an *automatic*

instance) is the database that will be used to perform the TSPITR. It is a transient database, used just long enough to restore the tablespaces, export the database, and finish the TSPITR. The main difference here is that once RMAN is done with the TSPITR, the auxiliary instance will no longer be needed.

TSPITR transport-set check   When you start the TSPITR with the `recover tablespace` command, RMAN will check that the tablespace you want to recover can actually be recovered. It does this by checking the transport set to ensure that it's wholly self-contained. See the next section, "Checking the Transport Set," for more information on this process and why it's needed.

Create the auxiliary instance   Once RMAN confirms that the tablespace set can be transported, it will create the auxiliary instance, start it, and connect to it. This is nice since you will not have to create the auxiliary instance. You can opt to create the auxiliary instance yourself if there are specific reasons to do so. RMAN will create a control file for the auxiliary instance.

Target database tablespaces are taken offline   Once the auxiliary instance has been created, the tablespaces on the target database to be moved will be taken offline. This implies that the data in these databases will not be available to users until the tablespaces are brought back online. Since you are restoring these tablespaces to a different point in time, the data the users will see the next time the tablespaces are brought back online will possibly be very different. Keep this in mind when doing a TSPITR: You are impacting the entire tablespace or set of tablespaces. If someone is not aware of what you are doing, you might get a very nasty phone call.

Transport the source tablespaces   Now that the tablespace(s) has been taken offline, RMAN will restore the recovery set and the auxiliary set from the target database to the auxiliary instance. The *recovery set* is the set of tablespaces that you are going to recover with TSPITR. The *auxiliary set* is the set of datafiles that are required to get the auxiliary instance running. This includes files for the SYSTEM tablespace, the UNDO tablespace, and the SYSAUX tablespace and temporary tablespace tempfiles.

Recover the auxiliary-instance database   Once the auxiliary set and the recovery set are restored, RMAN will proceed to recover the auxiliary-instance database to the point in time identified when the RMAN `recover` command was issued. Once the restore is complete, the auxiliary-instance database will be opened.

Transport the tablespace set   TSPITR uses transportable tablespaces to facilitate the movement of the tablespace datafiles from the auxiliary database instance to the target database instance. To perform this action, RMAN will first export needed metadata from the auxiliary database instance. It will then shut down the auxiliary database instance. On the target system, RMAN `switch` commands are executed to cause the datafile locations in the target database control file to be switched to the newly recovered datafiles. Finally, the backed-up metadata will be restored to the target database so the data in the restored tablespaces will be accessible to the target database.

Complete the operation   The auxiliary database files will be removed after the operation is completed. The target database tablespaces will be offline. You should back up those tablespaces, and then you will need to bring those tablespaces online manually. Once you do, you will find that the tablespaces contain the data in the version it existed in at the restore time indicated in the `recover` command.

TSPITR does not restore the point-in-time statistics for the objects contained in the restored tablespaces. Thus, you should analyze the objects in the tablespaces after completing the TSPITR.

Checking the Transport Set

When you perform a TSPITR, you want a transport set that is self-contained. This means that the tablespaces in the transport set do not have external object references; that is, they don't refer to objects that are not in the transport set. For example, suppose you are transporting the USERS tablespace, and a table in that tablespace has an index in the INDEX tablespace. In this case, you will not be able to transport the USERS tablespace unless you also transport the INDEX tablespace. When you transport both the USERS and the INDEX tablespace, you are transporting a wholly self-contained transport set.

RMAN will determine if the transport set is fully self-contained, but you may want to check beforehand to save some time. You can query the TS_PITR_CHECK view. In our example, USERS and INDEX_TBS are self-contained. If USERS is not transported with INDEX_TBS, then the TSPITR will error out. To determine if USERS and INDEX_TBS are self-contained, we would issue this query:

```
SQL> SELECT ts1_name, ts2_name, reason
  2  FROM SYS.TS_PITR_CHECK
  3  WHERE (
  4          TS1_NAME IN ('USERS','INDEX_TBS')
  5          AND TS2_NAME NOT IN ('USERS','INDEX_TBS')
  6         )
  7  OR    (
  8          TS1_NAME NOT IN ('USERS','INDEX_TBS')
  9          AND TS2_NAME IN ('USERS','INDEX_TBS')
 10*        )
SQL> /
no rows selected
```

If you were to plan to transport only the USERS tablespace, then you would see the following error:

```
SQL> SELECT ts1_name, ts2_name, reason
  2  FROM SYS.TS_PITR_CHECK
```

```
 3  WHERE (
 4          TS1_NAME IN ('USERS')
 5          AND TS2_NAME NOT IN ('USERS')
 6        )
 7  OR    (
 8          TS1_NAME NOT IN ('USERS')
 9          AND TS2_NAME IN ('USERS')
10*       )
SQL> /


TS1_NAME   TS2_NAME
---------- ----------
REASON
-------------------------------------------------------------------
USERS      INDEX_TBS
Tables and associated indexes not fully contained in the recovery set
```

Lost Objects

When you perform a TSPITR recovery, it is possible that you will lose objects in the tablespace that were created after the point in time to which you restore the tablespace. You can export these objects before the TSPITR with Oracle Data Pump and then import them after the TSPITR has completed.

By querying the view TS_PITR_OBJECTS_TO_BE_DROPPED, you can determine which objects will be lost, as shown in this example:

```
SQL> SELECT OWNER, NAME, TABLESPACE_NAME,
  2          TO_CHAR(CREATION_TIME, 'YYYY-MM-DD:HH24:MI:SS')
  3          FROM TS_PITR_OBJECTS_TO_BE_DROPPED
  4  WHERE TABLESPACE_NAME IN ('USERS')
  5  AND CREATION_TIME >
  6  TO_DATE('07-OCT-08:22:35:30','YY-MON-DD:HH24:MI:SS')
  7  ORDER BY TABLESPACE_NAME, CREATION_TIME;
OWNER                               NAME
----------------------------------- ----------------------------
TABLESPACE_NAME                     TO_CHAR(CREATION_TI
----------------------------------- -------------------
SCOTT                               TESTTABLE
USERS                               2008-10-07:19:34:39
```

Rules, Rules, and More Rules

Finally, TSPITR involves a few rules you need to be aware of:

- The target database must be in ARCHIVELOG mode.

- You must have a backup that was taken before the point in time that you want to perform the TSPITR.

- You must have all archived redo logs generated since the last backup (complete or incremental) up to the point to which you want to restore the transport set.

- If you rename a tablespace, you cannot perform a TSPITR to any point in time before that rename operation occurred.

- If you have tables in `tablespace_1` that have associated constraints in `tablespace_2`, then you must transport both tablespaces.

- If a tablespace contains the following objects, then that tablespace can not be used during a TSPITR.

  - Replicated master tables.

  - Incomplete tables; you must transport complete tables, including all partitions of a partitioned table.

  - Any tables that contain `VARRAY` columns, nested tables, or external tables.

  - Snapshot-related objects (snapshot logs and snapshots).

  - Tablespaces with `UNDO` or rollback segments.

  - Any tablespace with objects owned by the `SYS` schema.

TSPITR Aftereffects

Some interesting things happen after a TSPITR:

- If a datafile was added to the tablespace on the target database after the point in time for the recovery, then the resulting tablespace after the TSPITR process will have an empty datafile restored.

- Once the TSPITR is complete, all backups associated with tablespaces in the transport set taken before the point in time that you restored the tablespaces to are no longer valid. You should run a backup after the TSPITR.

- Once a TSPITR is complete, you will not be able to run another TSPITR on that tablespace to any time before the point to which you restored the tablespace.

- Once a TSPITR is complete, you will not be able to use the control file to restore any part of the database to any point in time before the time that you restored the tablespaces to during the TSPITR.

  In Exercise 8.2, you'll perform a tablespace point-in-time recovery with RMAN.

EXERCISE 8.2

Performing a Tablespace Point-in-Time Recovery

In this exercise, you will perform a tablespace point-in-time recovery of the USERS tablespace.

1. Log into the scott account in the database with SQL*Plus:

```
C:\Documents and Settings\Robert>set oracle_sid=orcl
C:\Documents and Settings\Robert>sqlplus scott/tiger
SQL*Plus: Release 11.1.0.6.0 - Production on Thu Oct 9 21:06:00 2008
Copyright (c) 1982, 2007, Oracle.  All rights reserved.
Connected to:
Oracle Database 11g Enterprise Edition Release 11.1.0.6.0 - Production
With the Partitioning, OLAP, Data Mining and
Real Application Testing options
SQL>
```

2. Create a table called TSPITR for this exercise. It will be created in the USERS tablespace (create the USERS tablespace if required):

```
SQL> create table tspitr (id number, the_date date)  tablespace users;
Table created.
```

3. Exit SQL*Plus and start RMAN. Back up the database with RMAN:

```
RMAN> backup as compressed backupset database plus archivelog delete input;
```

4. Exit RMAN and connect to the scott schema again with SQL*Plus:

```
RMAN> exit
Recovery Manager complete.
C:\Documents and Settings\Robert>sqlplus scott/tiger
SQL*Plus: Release 11.1.0.6.0 - Production on Thu Oct 9 21:15:39 2008
Copyright (c) 1982, 2007, Oracle.  All rights reserved.
Connected to:
Oracle Database 11g Enterprise Edition Release 11.1.0.6.0 - Production
With the Partitioning, OLAP, Data Mining and
Real Application Testing options
SQL>
```

5. Insert a record into the TSPITR table and commit:

```
SQL> insert into tspitr values (1,sysdate);
1 row created.
SQL> commit;
```

```
Commit complete.
SQL>
```

6. Wait a minute and insert another record into TSPITR. Commit the record:

```
SQL> insert into tspitr values (2,sysdate);
1 row created.
SQL> commit;
Commit complete.
SQL>
```

7. Select from the TSPITR table. Record the time/date of both records for a later step:

```
SQL> select * from tspitr;

        ID THE_DATE
---------- -------------------
         1 10/09/2008 22:09:02
         1 10/09/2008 22:10:04
```

8. Exit SQL*Plus.

9. From the operating system, create a directory for the auxiliary database files. In our case we are using c:\oracle\oradata\auxiliary.

```
c:>mkdir c:\oracle\oradata\auxiliary
```

10. Start RMAN. Connect to the target database:

```
C:\Documents and Settings\Robert>rman target=/
Recovery Manager: Release 11.1.0.6.0 -
Production on Thu Oct 9 21:30:01 2008
Copyright (c) 1982, 2007, Oracle.  All rights reserved.
connected to target database: ORCL (DBID=1194923408)
RMAN>
```

11. Perform a tablespace point-in-time recovery of the USERS tablespace to a point in time between insert #1 and insert #2.

```
RMAN> recover tablespace users
2> until time '10/09/2008:22:09:20' auxiliary destination 'c:\oracle\
auxiliary';
< we have decided to remove the output here to save a few trees.>
```

12. Back up the USERS tablespace:

```
RMAN> backup tablespace users;
```

```
Starting backup at 10/09/2008 22:28:51
using channel ORA_DISK_1
channel ORA_DISK_1: starting full datafile backup set
channel ORA_DISK_1: specifying datafile(s) in backup set
input datafile file number=00004
name=C:\ORACLE\ORADATA\ORCL\USERS01.DBF
channel ORA_DISK_1: starting piece 1 at 10/09/2008 22:28:58
channel ORA_DISK_1: finished piece 1 at 10/09/2008 22:28:59
piece handle=C:\ORACLE\FLASH_RECOVERY_AREA\ORCL\BACKUPSET\2008_10_09
\01_MF_NNNDF_TAG20081009T222851_4GXPJB5V_.BKP
tag=TAG20081009T222851 comment=NONE
channel ORA_DISK_1: backup set complete, elapsed time: 00:00:01
Finished backup at 10/09/2008 22:28:59
Starting Control File and SPFILE Autobackup at 10/09/2008 22:28:59
piece handle=C:\ORACLE\FLASH_RECOVERY_AREA\ORCL\AUTOBACKUP\2008_10_09
\01_MF_S_667693739_4GXPJMNZ_.BKP comment=NONE
Finished Control File and SPFILE Autobackup at 10/09/2008 22:29:14.
```

13. Connect to SYS with SQL*Plus:

```
C:\Documents and Settings\Robert>sqlplus sys/robert as sysdba
SQL*Plus: Release 11.1.0.6.0 - Production on Thu Oct 9 22:31:40 2008
Copyright (c) 1982, 2007, Oracle.  All rights reserved.
Connected to:
Oracle Database 11g Enterprise Edition Release 11.1.0.6.0 - Production
With the Partitioning, OLAP, Data Mining and
Real Application Testing options
```

14. Bring the USERS tablespace online:

```
SQL> alter tablespace users online;
Tablespace altered.
```

15. Select from the TSPITR table. Notice that only the first record is now in the table. This concludes this exercise.

```
SQL> select * from tspitr;

        ID THE_DATE
---------- -------------------
         1 10/09/2008 22:09:02
```

Performing a Database Disaster Recovery

In the previous several chapters, we discussed user-based backup and recovery and RMAN-based (or server-based) backup and recovery. So what happens if there is a complete disaster and you lose everything? First, you need to plan for such an event. Taking backups and moving them offsite is the first step. You will need to make sure that you not only have backups of your database offsite, but that you have copies of the Oracle software available offsite too. Any parameter files that are not backed up by RMAN (say, your `tnsnames.ora` or your `listener.ora` files) should be backed up offsite.

We thought we would close this chapter with a review of what you would need to do if you had to recover from offsite backups following a disaster. If you are using RMAN and you find you need to do a complete database recovery, you would follow the steps listed below. Chapter 6 provides more detail on the individual RMAN recovery steps and how to execute them:

1. Restore the OS.

2. Restore the Oracle software.

3. Configure Oracle networking.

4. Ensure that you have access to the RMAN backup set pieces that you need.

5. Restore the database spfile from the control-file autobackup. We assume that if you are doing control-file autobackups to disk, you will move those backups to tape and offsite them.

6. Once the database spfile is restored, you can mount the database and restore the control files of the database from the autobackups.

7. Once the database control file is restored, you would begin the restore and recovery of the database proper. This would complete your disaster-recovery operation. If you need to restore database files to a different location, you would use the `set newname` RMAN command as discussed in Chapter 6.

8. After you have completed the restore and recovery of the database datafiles, you would open the database with the `alter database open resetlogs` command.

If you are doing user-managed backup and recovery, the process is not all that different, as you can see here:

1. Restore the OS.

2. Restore the Oracle software.

3. Configure Oracle networking.

4. Ensure that you have access to the database backups that you will be restoring.

5. Restore the database parameter file or spfile from your backup media.

6. Once the database parameter file or spfile is restored, you can mount the database with the `alter database mount` command. You would then use a backup control file or the `create controlfile` command to re-create the control file of the database.

7. Once the database control file is restored, you would move the backups of the database datafiles from the backup media.

8. If you are restoring the database datafiles to a different location, you would need to rename them in the database control file. Use the `alter database rename file` command for this operation.

9. You will need to restore the needed archived redo logs from the backup media.

10. Use the `recover database` command to complete the database recovery. You will need to perform an incomplete recovery, since the online redo logs are not available. See Chapter 3 for more on incomplete user-managed recoveries.

11. Once the `recover database` command has completed its work, open the database with the `alter database open resetlogs` command.

Summary

In this chapter, we talked about some advanced RMAN recovery concepts. First we talked about changing database incarnations. You will want to know how to change incarnations of your database, as this provides the ability to restore your database from previous incarnations in certain cases.

The ability of RMAN to duplicate databases is very powerful. The Oracle OCP exam will include questions about this functionality, and we strongly suggest you go through the exercise of actually performing database duplication. The first few times, it can be a frustrating exercise, but it's well worth the experience.

Tablespace point-in-time recovery is an RMAN feature that makes recovering tablespaces to specific points in time easy to do. We covered the basics of TSPITR, which you will need to know for your OCP exam, but we encourage you to do further research into more customized methods of doing TSPITR that might meet your unique needs.

Finally, we concluded this chapter with a discussion of disaster recovery. This is the end game of backup and recovery (or as one person once told us, it should be called recovery and backup since *recovery* is the really important part). We gave you an outline of the process to follow to get your database back up to speed should you lose the whole database server.

Exam Essentials

Describe database incarnations.   Understand how to use the `set database incarnation` command. Know what a database incarnation is and when a given incarnation changes.

Describe database duplication.   There are two kinds of database duplication, active and backup-based. Understand that when you use backup-based duplication, the backup set pieces must be available on the host to which you are duplicating. Understand that active database duplication occurs over the network. Know how to set up for database duplication.

Describe tablespace point-in-time recovery.   Be able to list the benefits of tablespace point-in-time recovery. Understand how to perform a tablespace point-in-time recovery and what the restrictions are.

Describe disaster-recovery basics.   Understand how to restore a system from a complete disaster using both RMAN-based backup sets and user-managed recovery.

Review Questions

1. True or false: tablespace point-in-time recovery is possible only with RMAN.

   A. True

   B. False

2. Which command is used to begin a tablespace point-in-time recovery?

   A. `Restore tablespace`

   B. `Recover tablespace`

   C. `Tablespace recover`

   D. `Recover to time`

   E. `recover datafile`

3. When you're performing active database duplication, a backup of what kind is required?

   A. A current RMAN backup-set backup is required.

   B. No backup is required.

   C. An RMAN image backup is required.

   D. A manual backup is required.

   E. A "duplicate" preparatory backup is required.

4. Which of the following commands will perform an active database duplication of the ORCL database to the ORCL2 database?

   A.
   ```
   Set oracle_sid=orcl
   rman target=sys/robert auxname=sys/Robert@orcl2
   create duplicate target database to neworcl from
   active database nofilenamecheck
   spfile set control_files 'c:\oracle\oradata\neworcl\control01.ctl',
   'c:\oracle\oradata\neworcl\control02.ctl'
   set db_file_name_convert
   'c:\oracle\oradata\orcl','c:\oracle\oradata\neworcl'
   set log_file_name_convert
   'c:\oracle\oradata\orcl','c:\oracle\oradata\neworcl';
   ```

   B.
   ```
   Set oracle_sid=orcl
   rman target=sys/robert auxname=sys/Robert@orcl2
   duplicate target database nofilenamecheck
   spfile set control_files 'c:\oracle\oradata\neworcl\control01.ctl',
   'c:\oracle\oradata\neworcl\control02.ctl'
   ```

```
set db_file_name_convert
'c:\oracle\oradata\orcl','c:\oracle\oradata\neworcl'
set log_file_name_convert
'c:\oracle\oradata\orcl','c:\oracle\oradata\neworcl';
```

C.
```
Set oracle_sid=orcl
rman target=sys/robert auxname=sys/Robert@orcl2
duplicate target database to neworcl nofilenamecheck
spfile set control_files 'c:\oracle\oradata\neworcl\control01.ctl',
'c:\oracle\oradata\neworcl\control02.ctl'
set db_file_name_convert
'c:\oracle\oradata\orcl','c:\oracle\oradata\neworcl'
set log_file_name_convert
'c:\oracle\oradata\orcl','c:\oracle\oradata\neworcl';
```

D.
```
Set oracle_sid=orcl
rman target=sys/robert auxname=sys/Robert
duplicate target database to neworcl from active database nofilenamecheck
spfile set control_files 'c:\oracle\oradata\neworcl\control01.ctl',
'c:\oracle\oradata\neworcl\control02.ctl'
set db_file_name_convert
'c:\oracle\oradata\orcl','c:\oracle\oradata\neworcl'
set log_file_name_convert
'c:\oracle\oradata\orcl','c:\oracle\oradata\neworcl';
```

E.
```
Set oracle_sid=orcl
rman target=sys/robert auxname=sys/Robert@orcl2
duplicate target database to neworcl from active database nofilenamecheck
spfile set control_files 'c:\oracle\oradata\neworcl\control01.ctl',
'c:\oracle\oradata\neworcl\control02.ctl'
set db_file_name_convert
'c:\oracle\oradata\orcl','c:\oracle\oradata\neworcl'
set log_file_name_convert
'c:\oracle\oradata\orcl','c:\oracle\oradata\neworcl';
```

5. How many database instances are used during a database-duplication process?

    A. One

    B. Two

    C. Three

    D. Four

    E. Five

6. What command is used to reset a database to a previous incarnation?

A. `reset incarnation`

B. `incarnation reset`

C. `reset database to incarnation`

D. `reset database incarnation`

E. `reset databse incarnation number`

7. What view would you use to determine if a given tablespace is fully self-contained for the execution of a tablespace point-in-time recovery?

A. TS_CHECK

B. TPITR_CHECK

C. TS_PITR_CHECK

D. CHECK_TSPITR

E. PITR_TS_CHECK

8. When performing a full database disaster recovery with RMAN, in what order would you execute these steps?

a. Restore the control file from autobackups.

b. Run the RMAN restore and recover command.

c. Restore the database spfile from autobackups.

d. Make the RMAN backup set pieces available.

e. Open the database with the `alter database open resetlogs` command.

f. Open the database with the `alter database open` command.

A. a, b, c, d, e, f

B. c, d, a, b, f

C. d, c, a, b, f

D. d, b, d, c, e

E. d, c, a, b, e

9. When performing a database duplication, which `duplicate database` parameter would you set to ensure that the online redo logs are created in the correct location?

A. `log_file_name_convert`

B. `convert_log_file_name`

C. `file_name_convert_log`

D. `redo_log_file_name_convert`

E. `logfile_convert_directory`

10. Which command would correctly start a TSPITR of the USERS tablespace?

A.

```
recover tablespace users
until time '10/06/2008:22:42:00' auxiliary 'c:\oracle\auxiliary';
```

B.

```
recover tablespace users
time '10/06/2008:22:42:00' auxiliary destination 'c:\oracle\auxiliary';
```

C.

```
recover tablespace users
to point-in-time '10/06/2008:22:42:00'
auxiliary destination 'c:\oracle\auxiliary';
```

D.

```
recover tablespace users
except time '10/06/2008:22:42:00'
 auxiliary destination 'c:\oracle\auxiliary';
```

E.

```
recover tablespace users
until time '10/06/2008:22:42:00'
auxiliary destination 'c:\oracle\auxiliary';
```

11. True or false: you can perform an active database duplication when the database is in NOARCHIVELOG mode.

A. True

B. False

12. When running the tablespace point-in-time command

```
recover tablespace users
until time '10/06/2008:22:42:00'
auxiliary destination 'c:\oracle\auxiliary';
```

you receive the following error:

```
RMAN-00571: ===========================================================
RMAN-00569: =============== ERROR MESSAGE STACK FOLLOWS ===============
RMAN-00571: ===========================================================
RMAN-03002: failure of recover command at 10/08/2008 16:00:30
RMAN-20202: Tablespace not found in the recovery catalog
RMAN-06019: could not translate tablespace name "USERS"
```

What is the likely cause of the error?

A. The database is in ARCHIVELOG mode.

B. There is not a current backup of the database available.

C. The USERS tablespace has dependent objects in other tablespaces and can not be a part of a TSPITR alone.

D. The USERS tablespace is not eligible for TSPITR because it has invalid objects.

E. The `recover tablespace` command is incorrect and generates the error.

13. Which of the following restrictions are not true with respect to tablespace point-in-time recovery? (Choose all that apply.)

A. The target database must be in NOARCHIVELOG mode.

B. No backup is required of the database before you perform a TSPITR.

C. You must have all archived redo logs generated since the last backup up to the point to which you want to restore the transport set.

D. If you rename a tablespace, you can not perform a TSPITR to any point in time before that rename operation occurred.

E. If you have tables in `tablespace_1` that have associated constraints in `tablespace_2`, then you must transport both tablespaces.

14. If you are going to run a TSPITR recovery, which view will help you to determine which objects will be lost during the TSPITR?

A. TS_OBJECTS_TO_BE_DROPPED

B. TS_PTTR_OBJECT_DROPPED

C. TS_PITR_OBJECTS_TO_BE_DROPPED

D. TS_OBJECTS_DROPPED

E. TS_DROPPED_OBJECTS

15. You're performing tablespace point-in-time recovery on a tablespace called USERS. If an object in that tablespace has a foreign key constraint owned by another object in the INDEX_TBS, which statement is true?

A. You cannot perform the TSPITR with the constraints enabled.

B. You must perform the TSPITR recovery of both tablespaces for it to be successful.

C. You can perform TSPITR only on the USERS tablespace.

D. RMAN will determine if the INDEX_TBS tablespace must also be duplicated and will duplicate it automatically.

E. The TSPITR will only be successful if the constraint is enabled.

16. When issuing the `duplicate database` command, you use the parameter `DB_FILE_NAME_CONVERT`. For what purpose do you use this parameter?

    A. To indicate the location of the auxiliary-instance online redo logs.

    B. To indicate the location of the target database datafiles.

    C. To indicate the location of the auxiliary-instance control file and online redo logs.

    D. To indicate the location of the auxiliary-instance database datafiles.

    E. This is not a valid parameter when duplicating a database.

17. What is the end result of the following commands?

```
recover tablespace users
until time '10/06/2008:22:42:00'
auxiliary destination 'c:\oracle\auxiliary';
sql 'alter tablespace users online';
recover tablespace users
until time '10/06/2008:20:40:00'
auxiliary destination 'c:\oracle\auxiliary';
sql 'alter tablespace users online';
```

    A. The commands will be successful. The USERS tablespace will be recovered until 10/06/2008 at 20:40.

    B. The first `recover tablespace` command will fail because the syntax is incorrect.

    C. The first `alter tablespace users online` command will fail because the tablespace will already be online after the `recover` command.

    D. The second `recover tablespace` command will fail because it will be unable to complete the recovery.

    E. The second `alter tablespace users online` command will fail because you cannot perform two TSPITRs in a row without backing up the database between the first and the last recovery.

18. Why should you back up a duplicated tablespace after a TSPITR is complete?

    A. The tablespace cannot be duplicated or restored to any point in time after the duplication.

    B. The tablespace cannot be duplicated or restored to the point in time before the duplication.

    C. The entire database cannot be restored after a TSPITR, so a backup is required.

    D. You cannot bring the tablespace online until it's been backed up.

    E. There is no requirement to do so, as RMAN will back up the tablespace after the TSPITR.

19. In what state are the datafiles of a tablespace after a TSPITR has been successfully completed?

   A. The datafiles have an ONLINE status.

   B. The datafiles have an OFFLINE status.

   C. The datafiles have an ONLINE status and are in hot backup mode prepared for an online backup.

   D. The datafiles have an OFFLINE status and are in hot backup mode for an online backup.

   E. The datafiles are in STANDBY mode.

20. Which command do you use to generate a report of database incarnations?

   A. `list incarnation of database`

   B. `report incarnation of database`

   C. `list database incarnation`

   D. `database incarnation list`

   E. `report database incarnation`

Answers to Review Questions

1. B. Tablespace point-in-time recovery has been done in Oracle for some time, using various means and methods. RMAN simply automates and simplifies the process for you.

2. B. The `recover tablespace` command is used to start a TSPITR recovery.

3. B. Active database duplication does not require any backup before the duplication is run.

4. E. The commands in option E are the correct commands to perform an active database duplication given the conditions listed.

5. B. You will use two databases. The first is be the target database, and the second is the auxiliary database instance.

6. C. The `reset database to incarnation` command is used to reset the database incarnation.

7. C. The `TS_PITR_CHECK` view is used to determine if a given tablespace (or tablespaces) can be independently transported or if there are other dependencies that will require the transport of additional tablespaces.

8. E. You would first need to restore the RMAN backup set pieces. Then you would restore the database spfile followed by the database control file. You would then run the RMAN `restore` and `recover` command. Finally, you would open the database with the `alter database open resetlogs` command.

9. A. The correct answer is `log_file_name_convert`. This setting will direct RMAN to the directory in which it should create the online redo logs.

10. E. The correct command is shown in option E. You would issue the `recover tablespace` command and list the tablespaces to be recovered. You would then use the `until time` parameter to define the point in time to restore the tablespace to. Finally, you would define the location for the auxiliary database instance with the `auxiliary destination` parameter.

11. B. Any database to be duplicated in active mode must be in ARCHIVELOG mode.

12. B. This error message alludes to the fact that there is not a backup of the database available to perform TSPITR. A backup before the point in time of the recovery is required to perform TSPITR.

13. A, B. The database must be in ARCHIVELOG mode to perform a TSPITR. Additionally, you must have a backup of the database that occurred at a point in time before the point in time to which you want to perform the TSPITR.

14. C. Use the `TS_PITR_OBJECTS_TO_BE_DROPPED` view to determine which objects will be lost as a result of the pending tablespace point-in-time recovery operation. To preserve the objects, you will want to export them before the TSPITR and import them after the recovery is complete with the Oracle Data Pump or Imp/Exp utility.

15. B. If there is a constraint between two objects in two different tablespaces, you must perform a TSPITR between the two tablespaces. As an alternative, you could disable or drop the constraint. You may not be able to reenable the constraint with validation after the TSPITR, however.

16. D. The DB_FILE_NAME_CONVERT parameter is used to define the location in which the datafiles for the auxiliary-database datafiles should be created.

17. D. The second `recover tablespace` command will fail because it is trying to perform a recovery to a point in time before the time to which the tablespace was recovered during the first recovery.

18. B. After you perform a TSPITR, you should back up the tablespace/datafile. If you do not, you will not be able to do a TSPITR to any point in time before the original TSPITR.

19. B. After a TSPITR each datafile associated with the TSPITR will be offline. Oracle recommends you back up the datafile before bringing it online.

20. A. The `list incarnation of database` command is used to produce a report of database incarnations.

Chapter

9

Understanding Flashback Technology

ORACLE DATABASE 11*g*: ADMINISTRATION II EXAM OBJECTIVES COVERED IN THIS CHAPTER:

✓ **Using Flashback Technology**

- ▪ Restore dropped tables from the Recycle Bin
- ▪ Perform Flashback Query
- ▪ Use Flashback Transaction Query

✓ **Additional Flashback Operations**

- ▪ Perform Flashback Table Operations
- ▪ Configure, Monitor Flashback Database and perform Flashback Database operations
- ▪ Set up and use a Flashback Data Archive

If you have been working through this book chapter by chapter, you should have a pretty firm grasp of Oracle backup and recovery methods available through RMAN. For the most part, RMAN works in the physical realm. It provides recovery from physical problems such as physical block corruption, failed hardware, missing files, and so on. It is vital for a database administrator to be able to recover from these types of problems, and RMAN is definitely the tool for the job.

But database administrators must also have tools to deal with *logical corruption* in the database. Logical corruption, for the most part, is synonymous with the term *user error*. Rather than having a physical problem with your database, you have a problem with the data in your database. Here are some examples:

- A developer accidentally drops a table.

- A programming bug causes data updates to populate the wrong records.

- The DBA is purging data and accidentally deletes the wrong rows.

- An inadvertent table TRUNCATE takes place.

Logical corruption is far more common than physical corruption. And although RMAN could certainly be used to recover from logical corruption, a full-blown recovery effort is time-consuming and generally involves database downtime.

In these situations, Flashback technology provides the solution. It allows dropped objects to be recovered. It allows queries to view data as it existed at a point in time in the past, and it allows queries to view a history of changes made to data. It even allows returning the entire database to a point in time or SCN. Having a thorough understanding of the many Flashback options will not only help you pass your OCP exam; it will help you to be a better DBA.

This chapter offers a detailed explanation of the functionality provided by Flashback technology as it exists in Oracle Database 11*g* (Oracle 11*g*).

Initially, we will provide a brief overview of Flashback functionality and where it fits in the database administrator's arsenal. We will also examine Automatic Undo Management, the cornerstone upon which key Flashback technologies rely. Next, we will examine the various Flashback options:

- Flashback Drop (and the Recycle Bin)

- Flashback Query

- Flashback Versions Query

- Flashback Transaction

- Flashback Table

- Flashback Database
- Flashback Data Archive

For each of these options, we will discuss the requirements, capabilities, and limitations in detail.

> Exam objectives are subject to change at any time without prior notice and at Oracle's sole discretion. Please visit Oracle's Training and Certification website (http://www.oracle.com/education/certification/) for the most current exam-objectives listing.

Overview of Flashback Technology

Flashback technology was first introduced in Oracle Database 9*i*. Since then, it has been steadily improved with each successive Oracle release. In Oracle Database 11*g*, it represents a mature and time-tested technology.

Flashback technology consists of a set of tools that allow users to recover from logical data errors without resorting to a database recovery. However, Flashback can do much more.

The Recycle Bin allows dropped objects to persist in the database, and the Flashback Drop option allows the objects to be restored.

The Flashback Query option allows the user to query tables as they looked at a specific point in the past.

The Flashback Versions Query option allows the user to retrieve a historical view of data as it changed over time. In other words, if a column had been updated multiple times, Flashback Versions Query could provide a list of each of the values and the date and time that they were changed.

Flashback Transaction Query is a useful diagnostic tool that allows the user to retrieve detailed transaction information for previously executed transactions. It can run for a single transaction or for all transactions that occurred during a specified time frame.

Flashback Table allows point-in-time recovery (recovering one or more tables to a specified point in the past) without the need to take any part of the database offline. This offers a very desirable alternative to performing a full-blown point-in-time recovery.

Flashback Database is best used as a replacement for incomplete recovery of the entire database. The main benefit of Oracle Flashback Database over incomplete database recovery is that Flashback Database is much quicker and more efficient. Flashback Database is not based on undo data but on flashback logs. It is best suited to recover from errors such as truncating a large table, an incomplete batch job, or a dropped user.

As you can see, Flashback offers a wide variety of tools for the DBA. However, these options are not exclusive to the DBA. In fact, one of the key advantages to the various Flashback technologies is that they do not require DBA-level privileges. Users and developers can utilize them to recover from their own errors without DBA intervention (except for Flashback Database).

Using Automatic Undo Management

Before we can delve too deeply into Flashback technologies, it is important to understand that all of the Flashback options covered in this chapter, except for Flashback Database and Flashback Drop, work in conjunction with Oracle's undo functionality. Without undo, there would be no Flashback. In fact, without undo, transaction processing as we know it would not exist.

The topics of undo and undo management should not be new to you and will not be covered in depth here. However, we believe that a brief overview of the subject will be helpful in better understanding Flashback technologies and how they work.

In the following sections, you will take a look at undo and *Automatic Undo Management (AUM)*. First we will define undo and its purpose. You will discover how Oracle can automatically manage undo on your behalf. Then you will learn how undo sizing and undo record retention play a key role in Flashback technologies.

Uncovering Undo

So what exactly is "undo" and why does it need to be managed? Undo is a key component of the Oracle database that stores a record of every change made to data in the database. This record contains the data necessary to "undo" the change (in other words, roll back the transaction) and restore the data to its previous condition. For example, when a row in a table is updated, Oracle will create an undo record that stores the data that was changed. If a new row is inserted into a table, an undo record will be created that would effectively delete the row.

Maintaining undo records serves multiple purposes in the database:

- Transaction processing
- Failed-transaction recovery
- Read consistency
- Flashback functionality

Let's look at each of these individually.

Transaction Processing

Transaction processing allows SQL statements to be grouped into discrete units of work that can be committed or rolled back as one. The classic example is that of woman walking into a bank and asking to transfer $500 from her checking account to her savings account. Behind the scenes, two SQL statements are executed: one that subtracts $500 from her checking-account balance and one that adds $500 to her savings-account balance.

Now, suppose the bank's computer system crashed after completing the first statement but not the second. The money would be gone from her checking account but never added to her savings account. She would be out $500 on the deal. Instead, the two statements must be treated as a single, logical unit of work (in other words, a transaction). Only when both statements have completed successfully should the changes be committed. If either fails, they must both be rolled back.

When a user changes data in a table (via insert, update, or delete), the change does not occur immediately. The user must either commit the change (finalize it) or roll it back (undo it). Until they do, the database must keep track of both versions of the data (before the change and after the change).

In order to meet this requirement, the database will modify the data in the table to reflect the change. It will then create an *undo record* in the undo tablespace that contains any data needed to undo the change.

Although the transaction remains in limbo (neither committed nor rolled back), other users who query the table will see the data as it looked prior to the change. If the user decides to roll back the transaction, the undo information is used to modify the table data to revert it to its previous value. If the user decides to commit the transaction, the change becomes permanent.

From strictly a transaction-processing standpoint (allowing a transaction the option of committing or rolling back), the undo records for a transaction are useless after the transaction finishes. They have served their purpose and could be deleted. However, by retaining undo information for a period of time after a commit, many new options become available to us.

As you will see, as you continue through this chapter, the whole host of Flashback options becomes available by the simple act of retaining undo records for a period of time after they have been committed.

Failed-Transaction Recovery

A failed transaction is a transaction that never completes; that is, it never commits or rolls back. This can happen for a variety of reasons, but they all boil down to a session closing with a transaction still in progress.

Since most (if not all) Oracle clients are designed to either commit or roll back automatically when a session is closed, simply forgetting to finish a transaction before exiting will rarely result in a failed transaction. In general, a failed transaction occurs because of an abnormal server shutdown (because of hardware failure, loss of power, or even a `shutdown abort`).

When a failed transaction is discovered (generally at startup time following an abnormal shutdown), Oracle will undo the transaction automatically using the data stored in the undo tablespace.

Read Consistency

When a user issues a query, the database is required to process the query and return the data as it looked at the moment the query started. In other words, if you kicked off a long-running query at 10 a.m. and it finished at 10:15 a.m., the data should not reflect changes (committed or uncommitted) made by other users in the interim.

To fulfill this requirement, Oracle must retain undo records after their associated transaction has been committed. The length of time that it chooses to retain this data is governed by the undo retention period, which will be covered later in this chapter.

Flashback Functionality

Flashback functions allow users to view elements of the database as they appeared at a certain point in time. These functions will be described in much more detail later in this chapter.

Much like the read-consistency requirements, Flashback requires that undo records be retained for a period of time after the associated transaction has completed.

In short, the undo feature creates and maintains records of all transactions that occur in the database and stores the data necessary to undo them. By maintaining these records throughout the life of a transaction, undo provides transaction management and read-consistency capabilities. By maintaining these records after the transaction has been committed, undo provides read-consistency and Flashback options.

Working with Automatic Undo Management

Undo data is temporary. In that respect, the undo tablespace is similar to a temporary tablespace. Information is written there to fulfill a temporary need. As soon as the information is no longer needed, it can be removed to make room for new undo data. To keep things running smoothly requires a considerable amount of management. Luckily, Oracle offers the Automatic Undo Management feature.

Automatic Undo Management (AUM) is a feature whereby Oracle will handle all undo management tasks without interaction from the DBA. Although this is not a new feature in Oracle Database 11g, one important aspect has changed. In previous Oracle versions, manual undo management was the default setting. In order to enable AUM, configuration changes were required by the DBA. Beginning with Oracle Database 11g, AUM will be enabled by default.

When creating a new database with the Database Configuration Assistant (DBCA), Oracle will perform the following actions:

- Create an undo tablespace named UNDOTBS1
- Configure the undo tablespace to auto-extend.
- Add an UNDO_MANAGEMENT=AUTO initialization parameter

These three steps ensure that Oracle will automatically manage the undo needs for the database

Automatic Undo Management must ensure that Oracle can store undo information for all new transactions as they occur. This means that adequate space must be available in the undo tablespace.

By creating an auto-extending undo tablespace, Oracle can extend the size as needed to maintain adequate undo information.

So how long should Oracle retain committed undo information? The simple answer is, long enough to satisfy the undo retention period. The undo retention period represents the minimum amount of time that Oracle will attempt to retain committed undo information before allowing it to be overwritten.

Please note that it is still possible to run the database in manual undo management mode. This can be done by changing the initialization parameter to UNDO_MANAGEMENT=MANUAL. However, Oracle strongly advises against it.

In Oracle Database 11*g*, if the UNDO_MANAGEMENT initialization parameter is set to NULL, the database will default to AUTO. However, it was just the opposite in earlier Oracle versions. Therefore, if you are upgrading to version 11*g*, be aware that a NULL setting will have the opposite effect that it had in the prior version.

Understanding Undo Retention

The undo functionality of Oracle Database 11*g* is governed by a setting known as the undo retention period. The undo retention period represents the minimum time (expressed in seconds) that committed undo information should be retained in the undo tablespace.

To ensure read consistency, the undo retention period should be set to a value larger than the runtime of your longest-running query. If your longest-running query takes 60 minutes to run and you retain undo information for 65 minutes, your system should not encounter any ORA-01555 Snapshot too old errors.

To ensure that undo data is available for Flashback operations, the undo retention period should be set long enough to retain adequate data to support your Flashback needs. For example, if you want to always maintain a 4-hour window in which to undo data changes, then the setting should be at least 14400 (4 hours expressed in seconds).

It is important to understand that the undo retention setting is actually a target for AUM to achieve; it does not guarantee that data will actually be retained for the entire time. There are circumstances under which AUM may choose to violate the undo retention period.

Undo data is considered to be in one of three possible states at any given time: uncommitted, unexpired, or expired.

Uncommitted data is undo data corresponding to a transaction that has been neither committed nor rolled back. Undo data in this state will remain in the undo tablespace indefinitely. It will never be removed based on the retention period.

Once data has been committed, it enters the unexpired state. This effectively starts the timer running on the retention-period clock. It will remain in this state until the retention period has elapsed.

When the retention period has elapsed, the data will enter the expired state, meaning the data has been retained for the requested amount of time. The expired state tells Oracle that the data is now eligible to be purged from the Undo tablespace to make room for new data.

By keeping track of the state of all undo data, AUM can manage the space and ensure adequate space for new transactions. But suppose a new transaction begins when the undo tablespace is full and none of the undo data is expired? Oracle will attempt to extend the tablespace (if it is enabled) to make more space. If auto-extend is not possible (because it is not enabled or it has reached the MAXSIZE), Oracle must make a choice. It can either forego the retention period by removing unexpired data or honor the retention period, thereby causing the new transaction to fail. By default, Oracle will choose to sacrifice the unexpired data to make room for the new transaction.

In the following sections, you will learn how an undo retention period can be established and what effect it will have. You will also learn about the power and the pitfalls of guaranteeing undo retention.

Establishing an Undo Retention Period

As part of its management duties, AUM monitors system activity and available undo space to derive an optimum undo retention time. This setting may change over time as activity and available space change. Since AUM takes care of this, there is no action required by the DBA to establish an undo retention period.

However, AUM will also allow you to specify the retention period yourself. It can be done by setting the UNDO_RETENTION initialization parameter, as shown here:

```
SQL> ALTER SYSTEM SET UNDO_RETENTION=14400
     SCOPE=BOTH;
```

```
System altered
```

When AUM encounters a manual undo retention setting, it will honor the setting *only if it is using an auto-extending tablespace*. If AUM is configured with a fixed-size tablespace, it will ignore the setting and will instead follow its default behavior of dynamically setting the retention time based on system activity and available disk space.

Because of this behavior, it is highly recommended that you allow AUM to use an auto-extending undo tablespace. If you are concerned that an errant long-running query could cause it to extend too much, use the MAXSIZE option to limit its growth.

Guaranteeing Retention

As mentioned previously, Oracle will violate the undo retention period if it is required to prevent transactions from failing. For most users, it is a fair trade-off. However, there may be situations where it is more important to guarantee the retention period, even at the expense of failed transactions. This can be accomplished by specifying the RETENTION GUARANTEE clause on the undo tablespace. This can either be done when initially creating the tablespace or by altering the tablespace, as shown here:

```
SQL> ALTER TABLESPACE UNDOTBS1 RETENTION
     GUARANTEE;
```

```
System altered
```

When the RETENTION GUARANTEE clause is invoked on the undo tablespace, Oracle will never remove unexpired data from the undo tablespace, even if it means allowing new transactions to fail.

Using the RETENTION GUARANTEE option is a mixed blessing, and one that must be carefully considered. On the one hand, you ensure that undo records necessary for all of your Flashback and read-consistency needs will be retained. On the other hand, if space runs out and the undo tablespace cannot be extended, Oracle will stubbornly enforce the guarantee and allow new transactions to fail.

To summarize, these sections offered you a brief overview of undo and AUM. First you learned about undo and its purpose. You saw how Oracle automatically manages undo on your behalf. And you learned how undo sizing and undo record retention play a key role in Flashback technologies. But what exactly are Flashback technologies? You are about to find out.

Using Flashback Technologies

In the following sections, we will explore each of the various Flashback options and provide examples of how they can be used in the real world. First, we will discuss the Flashback Drop option and the Recycle Bin and how the two work together to recover dropped objects in the database. Next, we will use the Flashback Query option to view data as it existed at a point in the past.

We will continue on to discuss Flashback Versions Query, and you'll learn how to retrieve a historical view of changes made to the database. We will show how to use the Flashback Transaction Query option to retrieve information about past transactions and then show how to use the Flashback Transaction functionality to reverse those transactions.

Using Flashback Drop and the Recycle Bin

In Oracle Database 10*g*, the *Recycle Bin* feature was added to the Oracle Database. This feature enabled tables (and their associated objects) to persist in the database after they were dropped. Oracle 10*g* also introduced the Flashback Drop feature, which allows objects to be recovered from the Recycle Bin. These features remain largely unchanged in Oracle Database 11*g*.

In the following sections, we will provide an overview of the Recycle Bin feature. We will also demonstrate how to use the *Flashback Drop* feature to recover objects from the Recycle Bin.

Using the Recycle Bin

The Recycle Bin is a logical container for dropped tables and their associated objects (indexes, constraints, triggers, nested tables, large-object [LOB] segments, and LOB index segments).

When a table is dropped in Oracle Database 11*g*, it is not actually removed from the database. Instead, it is moved into the Recycle Bin. These objects remain in the Recycle Bin until they are purged explicitly or due to space pressure (permanently removed) or restored via the Flashback Drop feature.

In this section, we will cover the usage of the Recycle Bin, including how to use it, how to purge objects from it, how to enable and disable it, and how to recover objects from it using Flashback Drop.

The Recycle Bin is a logical container, as opposed to a physical container. There is no Recycle Bin tablespace or datafile into which the dropped objects are moved. Instead, the objects remain in their original tablespace and are simply renamed using a special naming convention. This naming convention ensures that database objects with the same name will not be assigned duplicate identifiers when they are moved into the Recycle Bin.

To demonstrate how objects interact with the Recycle Bin, this section will provide a series of examples showing how a dropped table is represented in the Recycle Bin. To begin, we first must drop a table, as shown here:

```
SQL> drop table job_history;

Table dropped.
```

Once the table has been dropped, our next step is to view the contents of the Recycle Bin to verify that the table is truly there. One simple way to do this is to use the SHOW RECYCLEBIN command, as shown here:

```
SQL> show recyclebin
ORIGINAL NAME    RECYCLEBIN NAME
OBJECT TYPE  DROP TIME
---------------- ------------------------------
------------ -------------------

JOB_HISTORY      BIN$F2JFfMq8Q5unbC0ceE9eJg==$0
TABLE        2008-04-07:11:52:36
```

The SHOW RECYCLEBIN command confirms that our table now resides in the Recycle Bin, as expected. It also provides several other pieces of useful information. These are described in Table 9.1.

TABLE 9.1   SHOW RECYCLEBIN Columns

Column Name	Description
ORIGINAL NAME	This column stores the original name of the object (at the time when it was dropped).
RECYCLEBIN NAME	This column shows the system-assigned name of the object. This is the object's unique identifier within the Recycle Bin.
OBJECT TYPE	This column shows the type of the object (TABLE, INDEX, and so on).
DROP_TIME	This column shows the timestamp corresponding to the dropping of the object.

Next, we will create a new table named JOB_HISTORY, insert some data, and then drop it. We will then look in the Recycle Bin to verify that both tables are there, even though both tables had the same name.

```
SQL> create table job_history (job_id number);

Table created.

SQL> insert into job_history values(1);

1 row created.

SQL> commit;

Commit complete.

SQL> drop table job_history;

Table dropped.

SQL> show recyclebin
ORIGINAL NAME    RECYCLEBIN NAME
OBJECT TYPE  DROP TIME
---------------- -----------------------------
------------ ------------------

JOB_HISTORY      BIN$XwEOKAONSRGwYREWXnjkKw==$0
TABLE        2008-04-07:12:16:55

JOB_HISTORY      BIN$F2JFfMq8Q5unbCOceE9eJg==$0
TABLE        2008-04-07:11:52:36
```

As promised, Oracle assigned the second version of the JOB_HISTORY table a unique identifier (RECYCLEBIN NAME). This ensures that either version of the table could be restored if required.

Besides the SHOW RECYCLEBIN command, Oracle also offers views named USER_RECYCLEBIN and DBA_RECYCLEBIN, which can be used to query objects in the Recycle Bin. These views offer much more information than the simple SHOW RECYCLEBIN command. For example, look at the following query:

```
SQL> select original_name, object_name, type, droptime from user_recyclebin;
```

```
ORIGINAL_NAME       OBJECT_NAME
------------------- ------------------------------
TYPE        DROPTIME
---------- -------------------
JHIST_JOB_IX        BIN$1h6Ja8caSluy+7vvQjANHA==$0
INDEX       2008-04-07:11:52:35

JHIST_EMPLOYEE_IX  BIN$Ju6REfJiTYagKJqj5OPgUQ==$0
INDEX       2008-04-07:11:52:35

JHIST_DEPT_IX       BIN$ZX4rQYBwTgyHPpT1C8JH+Q==$0
INDEX       2008-04-07:11:52:35

JHIST_EMP_ID_PK     BIN$ngQEsBNrRqSUadOWnyBQUg==$0
INDEX       2008-04-07:11:52:35

JOB_HISTORY         BIN$F2JFfMq8Q5unbCOceE9eJg==$0
TABLE       2008-04-07:11:52:36

JOB_HISTORY         BIN$XwEOKAONSRGwYREWXnjkKw==$0
TABLE       2008-04-07:12:16:55

6 rows selected.
```

Upon first glance, you might have assumed that this query would have returned the exact same results as the SHOW RECYCLEBIN command. Instead we see four additional rows showing the indexes that were moved to the Recycle Bin when we dropped the first JOB_HISTORY table.

The SHOW RECYCLEBIN command shows only tables that reside in the Recycle Bin. It filters out the dependent objects such as indexes and constraints. Furthermore, the USER_RECYCLEBIN view also offers many other columns, as listed in Table 9.2.

TABLE 9.2   USER_RECYCLEBIN Columns

Column Name	Description
OBJECT_NAME	The system-assigned name of the object. This is the object's unique identifier within the Recycle Bin.
ORIGINAL_NAME	The original name of the object (at the time when it was dropped).
OPERATION	The type of operation that occurred to move the object into the Recycle Bin (in other words, DROP, TRUNCATE). Currently, only dropped objects can be restored.

TABLE 9.2   USER_RECYCLEBIN Columns *(continued)*

Column Name	Description
OBJECT_NAME	The system-assigned name of the object. This is the object's unique identifier within the Recycle Bin.
ORIGINAL_NAME	The original name of the object (at the time when it was dropped).
OPERATION	The type of operation that occurred to move the object into the Recycle Bin (in other words, DROP, TRUNCATE). Currently, only dropped objects can be restored.
TYPE	The type of object (TABLE, INDEX, and so on).
TS_NAME	The name of the tablespace where the object resides.
CREATETIME	Timestamp reflecting when the object was created.
DROPTIME	Timestamp reflecting when the object was dropped.
DROPSCN	The system change number (SCN) corresponding to the dropping of the object.
PARTITION_NAME	If the dropped object was partitioned, the name of the partition.
CAN_UNDROP	This object can be undropped (restored) using the Flashback Drop option. This is true only for table objects. Dependent objects can be restored, but not by themselves. They will be restored only if their related table is restored.
CAN_PURGE	This object can be purged from the Recycle Bin.
RELATED	Object number of the parent object.
BASE_OBJECT	Object number of the base object (in other words, the original table that was dropped).
PURGE_OBJECT	Object number of the current Recycle Bin object. This is the object number that will be purged.
SPACE	Number of blocks used by the object.

Tables residing in the Recycle Bin can be queried directly, just like any other table. The only caveat is that they cannot have any Data Definition Language (DDL) or Data Manipulation Language (DML) statements performed on them. Any attempt to do so will result in an error.

To query a table currently residing in the Recycle Bin, simply use the system-assigned name (OBJECT_NAME), not the original name. Also, since this name consists of mixed-case characters, you must enclose the name in double quotes in your select statement. Here's an example:

```
SQL> select * from "BIN$XwEOKAONSRGwYREWXnjkKw==$0";


      JOB_ID
----------
         1
```

Purging the Recycle Bin

As was mentioned previously, objects are never physically moved into the Recycle Bin. Therefore, there is no tablespace associated with it. Instead, the objects remain in their respective tablespaces but are no longer listed in the data dictionary. So, they appear to have been dropped, yet they are still available for recovery.

However, this poses a problem for a user who is dropping tables to reclaim tablespace. Or perhaps you have a temporary table that you have no further need for and will never need to restore. For situations like these, the purge option should be used. Purging objects from the Recycle Bin will remove them permanently and release the storage space that they were occupying. However, it also means that they cannot be restored.

Purging can be accomplished in several ways. The first is by adding the PURGE option to the DROP command, as shown here:

```
SQL> drop table employees purge;
Table dropped
```

By adding PURGE to the end of the DROP command, you make the table will bypass the Recycle Bin altogether. It will not be recoverable, so proceed with caution.

To purge objects that already reside in the Recycle Bin, you have several options. First, you can purge a specific table, as shown:

```
SQL> purge table employees;


Table purged
```

When purging a single table, you can reference the table by using either the original table name or the system-assigned name. If you use the system-assigned name, be sure to use double quotes around the name.

You can also purge all objects from a specific tablespace by using the TABLESPACE option, as shown:

```
SQL> purge tablespace users;


Tablespace purged
```

You can also purge the entire Recycle Bin (all objects you have dropped, regardless of tablespace) as shown here:

```
SQL> purge recyclebin;
```

```
Recyclebin purged
```

This command will purge all of the objects from the Recycle Bin. By the same token, a DBA can purge all of the objects from all users' Recycle Bins at once using the following:

```
SQL> purge dba_recyclebin;
```

```
DBA Recyclebin purged
```

There may also be times when Oracle itself will purge objects from the Recycle Bin. This will occur when Oracle can no longer allocate new extents in a tablespace where the dropped objects reside without extending the tablespace. This is referred to as *space pressure*. Before extending the tablespace, Oracle will choose to purge Recycle Bin objects.

When space pressure occurs, Oracle will purge the oldest objects first, and it will purge dependent objects (in other words, indexes and triggers) before purging the table itself.

Because of the threat of space pressure, objects in the Recycle Bin are not guaranteed to be recoverable.

In Exercise 9.1, you'll purge a table from the Recycle Bin.

EXERCISE 9.1

Purging a Table from the Recycle Bin

To purge a table from the recycle bin, do the following:

1. Create a table and add rows of data.

2. Drop the table.

3. Purge the table from the Recycle Bin.

4. Verify that the table is no longer in the Recycle Bin:

   ```
   SQL> create table foo (x number, y varchar2(10));
   Table created.

   SQL> insert into foo values (1,'test1');
   1 row created.
   SQL> insert into foo values (2,'test2');
   1 row created.
   SQL> insert into foo values (3,'test3');
   1 row created.
   ```

```
SQL> commit;
Commit complete.
SQL> drop table foo;
Table dropped.
SQL> select * from recyclebin;

OBJECT_NAME                        ORIGINAL_NAME
OPERATION
--------------------------- ---------------------------------
---------
TYPE                    TS_NAME
CREATETIME
----------------------- -------------------------------
-------------------
DROPTIME              DROPSCN PARTITION_NAME               CAN CAN
------------------- ---------- ------------------------------- --- ---
    RELATED BASE_OBJECT PURGE_OBJECT       SPACE
---------- ----------- ------------ ----------
BIN$dKC+/rixR5GZmNzTPnUNnw==$0 FOO                         DROP
TABLE                     USERS
2008-11-04:20:50:28
2008-11-04:20:50:37    6048081                            YES YES
      72654       72654        72654            8


SQL> purge table foo;
Table purged.
SQL> select * from recyclebin;
no rows selected
SQL>
```

Disabling and Enabling the Recycle Bin

It is important to understand that even though the Recycle Bin is extremely useful, its use is entirely optional. Though it is enabled by default, it can be turned off at either the system or session level to suit the users' needs. For instance, if you work in an environment that is very tight on space, the Recycle Bin might be more of a hindrance than a help.

The Recycle Bin feature is governed by an initialization parameter named RECYCLEBIN. As with other initialization parameters, it can be set in the INIT.ORA file as shown:

```
RECYCLEBIN=OFF
```

For a database using spfiles, the same thing can be accomplished as shown here:

```
SQL>  alter system set recyclebin = off scope=spfile;

System altered.
```

It can also be set at the session level, as shown in the following example:

```
SQL>  alter session set recyclebin = off;

Session altered.
```

And, as you can probably guess, the Recycle Bin feature can be reenabled by all the same methods; just substitute ON for OFF.

Using Flashback Drop

Now that you've seen how the Recycle Bin works, it's time to use the Flashback Drop feature to restore objects from it. The syntax for the Flashback Drop command is as follows:

```
FLASHBACK TABLE table_name
TO BEFORE DROP
[RENAME TO new_table_name];
```

By default, a Flashback Table operation will restore the table using the same name it had originally. The optional rename clause allows you to restore the table under a different name. This may be required if an object with the original name already exists in your schema.

Let's take a look at how it all works. In this example, we will restore the JOB_HISTORY table and rename it JOB_HIST:

```
SQL> flashback table job_history to before drop rename to job_hist;

Flashback complete.
```

Now we'll query the restored table, as shown here:

```
SQL> select * from job_hist;

    JOB_ID
----------
         1
```

As you can see, the Flashback Drop feature was successful in restoring the table. However, we had two different versions of the JOB_HISTORY table in the Recycle Bin. Why did Oracle choose to restore this one instead of the other one? The answer is that Oracle will always choose to restore the most recently dropped version of the table (if it has two identically named tables).

To recover the previous version of the JOB_HISTORY table, we have two options. Since we already recovered the first one, we can simply execute the Flashback Drop command again to restore the second version (however, we must rename one of them). However, a better alternative is to use the system-assigned object name whenever you want to recover a specific version of a table. Here's an example:

```
SQL> flashback table "BIN$F2JFfMq8Q5unbCOceE9eJg==$0" to before drop;


Flashback complete.
```

By specifying the system-assigned object name in your Flashback Drop, you avoid duplicate-name issues and ensure that only the specific table that you've selected (and the specific version of that table) will be restored.

Flashback Drop functionality offers a simple way to recover from logical corruption caused when a table has been dropped in error. It is simple, fast, and works well. But there are other types of logical corruption that you must also be able to deal with, and those will require different tools. In the next section, we will introduce you to the next one: Flashback Query.

Regarding the Behavior of Dependent Objects after Undropping

When you recover a table from the Recycle Bin, the triggers, constraints, and indexes are also brought back; however, the names of the dependent objects remain as they were in the Recycle Bin. For example, if table T has an index IN_T, a primary key constraint PK_T, and a trigger named TR_T and the table is dropped and later flashed back, all these dependent objects will revert back to table T but with different names:

```
SQL> select trigger_name from user_triggers where table_name = 'T';
 TRIGGER_NAME
-----------------------------
BIN$VJSEh1G2cMngQA4KH2h7+A==$0
 SQL> select index_name from user_indexes where table_name = 'T';
 INDEX_NAME
-----------------------------
BIN$VJSEh1G0cMngQA4KH2h7+A==$0
BIN$VJSEh1G1cMngQA4KH2h7+A==$0
 SQL> select constraint_name from user_constraints where table_name = 'T';
 CONSTRAINT_NAME
-----------------------------
BIN$VJSEh1GzcMngQA4KH2h7+A==$0
```

You will need to explicitly rename these objects to their former names, if you so choose. Additionally, the following statements are true:

- Some constraints, such as FK, can't be flashed back; they are lost.

- Bitmap join indexes are not flashed back.

- Materialized view logs are not placed in the Recycle Bin, so they are lost.

- It's possible that some indexes may have been erased from the Recycle Bin, even when the table remained (typically under space pressure). So, it's not guaranteed that all the indexes will be reverted back when the table is flashed back before drop.

Using Flashback Query

In the previous section you learned how to restore tables that had been dropped by accident. But oftentimes, logical corruption issues are not as blatant as a dropped table. It is much more common that a user will make a mistake on a data-entry form, delete a row by accident, or make any of a number of other mistakes. When a problem like this occurs, wouldn't it be nice to be able to go back in time to fix it? Flashback Query allows you to do just that—in a manner of speaking.

Flashback Query provides a method of viewing data as it existed at a prior point in time. So when a user makes a mistake, you can just go back in time and fix it.

Flashback Query is implemented through the AS OF clause of the SELECT statement. The AS OF clause is used to specify a particular point in time (either a timestamp or an SCN number) for one or more tables in the query. When the query is executed, Flashback Query will return the data exactly as it existed at a specified point in time. It is important to note that Flashback Query will return only committed data. It will never return uncommitted data. So if the query happened to specify a point in time that fell in the middle of a transaction, Flashback Query will ignore the transaction and simply return the committed data.

As you can imagine, Flashback Query can be used in many situations encountered by a DBA in the course of their duties:

- Recovering from data changes that were committed by mistake

- Comparing current data values to past values

- Simplifying certain programming tasks by alleviating the need to store certain types of temporary data

- Allowing users to correct their own mistakes

In the past, these types of problems could be addressed only through a costly and time-consuming recovery process. With Flashback Query, they can be handled with ease. Also, Flashback Query functionality is not limited to the DBA. Any user who has been granted SELECT and FLASHBACK privileges can take advantage of it.

Let's take a look at Flashback Query in action. To begin with, we will look at the JOB_HISTORY table:

```
SQL> select * from job_history;

EMPLOYEE_ID START_DAT END_DATE  JOB_ID      DEPARTMENT_ID
----------- --------- --------- ----------- -------------
        102 13-JAN-93 24-JUL-98 IT_PROG                60
        101 21-SEP-89 27-OCT-93 AC_ACCOUNT            110
        101 28-OCT-93 15-MAR-97 AC_MGR               110
        201 17-FEB-96 19-DEC-99 MK_REP                20
        114 24-MAR-98 31-DEC-99 ST_CLERK              50
        122 01-JAN-99 31-DEC-99 ST_CLERK              50
        200 17-SEP-87 17-JUN-93 AD_ASST               90
        176 24-MAR-98 31-DEC-98 SA_REP                80
        176 01-JAN-99 31-DEC-99 SA_MAN                80
        200 01-JUL-94 31-DEC-98 AC_ACCOUNT            90
```

10 rows selected.

Now, let's simulate a user accidentally dropping a row:

```
SQL> delete from job_history where employee_id = 102;

1 row deleted.

SQL> commit;

Commit complete.
```

You can see that the row has indeed been deleted:

```
SQL> select * from job_history;

EMPLOYEE_ID START_DAT END_DATE  JOB_ID      DEPARTMENT_ID
----------- --------- --------- ----------- -------------
        101 21-SEP-89 27-OCT-93 AC_ACCOUNT            110
        101 28-OCT-93 15-MAR-97 AC_MGR               110
        201 17-FEB-96 19-DEC-99 MK_REP                20
        114 24-MAR-98 31-DEC-99 ST_CLERK              50
        122 01-JAN-99 31-DEC-99 ST_CLERK              50
        200 17-SEP-87 17-JUN-93 AD_ASST               90
        176 24-MAR-98 31-DEC-98 SA_REP                80
```

```
        176 01-JAN-99 31-DEC-99 SA_MAN                80
        200 01-JUL-94 31-DEC-98 AC_ACCOUNT            90
```

9 rows selected.

Now, we can use Flashback Query to view the data that existed prior to the delete, as shown here:

```
SQL> select *
from job_history as of timestamp(
to_timestamp('08-MAY-2008 11:50:00','DD-MON-YYYY HH24:MI:SS'))
where employee_id = 102;


EMPLOYEE_ID START_DAT END_DATE  JOB_ID      DEPARTMENT_ID
----------- --------- --------- ----------  -------------
        102 13-JAN-93 24-JUL-98 IT_PROG               60
```

The Flashback Query successfully returned the missing row, but we have only displayed it. We haven't actually recovered it. To do so, we can simply run the same query but wrap it inside an INSERT statement as shown here:

```
SQL> insert into job_history
(select * from job_history
as of timestamp(
to_timestamp('08-MAY-2008 11:50:00','DD-MON'))
where employee_id = 102);


1 row created.


SQL> commit;


Commit complete.


SQL> select * from job_history;


EMPLOYEE_ID START_DAT END_DATE  JOB_ID      DEPARTMENT_ID
----------- --------- --------- ----------  -------------
        102 13-JAN-93 24-JUL-98 IT_PROG               60
        101 21-SEP-89 27-OCT-93 AC_ACCOUNT           110
        101 28-OCT-93 15-MAR-97 AC_MGR               110
        201 17-FEB-96 19-DEC-99 MK_REP                20
        114 24-MAR-98 31-DEC-99 ST_CLERK              50
        122 01-JAN-99 31-DEC-99 ST_CLERK              50
```

```
   200 17-SEP-87 17-JUN-93 AD_ASST                  90
   176 24-MAR-98 31-DEC-98 SA_REP                   80
   176 01-JAN-99 31-DEC-99 SA_MAN                   80
   200 01-JUL-94 31-DEC-98 AC_ACCOUNT               90
```

```
10 rows selected.
```

We have now successfully recovered from the accidental deletion and, as you can see, the effort was minimal.

In the example, our Flashback query pulled data only from a single table, and at a single point in time. Flashback Query is not limited to such simple queries. It can be used in multi-table join queries as well. It can also be mixed and matched with tables that are not flashed back as well as tables that are flashed back to a different point in time. Look at the following example:

```
SQL> select e.last_name, d.department_name, j.job_title
from employees as of timestamp(to_timestamp(
'08-MAY-2008 11:50:00','DD-MON-YYYY HH24:MI:SS')) e,
departments as of timestamp(
to_timestamp('08-MAY-2008 11:53:00','DD-MON-YYYY
HH24:MI:SS')) d,
jobs j
where e.department_id = d.department_id
and e.job_id = j.job_id
and e.employee_id = 200;


LAST_NAME  DEPARTMENT_NAME      JOB_TITLE
---------- -------------------- ----------------------
Whalen     Administration       Administration Assistant
```

This query joined a total of three tables. Two of these tables were flashed back to different points in time. The third table was not flashed back at all. This demonstrates the flexibility of Flashback Query. In fact, a single table could even be joined multiple times, each join flashed back to a different point in time. As has been discussed before, the only limitation is how far back in time you can flash back, and that is determined by the undo retention period.

It is important to understand that the data present in the undo segment governs the ability to flash back to a point in time. Undo retention is only a guideline.

In this section, you've seen a sample of what Flashback Query can do and what a powerful tool it can be in a DBA's arsenal. It allows you to look into the past to view data as it existed at a specific point in time. But what if you're not sure exactly when a change was made? Or suppose you wanted to see all the changes that were made to a column over a period of time. Those are different types of problems and require a different type of tool—Flashback Versions Query.

In Exercise 9.2, you'll practice using the Flashback Query feature.

Using Flashback Query

To practice using the Flashback Query feature, perform the following:

1. Create a table, insert rows of data, and commit.

2. Select all rows from the table.

3. Select the system time.

4. Insert more rows of data into the table, and commit.

5. Select all rows from the table prior to the system time returned in step 3:

```
SQL> create table foo (x number, y varchar2(10));

Table created.

SQL> insert into foo values (1,'test1');

1 row created.

SQL> insert into foo values (2,'test2');

1 row created.

SQL> insert into foo values (3,'test3');

1 row created.

SQL> commit;

Commit complete.

SQL> alter session set nls_date_format = 'DD-MON-YY HH24:MI:SS';

Session altered.

SQL> select sysdate from dual;

SYSDATE
------------------
04-NOV-08 20:31:19
```

```
SQL> insert into foo values (4,'test4');

1 row created.

SQL> insert into foo values (5,'test5');

1 row created.

SQL> commit;

Commit complete.

SQL> select * from foo;

        X Y
---------- ----------
        1 test1
        2 test2
        3 test3
        4 test4
        5 test5
SQL> select * from foo as of timestamp(to_timestamp(
'04-NOV-08 20:31:19','DD-MON-YY HH24:MI:SS'));
        X Y
---------- ----------
        1 test1
        2 test2
        3 test3
SQL>
```

Using Flashback Versions Query

Flashback Versions Query allows you to query a table and retrieve all of the versions of the data that have existed between two specific points in time (specified by a timestamp or an SCN). What's more, Flashback Versions Query offers a host of metadata columns that can also be included in your query, allowing you to view details regarding each change, such as the date/time that the change took place and the SCN that governed the change.

Like Flashback Query, Flashback Versions Query returns only the committed occurrences of the data. Uncommitted data will be ignored. Also just like Flashback Query, Flashback Versions Query works by retrieving data from the UNDO tablespace and is therefore limited by the undo retention period. It also requires the same privileges as Flashback Query: SELECT and FLASHBACK.

Flashback Versions Query is implemented by adding a VERSIONS BETWEEN clause to a SELECT statement. Just like the AS OF clause in Flashback Query, the VERSIONS BETWEEN clause allows the starting point in time to be expressed as either a timestamp or as an SCN.

Let's look at Flashback Versions Query in action. First, we will update a single row in our table several times to simulate changes that may have occurred over time:

```
SQL> update employees
    set salary=salary*1.03
    where employee_id = 193;

1 row updated.

SQL> commit;

Commit complete.

SQL> update employees
    set salary=salary*1.05
    where employee_id = 193;

1 row updated.

SQL> commit;

Commit complete.

SQL> update employees
    set salary=salary/2
    where employee_id=193;

1 row updated.

SQL> commit;

Commit complete.
```

As you can see, our sample employee received a 3 percent raise, a 5 percent raise, and then had his salary cut in half. Next, we will query the table using the versions between clause to view the history of changes:

```
SQL> select salary
  from employees
  versions between scn minvalue and maxvalue
  where employee_id = 193;


    SALARY
----------
   2108.93
   4217.85
      4017
      3900
```

The results show us, from most to least recent, the history of our employee's salary changes. He started off at a salary of $3,900, his 3 percent raise boosted him to $4,017, and his 5 percent raise boosted him to $4,217.85. Finally, our hapless employee's salary was cut in half, to $2,018.93 (presumably after he was unable to quickly restore the rows his boss deleted since he didn't know about Flashback technologies).

You will also notice that the sample query used the clause between scn minvalue and maxvalue to identify the range of versions to select. This construct allows the user to quickly select all versions that are available in the undo tablespace. This is a much cleaner solution than using artificially low and high date ranges such as BETWEEN TIMESTAMP TO_TIMESTAMP('01-JAN-1700','DD-MON-YYYY')

AND

TO_TIMESTAMP('31-DEC-2999', 'DD-MON-YYYY').

As mentioned earlier, there are several pseudocolumns available in conjunction with Flashback Versions Query that can be used to identify when and how the changes were originally made. These columns are identified in Table 9.3.

TABLE 9.3 Flashback Versions Query Pseudocolumns

Column Name	Description
VERSIONS_STARTTIME	The timestamp of the first version of the rows returned from the query.
VERSIONS_ENDTIME	The timestamp of the last version of the rows returned from the query.

TABLE 9.3 Flashback Versions Query Pseudocolumns *(continued)*

Column Name	Description
VERSIONS_STARTSCN	The SCN of the first version of the rows returned from the query.
VERSIONS_ENDSCN	The SCN of the last version of the rows returned from the query.
VERSIONS_XID	The unique transaction ID under which the data was originally changed. In Oracle 11*g* this is a raw value, whereas in 10*g* it was a character value.
VERSIONS_OPERATION	The type of operation that caused the change. Valid values are as follows: I - Insert U - Update D - Delete

In our next example, we will use some of these pseudocolumns to create a simple history report covering the salary changes of our sample employee. The query is shown here:

```
SQL> select to_char(versions_starttime,'DD-MON HH:MI') "START DATE",
    to_char (versions_endtime, 'DD-MON HH:MI') "END DATE",
    versions_operation,
    employee_id,
    salary
    from employees
    versions between scn minvalue and maxvalue
    where employee_id = 123;

START DATE    END DATE     V EMPLOYEE_ID SALARY
------------- ------------ - ----------- ----------
08-MAY 09:13               U         123    2108.93
08-MAY 09:12 08-MAY 09:13  U         123    4217.85
08-MAY 09:08 08-MAY 09:12  U         123       4017
08-MAY 08:15 08-MAY 09:08  I         123       3900
```

This simple query has produced a comprehensive report showing a wealth of information regarding this employee's salary history. By reading from the bottom up, you can see the date and time that the employee was first inserted into the EMPLOYEES table (presumably the day he was hired), as well as his starting salary.

The next lines show the dates, times, amounts, and durations of each salary change for the employee. You will notice that the last line (the top one) has no value for END DATE. This shows that this value still represents the current salary for the employee.

 The Flashback Versions Query can also be used in DDL and DML subqueries.

So, in conclusion, Flashback Versions Query allows you to see into the past to view the history of data changes in the database. It takes the power of Flashback Query a step further and provides you with additional metadata to identify changes in further detail. It even allows you to identify the specific transaction that made the change.

But wouldn't it be nice if you could drill down even further, to see specific details about that transaction? Unfortunately, Flashback Versions Query does not allow you to do that. Instead, you need to move ahead to the next section and learn about the tool that *will* allow you to do that: Flashback Transaction Query.

Using Flashback Transaction Query

Flashback Transaction Query is a diagnostic tool used to identify changes made to the database at the transaction level. Much like Flashback Versions Query, Flashback Transaction Query allows you to identify all changes made between two specific points in time. But Flashback Transaction Query goes a step further, allowing you to perform transactional recovery of tables. In other words, it provides you with the SQL that could be used to undo the transaction.

Before you can begin using Flashback Transaction Query functionality, there are two configuration steps that must be completed.

1. Ensure that the database is running with version 10.0 compatibility.

2. Supplemental logging must be enabled (in other words, ALTER DATABASE ADD SUPPLEMENTAL LOG DATA;).

In addition to these systemwide settings, users who want to take advantage of this feature must be granted the SELECT ANY TRANSACTION privilege. They must also be granted the FLASHBACK privilege on the specific tables they want to flash back, or they must have the broader FLASHBACK ANY TABLE privilege.

Flashback Transaction Query is implemented through the use of the FLASHBACK_TRANSACTION_QUERY view. The data in this view allows analysis of a specific transaction to identify what changes were made to the data. This view can be large, so it is helpful to use a filter when querying the view. This will generally be the transaction identifier (XID column).

Be sure to note that the transaction identifier is stored as a raw value in Oracle 11*g*. This is a change from Oracle 10*g*, which stored it as a character value. Because of this, you can't simply pass in a string representation of a transaction identifier; you must provide a raw value. You can use Flashback Versions Query to provide it for you. For example, let's use the FLASHBACK_TRANSACTION_QUERY view to analyze the transactions that created the changes we viewed in the previous section. To do this, we will join a Flashback Versions Query with the FLASHBACK_TRANSACTION_QUERY view as shown here:

```
SQL> select table_name, operation, undo_sql
from flashback_transaction_query t,
(select versions_xid as xid
 from employees versions between scn minvalue and maxvalue
 where employee_id = 123) e
where t.xid = e.xid
and operation = 'UPDATE';


TABLE_NAME OPERATION UNDO_SQL
---------- --------- -------------------------------------
EMPLOYEES  UPDATE    update "HR"."EMPLOYEES" set "SALARY" =
                     '2108.93' where ROWID =
                     'AAARAgAAFAAAABYABd';
EMPLOYEES  UPDATE    update "HR"."EMPLOYEES" set "SALARY" =
                     '4217.85' where ROWID =
                     'AAARAgAAFAAAABYABd';
EMPLOYEES  UPDATE    update "HR"."EMPLOYEES" set "SALARY" =
                     '4017' where ROWID =
                     'AAARAgAAFAAAABYABd';

3 rows selected.
```

This query shows you the three update transactions you ran earlier to modify our employee's salary. It also provides you with a SQL statement that could be run to effectively offset the transaction.

The example query selected only a few of the columns available in the view. Table 9.4 shows the complete list.

TABLE 9.4 FLASHBACK_TRANSACTION_QUERY View Columns

Column Name	Description
XID	Transaction identifier.
START_SCN	Current SCN at start of transaction.
START_TIMESTAMP	Timestamp at start of transaction.
COMMIT_SCN	SCN at commit of transaction. This is the SCN associated with the transaction.

TABLE 9.4 FLASHBACK_TRANSACTION_QUERY View Columns *(continued)*

Column Name	Description
COMMIT_TIMESTAMP	Timestamp at commit of transaction.
LOGON_USER	User who executed the transaction.
UNDO_CHANGE#	Link to the related undo information.
OPERATION	DML operation performed by the transaction.
TABLE_NAME	Name of the table to which the DML is being applied.
TABLE_OWNER	Owner of the table to which the DML is being applied.
ROW_ID	Row ID of the row modified by the DML.
UNDO_SQL	SQL to undo the transaction.

If you've ever used Oracle Log Miner, the columns listed in Table 9.4 may look familiar to you. In fact, Flashback technology offers functionality that is very similar to Log Miner, but is much simpler to use. It allows you to drill down to the transactional level to analyze data changes. It also provides the SQL necessary to undo any transaction, provided the necessary undo records still exist in the undo tablespace.

Using Additional Flashback Operations

In the following sections, you will first learn how to perform Flashback Table operations and then learn how to perform point-in-time recovery on tables in a live database. Then you will learn how to configure, monitor, and perform Flashback Database operations. Lastly, you will learn to set up and use a Flashback Data Archive.

Using Flashback Table

All of the previous Flashback options we've covered in this chapter have allowed you to view and correct specific data elements within a table. They have not affected the table as a whole. Flashback Table is a little different in that regard.

Flashback Table is a Flashback technology that allows you to recover an entire table (or set of tables) to a specific point in time without the hassle of performing an incomplete recovery. This means that rather than rolling back a single transaction, the entire table will be rolled back. If the table has dependent objects associated with it, they are also rolled back automatically.

So why would you choose to use Flashback Table instead of performing an incomplete recovery? There are several reasons:

Speed   It is much faster than incomplete recovery.

Simplicity   It is much easier than incomplete recovery.

Availability   Flashback Table does not impact the availability of the database. Unlike with other recovery methods, the database remains available, and the tablespace remains online the entire time.

Accessibility   Users can flash back their own tables, so DBA involvement is not required.

Like other Flashback technologies, Flashback Table is limited only by the availability of undo data. Flashback Table also uses RETENTION GUARANTEE in the same manner as the previously discussed Flashback options.

There are two main clauses that are used with the Flashback Table:

- The TO SCN clause can recover the Flashback Table to a certain SCN.

- The TO TIMESTAMP clause can recover the Flashback Table to a certain point in time.

 To flash back a table, the table must have ROW MOVEMENT enabled. This can be accomplished with the following command: ALTER TABLE *tablename* ENABLE ROW MOVEMENT.

It is important to get the current SCN from the database. The current SCN can be identified by querying the CURRENT_SCN column in the V$DATABASE view. To show that Flashback Table is recovered, you can create a change to the data. In the following example, you will update the SALARY value for an employee and commit the transaction. Then you will perform a Flashback Table operation to recover the table to its state prior to the update. This change will be missing if the table is recovered to an SCN before the change is introduced.

Let's walk through performing a Flashback Table operation with SCN:

1. Enable row movement on the employees table:

```
SQL> alter table employees enable row movement;

Table altered.
```

2. Retrieve the current SCN from the database. This is for reference, so make a note of it:

```
SQL> select current_scn from v$database;

CURRENT_SCN
-----------
     623411
```

3. Query the employees table to verify the current salary for the employee with an employee_id = 110:

```
SQL> select employee_id, salary
from employees
where employee_id = 110;


EMPLOYEE_ID SALARY
----------- ----------
110                3000
```

4. Update the employees table as shown. Be sure to commit the change too:

```
SQL> update employees set salary=4000 where
    employee_id = 110;


1 row updated.


SQL> commit;


Commit complete.
```

5. Query the employees table to verify the new salary for our sample employee:

```
SQL> select employee_id, salary
from employees
where employee_id = 110;


EMPLOYEE_ID SALARY
----------- ----------
110                4000
```

6. Perform a Flashback Table operation to recover the table to the SCN retrieved in step 2:

```
SQL> flashback table employees
        to scn 623411;
```

7. Query the employees table again to verify that the change was eliminated because of the Flashback Table operation:

```
SQL> select employee_id, salary
from employees
where employee_id = 110;
```

```
EMPLOYEE_ID SALARY
----------- ----------
110                3000
```

As the example shows, the table has been recovered to its previous state, as it existed back at SCN 623411. Also, if any dependent objects such as indexes existed on the table, they would have also been recovered to maintain consistency.

If a table contains triggers, however, there are some special rules that apply when a Flashback Table operation is performed. All triggers are disabled during a Flashback Table operation. By default, they will remain disabled after the operation is complete, regardless of whether the trigger was previously enabled or not.

If a table has one or more enabled triggers and you want them to remain enabled after the Flashback Table operation is complete, you can add the ENABLE TRIGGERS clause to the statement, as shown here:

```
SQL> flashback table employees
  to scn 623411
    enable triggers;
```

When you specify the ENABLE TRIGGERS option, all triggers that were previously enabled will be reenabled after the operation is complete. Note that the trigger did not remain enabled during the Flashback Table operation. As stated before, all triggers are disabled during the operation (they will not fire in conjunction with the recovery operation). They are then reenabled only after the operation is complete.

As you can see, the Flashback Table operation is a valuable recovery method. Now when a user updates a table using an incorrect WHERE clause, you can simply undo the change using Flashback Table. They could even do it themselves. And, best of all, the availability of the database is not impacted by the operation. Please keep in mind that more complex flashback operations may be required, depending on the number of objects and relations impacted.

In Exercise 9.3, you'll practice using the Flashback Table feature; continue using the table created in Exercise 9.2.

EXERCISE 9.3

Using Flashback Table

To practice using the Flashback Table feature, continue using the table created in Exercise 9.2, and perform the following:

1. Select all rows from the table.

2. Verify the system time at which the last two rows were inserted.

3. Flash back the table to the system time returned in step 2:

   ```
   SQL> alter table foo enable row movement;
   Table altered.
   ```

```
SQL> select * from foo;

        X Y
---------- ----------
         1 test1
         2 test2
         3 test3
         4 test4
         5 test5

SQL> flashback table foo to timestamp to_timestamp(
'04-NOV-08 20:31:19','DD-MON-YY HH24:MI:SS');

Flashback complete.

SQL> select * from foo;

        X Y
---------- ----------
         1 test1
         2 test2
         3 test3

SQL>
```

Configuring and Monitoring Flashback Database and Performing Flashback Database Operations

Flashback Database was introduced in Oracle 10g. There is one main difference between the other Flashback technologies and Flashback Database: Flashback Database relies on "before" images in the flashback logs, whereas the other Flashback features rely on the undo data.

Flashback Database allows you to flash the entire database back to a specific point in time. This is extremely useful to recover from errors such as truncating a large table, not completing a batch job, or dropping a user. Flashback Database recovery is also the best choice for most logical corruptions such as a bad complex transaction that gets propagated throughout the database.

Before you can use Flashback Database, you must set up the *flash recovery area*. Please refer to Chapter 2 for an introduction to the flash recovery area, and refer to Chapter 3 to learn how to configure it.

One major technological benefit of Flashback Database is that it allows you to reverse user errors or logical corruption much quicker than performing a traditional incomplete recovery or using the Oracle Log Miner utility. The reason Flashback Database recovery is much quicker than traditional recovery operations is that recovery is no longer impacted by the size of the database. The mean time to recovery (MTTR) for traditional recovery is dependent on the size of the datafiles and archive logs that need to be restored and applied. Using Flashback Database recovery, recovery time is proportional to the number of changes that need to be backed out of the recovery process, not the size of datafiles and archive logs. This makes the Flashback Database recovery process the most efficient recovery process in most user-error or logical-corruption situations.

The Flashback Database architecture consists of the recovery writer *RVWR* background process and Flashback Database logs. When the Flashback Database is enabled, the RVWR process is started. *Flashback Database logs* are a new type of log file that contain a "before" image of physical database blocks. The RVWR writes the Flashback Database logs in the flash recovery area. Enabling the flash recovery area is a prerequisite to using Flashback Database because the Flashback Database logs are written to the flash recovery area.

Configuring the Flashback Database

The database must have multiple features configured prior to configuring Flashback Database. The database must have ARCHIVE LOG enabled. As mentioned earlier, the flash recovery area must be configured to store the Flashback Database logs.

First, make sure the database is shut down. Next, the database must be started in MOUNT mode. Then, the database parameter DB_FLASHBACK_RETENTION_TARGET can be set to the desired value, which is based on minutes. This value determines how far back in time you can flash back the database. This is like a baseline for Flashback Database. Next, Flashback Database can be enabled with the ALTER DATABASE FLASHBACK ON command. Finally, the database can be opened for normal use.

Let's walk through these steps in more detail:

1. Start the database in MOUNT mode:

```
SQL> connect / as sysdba
SQL> startup mount
ORACLE instance started.
Total System Global Area  535662592 bytes
Fixed Size                  1334380 bytes
Variable Size             171967380 bytes
Database Buffers          356515840 bytes
Redo Buffers                5844992 bytes
```

```
Database mounted.
```

2. Set the DB_FLASHBACK_RETENTION_TARGET parameter to the desired value. This value is in minutes, which equates to three days:

```
SQL> alter system set db_flashback_retention_target=4320;
```

3. Enable the flashback capability:

```
SQL> alter database flashback on;
```

4. Now the database can be opened for normal use:

```
SQL> alter database open;
```

As you can see, enabling Flashback Database is fairly simple. A key point for you to know is how far back in time you need to be able to flash back from, or know the DB_FLASHBACK_RETENTION_TARGET parameter value. The DB_FLASHBACK_RETENTION_TARGET value will determine how far you can flash back the database in minutes. In the preceding example, you specified the value of 4,320, which is for three days; the default value is 1,440, or one day.

Monitoring Flashback Database

The Flashback Database can be monitored by using a few dynamic views: V$DATABASE, V$FLASHBACK_DATABASE_LOG, and V$FLASHBACK_DATABASE_STAT. These views provide some valuable information regarding the status of the Flashback Database and the supporting operations.

The V$DATABASE view displays if the Flashback Database is on or off. This tells you whether the Flashback Database is enabled or not.

Let's query the V$DATABASE view and see the results:

```
SQL> select flashback_on from v$database;


FLASHBACK_ON
------------
YES
SQL>
```

Query the V$FLASHBACK_DATABASE_LOG to determine the amount of space required in the recovery area to support the flashback activity generated by changes in the database. The values in the OLDEST_FLASHBACK_SCN and OLDEST_FLASHBACK_TIME columns give you information regarding how far back you can use Flashback Database. This view also shows the size of the flashback data in the FLASHBACK_SIZE column. The column ESTIMATED_FLASHBACK_SIZE can be used to identify the estimated size of flashback data that you need for your current target retention. Shown next is an example of querying the V$FLASHBACK_DATABASE_LOG:

```
SQL> select
  2.   oldest_flashback_scn,
  3.   oldest_flashback_time,
  4.   retention_target,
  5.   estimated_flashback_size
  6.   from v$flashback_database_log;
```

OLDEST_FLASH_SCN	OLDEST_FLASH_TIME	RET_TARGET	EST_FLASHBACK_SIZE
979720	20-JUL-08	4320	298967040

```
SQL>
```

The V$FLASHBACK_DATABASE_STAT view is used to monitor the overhead of maintaining the data in the Flashback Database logs. This view allows you to make estimates regarding future Flashback Database operations. This is done by coming up with an estimate about potential required space.

Let's look at the V$FLASHBACK_DATABASE_STAT:

```
SQL> select * from v$flashback_database_stat;
```

BEGIN_TIM	END_TIME	FLASHBACK_DATA	DB_DATA	REDO_DATA
ESTIMATED_FLASHBACK_SIZE				
20-JUL-08	20-JUL-08	61784064	35880960	99203072
0				

```
SQL>
```

As you can see, the V$FLASHBACK_DATABASE_STAT dynamic view shows the utilization of the Flashback Database log. This is determined by the begin and end times.

Using Flashback Database

The Flashback Database can be used with SQL*Plus to perform recoveries. Once the database is configured for the Flashback Database, you just need to start the database in MOUNT mode, and you are ready to perform a Flashback Database recovery. You also need to get either OLDEST_FLASHBACK_SCN or OLDEST_FLASHBACK_TIME from the V$FLASHBACK_DATABASE_LOG view. This will allow you to utilize the TO SCN or TO TIME clause in the FLASHBACK DATABASE clause. If you have established a *restore point*, you can recover to it if it is newer than the oldest_flashback_scn.

Let's walk through performing a Flashback Database recovery to an SCN:

1. First, query the V$FLASHBACK_DATABASE_LOG view to retrieve the OLDEST_FLASHBACK_SCN:

```
SQL> select oldest_flashback_scn, oldest_flashback_time
  2  from v$flashback_database_log;


OLDEST_FLASHBACK_SCN OLDEST_FLASHBACK_TIME
-------------------- --------------------
              979720 20-JUL-08

SQL>
```

2. Next, shut down and start the database in MOUNT mode:

```
SQL> shutdown
Database closed.
Database dismounted.
ORACLE instance shut down.
SQL>
SQL> startup mount
ORACLE instance started.
Total System Global Area  535662592 bytes
Fixed Size                  1334380 bytes
Variable Size             171967380 bytes
Database Buffers          356515840 bytes
Redo Buffers                5844992 bytes
Database mounted.
SQL>
```

3. Next, issue the Flashback Database recovery command:

```
SQL> flashback database to scn 979721;
Flashback complete.
SQL>
```

4. Finally, open the database with the RESETLOGS option, because you recovered to a time prior to the current database:

```
SQL> alter database open resetlogs;
Database altered.
SQL>
```

As you can see, the Flashback Database recovery is a fairly simple process. The V$FLASHBACK_DATABASE_LOG dynamic view is useful for both TO SCN and TO TIME recoveries. The Flashback Database recovery is a quick and efficient method for recovering from user errors or logical corruptions in the database. This is a great alternative to performing a traditional incomplete recovery.

 Flashback Database recovery can also be performed in SQL*Plus with the FLASHBACK DATABASE command as well as with RMAN.

Limitations with the Flashback Database

Flashback Database recovery cannot recover through some common occurrences such as resizing a datafile to a smaller size or a deleted datafile. In these cases, the datafile would need to be restored with traditional methods to a point in time prior to its deletion or resizing. Then you could use Flashback Database recovery to recover the rest of the database.

Flashback Database is a nice substitute for incomplete recovery for logical corruption and user errors. However, there are some limitations to Flashback Database that you should be aware of:

- Media failure cannot be resolved with Flashback Database. You will still need to restore datafiles and recover archived redo logs to recover from media failure.

- Resizing datafiles to a smaller size, also called shrinking datafiles, cannot be undone with the Flashback Database.

- You cannot use Flashback Database if the control file has been restored or re-created.

- Dropping a tablespace and recovery through resetlogs cannot be performed.

- You cannot flash back the database to an SCN prior to the earliest available SCN in the flashback logs.

Setting Up and Using a Flashback Data Archive

The *Flashback Data Archive*, also known as *Oracle Total Recall*, allows you to retain and track all transactional changes to a record over its lifetime. This eliminates the need to write custom programs to archive all transactional changes to data. The uses of the Flashback Data Archive are many, but auditing and compliance are two key areas where this technology can be useful.

To utilize the Flashback Data Archive capabilities, create one or more tablespaces as an archive. Each archive has a retention time that determines how long data is retained within it. The DBA can designate a default Flashback Data Archive for the database.

Once you have a created a Flashback Data Archive, you can enable flashback data archiving on a per-table basis. By default, flashback archiving is turned off.

Configuring the Flashback Data Archive

Setting up the Flashback Data Archive is straightforward. Simply name the archive and assign a tablespace, an optional space quota, and the retention time:

```
SQL> create flashback archive audit_flash_archive
tablespace audit_archive quota 20g retention 7 year;


SQL> create flashback archive audit_flash_archive_2
Tablespace audit_archive quota 10m retention 90 day;
SQL>
```

To establish a default Flashback Data Archive, simply add the `default` keyword in the `create` clause:

```
SQL> create flashback archive default default_flash_archive
Tablespace audit_archive quota 10m retention 90 day;
SQL>
```

After you've created a Flashback Data Archive, of course you will need to alter it. As DBA, you may alter the storage quota and retention time and add, drop, or modify tablespaces in a data archive using the `alter flashback archive` command. Here are a few examples:

```
SQL> alter flashback archive default_flash_archive
Modify tablespace audit_archive quota 100m;
SQL>
SQL> alter flashback archive default_flash_archive
retention 180 day;
SQL>
SQL> alter flashback archive default_flash_archive
Remove Tablespace audit_archive;
SQL>
```

To clean up or purge data to an SCN or timestamp from a Flashback Data Archive, use the `alter` command with the purge clause:

```
SQL> alter flashback archive default_flash_archive
Purge before SCN 979271;
SQL>
```

```
SQL> alter flashback archive default_flash_archive
Purge before timestamp (SYSDATE - 180);
SQL>
```

And if you have established a deletion policy for archives, you can drop an archive quite easily:

```
SQL> drop flashback archive default_flash_archive;
SQL>
```

Using the Flashback Data Archive

Once the Flashback Data Archive is created, you can begin archiving data from specific tables. To enable archiving for an existing table, use the ALTER TABLE command with the FLASHBACK ARCHIVE clause:

```
SQL> alter table employee_history flashback archive audit_flash_archive;
SQL>
```

If you have created a default flashback archive and want to use it, then you don't need to specify the name of the archive.

Equally straightforward, create a new table with the archive feature to utilize the default Flashback Data Archive:

```
SQL> create table shipments (ship_id number(9),
shipper number(9), ship_date date),
flashback archive;
SQL>
```

To disable archiving for a table, simply alter the table using the NO FLASHBACK ARCHIVE clause:

```
SQL> alter table shipments no flashback archive;
SQL>
```

Now that you have established all the structures, query the base table to retrieve archive data using the AS OF TIMESTAMP clause:

```
SQL> select * from shipments AS OF TIMESTAMP
('2008-05-01 12:00:00', 'YYYY-MM-DD HH24:MI:SS');
SQL>
```

Certain DDL is not allowed on archived tables: TRUNCATE, DROP, and RENAME as well as ALTER commands that drop, rename, or modify a column, change a long raw to a LOB, perform a partition or subpartition operation, or use the UPGRADE TABLE clause.

Monitoring the Flashback Data Archive

The Flashback Data Archiver process, FBDA, archives the historical rows of tables enabled for archiving to the Flashback Data Archive. FBDA writes a pre-image of a row and metadata on current rows into the flashback archive when a transaction that changes data commits. FBDA manages the Flashback Data Archive retention and space.

Several views are available for monitoring the Flashback Data Archive. See Table 9.5 for an description of the views.

TABLE 9.5　Flashback Data Archive Views

View Name	Description
DBA_FLASHBACK_ARCHIVE	Information about Flashback Data Archive
DBA_FLASHBACK_ARCHIVE_TS	Tablespaces used for Flashback Data Archive
DBA_FLASHBACK_ARCHIVE_TABLES	Tables that are enabled for archive

Summary

In this chapter, you learned about Flashback technologies and their dependence on Oracle's undo functionality. You learned about Automatic Undo Management (AUM) and how it aids the DBA in managing undo information.

We discussed the Recycle Bin in detail, and you learned how dropped objects are moved to the Recycle Bin. We showed you how to query the contents of the Recycle Bin and how to recover objects using the Flashback Drop feature.

Next, you learned about Flashback Query and its ability to show you data as it appeared at a specific time in the past.

The next section discussed the Flashback Versions Query, which retrieves all versions of the rows that existed between two specific points in time.

You then used the Flashback Transaction Query to view transactional changes in data. You saw examples of how you can use this tool to perform transactional analysis, including producing SQL statements that will undo the transaction.

You used Flashback Table to recover a table to a specific point in time without performing an incomplete recovery. You also learned how all dependent objects are recovered when using Flashback Table.

The Flashback Database is best used to recover from logical corruption and user error. This is an alternative to incomplete recovery or the Log Miner utility. The Flashback Database can be enabled and configured fairly easily. You must have the flash recovery area enabled to implement the Flashback Database.

The last Flashback technology discussed in this chapter was the Flashback Data Archive, which Flashback Data Archive can be used to track all DML changes to a table and keep the changes for a specific retention period.

Exam Essentials

Know how to restore dropped tables from the Recycle Bin. Make sure that you understand how the Recycle Bin handles dropped objects. You should be able to locate objects in the Recycle Bin. You should be able to perform a Flashback Drop recovery of a dropped object.

Know how to perform a Flashback query. You must understand how Flashback Query works. Know which options are available in the AS OF clause (timestamp and SCN). Be able to execute a Flashback query and understand what the results represent.

Know how to use Flashback Transaction Query. Know how to use Flashback Transaction Query to expose transactional information relating to changes in the database. Be sure that you are familiar with the contents of the FLASHBACK_TRANSACTION_QUERY view. Be able to access the undo SQL required to roll back a transaction.

Understand how to perform Flashback Table operations. Understand the basics of how Flashback Table works. Know how to perform a Flashback Table operation with a time-stamp or an SCN. Be aware of how undo data is used in Flashback Table and how to protect this data.

Understand the Flashback Database architecture. Make sure you are aware of the components that make up the Flashback Database architecture. Understand the Flashback Database logs and RVWR background-process functionality.

Understand how to enable and disable the Flashback Database. Know how to configure the Flashback Database. Understand the flash recovery area and how it is configured.

Know how to monitor the Flashback Database. Know the dynamic views that monitor the Flashback Database. Understand what each view contains.

Know how to create and use a Flashback Data Archive. Know the syntax to create a Flashback Data Archive in a tablespace, alter the storage and retention parameters, purge and drop, archive a table, and query the results.

Review Questions

1. Which of the following Oracle features utilize the undo tablespace? (Choose all that apply)

   A. Flashback Query

   B. Flashback Drop

   C. Flashback Table

   D. Flashback Database

   E. Transaction Processing

   F. Recycle Bin

2. Which of the following statements are true regarding the Recycle Bin? (Choose all that apply.)

   A. The Recycle Bin is a physical storage area for dropped objects.

   B. The Recycle Bin is a logical container for dropped objects.

   C. The Recycle Bin stores the results of a Flashback Drop operation.

   D. The objects in the Recycle Bin are stored in the tablespace in which they were created.

3. Over the course of a day, a department performed multiple DML statements (inserts, updates, deletes) on multiple rows of data in multiple tables. The manager would like a report showing the time, table name, and DML type for all changes that were made. Which Flashback technology would be the best choice to produce the list?

   A. Flashback Drop

   B. Flashback Query

   C. Flashback Transaction Query

   D. Flashback Versions Query

   E. Flashback Table

4. A user named Arren is executing this query:

   ```
   select table_name, operation, undo_sql
       from
       flashback_transaction_query t,
         (select versions_xid as xid
      from employees versions between scn minvalue
      and maxvalue
         where employee_id = 123) e
         where t.xid = e.xid;
   ```

   When the query runs, he receives an ORA-01031: insufficient privileges error. Since the user owns the employees table, you know that it is not the problem. Which of the following SQL statements will correct this problem?

A. GRANT SELECT ANY TRANSACTION TO ARREN;

B. GRANT SELECT ON FLASHBACK_TRANSACTION_QUERY TO ARREN;

C. GRANT SELECT_ANY_TRANSACTION TO ARREN;

D. GRANT FLASHBACK TO ARREN;

E. GRANT SELECT ANY VIEW TO ARREN;

5. AUM has been retaining about 15 minutes' worth of undo. You want to double the retention period, but not at the expense of new transactions failing. You decide to alter the system to set the parameter UNDO_RETENTION=18000. However, AUM still retains only about 15 minutes' worth of undo. What is the problem? (Choose the best answer.)

    A. You need to alter the undo tablespace to add the RETENTION GUARANTEE setting.

    B. You need to increase the size of the undo tablespace.

    C. The undo tablespace is not set to auto-extend.

    D. You need to alter the Recycle Bin to add the RETENTION GUARANTEE setting.

6. In order to perform Flashback Transaction Query operations, which of these steps are required? (Choose all that apply.)

    A. Ensure that database is running with version 10.1 compatibility.

    B. Enable Flashback Logging.

    C. Enable Supplemental Logging.

    D. Ensure that the database is running with version 10.0 compatibility.

    E. Ensure that the database is in ARCHIVELOG mode

7. Users notify you that their application is failing every time they try to add new records. Because of poor application design, the actual ORA error message is unavailable. What might be the problem? (Choose the best answers.)

    A. The application user has exceeded their undo quota.

    B. The FLASHBACK GUARANTEE option is set on the undo tablespace.

    C. The table is currently being queried by a Flashback Transaction Query operation.

    D. The table is currently being queried by a Flashback Versions Query operation.

    E. The RETENTION GUARANTEE option is set on the undo tablespace.

8. Which of the following statements best describes Flashback Versions Query?

    A. Flashback Versions Query is used to make changes to multiple versions of data that existed between two points in time.

    B. Flashback Versions Query is used to view all version changes on rows that existed between the time the query was executed and a point in time in the past.

    C. Flashback Versions Query is used to view version changes and the SQL to undo those changes on rows that existed between two points in time.

    D. Flashback Versions Query is used to view all version changes on rows that existed between two points in time.

9. Which pseudocolumn could you use to identify a unique row in a Flashback Versions Query?

   A. XID

   B. VERSIONS_PK

   C. VERSIONS_XID

   D. VERSIONS_UNIQUE

10. Which of the following can be used in conjunction with a Flashback Versions Query to filter the results? (Choose all that apply.)

   A. A range of SCN values

   B. A list of SCN values

   C. A starting and ending timestamp

   D. Minimum and maximum sequence values

   E. A list of sequence values

11. At the request of a user, you issue the following command to restore a dropped table:

```
flashback table "BIN$F2JFfMq8Q5unbC0ceE9eJg==$0" to
```

before drop; Later, the user notifies you that the data in the table seems to be very old and out of date. What might be the problem?

   A. Because a proper range of SCNs was not specified, the wrong data was restored.

   B. A proper range of timestamps was not specified, so the wrong data was restored.

   C. A previous Flashback Drop operation had been performed, resulting in multiple versions of the table being stored in the Recycle Bin.

   D. Either option A or B could be correct. Not enough information was provided to determine which.

   E. None of the above.

12. Which of the following statements is true regarding the VERSIONS BETWEEN clause?

   A. The VERSIONS BETWEEN clause may be used in DML statements.

   B. The VERSIONS BETWEEN clause may be used in DDL statements.

   C. The VERSIONS BETWEEN clause may not be used to query past DDL changes to tables.

   D. The VERSIONS BETWEEN clause may not be used to query past DML statements to tables.

13. Which of the following statements is true regarding implementing a Flashback Table recovery?

   A. An SCN is never used to perform a Flashback Table recovery.

   B. If a significant number of changes have been made to the table, row movement must be enabled.

   C. The tablespace must be offline before performing a Flashback Table recovery.

   D. Flashback Table recovery is completely dependent on the availability of undo data in the undo tablespace.

14. You have just performed a FLASHBACK TABLE operation using the following command:

```
flashback table employees
to scn 123456;
```

The `employees` table has triggers associated with it. Which of the following statements is true regarding the state of the triggers during the Flashback Table operation?

A. All the triggers are disabled.

B. All the triggers are enabled by default.

C. Enabled triggers remain enabled and disabled triggers remain disabled.

D. Triggers are deleted when a Flashback Table operation is performed.

15. Which method could be utilized to identify both DML operations and the SQL statements needed to undo those operations for a specific schema owner? (Choose all that apply.)

A. Query DBA_TRANSACTION_QUERY for TABLE_NAME, OPERATION, and UNDO_SQL. Limit rows by START_SCN and TABLE_OWNER.

B. Query FLASHBACK_TRANSACTION_QUERY for TABLE_NAME, OPERATION, and UNDO_SQL. Limit rows by START_SCN and TABLE_OWNER.

C. Query FLASHBACK_TRANSACTION_QUERY for TABLE_NAME, OPERATION, and UNDO_SQL. Limit rows by START_TIMESTAMP and TABLE_OWNER.

D. Query DBA_TRANSACTION_QUERY for TABLE_NAME, OPERATION, and UNDO_SQL. Limit rows by START_SCN and TABLE_OWNER.

16. Flashback Database relies on which technologies to recover to a point in time?

A. Flashback Data Archive

B. Flashback logs in the flash recovery area

C. Undo tablespace

D. RMAN command line

E. None of the above

17. The _____ writes the Flashback Database logs in the flash recovery area.

A. FLSH

B. FLDB

C. RVWR

D. RVRW

E. FBDA

18. Which of these are valid Flashback Database recovery point parameters? (Choose all that apply.)

    A. SCN

    B. Timestamp

    C. Named recovery point

    D. Transaction ID

    E. Session ID

19. When setting up the Flashback Data Archive, which of these key parameters are required? (Choose all that apply.)

    A. Tablespace name

    B. Storage quota

    C. Retention

    D. Table name

    E. Create a default archive

20. To clean up old records that are in a Flashback Data Archive and are past the retention period, what must the DBA do?

    A. TRUNCATE the archive table.

    B. DROP the Flashback Data Archive.

    C. Nothing; expired rows are automatically removed.

    D. Nothing; expired rows are moved to an archive table.

    E. Delete entries from the archive where the metadata date retained is greater than the retention period.

Answers to Review Questions

1. A, C, E. Flashback Drop utilizes the Recycle Bin, which does not use the undo tablespace; therefore options B and F are incorrect. Flashback Database is a physical recovery method and does not use undo; therefore option D is incorrect.

2. B, D. The Recycle Bin is a logical container of Flashback dropped objects. The objects in the Recycle Bin are stored in the tablespace they were created in.

3. C. Flashback Transaction Query could provide the data requested in a single query. Option A is an invalid choice because the table wasn't dropped. Option B is incorrect because Flashback Query returns data at only a specific point in time, not for a range of times. Option D is incorrect because, although it could produce the data needed for the report, Flashback Versions Query would have to be run for each table individually. Option E is incorrect because the user does not want to recover the table at all.

4. A. The user needs to have the SELECT ANY TRANSACTION privilege granted to him. All of the other choices are incorrect.

5. C. AUM will ignore the UNDO_RETENTION parameter if the undo tablespace is not set to auto-extend. Option A is incorrect because guaranteeing retention could result in failed transactions, which you are specifically wanting to avoid. Option B is not the best answer because the size of the undo tablespace is not the cause of the issue, but increasing the size of the undo tablespace could increase the amount of undo retained. Option D is wrong because this question is not dealing with the Recycle Bin and because it has no guaranteed retention setting.

6. C, D. Version 10.0 compatibility must be set, so option A is incorrect. Option B is incorrect because there is no such thing as Flashback Logging. Option E is incorrect because ARCHIVELOG mode has no effect on Flashback Transaction Query functionality.

7. A, E. The likely causes are that the RETENTION GUARANTEE option has been set on the undo tablespace and there are no expired transactions to remove to make room for new transactions, or that the user has exceeded the undo quota that has been set by the database resource manager. FLASHBACK GUARANTEE is not a valid option, so option B is incorrect. Flashback queries would not interfere with transactions entering the system, so options C and D are incorrect.

8. D. Flashback Versions Query does not change data at all, so option A is incorrect. B could be correct, but only if one of the specified points in time was the current timestamp. Therefore, B is not the best description. Option C is incorrect because Flashback Versions Query does not provide the SQL to undo the changes.

9. C. The VERSIONS_XID column contains the unique transaction identifier for the row. None of the other choices are valid column names.

10. A, C. Lists of values are not valid, so both B and E are incorrect. Also, sequence values are not valid, so D is also incorrect.

11. E. A Flashback Drop operation restores dropped objects from the Recycle Bin. It does not use SCN or timestamp ranges, so options A, B, and D are incorrect. Also, Flashback Drop operations don't create objects in the Recycle Bin (they move them out of the Recycle Bin), so C is incorrect. The likely cause is that multiple versions of the table existed in the Recycle Bin and the wrong one was restored.

12. C. The VERSIONS BETWEEN clause of the Flashback Versions Query cannot query past table modifications or DDL changes to a table.

13. D. Like the other Flashback options, Flashback Table must be able to find the necessary undo records in order to recover. The use of SCNs is valid in Flashback Table; therefore option A is incorrect. Row Movement must be enabled in all cases, not just when a significant number of changes have been made. Therefore option B is incorrect. One of the main features of Flashback Table is that the tablespace can remain online, so option C is incorrect.

14. A. The default action for the FLASHBACK TABLE command is to disable all triggers regardless of their previous state. If the ENABLE TRIGGER clause is added to the FLASHBACK TABLE command, then triggers that were previously enabled will be reenabled after the operation completes.

15. B, C. FLASHBACK_TRANSACTION_QUERY is the correct view to query, and it can be done using either timestamps or SCN ranges. DBA_TRANSACTION_QUERY is not a valid view; therefore options A and D are incorrect.

16. B. Flashback Database relies on flashback logs in the flash recovery area. The Flashback Data Archive and Undo tablespace are not required. The RMAN command line is not required to recover to a flashback point; the DBA can execute the Flashback Database command from within SQL Plus.

17. C. The Flashback Database architecture consists of the recovery writer RVWR background process and Flashback Database logs. When the Flashback Database is enabled, the RVWR process is started. The RVWR writes the Flashback Database logs in the flash recovery area. FBDA is the Flashback Data Archive background process; the remaining options are fictitious.

18. A, B, C. The DBA can use Flashback Database to recover to an SCN, a point in time, or a named recovery point that is within the recovery window. Transaction ID and Session ID will not help you recover using the Flashback Database feature.

19. A, C. When creating a Flashback Data Archive, you need to specify the tablespace name and a retention period. The storage quota is optional. You add tables to an archive after the archive is created, not as a prerequisite. You don't need to name a default Flashback Data Archive.

20. C. Do nothing. Once the retention period has passed, rows will be automatically removed from the Flashback Data Archive. TRUNCATE on a table that is archived is not allowed. Dropping the archive will definitely clear the old records, but it will also eliminate the ones you wanted to keep.

Chapter

10

Diagnosing the Database and Managing Performance

ORACLE DATABASE 11*g*: ADMINISTRATION II EXAM OBJECTIVES COVERED IN THIS CHAPTER:

✓ **Diagnosing the Database**

- Set up Automatic Diagnostic Repository

- Using Support Workbench

- Perform block media recovery

✓ **Managing Database Performance**

- Use the SQL Tuning Advisor

- Use the SQL Access Advisor to tune a workload

- Understand Database Replay

This chapter is divided into two sections; the first section is dedicated to tools that help the DBA diagnose problems in the database, and the second part is dedicated to tools that assist with detecting and resolving performance issues.

In the first part, we introduce the Automatic Diagnostic Repository, the new central repository for all database diagnostic information, and the Support Workbench, which the DBA uses for problem recognition, reporting, and resolution. We also discuss and demonstrate block media recovery.

In the second part, we introduce the SQL Tuning Advisor and the SQL Access Advisor and also teach you the fundamentals of Database Replay. The SQL Tuning Advisor may recommend SQL profiles and indexes, rewriting your SQL statements, or using statistics to improve query performance. The SQL Access Advisor may recommend indexes, partitioning, and materialized views to improve the performance of a workload. Database Replay allows the DBA to capture a workload on a production system and replay it on a different system, simulating the behavior of the production application in a different environment.

Exam objectives are subject to change at any time without prior notice and at Oracle's sole discretion. Please visit Oracle's Training and Certification website (http://www.oracle.com/education/certification/) for the most current exam-objectives listing.

Diagnosing the Database

One of the most important day-to-day tasks of the DBA is to monitor system activity and diagnose, report, and repair problems. In Oracle 11g, the toolset has improved dramatically. The Automatic Diagnostic Repository provides a central location for storing problem-incident-related information. The Support Workbench improves DBA productivity when it is time to report, analyze, and seek help from Oracle Support to resolve a problem. Block media recovery improvements in 11g make it easier for the DBA to recognize and recover from a data-corruption incident.

Setting Up the Automatic Diagnostic Repository

The Automatic Diagnostic Repository (ADR) is a hierarchical file-based systemwide and system-managed repository for storing and organizing dump files, trace files, alert logs, health monitor reports, network tracing, and all other error diagnostic data. In Oracle 11*g*, ADR is the diagnostic data repository for Automatic Storage Management (ASM), the database, and all other Oracle products.

The ADR stores information in files outside the database so the information is available whether or not the database is up. The files are stored in a directory structure that includes a home directory for each instance of each product.

ADR Initialization Parameters

Since the Oracle 11*g* ADR provides a single repository location for the alert log and all dump files and trace files, there is no longer a need for the BACKGROUND_DUMP_DEST, CORE_DUMP_DEST, and USER_DUMP_DEST initialization parameters. They are deprecated and ignored. Now you use the initialization parameter DIAGNOSTIC_DEST to designate the location of the ADR.

```
SQL> show parameter diag
NAME                                   TYPE        VALUE
------------------------------------   ----------  ---------
diagnostic_dest                        string      C:\ORACLE
```

The default value for DIAGNOSTIC_DEST is $ORACLE_BASE. If the ORACLE_BASE environment variable is not set, then $ORACLE_HOME is used for DIAGNOSTIC_DEST.

Directory Structure of the Automatic Diagnostic Repository

Within the DIAGNOSTIC_DEST directory, Oracle builds the hierarchy of directories to support the ADR. The ADR home directory is located in this directory structure:

```
<diagnostic_dest>/diag/rdbms/<dbname>/<instname>
```

For the examples used in this chapter, the following represents the correct ADR home:

```
C:\oracle\diag\rdbms\orcl\orcl
```

These are some important directories that you need to know about:

- Incident: Each incident gets its own subdirectory within the incident directory.
- Alert: The alert log is written to the alert directory.
- Cdump: Core dumps are written to this directory.
- Trace: Trace files are written to the trace directory.

See Figure 10.1 for an example directory structure.

The DBA can set the value of DIAGNOSTIC_DEST on each instance in Real Application Clusters. The recommendation from Oracle is for each instance in a cluster to have the same value for DIAGNOSTIC_DEST.

FIGURE 10.1   Folders within the ADR home directory

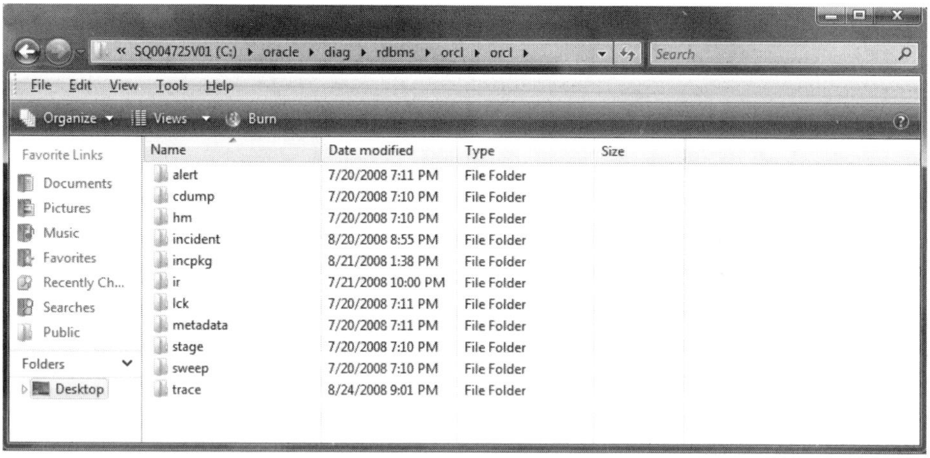

In Exercise 10.1, you'll set the diagnostic destination.

EXERCISE 10.1

Setting the Diagnostic Destination

To set the value for the diagnostic destination, do the following:

1. Verify the current setting for DIAGNOSTIC_DEST.

2. Determine the new destination.

3. Set the value for DIAGNOSTIC_DEST.

4. Verify that the directory structure has been created.

5. Verify the current setting for DIAGNOSTIC_DEST.

    ```
    SQL> show parameter diag
    ```

NAME	TYPE	VALUE
diagnostic_dest	string	C:\ORACLE

6. Determine the new destination. Check the new destination for security, access, and sufficient space. In this example, we're moving the diagnostic destination from c:\ oracle to c:\temp.

7. Set the value for DIAGNOSTIC_DEST.

8. Use the ALTER SYSTEM command to change the value of DIAGNOSTIC_DEST:

    ```
    SQL> alter system set diagnostic_dest="c:\temp";
    ```

EXERCISE 10.1 *(continued)*

9. Verify that the directory structure has been created.

10. Oracle creates the `diag` directory under the `diagnostic_dest` directory and creates the directory tree under the `diag` directory:

```
SQL> host

c:\temp>cd diag

c:\temp\diag>tree
Folder PATH listing for volume SQ004725V01
Volume serial number is 000DF7CC 8E02:02B8
C:.
rdbms
    orcl
        orcl
            alert
            cdump
            hm
            incident
            incpkg
            ir
            lck
            metadata
            stage
            sweep
            trace

c:\temp\diag>
```

Using the Support Workbench

New to Oracle 11g, the Enterprise Manager Support Workbench (Support Workbench) is a central location for the DBA to see reported problems, investigate the problems, report the problem to Oracle support, and follow up through problem resolution. This is a vast improvement over previous versions, where there was no central location and no defined process for reporting, tracking, and resolving problem incidents.

To access the Support Workbench, start from the Enterprise Manager Database home page, click the Software and Support tab, and then in the Support section, click Support Workbench.

Fundamental Tasks of the Support Workbench

The Support Workbench provides a framework for problem resolution: investigate, report, and resolve a problem. The following are the basic tasks within the Support Workbench:

- View critical error alerts.
- View problem details.
- Gather additional diagnostic information.
- Create a service request.
- Package and upload diagnostic data to Oracle Support.
- Track the service request and implement any repairs.
- Close the incident.

Task 1: View Critical Error Alerts

In most cases, you'll discover a critical alert on the Enterprise Manager home page and then work your way to the Support Workbench page. On the EM Database Instance home page, critical-error alerts and warnings will be displayed in the Alerts section. A red X in the Severity column and an incident in the Category column indicate a critical-error alert. See Figure 10.2 for an example.

FIGURE 10.2   Alerts on the Enterprise Manager home page

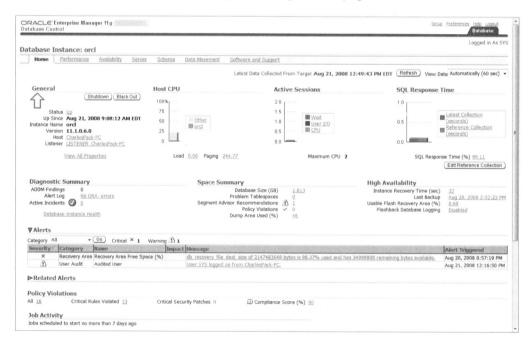

When you select the Message link, EM will direct you to the details for the critical alert, indicating by default any incidents in the last 24 hours. As you can see in Figure 10.3, changing the View Data option to Last 7 Days shows a lingering problem that needs to be addressed. You can add a comment to the most recent alert, or you can click one of the alert messages and add a comment to that specific alert.

FIGURE 10.3   Critical alert

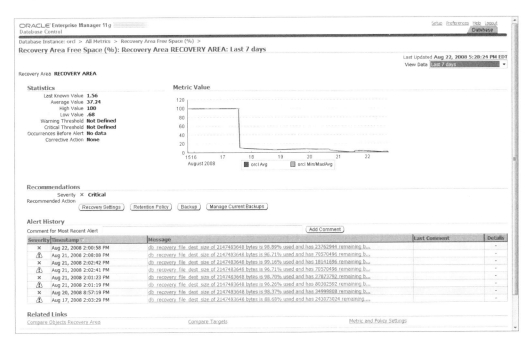

Return to the Database home page and go to the Support Workbench home page as described previously. Figure 10.4 shows one problem and two incidents. In Oracle 11*g*, a *problem* is a critical error in the database. An *incident* is a single occurrence of a *problem*. By default, incidents of a problem that have occurred within the last 24 hours are displayed on the page. To change the date range displayed, click the View drop-down menu and select your preference. To view all of the incidents for a problem, click the Details column's Show icon or the Show All Details link.

Task 2: View Problem Details

Click the Select check box for the problem, and click the View button to see the problem details and, by default, all open incidents of the problem. To view all open, all closed, or all incidents associated with the problem, select the appropriate values from the Status drop-down menu options. There is also a Data Dumped drop-down menu; the options are yes and no. For the example shown in Figure 10.5, we want to see open incidents with data dumped.

FIGURE 10.4   Support Workbench

FIGURE 10.5   Problem details

You can view the details for an incident of this problem by clicking the Show icon in the Details column of the Incidents section.

Task 3: Gather Additional Diagnostic Information

With this problem, the DBA needs to generate additional dumps and test cases before engaging Oracle Support, as noted at the top of the Problem Details subpage. Now would be a good time to perform self-service. In the Investigate and Resolve Section on the Self Service tab, select Run Checkers. For the example shown in Figure 10.6, there are no recommended checkers to run.

FIGURE 10.6   Run Checkers

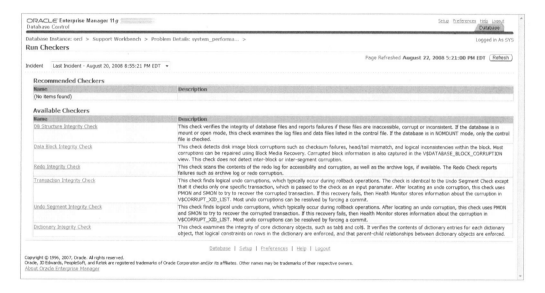

Task 4: Create a Service Request

If you would like to open a service request with Oracle Support, click the Go to Metalink button in the Investigate and Resolve section; your browser will take you to Oracle's Metalink home page. From there, you can open a service request and then return to EM.

Task 5: Package and Upload Diagnostic Data to Oracle Support

The Support Workbench has solved one very annoying problem for the active DBA: packaging all of the related data for an incident and getting it to Oracle. In the past, we searched for relevant files, compressed them, batched them, and either FTPed them to Oracle Support or attached the files to the Technical Assistance Request (TAR). Oracle 11*g* Incident Packaging Service (IPS) makes it easy. It identifies all files associated with a critical error and adds them to a zip file so you can easily send it to Oracle Support.

IPS is built into the Support Workbench, meant to make the DBA more productive and help Oracle Support to receive a complete set of data before advising on action steps.

From the Investigate and Report section on the Problem Details page, click Quick Package. This will allow you to zip files related to the problem and send them to Oracle Support. We start the process in Figure 10.7.

Enter your package description, Metalink credentials, and customer-support identifier. Click Next to view the package contents, shown in Figure 10.8.

FIGURE 10.7 Quick Packaging: Create New Package

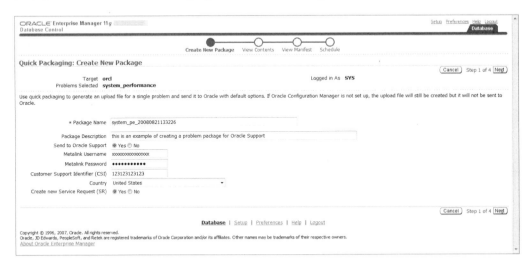

FIGURE 10.8 Viewing the package contents

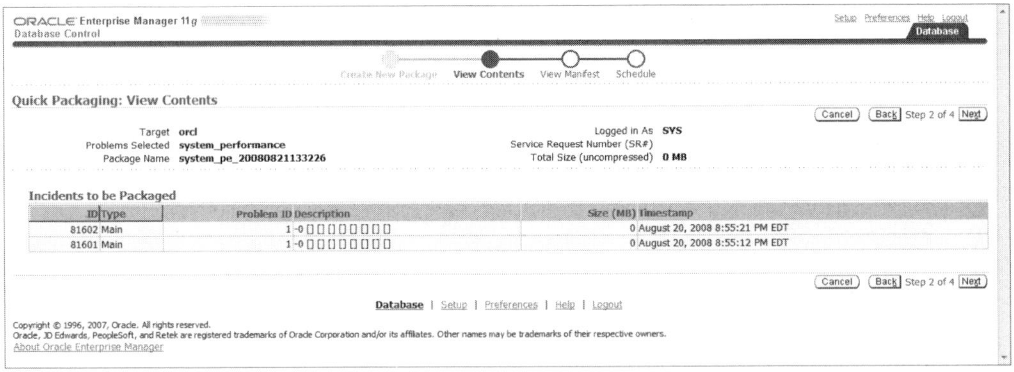

The View Manifest screen, shown in Figure 10.9, displays the package information that will be sent to Oracle Support.

After you verify that the information is correct, click Next to schedule the job that will submit the information to Oracle Support. Once you verify the job send time, click the final Submit button. Then click the OK button to return to the Problem Details page.

To view the details of a package in the Support Workbench, choose packages from the Support Workbench home page, and then choose a package by clicking on the package name. You can view the list of files included in the package, as shown in Figure 10.10, by clicking the Files tab from the Incident Package Details screen.

FIGURE 10.9   The View Manifest screen

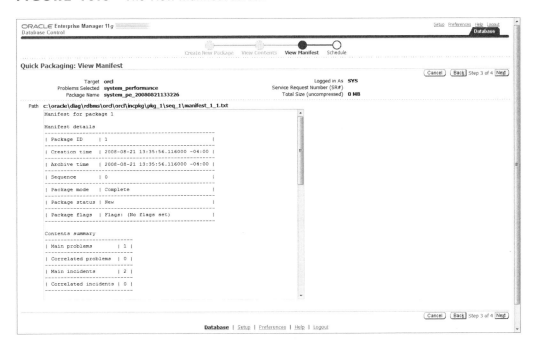

FIGURE 10.10   The Customize Package screen

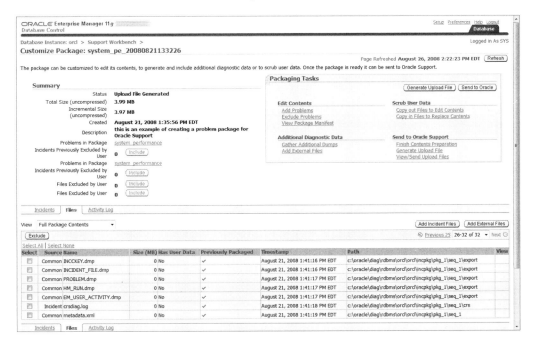

Task 6: Track the Service Request and Implement Any Repairs

From the Problem Details page, click the Activity Log link to view the list of activities performed in response to this problem, as shown in Figure 10.11. On the Problem Details page, you can add the Oracle SR number as well as the Oracle bug number related to the problem by clicking on the Edit button next to the item.

FIGURE 10.11 Viewing the activity log

Task 7: Close the Incident

From the Problem Details page in the Incidents section, select the incident close, then click the Close button. You will be asked to confirm.

Performing Block Media Recovery

Block media recovery (BMR) is used to repair corrupt blocks within a datafile. It allows you to recover corrupt blocks while keeping the datafile online, as opposed to datafile media recovery, which requires taking the file offline during the restore and recovery operation. You can perform BMR only on blocks that are identified as corrupt. Block media recovery requires Enterprise Edition.

Advantages of Block Media Recovery

The advantages of block media recovery are straightforward:

- The mean time to recovery (MTTR) is reduced.
- Datafiles remain online while corrupt blocks are repaired.

These advantages are related to recovery performance and returning the customer to normal operating mode.

Detecting Block-level Corruption

Data-block corruption can occur because of memory corruption that is written to disk or because of I/O errors. Corruption is detected by dbv, SQL that accesses corrupt blocks, RMAN, ANALYZE operations, and any other operation that attempts to read data from a corrupt block, including DBMS_REPAIR.CHECK_OBJECT. Once a corrupt block is detected, the database will not allow access to that block until it is repaired.

The aid the DBA in diagnosis of datafile corruption, Oracle provides the dbv "DB Verify" OS utility program. The dbv program takes, for example, a database file name as a command-line parameter, and performs an analysis of the structure and contents of the file and determines if there is any block corruption. At the command line, execute dbv to see the following help screen:

```
C:\>dbv

DBVERIFY: Release 11.1.0.6.0 - Production on Sun Nov 23
18:30:28 2008

Copyright (c) 1982, 2007, Oracle.  All rights reserved.

Keyword      Description                      (Default)
-----------------------------------------------------
FILE         File to Verify                   (NONE)
START        Start Block                      (First Block of
File)
END          End Block                        (Last Block of File)
BLOCKSIZE    Logical Block Size               (8192)
LOGFILE      Output Log                       (NONE)
FEEDBACK     Display Progress                 (0)
PARFILE      Parameter File                   (NONE)
USERID       Username/Password                (NONE)
SEGMENT_ID   Segment ID (tsn.relfile.block)   (NONE)
HIGH_SCN     Highest Block SCN To Verify      (NONE)
             (scn_wrap.scn_base OR scn)
```

Physical and logical block corruption are recorded in V$DATABASE_BLOCK_CORRUPTION. Physical block corruption is when the database does not recognize the block because the block header is damaged, the checksum is invalid, or the block contains all zeros. This is often due to disk hardware or OS failures and often is not acknowledged as corruption by the OS or underlying storage devices. Logical block corruption is when the contents of the block are logically inconsistent, sometimes the result of an Oracle internal error. Logical block corruption checking is enabled by using the RMAN BACKUP, RESTORE, RECOVER, or VALIDATE command with the CHECK LOGICAL clause. Logical block corruption is not repairable by BMR.

Performing Block Media Recovery

Oracle 11g can restore prior uncorrupted versions of the corrupt block from the flashback logs, improving recovery performance over restore from tape or disk backups. In previous versions of the database, block media recovery required restoring the uncorrupted blocks from a backup and then applying any necessary archive logs. A gap in archive logs meant the end of the recovery process. In Oracle 11g, if BMR encounters a gap in archive logs, it will continue forward to search for newer versions of the corrupted blocks. If a newer version is available, the restore and recovery can continue. If there are no uncorrupted newer versions of the block, the operation will fail.

To perform BMR, the database must be open or mounted and in ARCHIVELOG mode, and must have a current, usable control file. The database must not be a standby database. You must use level 0 or full backups for the restore. All of the required archived redo logs must be available for the recovery process.

If you have enabled Flashback Database and logging, then RMAN will search the flashback logs for uncorrupted versions of the required blocks.

The steps to recover blocks using BMR are fairly simply. From SQL*Plus, determine which blocks need recovery by viewing the alert log or querying the V$DATABASE_BLOCK_ CORRUPTION view:

```
SQL> SELECT NAME, VALUE FROM V$DIAG_INFO;
```

```
SQL> SELECT FILE#, BLOCK#, BLOCKS, CORRUPTION_TYPE "TYPE"
FROM V$DATABASE_BLOCK_CORRUPTION;


    FILE#      BLOCK#     BLOCKS CORRUPTION_CHANGE# TYPE
---------- ---------- ---------- ------------------ ---------
    1201       1968          2                      PHYSICAL
```

Now that you have the blocks required for recovery, connect to the target database with RMAN and begin the recovery:

```
RMAN> RECOVER DATAFILE 1201 BLOCK 1968;
```

RMAN also allows you to recover all corrupt blocks in a database using BMR. Query the V$DATABASE_BLOCK_CORRUPTION view to measure the extent of the damage, then launch RMAN to perform the recovery:

```
RMAN> RECOVER CORRUPTION LIST;
```

When a block is repaired, it is removed from the V$DATABASE_BLOCK_CORRUPTION view.

Block media recovery will fail if there is physical corruption in the redo logs that results in a checksum failure.

Managing Database Performance

In the following sections, you will learn how to use the SQL Tuning Advisor, the SQL Access Advisor, and Database Replay. Each of these tools can be used by the DBA to analyze and improve database performance. The Advisors operate directly on the database you wish to tune, while the Database Replay feature allows you to test a production workload on a test system to determine ways to improve performance without directly impacting the production system.

Using the SQL Tuning Advisor

The SQL Tuning Advisor is a tool that you can use to analyze the performance of one or more SQL statements. To improve SQL performance, the Advisor may suggest new or modified indexes, SQL profiles, restructuring your SQL statements, or gathering statistics. The SQL Tuning Advisor runs in one of two modes, Automatic or Manual. The Automatic Tuning Advisor is scheduled to run during the maintenance window, finds ways to improve high-load SQL statements, and automatically takes action. Use the SQL Tuning Advisor in Manual mode to analyze collections of SQL statements or individual SQL statements. In Manual mode, the SQL Tuning Advisor is used to analyze a collection of SQL statements called a SQL Tuning Set.

From the database home page in EM, in the Related Links section, choose the Advisor Central link, then SQL Advisors, and you'll see the page in Figure 10.12.

Automatic SQL Tuning Advisor

From the SQL Advisors page, click the Automatic SQL Tuning Results Summary link. The page that appears, shown in Figure 10.13, will display the results from the most recent Automatic SQL Tuning Advisor job.

From the results page, you can click the Configure button to configure the Automatic SQL Tuning tasks that will run during each daily maintenance window, as shown in Figure 10.14.

FIGURE 10.12   SQL Advisors home page

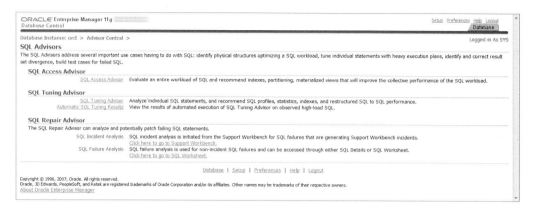

FIGURE 10.13   Automatic SQL Tuning results

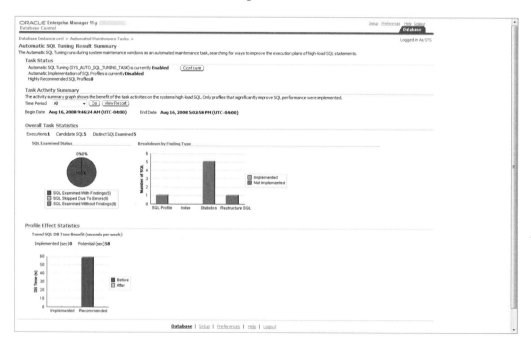

You can view the Automatic SQL Tuning result details, shown in Figure 10.15, by clicking the View Report button in the Task Activity Summary section of the Automatic SQL Tuning Result Summary page.

And you can view the recommendations made by the Tuning Advisor, as shown in Figure 10.16.

FIGURE 10.14   Automatic Maintenance Task Configuration page

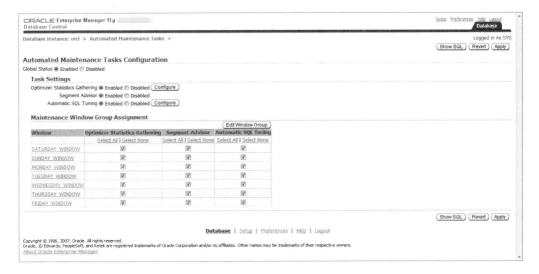

FIGURE 10.15   Automatic SQL Tuning Result Details page

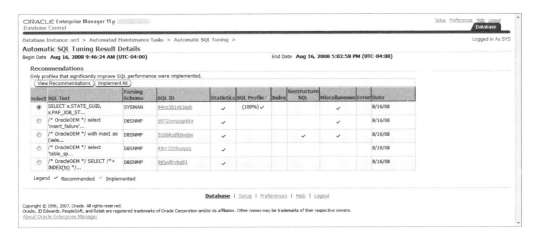

FIGURE 10.16   Automatic SQL Tuning recommendations

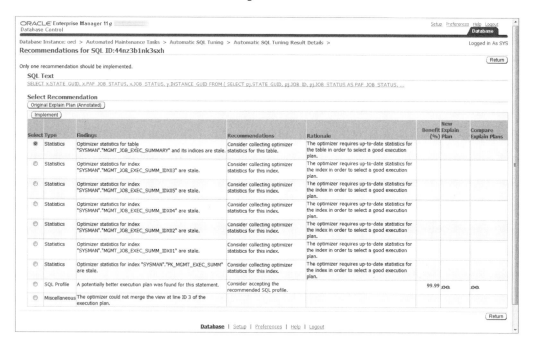

Manual SQL Tuning Advisor

From the SQL Advisors page, select the SQL Tuning Advisor to configure manual tuning. On the SQL Tuning Advisor page you will input the parameters for collecting SQL statement information, including scheduling information for task-data collection.

If there are no defined SQL tuning sets, then you have the opportunity to create a new one. On the SQL Tuning Sets page, click the Create button; this will begin a five-step process to create a new SQL tuning set, as shown in Figure 10.17.

FIGURE 10.17   Creating a new SQL tuning set

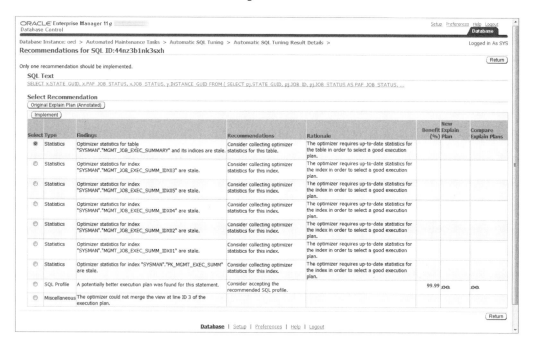

Step 1 is to type a name for your tuning set, the schema owner, and a description, as shown in Figure 10.18.

Step 2 is to choose the load methods; in the case, as shown in Figure 10.19, a duration of 24 hours with samples taken at 5-minute intervals.

FIGURE 10.18   SQL tuning set options

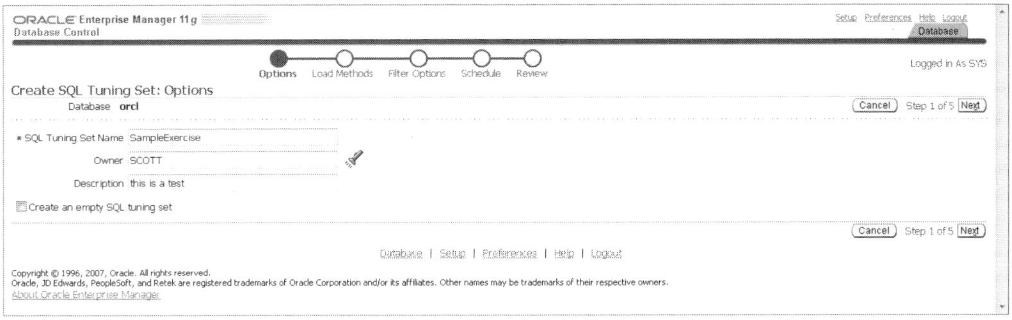

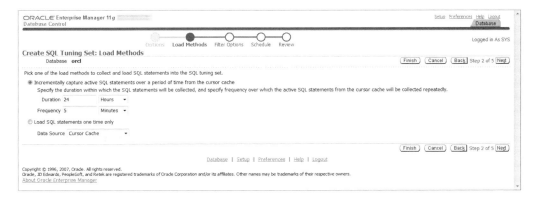

FIGURE 10.19   SQL tuning set load methods

In step 3 you set criteria for SQL statements to include in the tuning set, as shown in Figure 10.20. The drop-down menu allows you to select from a predefined list to add additional filter attributes.

In step 4 (Figure 10.21), you create and schedule a job to collect the SQL statement information and load it into a SQL tuning set. We want to start collecting immediately for this example. Click Next for the final review.

In step 5 we review, confirm, and submit to begin collection to the tuning set, shown in Figure 10.22.

FIGURE 10.20 SQL tuning set filter options

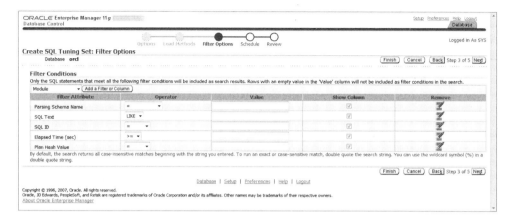

FIGURE 10.21 SQL tuning set schedule

FIGURE 10.22 SQL tuning set review

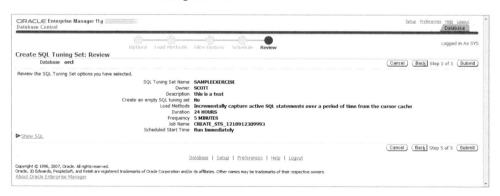

The confirmation page, shown in Figure 10.23, indicates that the SQL tuning set and collection job have been successfully created.

Return to the SQL Advisor page and select the name of this SQL tuning set; you should receive quick confirmation that SQL collection is in progress—the SQL statements count will increase. After you have collected SQL statements in a set, you can run the SQL Tuning Advisor using the tuning set. In Figure 10.24, we identify which SQL tuning set to process, the scope of analysis, and when to schedule the Advisor process. For this example, we will use a comprehensive scope of analysis and schedule it to run immediately.

FIGURE 10.23   SQL tuning set confirmation

FIGURE 10.24   SQL tuning advisor schedule

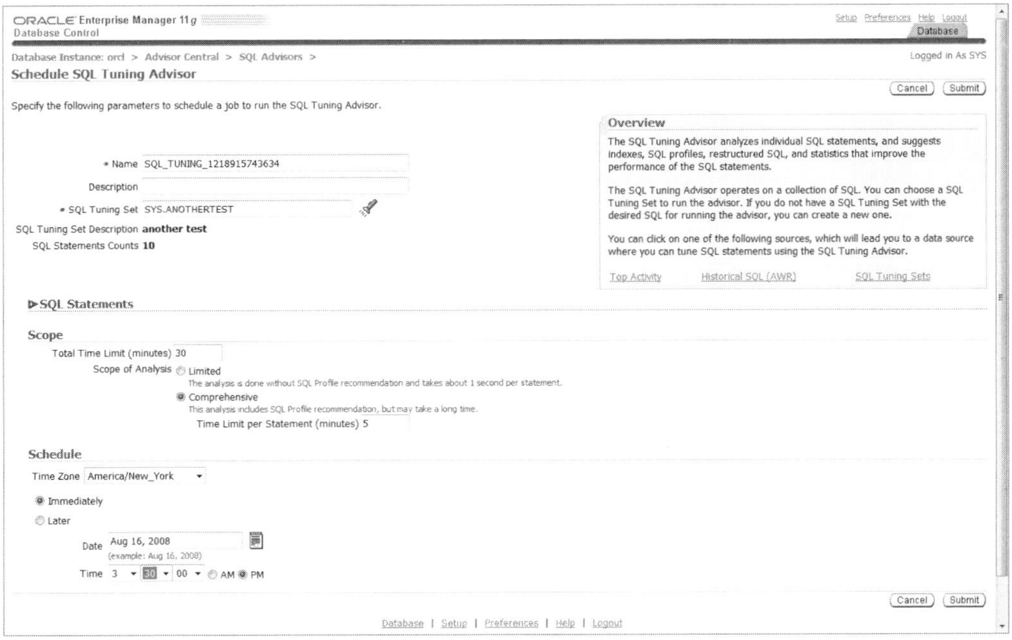

When you submit the analysis, you will be directed to the SQL Tuning Advisor task status page, shown in Figure 10.25. The page will refresh automatically.

When the task completes, the status will change to completed and the SQL information will be displayed on the SQL Tuning Results page. See Figure 10.26 for the Tuning Advisor results for this example.

FIGURE 10.25   SQL Tuning Advisor task processing

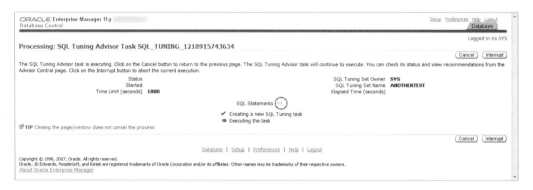

FIGURE 10.26   SQL Tuning Advisor results

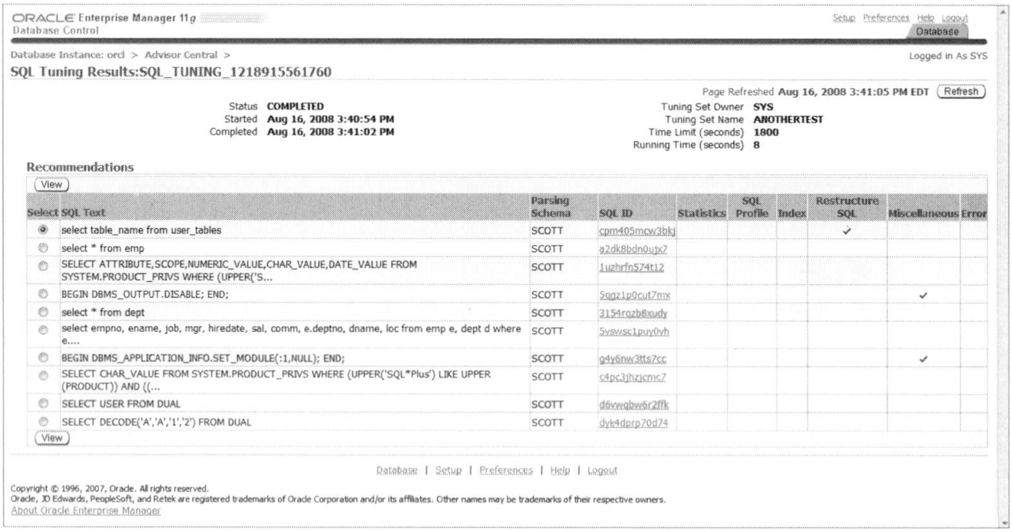

Select a SQL statement to view, and as shown on the details page in Figure 10.27, the Advisor will recommend a course of action. We selected the first query listed in Figure 10.26, and in Figure 10.27 the Advisor cautions that we have a Cartesian product.

If we then click the findings, we can see the detailed execution plan, as shown in Figure 10.28, and determine an action plan.

FIGURE 10.27   SQL Tuning Advisor recommendations for a SQL statement

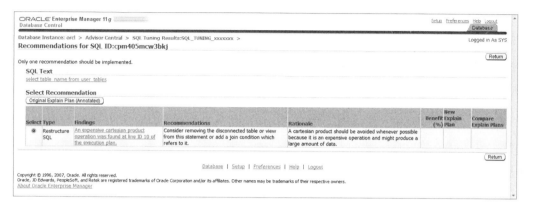

FIGURE 10.28   SQL Tuning Advisor recommendations: SQL statement original explain plan

Operation	Line ID	Object	Object Type	Order	Rows	Bytes	Cost	Time	CPU Cost	I/O Cost
▼ SELECT STATEMENT	0			20		401.060	510	7	151,334,400	503
▼ HASH JOIN RIGHT OUTER	1			19		401.060	510	7	151,334,400	503
INDEX FULL SCAN	2	SYS.I_USER2	INDEX (UNIQUE)	1		0.352	1	1	7,321	1
▼ HASH JOIN OUTER	3			18		391.337	508	7	139,989,232	502
▼ HASH JOIN OUTER	4			16		371.892	452	6	120,174,920	447
▼ HASH JOIN RIGHT OUTER	5			14		359.738	396	5	100,360,608	392
TABLE ACCESS FULL	6	SYS.SEG$	CLUSTER	2		79.138	61	1	2,945,082	61
▼ HASH JOIN	7			13		333.001	335	5	84,986,120	331
TABLE ACCESS FULL	8	SYS.TS$	CLUSTER	3		0.021	4	1	50,900	4
▼ NESTED LOOPS	9			12		325.709	330	4	73,609,816	327
▼ MERGE JOIN CARTESIAN	10			9		252.789	237	3	68,125,304	234
▼ HASH JOIN	11			6		0.066	1	1	11,790,607	0
FIXED TABLE FULL	12	SYS.X$KSPPI	TABLE (FIXED)	4		0.054	0	1	355,000	0
FIXED TABLE FULL	13	SYS.X$KSPPCV	TABLE (FIXED)	5		1.270	0	1	350,000	0
▼ BUFFER SORT	14			8		87.504	237	3	67,775,304	234
TABLE ACCESS FULL	15	SYS.OBJ$	TABLE	7		87.504	237	3	56,334,696	234
▼ TABLE ACCESS CLUSTER	16	SYS.TAB$	CLUSTER	11		0.029	1	1	10,051	1
INDEX UNIQUE SCAN	17	SYS.I_OBJ#	INDEX (CLUSTER)	10			0	1	1,900	0
INDEX FAST FULL SCAN	18	SYS.I_OBJ1	INDEX (UNIQUE)	15		340.317	55	1	1,395,802	55
INDEX FAST FULL SCAN	19	SYS.I_OBJ1	INDEX (UNIQUE)	17		544.508	55	1	1,395,802	55

SQL Tuning Advisor Supplied Package and Views

Oracle 11g includes the DBMS_SQLTUNE package to manually execute the SQL Tuning Advisor. Instead of point and click from Oracle EM, you can manually configure the steps from SQL*Plus or another SQL front end.

Oracle also provides SQL tuning informational views, if you prefer to use them instead of EM:

- DBA_ADVISOR_TASKS

- DBA_ADVISOR_EXECUTIONS

- DBA_ADVISOR_FINDINGS

- DBA_ADVISOR_RECOMMENDATIONS

- DBA_ADVISOR_RATIONALE

- DBA_SQLTUNE_STATISTICS

- DBA_SQLTUNE_BINDS

- DBA_SQLTUNE_PLANS

- DBA_SQLSET

- DBA_SQLSET_BINDS

- DBA_SQLSET_STATEMENTS

- DBA_SQLSET_PREFERENCES

- DBA_SQLSET_PLANS

- USER_SQLSET_PLANS

- DBA_SQL_PROFILES

Using the SQL Access Advisor to Tune a Workload

The SQL Access Advisor is a tuning tool that assists the DBA by offering recommendations for indexes, partitioning, and materialized view logs for a workload.

Indexing recommendations may include B-tree, bitmap, and function-based indexes. The SQL Access Advisor may recommend partitioning tables, new partitioned indexes, and new partitioned materialized views. It also provides recommendations on how to improve the performance of materialized views by using Fast Refresh and Query Rewrite.

You can manually execute the SQL Access Advisor functions and procedures included in the DBMS_ADVISOR package. For this exercise, we will use Enterprise Manager. From the database home page in EM, in the Related Links section, chose the Advisor Central link, then SQL Advisors. From the SQL Advisors home page, shown in Figure 10.29, choose the SQL Access Advisor.

From the Initial Options page, shown in Figure 10.30, choose the Recommend New Access Structures option.

First, select the workload source. We'll use a tuning set that we've already created, shown in Figure 10.31.

Next, choose the depth and breadth of recommendation options, shown in Figure 10.32. For this exercise, we just want to view index recommendations. The Advanced Options link allows you to select space restrictions, tuning prioritization, workload scope and volatility, default storage schema and tablespace names for indexes and materialized views, and tablespace names for materialized view logs and partitions.

FIGURE 10.29 SQL Advisors home page

FIGURE 10.30 SQL Access Advisor initial options

FIGURE 10.31 Choose Workload Source for SQL Access Advisor

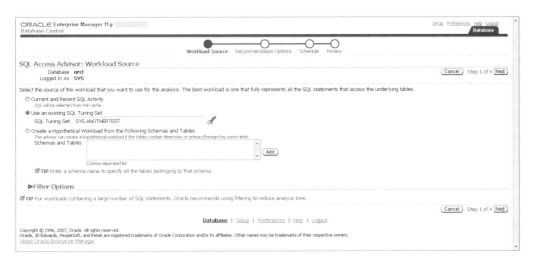

FIGURE 10.32 Recommendation options for SQL Access Advisor task

Step 3 is to schedule the SQL Access Advisor task, shown in Figure 10.33.

FIGURE 10.33 Scheduling the SQL Access Advisor task

In step 4, we review, verify, and submit, as shown in Figure 10.34.

Once the task is submitted, you receive confirmation that the task was submitted successfully. You can monitor the task through completion from the Advisor Central home page, shown in Figure 10.35.

Once the task is complete, in the Advisor Tasks section, click the Results Name link to view the detailed recommendations for the task. The results of our task are shown in Figure 10.36.

FIGURE 10.34   Review and submit the SQL Access Advisor task

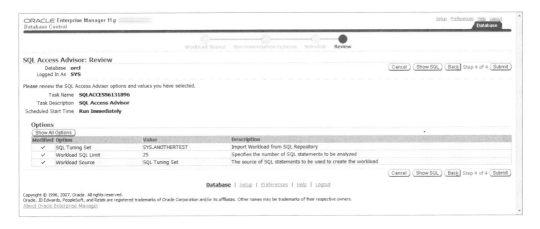

FIGURE 10.35   Monitor the SQL Access Advisor task

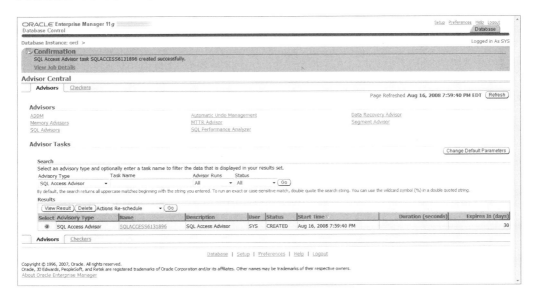

FIGURE 10.36   Results for SQL Access Advisor task

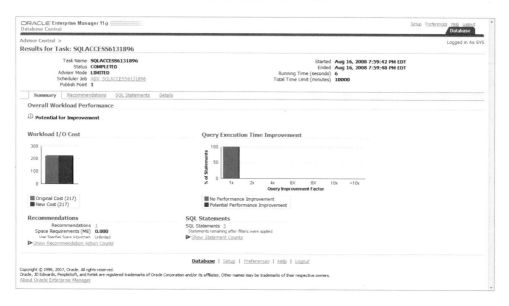

For this simplified example, there were no recommendations, as shown in Figure 10.37, because the sample tables are too small. With larger tables and more SQL statements to work with, we would see legitimate recommendations.

FIGURE 10.37   Recommendations for the SQL Access Advisor task

To implement the recommendations, select the recommended items and then click the Schedule Implementation button. Figure 10.38 shows the Schedule Implementation page.

Click the Submit button to implement the recommendations. The confirmation note will appear on the Results page, shown in Figure 10.39.

FIGURE 10.38   Implement recommendations for the SQL Access Advisor task

FIGURE 10.39   Results confirmed for the SQL Access Advisor task

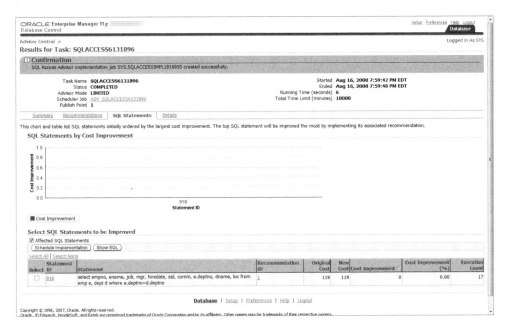

When implementing recommendations in SQL Access Advisor, be aware that certain operations will take time to complete. Partitioning an existing large table may take a long time, so keep that in mind before implementing it. The partitioning process creates a copy of the existing unpartitioned table, so make sure you have sufficient disk space for the operation.

In Exercise 10.2, you will run the SQL Access Advisor on your database instance and determine which tuning steps should be applied.

EXERCISE 10.2

Using the SQL Access Advisor

In this exercise, you will utilize the SQL Access Advisor to tune a workload. Since the workload is highly dependent on your database configuration, you will need to provide a workload, execute the advisor, and take the recommended actions.

1. Select a workload that you've already created, or create a new workload.

2. For the depth and breadth of recommendation options, you want to review only indexing recommendations.

3. Review the recommendations. If they make sense to you for your database, then implement them.

Understanding Database Replay

One of the most difficult tasks for the professional DBA is setting up and conducting valid workload performance tests. It's easy to test the performance of a single query but often very challenging to test how an entire workload will perform in a different environment. For many organizations, the cost to test a platform migration is prohibitive, and the perceived risk of not testing is too high. Organizations need to know how infrastructure changes will affect database application performance and if there's any impact to service-level agreements.

Database Replay allows the DBA to capture a workload on one database and replay it on another. Database Replay is platform-independent, so it is very useful when planning a hardware or operating-system change to understand how workload performance might also change. If you have multiple platforms or components available to test, you can conduct a valid and repeatable performance comparison. The DBA and team can utilize Database Replay to identify performance bottlenecks in the workload; determine if storage, CPU, memory, or OS changes can remove the bottlenecks; then run additional comparisons after the changes are made.

These are the basic steps of Database Replay:

- Capture the database workload.
- Preprocess the workload.
- Replay the workload.
- Analyze the workload.

Let's look at each of these individually.

Capture a Workload

We start by capturing all the external client requests performed against a database and writing the information to a platform-independent binary capture file. The workload capture contains the following client request info:

- SQL text
- Bind variable values
- Information about transactions

Workload capture can be initiated from Oracle Enterprise Manager or through the DBMS_WORKLOAD_CAPTURE package. For this text, we will focus on EM.

There a few basic steps that should be followed before capturing a workload:

- Make sure you have a replay database that is similar in data content to the capture system. You can accomplish this by using Oracle or third-party tools to keep the data synchronized close to the capture start time. Consider RMAN, a standby database, or export/import.

- Oracle recommends a clean shutdown and restart of the capture database before beginning workload capture. Start the database instance in RESTRICTED mode, start the capture, and the instance will automatically switch to UNRESTRICTED. If a database instance restart is not feasible, then quiesce the database or verify that there are no transactions running at the time the workload capture begins.

- Define either inclusion or exclusion workload filters to include or exclude specific user sessions. The default is to capture all user sessions; you can use include or exclude filters, but not both.

- Set up a capture directory, and make sure it's empty and has plenty of space. The workload capture will stop if it runs out of space.

Using Enterprise Manager, click the Software and Support tab. From the page shown in Figure 10.40, choose the Database Replay link under the Real Application Testing heading.

Note that EM provides an overview and lists the typical steps to perform a database replay, as shown in Figure 10.41.

Once all of the prerequisites are verified, you can start the workload capture by clicking on the Go to Task icon in the rightmost column of task 1, shown in Figure 10.41. In step 1, you acknowledge that the prerequisites have been met (see Figure 10.42).

Restrictions and Limitations of Workload Capture

- Only one workload capture can run at a time.

- Distributed transactions will be replayed as local transactions

The following are not captured:

- Background activities and database scheduler jobs

- Direct path load of data from external files using utilities such as SQL*Loader

- Shared server requests (Oracle MTS)

- Oracle streams

- Advanced replication streams

- Non-PL/SQL-based Advanced Queuing (AQ)

- Flashback queries

- Object navigations based on Oracle Call Interface (OCI)

- Non-SQL-based object access

- Remote DESCRIBE and COMMIT operations

In an Oracle Real Application Cluster (RAC) database, workload capture is for the database, not for a single instance. Following Oracle's recommendation to capture a clean workload, you will need to shut down and restart all instances in this manner:

1. Shut down all instances associated with the database.
2. Start one of the instances.
3. Begin the workload capture.
4. Start the remaining instances.

In step 2, you choose to restart the database and select workload filters, as shown in Figure 10.43.

In step 3, shown in Figure 10.44, you specify the name of the capture file, the directory object, and the database-instance shutdown and startup options. If the directory doesn't exist, you can create it using an OS program, and then click the Create Directory button to assign the directory to a directory object. Figure 10.44 shows confirmation that the directory object was created successfully.

FIGURE 10.40   Software and support home page

FIGURE 10.41   Database replay home page

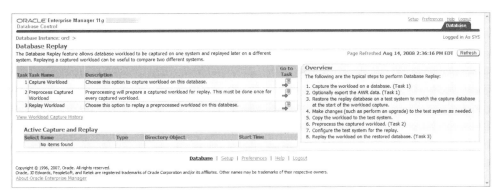

FIGURE 10.42   The Capture Workload: Plan Environment screen

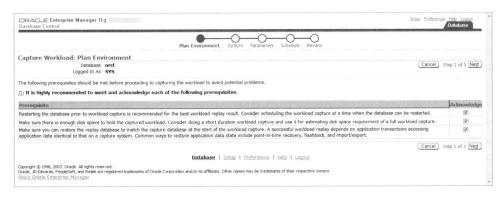

FIGURE 10.43 The Capture Workload: Options screen

FIGURE 10.44 The Capture Workload: Parameters screen

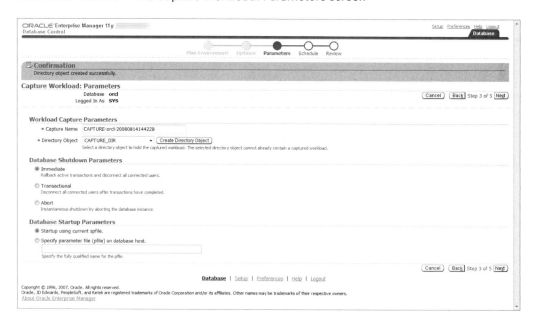

Specify the job schedule, parameters, and credentials in step 4, shown in Figure 10.45.

Step 5 is the final review and acknowledgement, shown in Figure 10.46. Click the Submit button to begin the workload capture. You will be asked to confirm that you wish to restart the database and begin the capture. If you wish to continue, click the Yes button.

FIGURE 10.45   The Capture Workload: Schedule screen

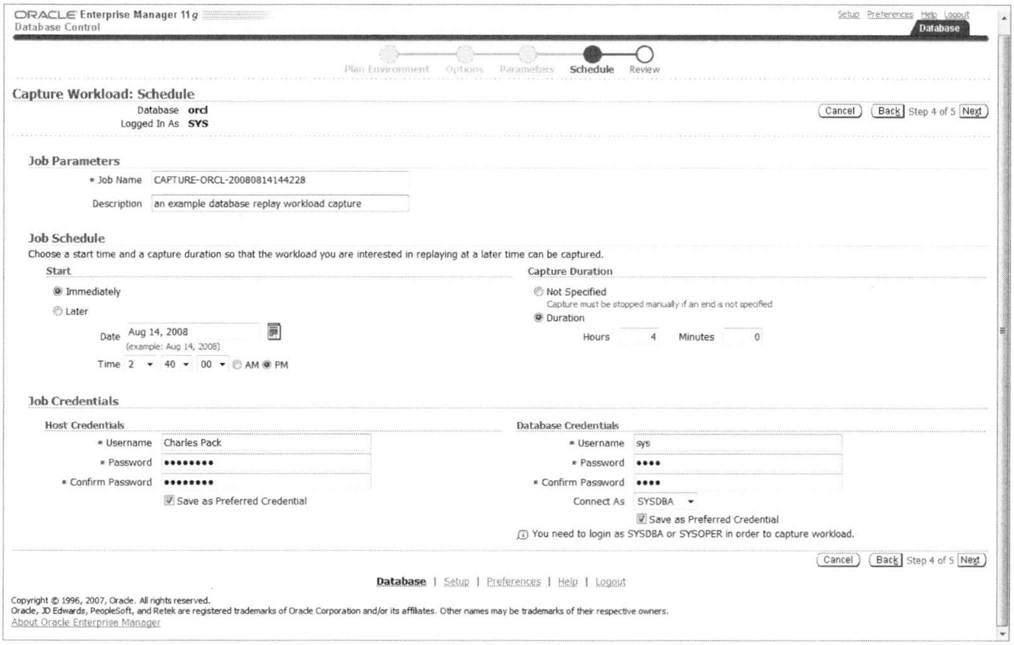

FIGURE 10.46   The Capture Workload: Review screen

After you select yes, you will be directed to an information page (see Figure 10.47) while the database is restarted.

Click Refresh to log on to the database after it has restarted. When you log on, you will be directed to the View Workload Capture screen, shown in Figure 10.48, where you may observe the capture in progress. Click the summary icon to change the view. Click the Report button to see the detailed workload capture report. Click Stop Capture to end the workload capture. You will be asked to acknowledge before the capture is stopped. Once you stop the capture, you will be presented with the option to export the workload to the AWR workload directory. If you choose not to save the AWR data at this time, you may do so later. Click the OK button to return to the Database Replay page.

FIGURE 10.47   The Confirmation screen

FIGURE 10.48   The View Workload Capture screen

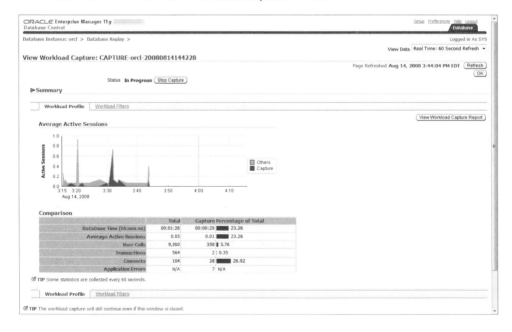

For this example, we used the general-purpose database supplied with Oracle 11*g*. We ran queries from three SQL*Plus sessions and from an MS-Access session.

Preprocess a Captured Workload

The next task is to preprocess the captured workload. Launch the task by clicking the Go to Task icon at the end of the row on task 2 (see Figure 10.49).

To preprocess a workload, select a workload directory and the relevant data will be populated to the EM screen, as shown in Figure 10.50. Once you have acknowledged the correct workload, click Preprocess Workload

FIGURE 10.49   Database Replay preprocess

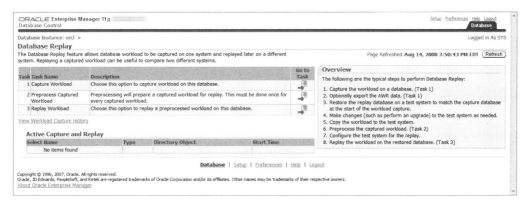

FIGURE 10.50   The Preprocess Captured Workload screen

The next screen is shown in Figure 10.51; in step 1, you confirm the capture database version, username, and instance name.

In step 2, you schedule the preprocess job, as shown in Figure 10.52. For this exercise, we will start immediately upon completion of these steps. You will need to provide host OS credentials for the host machine where the database replay capture directory object resides.

In step 3, you review the preprocess job and submit it, as shown in Figure 10.53.

When the job is submitted, you will be returned to the Database Replay screen and receive confirmation that the preprocess job has been submitted, as seen in Figure 10.54. Click the refresh button to verify that the job has completed successfully.

FIGURE 10.51 The Preprocess Captured Workload: Database Version screen

FIGURE 10.52 The Preprocess Captured Workload: Schedule screen

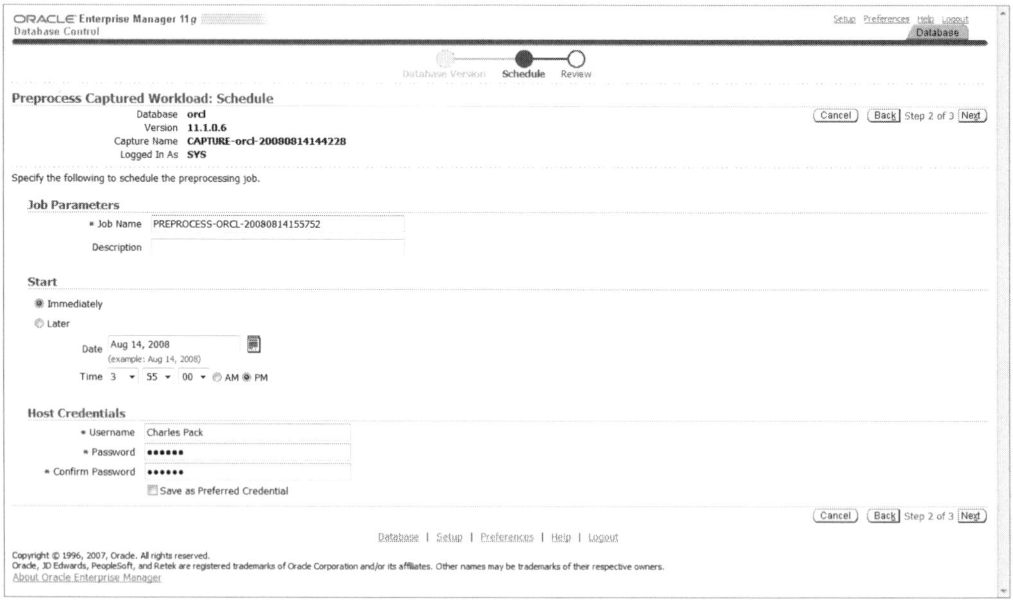

FIGURE 10.53   The Preprocess Captured Workload: Review screen

FIGURE 10.54   The job Confirmation screen

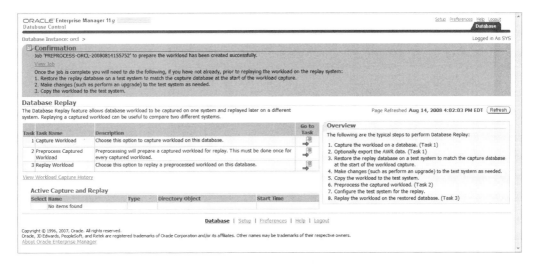

From the Database Replay home page, click the View Workload Capture History link to see the status of captured workloads, shown in Figure 10.55.

FIGURE 10.55   The View Workload Capture History screen

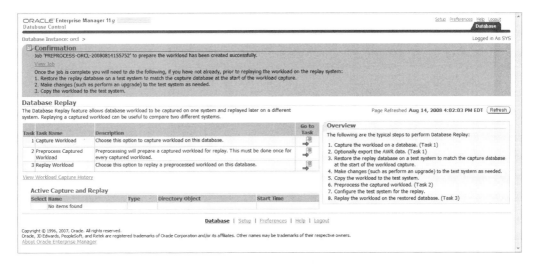

Replay a Captured Workload

To replay a workload, you need a test database that has data that's similar to the data in the capture database. We created a general-purpose database named STDB using the Database Configuration Assistant, and it is basically the same as the ORCL database we used to capture the workload.

You can perform Workload Replay using the DBMS_WORKLOAD_REPLAY supplied package, but for this example, we will use EM. From the test database EM home page, choose the Software and Support tab, and under Real Application Testing, click the Database Replay. The next page presented is the Database Replay page; in this example, we chose task 3, replay workload. Note that in Figure 10.56, there are no active captures or replays at this time.

As we did during workload capture, we need to specify a directory object, as shown in Figure 10.57, and provide OS credentials to create the directory. Once it's created, click the Test File System button to verify and then click OK.

The confirmation page in Figure 10.58 gives you the chance to verify the playback information before continuing. Click the Setup Replay button to continue.

FIGURE 10.56 Database Replay home page

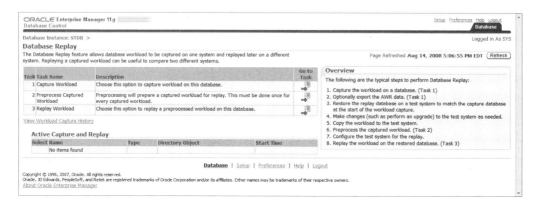

FIGURE 10.57 The Create Directory Object screen

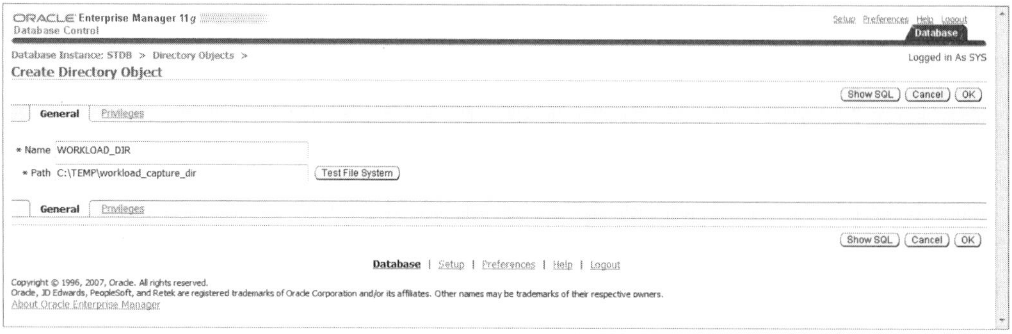

FIGURE 10.58   The Database Replay Confirmation page

The next page, shown in Figure 10.59, reminds you to verify each of the prerequisites before continuing. If you have verified that each of the prerequisites has been met and you're ready to continue, click the Continue button.

The page shown in Figure 10.60 reminds you that Database Replay should be performed on an isolated test system and to make sure there are no external references on the target test database. Verify that there are no DB links, directory objects, or streams. When you're ready to proceed, click the Continue button.

FIGURE 10.59   Database Replay prerequisites

FIGURE 10.60 Database Replay external references

Step 1 of the replay options, Choose Initial Options, allows you to add a custom name for the replay. See Figure 10.61.

In step 2, Customize Options, you can modify the connection mappings on the first page, shown in Figure 10.62, and choose the replay parameters on the second page, shown in Figure 10.63. On the Connection Mappings page, you can designate a connect descriptor and test it; use a single TNS net service name for each client, or use separate connect descriptors for each client.

In step 3, shown in Figure 10.64, you are reminded to prepare the replay clients. You will run the replay clients from the OS, not within Enterprise Manager, so now is a good time to make sure you're ready to run the clients. Click Next to continue.

FIGURE 10.61 The Choose Initial Options screen

FIGURE 10.62 Database Replay connection mappings

FIGURE 10.63 Database Replay replay parameters

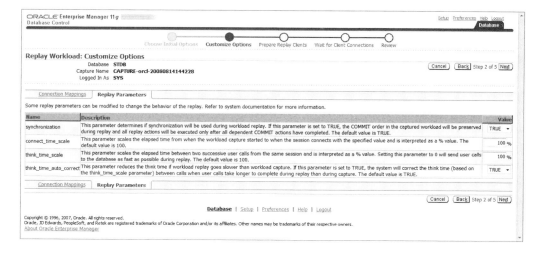

FIGURE 10.64 The Prepare Replay Clients screen

In step 4, shown in Figure 10.65, you start the replay clients externally, wait on them to connect, and confirm when they do. To start a replay client, you'll need to execute the $ORACLE_HOME\bin\wrc program with the appropriate parameters. For this basic exercise, we'll pass the username and password parameters as well as the replay directory:

```
c:\oracle\bin\WRC system/stdb@stdbreplaydir=c:\temp\workload_capture_dir
Workload Replay Client: Release 11.1.0.6.0 - Production
on Thu Aug 14 19:10:56 2008
Copyright (c) 1982, 2007, Oracle. All rights reserved.
Wait for the replay to start (19:10:56)
```

FIGURE 10.65 Database Replay client connections

Once the clients have connected, click Next to continue.

On the Review page, shown in Figure 10.66, you are instructed to reset the system time on the test database server to match the start time of the workload capture. You then begin the replay by clicking the Submit button.

FIGURE 10.66   Database Replay review

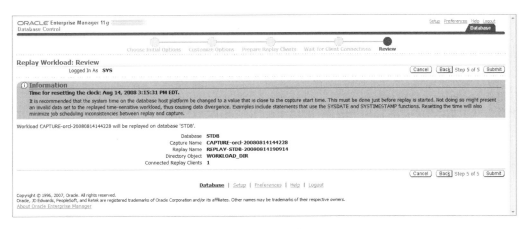

Once the replay has begun, you can monitor the progress, as shown in Figure 10.67. At the OS prompt where you ran the wc command, you'll notice an acknowledgement that the replay has started, and the replay start time matches the system time:

```
Replay started (15:16:51)
```

FIGURE 10.67   The View Workload Replay screen

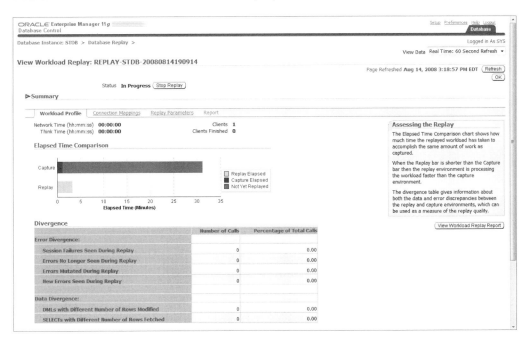

When the replay is complete, the command window will indicate replay completion time. You can then view the report and analyze the results:

```
Replay finished (15:51:19)
```

Analyze the Workload Replay Results

The basic steps to analyze the results are to view the capture report, view the replay report, and compare the results. To view the capture report from the database replay page in EM, click the View Workload Capture History link, select the capture report you wish to analyze, and then click the View button. On the subsequent capture summary page, click the View Workload Capture Report button.

We will not go into a detailed analysis of the report, but there are a few key sections of the report to review:

- Workload Captured
- Workload Not Captured
- SQL Text
- Workload Filters

To view the replay report, connect to the replay database using EM. From the database replay page, click the replay workload Go to Task icon. From the drop-down box, choose the directory object for the replay. When the Replay Workload page is populated with capture summary and replay history information, select the appropriate replay name and then click the Replay History View button. Once the workload replay summary is presented, click the View Workload Replay Report button, shown in Figure 10.68.

FIGURE 10.68   The View Workload Replay summary

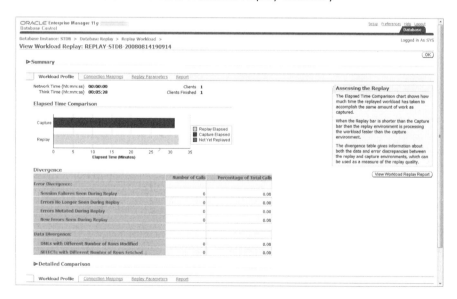

Key items to look for in the replay report are top SQL statements, performance divergence, data divergence, and error divergence. Performance divergence is usually due to infrastructure or configuration differences between the capture and replay environments. In this example, the replay took longer than the capture, so we need to further investigate to determine the bottlenecks in the test system. Data divergence occurs when the DML and SQL statement results in the replay system and capture system do not match. Error divergence is when the errors that occur do not match.

In Exercise 10.3, you will capture a Database Replay workload on a source database and replay it on a destination database.

EXERCISE 10.3

Performing Database Replay

In this exercise you will use the Database Replay feature to compare workload performance between a source database and a destination database.

1. Create a replay database as a copy of the capture database. One method is to use RMAN to make a clone. You could also use the DBCA to create a new capture database and a replay database.

2. Capture a workload on the source database.

3. Preprocess the workload capture.

4. Replay the workload on the destination database.

5. Analyze the results.

Summary

In this chapter, you learned about tools that help the DBA diagnose problems in the database and tools that assist with detecting and resolving performance issues.

In the first part, we introduced the Automatic Diagnostic Repository (ADR), the new central repository for storing all database diagnostic information, and the Support Workbench, which the DBA uses for problem recognition, reporting, and resolution. The Support Workbench improves DBA productivity by providing a process and web pages to report, analyze, and send diagnostic information to Oracle Support for problem resolution. Block media recovery improvements in 11g include faster automatic recognition of corrupt blocks and faster block recovery using the flashback logs.

In the second part, we introduced the SQL Tuning Advisor, the SQL Access Advisor, and Database Replay. To help improve the performance of SQL statements, the SQL Tuning Advisor recommends new or modified indexes, SQL profiles, rewriting your SQL statements, or using statistics. The SQL Access Advisor looks at workgroups and recommends indexes, partitioning, and materialized views to improve the performance of a workload. Database Replay is an extremely useful tool that allows the DBA to capture and replay a workload to compare the performance of one system to another.

Exam Essentials

Know how to set up the Automatic Diagnostic Repository.   Make sure you understand the new initialization parameter for ADR, which parameters are deprecated, and the basic directory structure of the ADR.

Know how to use the Support Workbench to report an incident.   Know the steps required to open a service request with Oracle Support. Know how to package and submit the files related to a problem incident.

Know how to perform block media recovery.   Know how to discover corrupt data blocks, what causes data corruption, and how to repair corrupt data blocks. Know what can contribute to faster recoveries. Know what is required to perform block media recovery.

Understand automatic and manual SQL tuning.   Understand the differences between automatic and manual SQL tuning using the Tuning Advisor. Understand the advantages and potential dangers of automatic SQL tuning. Understand how to use the SQL Tuning Advisor in manual mode.

Understand the SQL Access Advisor.   Know what types of changes and types of indexes the SQL Access Advisor may recommend. Understand the impact of implementing recommendations.

Know when to use Database Replay.   Know the purpose and uses for Database Replay. Know what is required to set up and perform Database Replay. Know how to compare results from the production workload and the replay workload.

Review Questions

1. Which of the following initialization parameters have been deprecated in Oracle 11g because of the introduction of the Automatic Workload Repository? (Choose all that apply.)

   A. BACKGROUND_DUMP_DEST

   B. FOREGROUND_DUMP_DEST

   C. CORE_DUMP_DEST

   D. USER_DUMP_DEST

   E. DIAGNOSTIC_DEST

   F. All of the above

2. Which of the following statements is true regarding the initialization parameter DIAGNOSTIC_DEST?

   A. The default value is the value of the environment variable $ORACLE_HOME; if $ORACLE_HOME isn't set, then the default is set to $ORACLE_BASE.

   B. The default value is the value of the environment variable $ORACLE_BASE; if $ORACLE_BASE isn't set, then it is set to $ORACLE_HOME.

   C. DIAGNOSTIC_DEST is always equal to $ORACLE_HOME.

   D. DIAGNOSTIC_DEST is always equal to $ORACLE_BASE.

3. Which of these formats represents the correct hierarchy for the ADR?

   A. <diagnostic_dest>/rdbms/diag/<dbname>/<instname>

   B. <diagnostic_dest>/diag/rdbms/<instname>/<dbname>

   C. <diagnostic_dest>/diag/rdbms/<dbname>/<instname>

   D. None of the above

4. Which of the following are not fundamental tasks of the Support Workbench? (Choose all that apply.)

   A. View long-running SQL workloads

   B. View problem details

   C. Gather additional diagnostic information

   D. Create a Service Request

   E. Clean up incident data after upload to Oracle Support

5. Which of the following tasks does the tool Incident Packaging Service (IPS) perform?

   A. Cleans up the ADR by deleting files not associated with an incident uploaded to Oracle Support.

   B. Identifies all files associated with a critical error and adds them to a zip file to be sent to Oracle Support.

   C. Automatically opens a Service Request with Oracle Support for each critical error and sends all relevant files.

   D. Displays a high-level view of critical errors on the database home page.

6. Choose the correct order to package and upload data for an incident to Oracle Support.

   A. Schedule, create new package, view manifest, view contents

   B. Create new package, view manifest, view contents, schedule

   C. Schedule, create new package, view contents, view manifest

   D. Create new package, view contents, view manifest, schedule

   E. None of the above.

7. Which of the following is *not* an advantage of block media recovery (BMR)?

   A. Reduced MTTR.

   B. Datafiles remain offline while corrupt blocks are repaired.

   C. Datafiles remain online while corrupt blocks are repaired.

   D. A and C

8. Which of the following methods can be used to detect block corruption?

   A. ANALYZE operations

   B. dbv

   C. SQL queries that access the potentially corrupt block

   D. RMAN

   E. All of the above

9. Which of the following are correct about block media recovery? (Choose all that apply.)

   A. Physical and logical block corruption is recorded automatically in V$DATABASE_BLOCK_CORRUPTION.

   B. Logical corruptions are repairable by BMR.

   C. Physical corruptions are repairable by BMR.

   D. RMAN can use any backup for a BMR restore.

   E. ARCHIVELOG mode is not required if you have both a full and incremental backup for restore.

10. While querying the EMPLOYEES table, you receive an ORA-01578 message indicating block corruption in File# 1201 and Block# 1968. You analyze the table and the corruption is verified. Which RMAN command do you use to perform BMR and repair the corrupt block?

   A. `RECOVER FILE=1201 BLOCK=1968;`

   B. `RECOVER CORRUPTION LIST;`

   C. `RECOVER DATAFILE 1201 BLOCK 1968;`

   D. `RECOVER BLOCK CORRUPTION LIST;`

   E. None of the above

11. To view the results of the most recent Automatic SQL Tuning Advisor task, which sequence should you follow?

   A. EM Database home page, Software and Support, SQL Advisors, Automatic SQL Tuning Advisor.

   B. EM Database home page, Software and Support, Advisor Central, SQL Advisors, Automatic SQL Tuning Advisor.

   C. EM Database home page, Software and Support, Support Workbench, Advisor Central, SQL Advisors, Automatic SQL Tuning Advisor.

   D. Either B or C.

   E. All of the above

12. When creating a SQL tuning set, which of the following steps allows the DBA to reduce the size of the SQL set by selecting specific operators and values?

   A. Filter versions

   B. Filter loads

   C. Filter tasks

   D. Filter options

13. To view the results of a manual SQL Tuning Advisor task, which steps should the DBA take?

   A. From the Advisor Central home page, select the tuning task from the Advisor Tasks section.

   B. From Advisor Central, choose SQL Advisors, SQL Tuning Advisors, Manual Tuning Task Results.

   C. From Advisor Central, choose SQL Advisors, Manual SQL Tuning Advisors, Tuning Task Results.

   D. Either B or C.

14. Which of these appropriately describes the results of a manual SQL Tuning Advisor task?

   A. A list of SQL statements and recommendations for tuning

   B. A list of SQL statements that have been tuned by the Advisor, with before and after metrics

   C. Graphs showing the actual performance improvement made by the Advisor after it implemented the recommended changes

   D. All of the above

15. Which of the following is a potential performance tuning recommendation from the SQL Access Advisor?

   A.   Create new indexes.

   B.   Modify existing indexes.

   C.   Implement partitioning on a nonpartitioned table.

   D.   Create materialized views.

   E.   All of the above

16. Which statement most accurately describes the implementation of a SQL Access Advisor recommendation?

   A.   SQL Access Advisor recommendations are automatically implemented.

   B.   Individual SQL Access Advisor recommendations can be scheduled for implementation.

   C.   All SQL Access Advisor recommendations for a specific task must be implemented at the same time.

   D.   SQL Access Advisor recommendations are automatically scheduled for implementation during the maintenance window.

   E.   None of the above.

17. Which of the following represents the correct sequence of events for Database Replay?

   A.   Capture, analyze, preprocess, replay

   B.   Capture, preprocess, analyze, replay

   C.   Capture, preprocess, replay, analyze

   D.   Analyze, capture, preprocess, replay

   E.   None of the above

18. Which of these recommendations should be followed before capturing a workload? (Choose all that apply.)

   A.   Make sure your replay database has the same structure as the capture database, except without data.

   B.   Make sure the replay and capture databases are similar in data content.

   C.   Perform a clean shutdown and restart of the capture database before beginning a workload capture.

   D.   Start the capture database in UNRESTRICTED mode, then start the capture.

   E.   Define inclusion and exclusion filters.

19. Which is true concerning Database Replay in an Oracle Real Application Cluster (RAC) database?

    A. Workload capture is per instance.

    B. You only need to restart one instance to begin workload capture.

    C. Specifically in RAC, you shut down all instances, restart them individually, and begin workload capture with the last instance started.

    D. RAC does not support workload capture, but it does support workload replay.

    E. None of the above.

20. Performance divergence indicated in the Workload Replay report is most likely due to what?

    A. DML and SQL statement results that do not match between the capture and replay systems

    B. When errors that occur in the capture system don't occur in the replay system

    C. Top SQL statements

    D. Infrastructure or system-configuration differences

    E. Time-of-day differences between capture and replay systems

Answers to Review Questions

1.   A, C, D. FOREGROUND_DUMP_DEST is not a valid initialization parameter, so option B is incorrect. DIAGNOSTIC_DEST is the new parameter that replaces the parameters in options A, C, and D, so E is incorrect.

2.   B. When $ORACLE_BASE is set, it is the default value for DIAGNOSTIC_DEST.

3.   C. Option A is incorrect because the correct order is diag/rdbms. Option B is incorrect because the correct order is <dbname>/<instname>.

4.   A, E. Options B, C, and D are each fundamental tasks of the Support Workbench problem-resolution process.

5.   B. Option A is incorrect because IPS does not delete files not associated with a package that will be sent to Oracle Support. Option C is incorrect because IPS does not open an Oracle service request for each critical error. D is incorrect because IPS does not display critical errors on the database home page.

6.   D. All other sequences are incorrect. D is the correct sequence. First create the new package, then view the package contents. Next view the manifest, then schedule the job to upload the data for the incident to Oracle Support.

7.   B. Option A is incorrect because reduced MTTR is an advantage of BMR. Option C is incorrect because the datafiles remaining online is an advantage of BMR. Since A and C are advantages, D is also incorrect. Option B is the correct choice because it is not an advantage of BMR.

8.   E. Option A is correct because if you attempt to analyze a table or index that has a corrupt block, the ANALYZE command will indicate it. Option B is correct because the dbv command (DBVERIFY utility) is used to verify the data-structure integrity of an offline datafile. DBVERIFY will let you know if the datafile fails the integrity check. Option C is correct unless you have used DBMS_REPAIR.SKIP_CORRUPT_BLOCKS to permit queries to skip corrupt blocks. D is correct because the RMAN BACKUP command will detect corruption by default.

9.   A, C. Option B is incorrect because logical corruptions are not repairable by BMR. Option D is incorrect because you must use a level 0 or full backup for the restore. Option E is incorrect because ARCHIVELOG mode is a requirement for BMR.

10. B, C. Option A is incorrect because the syntax is wrong. Option D is incorrect because BLOCK doesn't belong. B is how we recover all corrupt blocks listed in V$DATABASE_BLOCK_ CORRUPTION. C is the correct syntax to recover just the one block that we've identified as corrupt.

11. D. Option A is incorrect because there is no direct link on the Software and Support home page to the SQL Advisors. You use either sequence B or C to get to the SQL Advisors and to the Automatic SQL Tuning Advisor page; from there, you can see the results of the most recent Automatic SQL Tuning Advisor task.

12. D. Options A, B, and C are not valid choices when creating a SQL tuning set. During the filter options step, the DBA can choose the SQL attributes, the operator, and the values to use as filter conditions.

13. A. Option B is incorrect because there is no Manual Tuning Task Results option. C is incorrect because there is no Manual SQL Tuning Advisors option.

14. A. Option B is incorrect because the manual SQL Tuning Advisor task does not tune the SQL statements. C is incorrect for the same reason.

15. E. All of the options are correct. The SQL Access Advisor recommends indexing, partitioning, and materialized view changes to improve performance.

16. B. Option A is incorrect because SQL Access Advisor recommendations are not automatically implemented. Option C is incorrect because the DBA can choose which recommendations to schedule and implement from the task result set. D is incorrect because the recommendations are not automatically scheduled for implementation.

17. C. The correct sequence is capture, preprocess, replay, analyze.

18. B, C. Option A is incorrect because the data divergence between the capture and replay databases should be minimized. Option D is incorrect because the database should be started in RESTRICTED mode, and then the workload capture process will switch the database to UNRESTRICTED. Option E is incorrect because you can define either inclusion or exclusion filters for a workload capture, but not both.

19. E. Option A is incorrect because workload capture is for the database, not for individual instances. B is incorrect because the correct procedure is to shut down all instances before you begin workload capture. Option C is incorrect; after the shutdown of all instances, start one instance to begin workload capture, and then start the remaining instances after capture begins. Workload capture and replay are supported in RAC, so D is incorrect.

20. D. Option A is incorrect; DML and SQL results drive data divergence. Option B is incorrect because error divergence, not performance divergence, happens when errors that occur in the capture system don't occur in the replay system. Top SQL statements should behave the same in the capture and replay systems, unless there is a data-divergence issue, so C is incorrect. E is incorrect because the time of day should have no impact on differences between the capture and replay systems. It is possible that other workloads running on the capture and replay systems that have a time-of-day trend might impact performance, but that is an extraneous variable, not a cause.

Chapter

11

Managing Database Resources

ORACLE DATABASE 11*g*: ADMINISTRATION II EXAM OBJECTIVES COVERED IN THIS CHAPTER:

✓ **Managing Memory**

- Implementing Automatic Memory Management

- Manually configure SGA parameters

- Configuring automatic PGA memory management

✓ **Space Management**

- Managing resumable space allocation

- Describe the concepts of transportable tablespaces and databases

- Reclaim wasted space from tables and indexes by using the segment shrink functionality

✓ **Managing Resources**

- Understand the Database Resource Manager

- Create and use Database Resource Manager Components

In this chapter, we will discuss how to most effectively manage memory, space, and resources. For memory management, we will discuss the Oracle 11g feature Automatic Memory Management, which enables the DBA to set one memory parameter for management of the instance memory. For space management, we will discuss resumable space allocation, transportable tablespaces and databases, and shrinking segments. For resource management, we will discuss the Database Resource Manager functionality and components.

Memory management is critical to database instance performance and has often been a source of frustration for Oracle DBAs. With Oracle 11g, much of the manual memory management has been replaced with automatic memory options—either to automatically manage all of the instance memory or to automatically manage the SGA and PGA as two separate pools.

We'll cover two features (resumable space allocation and shrinking segments) for managing the efficient utilization of space resources and two features (transportable tablespaces and transportable databases) for managing large-scale data movement. The resumable space allocation feature allows you to efficiently utilize space resources and prevent transaction aborts when space limitations are encountered. Shrinking segments allow you to eliminate white space in a segment in place while the segment remains online and available for application use. For large-scale movement of tablespaces from one database to another, the DBA can use the transportable tablespaces feature. To move an entire database, even to another platform, you can use the transportable database feature.

The Database Resource Manager is a robust and mature feature that allows the DBA to manage scarce session, I/O, and CPU resources within an Oracle instance. The Database Resource Manager allows you to create groups, policies, and plans to control the utilization of system resources.

Throughout this chapter, we will show command-line and Oracle Enterprise Manager methods for managing memory, space, and resources.

Exam objectives are subject to change at any time without prior notice and at Oracle's sole discretion. Please visit Oracle's Training and Certification website (http://www.oracle.com/education/certification/) for the most current exam-objectives listing.

Managing Memory

In the following sections, we will first cover Automatic Memory Management, new to Oracle 11g, which allows the DBA to set one initialization parameter and then leave the memory management up to the Oracle instance. Our next topic for memory management is manually configuring System Global Area (SGA) parameters. DBAs who need more granular control over the SGA pools will find this discussion useful. We will then discuss configuring automatic Program Global Area (PGA) memory management.

Implementing Automatic Memory Management

In Oracle 11g, the DBA has the opportunity to set one initialization parameter and allow Oracle to manage the size of the SGA and instance PGA automatically. When you set the value of MEMORY_TARGET, Oracle will automatically resize the SGA and PGA components dynamically based on processing demands for optimal database performance. The instance will automatically deallocate and allocate memory between the SGA and instance PGA as needed. Automatic Memory Management, when enabled, automatically adjusts the cache and pool sizes as needed to keep the database performing optimally.

Automatic Memory Management is supported on Linux, Solaris, Windows, HP-UX, and AIX.

When you create a new database in Oracle 11g, the default is to use Automatic Memory Management. You can adjust individual SGA component minimum values to ensure that minimum performance thresholds are not compromised. However, the instance monitors the performance of each memory component and adjusts as necessary as workloads change to provide optimal performance.

Automatic Memory Management Options

To enable Automatic Memory Management for the instance, set the value of MEMORY_TARGET in the spfile. Also, MEMORY_MAX_TARGET sets the upper bound for MEMORY_TARGET. You can adjust MEMORY_TARGET dynamically up to the value of MEMORY_MAX_TARGET; however, MEMORY_MAX_TARGET is not a dynamic initialization parameter and will require an instance restart for a modification to take effect.

```
NAME                                TYPE        VALUE
----------------------------------- ----------- ------
...
memory_max_target                   big integer 1000M
memory_target                       big integer 816M
...
SQL>
```

If you don't set MEMORY_MAX_TARGET, it will default to the value of MEMORY_TARGET. By setting these values, you have set the maximum memory size that will be used by Oracle to manage all instance PGA and SGA objects.

If you would like more granular control over the SGA or instance PGA, Oracle will allow you to manage them manually with the Automatic Shared Memory Management, Manual Shared Memory Management, Automatic PGA Memory Management, or Manual PGA Memory Management option.

> Oracle strongly recommends that you enable Automatic Memory Management and let the Oracle instance manage the memory components on your system. If you choose not to use Automatic Memory Management, use the Memory Advisor in Enterprise Manager to assist you with your instance memory configuration.

Automatic Shared Memory Management

To exercise control over the SGA, you'll need to disable Automatic Memory Management and enable Automatic Shared Memory Management for the SGA by setting MEMORY_TARGET to zero and setting the values for SGA_MAX_SIZE and SGA_TARGET. You will also need to verify that the value of STATISTICS_LEVEL is set to TYPICAL or ALL. These parameters are dynamic, with the exception of SGA_MAX_SIZE, which requires an instance restart to take effect.

```
NAME                                TYPE        VALUE
----------------------------------- ----------- -----
lock_sga                            boolean     FALSE
...
sga_max_size                        big integer 600M
sga_target                          big integer 0
SQL>
```

Now that you have set the values for SGA_TARGET and SGA_MAX_SIZE, Oracle will manage the individual components of the SGA for optimal performance up to the SGA_TARGET value. You can dynamically increase the size of the SGA up to the value of SGA_MAX_SIZE, and Oracle will resize the pools as needed to take advantage of the additional memory.

When setting the value for SGA_TARGET, you'll need to consider the combined sizes of the different SGA memory pools:

- Default pool of database buffer cache DB_CACHE_SIZE
- Shared pool SHARED_POOL_SIZE
- Large pool LARGE_POOL_SIZE
- Java pool JAVA_POOL_SIZE
- Streams pool STREAMS_POOL_SIZE

You can set the value for each of the associated initialization parameters to a nonzero value, and that value will indicate the minimum size for each pool. If you dynamically set SGA_TARGET to zero, you will disable Automatic Shared Memory Management and the current sizes of the pools will not change dynamically. You can manually change the sizes of the pools as needed by using the ALTER SYSTEM command.

The following pools are not impacted by Automatic Shared Memory Management; they are manually sized:

- KEEP, RECYCLE, and non-default block-size buffer cache pools
- Fixed SGA and other internal memory structures
- Log buffer

The values of these manually configured pools are subtracted from the value of SGA_TARGET.

> When you disable Automatic Memory Management and enable Automatic Shared Memory Management, you also enable Automatic PGA Memory Management. We'll discuss Automatic PGA Memory Management later in this chapter.

Automatic Memory Management and Enterprise Manager

To use Enterprise Manager to configure and manage the Automatic Memory Management features, access the Memory Advisors page from the Advisor Central home page. You'll see the following information, also displayed in Figure 11.1:

- Whether Automatic Memory Management is enabled and the ability to toggle between enabled and disabled
- The current total and maximum memory size and advice
- Memory allocation history
- Tabs for SGA and PGA memory configuration details

FIGURE 11.1 Memory Advisors page

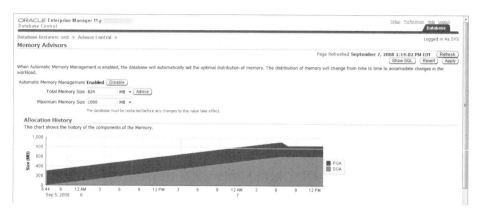

In Figure 11.2, we show the default lower half of the page displayed in Figure 11.1. This half of the page displays the detailed SGA configuration, which includes the SGA allocation history chart, the current SGA component MB allocated, and a pie chart showing the current SGA pool percentages:

- Shared pool
- Buffer cache
- Large pool
- Java pool
- Other

FIGURE 11.2 Memory Advisor SGA detail

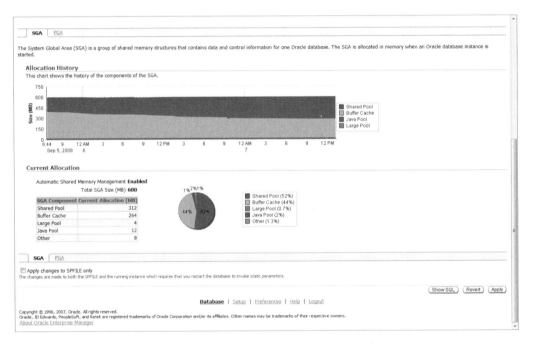

In Figure 11.3, we show the PGA details, which are viewed by clicking the PGA tab of the Memory Advisors page. Shown are the aggregate PGA target, current PGA allocated, maximum PGA allocated, and the cache hit percentage.

You can click the PGA Memory Usage Details button to see the current work area size executions, as shown in Figure 11.4. The chart shows the following:

- Optimal executions
- One-pass executions
- Multipass executions

On this page you have the options to change the chart view to see execution percentages and number of executions and also show memory-usage details for the PGA target that you choose from the drop-down list.

FIGURE 11.3 Memory Advisor PGA detail

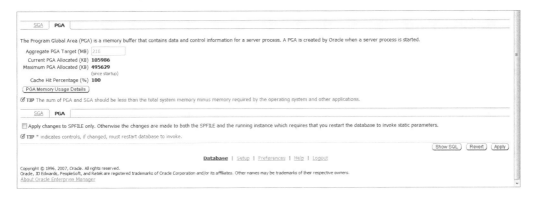

FIGURE 11.4 PGA work area size detail

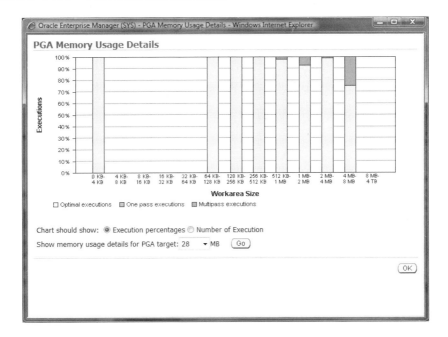

Disabling Automatic Memory Management Using Enterprise Manager

From the Memory Advisors page, you can disable Automatic Memory Management by clicking the Disable button. The change takes effect immediately. You can revert to

Automatic Memory Management by clicking the Enable button. We'll discuss enabling in a later section titled "Enabling Automatic Memory Management Using Enterprise Manager."

When you disable Automatic Memory Management, the Memory Advisors page changes to reflect that Automatic Memory Management is disabled, as shown in Figure 11.5. Now you have an SGA tab that gives you the ability to enable or disable Automatic Shared Memory Management as well as request advice (see Figure 11.6) and modify the total and maximum SGA sizes.

FIGURE 11.5   Automatic Memory Management SGA configuration

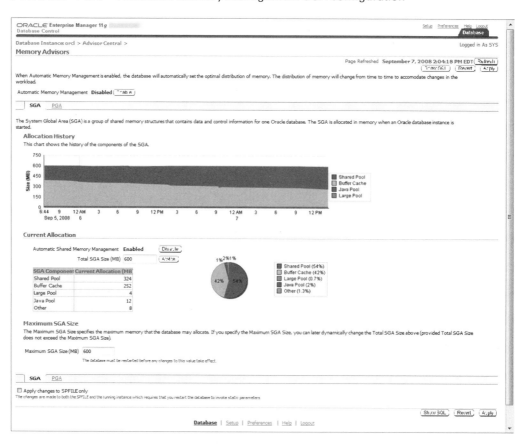

If you click the PGA tab, you'll see (Figure 11.7) that you can now request advice, as shown in Figure 11.8, and modify the aggregate PGA target based on the recommendations.

FIGURE 11.6   Automatic Memory Management SGA size advice

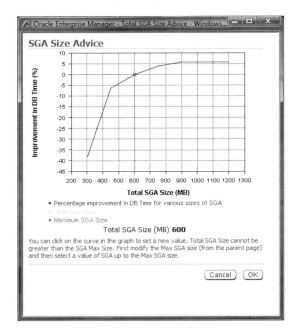

FIGURE 11.7   Automatic Memory Management PGA configuration

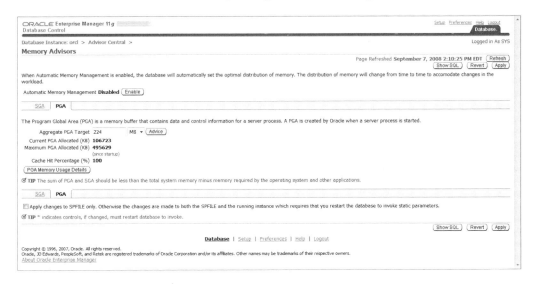

FIGURE 11.8   Automatic Memory Management PGA size advice

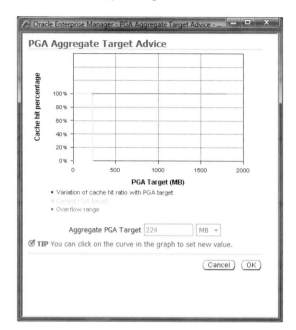

Disabling Automatic Shared Memory Management Using Enterprise Manager

If you now want to disable Automatic Shared Memory Management and manually set the values for the various SGA pools, you can do so by clicking the Disable button in the Current Allocation section on the SGA tab. This action opens the Disable Automatic Shared Memory Management page, shown in Figure 11.9, where you can manually set the values for each component. You may revert to Automatic Shared Memory Management by canceling from this page, or click OK to continue and begin manually managing the SGA.

FIGURE 11.9   Manually configuring the SGA

> If you disable Automatic Shared Memory Management, you will manually configure and manage each of the SGA pools. We'll discuss manual SGA memory management later in this chapter, in the section titled "Manually Configuring SGA Parameters."

Enabling Automatic Shared Memory Management Using Enterprise Manager

Stepping back from full manual configuration of the SGA to Automatic Shared Memory Management is straightforward; simply click the Enable button presented next to the Automatic Shared Memory Management Disabled header in the SGA section of the Memory Advisors page, as shown in Figure 11.10.

FIGURE 11.10   Enabling Automatic Shared Memory Management

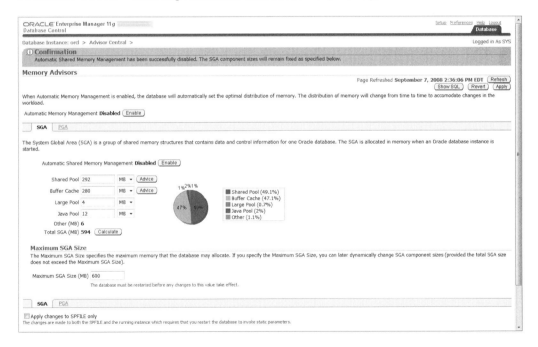

Enabling Automatic Memory Management Using Enterprise Manager

You can also go directly from manual SGA management to Automatic Memory Management by clicking the Enable button next to the Automatic Memory Management Disabled line directly under the Memory Advisors header on the Memory Advisors page (shown earlier, in Figure 11.10).

If you are currently running the instance in Automatic Shared Memory Management mode and want to enable Automatic Memory Management, click the Enable button, shown in Figure 11.11.

You'll have the opportunity to modify the maximum memory size and the total size of automatic shared memory, as shown in Figure 11.12.

Figure 11.13 shows confirmation that the instance is now running in Automatic Memory Management mode.

FIGURE 11.11   Enabling Shared Memory Management

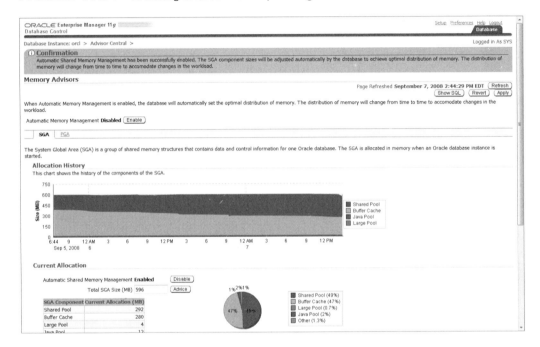

FIGURE 11.12   Configuring Automatic Memory Management

FIGURE 11.13   Automatic Memory Management enabled

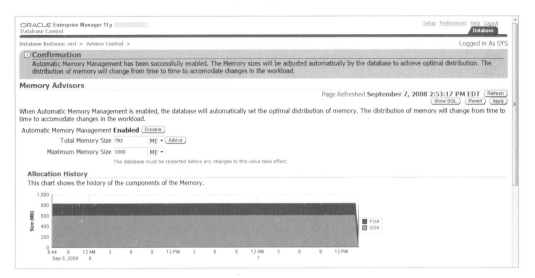

Manually Configuring SGA Parameters

If you don't want to let the Oracle instance manage the SGA memory allocations for you and you want greater control over the individual pools, Oracle provides the option for you to bypass both Automatic Memory Management and Automatic Shared Memory Management. By setting MEMORY_TARGET and SGA_TARGET initialization parameters to zero, you in effect force the manual configuration of each of the SGA memory pools and enable manual shared memory management.

While Oracle strongly recommends that you allow the instance to manage memory automatically, Oracle also understands that the DBA in some cases needs to manually configure specific pools based on specific knowledge of the application workload.

So when manually setting the SGA components, you'll need to plan and verify that each pool is given sufficient memory to meet performance requirements. As shown previously, in Figure 11.9, you can specify values for the following SGA components:

- Default pool of database buffer cache DB_CACHE_SIZE

- Shared pool SHARED_POOL_SIZE

- Large pool LARGE_POOL_SIZE

- Java pool JAVA_POOL_SIZE

Additionally, you'll need to set the value of SGA_MAX_SIZE to a value that represents the maximum amount of memory you would use for the SGA.

If you choose to manually configure the SGA components using Enterprise Manager after you have been running with Automatic Shared Memory Management, the SGA components are sized based on the current Memory Advisors advice. Additionally, you may seek advice after you have manually set the values, as shown earlier, in Figure 11.10. Figure 11.14 shows the advice for the shared pool, launched by clicking the Advice button next to the Shared Pool line on the Memory Advisors page.

Figure 11.15 shows the same exercise for the default database buffer pool, also known as the *buffer cache.*

FIGURE 11.14   Shared pool size advice

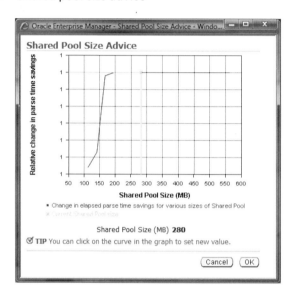

FIGURE 11.15   Buffer cache size advice

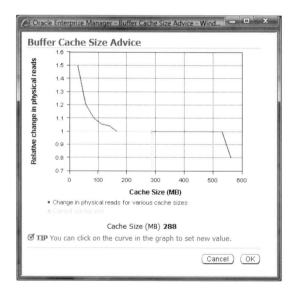

NOTE If you attempt to manually size the SGA pools to a total SGA size greater than or equal to the value for Maximum SGA Size (SGA_MAX _SIZE), you will receive the messages "ORA-02097: Parameter cannot be modified because specified value is invalid" and "ORA-04033: Insufficient memory to grow pool." If you attempt to grow the buffer cache too large, you will receive the ORA-02097 error and the message "ORA-00384: Insufficient memory to grow cache." In either case, you will not be able to make the total size of the SGA greater than or equal to the Maximum SGA Size value. See Figure 11.16.

FIGURE 11.16 Attempting to manually resize beyond the maximum SGA size

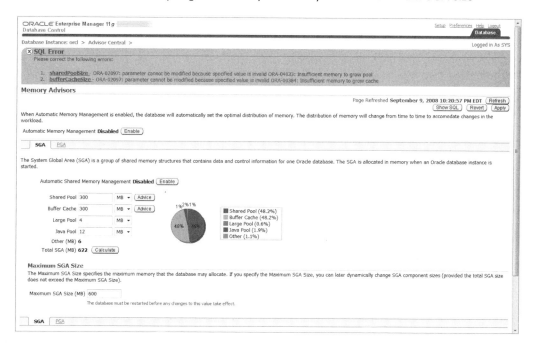

Also note in Figure 11.16 that you can change the Maximum SGA Size value, SGA_MAX_SIZE, but this will require a database-instance restart to take effect. Also on this screen you have the option to apply changes to the spfile only. If you do so, you will receive an update message indicating that changes were made to the spfile, as shown in Figure 11.17.

FIGURE 11.17   Save SGA size changes to the spfile

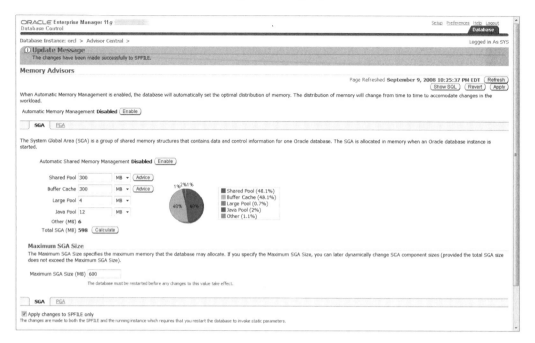

Configuring Automatic PGA Memory Management

Remember that when you configure the database instance for Automatic Memory Management, PGA memory is automatically allocated and deallocated from MEMORY_TARGET as needed. If you determine that you need greater control over the PGA, then you can go to Automatic Shared Memory Management or manual shared memory management, thereby being forced to choose between automatic or manual PGA memory management. In Automatic PGA Memory Management, you set the value of PGA_AGGREGATE_TARGET and the Oracle instance manages memory allocation to work areas as needed. If you choose manual PGA memory management, you will need to configure each of the work areas manually, which requires you to keep up with workload changes and modify the work areas accordingly.

If you choose to not utilize Automatic Memory Management for the instance, Oracle strongly recommends that you enable Automatic PGA Memory Management and let the Oracle instance manage the PGA components on your system. If you choose not to use Automatic PGA Memory Management, use the Memory Advisor in Enterprise Manager to assist you with your instance PGA memory configuration.

Automatic PGA Memory Management

In the following sections, we'll discuss how to enable Automatic PGA Memory Management in Enterprise Manager, how to monitor Automatic PGA Memory Management, and how you can tune Automatic PGA Memory Management. We will also discuss how you can disable Automatic PGA Memory Management and tune the individual work areas manually.

Enabling Automatic PGA Memory Management Using Enterprise Manager

If you're currently running your instance in Automatic or manual Shared Memory Management mode, then you are by default running Automatic PGA Memory Management. You can verify that the instance is in Automatic PGA Memory Management mode, and not manual mode, by viewing the PGA tab in the Memory Advisors page, as shown in Figure 11.18. On this page you can change the value of the PGA aggregate target based on the recommendations received when you click the Advice button.

FIGURE 11.18   Automatic PGA Memory Management

The minimum value for PGA_AGGREGATE_TARGET is 10MB, and the maximum value is 256GB.

If your database instance was running in Automatic Memory Management mode and you converted to Automatic Shared Memory Management mode, then the PGA_AGGREGATE_TARGET was set at the value determined by the instance when it was running in Automatic Memory Management mode.

For an online transaction processing (OLTP) system, a good starting point for the PGA size, the value of the PGA_AGGREGATE_TARGET, should be approximately 20 percent of the memory available on the system; conversely, the value of the SGA should be about 80 percent of the available memory. For a decision support system, data warehouse, or analytical database, a good starting point is 50 percent of available memory for PGA and 50 percent for SGA. Of course, you will need to tune the PGA_AGGREGATE_TARGET value based on advice from the Memory Advisors page or by querying dynamic views. Also note that if you run multiple instances on the same server, it is easy to overallocate the SGA and PGA so that the combined memory used by all the instances is larger than real memory on the server, which can lead to memory paging and significant performance degradation.

Monitoring Automatic PGA Memory Management

You can monitor the PGA performance using several dynamic performance views:

- V$PGASTAT
- V$PROCESS
- V$PROCESS_MEMORY
- V$SQL_WORKAREA_ACTIVE
- V$SQL_WORKAREA
- V$SQL_WORKAREA_HISTOGRAM

A key statistic to look for in the V$PGASTAT view is the overallocation count, which tells you the cumulative number of times you have overallocated the PGA since instance startup; a large number indicates that the PGA_AGGREGATE_TARGET may be too small.

The V$PROCESS view has one row for each Oracle process for this instance. You can monitor PGA usage by observing the columns that start with PGA_*.

The V$PROCESS_MEMORY view goes into greater detail for each process, showing PGA memory used for these six categories: PL/SQL, SQL, Java, OLAP, Freeable, and "other."

V$SQL_WORKAREA_ACTIVE shows currently active work areas in the instance, excluding sorts that are less than 64KB. When a SQL operation is complete, the work area is deallocated from V$SQL_WORKAREA_ACTIVE and the V$SQL_WORKAREA view is updated to include the cumulative execution statistics for each work area.

The V$SQL_WORKAREA_HISTOGRAM view shows the cumulative statistics for the number of work areas executed since instance startup for optimal, one-pass, and multipass memory sizes. The columns for low and high optimal size bytes represent the work-area size buckets that were used. Your expectation should be to run as many work areas as possible in the OPTIMAL_EXECUTIONS column.

Tuning Automatic PGA Memory Management

The PGA advice performance views are available to help you tune the value of PGA_AGGREGATE_TARGET. The dynamic views V$PGA_TARGET_ADVICE and V$PGA_TARGET_ADVICE_HISTOGRAM are supplied to help you tune Automatic PGA Memory Management.

Set the value of STATISTICS_LEVEL to TYPICAL or ALL and set the value of PGA_AGGREGATE_TARGET to between 10MB and 256GB to enable the automatic generation of PGA advice statistics and population of the advice views.

The V$PGA_TARGET_ADVICE view shows the predicted cache hit-ratio improvement as you increase the size of the PGA_AGGREGATE_TARGET. In this case, the small workload indicates you could reduce the size of the 200MB PGA_AGGREGATE_TARGET and still have a good PGA hit ratio.

```
SQL> SELECT PGA_TARGET_FOR_ESTIMATE/1024/1024 "target mb",
  2  ESTD_PGA_CACHE_HIT_PERCENTAGE "cache_hit%"
  3  FROM V$PGA_TARGET_ADVICE
  4  /


target mb cache_hit%
---------- ----------
        25         99
        50         99
       100        100
       150        100
       200        100
       240        100
       280        100
       320        100
       360        100
       400        100
       600        100
       800        100
      1200        100
      1600        100
14 rows selected.
SQL>
```

Similarly, the V$PGA_TARGET_ADVICE_HISTOGRAM view forecasts how the V$SQL_WORKAREA_HISTOGRAM will change if you modify the value of PGA_AGGREGATE_TARGET. It shows the predicted number of executions in each of the optimal, one-pass, and multipass work areas for each setting of PGA_AGGREGATE_TARGET.

Disabling Automatic PGA Memory Management Using Enterprise Manager

If you want to manually control the sizes of the individual work areas, going against the strong recommendation from Oracle, you will need to set the value of PGA_AGGREGATE_TARGET to zero and set the following parameters to a positive value:

- SORT_AREA_SIZE
- HASH_AREA_SIZE
- BITMAP_MERGE_AREA_SIZE
- CREATE_BITMAP_AREA_SIZE

Then restart the instance and enjoy tuning the work areas manually.

If you're using OEM, set the PGA Aggregate Target value to zero and choose to make the changes to the spfile, as shown in Figure 11.19.

Once you've stopped and started the instance and returned to the PGA tab of the OEM Memory Advisor, you'll notice that the page has changed from the view in Figure 11.18 to what you see in Figure 11.20.

FIGURE 11.19 Disabling Automatic PGA Memory Management

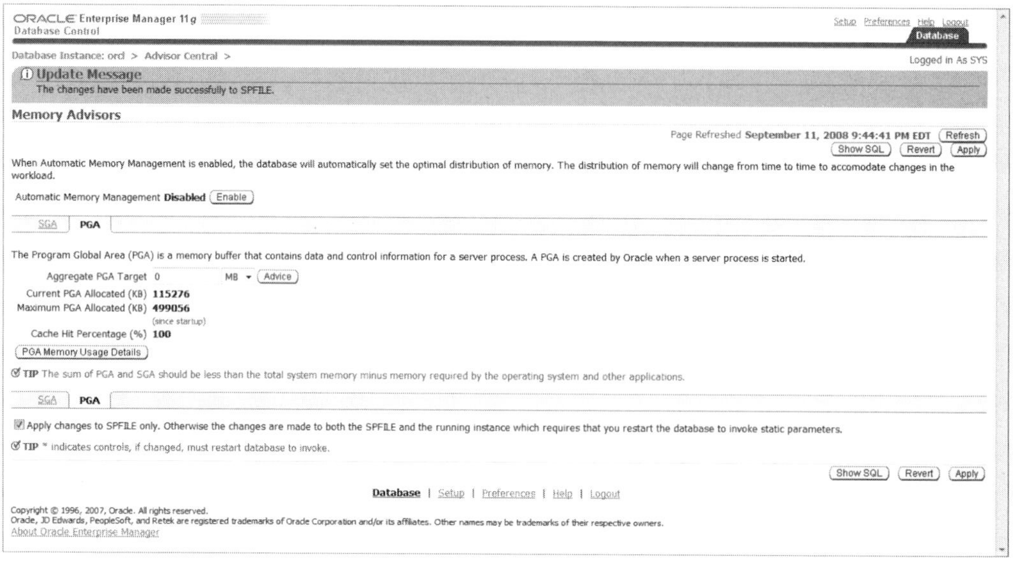

FIGURE 11.20 Manual PGA Memory Management

You'll note that the only work area that you can modify with OEM is the SORT_AREA_ SIZE, but you can also set the value for the maximum number of concurrent users; the product of the two determines the maximum total size of memory that will be used for the sort work area. Also, from the command-line interface you can show the *_AREA_SIZE parameters and modify them in the spfile as needed. Please note that HASH_AREA_SIZE and SORT_AREA_SIZE can be modified at the session level and that they are not dynamically modifiable for the instance.

```
SQL> show parameter area_size

NAME                                TYPE        VALUE
----------------------------------- ----------- -------
bitmap_merge_area_size              integer     1048576
create_bitmap_area_size             integer     8388608
hash_area_size                      integer     131072
sort_area_size                      integer     65536
```

You can very easily return to Automatic PGA Memory Management mode by clicking the Enable Automatic Mode button and then Apply.

Managing Space

In the following sections, we will explore resumable space allocation, transportable tablespaces, transportable databases, and shrinking segments. Resumable space allocation allows you to temporarily suspend operations that run out of space while you correct the space issue without aborting the operation. With the transportable tablespace feature, you can copy a set of tablespaces from a source database to a destination database. With the transportable database feature, you can copy an entire database from one platform to another. And finally, you'll learn how to shrink segments dynamically.

Managing Resumable Space Allocation

If the Oracle database encounters a space problem during the execution of an operation, it can suspend the operation and then later resume the operation. This feature is called *resumable space allocation*, and it allows the DBA to fix a problem prior to the database returning an error message to the user process. Once you've fixed the problem, the database automatically resumes the suspended operation.

Enabling resumable space allocation is simple: you can set the initialization parameter RESUMABLE_TIMEOUT to a value greater than zero, or you can issue the ALTER SESSION ENABLE RESUMABLE statement.

Understanding Resumable Space Allocation

A resumable statement suspends when an object runs out of space, it reaches the maximum number of extents, or a space quota is exceeded. An object running out of space or reaching maximum extents applies to tables, indexes, temporary segments, undo segments, large objects (LOBs), clusters, and table or index partitions. When a resumable statement is suspended, an error is reported in the alert log and the system issues the resumable session suspended alert, and if an AFTER SUSPEND trigger is in place, it will be executed. When the statement is suspended, the transaction will be suspended and all transaction resources held until rolled back or the suspend operation is resumed to completion. When the suspend condition is resolved, it will automatically resume and the associated resumable session suspended alert is cleared; of course, the original error message logged in the alert log remains.

In a distributed transaction, the remote RESUMABLE_TIMEOUT initialization parameter applies to the remote part of the transaction, and the remote session resumable setting applies. Also, local resumable settings do not apply to the remote part of the distributed transactions.

Resumable Space Operations

Specific Data Definition Language (DDL), Import/Export, Data Manipulation Language (DML), and query statements are candidates for resumable executions:

- SELECT statements that run out of sort area temporary space
- INSERT, UPDATE, DELETE, and INSERT INTO...SELECT
- Export/import and SQL*Loader
- The following DDL statements:
  CREATE TABLE AS SELECT
  CREATE INDEX
  ALTER TABLE MOVE PARTITION
  ALTER TABLE SPLIT PARTITION
  ALTER INDEX REBUILD
  ALTER INDEX REBUILD PARTITION
  ALTER INDEX SPLIT PARTITION
  CREATE MATERIALIZED VIEW
  CREATE MATERIALIZED VIEW LOG

For parallel operations, each process is handled independently. If one suspends, an error is logged and the associated AFTER SUSPEND trigger is executed. Meanwhile, the other parallel processes continue. However, if one aborts, the parallel operation aborts. As with all resumable processing, when a suspend condition is repaired, it will continue and join up with the others.

Enabling and Disabling Resumable Operations

You enable resumable operations and configure the suspend time-out for the instance and for a session. For the instance, configure the initialization parameter RESUMABLE_TIMEOUT. For the session, set the session parameter RESUMABLE_TIMEOUT to a numeric value greater than zero, or issue the ALTER SESSION command.

Enabling and Disabling Resumable Operations for an Instance

To enable resumable operations for the instance, alter the instance parameter RESUMABLE_TIMEOUT to a numeric value greater than zero. The default value is 0, which in effect initially disables resumable operations for all sessions. This represents the number of seconds that an operation may suspend while you take corrective action. After the time-out is reached, the operation will abort. In this example, we alter the system RESUMABLE_TIMEOUT from 1 minute to 10 minutes:

```
SQL> show parameter resumable


NAME                                 TYPE        VALUE
------------------------------------ ----------- -------
resumable_timeout                    integer     60
SQL> alter system set resumable_timeout=600 scope=both;

System altered.
```

Enabling and Disabling Resumable Operations for a Session

Before you can enable or disable resumable operations at the session level, the user must have been granted the RESUMABLE system privilege. Once that's granted, resumable operations are enabled within a session when the following command is issued:

```
SQL> alter session enable resumable;

Session altered.
```

The default resumable time-out for a session is 7,200 seconds. To disable resumable operations within a session, issue the following command:

```
SQL> alter session disable resumable;

Session altered.
```

Additionally, the user session can control the suspend time-out in one of three ways: by altering the RESUMABLE_TIMEOUT parameter for the session, by executing the DBMS_RESUMABLE. SET_TIMEOUT procedure (covered later, in the section "The DBMS_RESUMABLE Supplied Package") or by appending to the ALTER SESSION ENABLE RESUMABLE command as follows:

```
SQL> alter session set resumable_timeout=3600;
```

```
Session altered.

SQL> show parameter resumable;

NAME                                TYPE        VALUE
----------------------------------- ----------- -----
resumable_timeout                   integer     3600
SQL>


SQL> alter session enable resumable timeout 7200;

Session altered.
SQL> show parameter resumable;

NAME                                TYPE        VALUE
----------------------------------- ----------- -----
resumable_timeout                   integer     3600
SQL>
```

The alter session enable resumable timeout nnnn command does not alter the value of the session-initialization parameter RESUMABLE_TIMEOUT.

Procedurally, you can also enable resumable operations for a session with a logon trigger.

Identifying Resumable Sessions

By default, if a session is enabled for resumable space allocation, the session is identified in the NAME column of the DBA_ and USER_RESUMABLE views by the username, session ID, and instance number, as follows:

```
SQL> select name from user_resumable;

NAME
-----------------------------------
User SYS(0), Session 108, Instance 1

SQL>
```

You can alter the session identifier by issuing the ALTER SESSION command and adding the NAME clause, as follows:

```
SQL> alter session enable resumable name 'LEB test';
Session altered.
SQL> select name from user_resumable;
NAME
```

```
--------------------------------------------------
LEB test
SQL>
```

This changed name remains in effect until it's altered by the ENABLE RESUMABLE NAME command, until resumable is disabled by the session, or until the session ends.

Working with Resumable Operations

Once you've enabled resumable operations, you'll need to monitor and take action on suspended resumable operations. You'll monitor specific views to determine the status of resumable operations, and you'll write AFTER SUSPEND triggers and utilize the DBMS_RESUMABLE supplied package to take action within a session when a suspend occurs.

Additionally, Enterprise Manager reports resumable alerts and provides the mechanism for resolving resumable space issues.

Views for Monitoring Resumable Space Allocation

The DBA_RESUMABLE and USER_RESUMABLE views contain rows for suspended resumable statements as well as those that are executing as normal. The key information columns are described in Table 11.1. The USER_ID column is not included in the USER_RESUMABLE view, and as with all USER_ views, only the current session information is shown.

TABLE 11.1   DBA_RESUMABLE Columns

Column Name	Description
STATUS	Status of the RESUMABLE statement: RUNNING, SUSPENDED, TIMEOUT, ERROR, ABORTED.
TIMEOUT	Time-out value of the resumable statement.
START_TIME	Start time of the resumable statement.
SUSPEND_TIME	The last time the resumable statement was suspended.
RESUME_TIME	The last time the statement resumed.
SQL_TEXT	The resumable statement.
ERROR_NUMBER	The error number of the last error logged or this resumable statement. If no errors, the value will be NULL.
ERROR_PARAMETERn	Error parameter columns 1 through 5.
ERROR_MSG	The error message associated with the ERROR_NUMBER.

The DBA can also use the V$SESSION_WAIT view to catch suspended resumable operations. The EVENT column will contain a statement indicating that the operation is suspended and waiting for the error to be cleared.

Monitoring Resumable Space Alerts with Enterprise Manager

Oracle Enterprise Manager will display alerts on the database home page when there are resumable space suspends. In the example shown in Figure 11.21, we have created a suspend condition by attempting to insert into a table that is in a space-constrained tablespace.

FIGURE 11.21 Resumable space suspend alert on database home page

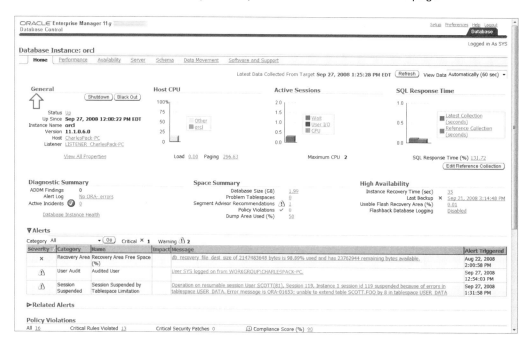

Click the Message link to see the details, shown in Figure 11.22.

Now from the database home page, under the Space Summary caption, click on the value to the right of Database Size" to display the database tablespaces, shown in Figure 11.23.

Choose the constrained tablespace, shown in Figure 11.24. From there, choose to add a new datafile to the tablespace or edit the datafile and increase the size.

For this example, we will click the link on the datafile name, and we can either increase the size of the datafile or change the datafile to AUTOEXTEND ON to resolve the suspend issue.

FIGURE 11.22   Resumable space suspended session details

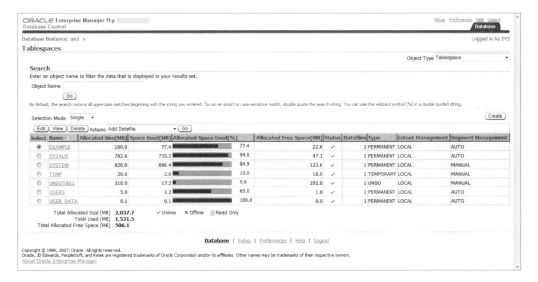

FIGURE 11.23   Database tablespaces

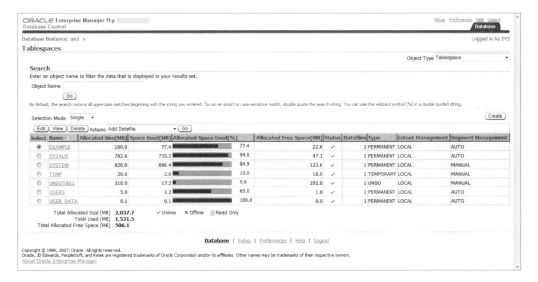

FIGURE 11.24 Tablespaces datafile details

The *DBMS_RESUMABLE* Supplied Package

The DBMS_RESUMABLE package allows you to get and set time-out parameters for a session, abort a suspended resumable session, and query the error stack for specific resumable space errors. Table 11.2 describes the package functions and subprograms.

TABLE 11.2 DBMS_RESUMABLE Package Programs

Program Name	Description
ABORT	Procedure that allows you to abort a suspended resumable operation
GET_SESSION_TIMEOUT	Function that when passed the session ID returns the current resumable time-out
GET_TIMEOUT	Function that returns resumable time-out for the current session
SET_SESSION_TIMEOUT	Procedure that when passed the session ID and time-out value sets the time-out for a session
SET_TIMEOUT	Procedure that sets the time-out for the current session
SPACE_ERROR_INFO	Function that allows you to search the error stack on error_type, object_type, object_owner, object_name, sub_object_name, and table_space_name

In the following code, you see an example that enables resumable for the session, gets the session time-out value; changes the value; queries the value; disables resumable; and then queries, modifies, and enables it. You'll note that the resumable time-out value is retained by the session even though resumable was disabled. Also note that the default time-out is 7,200 seconds.

```
SQL> alter session enable resumable;

Session altered.

SQL> select dbms_resumable.get_timeout from dual;

GET_TIMEOUT
-----------
       7200

SQL> exec dbms_resumable.set_timeout (9600);

PL/SQL procedure successfully completed.

SQL> select dbms_resumable.get_timeout from dual;

GET_TIMEOUT
-----------
       9600

SQL> alter session disable resumable;

Session altered.

SQL> select dbms_resumable.get_timeout from dual;

GET_TIMEOUT
-----------
       9600

SQL> alter session enable resumable timeout 7200;

Session altered.

SQL> select dbms_resumable.get_timeout from dual;
```

```
GET_TIMEOUT
-----------
       7200
```

SQL>

Triggered Events to Respond to Suspends

Oracle has created the AFTER SUSPEND trigger to help you resolve suspend conditions program-
matically. By registering an AFTER SUSPEND trigger on the database as user SYS using the ON
DATABASE clause, you can take action regardless of who owns the resumable operation.

Managing Transportable Tablespaces

The transportable tablespace feature allows you to copy or move a tablespace from one database to another. Using transportable tablespaces is faster than copying rows or using export/
import or unload/load. With Oracle 10g or higher, it is possible to transport tablespaces across
some but not all platforms. Transportable tablespaces are useful for, but not limited to, the
following:

- Database migrations

- Sharing tablespaces with other database users (for example, remote customers)

- Tablespace point-in-time recovery (TSPITR)

- Archiving data from one database to another

- Exporting and importing partitions

Transporting a tablespace is straightforward, but there are caveats and limitations. You
can use Enterprise Manager, or you can use SQL*Plus and the OS command line. We will
take you through the basic process and list the major considerations.

The first step is to determine what will be transported. If your intent is to transport
objects that exist only in one tablespace and have no dependencies in other tablespaces,
then the process is simplified. If, however, you intend to transport a set of objects that are
spread across multiple tablespaces or have dependencies on objects in other tablespaces,
then the task becomes slightly more complex.

Transportable Tablespace Sets

A transportable tablespace set is a self-contained group of tablespaces that encapsulate the
objects that you wish to transport from one database to another. For example, if you wish to
transport several tables that reside in different tablespaces, then you would include each of the
tablespaces in the tablespace set. If you wish to transport a partitioned table and the different
partitions are in different tablespaces, then you would need to include each of the tablespaces
in the tablespace set.

We'll discuss tablespace sets in detail and show examples a bit later.

Requirements of Transportable Tablespaces

Transportable tablespaces must meet the following requirements:

- The tablespaces can be locally managed or dictionary managed.

- In Oracle9*i* or higher, the transported tablespace does not have to be the same block size as the target database's standard block size. However, the target database must have a *DB_nK_CACHE_SIZE* initialization parameter set, where *n* is the block size of the transportable tablespace.

- The tablespace must be placed in read-only mode during the transport process.

- Starting with Oracle 11*g*, data pump is used instead of export/import to move the metadata from the source to the target.

- You can't import a transported tablespace that has the same name as an existing tablespace in the target database. You can rename the transported tablespace as part of the import process.

- In order for an object to be transportable, all of the partitions that contain its dependent objects such as indexes, materialized views, and partitioned tables must be included in the tablespace set.

- Tablespaces that do not use block encryption but have tables that have encrypted columns are not transportable.

- You can't transport the SYSTEM tablespace or objects owned by the SYS user.

- Tablespaces with 8.0-compatible advanced queues with multiple recipients are not transportable.

- If you're transporting across platforms, RAW, BFILE, and AnyTypes are not converted from one endian type to another as part of the transport process.

Manually Transporting a Tablespace

In this section, we will demonstrate how to manually transport a tablespace using a combination of SQL*Plus, the OS command line, and data pump.

The basic steps are as follows:

1. Check compatibility and endian format.
2. Choose the transportable tablespace set.
3. Generate the transportable tablespace set.
4. Transport the tablespace set.
5. Import the tablespace set.

Database Requirements for Transportable Tablespaces

To utilize the transportable tablespace feature, you must make sure the database meets the following criteria:

- To create a transportable tablespace set, the source database must be Oracle 8*i* or later, and it must be Enterprise Edition.

- To import a tablespace set from the same platform, the target database can be any edition of Oracle8*i* or higher.

- To create a transportable tablespace set for import into a database on a different platform, the source database must have compatibility set to 10.0 or higher.

- To import a transportable tablespace set from a different platform, both the source and target databases must have compatibility set to 10.0 or higher.

- The source and target database must have the same character set and national character set.

Step 1: Check Compatibility and Endian Format

If the source and target are different versions of the database, you'll need to verify the minimum compatibility for transportable tablespaces. When you create a transportable tablespace set, Oracle determines the minimum compatibility level for the target. Oracle throws an error if the target database's compatibility level is lower than the minimum compatibility. If you're transporting a tablespace to the same platform, the minimum compatibility must be 8.0 for both the source and target. Both source and target must have a minimum compatibility of 9.0 if the transportable tablespace's block size is different than the target's standard block size. For different platforms, the minimum compatibility must be 10.0 for both source and target.

If your source and target are different platforms, it will be necessary to check for endian compatibility. If the source and target are not directly compatible—for example, the source is big endian and the target is little endian—then you will need to use RMAN to convert the copy of each tablespace datafile on either the source or target platform. To determine which platforms you can transport to, run this query:

```
SQL> select * from v$transportable_platform;
PLATFORM_ID PLATFORM_NAME                      ENDIAN_FORMAT
----------- ---------------------------------- --------------
          1 Solaris[tm] OE (32-bit)            Big
          2 Solaris[tm] OE (64-bit)            Big
          7 Microsoft Windows IA (32-bit)      Little
         10 Linux IA (32-bit)                  Little
```

```
    6 AIX-Based Systems (64-bit)        Big
    3 HP-UX (64-bit)                    Big
    5 HP Tru64 UNIX                     Little
    4 HP-UX IA (64-bit)                 Big
   11 Linux IA (64-bit)                 Little
   15 HP Open VMS                       Little
    8 Microsoft Windows IA (64-bit)     Little
    9 IBM zSeries Based Linux           Big
   13 Linux 64-bit for AMD              Little
   16 Apple Mac OS                      Big
   12 Microsoft Windows 64-bit for AMD  Little
   17 Solaris Operating System (x86)    Little
   18 IBM Power Based Linux             Big
   19 HP IA Open VMS                    Little
   20 Solaris Operating System (AMD64)  Little

19 rows selected.
SQL>
```

If you only want to see target platforms that are endian-compatible with the source platform, run this query at your source database:

```
SQL> COL "Source" FORM A32
SQL> COL "Compatible Targets" FORM A32
SQL> BREAK ON "Source"

SQL> select d.platform_name "Source", t.platform_name
 "Compatible Targets", endian_format
 from v$transportable_platform t, v$database d
 where t.endian_format = (select endian_format
                          from v$transportable_platform t,
                          v$database d
                          where d.platform_name =
                          t.platform_name)
SQL> /

Source                          Compatible Targets
           ENDIAN_FORMAT
------------------------------- -------------------------
------ -------------

Microsoft Windows IA (32-bit)   Microsoft Windows IA (32-bit)   Little
```

```
                              Linux IA (32-bit)              Little
                              HP Tru64 UNIX                  Little
                              Linux IA (64-bit)              Little
                              HP Open VMS                    Little
                              Microsoft Windows IA (64-bit)  Little
                              Linux 64-bit for AMD           Little
                              Microsoft Windows 64-bit for AMD Little
                              Solaris Operating System (x86) Little
                              HP IA Open VMS                 Little
                              Solaris Operating System (AMD64) Little

11 rows selected.

SQL>
```

If the source and target have the same endian format, no RMAN conversion is necessary. If they are different, you will need to use RMAN to convert the tablespace datafiles in the transportable set to the correct endian format.

Step 2: Choose the Transportable Tablespace Set

In order for a tablespace set to be transportable, it must be self-contained; that is, objects in the tablespace set must have no dependencies in tablespaces outside the tablespace set. Here are some basic rules:

- The tablespace set must contain all of the partitions of a partitioned table if any of the table's partitions are included in the tablespace set.

- If an index is included in a tablespace set, its corresponding table must also be included in the tablespace set.

- If you choose to include referential integrity constraints in the tablespace set, then all tablespaces required to support the constraints must be included in the set.

- If you have tables with LOB columns in the set, the tablespace that contains the LOBs must be included.

The easy way to determine if the set of tablespaces is self-contained is to execute the DBMS_TTS.TRANSPORT_SET_CHECK procedure, supplying the list of tablespaces in the tablespace set, as in this example:

```
SQL> create table scott.foo_1 (x number, y varchar2(20)) tablespace users;
Table created.
SQL> create index scott.foo_1_indx on scott.foo_1 (x) tablespace user_data;
Index created.
SQL> SET SERVEROUTPUT ON
SQL> exec dbms_tts.transport_set_check ('USER_DATA');
```

```
PL/SQL procedure successfully completed.
SQL> SELECT * FROM TRANSPORT_SET_VIOLATIONS;
VIOLATIONS
ORA-39907: Index SCOTT.FOO_1_INDX in tablespace USER_DATA points to table
SCOTT.FOO_1 in tablespace USERS.
SQL>
```

This simple verification showed that the index foo_1_indx was built in the USER_DATA tablespace but the corresponding foo_1 table is in the USERS tablespace, which is not included in the transportable tablespace set. You must remedy this situation before you can transport tablespace USER_DATA.

It is important at this time to discuss the concept of referential integrity constraints relative to transportable tablespace sets. By default, referential integrity constraints are not required to be included in the transportable set; however, you can test for constraint containment with the DBMS_TTS.TRANSPORT_SET_CHECK procedure. For the following example, we have created the table FOO in the USER_DATA tablespace and checked the transportability. We then add an index on FOO in the USERS tablespace and create a primary key constraint on the indexed column. We check the transportability of the USER_DATA tablespace as follows:

```
SQL> exec dbms_tts.transport_set_check ('USER_DATA',TRUE);
PL/SQL procedure successfully completed.

SQL> SELECT * FROM TRANSPORT_SET_VIOLATIONS;
no rows selected
SQL>
SQL> CREATE INDEX SCOTT.FOO_INDX
  2  ON SCOTT.FOO (X)
  3  TABLESPACE USERS;
Index created.
SQL> ALTER TABLE SCOTT.FOO ADD (PRIMARY KEY (x));
Table altered.
SQL> exec dbms_tts.transport_set_check ('USER_DATA',TRUE);
PL/SQL procedure successfully completed.
SQL> SELECT * FROM TRANSPORT_SET_VIOLATIONS;

VIOLATIONS
----------------------------------------------------------

ORA-39908: Index SCOTT.FOO_INDX in tablespace USERS
 enforces primary constraints
of table SCOTT.FOO in tablespace USER_DATA.
SQL>
```

Before we can transport the USER_DATA tablespace, we need to resolve this constraint issue by including the USERS tablespace, by rebuilding the index into the USER_DATA tablespace, by dropping the primary key constraint, or by deciding not to include constraints in the transportable set.

The SYSAUX tablespace is not transportable. Also, if the SYSTEM tablespace is locally managed, you can plug in a dictionary-managed tablespace, but it will be read-only and cannot be made writable.

Step 3: Generate the Transportable Tablespace Set

As introduced earlier, a transportable tablespace set is a self-contained group of tablespaces that encapsulate the objects that you wish to transport from one database to another. The transportable set must include all datafiles for each of the tablespaces to transport. The remaining component of the transportable set is a data pump export file that contains metadata about the transportable set. Here are the basic steps required to generate the transportable set:

1. Make all of the tablespaces in the transportable set read-only.

2. Use data pump on the source system to specify which tablespaces are included in the transportable set.

3. If converting to a different endian format, use the RMAN convert command to convert the files in a temporary location on the source system.

With these basic steps, we can show you a straightforward example. Remember, the tablespaces are placed in read-only mode and remain read-only until the files have been copied to the target or to their temporary location for endian conversion.

You must have the EXP_FULL_DATABASE role to export a transportable tablespace. You must use a valid DIRECTORY in your data pump export command.

First, place the tablespaces in the transportable set in read-only mode:

```
SQL>alter tablespace user_data read only;
Tablespace altered.
```

Now exit or "host" to the command line and execute the data pump export command:

```
SQL>host
C:\>expdp dumpfile=expdat.dmp DIRECTORY=exp_dir
 TRANSPORT_TABLESPACES= user_data

Export: Release 11.1.0.6.0 - Production on Sunday, 28 September, 2008 14:40:19
```

```
Copyright (c) 2003, 2007, Oracle.  All rights reserved.

Username: sys as sysdba
Password:

Connected to: Oracle Database 11g Enterprise Edition
 Release 11.1.0.6.0 - Production
With the Partitioning, OLAP, Data Mining and Real Application Testing options
Starting "SYS"."SYS_EXPORT_TRANSPORTABLE_01":
sys/******** AS SYSDBA dumpfile=e
xpdat.dmp DIRECTORY=EXP_DIR TRANSPORT_TABLESPACES= user_data
Processing object type TRANSPORTABLE_EXPORT/PLUGTS_BLK
Processing object type TRANSPORTABLE_EXPORT/TABLE
Processing object type TRANSPORTABLE_EXPORT/INDEX
Processing object type TRANSPORTABLE_EXPORT/CONSTRAINT/CONSTRAINT
Processing object type TRANSPORTABLE_EXPORT/INDEX_STATISTICS
Processing object type TRANSPORTABLE_EXPORT/TABLE_STATISTICS
Processing object type TRANSPORTABLE_EXPORT/POST_INSTANCE/PLUGTS_BLK
Master table "SYS"."SYS_EXPORT_TRANSPORTABLE_01" successfully loaded/unloaded
******************************************************************************
Dump file set for SYS.SYS_EXPORT_TRANSPORTABLE_01 is:
  C:\TEMP\EXPDAT.DMP
******************************************************************************
Datafiles required for transportable tablespace USER_DATA:
  C:\ORACLE\ORADATA\ORCL\USER_DATA01.DBF
Job "SYS"."SYS_EXPORT_TRANSPORTABLE_01" successfully completed at 14:41:47
```

Once the export is complete, if no endian conversion is required you can move on to the step of transporting the tablespace set. If endian conversion is required and you want to run the conversion on the target system, move on to that step. Otherwise, endian conversion is required locally and you'll need to invoke RMAN on the source system as follows:

```
C:\>RMAN TARGET /
RMAN> convert tablespace user_data
2> to platform 'Solaris[tm] OE (32-bit)'
3> format 'c:\temp\%U';

Starting conversion at source at 28-SEP-08
using channel ORA_DISK_1
channel ORA_DISK_1: starting datafile conversion
input datafile file number=00006 name=C:\ORACLE\ORADATA\ORCL\USER_DATA01.DBF
converted datafile=C:\TEMP\DATA_D-ORCL_I-1190467526_TS-
```

```
USER_DATA_FNO-6_3RJRNU8G
channel ORA_DISK_1: datafile conversion complete, elapsed time: 00:00:01
Finished conversion at source at 28-SEP-08

RMAN>
```

At this point you can exit from RMAN and return to SQL*Plus; you have a transportable set that consists of the export dump file and the converted tablespace datafile on the local source system. You can exit to SQL*Plus and return the tablespaces in the transportable set to read-write mode:

```
SQL>alter tablespace user_data read write;
Tablespace altered.
SQL>
```

Step 4: Transport the Tablespace Set

Now you will need to copy the export dump file and datafiles in the tablespace set to the target system. If the datafiles didn't need endian conversion or if you converted the data-files using RMAN on the source system, copy the datafiles from the source to the target destination using an operating-system copy utility or FTP binary mode, RMAN, or the DBMS_FILE_TRANSFER package. If the files require target-side conversion, copy the files into the temporary staging directory on the target.

Once you have copied the datafiles from the source system, you can return to SQL*Plus on the source and return the tablespaces in the transportable set to read-write mode:

```
SQL>alter tablespace user_data read write;
Tablespace altered.
SQL>
```

If the files do not need conversion, move on to step 5 at this time. If the datafiles require target-side endian conversion, invoke RMAN to perform the conversion, as in this example:

```
RMAN> CONVERT DATAFILE
'/orastage/user_data01.dbf'
TO PLATFORM="Solaris[tm] OE (32-bit)"
FROM PLATFORM="Microsoft Windows IA (32-bit)"
DB_FILE_NAME_CONVERT="/oracle/oradata/LNEB/";
```

Now that the datafiles are converted locally and in the correct target destination, you can move on to step 5.

Step 5: Import the Tablespace Set

As mentioned in an earlier note, either the transportable tablespace's block size must match the standard block size of the target database or the target database must have a cache con-figured for the same block size as the transportable set.

In the previous target-side endian conversion example, we copied the tablespace datafile and converted it into the /oracle/oradata/LNEB directory. Make sure that you have a DIRECTORY created for the target database and that you have copied the export metadata file referenced by DUMPFILE into that location. Now we'll import the datafiles:

```
IMPDP DUMPFILE=expdat.dmp DIRECTORY=imp_dir
TRANSPORT_DATAFILES=/oracle/oradata/LNEB/user_data01.dbf
```

> **NOTE**   If the schema owner on the source does not exist on the target, you must either create the schema owner on the target or use the REMAP_SCHEMA import clause to specify a new schema owner. You must use a valid Directory object in your data pump import command.

Once you have verified that the import completed successfully, it would be a good time to verify that the source tablespaces are in read-write mode.

In Exercise 11.1, you will see how to export a transportable tablespace set.

EXERCISE 11.1

Exporting a Transportable Tablespace Set

To export a transportable tablespace set, do the following:

1. Check source and destination compatibility.

2. Select the tablespaces for the transportable tablespace set and verify that the set is self-contained.

3. Generate the transportable tablespace set.

Using Enterprise Manager to Transport a Tablespace

In this section we will show you how to transport a tablespace using Enterprise Manager. From the Enterprise Manager database home page, click the Data Movement tab, then click the Transport Tablespaces link under Move Database Files, shown in Figure 11.25.

From the Transport Tablespaces page, select the Generate a Transportable Tablespace Set option, provide the host credentials, then click the Continue button, all shown in Figure 11.26.

Now, in the screen shown in Figure 11.27, add the tablespaces required in the transportable tablespace set, and choose Self or Full under Containment Type. For self-contained, determine if you need to include constraints. You can also check containment at this time.

Once you have checked containment, you will be given the opportunity to select the destination database platform and character set, shown in Figure 11.28.

FIGURE 11.25   The Transport Tablespace link in Enterprise Manager

FIGURE 11.26   Transport tablespaces using Enterprise Manager.

FIGURE 11.27   Generate Transportable Tablespaces: Select Tablespaces

FIGURE 11.28 Generate Transportable Tablespaces: Destination Characteristics

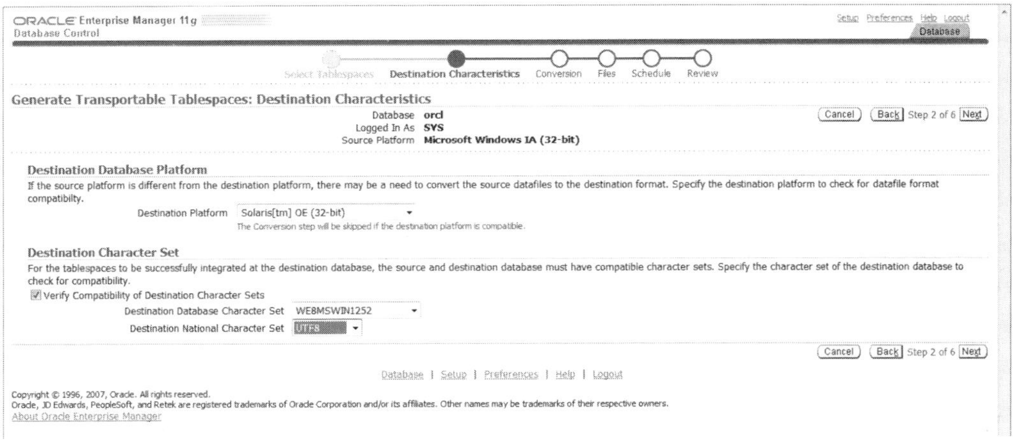

The next step is to choose the conversion process, either convert at destination or convert at source, as shown in Figure 11.29. For this exercise, we'll choose to convert at the source.

Now we choose the dump-file directory and dump-file name, as shown in Figure 11.30.

Now you can schedule the export and conversion, and then review as shown in Figure 11.31.

Submit the job. You will be returned to the Data Movement home page, and you can view the job details if you choose. At this point, you have a transportable tablespace set that you can import into a target database using Enterprise Manager or the command line.

FIGURE 11.29 Generate Transportable Tablespaces: Conversion

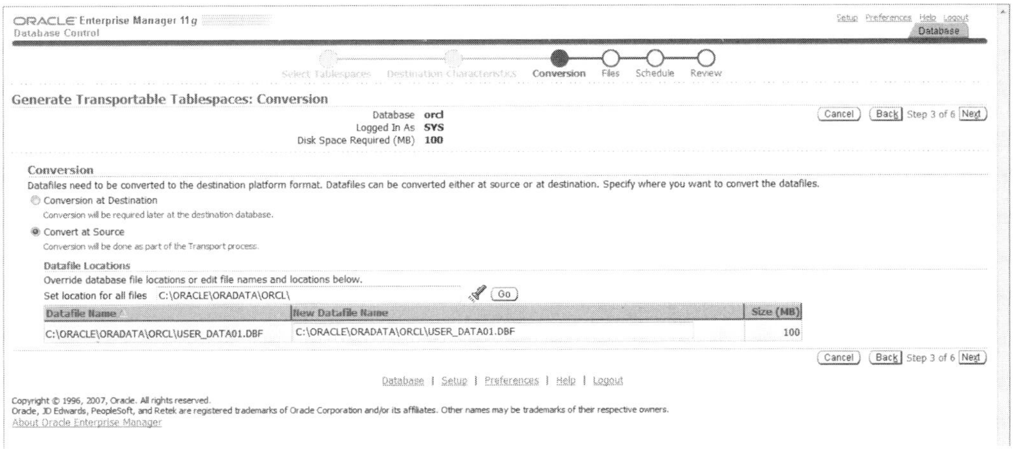

FIGURE 11.30 Generate Transportable Tablespaces: Files

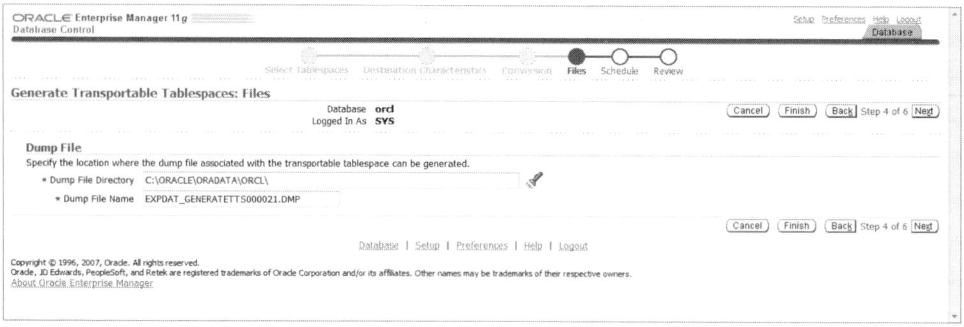

FIGURE 11.31 Generate Transportable Tablespaces: Review

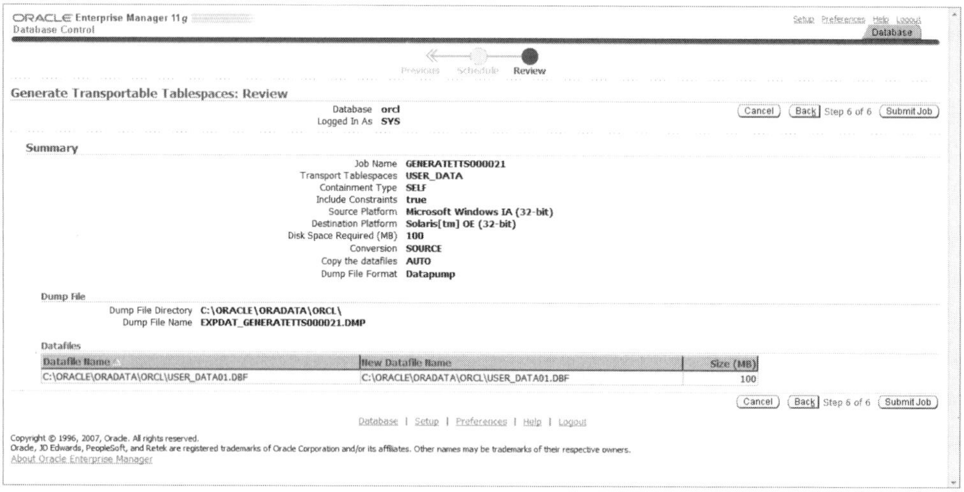

Managing Transportable Databases

Transportable Database (TDB) allows you to migrate an entire database from one platform to another as long as the source and destination platforms have the same endian format. You must use a tool other than TDB for database migration if the source and destination are not of the same endian format.

TDB utilizes RMAN to convert all datafiles from the source to the destination platform. You can use TDB to create a copy of the database on the source system in the format of the destination system and then copy to the files to the destination, or you can copy the source files to the destination system into a staging area and then use RMAN to convert the datafiles and copy them to their intended final destination.

The basic steps for TDB to migrate a database to a new platform are as follows:

1. Verify the prerequisites.

2. Identify all external files and directories.

3. Start the source database in read-only mode.

4. Verify that the source database is ready for migration.

5. Run RMAN CONVERT DATABASE.

6. Move files to the destination system.

7. Complete the migration.

 A large amount of the time required to complete the migration will be spent writing files, with RMAN converting files and transferring files from the source to the destination. If you have a time constraint, consider manually copying files across a LAN instead; utilize your storage area network (SAN)–attached storage, network attached storage (NAS), or network file system (NFS)–mounted file systems to speed the process. Allowing source and destination to share the staging area will reduce your transfer time. Also consider running the RMAN CONVERT process on the system that has the better throughput.

Checking Prerequisites

Before you begin TDB, you'll need to verify that your source and destination database platforms are supported. From your source database, query the V$DB_TRANSPORTABLE_PLATFORM view. If you don't see the destination platform, you'll need to skip TDB and choose another migration method.

```
SQL> select platform_name from v$db_transportable_platform;

PLATFORM_NAME
------------------------------
Microsoft Windows IA (32-bit)
Linux IA (32-bit)
HP Tru64 UNIX
Linux IA (64-bit)
HP Open VMS
Microsoft Windows IA (64-bit)
Linux 64-bit for AMD
Microsoft Windows 64-bit for AMD
Solaris Operating System (x86)
HP IA Open VMS
Solaris Operating System (AMD64)

11 rows selected.

SQL>
```

The query results show that you can transport the database on this server to any of those platforms listed.

The remaining prerequisite steps are as follows:

1. Verify that there are no restrictions or limitations that the source or destination database may encounter.

2. Verify that the destination and source systems have the same Oracle version, critical patch updates, patch-set version, and patch-set exceptions. Verify using the OPatch utility.

3. Determine if you will use the source or destination system to perform the conversion.

Identifying all External Files and Directories

Verify that you have created all necessary directories on the destination system as well as determined which external database files, such as BFILES and external tables, need to migrate to the destination. Query DBA_DIRECTORIES to report file system locations. Execute the supplied function DBMS_TDB.CHECK_EXTERNAL to identify external tables, directories, and BFILES that you'll need to move as part of the migration. Here's an example:

```
SQL> set serveroutput on
SQL> declare
        tdb_check boolean;
    begin
        tdb_check := dbms_tdb.check_external();
    end;
/
The following external tables exist in the database:
SYS.WRR$_REPLAY_CONN_DATA_EXT, SYS.WRR$_REPLAY_SEQ_DATA_EXT,
SYS.WRR$_REPLAY_SCN_ORDER_EXT, SH.SALES_TRANSACTIONS_EXT
The following directories exist in the database:
SYS.EM_TTS_DIR_OBJECT, SYS.EXP_DIR, SYS.IDR_DIR, SYS.CAPTURE_DIR, SYS.SUBDIR,
SYS.XMLDIR, SYS.MEDIA_DIR, SYS.LOG_FILE_DIR, SYS.DATA_FILE_DIR, SYS.AUDIT_DIR,
SYS.DATA_PUMP_DIR
The following BFILEs exist in the database:
PM.PRINT_MEDIA

PL/SQL procedure successfully completed.

SQL>
```

Once you start the migration, don't create any new external objects in the source database.

Starting the Source Database in Read-Only Mode

When you're ready to start the migration, you'll need to shut down the source database and open it in read only mode.

```
SQL> shutdown immediate;
SQL> startup mount;
SQL> alter database open read only;
```

At this point in time you have not started the migration to the destination system, and you haven't made any changes to the source system. If you run into problems and need to return to normal operations in the source system, this would be your "rollback" point.

Verifying that the Database Is Ready for Migration

Now you need to verify that the source database is in fact ready for migration to the destination. Execute the DBMS_TDB.CHECK_DB function, providing the destination system PLATFORM_NAME exactly as shown in the V$DB_TRANSPORTABLE_PLATFORM view. If the CHECK_DB function returns an error condition, you must fix it before you can continue the migration.

```
SQL> set serveroutput on
SQL> declare
        tdb_check boolean;
    begin
        tdb_check := dbms_tdb.check_db
        ('Linux IA (64-bit)',dbms_tdb.skip_none);
    end;
Database is not open in READ-ONLY mode. Open the database
 in READ-ONLY mode and retry.
PL/SQL procedure successfully completed.
```

The results show that you didn't start the database in read-only mode, so you must fix that and rerun the PL/SQL block before moving to the next step.

> If you're using a physical standby database for the migration source, run the DBMS_TDB.CHECK_DB function on the standby, not the primary. Follow this general rule for the remainder of this section unless otherwise indicated. If you're migrating from a physical standby database, use the physical standby, not the primary database, wherever we refer to the source.

Running RMAN *CONVERT DATABASE*

With the RMAN conversion, you'll run either a source-system or destination-system conversion. We'll describe the process for both, starting with the source-system, then the destination-system approach.

Database Conversion on the Source System

To create the converted copy of the source database on the source system, connect to RMAN on the source system and execute the CONVERT DATABASE command. In this example, we converted the small orcl sample database on a Windows 32-bit system to Linux 64-bit. The database files are converted and placed into the c:\temp\stage directory on the source system, and the transport script and the init.ora file are placed in the c:\temp directory.

```
RMAN> convert database
2> transport script 'c:\temp\transport_db_orclnx.sql'
3> new database 'orclnx'
4> to platform 'Linux IA (64-bit)'
5> parallelism 4
6> format 'c:\temp\%d%f'
7> db_file_name_convert 'c:\oracle\oradata\orcl\','c:\temp\stage\';

Starting conversion at source at 31-AUG-08
using channel ORA_DISK_1
using channel ORA_DISK_2
using channel ORA_DISK_3
using channel ORA_DISK_4

External table SYS.WRR$_REPLAY_CONN_DATA_EXT found in the database
External table SYS.WRR$_REPLAY_SEQ_DATA_EXT found in the database
External table SYS.WRR$_REPLAY_SCN_ORDER_EXT found in the database
External table SH.SALES_TRANSACTIONS_EXT found in the database

Directory SYS.IDR_DIR found in the database
Directory SYS.CAPTURE_DIR found in the database
Directory SYS.SUBDIR found in the database
Directory SYS.XMLDIR found in the database
Directory SYS.MEDIA_DIR found in the database
Directory SYS.LOG_FILE_DIR found in the database
Directory SYS.DATA_FILE_DIR found in the database
Directory SYS.AUDIT_DIR found in the database
Directory SYS.DATA_PUMP_DIR found in the database
Directory SYS.ORACLE_OCM_CONFIG_DIR found in the database

BFILE PM.PRINT_MEDIA found in the database

User SYS with SYSDBA and SYSOPER privilege found in password file
channel ORA_DISK_1: starting datafile conversion
```

```
input datafile file number=00005 name=C:\ORACLE\ORADATA\ORCL\EXAMPLE01.DBF
channel ORA_DISK_2: starting datafile conversion
input datafile file number=00002 name=C:\ORACLE\ORADATA\ORCL\SYSAUX01.DBF
channel ORA_DISK_3: starting datafile conversion
input datafile file number=00001 name=C:\ORACLE\ORADATA\ORCL\SYSTEM01.DBF
channel ORA_DISK_4: starting datafile conversion
input datafile file number=00003 name=C:\ORACLE\ORADATA\ORCL\UNDOTBS01.DBF
converted datafile=C:\TEMP\STAGE\EXAMPLE01.DBF
channel ORA_DISK_1: datafile conversion complete, elapsed time: 00:00:41
channel ORA_DISK_1: starting datafile conversion
input datafile file number=00004 name=C:\ORACLE\ORADATA\ORCL\USERS01.DBF
converted datafile=C:\TEMP\STAGE\USERS01.DBF
channel ORA_DISK_1: datafile conversion complete, elapsed time: 00:00:26
converted datafile=C:\TEMP\STAGE\UNDOTBS01.DBF
channel ORA_DISK_4: datafile conversion complete, elapsed time: 00:02:18
converted datafile=C:\TEMP\STAGE\SYSAUX01.DBF
channel ORA_DISK_2: datafile conversion complete, elapsed time: 00:03:17
converted datafile=C:\TEMP\STAGE\SYSTEM01.DBF
channel ORA_DISK_3: datafile conversion complete, elapsed time: 00:03:15
Edit init.ora file C:\TEMP\INIT_ORCLNX4294967295.ORA.
This PFILE will be used to
 create the database on the target platform
Run SQL script C:\TEMP\TRANSPORT_DB_ORCLNX.SQL on the
 target platform to create
database
To recompile all PL/SQL modules, run utlirp.sql and
 utlrp.sql on the target plat
form
To change the internal database identifier, use DBNEWID Utility
Finished conversion at source at 31-AUG-08

RMAN>
```

 Verify the accuracy of the filenames and directories in the script files before you run them and attempt to start up your new destination database.

Database Conversion on the Destination System

To create the converted copy of the source database on the destination system, run RMAN on the destination system and execute the CONVERT DATABASE ON DESTINATION PLATFORM command. The command produces the convert script necessary to convert the database files on the destination system, the pfile, and a transport script.

```
rman connect target /
RMAN> convert database on destination platform
2>convert script '/tmp/convert_orclnx.rman'
3>transport script '/tmp/transport_orclnx.sql'
4>new database 'orclnx'
5>format '/tmp/orclnx%U'
6>db_file_name_convert '/ora100/oradata/orclnx/datafile','/tmp/stage/';
```

Moving Files to the Destination System

If you converted the datafiles at the source, you should now copy them to the destination system. If you used your SAN, NAS, or NFS storage, now's the time for the destination system to take ownership of the database files. Copy the transport SQL script, pfile, external table files, and BFILES to the destination.

If you chose to convert the files at the destination, you will now need to copy the convert script to the destination and move the unconverted datafiles to the staging area. Again, SAN, NAS, and/or NFS storage should be made read/write for the destination at this time.

Completing the Migration

If you converted the datafiles at the destination, you'll need to run the RMAN convert script on the destination system.

Whether you converted at the source or at the destination, review and modify the pfile as required. Now review the transport script created by the RMAN CONVERT DATABASE command. Verify that the directory locations are correct for the pfile, datafiles, log files, and tempfile. After you make corrections and verify, execute the transport script and check for any error messages.

Using Shrinking Segments

As with the files on the hard drive in your personal computer, the data within Oracle database segments can become fragmented with use. Data Manipulation Language (DML) operations—namely delete, update, and insert—can cause fragmentation of data and free space. Fragmentation of free space leads to wasted free space as well as performance issues such as the following:

Cache utilization   Sparsely populated (fragmented) data blocks in memory require more reads to get the same amount of data as densely populated (defragmented) data blocks.

Table and index scans   A full segment scan of fragmented data blocks requires more physical reads than a scan of defragmented blocks, so full table scans must read more fragmented blocks than defragmented blocks to get the same results.

There are two methods to defragment a segment online; use either Table Redefinition, also referred to as *reorganization*, or Segment Shrink. Table Redefinition copies a table to a new location and consolidates the data. This operation requires space for the new copy of the table and its dependent objects. Also worth mentioning is the method to deallocate unused space above the high-water mark by issuing the DEALLOCATE UNUSED command. See Table 11.3 for a comparison of these methods.

TABLE 11.3   Comparing Space-Reclamation Methods

Method	Reclamation Method
Segment Shrink	Reclaims space above and below the high-water mark without using additional space
Reorganization	Moves rows to a new physical location, resetting the high-water mark but using additional space during the operation
Deallocate Unused	Deallocates space above the high-water mark that is currently not in use

For segments in dictionary-managed tablespaces or for locally managed tablespaces with manual segment space management, segment reorganization is the only permitted operation for reclaiming fragmented free space.

Online Segment Shrink compacts the segment in place and does not require additional space to perform the operation. Segment Shrink can be performed on the dependent objects like indexes and partitions. Segment Shrink works on the following objects:

- Heap tables
- Index-organized tables and their overflow segments
- LOBs and LOB segments
- Materialized views and materialized view logs
- Indexes
- Partitions and subpartitions

To be eligible for segment shrink, the segment must have row movement enabled and reside in a tablespace that is locally managed and utilizes Automatic Segment Space Management (ASSM). The following objects in an ASSM tablespace are not eligible for Segment Shrink:

- SecureFile LOBs
- Index-organized table mapping tables
- Tables that have ROWID-based materialized views
- Tables with function-based indexes

> To enable row movement for a table, issue the ALTER TABLE … ENABLE ROW MOVEMENT command.

Performing an Online Segment Shrink Operation

Because Segment Shrink moves rows and changes the ROWIDs, before you perform the online Segment Shrink operation, you will need to do the following:

- Enable row movement.
- Disable any ROWID-based triggers defined on the object.
- Determine if the application uses any ROWID-based DML or queries.

By default, online Segment Shrink performs the following:

- Compacts the segment
- Resets the high-water mark
- Releases the reclaimed free space

Since Segment Shrink is an online operation, DML and queries can continue as normal. There is a brief block of concurrent DML operations on the segment when the space is released at the end of the shrink operation. Indexes remain usable throughout the operation.

Here's an example of shrinking a table:

```
SQL> ALTER TABLE HR.EMPLOYEES SHRINK SPACE;
ALTER TABLE HR.EMPLOYEES SHRINK SPACE
*
ERROR at line 1:
ORA-10636: ROW MOVEMENT is not enabled
SQL> ALTER TABLE HR.EMPLOYEES ENABLE ROW MOVEMENT;
Table altered.
SQL> ALTER TABLE HR.EMPLOYEES SHRINK SPACE;
Table altered.
```

There are two optional clauses with the SHRINK SPACE command: COMPACT and CASCADE. The COMPACT clause defragments and compacts but does not reset the high-water mark or return the free space. Execute the SHRINK SPACE command without the COMPACT clause at a later time to complete the task.

The CASCADE clause performs the Shrink Space operation on all dependent objects, as reported by the DBMS_SPACE.OBJECT_DEPENDENT_SEGMENT procedure.

> Partitions in a partitioned table are automatically shrunk with the SHRINK SPACE command, so you don't need to specify the CASCADE clause.

Here's an example of a small sample table called HR.EMPLOYEES_HIST, built as a copy of the Oracle-provided HR.EMPLOYEE table. We've inserted rows until we've allocated 40 blocks, then deleted about 70 percent of the rows. The shrink operation should reduce the number of blocks to 16. We'll perform the two-step COMPACT process and CASCADE so that you can see how they work:

```
SQL> SELECT COUNT(1) from hr.employees_hist;

  COUNT(1)
----------
      2943

SQL> SELECT SEGMENT_NAME, BLOCKS FROM DBA_SEGMENTS
WHERE OWNER = 'HR' and SEGMENT_NAME LIKE 'EMPL%';

SEGMENT_NAME                 BLOCKS
------------------------ ----------
EMPLOYEES                         8
EMPLOYEES_HIST                   40
EMPLOYEES_HIST_IX                16

SQL> ALTER TABLE HR.EMPLOYEES_HIST SHRINK SPACE COMPACT;
Table altered.
SQL> SELECT SEGMENT_NAME, BLOCKS FROM DBA_SEGMENTS
WHERE OWNER = 'HR' and SEGMENT_NAME LIKE 'EMPL%';

SEGMENT_NAME                 BLOCKS
------------------------ ----------
EMPLOYEES                         8
EMPLOYEES_HIST                   40
EMPLOYEES_HIST_IX                16

SQL> ALTER TABLE HR.EMPLOYEES_HIST SHRINK SPACE;
Table altered.
SQL> SELECT SEGMENT_NAME, BLOCKS FROM DBA_SEGMENTS
WHERE OWNER = 'HR' and SEGMENT_NAME LIKE 'EMPL%';

SEGMENT_NAME                 BLOCKS
------------------------ ----------
EMPLOYEES                         8
EMPLOYEES_HIST                   16
```

```
EMPLOYEES_HIST_IX                    16

SQL> ALTER TABLE HR.EMPLOYEES_HIST SHRINK SPACE CASCADE;
Table altered.
SQL> SELECT SEGMENT_NAME, BLOCKS FROM DBA_SEGMENTS
WHERE OWNER = 'HR' and SEGMENT_NAME LIKE 'EMPL%';

SEGMENT_NAME                    BLOCKS
----------------------- ----------
EMPLOYEES                            8
EMPLOYEES_HIST                      16
EMPLOYEES_HIST_IX                    8

SQL> SELECT COUNT(1) from hr.employees_hist;

  COUNT(1)
----------
       910

SQL>
```

Using Enterprise Manager Segment Space Advisor to Perform an Online Segment Shrink Operation

After repopulating and deleting from our test table HR.EMPLOYEES_HIST, we want to use EM to shrink the segment. From the Enterprise Manager database home page, in the Related Links section, find the Advisor Central. From the Advisor Central, choose the Segment Advisor. From the Segment Advisor Scope page, shown in Figure 11.32, choose Schema Objects and then click Next.

FIGURE 11.32 The Automatic Segment Advisor: Scope page

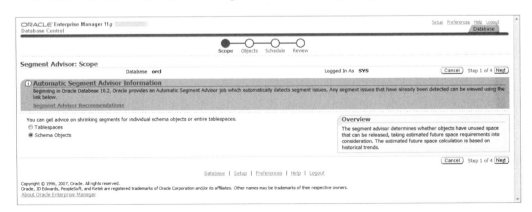

Next choose the objects to add to the advisor by clicking the check box in the Select column next to the object name on the Schema Objects page, shown in Figure 11.33. You can also set the time limit for analysis under the advanced options, shown in Figure 11.34.

FIGURE 11.33 The Automatic Segment Advisor: Schema Objects page

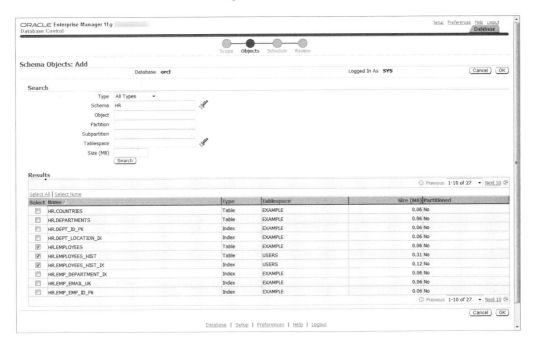

FIGURE 11.34 The Automatic Segment Advisor: Schema Objects page

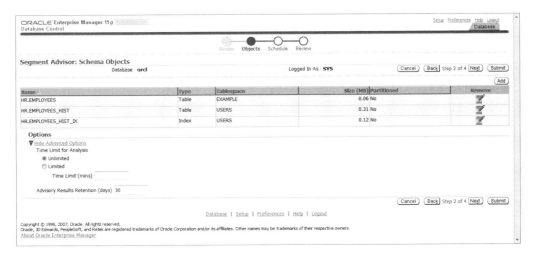

Once you set the schedule and review it, return to the Advisor Central page to monitor the Auto Space Advisor task results. For the example, the Segment Space Advisor chose not to shrink our HR.EMPLOYEES_HIST table. Since we're really persistent about shrinking this table, from the EM database home page we will go to the Schema page, click Tables, enter the schema and object information for HR.EMPLOYEES_HIST, and then click the Go button. The basic information for the object will be displayed as in Figure 11.35.

Figure 11.36 shows that we chose the Shrink Segment operation from the Actions drop-down menu.

FIGURE 11.35   Selecting a table

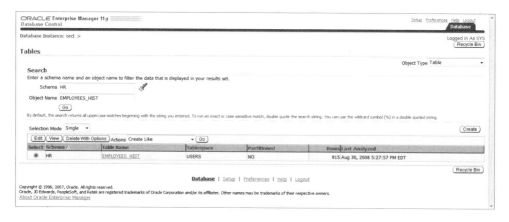

FIGURE 11.36   Selecting the shrink operation

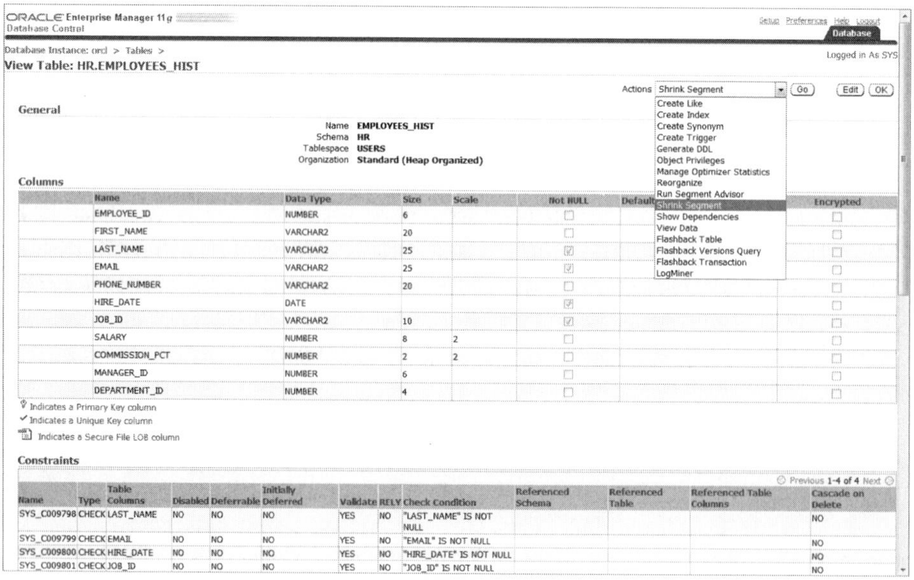

Managing Space 509

Under Shrink Options (shown in Figure 11.37), choose to compact only or to compact and release freed space, and also choose an option under Segment Selection, synonymous with the CASCADE clause we used at the command line. Schedule a job to shrink the table by clicking the Continue button; then submit the job. You can see in Figure 11.38 that the job completed successfully, and you can view the SQL statement executed to shrink the segment.

FIGURE 11.37 Selecting the shrink options

FIGURE 11.38 Viewing the shrink job

We want to verify the operation was successful, so in SQL*Plus, run the query we ran before to validate the results.

```
SQL> SELECT SEGMENT_NAME, BLOCKS FROM DBA_SEGMENTS
WHERE OWNER = 'HR' and SEGMENT_NAME LIKE 'EMPL%';

SEGMENT_NAME                    BLOCKS
------------------------    ----------
EMPLOYEES                         8
EMPLOYEES_HIST                   16
EMPLOYEES_HIST_IX                 8
```

In Exercise 11.2, you'll learn how to shrink a segment.

EXERCISE 11.2

Shrinking a Segment

For this exercise, you'll create a table, populate it, delete rows, and then shrink the table segment:

1. Create a table named shrink_test with two columns: a NUMBER column named X and a VARCHAR2 (10) column named Y. Enable row movement for the table.

2. Insert two rows with a unique value for X for each row.

3. Now, using the insert into shrink_test select * from shrink_test SQL statement repeatedly, grow the table to 1 million rows (or more), and commit. Verify that every other row has the same value.

4. Query DBA_SEGMENTS to determine the size of the segment.

5. Delete half the rows from the table, using one of the values of X as the delete criteria.

6. Now shrink the segment online, and verify that the number of blocks decreases.

Managing Resources

As a database administrator, it is your job to maintain a given level of performance from the database. Successfully accomplishing this mission requires close management of scarce hardware resources.

In the past, management of Oracle resources fell upon the operating system. The operating system had to juggle resources not only between the different Oracle processes, but also between Oracle and all other processes running on the system. As if that weren't enough, it also had no way of differentiating one Oracle process from another. Therefore, allocating resources between user groups or applications was impossible.

In addition, resource management performed by the operating system has a tendency to cause certain performance problems. Excessive context switching can occur when the number of server processes is high. Server processes holding latches can be descheduled, resulting in further inefficiency. And inappropriate resource allocation is common due to the inability to prioritize Oracle tasks.

Oracle's Database Resource Manager (DRM) circumvents the inefficient operating system management process by giving the Oracle database server more control over resource-management decisions. It also allows you to distribute available system resources among your users and applications based on business needs (or whatever criteria you wish to base it on).

The following sections describe the different elements of DRM and how to use them. In the overview section, you'll learn about the elements that DRM comprises and see, at a high level, how they interact. You will be introduced to the pending area, a work area that must be established prior to the creation or modification of DRM objects.

Next, you will learn about resource consumer groups, which allow you to classify users based on their resource requirements. You'll learn how to set up resource plans that direct the allocation of resources among the resource consumer groups. You'll learn about resource-allocation options offered by the database, and the methods you can define to apply them.

You will also learn about resource-plan directives that associate resource consumer groups, resource plans, and resource-allocation methods. Finally, you'll learn the PL/SQL interface to manage DRM as well as the views available to query DRM information.

Keep in mind that the elements of DRM constitute a "chicken or the egg" situation in terms of the ordering of the topics. For instance, the pending area must be established before anything else is done. However, discussion of the pending area assumes knowledge of the objects defined later. In the interest of organization and ease of use, each topic will be covered separately in its own section. Then, a final section will show how the elements integrate.

The DRM offers a component-based approach to resource allocation management. When you define distinct, independent components representing the DRM elements, the result is an extremely flexible and easy-to-use system.

There are three main elements that make up the DRM:

- Resource consumer groups
- Resource plans
- Resource-plan directives

DRM allocates resources among resource consumer groups based on a resource plan. A resource plan consists of resource-plan directives that specify how resources should be distributed among the groups. Resource consumer groups are categories to which user sessions can be assigned. These groups can then be allocated resources through plan directives.

Plan directives define resource-allocation rules by assigning resource-allocation methods to specific resource consumer groups. They connect resource plans to consumer groups and define the resource-allocation method to be used.

Resource-allocation methods are methods that can be used to allocate resources such as CPU usage, number of sessions, idle time, operation execution time, and so on. Resource-allocation methods are predefined by Oracle, but plan directives determine which ones to apply and the allocation amounts. For example, a plan named NIGHT_PLAN may contain a directive allocating a percentage of CPU to a consumer group named MANAGERS.

Working with the Pending Area

Before defining or updating any DRM objects, you must first establish a pending area. A *pending area* is a staging area where resource-management objects can be defined and validated before they are activated. If you forget to create the pending area, you will receive the following error message if you try to create or update a DRM object:

```
ERROR at line 1:
ORA-29371: pending area is not active
ORA-06512: at "SYS.DBMS_RMIN", line 115
ORA-06512: at "SYS.DBMS_RESOURCE_MANAGER", line 108
ORA-06512: at line 1
```

The next sections explain how to manage pending areas. You will learn to create, validate, submit, and clear them.

Creating a Pending Area

To create a pending area, simply execute the DBMS_RESOURCE_MANAGER.CREATE_PENDING_AREA procedure. This procedure accepts no parameters, so it can be called as follows:

```
SQL> exec dbms_resource_manager.create_pending_area();

PL/SQL procedure successfully completed.
```

Once a pending area has been created, all changes will automatically be stored there until they are validated and submitted.

Validating Changes to the Pending Area

After changes have been made in the pending area, they need to be checked for validity before being activated. This can be accomplished through the DBMS_RESOURCE_GROUP.VALIDATE_ PENDING_AREA procedure.

The validation process verifies that any changes in the pending area will not result in a violation of any of the following rules:

- No plan schema can contain a loop.
- All DRM objects identified in a plan directive must exist.
- All plan directives refer to either plans or resource groups.
- Allocation percentages for a given level cannot exceed 100.

- Deletes are not allowed for top plans being used by an active instance.
- Only plan directives that refer to resource consumer group are allowed to set the following parameters:
    - ACTIVE_SESS_POOL_P1
    - MAX_EST_EXEC_TIME
    - MAX_IDLE_BLOCKER_TIME
    - MAX_IDLE_TIME
    - PARALLEL_DEGREE_LIMIT_P1
    - QUEUEING_P1
    - SWITCH_ESTIMATE
    - SWITCH_GROUP
    - SWITCH_TIME
    - SWITCH_FOR_CALL
    - SWITCH_IO_MEGABYTES
    - SWITCH_IO_REQS
    - UNDO_POOL
- An active plan schema can contain no more than 32 resource consumer groups.
- Plan names cannot conflict with resource consumer group names.
- There must be a plan directive for the OTHER_GROUPS group to allocate resources for sessions not identified in the active plan.

If any of the preceding rules are violated, the VALIDATE_PENDING_AREA procedure will return errors for each violation. Here's an example:

```
SQL> exec dbms_resource_manager.validate_pending_area;
BEGIN dbms_resource_manager.validate_pending_area; END;

*
ERROR at line 1:
ORA-29382: validation of pending area failed
ORA-29377: consumer group OTHER_GROUPS is not part of top-plan OLTP_PLAN
ORA-29383: all leaves of top-plan OLTP_PLAN must be consumer groups
ORA-29374: resource plan OLTP_PLAN in top-plan OLTP_PLAN
 has no plan directives
ORA-29377: consumer group OTHER_GROUPS is not part of top-plan OFF_HOURS_PLAN
ORA-29383: all leaves of top-plan OFF_HOURS_PLAN must be consumer groups
ORA-29374: resource plan OFF_HOURS_PLAN in top-plan OFF_HOURS_PLAN has no plan
  directives
```

```
ORA-29377: consumer group OTHER_GROUPS is not part of top-plan DAY_PLAN
ORA-29383: all leaves of top-plan DAY_PLAN must be consumer groups
ORA-29374: resource plan DAY_PLAN in top-plan DAY_PLAN has no plan directives
ORA-06512: at "SYS.DBMS_RMIN", line 402
ORA-06512: at "SYS.DBMS_RESOURCE_MANAGER", line 437
ORA-06512: at line 1
```

If validation is successful, no error messages will be returned.

Submitting the Pending Area

When you are ready to make your changes active, you can use the DBMS_RESOURCE_MANAGER
.SUBMIT_PENDING_AREA procedure, as shown here:

```
SQL> exec dbms_resource_manager.submit_pending_area;
```

```
PL/SQL procedure successfully completed.
```

As you can see, no parameters are required when submitting the pending area.

Submitting the contents of the pending area will activate those objects (move them to the
data dictionary). Active objects are stored in the data dictionary and can be enabled by DRM.

 WARNING Just because a DRM object is active does not mean it is enabled. It simply
means it can be enabled or be included in an enabled plan.

Submitting the pending area actually performs three distinct actions: it validates, submits,
and clears the pending area. Therefore, it is not required to perform a separate validation
before submitting. However, from a debugging standpoint, it is beneficial to validate changes
on an incremental basis rather than waiting until submit time.

Clearing the Pending Area

To clear the pending area without submitting your changes, you can use the DBMS_RESOURCE_
MANAGER.CLEAR_PENDING_AREA procedure, as shown here:

```
SQL> exec dbms_resource_manager.clear_pending_area;
```

```
PL/SQL procedure successfully completed.
```

Clearing the pending area drops everything in the pending area irretrievably, so use
this procedure with caution. As mentioned earlier, submitting the pending area also clears
the pending area, so it is not necessary to use this procedure after a successful submit is
performed.

The name of this procedure is somewhat misleading. It seems to imply that the objects
in the pending area will be cleared but that the pending area will remain intact. This is
not true. Once the pending area is cleared, a new pending area must be created before you
make any new changes.

Resource Consumer Groups

Resource consumer groups represent the next step in defining a DRM strategy. They allow you to classify users into logical groupings based on resource-consumption requirements or business needs.

There are two ways to define *resource consumer groups*:

- A resource consumer group is a method of classifying users based on their resource-consumption tendencies or requirements.

- A resource consumer group is a method of prioritizing database resource usage by classifying users based on business needs.

For instance, in most companies, payroll users tend to have high priority because no one wants their paychecks to be late. Therefore, a resource consumer group named PAYROLL can be created and all payroll users assigned to it.

This does not imply anything about the resource-consumption tendencies or the requirements of payroll users. Instead, it identifies them based on a business need.

On the other hand, a group of inexperienced users may have a habit of executing queries without first checking join conditions. Their resultant Cartesian products tend to run for hours, wasting system resources. For these users, a group named NOVICE could be created. This group could then have resource limitations placed upon it.

In this situation, group classification is directly related to the consumption tendencies of the users.

In either situation, users can be assigned to one or more resource consumer groups, although each active session can be assigned to only one resource consumer group at a time. A user may, for example, use the system in an online transaction processing (OLTP) capacity for part of the day, perhaps entering orders or doing account maintenance. The rest of the day, the same user may switch to an online analytical processing (OLAP) capacity, running reports and statistical queries. This user could be a member of both the OLTP and OLAP resource consumer groups but could be assigned to only one for any session.

The following sections explain how to manage resource consumer groups using PL/SQL packages.

Managing Resource Consumer Groups

Resource consumer groups can be managed by using the DBMS_RESOURCE_MANAGER PL/SQL package. This package offers procedures that allow the creation, deletion, and modification of resource consumer groups. It also provides functionality for assigning users to groups and switching the group for user sessions.

In the next few sections, you'll learn how to add, modify, and delete resource consumer groups using the DBMS_RESOURCE_MANAGER package. You will also learn to assign users to groups as well as how to switch user sessions between groups.

You must have the ADMINISTER_RESOURCE_MANAGER system privilege to administer Database Resource Manager. This privilege is granted by default to the DBA role.

Creating Resource Consumer Groups

To create a new resource consumer group, use the DBMS_RESOURCE_MANAGER.CREATE_CONSUMER_GROUP procedure. All that is required when defining a new group is a unique name and a description. It is not necessary (nor possible) to define how this group will be used at this point.

There are three parameters that you can specify when creating a resource consumer group. Table 11.4 describes these parameters.

TABLE 11.4: CREATE_CONSUMER_GROUP **PARAMETERS**

Parameter	Description
CONSUMER_GROUP	Consumer group name.
COMMENT	Any comment (usually a description of the group).
CPU_MTH	Deprecated. Use MGMT_MTH.
MGMT_MTH	Method used to schedule CPU resources between sessions in the group. Valid values are as follows: ROUND_ROBIN (the default) ensures fair distribution by using a round-robin schedule; RUN_TO_COMPLETION schedules the most active sessions ahead of other sessions.

The CPU_MTH parameter defines the resource scheduling method used between sessions within a resource group. This method governs only CPU resources between group members.

Be aware that a CPU-allocation method can also be defined at the plan level. Therefore, the total CPU available to the resource group may already have been limited by the active resource plan.

To create a new resource consumer group named DEVELOPERS that uses a round-robin CPU methodology, see the following example:

```
SQL> begin
  dbms_resource_manager.create_consumer_group('developers',
    'application developers');
 end;
SQL>/

PL/SQL procedure successfully completed.
```

To verify that the command succeeded, you can use the DBA_RSRC_CONSUMER_GROUPS view:

```
SQL>  select consumer_group, cpu_method, comments from
```

```
dba_rsrc_consumer_groups
 where consumer_group = 'DEVELOPERS';
```

```
CONSUMER_GROUP   CPU_METHOD        COMMENTS
---------------  ---------------   ------------------------

DEVELOPERS       ROUND-ROBIN       application developers
```

By default, there are 14 resource consumer groups predefined in the database. They are described in Table 11.5.

TABLE 11.5 Predefined Resource Consumer Groups

Group Name	Description
DEFAULT_CONSUMER_GROUP	Default group for all users/sessions not assigned to an initial consumer group.
OTHER_GROUPS	Catchall group for users assigned to groups that are not part of the currently active plan. This group cannot be explicitly assigned to users.
SYS_GROUP	Used by the Oracle-provided SYSTEM_PLAN plan.
LOW_GROUP	Used by the Oracle-provided SYSTEM_PLAN plan.
BATCH_GROUP	Consumer group for batch operations.
ORA$DIAGNOSTICS	Consumer group for diagnostics.
ORA$AUTOTASK_HEALTH_GROUP	Consumer group for health checks.
ORA$AUTOTASK_SQL_GROUP	Consumer group for SQL tuning.
ORA$AUTOTASK_SPACE_GROUP	Consumer group for space-management advisors.
ORA$AUTOTASK_STATS_GROUP	Consumer group for gathering optimizer statistics.
ORA$AUTOTASK_MEDIUM_GROUP	Consumer group for medium-priority maintenance tasks.
INTERACTIVE_GROUP	Consumer group for interactive OLTP operations.
AUTO_TASK_CONSUMER_GROUP	System-maintenance task consumer group.
ORA$AUTOTASK_URGENT_GROUP	Consumer group for urgent maintenance tasks.

As you can see in the description, all users who are not assigned to a group will become part of the DEFAULT_CONSUMER_GROUP group. And users who are not assigned to a group in the currently active plan will be assigned to the OTHER_GROUPS group.

The remaining groups were defined to support predefined resource plans provided by Oracle.

Updating Resource Consumer Groups

Resource consumer groups can be updated using the DBMS_RESOURCE_MANAGER.UPDATE_CONSUMER_GROUP procedure. This procedure allows you to change the comment and/or the CPU-allocation method for a particular group. Table 11.6 describes the parameters for the DBMS_RESOURCE_MANAGER.UPDATE_CONSUMER_GROUP procedure.

TABLE 11.6: UPDATE_CONSUMER_GROUP Procedure Parameters

Parameter	Description
CONSUMER_GROUP	Name of the consumer group.
NEW_COMMENT	Updated comment.
NEW_CPU_MTH	Deprecated. Use NEW_MGMT_MTH.
NEW_MGMT_MTH	Updated method for CPU resource allocation.

For instance, to change the CPU-allocation method for the DEVELOPERS group, the following SQL could be used:

```
SQL> begin
  dbms_resource_manager.update_consumer_group(
  CONSUMER_GROUP => 'DEVELOPERS',
  NEW_MGMT_MTH => 'RUN-TO-COMPLETION');
  end;
SQL> /

PL/SQL procedure successfully completed.
```

As you can see in this example, the NEW_COMMENT parameter was omitted because no change was being made to it. By the same token, the NEW_MGMT_MTH parameter could be omitted if only the comment was being updated.

Deleting a Resource Consumer Group

Resource consumer groups can be deleted using the DBMS_RESOURCE_MANAGER.DELETE_ CONSUMER_GROUP procedure. Deleting a resource group has a couple of implications that are important to understand:

- Users assigned to the deleted group as their initial resource consumer group will be assigned to the DEFAULT_CONSUMER_GROUP group.

- Current sessions assigned to the deleted group will be switched to the DEFAULT_ CONSUMER_GROUP group.

> Don't worry if you don't understand the implications of these changes right now. They will be made clear as this chapter progresses.

The single parameter required by the DBMS_RESOURCE_MANAGER.DELETE_CONSUMER_GROUP procedure is CONSUMER_GROUP, the name of the consumer group to be deleted.

Only the name of the group to be deleted needs to be passed to the procedure, as you can see in this example:

```
SQL> begin
  dbms_resource_manager.delete_consumer_group('DEVELOPERS');
 end;
SQL>/
```

```
PL/SQL procedure successfully completed.
```

The DEVELOPERS group should now be deleted from the system.

Assigning User Sessions to Consumer Groups

Creating resource consumer groups is only half the battle. You still need a method of assigning consumer groups to user sessions. DRM can be configured to automatically assign consumer groups to sessions based on specific session attributes. This process is called *consumer group mapping*. In the following sections, you will learn how to create consumer group mappings. You will also learn how to set priorities so DRM knows which mapping has precedence in case of conflicts.

CREATING CONSUMER GROUP MAPPINGS

Consumer group mappings can be created by using the DBMS_RESOURCE_MANAGER.SET_ CONSUMER_GROUP_MAPPING procedure to create the mapping and the DBMS_RESOURCE_ MANAGER.SET_CONSUMER_GROUP_MAPPING_PRI procedure to create the attributes for the mapping. These procedures allow you to map sessions to consumer groups based on login or runtime *session attributes*. Table 11.7 shows the available attributes that can be mapped.

TABLE 11.7: SET_CONSUMER_GROUP_MAPPING_PRI Session Attributes

Attribute	Type	Description
ORACLE_USER	Login	Oracle Database username.
SERVICE_NAME	Login	Service name used by the client to establish a connection.
CLIENT_OS_USER	Login	Operating-system username of the client that is logging in.
CLIENT_PROGRAM	Login	Name of the client program used to log in to the server.
CLIENT_MACHINE	Login	Name of the computer from which the client is making the connection.
MODULE_NAME	Runtime	Module name that is currently executing, as defined by the DBMS_APPLICATION_INFO.SET_MODULE_NAME procedure.
MODULE_NAME_ACTION	Runtime	Module name and module action that are currently executing, as defined by the DBMS_APPLICATION_INFO.SET_MODULE_NAME/SET_ACTION procedures. Attribute is specified in the format *SERVICE_NAME.ACTION*.
SERVICE_MODULE	Runtime	Service name and module name in the format *SERVICE_NAME.MODULE_NAME*.
SERVICE_MODULE_ACTION	Runtime	Service name, module name, and action name in the format *SERVICE_NAME.MODULE_NAME.ACTION_NAME*.

Mappings simply define a session attribute, a value for the attribute, and a consumer group. For example, if the session attribute CLIENT_OS_USER has a value of graciej, then assign the OLAP_GROUP to the session. The following code would create this mapping:

```
SQL> begin
  dbms_resource_manager.set_consumer_group_mapping(
ATTRIBUTE => CLIENT_OS_USER,
    VALUE => 'graciej', CONSUMER_GROUP => 'OLAP_GROUP');
 end;
SQL>/

PL/SQL procedure successfully completed.
```

> Note that session attributes are defined as Oracle constants and are therefore specified without surrounding single quotes.

ESTABLISHING MAPPING PRIORITIES

It is possible that a session may map to more than one consumer group based on mapping rules. Therefore, Oracle allows the creation of *mapping priorities* through the use of the DBMS_RESOURCE_MANAGER.SET_CONSUMER_GROUP_MAPPING_PRI procedure, as follows:

```
SQL> begin
  dbms_resource_manager.set_consumer_group_mapping_pri(
    EXPLICIT => 1,
    CLIENT_OS_USER => 2,
    CLIENT_MACHINE => 3,
    CLIENT_PROGRAM => 4,
    ORACLE_USER => 5,
    MODULE_NAME => 6,
    MODULE_NAME_ACTION => 7,
    SERVICE_NAME => 8,
    SERVICE_MODULE => 9,
    SERVICE_MODULE_ACTION => 10);
  end;
SQL>/


PL/SQL procedure successfully completed.
```

The priorities defined in the SET_CONSUMER_GROUP_MAPPING_PRI procedure are used to resolve any conflicting mapping rules. The EXPLICIT attribute refers to an explicit consumer-group switch (using one of the switching methods described in the next section).

Changing Resource Consumer Groups

Two procedures are provided in the DBMS_RESOURCE_MANAGER package to allow you to explicitly change consumer groups for currently active user sessions: the SWITCH_CONSUMER_GROUP_FOR_SESS and SWITCH_CONSUMER_GROUP_FOR_USER procedures.

In addition, users can be granted the privilege to change their own consumer group. When a user is granted the *switch privilege*, they can use the DBMS_SESSION.SWITCH_CURRENT_CONSUMER_GROUP procedure to change the consumer group for their current session.

In the following sections, you will learn how to use each of these methods to explicitly change consumer groups. You will also learn how to grant and revoke the switch privilege.

SWITCHING GROUPS USING *DBMS_RESOURCE_MANAGER PROCEDURES*

The first procedure, SWITCH_CONSUMER_GROUP_FOR_SESS, explicitly assigns an active session to a new consumer group. The session is identified by the session identifier (SID) and serial number (SERIAL#), both of which can be derived from the V$SESSION table. This procedure is described in Table 11.8.

TABLE 11.8: SWITCH_CONSUMER_GROUP_FOR_SESS Procedure Parameters

Parameter	Description
SESSION_ID	Session identifier (SID column from the view V$SESSION)
SESSION_SERIAL	Serial number of the session (SERIAL# column from view V$SESSION)
CONSUMER_GROUP	Name of the target consumer group

For example, the following SQL switches a session to the LOW_GROUP group:

```
SQL> begin
  dbms_resource_manager.switch_consumer_group_for_sess (
     SESSION_ID => '56',
     SESSION_SERIAL=> '106',
     CONSUMER_GROUP => 'LOW_GROUP');
 end;
SQL>/


PL/SQL procedure successfully completed.
```

The second method of changing the consumer group for an active session is the SWITCH_ CONSUMER_GROUP_FOR_USER procedure. This procedure changes all active sessions for a given Oracle username. Here's an example:

```
SQL> begin
  dbms_resource_manager.switch_consumer_group_for_user (
     USER => 'BRANDON',
     CONSUMER_GROUP => 'LOW_GROUP');
 end;
SQL>/


PL/SQL procedure successfully completed.
```

This procedure identifies all sessions running under the username of BRANDON and switches them to the LOW_GROUP.

Both of these procedures also switch all parallel sessions that may have been spawned by the session or user.

Explicit consumer-group changes are not persistent. They affect only current sessions.

SWITCHING GROUPS USING *DBMS_SESSION*

If a user has been granted the switch privilege, they can use the DBMS_SESSION.SWITCH_CURRENT_CONSUMER_GROUP procedure to explicitly change the group for their current session. Table 11.9 describes the parameters for this procedure.

TABLE 11.9:   SWITCH_CURRENT_CONSUMER_GROUP Procedure Parameters

Parameter	Description
NEW_CONSUMER_GROUP	The name of the consumer group to which the session is switching.
OLD_CONSUMER_GROUP	An output parameter that returns the name of the original consumer group (before the switch).
INITIAL_GROUP_ON_ERROR	If the switch fails, this parameter controls the outcome. If TRUE, the session reverts to its original group. If FALSE, an error is raised.

When this procedure completes, it returns the name of the original consumer group back to the calling program. This is presumably so the program can retain the original group and use it to revert later in the program, if so desired. The following example shows how to call this procedure from a PL/SQL block:

```
DECLARE
   original_group varchar2(30);
   junk           varchar2(30);
BEGIN
  DBMS_SESSION.SWITCH_CURRENT_CONSUMER_GROUP(
  'MARKETING', original_group, FALSE);

< execute some SQL>

  DBMS_SESSION.SWITCH_CURRENT_CONSUMER_GROUP(
  original_group, junk, FALSE);

END;
```

This PL/SQL block switches from the current consumer group to the MARKETING group and saves the original group name in a variable named ORIGINAL_GROUP. After executing some SQL, it uses the ORIGINAL_GROUP variable to switch back to the original group.

MANAGING THE SWITCH PRIVILEGE

Before a user can switch their own consumer group, they must have been granted the switch privilege directly or have been granted a role that has been granted the switch privilege.

The switch privilege is granted to users and/or to roles through the DBMS_RESOURCE_MANAGER_ PRIVS.GRANT_SWITCH_CONSUMER_GROUP procedure. The parameters for this procedure are described in Table 11.10.

TABLE 11.10:   **GRANT_SWITCH_CONSUMER_GROUP** Procedure Parameters

Parameter	Description
GRANTEE_NAME	Username or role name receiving the grant.
CONSUMER_GROUP	Name of the consumer group to which the grantee will be allowed to switch.
GRANT_OPTION	Determines whether the grantee can, in turn, grant the switch privilege to another user. If TRUE, the grantee can grant the switch privilege to another user. If FALSE, the grantee cannot grant the switch privilege to another user.

By granting the switch privilege to roles, it is much easier to grant the privilege to entire groups of users, as shown here:

```
SQL> begin
  dbms_resource_manager_privs.grant_switch_consumer_group(
    'PROG_ROLE', 'DEVELOPERS', FALSE);
 end;
SQL>/

PL/SQL procedure successfully completed.
```

In this example, the switch privilege is granted to the PROG_ROLE role. Any user granted that role will be able to switch to the DEVELOPERS group, but they cannot grant the privilege to any other users. If the GRANT_OPTION parameter was set to TRUE, the user could, in turn, grant the same privilege to another user.

If the switch privilege is granted to PUBLIC for any consumer group, any user will be able to switch to the specified consumer group.

The switch privilege can also be revoked by using the DBMS_RESOURCE_MANAGER_PRIVS .REVOKE_SWITCH_CONSUMER_GROUP procedure. The parameters for this procedure are described in Table 11.11.

TABLE 11.11:   **REVOKE_SWITCH_CONSUMER_GROUP** Procedure Parameters

Parameter	Description
REVOKEE_NAME	Name of user or role with privileges being revoked
CONSUMER_GROUP	Name of consumer group being revoked

This procedure revokes a user's or role's privilege to switch to the specified consumer group. Here's an example:

```
SQL> begin
  dbms_resource_manager_privs.revoke_switch_consumer_group(
    'PROG_ROLE', 'DEVELOPERS');
 end;
SQL>/

PL/SQL procedure successfully completed.
```

This example revokes the privileges granted in the preceding example.

Resource Plans

DRM allocates resources among resource consumer groups based on a resource plan. A *resource plan* consists of directives specifying how resources should be distributed among resource consumer groups or other resource plans.

Resource plans prioritize resource allocation through the use of levels, with level 1 being the highest priority and level 8 being the lowest.

Simple resource plans are limited to allocating only CPU resources to a small number of consumer groups. However, they are very simple to set up, and they represent a good starting place if you're new to DRM. Simple resource plans define the resource plan, resource plan directives, and resource consumer groups all with one procedure, whereas complex plans define each separately. Simple resource plans are also classified as *single-level resource plans* because there are no subplans involved.

Complex resource plans can use any of Oracle's predefined resource-allocation methods and can include up to 32 consumer groups. Complex resource plans can also contain *subplans*. If subplans are defined, the plan would be classified as a multilevel resource plan.

There is no difference between a plan and a subplan. They are defined in exactly the same manner. A subplan is simply a plan that is nested within the scope of a top-level plan, so it is allocated resources from the top-level plan.

Resource plans have two options regarding the CPU-allocation method—EMPHASIS and RATIO—as described in Table 11.12.

TABLE 11.12 Resource Plan CPU-Allocation Methods

CPU-Allocation Method	Description
EMPHASIS	The allocated amount is treated as a percentage (in other words, 80 = 80 percent) of available CPU. EMPHASIS is valid for both single- and multilevel plans and is the only option for simple resource plans (the default).
RATIO	The allocated amount is treated as a ratio of the total CPU resources. The RATIO method can be defined only on single-level plans.

The EMPHASIS method is used most often and can be used for either single- or multilevel plans. Under the EMPHASIS method, CPU resource allocations are expressed as percentages in the plan directives.

The RATIO method can be used only on single-level plans (plans that contain directives that allocate CPU resources at level 1 only). Under the RATIO method, the CPU resource allocations are expressed as a weight in the plan directives.

For example, assume a plan containing plan directives for the PAYROLL, MARKETING, and OTHER_GROUPS consumer groups. The plan is defined to use the RATIO method for CPU allocation. Assume that the directives contain the allocations listed in Table 11.13.

TABLE 11.13 Plan Directives Using the RATIO Method

Consumer Group	CPU_P1 Parameter Setting
PAYROLL	10
MARKETING	2
OTHER_GROUPS	1

The result of these directives will allocate CPU resources using a 10:2:1 ratio. The MARKETING group will get only two CPU cycles for every 10 that the PAYROLL group receives. The OTHER_GROUPS group will get one cycle for every for every two that the MARKETING group receives.

 Examples of resource directives using both the EMPHASIS and RATIO methods are provided in the section "Resource Plan Directives" later in this chapter.

In the following sections, you will learn how to create both simple and complex resource plans. You'll also learn how to update and delete resource plans.

Creating Simple Resource Plans

Simple resource plans, though limited in their abilities and scope, offer an adequate solution for environments with only basic resource-management needs. They are distinct from complex plans in that they create a resource plan, resource-plan directives, and resource consumer groups in one simple procedure.

Simple resource plans are limited to using only the CPU resource-plan directive. This means that the only resource that can be allocated is the CPU. Simple plans also limit the total number of resource groups to eight.

Oracle provides the DBMS_RESOURCE_MANAGER.CREATE_SIMPLE_PLAN procedure for creating a simple resource plan; its parameters are described in Table 11.14 (deprecated parameters not listed).

TABLE 11.14:   CREATE_SIMPLE_PLAN Procedure Parameters

Parameter	Description
SIMPLE_PLAN	The name assigned to the plan
CONSUMER_GROUP1	The name of the first consumer group
GROUP1_PERCENT	The CPU allocation for the first consumer group
CONSUMER_GROUP2	The name of the second consumer group
GROUP2_PERCENT	The CPU allocation for the second consumer group
CONSUMER_GROUP3	The name of the third consumer group
GROUP3_PERCENT	The CPU allocation for the third consumer group
CONSUMER_GROUP4	The name of the fourth consumer group
GROUP4_PERCENT	The CPU allocation for the fourth consumer group
CONSUMER_GROUP5	The name of the fifth consumer group
GROUP5_PERCENT	The CPU allocation for the fifth consumer group
CONSUMER_GROUP6	The name of the sixth consumer group
GROUP6_PERCENT	The CPU allocation for the sixth consumer group
CONSUMER_GROUP7	The name of the seventh consumer group
GROUP7_PERCENT	The CPU allocation for the seventh consumer group

TABLE 11.14: **CREATE_SIMPLE_PLAN** Procedure Parameters *(continued)*

Parameter	Description
CONSUMER_GROUP8	The name of the eighth consumer group
GROUP8_PERCENT	The CPU allocation for the eighth consumer group

This procedure allows for the creation of up to eight consumer groups, along with their CPU allocations.

Simple resource plans always use the EMPHASIS CPU resource-allocation policy. This means that the value entered for the CPU allocations will be interpreted as a percentage of total CPU. For example, if you want to implement the specifications shown in Table 11.15, a simple resource plan can be created as in the example that follows.

```
SQL> begin
DBMS_RESOURCE_MANAGER.CREATE_SIMPLE_PLAN(
   SIMPLE_PLAN => 'DEPARTMENTS',
   CONSUMER_GROUP1 => 'PAYROLL',
   GROUP1_PERCENT => 50,
   CONSUMER_GROUP2 => 'SALES',
   GROUP2_PERCENT => 25,
   CONSUMER_GROUP3 => 'MARKETING',
   GROUP3_PERCENT => 25);
end;
SQL> /

PL/SQL procedure successfully completed.
```

TABLE 11.15: **DEPARTMENTS** Plan Specification

Group	CPU Allocation
PAYROLL	50%
SALES	25%
MARKETING	25%

When a simple plan is created, the results might be somewhat surprising. Table 11.16 shows the finished plan, and you can see that Oracle has added two additional consumer groups to it: SYS_GROUP and OTHER_GROUPS.

TABLE 11.16 Final DEPARTMENTS Plan

Level	SYS_GROUP	PAYROLL	SALES	MARKETING	OTHER_GROUPS
1	100%				
2		50%	25%	25%	
3					100%

SYS_GROUP represents the users SYS and SYSTEM.

OTHER_GROUPS is a required group that must be included in any resource plan. It ensures that users who are not assigned to any group in the active resource plan will still have resources allocated.

Notice also that the final plan is a multilevel plan and the elements that you defined are assigned to the second level. This ensures that members of the SYS_GROUP (at level 1) will have no CPU restrictions. Groups at level 2 will share CPU resources not used by level-1 groups. Likewise, users not assigned to any group in the plan (at level 3) will receive CPU time only after levels 1 and 2 have satisfied their requirements.

Creating Complex Resource Plans

Complex resource plans differ from simple resource plans in how they are defined. When you create a simple plan, you can create the plan, resource groups, and plan directives in one operation. For complex plans, each of these elements is defined and stored separately. This method offers more flexibility when building resource plans.

This method also allows for the nesting of plans, so one plan can act as a subplan of another. When plans are nested in this manner, it is referred to as a multilevel plan.

Creating a plan involves defining the name of the plan, a comment or description regarding the plan, and the methods that the plan will follow when allocating specific resources. Notice that the plan does not determine which resources it will manage. Those are predefined by Oracle. A plan defines only the method it will apply when allocating those resources.

To create a new plan, use the DBMS_RESOURCE_MANAGER.CREATE_PLAN procedure, whose parameters are described in Table 11.17.

TABLE 11.17: CREATE_PLAN Procedure Parameters

Parameter	Description
PLAN	The name of the resource plan.
COMMENT	A comment or a description of the plan.

TABLE 11.17: **CREATE_PLAN** Procedure Parameters *(continued)*

Parameter	Description
CPU_MTH	Deprecated. Use MGMT_MTH.
ACTIVE_SESS_POOL_MTH	The method of allocating session pool resources (limiting the number of active sessions). ACTIVE_SESS_POOL_ABSOLUTE is the only method available. Treats the number specified in a plan directive as the maximum number of active sessions allowed.
PARALLEL_DEGREE_LIMIT_MTH	The method of specifying degree of parallelism for any operation. PARALLEL_DEGREE_LIMIT_ABSOLUTE is the only method available. Treats the number specified in plan directives as the maximum degree of parallelism that will be allowed.
QUEUEING_MTH	The Method of allocating execution of queued sessions. FIFO_TIMEOUT is the only method available. Uses a first-in/first-out method for prioritizing sessions waiting in queue due to resource limitations.
MGMT_MTH	The method of allocating CPU resources. EMPHASIS (default): CPU will be distributed on a percentage basis for single and multilevel plans. RATIO: CPU will be distributed on a ratio basis for single-level plans.
SUB_PLAN	If TRUE, the plan can't be used as the top-level plan. Default is FALSE.

As you can see, only the PLAN, COMMENT, and MGMT_MTH parameters actually have any effect on the plan. The others (ACTIVE_SESS_POOL_MTH, PARALLEL_DEGREE_LIMIT_MTH, and QUEUEING_MTH) offer only one option, which is also the default. It is expected that future releases will expand the choices for these parameters. For the SUB_PLAN parameter, you can specify if this plan cannot be used as a top-level plan.

Therefore, a plan can be created as follows:

```
SQL> begin
  dbms_resource_manager.create_plan(
    PLAN => 'DAY',
    COMMENT => 'Use during daytime');
  end;
SQL>/

PL/SQL procedure successfully completed.
```

To verify that the resource plan was actually created, you can use the DBA_RSRC_PLANS view:

```
SQL> select plan, num_plan_directives, cpu_method
  2  from dba_rsrc_plans;

PLAN                 NUM_PLAN_DIRECTIVES CPU_METHOD
-------------------- ------------------- ----------
SYSTEM_PLAN                            3 EMPHASIS
INTERNAL_QUIESCE                      2 EMPHASIS
INTERNAL_PLAN                         1 EMPHASIS
DAY                                   1 EMPHASIS
```

As you can see, the plan was indeed created, and in fact it already has one plan directive assigned to it. Remember that Oracle requires all plans to have a directive for the OTHER_GROUPS resource group. Therefore, Oracle automatically creates this directive for you.

Creating Resource Subplans

A resource subplan is created in exactly the same manner as a resource plan. That's because there is no difference between them. A subplan is a plan. It becomes a subplan only if a higher-level plan allocates resources to it (through a resource plan directive) or if you explicitly define that it can be only a subplan when you create the plan.

For example, plan A can allocate resources to consumer groups X and Y and to plan B. Plan B is now classified as a subplan. The difference is that a top-level plan always has 100 percent of the resources available to allocate, whereas a subplan can allocate only the resources that have been allocated to it by the top-level plan.

Modifying Resource Plans

Resource plans can be modified by using the DBMS_RESOURCE_MANAGER.UPDATE_PLAN procedure. The parameters for this procedure are described in Table 11.18.

TABLE 11.18: UPDATE_PLAN Procedure Parameters

Parameter	Description
PLAN	Name of the resource plan
NEW_COMMENT	New comment
NEW_CPU_MTH	Deprecated. Use NEW_MGMT_MTH
NEW_ACTIVE_SESS_POOL_MTH	New method of allocating session pool resources
NEW_PARALLEL_DEGREE_LIMIT_MTH	New method of specifying the degree of parallelism for any operation

TABLE 11.18: UPDATE_PLAN Procedure Parameters *(continued)*

Parameter	Description
NEW_QUEUEING_MTH	New method of allocating the execution of queued sessions
NEW_MGMT_MTH	New method of allocating CPU resources

Again, keep in mind that only the first three parameters in the UPDATE_PLAN procedure will have any effect on resource plans because there are no other valid options for the others. To verify this, you can use any of the following views:

- V$ACTIVE_SESS_POOL_MTH
- V$PARALLEL_DEGREE_LIMIT_MTH
- V$QUEUEING_MTH
- V$RSRC_PLAN_CPU_MTH

These views display the valid values for each of the resource-plan allocation methods.

To change the comment on the DAY plan, see the following example:

```
SQL>  exec dbms_resource_manager.update_plan(
  PLAN => 'DAY',
  NEW_COMMENT => 'Plan for scheduled work hours');

PL/SQL procedure successfully completed.
```

Deleting Resource Plans

Resource plans can be deleted by using either the DBMS_RESOURCE_MANAGER.DELETE_PLAN procedure or the DBMS_RESOURCE_MANAGER.DELETE_PLAN_CASCADE procedure. The former removes the resource plan but leaves all subordinate objects (consumer groups, plan directives, and subplans) intact. The latter removes the resource plan, along with all subordinate objects.

If the DELETE_PLAN_CASCADE procedure attempts to delete a subordinate object that happens to also be part of the currently active plan, the delete will fail and the entire plan will be restored.

The only parameter accepted by these procedures is a valid resource plan name, as shown in this example:

```
SQL>  exec dbms_resource_manager.delete_plan('DAY');

PL/SQL procedure successfully completed.
```

Resource-Plan Directives

Resource-plan directives are the key element in creating complex resource plans. As you saw earlier in this chapter, a resource plan by itself does very little until it has resource-plan directives assigned to it. Resource-plan directives assign consumer groups to resource plans and define the resource allocations for each. In addition to consumer groups, plan directives can allocate resources to subplans.

Resource-plan directives work by specifying the owning resource plan, the target consumer group or subplan, and the resource allocations assigned to the target. Resources are allocated to the target by setting parameters for the various resource-allocation methods.

Resource-allocation methods are predefined by Oracle and, as such, are not modifiable. They represent the various methods available to DRM to allocate resources. The following methods are available:

CPU The CPU method specifies how CPU resources are to be allocated among consumer groups or subplans. Up to eight levels can be defined, allowing for the prioritization of CPU resources. For example, level 2 gets CPU only if level 1 is unable to utilize all of its allocated CPU. Therefore, level 1 has the highest priority, while level 8 has the lowest priority.

Active session pool with queuing This method limits the number of concurrent active sessions available to a consumer group. If the allocated number of sessions is reached, new session requests will be placed in a queue until an active session completes.

Degree of parallelism limit This method specifies the maximum parallel degree for any operation within a consumer group. If a higher degree is specified, it will automatically be altered down to the value specified for this parameter.

Automatic consumer-group switching This switching method allows sessions exceeding certain execution-time criteria to be dynamically switched to a different group. For example, if a session exceeds the defined execution-time threshold, it can be automatically switched to a lower priority group. This method can also be used to automatically cancel the operation or even kill the offending session.

Canceling SQL and terminating sessions This method specifies that long-running queries or long-running sessions will be automatically terminated if the execution-time threshold is exceeded.

Execution time limit The execution time-limit method specifies the maximum estimated execution time allowed for any operation. If Oracle estimates that an operation will exceed the specified execution time, it will terminate the operation and return an error. It does this before actual execution begins.

Undo pool The undo-pool method specifies the amount of undo that can be generated by a consumer group. If the group exceeds the allocated amount, the current DML statement is terminated and no other group members may perform data manipulation until undo space is freed.

Idle time limit This method specifies the maximum amount of time that a session can remain idle. If this limit is exceeded, the session will automatically be terminated. This method can also be limited to terminating only idle sessions that are blocking other sessions.

Resource-plan directives can set levels for one or more of these methods for each consumer group or subplan. However, only CPU methods may be defined for subplans. The other methods are invalid for assigning resources to subplans.

In the following sections, you will learn how to create the various types of resource-plan directives. You'll also learn how plan directives can be used to monitor and manage long-running operations. Finally, you'll learn to update and delete plan directives.

Creating Resource-Plan Directives

To create a resource-plan directive, the DBMS_RESOURCE_MANAGER.CREATE_PLAN_DIRECTIVE procedure is used. Table 11.19 describes the interface for this procedure.

TABLE 11.19: CREATE_PLAN_DIRECTIVE Procedure Parameters

Parameter	Description
PLAN	The name of the resource plan to which this directive belongs.
GROUP_OR_SUBPLAN	The name of the consumer group or subplan being allocated resources by this directive.
COMMENT	A comment or a description of the plan directive.
CPU_P1	Deprecated. Use MGMT_P1.
CPU_P2	Deprecated. Use MGMT_P2.
CPU_P3	Deprecated. Use MGMT_P3.
CPU_P4	Deprecated. Use MGMT_P4.
CPU_P5	Deprecated. Use MGMT_P5.
CPU_P6	Deprecated. Use MGMT_P6.
CPU_P7	Deprecated. Use MGMT_P7.
CPU_P8	Deprecated. Use MGMT_P8.
ACTIVE_SESS_POOL_P1	Specifies the maximum number of concurrently active sessions for a consumer group or subplan. The default is NULL, which means unlimited.

TABLE 11.19:   **CREATE_PLAN_DIRECTIVE** Procedure Parameters *(continued)*

Parameter	Description
QUEUEING_P1	The number of seconds before a job in the inactive session queue times out. The default is NULL, meaning that queued jobs will never time out.
PARALLEL_DEGREE_LIMIT_P1	The maximum degree of parallelism that can be defined for any operation. The default is NULL, meaning that no limit is imposed.
SWITCH_GROUP	The consumer group to which this session will be switched if the switch criteria is met. The default is NULL. Other options are CANCEL_SQL, which will kill the query when switch criteria is met, and KILL_SESSION, which will kill the session when the switch criteria is met.
SWITCH_TIME	The number of seconds for which a session can execute an operation before a group switch will occur. The default is NULL, meaning that there is no limit on execution time. After the operation is complete, the session remains in the new consumer group rather than reverting to its original consumer group.
SWITCH_ESTIMATE	Directs Oracle to estimate the execution time for an operation before execution begins. If the estimated time exceeds the value set for SWITCH_TIME, Oracle will perform the switch before execution of the query begins. Valid settings are TRUE and FALSE. The default is FALSE.
MAX_EST_EXEC_TIME	Directs Oracle to estimate the execution time for an operation before execution begins. If the estimated time exceeds the number of seconds defined in this parameter, the operation is not started and an ORA-07455 error is issued. The default is NULL, meaning that no estimate limit is imposed.
UNDO_POOL	Maximum kilobytes (KB) of undo that can be generated by the consumer group/subplan. The default is NULL, meaning that no limit is imposed.
MAX_IDLE_TIME	The number of seconds that a session can remain idle before the session is killed. The default is NULL, meaning that no idle time limit is imposed.
MAX_IDLE_BLOCKER_TIME	The number of seconds that a blocking session can remain idle before the session is killed. (A blocking session is a session that is locking a resource that is needed by another session.) The default is NULL, meaning that no idle time limit is imposed.

TABLE 11.19: **CREATE_PLAN_DIRECTIVE** Procedure Parameters *(continued)*

Parameter	Description
SWITCH_TIME_IN_CALL	Deprecated. Use SWITCH_FOR_CALL.
MGMT_P1	If the resource plan uses the EMPHASIS allocation method, this parameter defines the percentage of CPU allocated at level 1 for the group/subplan. If the plan uses the RATIO allocation method for CPU resources, this parameter defines the weight of CPU usage for the group/subplan. The default is NULL for all MGMT_Pn parameters, which provides no allocation of CPU resources.
MGMT_P2	The percentage of CPU allocated at level 2 for the group/subplan (if the plan uses the EMPHASIS method). Not applicable for the RATIO method. The default is NULL.
MGMT_P3	The percentage of CPU allocated at level 3 for the group/subplan (if the plan uses the EMPHASIS method). Not applicable for the RATIO method. The default is NULL.
MGMT_P4	The percentage of CPU allocated at level 4 for the group/subplan (if the plan uses the EMPHASIS method). Not applicable for the RATIO method. The default is NULL.
MGMT_P5	The percentage of CPU allocated at level 5 for the group/subplan (if the plan uses the EMPHASIS method). Not applicable for the RATIO method. The default is NULL.
MGMT_P6	The percentage of CPU allocated at level 6 for the group/subplan (if the plan uses the EMPHASIS method). Not applicable for the RATIO method. The default is NULL.
MGMT_P7	The percentage of CPU allocated at level 7 for the group/subplan (if the plan uses the EMPHASIS method). Not applicable for the RATIO method. The default is NULL.
MGMT_P8	The percentage of CPU allocated at level 8 for the group/subplan (if the plan uses the EMPHASIS method). Not applicable for the RATIO method. The default is NULL.
SWITCH_IO_MEGABYTES	The number of megabytes of I/O that a session can transfer (read and write) before action is taken. The default is UNLIMITED. Action specified by SWITCH_GROUP.
SWITCH_IO_REQS	Specifies the number of I/O requests that a session is allowed to execute before action is taken. The default is UNLIMITED. Action specified by SWITCH_GROUP.

TABLE 11.19: CREATE_PLAN_DIRECTIVE Procedure Parameters *(continued)*

Parameter	Description
SWITCH_FOR_CALL	When set to TRUE, a user session that was automatically switched to another consumer group (based on SWITCH_IO_MEGABYTES, SWITCH_IO_REQS, or SWITCH_TIME) is returned to its original consumer group when the top-level call completes. Default is NULL.

 Both SWITCH_TIME_IN_CALL and SWITCH_TIME cannot be specified in the same resource directive because they represent conflicting actions.

The following example creates a resource-plan directive for the DAY plan, which limits the parallel degree settings for the DEVELOPERS group:

```
SQL> begin
  dbms_resource_manager.create_plan_directive(
    PLAN => 'DAY',
    COMMENT => 'DEVELOPERS DAY PLAN',
    GROUP_OR_SUBPLAN => 'DEVELOPERS',
    PARALLEL_DEGREE_LIMIT_P1 => '4');
  end;
SQL> /

PL/SQL procedure successfully completed.
```

In the following sections, you will learn to create directives that define subplans. You'll also learn to create directives that create multilevel plans. Finally, you'll learn to create plans that use the consumer group switching method to manage long-running operations.

Creating Subplan Directives

To create a subplan directive, you first create a plan directive, which allocates CPU resources to another plan (which is then referred to as a subplan). The subplan still retains all of its original functionality. However, the total CPU resources it can allocate are limited to those it receives from the top-level plan.

For example, to define a subplan under the DAY plan, you would set the GROUP_OR_SUBPLAN parameter to the name of the target plan, as follows:

```
SQL> begin
  dbms_resource_manager.create_plan_directive(
    PLAN => 'DAY',
```

```
    COMMENT => 'DEPARTMENTS SUB-PLAN',
    GROUP_OR_SUBPLAN => 'DEPARTMENTS',
    MGMT_P2=> 50);
  end;
SQL> /


PL/SQL procedure successfully completed.
```

In this example, the plan DEPARTMENTS was defined as a subplan of the DAY plan and limited to 50 percent of the level-2 CPU resources.

 Subplan directives can allocate only CPU resources to a subplan.

Creating Multilevel Plan Directives

Multilevel plan directives are used to prioritize CPU allocation for consumer groups and subplans. When a plan directive is created, the parameters CPU to MGMT determine the level at which the CPU resources will be allocated to the specified group or subplan. The total resources allocated at any one level cannot exceed 100 percent.

Up to eight levels can be specified, with level 1 being the highest priority and level 8 being the lowest. Level-1 recipients share the total available CPU based on their respective MGMT_P1 parameter value. Level-2 recipients share only the CPU resources that are not consumed at level 1, and so on.

Consider this example:

```
SQL> begin
  dbms_resource_manager.create_plan_directive(
    PLAN => 'DAY',
    COMMENT => 'SYSTEM USERS',
    GROUP_OR_SUBPLAN => 'SYS_GROUP',
    MGMT_P1=> 100);
  end;
SQL> /


PL/SQL procedure successfully completed.

SQL> begin
  dbms_resource_manager.create_plan_directive(
    PLAN => 'DAY',
    COMMENT => 'DEPARTMENTS SUB-PLAN',
    GROUP_OR_SUBPLAN => 'DEPARTMENTS',
```

```
      MGMT_P2=> 50);
    end;
SQL> /

PL/SQL procedure successfully completed.

SQL> begin
  dbms_resource_manager.create_plan_directive(
    PLAN => 'DAY',
    COMMENT => 'DEVELOPERS GROUP CPU ALLOCATION',
    GROUP_OR_SUBPLAN => 'DEVELOPERS',
    MGMT_P2=> 50);
  end;
SQL> /

PL/SQL procedure successfully completed.

SQL> begin
  dbms_resource_manager.create_plan_directive(
    PLAN => 'DAY',
    COMMENT => 'OTHER_GROUPS CPU ALLOCATION',
    GROUP_OR_SUBPLAN => 'OTHER_GROUPS',
    MGMT_P3=> 100);
  end;
SQL> /

PL/SQL procedure successfully completed.
```

In this example, four directives are created for the DAY plan. The first directive allocates 100 percent of level-1 CPU resources to the SYS_GROUP group. The second directive allocates 50 percent of level-2 CPU resources to the DEPARTMENTS subplan. The third directive allocates the other 50 percent of level-2 CPU resources to the DEVELOPERS consumer group. Finally, the fourth directive allocates 100 percent of level-3 CPU resources to the OTHER_GROUPS group.

Creating Automatic Consumer Group Switching Directives

Plan directives can include options for automatically switching resource consumer groups for sessions that exceed defined thresholds. For example, a directive can dictate that any session that has an operation executing for more than 10 minutes should automatically be switched into a lower-priority group. They can also dictate that Oracle will automatically kill the query or even the session when switching thresholds are exceeded.

The key parameters in defining automatic consumer group switching are as follows:

SWITCH_TIME   The SWITCH_TIME parameter sets the maximum execution time (in seconds) allowed for any operation. A session violating this threshold is automatically switched to the group defined by the SWITCH_GROUP parameter.

The switch group is generally a group with lower priority so that the long-running operation will be allocated fewer resources. However, the switch group can also be set to the Oracle constant KILL_SESSION or CANCEL_SQL, which would result in the offending session being killed or the offending SQL operation being canceled.

Once a session has been switched to another group using this method, it will not switch back to its original consumer group, even after the offending operation has completed.

 The SWITCH_TIME and SWITCH_TIME_IN_CALL methods are mutually exclusive. Only one method may be defined in a plan directive.

SWITCH_ESTIMATE   The SWITCH_ESTIMATE parameter specifies that the Oracle optimizer should estimate the execution time of an operation before actually executing it. If the estimated time exceeds the value set in the SWITCH_TIME parameter, then the consumer group switch will occur prior to execution of the operation.

When a session is switched using this method, it will not revert to its original consumer group if the SWITCH_TIME parameter is set.

SWITCH_IO_MEGABYTES   The SWITCH_IO_MEGABYTES parameter specifies that the session that exceeds the number of megabytes transferred will be switched.

SWITCH_FOR_CALL   The SWITCH_FOR_CALL parameter, when TRUE, specifies that the session will be returned to the original consumer group after the PL/SQL block completes.

To create a plan directive that automatically cancels operations that execute for more than one hour, see the following example:

```
SQL> begin
  dbms_resource_manager.create_plan_directive(
    PLAN => 'DAY',
    COMMENT => 'LIMIT DEVELOPERS EXECUTION TIME',
    GROUP_OR_SUBPLAN => 'DEVELOPERS',
    SWITCH_GROUP => 'CANCEL_SQL',
    SWITCH_TIME => 3600);
  end;
SQL> /

PL/SQL procedure successfully completed.
```

To create a plan directive that temporarily moves DEVELOPERS sessions to a lower-priority group whenever the actual I/O transferred in exceeds 3,000 megabytes, then returns them to their original group following the completion of the PL/SQL block, see this example:

```
SQL> begin
  dbms_resource_manager.create_plan_directive(
    PLAN => 'DAY',
    COMMENT => 'SWITCH DEVELOPERS TEMPORARILY',
    GROUP_OR_SUBPLAN => 'DEVELOPERS',
    SWITCH_IO_MEGABYTES => 3000,
    SWITCH_GROUP => 'LOW_GROUP',
    SWITCH_FOR_CALL => TRUE);
  end;
SQL> /

PL/SQL procedure successfully completed.
```

This example switches the session to the LOW_GROUP consumer group prior to execution of any operation that Oracle estimates will exceed 15 minutes (900 seconds). When the operation has completed, the session will revert to the DEVELOPERS group.

Updating Resource Plan-Directives

Resource-plan directives can be updated using the DBMS_RESOURCE_MANAGER.UPDATE_PLAN_DIRECTIVE procedure. The parameters for this procedure are identical to the parameters for the CREATE_PLAN_DIRECTIVE procedure, except that the prefix NEW_ has been added to all of the modifiable parameters (for example, NEW_COMMENT, NEW_MGMT_P1, and so on).

The only parameters that cannot be modified are PLAN and GROUP_OR_SUBPLAN. All of the others can be updated.

Consider the following example:

```
SQL> begin
  dbms_resource_manager.update_plan_directive(
    PLAN => 'DAY',
    GROUP_OR_SUBPLAN => 'DEVELOPERS',
    NEW_SWITCH_ESTIMATE => FALSE);
  end;
SQL>/

PL/SQL procedure successfully completed.
```

In this example, the SWITCH_ESTIMATE setting is updated to a value of FALSE. Notice that the parameter used is NEW_SWITCH_ESTIMATE rather than SWITCH_ESTIMATE.

Real World Scenario

Runaway Processes

In our current job, our team administers (among other things) a data warehouse totaling approximately five billion rows. Due to the size of many of the tables, parallel queries drastically reduce runtime most of the time. However, we seem to encounter our share of Oracle bugs, resulting in runaway parallel processes.

For example, a query will spawn eight parallel processes and proceed normally until very near the end of the processing. Then, one process will slowly start spinning CPU cycles. If not caught early, it will eventually consume all CPU and bring the system grinding to a halt.

We've applied several patches that seem to fix the problem, but in reality we just encounter the bug (or a different one with similar effects) less often.

By using Database Resource Monitor, we were able to devise a relatively simple plan that killed sessions if they reached a very high CPU-percentage threshold. Now the runaway processes are automatically killed, and the beauty of it is that no DBA involvement is required.

Deleting Resource-Plan Directives

Resource-plan directives can be deleted using the DBMS_RESOURCE_MANAGER.DELETE_PLAN_ DIRECTIVE procedure. The only parameters required are the PLAN and GROUP_OR_SUBPLAN parameters, as shown here:

```
SQL> begin
  dbms_resource_manager.delete_plan_directive(
    PLAN => 'DAY',
    GROUP_OR_SUBPLAN => 'DEVELOPERS');
  end;
SQL>/

PL/SQL procedure successfully completed.
```

Creating and Using Database Resource Manager Components

Now that you've learned about all of the various elements of DRM individually, it's time to put them all together.

For most companies, database requirements differ depending on the time of day. For example, during normal daytime business hours, online transaction processing (OLTP) may be mission-critical, along with a small amount of report processing. After hours, however, bulk data loads and online analytical processing (OLAP) reports may take priority.

In the following sections, you'll learn how to develop complex multilevel resource plans to accommodate these types of business requirements. You'll see how all of the elements are created and associated to the plan. You'll also learn how to enable the finalized plan.

You will be provided step-by-step instructions for the creation of the plans. First, the pending area will be created. Next, the resource consumer groups will be created. After that, the resource plans will be created. And, finally, the resource-plan directives will be created to tie them all together.

Once all of the elements are in place, they will be validated and activated. Finally, you'll learn to enable the resource plans, as well as how to switch the enabled resource plan.

Creating the Pending Area

Before any new DRM elements are created, a pending area must be established to hold your new plans. The pending area is a development area where you can work on DRM elements without affecting the active DRM plan. It can be created as shown here:

```
SQL> exec dbms_resource_manager.create_pending_area();


PL/SQL procedure successfully completed.
```

Once the pending area is in place, new elements will reside there until the plan is enabled.

Creating the Resource Consumer Groups

Next, the resource consumer groups can be created. In this step, all resource consumer groups required by both resource plans will be created.

These groups can be created as follows:

```
SQL> begin
  dbms_resource_manager.create_consumer_group(
  'OLTP_GROUP','Incoming orders');
 end;
SQL>/


PL/SQL procedure successfully completed.


SQL> begin
  dbms_resource_manager.create_consumer_group(
  'DAY_REPORTS_GROUP','DAYTIME REPORTS');
 end;
SQL>/


PL/SQL procedure successfully completed.


SQL> begin
  dbms_resource_manager.create_consumer_group(
```

```
   'NIGHTLY_PROCESSING_GROUP','BULK LOADS, ETL, ETC.');
 end;
SQL>/


PL/SQL procedure successfully completed.

SQL> begin
  dbms_resource_manager.create_consumer_group(
  'OLAP_REPORTS_GROUP','OFF HOURS REPORTS');
 end;
SQL>/


PL/SQL procedure successfully completed.
```

Because the SYS_GROUP and the OTHER_GROUPS consumer groups are created automatically at Oracle installation time, there is no need to create them.

Creating the Resource Plans

Now that all the necessary consumer groups are in place, the next step is to create the resource plans. Three distinct plans are required. Both the DAY_PLAN and the OLTP_PLAN plan use the default EMPHASIS CPU-allocation method, whereas the OFF_HOURS_PLAN plan utilizes the RATIO method. Remember that the CPU resource-allocation method (CPU_MTH) sets the type of allocation used only if there is a resource-plan directive that specifies CPU allocation.

These plans can be created as shown here:

```
SQL> begin
  dbms_resource_manager.create_plan(
    PLAN => 'DAY_PLAN',
    COMMENT => 'GOVERNS NORMAL WORKING HOURS ');
  end;
SQL> /


PL/SQL procedure successfully completed.

SQL> begin
  dbms_resource_manager.create_plan(
    PLAN => 'OLTP_PLAN',
    COMMENT => 'ORDER ENTRY SUB-PLAN');
  end;
```

```
SQL> /

PL/SQL procedure successfully completed.

SQL> begin
  dbms_resource_manager.create_plan(
    PLAN => 'OFF_HOURS_PLAN',
    COMMENT => 'GOVERNS NON-WORKING HOURS',
    MGMT_MTH => 'RATIO');
  end;
SQL> /

PL/SQL procedure successfully completed.
```

Because the default CPU-allocation method is EMPHASIS, the MGMT_MTH parameter was left out when creating the first two plans. For the OFF_HOURS_PLAN plan, the CPU_MTH parameter was explicitly set.

Creating the Resource-Plan Directives

Next, the resource-plan directives need to be created. This will be done in three steps. First, the directives for the OFF_HOURS_PLAN plan will be created. Next, the directives for the OLTP_PLAN plan will be created. Finally, the directives for the DAY_PLAN plan will be created.

CREATING THE *OFF_HOURS_PLAN* PLAN DIRECTIVES

The OFF_HOURS_PLAN plan is a single-level plan using the RATIO method for CPU allocation. The plan directives can be created as follows:

```
SQL> begin
  dbms_resource_manager.create_plan_directive(
    PLAN => 'OFF_HOURS_PLAN',
    GROUP_OR_SUBPLAN => 'SYS_GROUP',
    COMMENT => 'CPU ALLOCATION FOR SYS_GROUP',
    MGMT_P1 => 10);
 end;
SQL>/

PL/SQL procedure successfully completed.

SQL> begin
   dbms_resource_manager.create_plan_directive(
     PLAN => 'OFF_HOURS_PLAN',
     GROUP_OR_SUBPLAN => 'NIGHTLY_PROCESSING_GROUP',
```

```
      COMMENT => 'CPU ALLOCATION FOR NIGHTLY JOBS',
      MGMT_P1 => 5);
  end;
SQL>/

PL/SQL procedure successfully completed.

SQL> begin
   dbms_resource_manager.create_plan_directive(
      PLAN => 'OFF_HOURS_PLAN',
      GROUP_OR_SUBPLAN => 'OLAP_REPORTS_GROUP',
      COMMENT => 'CPU ALLOCATION FOR NIGHTLY REPORTS',
      MGMT_P1 => 2);
  end;
SQL>/

PL/SQL procedure successfully completed.

SQL> begin
   dbms_resource_manager.create_plan_directive(
      PLAN => 'OFF_HOURS_PLAN',
      GROUP_OR_SUBPLAN => 'OTHER_GROUPS',
      COMMENT => 'CPU ALLOCATION FOR OTHER_GROUPS',
      MGMT_P1 => 1);
  end;
SQL>/

PL/SQL procedure successfully completed.
```

The CPU-allocation ratio for the OFF_HOURS_PLAN plan will be 10:5:2:1.

CREATING THE *OLTP_PLAN* PLAN DIRECTIVES

Next, the plan directives for the OLTP_PLAN plan can be created:

```
SQL> begin
  dbms_resource_manager.create_plan_directive(
    PLAN => 'OLTP_PLAN',
    GROUP_OR_SUBPLAN => 'OLTP_GROUP',
    COMMENT => 'CPU ALLOCATION FOR OLTP USERS',
    MGMT_P1 => 90);
  end;
SQL>/
```

```
PL/SQL procedure successfully completed.

SQL> begin
  dbms_resource_manager.create_plan_directive(
    PLAN => 'OLTP_PLAN',
    GROUP_OR_SUBPLAN => 'DAY_REPORTS_GROUP',
    COMMENT => 'CPU ALLOCATION FOR DAYTIME REPORTING',
    MGMT_P1 => 10);
 end;
SQL>/

PL/SQL procedure successfully completed.

SQL> begin
  dbms_resource_manager.create_plan_directive(
    PLAN => 'OLTP_PLAN',
    GROUP_OR_SUBPLAN => 'OTHER_GROUPS',
    COMMENT => 'CPU ALLOCATION FOR OTHER_GROUPS',
    MGMT_P2 => 100);
 end;
SQL>/

PL/SQL procedure successfully completed.
```

As you can see, the directives for the OLTP_PLAN plan allocate 90 percent of level-1 CPU resources to the OLTP_GROUP group and the other 10 percent to the DAY_REPORTS_GROUP group. One hundred percent of level-2 CPU resources are allocated to the OTHER_GROUPS group.

CREATING THE *DAY_PLAN* PLAN DIRECTIVES

Now the directives for the DAY_PLAN plan can be created:

```
SQL> begin
  dbms_resource_manager.create_plan_directive(
    PLAN => 'DAY_PLAN',
    GROUP_OR_SUBPLAN => 'SYS_GROUP',
    COMMENT => 'CPU ALLOCATION FOR SYS_GROUP',
    MGMT_P1 => 100);
 end;
SQL>/

PL/SQL procedure successfully completed.
```

```
SQL> begin
  dbms_resource_manager.create_plan_directive(
    PLAN => 'DAY_PLAN',
    GROUP_OR_SUBPLAN => 'OLTP_PLAN',
    COMMENT => 'CPU ALLOCATION FOR OLTP_PLAN SUB-PLAN',
    MGMT_P2 => 100);
 end;
SQL>/

PL/SQL procedure successfully completed.

SQL> begin
  dbms_resource_manager.create_plan_directive(
    PLAN => 'DAY_PLAN',
    GROUP_OR_SUBPLAN => 'OTHER_GROUPS',
    COMMENT => 'CPU ALLOCATION FOR OTHER_GROUPS',
    MGMT_P3 => 100);
 end;
SQL>/

PL/SQL procedure successfully completed.
```

You may have noticed that both the DAY_PLAN and OLTP_PLAN plans allocate resources to the OTHER_GROUPS group. Remember that *every* resource plan must have an allocation to the OTHER_GROUPS group. In fact, any consumer group can be assigned to more than one plan, as long as no loops are created as a result.

Validating the Pending Area

Now that all of the necessary elements have been created and defined, the contents of the pending area must be validated. Validation checks for any rule violations that may exist when the elements are grouped under their respective plans.

Validation will be done for all elements in the pending area, as shown here:

```
SQL> exec dbms_resource_manager.validate_pending_area;

PL/SQL procedure successfully completed.
```

When you're validating the pending area, no news is good news. As long as the procedure completes and no error messages are returned, the pending area has passed inspection.

WARNING If you are using SQL*Plus, make sure the SERVEROUTPUT option is on before validating. Otherwise, no error messages will be displayed onscreen. Use the SET SERVEROUTPUT ON statement to turn it on.

Submitting the Pending Area

The final step is to activate the plans by submitting the pending area. This step moves the DRM elements to the data dictionary. Once the elements are in the data dictionary, they are considered active and eligible to be enabled (resource plans) or referenced by enabled plans (resource consumer groups and resource-plan directives). Remember that this step does not actually enable a plan; it only makes it eligible to be enabled.

Also, when you're submitting a pending area, Oracle automatically performs the same validation that was done in the previous step. Therefore, the validation step discussed earlier is technically unnecessary. However, it is still a good idea from a debugging standpoint, especially when designing very complex plans.

The pending area can be submitted as shown:

```
SQL> exec dbms_resource_manager.submit_pending_area;

PL/SQL procedure successfully completed.
```

Again, the absence of error messages signifies successful submission of the pending area to the data dictionary. The plans are now active (in other words, residing in the data dictionary) and can be enabled at any time.

Enabling the Resource Plans

When a resource plan is enabled, it governs all resource allocation for the Oracle instance. Only one resource plan may be enabled at any given time, and the enabled plan can be switched at any time.

There are two methods in which resource plans can be enabled:

- Initialization parameter (at instance startup time)
- ALTER SYSTEM statement

Initialization parameter method   In the init.ora file, the RESOURCE_MANAGER_PLAN initialization variable can be set to the name of any active plan. For example, the following code can be added to the init.ora file:

```
RESOURCE_MANAGER_PLAN = DAY_PLAN;
```

When the instance is restarted, DAY_PLAN will be the enabled plan for the instance.

ALTER SYSTEM statement method   Resource plans can also be enabled dynamically by using the ALTER SYSTEM statement, as shown here:

```
ALTER SYSTEM SET RESOURCE_MANAGER_PLAN = 'DAY_PLAN' [SCOPE = BOTH];
```

This dynamically enables the DAY_PLAN plan for the instance. There is no need to shut down the instance in this case. The optional SCOPE clause can be used in an spfile environment to change the setting both in memory and in the spfile (to make the change persist through a shutdown).

Switching the Enabled Resource Plan

The top-level plans that were created in this section are designed to govern specific times of the day. The DAY_PLAN plan is to be used during normal business hours, while the OFF_HOURS_PLAN plan is to be used on nights and weekends.

The enabled plan can be changed at any time by using the ALTER SYSTEM command, as you saw earlier, but it would be very inconvenient to have to always make this change manually. Instead, you can use Oracle's scheduler to schedule the switch so that it is executed automatically based on a specific schedule.

One caveat of scheduling resource-plan switches, however, is that you may encounter a situation in which you don't want the plans to change.

For instance, if your nightly data loads are larger than normal and might exceed the cutoff time, you may want to delay the switch until the loads have finished. This will ensure that the loads have all the resources necessary to complete.

Rather than having to alter the job in the scheduler, you can simply execute the following statement:

```
SQL> ALTER SYSTEM
  SET RESOURCE_MANAGER_PLAN = 'FORCE:OFF_HOURS_PLAN';

System altered.
```

When the prefix FORCE: is added to the name of the plan, Oracle will restrict the active plan from being changed by the scheduler. The scheduler will still attempt to make the change, but it will fail.

When the nightly loads are finished, the restriction can be lifted by reissuing the identical ALTER SYSTEM statement without the FORCE: prefix, as shown here:

```
SQL> ALTER SYSTEM
  SET RESOURCE_MANAGER_PLAN = 'OFF_HOURS_PLAN';

System altered.
```

With the restriction lifted, the resource plan can now be changed manually (or by the scheduler).

I/O Calibration with DRM

Also included in the DRM is a procedure that enables the DBA to test the I/O performance of the database's storage system. The supplied DBMS_RESOURCE_MANAGER.CALIBRATE_IO procedure executes an I/O intense read of the database files and determines the maximum sustainable IOPS (I/O requests per second) and MBPS (megabytes of I/O per second). The results are written to the DBA_RSRC_IO_CALIBRATE table. Because it is an intense workload, choose to run this procedure when it will have the least impact on your customers. This tool is a valid representative of storage performance capabilities using the Oracle database engine.

Resource Manager Statistics in AWR

The Automatic Workload Repository (AWR) introduces new views for DRM statistics. The DBA_HIST_RSRC_PLAN and DBA_HIST_RSRC_CONSUMER_GROUP views retain historical versions of the statistics in V$RESOURCE_PLAN and V$RESOURCE_CONSUMER_GROUP. The view V$RSRCMGRMETRIC shows resource utilization and waits due to DRM.

DBRM is the background process for the Database Resource Manager.

Summary

In this chapter, you learned about Automatic Memory Management, Automatic Shared Memory Management, manually configuring SGA parameters, Automatic PGA Memory Management, resumable space operations, transportable tablespaces, transportable databases, Segment Shrink operations, and the Database Resource Manager.

With memory management, you learned that Oracle highly recommends that you configure Automatic Memory Management and leave memory tuning and management to the Oracle instance. If you as the DBA for a database understand the application and know how to tune the SGA and PGA to achieve better results, then choose Automatic Shared Memory Management and Automatic PGA Memory Management. If you need more granular control, then manually configure your SGA and/or PGA.

You learned about resumable space allocations and how to configure, detect, and remedy suspended transactions.

You learned about transportable tablespaces and transportable databases. With transportable tablespaces, you can convert a tablespace set to run on a different platform with a different endianness using the RMAN convert clause. You cannot transport an entire database to a different endian format, but you can convert it to run on a different platform with the same endianness.

The Segment Shrink feature can be used to reclaim space both above and below the high-water mark while a segment remains online and in use.

You learned about the Oracle Database Resource Manager (DRM) and how to configure it to manage resources on your Oracle database. You can set up a pending area to hold all of the DRM objects as they are created or modified. Objects in the pending area need to be validated before moving them into the data dictionary. We discussed the requirements that each object must pass before being declared valid by the DRM. You learned that submitting the pending area activates all the objects therein and moves them into the data dictionary. To put all of the elements together, you can build a complex resource-plan schema using PL/SQL packages and then enable the plan on the database.

Exam Essentials

Know the difference between Automatic Memory Management and Automatic Shared Memory Management. Be able to distinguish the characteristics, pros, and cons of Automatic Memory Management. Understand how to configure Automatic Memory Management vs. Automatic Shared Memory Management. Understand the difference between the MEMORY_TARGET and MAX_MEMORY_TARGET and the difference between SGA_TARGET and SGA_MAX_SIZE. Understand how to dynamically increase or decrease the amount of memory usable by the instance.

Know how to manually configure the SGA. Understand how to disable Automatic Memory Management and Automatic Shared Memory Management and how to manually configure the individual SGA pools. Know the names of the pools you can configure manually.

Know how to configure Automatic PGA Memory Management. Understand how to explicitly and implicitly configure Automatic PGA Memory Management. Understand what instance PGA memory is used for. Understand the meaning of and how to configure Automatic PGA Memory using PGA_AGGREGATE_TARGET.

Know how to configure the Database Resource Manager. Be able to create, update, and delete DRM objects. Be aware of the pending area and the need to validate and submit objects to the data dictionary to make them active. Know that submitting the pending area enforces validation, so it isn't strictly necessary to validate as a separate step. Know the various methods of enabling DRM (through ALTER SYSTEM and through initialization parameters). Understand the various allocation methods.

Be able to assign users to Database Resource Manager groups. Know all the methods of assigning user sessions to DRM groups. Know the names of the DBMS_RESOURCE_MANAGER procedures for assigning groups. Be aware of the switch privilege and how it is granted. Be aware of the DBMS_SESSION procedure that users can use to change their own group.

Know how to create resource plans within groups. Understand all the steps involved in creating resource plans, both simple and complex. Know the difference between single- and multilevel resource plans. Understand the allocation methods used. Know what constitutes a top-level plan and a subplan.

Be able to specify directives for allocating resources to consumer groups. Know how to create and manage plan directives to allocate resources to consumer groups and subplans. Understand which allocation methods are available for directives to groups as opposed to directives to subplans.

Review Questions

1. Which of the following Oracle features is enabled by setting a nonzero value for the MEMORY_TARGET initialization parameter?

    A. Automatic PGA Memory Management

    B. Automatic SGA Memory Management

    C. Automatic Shared Memory Management

    D. Automatic Memory Management

    E. Manual SGA Memory Management

    F. None of the above

2. By setting the value of MEMORY_TARGET to zero and setting the value of SGA_TARGET to a nonzero value, you will enable which of the following memory-management options?

    A. Automatic PGA Memory Management

    B. Automatic SGA Memory Management

    C. Automatic Shared Memory Management

    D. Automatic Memory Management

    E. Manual SGA Memory Management

    F. None of the above

3. For Oracle 11*g*, Oracle strongly recommends that you configure your database to use which of the following memory-management features?

    A. Automatic PGA Memory Management

    B. Automatic SGA Memory Management

    C. Automatic Shared Memory Management

    D. Automatic Memory Management

    E. Manual SGA Memory Management

    F. None of the above

4. To manually configure the SGA components using Oracle Enterprise Manager Memory Advisor, you can set values for which of the following initialization parameters? (Choose all that apply.)

    A. DB_CACHE_SIZE

    B. SHARED_POOL_SIZE

    C. LARGE_POOL_SIZE

    D. JAVA_POOL_SIZE

    E. SGA_MAX_SIZE

    F. SORT_AREA_SIZE

5. When manually configuring the SGA, which of the following parameter changes requires an instance restart to take effect?

   A. DB_CACHE_SIZE

   B. SHARED_POOL_SIZE

   C. LARGE_POOL_SIZE

   D. JAVA_POOL_SIZE

   E. SGA_MAX_SIZE

   F. SORT_AREA_SIZE

6. Using Oracle Enterprise Manager to set SGA pool values manually, for which of the following pools does Oracle EM offer advice to set the value appropriately? (Choose all that apply.)

   A. DB_CACHE_SIZE

   B. SHARED_POOL_SIZE

   C. LARGE_POOL_SIZE

   D. JAVA_POOL_SIZE

   E. SGA_MAX_SIZE

   F. SORT_AREA_SIZE

7. In Oracle 11g, by default which one of the following conditions implicitly enables Automatic PGA Memory Management?

   A. Setting a nonzero value for SGA_TARGET

   B. Configuring Automatic Shared Memory Management

   C. Configuring Automatic Memory Management

   D. Setting a nonzero value for SGA_MAX_SIZE and PGA_AGGREGATE_TARGET

   E. None of the above

8. Automatic PGA Memory Management eliminates the need to manually configure which of the following initialization parameters? (Choose all that apply.)

   A. SORT_AREA_SIZE

   B. HASH_AREA_SIZE

   C. BITMAP_MERGE_AREA_SIZE

   D. CREATE_BITMAP_AREA_SIZE

   E. PGA_AGGREGATE_TARGET

9. When tuning Automatic PGA Memory Management, which of the following views will provide the information specified?

    A. The V$PGA_TARGET_ADVICE view shows the predicted cache hit-ratio improvement if you increase PGA_AGGREGATE_TARGET.

    B. The V$PGA_TARGET_ADVICE view shows how the V$SQL_WORKAREA histogram will change if you change the value of PGA_AGGREGATE_TARGET.

    C. The V$PGA_TARGET_ADVICE_HISTOGRAM view shows how the V$SQL_WORKAREA_HIS-TOGRAM will change if you switch between Manual and Automatic PGA Memory Management.

    D. The V$PGA_TARGET_ADVICE view shows how performance will improve for the different work areas if you switch from Manual to Automatic PGA Memory Management.

10. To enable resumable space allocation for the instance, which of the following initialization parameters should you set to a nonzero value?

    A. RESUMABLE_SPACE_TIME

    B. RESUMABLE_SPACE

    C. RESUMABLE_TIME

    D. RESUMABLE_TIMEOUT

    E. TIME_RESUMABLE

11. Which of the following describes how a distributed resumable transaction behaves?

    A. The resumable setting on the initiating session determines the resumable conditions for the entire distributed transaction.

    B. The resumable setting for the initiating instance determines the resumable conditions for the entire distributed transaction.

    C. The resumable setting on the initiating session controls only that part of the transaction that occurs within the local instance; remote resumable settings determine the behavior of the distributed parts of the transaction.

    D. None of the above.

12. Which of these components correctly identify the unique value of the NAME column in the DBA_RESUMABLE view?

    A. Username, instance number, session ID

    B. Instance number, username, session ID

    C. Instance number, session ID, username

    D. Username, session ID, instance number

    E. None of the above

13. Which of the following are included in a transportable tablespace set? (Choose all that apply.)

   A.   The datafiles that make up a self-contained group of tablespaces required for copy

   B.   The system tablespace

   C.   An export of the tablespace metadata

   D.   The spfile

   E.   All of the above

14. The following query will provide what information about transportable tablespaces for the current database? (Choose all that apply.)

```
select d.platform_name "Source", t.platform_name
 "Compatible Targets", endian_format
 from v$transportable_platform t, v$database d
 where t.endian_format = (select endian_format
     from   v$transportable_platform t,
                             v$database d
                     where d.platform_name =
                     t.platform_name);
```

   A.   The list of target platforms having the same endian format as the source database

   B.   The list of target platforms requiring endian conversion

   C.   The list of target platforms that will not require endian conversion

   D.   The list of all target platforms that can receive transportable tablespaces from the source database

   E.   None of the above

15. When exporting metadata for the transportable tablespaces, what is the correct next step after confirming endian format?

   A.   Export the tablespaces using data pump.

   B.   Determine if the transportable set is self-contained.

   C.   Convert the datafiles using RMAN.

   D.   Copy the datafiles from source to destination.

16. Which of the following are prerequisite steps to transport a database? (Choose all that apply.)

   A.   Query the V$TRANSPORTABLE_PLATFORMS view in the source database to determine if the intended destination is listed.

   B.   Verify that there are no restrictions or limitations that the source or destination database may encounter.

   C.   Verify that the source and destination have the same Oracle version, critical updates, patch-set version, and patch-set exceptions.

   D.   Determine if you will perform the conversion on the source or destination platform.

   E.   None of the above.

17. Which of the following supplied functions is used to identify external tables, directories, and BFILES?

A. DBMS_TDB.CHECK_DIRECTORIES

B. DBMS_TDB.CHECK_EXTERNAL

C. DBMS_TDB.CHECK_BFILE

D. DBMS_TDB.CHECK_EXT

18. Which of the following is a prerequisite for running DBMS_TDB.CHECK_DB to a successful completion?

A. The database must be in read-write mode.

B. The database must have no external files.

C. The database must open in read-only mode.

D. The database must be mounted but not opened.

19. Which of the following options describes Segment Shrink?

A. Reclaims space above and below the high-water mark without using additional space

B. Moves rows to a new physical location, resetting the high-water mark, but uses additional space during the operation

C. Deallocates space above the high-water mark that is currently not in use

D. None of the above

20. For which of the following can you use Segment Shrink? (Choose all that apply.)

A. Heap tables

B. Tables with function-based indexes

C. Indexes

D. Partitions and subpartitions

E. None of the above

21. When shrinking a table segment, you choose to shrink all the indexes for that table using the SHRINK SPACE command. Which clause should you use?

A. INCLUDING DEPENDENCIES

B. INCLUDING DEPENDENCIES CASCADE

C. COMPACT

D. CASCADE

E. None of the above

22. Which of these represent the main components of Database Resource Manager? (Choose all that apply.)

    A. Resource consumer groups

    B. Resource plans

    C. Resource-plan groups

    D. Resource-plan directives

    E. All of the above

23. Every resource plan must contain an allocation to which consumer group?

    A. LOW_GROUP

    B. SYS_GROUP

    C. DEFAULT_GROUP

    D. BASE_GROUP

    E. OTHER_GROUPS

24. Which DBMS_RESOURCE_MANAGER procedure prioritizes consumer-group mappings?

    A. CREATE_MAPPING_PRIORITY

    B. SET_MAPPING_PRIORITY

    C. SET_MAPPING_ORDER

    D. PRIORITIZE_MAPPING_ORDER

    E. This functionality is not available through the DBMS_RESOURCE_MANAGER package.

25. Within a resource-plan definition, what differentiates a top-level plan from a subplan?

    A. A subplan has the PLAN_SUB parameter value set to SUB.

    B. A top-level plan has the GROUP_OR_PLAN parameter set to the name of the subplan in the resource-plan definition.

    C. There is no difference in the resource-plan definition.

    D. A subplan always has the CPU_MTH parameter value set to RATIO.

    E. The string TOP_LEVEL is appended to the name of top-level resource plans.

Answers to Review Questions

1. D. The MEMORY_TARGET initialization parameter is used to set the total memory shared between SGA and PGA for Automatic Memory Management.

2. C. The SGA_TARGET initialization parameter is used to set the total memory for the SGA for Automatic Shared Memory Management.

3. D. For Oracle 11*g*, Oracle highly recommends that you let the instance manage all the memory automatically, using the Automatic Memory Management feature.

4. A, B, C, D. Each of these are SGA components that are configured manually if you choose not to manage the SGA using Automatic Shared Memory Management or all memory using Automatic Memory Management. The SGA_MAX_SIZE is not an SGA component but represents the maximum value for the combined SGA pool sizes. The SORT_AREA_SIZE is a manual PGA initialization parameter.

5. E. The SGA_MAX_SIZE parameter can be changed in the spfile using OEM, but it cannot be changed dynamically for the instance. It requires an instance restart to take effect. You can change options A, B, C, and D without requiring a restart as long as the sum of the values remains less than the value for SGA_MAX_SIZE. SORT_AREA_SIZE is not an SGA parameter.

6. A, B. Advice can be obtained for the buffer cache DB_CACHE_SIZE parameter and the shared pool SHARED_POOL_SIZE parameter. Advice is not offered for the large pool, Java pool, or the maximum SGA size. SORT_AREA_SIZE is not an SGA parameter.

7. B. By default, Oracle 11*g* is configured for Automatic Memory Management. If you configure Automatic Shared Memory Management and make no other changes, you will implicitly enable Automatic PGA Memory Management. Setting SGA_TARGET to a nonzero value doesn't immediately enable Automatic Shared Memory Management because you may still have Automatic Memory Management enabled. Setting the parameter SGA_MAX_SIZE to nonzero puts a cap on manual SGA configuration, but again it does not implement Manual Shared Memory Management. The value of PGA_AGGREGATE_TARGET is relevant only if Automatic Memory Management is not configured, so you must also set MEMORY_TARGET to zero for it to take effect.

8. A, B, C, D. Each of these are work areas in the PGA is configured manually if Automatic PGA Memory Management is not enabled. You enable Automatic PGA Memory Management when you disable Automatic Memory Management and set a nonzero value for the PGA_AGGREGATE_TARGET parameter.

9. A. When operating in Automatic PGA Memory Management mode, you can seek advice on increasing or decreasing the value of PGA_AGGREGATE_TARGET to influence the hit ratio for the PGA work areas.

10. D. For the instance, set the initialization parameter RESUMABLE_TIMEOUT to a nonzero value, representing the number of seconds for which an operation will suspend until an action is taken to repair the condition or the operation aborts due to the condition.

11. C. In a distributed transaction, the remote RESUMABLE_TIMEOUT initialization parameter applies to the remote part of the transaction, and the remote-session resumable setting applies. Also, local resumable settings do not apply to the remote part of the distributed transactions.

12. D. For the DBA_RESUMABLE view, the NAME column is populated with the username, session ID, and instance number.

13. A, C. The transportable tablespace set is the self-contained group of tablespaces that encapsulate the objects that you wish to transport along with the exported metadata for the tablespaces.

14. A, C. The SQL query returns the list of target platforms that have the same endian format and do not require RMAN conversion between source and destination databases.

15. B. Execute the DBMS_TTS.TRANSPORT_SET_CHECK procedure using the proposed list of tablespaces for the transportable set. Optionally, the last parameter should be TRUE to verify referential integrity constraints.

16. B, C, D. Option A is incorrect because the correct view name is V$DB_TRANSPORTABLE_PLATFORM. You'll need to verify that there are no restrictions or limitations such as storage or memory, verify that the version levels are the same, and determine where you will perform the conversion.

17. B. The DBMS_TDB.CHECK_EXTERNAL function returns the list of external files that will need to be copied to the destination system. The other answers are not valid.

18. C. The DBMS_TDB.CHECK_DB function must execute with the database open and in read-only mode.

19. A. The Segment Shrink feature reclaims space above and below the high-water mark without using additional space to perform an operation.

20. A, C, D. The Segment Shrink feature can be used on tables, indexes, and partitions, but not on tables with function-based indexes.

21. D. The Segment Shrink SHRINK SPACE command specifying the table name, and then including the CASCADE clause, will reclaim space from the table segment and all dependent index segments, as reported by the DBMS_SPACE.OBJECT_DEPENDENT_SEGMENT function.

22. A, B, D. The main components are resource consumer groups, resource plans, and resource-plan directives. There is no such thing as a resource-plan group.

23. E. The OTHER_GROUPS consumer group is assigned to sessions whose assigned group is not contained in the enabled plan. Therefore, Oracle requires that an allocation be made so that no sessions will be completely deprived of resources.

24. B. The SET_MAPPING_PRIORITY procedure allows for prioritization based on the session attribute type.

25. C. There is no concept of a subplan in the resource-plan definition. Only in a resource-plan directive can a subplan be identified.

Chapter

12

Using the Scheduler to Automate Tasks

ORACLE DATABASE 11*g*: ADMINISTRATION II EXAM OBJECTIVES COVERED IN THIS CHAPTER:

✓ **Automating Tasks with the Scheduler**

    ▪ Create a job, program, and schedule

    ▪ Use a time-based or event-based schedule for executing Scheduler jobs

    ▪ Create lightweight jobs

    ▪ Use job chains to perform a series of related tasks

✓ **Administering the Scheduler**

    ▪ Create Windows and Job Classes

    ▪ Use advanced Scheduler concepts to prioritize jobs

As an Oracle database administrator, you might find that an inordinate amount of your time is spent performing routine tasks. Unfortunately, routine tasks come with the territory, and that is unlikely to change in the foreseeable future. Handling these routine tasks manually is an invitation for problems. Mistakes can be made, or even worse, the tasks will be forgotten and not run at all.

The Oracle Scheduler feature makes the scheduling of routine tasks a simple matter. The Oracle Scheduler is a major advancement over the old DBMS_JOB scheduling system found in previous Oracle versions. It corrects many of the nagging idiosyncrasies while adding powerful new features such as the calendaring syntax, a flexible method of defining repeat intervals for Scheduler jobs. DBMS_JOB is now deprecated, so we will focus on using the Scheduler to manage jobs in the Oracle database.

In this chapter, you will learn how the Scheduler works and how to create and manage Scheduler elements. First, you will get an overview of the terminology and components that make up the Scheduler. You will learn the underlying architecture of the Scheduler and how all the pieces fit together.

Next, you will learn about Scheduler jobs and how to create and manage them. You will also learn about job groups and how they can be used to simplify the management of jobs as well as to prioritize job execution.

You will also learn about Scheduler programs, which define the work that will be performed. You'll learn to create and manage schedules, which define when jobs will be run and how often they will be repeated. You'll learn how to define complex repeat intervals using Oracle's calendaring syntax.

Next, you will learn about windows and window groups, which allow you to switch resource plans based on a schedule. You'll learn about job classes, which allow you to group jobs together based on business requirements. You'll learn about lightweight jobs, which are used for high-frequency, low-utilization programs. We'll introduce the concept of the job chain, which allows you to implement dependency-based scheduling. And, last, you will learn about the Scheduler views that are available to you.

Automating Tasks with the Scheduler

The main functionality of any enterprise scheduling system is the ability to schedule tasks to execute at a specific date and time. These can be recurring tasks that run at preset intervals or one-time tasks set to execute immediately or at some point in the future.

To achieve this functionality, the Scheduler uses several distinct components to specify scheduled tasks:

Jobs   A *job* instructs the Scheduler to run a specific program at a specific time on a specific date.

Programs   A *program* contains the code (or a reference to the code) such as PL/SQL code or a binary executable that needs to be run to accomplish a task. It can also contain parameters that should be passed to the program at runtime. A program can be stored as an independent object that can be referenced by many jobs.

Schedules   A *schedule* contains a start date, an optional end date, and a repeat interval. With these elements, an execution schedule can be calculated. A schedule can be stored as an independent object that can be referenced by many jobs.

Windows   A *window* identifies a recurring block of time during which a specific resource plan should be enabled to govern resource allocation for the database. For instance, the weekend may be classified as a maintenance window, and you can enable a resource plan that allocates the bulk of the system resources to administrative users.

Job classes   A *job class* is a logical method of classifying jobs with similar attributes. Job groups define specific attributes that will be inherited by all jobs assigned to the group. They also simplify management by allowing collections of jobs to be manipulated as one object.

Window groups   A *window group* is a logical method of grouping windows. They simplify the management of windows by allowing the members of the group to be manipulated as one object. Unlike job groups, window groups don't set default characteristics for windows that belong to the group.

Chains   A *chain* consists of two or more Scheduler programs that are linked together to meet an objective. A chain is an implementation of dependency scheduling, where the outcome of one job determines which job or jobs will execute next.

These basic components make up the bulk of Oracle's Scheduler facility. Their design encourages building flexible, reusable components shared by many scheduled jobs.

The Scheduler also offers a powerful and flexible *calendaring syntax* that is used to specify recurring task executions. This new syntax allows for the specification of complex date and time requirements. It also eliminates many of the shortcomings of DBMS_JOB, such as schedule creep (where the start time of a task was directly affected by the start time of the previous execution of that task).

Last, the Scheduler allows the execution of non-Oracle-related programs and scripts. This means that the Scheduler can be used not only to execute SQL and PL/SQL, but also operating-system executable programs. Therefore, most of your tasks can be scheduled in a common place.

Exploring the Scheduler Architecture

Understanding how to use the Scheduler begins with understanding the underlying architecture upon which the Scheduler functionality is built. This is not to say that you have to be able to name every locking mechanism and memory structure used in the Scheduler, any more than a person needs to know the ignition sequence of their car in order to drive it. Rather, it implies that a high-level knowledge of the underlying Scheduler processes will help you create more logical Scheduler objects and enable you to troubleshoot problems associated with the Scheduler.

In the following sections, you will learn about these topics:

- The job table, which houses all the active jobs within the database

- The job coordinator, a key Oracle process that ensures that jobs are being run on schedule

- Job slaves, processes that carry out the execution of jobs under the guidance of the job coordinator

- The architecture in Real Application Clusters (RAC) environments and how it differs only slightly from a stand-alone database environment

- Special considerations for Data Guard

The Job Table

The Scheduler *job table* is the master container for all enabled jobs in the database. This table stores information about all jobs, including the objects referenced by the job, the owner of the job, and the next run date. It also stores statistical information about jobs, such as the number of times the job has run and the number of times the job has failed. And it contains the STATE column, which contains the current state of the job (for example, RUNNING, SCHEDULED, BROKEN).

The information stored in the job table can be viewed through the *_SCHEDULER_JOBS view. For example, the following query will show the state of all jobs in the table as well as their next run date:

```
SQL> select owner, job_name, state
  2  from dba_scheduler_jobs;


OWNER      JOB_NAME             STATE
---------- -------------------- ------------
SYS        PURGE_LOG            SCHEDULED
SYS        GATHER_STATS_JOB     RUNNING
```

As you can see in this example, the GATHER_STATS_JOB is currently running, while the PURGE_LOG job is scheduled to run at some point in the future. If you really want to know when the PURGE_LOG job will run, you could include the NEXT_RUN_DATE column in your query and see exactly when it will run next.

The Job Coordinator

The *job coordinator* is an Oracle background process with the responsibility of ensuring that jobs are run on schedule. The job coordinator regularly queries the job table and copies job information to a memory cache for improved performance when the job is executed.

The Oracle database itself monitors job schedules and starts the job-coordinator process (if it is not already started) when a job needs to be executed. The job coordinator pulls the job information from the memory cache and passes it to a job-slave (described in the next section) process for execution.

The job coordinator controls all aspects of the job-slave pool of processes, so it can remove dormant slave processes and spawn new processes as needed to meet the needs of the Scheduler.

 The background process for the job coordinator is cjqNNN. There is one job-coordinator process per instance.

The Job-Slave Processes

Job-slave processes are tasked with carrying out the execution of job programs assigned to them by the Scheduler. When a job slave receives the job information from the coordinator, it sets to work collecting all the metadata that it needs to carry out the request. This metadata includes things such as the program arguments and privilege information.

When it is ready to execute the program, the job slave creates a new session as the owner of the job, starts a transaction within the session, and then executes the job. When the job is complete, the transaction is committed and the session is closed by the job slave. Next, the slave performs the following actions:

- Reschedules the job if required.
- Updates the STATUS column to a value of COMPLETED in the job table for the current job.
- Updates the RUN_COUNT column to increment the current value by 1 in the job table for the current job. If necessary, updates the failure and retry count.
- Inserts an entry into the job log table.
- Cleans up.
- Looks for any new work that needs to be done.

If no new work is found, the job-slave process will sleep until it is called again by the coordinator or until it is removed from the system by the job coordinator.

RAC Considerations

The Scheduler architecture in an Oracle Real Application Clusters (RAC) environment is the same as in a stand-alone instance, with the following exceptions:

- Each instance in the cluster will have its own job coordinator.

- The job coordinators can communicate with one another to share information.

- Jobs can be defined with a service affinity (they should run on a specific service) as opposed to an instance affinity (they should run on a specific instance). If a job is assigned to a service consisting of two instances, even if one instance is down, the other can execute the job normally.

- If there is service affinity and more than one instance in the service is available, the Scheduler will attempt to balance job workload across instances in the service.

- If there is no service affinity, the Scheduler will attempt to balance the workload across all available instances.

- If there is instance affinity and the instance is down, none of the jobs with an affinity to that instance will run until the instance is back up.

Aside from these exceptions, the Scheduler architecture in a RAC environment is the same as described previously.

 As mentioned earlier, there is one job-coordinator process per instance. There is only one job table per database.

Data Guard Considerations

With Oracle 11g, the Scheduler can run jobs taking into consideration whether the database is a physical or logical standby in an Oracle Data Guard configuration.

- Changes made to the Scheduler on the primary database are applied to the physical standby.

- If you want the job to run on the logical standby only after it becomes the primary, then set the database_role attribute to PRIMARY using the DBMS_SCHEDULER.SET_ ATTRIBUTE procedure.

- If you want the job to run on the logical standby only if it is in the logical-standby role, then set the database_role attribute to LOGICAL STANDBY using the DBMS_SCHEDULER. SET_ATTRIBUTE procedure.

Aside from these exceptions, the Scheduler architecture in a RAC environment is the same as described previously.

Exploring Common Administration Tools

The Oracle Scheduler is implemented through a PL/SQL package named DBMS_SCHEDULER. This package offers a collection of procedures that are used to create and manage Scheduler objects (jobs, programs, schedules, windows, job classes, window groups, and chains). Each of these object types will be covered thoroughly in this chapter.

Most of the procedures in the DBMS_SCHEDULER package are specific to a certain object type. The object type can be derived from the name of the procedure. For example, the CREATE_PROGRAM procedure is obviously specific to program objects.

However, because all Scheduler objects share some common attributes, there are also procedures that work with any Scheduler object type. These procedures play an important role in the management of Scheduler objects, so they warrant thorough coverage. However, due to their "global" nature, they will be covered in the following sections, separate from any specific object type.

You will learn about the following DBMS_SCHEDULER procedures:

- ENABLE
- DISABLE
- SET_ATTRIBUTE
- SET_ATTRIBUTE_NULL

You will also learn about any special cases that may exist within the different Scheduler object types.

Using the *ENABLE* Procedure

With the exception of schedules, all Scheduler objects have a common attribute named ENABLED. The attribute is a Boolean (TRUE or FALSE) value that identifies whether the object is eligible for use by the Scheduler.

Because schedule objects do not have an ENABLED attribute, they cannot be enabled or disabled. They are always enabled by default.

Therefore, to be eligible for use in the Scheduler, the ENABLED attribute must be set to TRUE. By default, only schedule objects are enabled at creation time, because they cannot be disabled. All other objects will be disabled by default when they are created.

To enable an object, the DBMS_SCHEDULER.ENABLE procedure is used. The procedure accepts only one argument, NAME, which designates one of the following:

- The name of one specific object
- A comma-separated list of objects

For example, here's how to enable one specific object:

```
SQL> begin
  2  dbms_scheduler.enable('BACKUP_JOB');
  3  end;
  4  /
```

PL/SQL procedure successfully completed.

To enable multiple objects, a comma-separated list can be passed in. Note that the entire list is enclosed in single quotes. Therefore, the list is submitted as a single parameter, as shown here:

```
SQL> begin
  2  dbms_scheduler.enable(
  3   'BACKUP_PROGRAM, BACKUP_JOB, STATS_JOB');
  4  end;
  5  /
```

PL/SQL procedure successfully completed.

The list of objects can also contain both groups and individual objects:

```
SQL> begin
  2  dbms_scheduler.enable(
  3   'BACKUP_JOB_GROUP, STATS_JOB, SYS.WINDOW_GROUP_1');
  4  end;
  5  /
```

PL/SQL procedure successfully completed.

There are a couple of special cases that should be noted about enabling group objects:

- When a job group is enabled, all members of that job group will be enabled.
- When a window group is enabled, only the window group object is enabled. Windows that are members of the group are not enabled.
- When a window or window group is referenced in the ENABLE procedure, it must always be prefixed with the SYS schema name as shown in the preceding example (SYS.WINDOW_GROUP_1).

Using the *DISABLE* Procedure

When a Scheduler object is disabled, it is ineligible for use by the Scheduler. Disabling a Scheduler object is accomplished by setting the object's ENABLED attribute to FALSE.

To disable an object, the DBMS_SCHEDULER.DISABLE procedure is used. This procedure accepts two parameters: NAME and FORCE. The NAME parameter designates one of the following:

- The name of one specific object
- A comma-separated list of objects

The FORCE parameter is a Boolean (TRUE or FALSE) value that tells the procedure how to handle the request if dependencies exist. The default value is FALSE.

There are two situations that could be classified as dependencies:

- A job object that references a program object is considered to be dependent on that object.
- If an instance of an object is currently running (for example, a window is open or a job is running), there may be a dependency issue.

If any dependencies are found, the value of the FORCE parameter will determine the ultimate outcome of the DISABLE procedure.

WARNING   The purpose of the FORCE parameter is not to cascade the changes to dependent objects. The purpose is to make you aware of dependencies. No changes will be made to dependent objects.

The effect of the FORCE option varies between object types. The differences are listed in Table 12.1.

TABLE 12.1   Effects of DISABLE with the FORCE Option

Object Type	Effect
Job	If the FORCE attribute is FALSE: If an instance of the job is currently running, the procedure will fail. If the FORCE attribute is TRUE: The job is disabled, but the currently running instance is allowed to finish.
Schedule	N/A
Program	If the FORCE attribute is FALSE: If the program is referenced by any job, the procedure will fail. If the FORCE attribute is TRUE: The program will be disabled. Jobs that reference the program will not be disabled but will fail at runtime if the program is still disabled.
Window	If the FORCE attribute is FALSE: If the window is open or referenced by any job, the procedure will fail. If the FORCE attribute is TRUE: The procedure will succeed in disabling the window. If that window is open at the time the DISABLE procedure is called, it will not be affected. Jobs that reference the window will not be disabled.
Window group	If the FORCE attribute is FALSE: If any member windows are open or if any member windows are referenced by a job object, the DISABLE procedure will fail. If the FORCE attribute is TRUE: The window group will be disabled. Any open window that is a member of the group will continue to its end. Jobs that reference the window group as their schedule will not be disabled.

If an object has no dependencies, using the DISABLE procedure will disable any valid Scheduler object regardless of the value of the FORCE parameter.

For example, use the following command to disable one specific object:

```
SQL> begin
  2   dbms_scheduler.disable('BACKUP_JOB');
  3   end;
  4   /


PL/SQL procedure successfully completed.
```

To disable multiple objects, a comma-separated list can be passed in. Note that the entire list is enclosed in single quotes. Therefore, the list is submitted as a single parameter. In this example, the FORCE option is also set to TRUE:

```
SQL> begin
  2   dbms_scheduler.disable(
  3    'BACKUP_PROGRAM, BACKUP_JOB, STATS_JOB',TRUE);
  4   end;
  5   /


PL/SQL procedure successfully completed.
```

The list of objects can also contain both groups and individual objects:

```
SQL> begin
  2   dbms_scheduler.disable(
  3    'BACKUP_JOB_GROUP, STATS_JOB, SYS.WINDOW_GROUP_1');
  4   end;
  5   /


PL/SQL procedure successfully completed.
```

There are a couple of special cases that should be noted about disabling group objects:

- Disabling a window group does not disable jobs that reference the group. However, those jobs will fail when they try to execute.
- Disabling a window group does not affect members of the group. They will continue to function normally.

Setting Attributes

You might be surprised to find that the DBMS_SCHEDULER package does not have an ALTER procedure of any kind. This is because Scheduler objects are collections of attributes. To make a change to an object requires setting its *attributes*. Therefore, to alter a Scheduler object, the DBMS_SCHEDULER.SET_ATTRIBUTE and DBMS_SCHEDULER.SET_ATTRIBUTE_NULL procedures are used.

In the following sections, you will learn to use these procedures with all types of Scheduler objects.

The SET_ATTRIBUTE procedure sets an attribute for any type of Scheduler object. The SET_ATTRIBUTE_NULL procedure, on the other hand, sets any attribute to NULL for any type of Scheduler object. This is useful for "unsetting" an attribute.

The only attribute that cannot be altered (for any type of Scheduler object) is the name of the object.

When the attributes on an object are changed, Oracle will attempt to disable the object before making the changes. When the attribute has been successfully altered, Oracle will reenable the object automatically. If the SET_ATTRIBUTE procedure fails, the object will remain disabled (and an error message is returned).

Using the SET_ATTRIBUTE procedure does not affect instances of the object that are currently executing. Changes made will affect only future instantiations of the object.

The SET_ATTRIBUTE procedure accepts three parameters:

NAME   The name of the Scheduler object.

ATTRIBUTE   The name of the attribute to be changed.

VALUE   The new value for the attribute. The procedure is overloaded to accept a value of any applicable datatype, so no conversion is necessary when setting values for different datatypes.

The SET_ATTRIBUTE_NULL procedure accepts only two parameters:

NAME   The name of the Scheduler object.

ATTRIBUTE   The name of the attribute, which should be set to NULL.

In the preceding section, you learned that an object was considered enabled when the ENABLED attribute was set to a value of TRUE. Therefore, you can enable or disable an object by using the SET_ATTRIBUTE procedure, as shown here:

```
SQL> begin
  2  dbms_scheduler.set_attribute (
  3  name => 'TEST_JOB',
  4  attribute => 'ENABLED',
  5  value => TRUE);
  6 end;
  7 /

PL/SQL procedure successfully completed.
```

To remove the end date from a schedule, the SET_ATTRIBUTE_NULL procedure can be used to set the attribute to NULL, as shown here:

```
SQL> begin
  2   dbms_scheduler.set_attribute_null (
  3   name => 'TEST_SCHEDULE',
  4   attribute => 'END_DATE');
  5   end;
  6 /

PL/SQL procedure successfully completed.
```

Using Scheduler Jobs

A Scheduler job defines a specific program to be executed, the arguments (or parameters) to be passed to the program, and the schedule defining when the program should be executed. It also specifies other characteristics, such as logging options, job priority, and so on.

Many of these characteristics are explicitly set at job-creation time through the CREATE_JOB procedure. However, others are inherited from the job class to which the job is assigned. If a job is not explicitly assigned to a job class, these characteristics will be inherited from a job class named DEFAULT_JOB_CLASS.

In the following sections, you will learn how to administer the various aspects of Scheduler jobs. You will learn to create, copy, and alter jobs to achieve your scheduling needs. You will learn how to run jobs and how to stop jobs that are running. You will learn how to enable and disable jobs and, finally, how to drop jobs that are no longer needed.

Creating Jobs

Scheduler jobs can be created by using the DBMS_SCHEDULER.CREATE_JOB procedure. As you will recall, a job combines a program and a schedule for execution of that program. Therefore, these are the elements that you must define when creating a new job.

Depending on the program that the job uses, you may also need to set job arguments. These are parameters that will be passed to the program at execution time. Job arguments can be set by using the SET_JOB_ARGUMENT and/or SET_JOB_ANYDATA_VALUE procedures in the DBMS_SCHEDULER package.

Jobs also have *job attributes* that control certain behaviors of the job. Many of these can be set through the CREATE_JOB procedure, while others are inherited from the job class to which the job is assigned (or from the DEFAULT_JOB_CLASS class, as mentioned previously).

For example, job attributes such as JOB_TYPE, JOB_ACTION, and REPEAT_INTERVAL can all be defined at job-creation time. Other attributes, such as MAX_FAILURES, LOGGING_LEVEL, and JOB_PRIORITY, are inherited from the job class.

A job is stored like any other database object, so it is vital that a valid object name is used when creating jobs. The job name must also be unique within the schema in which it is created. Like other database objects, jobs can be created in a different schema by prefixing the job name with a schema name.

In the following sections, you will learn which attributes define a Scheduler job. You will also learn how to administer all aspects of Scheduler job objects.

Job Attributes

Scheduler jobs have a specific set of attributes that you can set to define the characteristics of the job. These attributes can be set at job-creation time through the following CREATE_JOB procedure parameters:

JOB_NAME   The JOB_NAME parameter specifies the name assigned to the new job. Because jobs are stored like any other database object, standard Oracle naming requirements are enforced for jobs. This means that the job name must not only be a valid Oracle object name; it must also be unique within the schema.

JOB_TYPE   The JOB_TYPE parameter specifies the type of job that will be created. This is a required parameter and cannot be excluded. It can be any one of the following:

PLSQL_BLOCK   The job will execute an anonymous PL/SQL block. Anonymous PL/SQL block jobs do not accept job or program arguments, so the number of arguments must be set to 0.

STORED_PROCEDURE   The job will execute a PL/SQL stored procedure. When you use PL/SQL's External Procedure feature, the PL/SQL procedure could be a wrapper to call a Java stored procedure or an external C routine.

EXECUTABLE   The job will execute a program that is external to the database. An external job is any program that can be executed from the operating system's command line. ANYDATA arguments are not supported with a job or program type of executable.

JOB_ACTION   The JOB_ACTION attribute specifies the code to be executed for this job.

For a PL/SQL block, the Scheduler will automatically wrap the JOB_ACTION code in its own PL/SQL block prior to execution. Therefore, JOB_ACTION can be a complete PL/SQL block or one or more lines of valid PL/SQL code. Therefore, both of the following examples are valid:

```
'BEGIN update employee set salary = salary*2
where employee_name like 'EVANS'; commit; END;'
```

```
'update employee set salary = salary*2
where employee_name like 'EVANS'; commit;'
```

For a stored procedure, the value should be the name of the stored procedure, as in this example:

```
'DBMS_SESSION.SET_ROLE(''PAYROLL_USER'');'
```

For an executable, the value is the name of the executable, including the full path name and applicable command-line arguments. If environment variables are required, we suggest that the executable be wrapped in a shell script that defines the environment before executing the program.

For example, specifying `'/prod/bin/big_load.sh full'` would execute the `big_load.sh` script and pass in one argument with the value of `full`.

NUMBER_OF_ARGUMENTS   The NUMBER_OF_ARGUMENTS parameter specifies the number of arguments that the job accepts. The range is 0 (default) to 255.

PROGRAM_NAME   The PROGRAM_NAME parameter specifies the name of the program associated with this job. The program name must be the name of an existing program object.

START_DATE   The START_DATE parameter specifies the first date that the job should be run. If both the START_DATE and REPEAT_INTERVAL parameters are NULL, the job will be run as soon as it is enabled.

The START_DATE parameter is used as a reference date when the REPEAT_INTERVAL parameter uses a calendaring expression. In this situation, the job will run on the first date that matches the calendaring expression *and* is on or after the date specified in the START_DATE parameter.

> The Scheduler cannot guarantee that a job will execute at an exact time because the system may be overloaded and thus resources may be unavailable.

REPEAT_INTERVAL   The REPEAT_INTERVAL parameter specifies how often the job should be repeated. This parameter can be specified using either a calendaring or a PL/SQL expression. If this parameter is NULL, the job will run only once (at the scheduled start time).

SCHEDULE_NAME   The SCHEDULE_NAME parameter specifies the name of the schedule associated with this job. It can optionally specify a window or window group associated with the job.

END_DATE   The END_DATE parameter specifies the date when the job will expire. After the date specified, the job will no longer be executed; the STATE of the job will be set to COMPLETED, and the ENABLED flag will be set to FALSE.

If this parameter is set to NULL, the job will repeat forever. However, if the MAX_RUNS or MAX_FAILURES parameters are set, the job will stop if either of these thresholds is met.

COMMENTS   The COMMENTS parameter allows the entry of a comment to document the job.

ENABLED   The ENABLED parameter specifies whether the job is created in an enabled state. A value of TRUE means the job will be enabled. By default, all jobs are created disabled, so the default value for this parameter is FALSE. A disabled job will exist as an object in the database, but it will never be processed by the job coordinator.

AUTO_DROP   The AUTO_DROP parameter specifies whether the job will be automatically dropped once it has been executed (for nonrepeating jobs) or when its status is changed to COMPLETED (for repeating jobs).

The default value for this parameter is TRUE, meaning the job will be dropped from the database. If it is set to FALSE, the jobs are not dropped and their metadata is retained in the database until they are explicitly dropped using the DBMS_SCHEDULER.DROP_JOB procedure.

Identifying the *CREATE_JOB* Procedure Options

Jobs are created by using the DBMS_SCHEDULER.CREATE_JOB procedure. The CREATE_JOB procedure is an *overloaded procedure*. If you are not familiar with procedure overloading, it simply means that the procedure can accept a variety of different parameter combinations. Oracle will execute the version of the procedure that matches the parameter list that is passed in. For a more thorough explanation, see the sidebar "Overloading Procedures and Functions."

Overloading Procedures and Functions

Overloading allows you to create multiple versions of a procedure or function. Each version has the same name but a different parameter list. When an overloaded procedure or function is called, Oracle will execute the version with the parameter list matching the parameters that have been passed in.

The power of overloading lies in the ability to make a single function or procedure that will work with differing datatypes or data elements. For example, if you want to create a function that returns a date in *DD-MM-YYYY* format, you could overload the function to accept date, string, or numeric datatypes. The function could be defined as shown here:

```
FUNCTION conv_date (dt IN DATE)
   <CODE GOES HERE>
   RETURN VARCHAR2;

FUNCTION conv_date (dt IN VARCHAR2)
   <CODE GOES HERE>
   RETURN VARCHAR2;

FUNCTION conv_date (
   mon IN NUMBER,
   day IN NUMBER,
   year IN NUMBER
   )
   <CODE GOES HERE>
   RETURN VARCHAR2;
```

By overloading the function, you can use the same function name regardless of how the date is passed in.

Using the *CREATE_JOB* Procedure

Now that you have been introduced to the options available with the CREATE_JOB procedure, you should have a feel for how Scheduler jobs are created. The following example creates a job that will run once every year to enact cost-of-living adjustments for all employees:

```
SQL> begin
  2   dbms_scheduler.create_job (
  3   job_name => 'LNE_job',
  4   job_type => 'PLSQL_BLOCK',
  5   job_action => 'update employee set salary = salary*1.05;',
  6   start_date => '10-OCT-2008 06:00:00 AM',
  7   repeat_interval => 'FREQ=YEARLY',
  8   comments => 'Cost of living adjustment');
  9   end;
 10   /

PL/SQL procedure successfully completed.
```

To verify that the job was created, you can query the DBA|ALL|USER_SCHEDULER_JOBS view, as shown here:

```
SQL> select job_name, enabled, run_count
  from user_scheduler_jobs;

JOB_NAME           ENABLED   RUN_COUNT
------------------------ ----------
LNE_JOB            FALSE         0
```

As you can see from the results, the job was indeed created, but it's not enabled because the ENABLE attribute was not explicitly set in the CREATE_JOB procedure.

 By default, jobs are created disabled. You must explicitly enable a job before it will become active and scheduled.

Copying Jobs

Jobs can be copied by using the DBMS_SCHEDULER.COPY_JOB procedure. This procedure accepts only two parameters: OLD_JOB and NEW_JOB. These parameters represent the name of the source and destination job names, respectively.

A copied job will be identical to the original job, with the following exceptions:

- The new job will have a different name.
- The new job will be created in a disabled state.

The COPY_JOB procedure can be used as shown in the following example:

```
SQL> begin
  2  dbms_scheduler.copy_job('LNE_JOB','RAISE_JOB');
  3  end;
  4  /


PL/SQL procedure successfully completed.
```

In the example, a new job named RAISE_JOB was created as a copy of the LNE_JOB job. To verify, the USER_SCHEDULER_JOBS view can be queried, as shown here:

```
SQL> select job_name, enabled
  2  from user_scheduler_jobs;


JOB_NAME                     ENABL
---------------------------- -----
LNE_JOB                      TRUE
RAISE_JOB                    FALSE
```

As you can see, the job was indeed created, and even though the LNE_JOB job is enabled, the RAISE_JOB job is disabled.

Running Jobs

The Scheduler allows scheduled jobs to be run outside of their normal schedule through the DBMS_SCHEDULER.RUN_JOB procedure. This procedure is useful for testing a newly created job or for re-executing a job that failed previously. It doesn't affect the existing schedule of the job, nor does it require the creation of a separate, one-time-only job.

The RUN_JOB procedure accepts the JOB_NAME and USE_CURRENT_SESSION parameters. The USE_CURRENT_SESSION parameter is a Boolean (TRUE or FALSE) value that determines the method in which the job will be run. If this parameter is set to FALSE (the default value), the job will be submitted to the job Scheduler for normal asynchronous execution.

If the parameter is set to TRUE, the job will be executed synchronously using the current user session. This means that as soon as the procedure is executed, the job will run. Therefore, control will not be returned to your user session until the job execution is complete, as you can see here:

```
SQL> begin
  2  dbms_scheduler.run_job('DAILY_ETL',TRUE);
  3  end;
  4  /


<JOB RUNS HERE>
```

```
PL/SQL procedure successfully completed.
SQL>
```

Keep in mind that only an enabled job may be run using the RUN_JOB procedure.

Stopping Jobs

A running job can be stopped by using the DBMS_SCHEDULER.STOP_JOB procedure. When a job is stopped in this manner, the Scheduler attempts to stop the job in a graceful manner by means of an interrupt mechanism. When that's successful, control is returned to the slave process running the job, which will set the status of the job to STOPPED.

Optionally, a user with the MANAGE_SCHEDULER privilege can set the FORCE parameter to TRUE. This causes Oracle to terminate the process running the job and stops the job much faster, in most cases.

The STOP_JOB procedure can be called as follows:

```
SQL> begin
  2  dbms_scheduler.stop_job(job_name => 'LNE_JOB',
  3  force => TRUE);
  4  end;
  5  /

PL/SQL procedure successfully completed.
```

WARNING   When a job is stopped using the STOP_JOB procedure, only the most recent transaction is rolled back. If the job has performed any commits prior to the time when it is stopped, data inconsistency may result.

Dropping Jobs

Jobs can be dropped by using the DBMS_SCHEDULER.DROP_JOB procedure. This procedure removes the job object completely from the database. If an instance of the job is running when you issue the DROP_JOB procedure, an error will result. If you set the FORCE option to TRUE, Oracle will issue an implicit STOP_JOB procedure to kill the current instance and then drop the job.

The DROP_JOB procedure can be called as follows:

```
SQL> begin
  2  dbms_scheduler.drop_job(job_name => 'LNE_JOB',
  3  force => TRUE);
  4  end;
  5  /

PL/SQL procedure successfully completed.
```

In Exercise 12.1, you'll create a job, copy it, run it, stop it, and then drop it.

EXERCISE 12.1

Getting Comfortable with Jobs

For this exercise, we'll create a job, copy it, run it, stop it, then drop it.

1. Create a table, and then create a job using dbms_scheduler.create_job.

```
create table LNE_TEST (x DATE);
begin
  dbms_scheduler.create_job (
  job_name => 'LNE_job',
  job_type => 'PLSQL_BLOCK',
  job_action => 'insert into LNE_TEST select sysdate from dual;',
  start_date => '30-NOV-2008 10:05:00 PM',
  repeat_interval => 'FREQ=YEARLY',
  comments => 'Cost of living adjustment');
end;
/
```

2. Copy the newly created job using dbms_scheduler.copy_job.

```
begin
   dbms_scheduler.copy_job('LNE_JOB','CSTAY_JOB');
end;
/
```

3. Now run the job using dbms_scheduler.run_job.

```
begin
  dbms_scheduler.run_job('LNE_JOB',TRUE);
end;
/
```

4. Try stopping the job using dbms_scheduler.stop_job. If the job already finished, modify the program so that the job will run longer so that you have the opportunity to stop it. (Hint, modify the program to loop, so that you have a chance to stop it).

```
begin
  dbms_scheduler.stop_job(job_name => 'LNE_JOB',
  force => TRUE);
end;
/
```

5. Now drop the job using `dbms_scheduler.drop_job`.

```
begin
  dbms_scheduler.drop_job(job_name => 'LNE_JOB',
  force => TRUE);
end;
/
```

Using Scheduler Programs

A program defines the action that will occur when a job runs. It can be a PL/SQL block, a stored procedure, or an operating-system executable. In the previous section, you learned to define a program within the confines of the `CREATE_JOB` procedure. However, programs can also be created as independent objects that can be reused by many different jobs. And because programs can also accept arguments, they offer flexibility and encourage reuse.

In the following sections, you will learn the different attributes that define a Scheduler program object. You will learn how to create new programs and how to drop them. You will also learn to define arguments for programs.

Program Attributes

Scheduler programs have a specific set of attributes that you can set to define their characteristics. These attributes can be set at creation time through the following `CREATE_PROGRAM` procedure parameters:

PROGRAM_NAME The `PROGRAM_NAME` parameter specifies the name assigned to the new program. Because programs are stored like any other database object, standard Oracle object-naming requirements are enforced for programs. This means that the program name must not only be a valid Oracle object name; it must also be unique within the schema.

PROGRAM_TYPE The `PROGRAM_TYPE` parameter specifies the type of program that will be created. This is a required parameter and cannot be excluded. It can be any one of the following:

PLSQL_BLOCK The program is an anonymous PL/SQL block. Anonymous PL/SQL block jobs do not accept job or program arguments, so the `NUMBER_OF_ARGUMENTS` attribute must be set to 0.

STORED_PROCEDURE The program is a PL/SQL stored procedure. When you use PL/SQL's External Procedure feature, the PL/SQL procedure could be a wrapper to call a Java stored procedure or an external C routine.

EXECUTABLE   The program is external to the database. An external program is any program that can be executed from the operating system's command line.

PROGRAM_ACTION   The PROGRAM_ACTION attribute specifies the code to be executed. For a PL/SQL block, the Scheduler automatically wraps the PROGRAM_ACTION code in its own PL/SQL block prior to execution. Therefore, this attribute can be a complete PL/SQL block or one or more lines of valid PL/SQL code.

NUMBER_OF_ARGUMENTS   The NUMBER_OF_ARGUMENTS parameter specifies the number of arguments that the job accepts. The range is 0 (the default) to 255.

ENABLED   The ENABLED parameter specifies whether the job is created in an enabled state. A value of TRUE means the program will be enabled. By default, all programs are created disabled, so the default value for this parameter is FALSE.

COMMENTS   The COMMENTS parameter allows the entry of a comment to document the program.

Creating Programs

New programs can be created by using the DBMS_SCHEDULER.CREATE_PROGRAM procedure. This procedure creates a new program object that can in turn be called by job objects. The procedure's parameters match the list of attributes described in the previous section.

Programs, like jobs, are stored as independent schema objects. Therefore, they must have unique names within the schema, and they must conform to Oracle's standards for valid object naming.

To create a program that executes a stored procedure, see the following example:

```
SQL> begin
  2  dbms_scheduler.create_program(
  3  program_name => 'STATS_PROGRAM',
  4  program_type => 'STORED_PROCEDURE',
  5  program_action => 'DBMS_STATS.GATHER_SCHEMA_STATS',
  6  number_of_arguments => 1,
  7  comments => 'Gather stats for a schema');
  8  end;
  9  /

PL/SQL procedure successfully completed.
```

This example creates a reusable program that will gather statistics for a schema. As you can see, the program requires one argument, which is the name of the schema. The argument can be defined by using the DEFINE_PROGRAM_ARGUMENT procedure, as shown here:

```
SQL> begin
  2  dbms_scheduler.define_program_argument(
```

```
 3  program_name => 'STATS_PROGRAM',
 4  argument_position => 1,
 5  argument_type => 'VARCHAR2');
 6  end;
SQL> /
```

PL/SQL procedure successfully completed.

 You may have noticed that the example of the DEFINE_PROGRAM_ARGUMENT procedure doesn't specify a name for the argument. The ARGUMENT_NAME parameter is available, but it's completely optional.

This program can now be used by a job object, and the schema name can be passed in as an argument. Therefore, the same program can be used by many jobs, each gathering statistics for a different schema.

Arguments can be dropped from programs as well. The DBMS_SCHEDULER.DROP_PROGRAM_ARGUMENT procedure allows arguments to be dropped either by name or by the position of the argument. The following examples show how an argument may be dropped by specifying its position:

```
SQL> begin
 2  dbms_scheduler.drop_program_argument(
 3  program_name => 'STATS_PROGRAM',
 4  argument_position => 1);
 5  end;
SQL> /
```

PL/SQL procedure successfully completed.

This example shows how an argument may be dropped by specifying its name:

```
SQL> begin
 2  dbms_scheduler.drop_program_argument(
 3  program_name => 'STATS_PROGRAM',
 4  argument_name => 'SCHEMA_NAME');
 5  end;
SQL> /
```

PL/SQL procedure successfully completed.

Dropping Programs

Program objects can be dropped through the use of the DBMS_SCHEDULER.DROP_PROGRAM procedure. This procedure removes the program entirely from the database. If existing job definitions include the program that you are attempting to drop, the drop will fail. However, if you set the FORCE parameter to TRUE, the program will be dropped and the referencing jobs will become disabled.

The following example drops the STATS_PROGRAM program and disables any referencing jobs:

```
SQL> begin
  2  dbms_scheduler.drop_program (
  3  program_name => 'STATS_PROGRAM',
  4  force => TRUE);
  5  end;
SQL> /

PL/SQL procedure successfully completed.
```

Using Schedules

Schedules define when jobs run as well as when windows are opened. (Windows will be covered later in this chapter.) Like jobs and programs, schedules are stored objects and follow all the same naming requirements. When schedules are saved as independent objects, they can be used by multiple jobs.

Schedules define not only when a job will start, but also how often the job will be repeated. This is known as the repeat interval. Oracle's Scheduler offers two ways to define the interval: using PL/SQL expressions or using the powerful new calendaring syntax introduced in Oracle 10g.

The Scheduler can schedule job execution based on the following methods:

- Time-based
- Event-based
- Dependency

In time-based scheduling, you define the time and date that you would like a job to run and repeat. Event-based scheduling allows you to start a job based on some event that signals the Scheduler. In dependency scheduling, the Scheduler runs jobs based on the results of previous jobs in a defined chain.

In the following sections, you will learn which attributes define a schedule object. You will learn how to create and drop schedules. You will also learn how to define repeat intervals using the calendaring syntax.

Schedule Attributes

Schedule objects have a specific set of attributes that you can set to define the characteristics of the schedule. These attributes can be set at creation time through the following CREATE_ SCHEDULE procedure parameters:

SCHEDULE_NAME   The SCHEDULE_NAME parameter specifies the name of the schedule. Because schedules are stored like any other database object, standard Oracle object-naming requirements are enforced for schedules. This means that the schedule name must not only be a valid Oracle object name it must also be unique within the schema.

START_DATE   The START_DATE parameter specifies the first date that the schedule is valid. The START_DATE parameter is used as a reference date when the REPEAT_INTERVAL parameter uses a calendaring expression. In this situation, the job runs on the first date that matches the calendaring expression *and* is on or after the date specified in the START_DATE parameter.

END_DATE   The END_DATE parameter specifies the date when the schedule will expire. After the date specified, the job will no longer be executed; the STATE of the job will be set to COMPLETED, and the ENABLED flag will be set to FALSE.

If this parameter is set to NULL, the job will repeat forever. However, if the MAX_RUNS or MAX_FAILURES parameter is set, the job will stop if either of these thresholds is met.

REPEAT_INTERVAL   The REPEAT_INTERVAL parameter specifies how often the schedule should be repeated. This parameter can be specified using either a calendaring or a PL/SQL expression. If this parameter is NULL, the job will run only once (at the scheduled start time).

COMMENTS   The COMMENTS parameter allows the entry of a comment to document the schedule.

Creating Schedules

Schedules are created using the DBMS_SCHEDULER.CREATE_SCHEDULE procedure. By default, schedules are created with access to the PUBLIC role. Therefore, no privileges need to be granted to allow other users to use the schedule.

The following example creates a schedule that repeats every night at 8:00 p.m.:

```
SQL> begin
  2  dbms_scheduler.create_schedule(
  3  schedule_name => 'NIGHTLY_8_SCHEDULE',
  4  start_date => SYSTIMESTAMP,
  5  repeat_interval => 'FREQ=DAILY; BYHOUR=20',
  6  comments => 'Runs nightly at 8:00 PM');
  7  end;
SQL> /

PL/SQL procedure successfully completed.
```

Setting Repeat Intervals

Oracle's calendaring syntax offers tremendous flexibility when it comes to defining repeat intervals. The syntax includes a set of elements that offer different methods of specifying repeating dates. By mixing and matching these elements, you can generate fairly complex repeat intervals. Table 12.2 describes the clauses and their usage.

TABLE 12.2 Calendaring Syntax Element Descriptions

Name	Description
FREQ	The FREQ parameter defines the frequency type. This parameter is required. The following values are valid: YEARLY, MONTHLY, WEEKLY, DAILY, HOURLY, MINUTELY, and SECONDLY.
INTERVAL	The INTERVAL element specifies how often the recurrence repeats. For example, if FREQ is set to DAILY, then an INTERVAL value of 1 (the default value) means that the job will execute every day. A value of 2 means that the job would execute every other day, and so on. The maximum value is 999.
BYMONTH	The BYMONTH element specifies the month or months in which you want the job to execute. The months can be represented numerically (1–12) or using three-letter abbreviations (JAN–DEC). Multiple months should be separated by commas.
BYWEEKNO	The BYWEEKNO element specifies the week of the year as a number. It follows the ISO-8601 standard, which defines the week as starting with Monday and ending with Sunday. It also defines the first week of a year as the first week in which most days fall within the Gregorian year.
BYYEARDAY	The BYYEARDAY element specifies the day of the year as a number. Positive numbers that are greater than 59 will be affected by leap day. For example, 60 would evaluate to March 1 on non-leap years but would evaluate to February 29 on leap years. Instead, negative numbers can be used. For example, –7 will always evaluate to December 25.
BYMONTHDAY	The BYMONTHDAY element specifies the day of the month as a number. Negative numbers can be used to count backward. For example, –1 will always evaluate to the last day of the month.
BYDAY	The BYDAY element specifies the day of the week using a three-letter abbreviation (MON, TUE, and so on). Monday is always the first day of the week. You can also prepend the BYDAY element with a number representing the occurrence of the specified day. For example, if FREQ is set to MONTHLY, you can specify the last Friday of the month by using –1FRI.
BYHOUR	The BYHOUR element specifies the hour on which the job is to run. Valid values are 0–23.

TABLE 12.2 Calendaring Syntax Element Descriptions *(continued)*

Name	Description
BYMINUTE	The BYMINUTE element specifies the minute on which the job is to run. Valid values are 0–59.
BYSECOND	The BYSECOND element specifies the second on which the job is to run. Valid values are 0–59.

Keep in mind that certain rules apply when using the calendaring syntax. These rules will aid you in creating accurate schedules:

- The first element defined must always be the frequency. All other elements are optional and can appear in any order.

- Elements should be separated by a semicolon, and each element can be represented no more than once.

- Lists of values within an element should be separated by commas. They do not need to be ordered.

- Calendaring statements are not case sensitive, and white space is allowed between elements.

- The BYWEEKNO element can be used only when the FREQ element is set to YEARLY. By default, it returns all days in the week, so a BYDAY setting would be required to limit the days.

- Negative numbers are allowed with certain BY elements. For example, months have different numbers of days, so defining the last day of every month is not possible by using a single, positive number. Instead, you can specify BYMONTHDAY=-1, which will always return the last day of the month. Fixed-size elements such as BYMONTH, BYHOUR, and so on do not support negative numbers.

- The BYDAY element generally specifies the day of the week. However, when used in conjunction with a frequency of YEARLY or MONTHLY, you can add a positive or negative number in front of the day to achieve greater specificity. For example, a FREQ value set to MONTHLY and a BYDAY value set to -1SAT would specify the last Saturday of every month.

- The calendaring syntax always considers Monday the first day of the week.

- The calendaring syntax does not allow you to specify time zones or daylight savings time adjustments. Instead, the region defined in the schedule's START_DATE attribute is used to determine the time zone/daylight savings time adjustments.

To help you get more familiar with the calendaring syntax, Table 12.3 provides examples that demonstrate different repeat intervals and the syntax used to achieve them.

TABLE 12.3   Calendaring Syntax Examples

Goal	Expression
Every Monday	FREQ=WEEKLY; BYDAY=MON;
Every other Monday	FREQ=WEEKLY; BYDAY=MON; INTERVAL=2;
Last day of each month	FREQ=MONTHLY; BYMONTHDAY=-1;
Every January 7	FREQ=YEARLY; BYMONTH=JAN; BYMONTHDAY=7;
Second Wednesday of each month	FREQ=MONTHLY; BYDAY=2WED;
Every hour	FREQ=HOURLY;
Every 4 hours	FREQ=HOURLY; INTERVAL=4;
Hourly on the first day of each month	FREQ=HOURLY; BYMONTHDAY=1;
15th day of every other month	FREQ=MONTHLY; BYMONTHDAY=15; INTERVAL=2

Testing Repeat Intervals

One issue inherent in defining schedule repeat intervals is testing. How do you make sure you didn't make a mistake in your logic? To address that issue, Oracle offers the DBMS_SCHEDULER .EVALUATE_CALENDAR_STRING procedure. This procedure allows you to pass in a calendaring syntax expression and a start date, and it will return the time and date that the job will execute next. Optionally, you can also instruct the procedure to show the next execution time after a certain date, thereby allowing you to see execution dates in the future. Table 12.4 lists the parameters for the EVALUATE_CALENDAR_STRING procedure and describes their usage.

TABLE 12.4:   **EVALUATE_CALENDAR_STRING** Procedure Parameters

Parameter	Description
CALENDAR_STRING	The calendar expression to be evaluated.
START_DATE	The date after which the repeat interval becomes valid.
RETURN_DATE_AFTER	Instructs the procedure to return only execution dates that will occur after the date specified in this parameter. This allows you to see dates and times far out into the future. By default, Oracle uses the current SYSTIMESTAMP.

Parameter	Description
NEXT_RUN_DATE	This is an out parameter (the procedure will return this value to the calling program) of type TIMESTAMP that shows the date and time of the next execution.

To use the EVALUATE_CALENDAR_STRING procedure, you will need to use PL/SQL that accepts a return value of type TIMESTAMP, as shown here:

```
SQL>  DECLARE
  2    start_date TIMESTAMP;
  3    return_date_after TIMESTAMP;
  4    next_run_date TIMESTAMP;
  5  BEGIN
  6    start_date := to_timestamp_tz(
  7  '10-OCT-2008 10:00:00','DD-MON-YYYY HH24:MI:SS');
  8    DBMS_SCHEDULER.EVALUATE_CALENDAR_STRING(
  9    'FREQ=MONTHLY; INTERVAL=2; BYMONTHDAY=15',
 10    start_date, null, next_run_date);
 11    DBMS_OUTPUT.PUT_LINE('next_run_date: ' ||
 12    next_run_date);
 13  END;
SQL> /
next_run_date: 15-OCT-08 10.00.00.000000 AM

PL/SQL procedure successfully completed.
```

As you can see, line 9 contains the actual calendar expression that is being evaluated. Also, because a value of NULL was submitted for the RETURN_DATE_AFTER parameter, Oracle uses the current date and time as the default.

The procedure returns only a single value for NEXT_RUN_DATE, but you may want to see more than one. If so, you can use the SQL shown here:

```
SQL>  DECLARE
  2    start_date TIMESTAMP;
  3    return_date_after TIMESTAMP;
  4    next_run_date TIMESTAMP;
  5  BEGIN
  6    start_date := to_timestamp_tz(
  7    '10-OCT-2008 10:00:00','DD-MON-YYYY HH24:MI:SS');
```

```
  8    return_date_after := start_date;
  9    FOR i IN 1..10 LOOP
 10    DBMS_SCHEDULER.EVALUATE_CALENDAR_STRING(
 11    'FREQ=MONTHLY; INTERVAL=2; BYMONTHDAY=15',
 12    start_date, return_date_after, next_run_date);
 13    DBMS_OUTPUT.PUT_LINE(
 14    'next_run_date: ' || next_run_date);
 15    return_date_after := next_run_date;
 16    END LOOP;
 17    END;
SQL> /
next_run_date: 15-OCT-08 10.00.00.000000 AM
next_run_date: 15-DEC-08 10.00.00.000000 AM
next_run_date: 15-FEB-09 10.00.00.000000 AM
next_run_date: 15-APR-09 10.00.00.000000 AM
next_run_date: 15-JUN-09 10.00.00.000000 AM
next_run_date: 15-AUG-09 10.00.00.000000 AM
next_run_date: 15-OCT-09 10.00.00.000000 AM
next_run_date: 15-DEC-09 10.00.00.000000 AM
next_run_date: 15-FEB-10 10.00.00.000000 AM
next_run_date: 15-APR-10 10.00.00.000000 AM

PL/SQL procedure successfully completed.
```

This example calls the procedure inside of a loop, and each time through, it uses the NEXT_RUN_DATE returned from the prior call as the value for the RETURN_DATE_AFTER parameter. This tells Oracle to only return a date that is farther in the future than the date specified. Therefore, you will get each successive execution date.

Creating Lightweight Jobs

New to Oracle 11g, a *lightweight job* is defined by indicating LIGHTWEIGHT as the value for job_style when creating the job. Lightweight jobs have the following characteristics:

- They are not schema objects
- Because they are not schema objects, they have lower overhead and better create and drop time when compared to regular jobs.
- They store less metadata and job runtime data than regular jobs.
- They must reference an enabled 'PLSQL_BLOCK' or 'STORED_PROCEDURE' program to specify a job action.

Lightweight jobs inherit their privileges from the program; you cannot grant privileges to lightweight jobs. Consider using a lightweight job when you have a high-frequency short-duration job.

Here's an example of a PL/SQL block that creates a lightweight job.

```
BEGIN
DBMS_SCHEDULER.CREATE_JOB (
    job_name => 'example_lightweight_job',
    program_name => 'lne_prog',
    repeat_interval => 'FREQ=SECONDLY;INTERVAL=30',
    job_style => 'LIGHTWEIGHT',
    comments => 'Heartbeat monitor job');
END;
/
```

In Exercise 12.2, you'll create a lightweight job and execute it.

EXERCISE 12.2

Creating and Executing a Lightweight Job

For this exercise, we'll create a lightweight job and execute it. Use the table LNE_TEST created in Exercise 12.1.

1. Create a stored procedure that inserts sysdate into a row in a table.

   ```
   create or replace procedure LNE_TEST_PROC
   as
   begin
   insert into LNE_TEST select sysdate from dual;
   end;
   /
   ```

2. Create and enable a program for the stored procedure using dbms_scheduler.create_program, and dbms_scheduler.enable.

   ```
   begin
     dbms_scheduler.create_program(
     program_name => 'LNE_PROGRAM',
     program_type => 'STORED_PROCEDURE',
     program_action => 'LNE_TEST_PROC',
     number_of_arguments => 0,
     comments => 'Insert SYSDATE into LNE_TEST table');
   end;
   ```

```
/

exec dbms_scheduler.enable('LNE_PROGRAM');
```

3. Create a lightweight job using dbms_scheduler.create_job to execute the stored procedure every 30 seconds.

```
begin
  dbms_scheduler.create_job (
  job_name => 'LNE_LIGHTWEIGHT_JOB',
  program_name => 'LNE_PROGRAM',
   repeat_interval => 'FREQ=SECONDLY;INTERVAL=30',
  job_style => 'LIGHTWEIGHT',
  comments => 'Lightweight job exercise');
end;
/
```

4. Now run the job using dbms_scheduler.run_job.

```
begin
  dbms_scheduler.run_job('LNE_LIGHTWEIGHT_JOB',TRUE);
end;
/
```

5. Finally, stop the job using dbms_scheduler.stop_job.

```
begin
  dbms_scheduler.stop_job(job_name => 'LNE_LIGHTWEIGHT_JOB',
  force => TRUE);
end;
/
```

Using Job Chains

Chains are used to implement dependency scheduling. A chain consists of two or more Scheduler programs that are linked together to meet an objective. These multiple steps, when combined with dependency rules or conditions, create a chain or decision tree. Here's an example:

- Run program A.
- If program A completes successfully, run program B.

- If both programs A and B complete successfully, run program C.
- If program A or B does not succeed, run program F.
- Run program ZZ.

Chains are useful for complex business transactions that require multiple dependent programs to complete successfully or take predefined steps when a step in the process fails. Financial reporting and a daily ETL load and report process are both examples of these kinds of business transactions.

A chain job is a type of scheduler job that references a job chain as the job action, can reference a chain instead of a program to start the process. Each step in the chain can be one of the following:

- A program
- Another chain
- An inline event or event schedule

When a chain job is running you can view its progress by querying the *_SCHEDULER_ RUNNING_JOBS, *_SCHEDULER_JOB_LOG, *_SCHEDULER_JOB_RUN_DETAILS, and *_SCHEDULER_ RUNNING_CHAINS views.

Creating a Chain

Create a chain by using the CREATE_CHAIN procedure, as follows:

```
BEGIN
DBMS_SCHEDULER.CREATE_CHAIN (
    chain_name => 'lne_chain',
    rule_set_name => NULL,
    evaluation_interval => NULL,
    comments => 'Never break the chain');
END;
/
```

Once you've created the chain, you'll define the steps and rules.

Defining Chain Steps

Now that you've created a chain, you need to add steps to it. Remember that each step can point to a program, another chain, an inline event, or an event schedule. Here's an example that adds three steps, each of which points to a specific program:

```
BEGIN
DBMS_SCHEDULER.DEFINE_CHAIN_STEP (
    chain_name => 'lne_chain',
```

```
    step_name => 'lne_step1',
    program_name => 'start_lne');
DBMS_SCHEDULER.DEFINE_CHAIN_STEP (
    chain_name => 'lne_chain',
    step_name => 'lne_step2',
    program_name => 'lne_run_stage1');
DBMS_SCHEDULER.DEFINE_CHAIN_STEP (
    chain_name => 'lne_chain',
    step_name => 'lne_step3',
    program_name => 'lne_run_stage2');
END;
/
```

It is not mandatory that the program exist when you define the chain step, but it must exist and be enabled before you execute the chain. If the program is an external executable, you must use the ALTER_CHAIN procedure to set the credentials for the step. If the program is a remote external executable, use ALTER_CHAIN to set the destination.

Defining a Chain That Waits for an Event

Use the DEFINE_CHAIN_EVENT_STEP procedure to define a step that waits for an event. In this example, we add a chain step to the previously defined lne_chain chain that will wait for a specific event to occur:

```
BEGIN
DBMS_SCHEDULER.DEFINE_CHAIN_EVENT_STEP (
    chain_name => 'lne_chain',
    step_name => 'lne_step4',
    event_schedule_name => 'lne_event_schedule');
END;
/
```

Adding Rules to a Chain

Chain rules define dependencies between steps and determine when steps run. A rule has a condition and an action. When a condition is evaluated true, the associated action is taken. The condition can contain a valid SQL WHERE clause or Scheduler chain condition syntax.

The Scheduler chain condition syntax takes one of the following two forms:

```
stepname [NOT] {SUCCEEDED|FAILED|STOPPED|COMPLETED}
stepname ERROR_CODE {comparision_operator|[NOT] IN} {integer|list_of_integers}
```

You can create complex conditions by using Boolean operators AND, OR, and NOT().

Step Attributes

When using the SQL WHERE clause to evaluate a condition, you can include the following step attributes: completed, state, start_date, end_date, error_code, and duration. When the state attribute is SUCCEEDED, FAILED, or STOPPED, the completed attribute is set to TRUE.

Conditions

Here are some examples of the chain condition syntax:

```
Credentials_confirm_step COMPLETED
Credentials_confirm_step SUCCEEDED
Credentials_confirm_step FAILED and
 credentials_confirm_step ERROR_CODE != 21000
```

In the first example, the step completed, with one of the following conditions: STOPPED, FAILED, or SUCCEEDED. In the second example, the step must have succeeded for the condition to be met. In the third example, the step must have failed and the returned error code must not be equal to 21000.

Defining Rules

In the following example, the rule starts the chain at step 1 and on completion starts step 2:

```
BEGIN
DBMS_SCHEDULER.DEFINE_CHAIN_RULE (
    chain_name => 'lne_chain',
    condition => 'TRUE',
    action => 'START lne step1',
    rule_name => 'lne_rule1',
    comments => 'start the chain');
DBMS_SCHEDULER.DEFINE_CHAIN_RULE (
    chain_name => 'lne_chain',
    condition => 'lne step1 completed',
    action => 'START lne step2',
    rule_name => 'lne_rule2');
END;
/
```

Starting and Ending the Chain

To start the chain, at least one rule must always evaluate to TRUE. The easiest way to do this is to simply set the condition to '1=1' if you're using SQL syntax or 'TRUE' if you using Scheduler chain condition syntax.

For the chain to end, at least one chain rule must have an action of 'END' when a condition evaluates to TRUE. If a chain has no more running steps and no END action has been determined to be TRUE, then the chain job will go into the CHAIN_STALLED state.

Enabling a Chain

Enabling a chain is straightforward:

```
BEGIN
DBMS_SCHEDULER.ENABLE ('lne_chain');
END;
/
```

The chain must be enabled before a job can run it.

Creating Jobs for Chains

There are two ways you can run a chain: either by using the RUN_CHAIN procedure or, as in this example, by creating and scheduling a job of type CHAIN:

```
BEGIN
DBMS_SCHEDULER.CREATE_JOB (
    job_name => 'lne_chain_job1',
    job_type => 'CHAIN',
    job_action => 'lne_chain',
    repeat_interval => 'freq=daily;byhour=7;byminute=30;bysecond=0',
    enabled => TRUE);
END;
/
```

The Scheduler creates a step job for each step of a chain job that is running. Each step job is uniquely identified by a job subname. To monitor the job steps, query the *_SCHEDULER_RUNNING_JOBS, *_SCHEDULER_JOB_LOG, and *_SCHEDULER_JOB_RUN_DETAILS views.

In Exercise 12.3, you'll create a job chain.

EXERCISE 12.3

Creating and Executing a Job Chain

For this exercise, you'll create a job chain. Reuse components from the previous exercises when possible.

1. Create a simple chain, and set up the starting chain step as described in the section "Starting and Ending the Chain."

```
BEGIN
DBMS_SCHEDULER.CREATE_CHAIN (
    chain_name => 'LNE_CHAIN',
    rule_set_name => NULL,
    evaluation_interval => NULL,
    comments => 'Never break the chain');
END;
/
```

2. Create chain steps for the stored procedures created earlier, and enable the job chain.

```
BEGIN
DBMS_SCHEDULER.DEFINE_CHAIN_STEP (
    chain_name => 'lne_chain',
    step_name => 'lne_step1',
    program_name => 'LNE_LIGHTWEIGHT_JOB');
DBMS_SCHEDULER.DEFINE_CHAIN_STEP (
    chain_name => 'lne_chain',
    step_name => 'lne_step2',
    program_name => 'LNE_JOB');
END;
/


BEGIN
DBMS_SCHEDULER.DEFINE_CHAIN_RULE (
    chain_name => 'LNE_CHAIN',
    condition => 'TRUE',
    action => 'START LNE_STEP1',
    rule_name => 'LNE_RULE1',
    comments => 'start the chain');
DBMS_SCHEDULER.DEFINE_CHAIN_RULE (
    chain_name => 'LNE_CHAIN',
    condition => 'LNE_STEP1 completed',
```

```
    action => 'START LNE_STEP2',
    rule_name => 'LNE_RULE2');
END;
/


BEGIN
    DBMS_SCHEDULER.ENABLE ('LNE_CHAIN');
END;
/
```

3. Execute the job chain, then drop the chain.

```
BEGIN
    DBMS_SCHEDULER.RUN_CHAIN (
    chain_name => 'LNE_CHAIN',
    job_name => 'impromptu_job_chain',
    start_steps => 'LNE_STEP1');
END;
/


BEGIN
    DBMS_SCHEDULER.DROP_CHAIN (
    chain_name => 'LNE_CHAIN',
    force => TRUE);
END;
/
```

Using Scheduler Windows

In Chapter 11, "Managing Database Resources," you learned to create and manage resource plans to allocate system resources. Scheduler windows allow you to change the active resource plan based on defined schedules. In general, resource plans tend to be created with specific time windows in mind. For instance, assume that your system performs heavy transaction processing between the hours of 8:00 a.m. and 5:00 p.m. but runs mostly batch processing and reports after hours. It would make sense to create a separate resource plan to govern resource allocation for each time period. Scheduler windows can then be used to switch automatically between the two.

Unlike most of the other Scheduler objects that you've seen so far, windows are created in the SYS schema. They are stored as database objects and therefore must have a valid name that is unique within the SYS schema.

In the following sections, you will learn to create, open, and close scheduler windows. You'll also learn about scheduler window logging and how to manage window logs. Last, you'll learn about purging scheduler logs.

Creating Windows

Windows can be created by using the DBMS_SCHEDULER.CREATE_WINDOW procedure. When creating a window, you have the choice of either using an existing schedule or defining an inline schedule. However, an existing schedule may not be used if the schedule has a repeat interval based on a PL/SQL expression.

The parameters for the CREATE_WINDOW procedure are described here:

WINDOW_NAME   The WINDOW_NAME parameter uniquely identifies the window in the SYS schema. The name has to be unique in the SYS schema.

RESOURCE_PLAN   The RESOURCE_PLAN parameter specifies the name of the resource plan that will govern the timeframe of the window. When the window opens, the system switches to the specified resource plan. When the window closes, the system either switches back to the prior resource plan or, if another window is opening, to the resource plan of the new window. If the current resource plan has been set through the use of the ALTER SYSTEM SET RESOURCE_ MANAGER_PLAN FORCE statement, the Scheduler will not be allowed to change the resource plan. If no resource plan is defined for the window, the current resource plan will remain in effect when the window opens and will stay in effect for the duration of the window.

START_DATE   The START_DATE parameter specifies the first date that the window is scheduled to open. If START_DATE is NULL or references a date in the past, the window will open as soon as it is created. The START_DATE parameter is used as a reference date when the REPEAT_INTERVAL parameter uses a calendaring expression. In this situation, the window will open on the first date that matches the calendaring expression *and* is on or after the date specified in the START_DATE parameter.

DURATION   The DURATION attribute specifies how long the window will remain open. There is no default value, so a value must be provided. The value should be specified as an INTERVAL DAY TO SECOND datatype (for example, interval '10' hour or interval '20' minute).

SCHEDULE_NAME   The SCHEDULE_NAME parameter specifies the name of the schedule associated with the window.

REPEAT_INTERVAL   The REPEAT_INTERVAL parameter specifies how often the window should repeat. It is defined using the calendaring syntax only; PL/SQL expressions cannot be used in conjunction with a window. If the REPEAT_INTERVAL parameter is NULL, the window will open only once at the specified start date.

END_DATE   The END_DATE parameter specifies the date when the window will be disabled. If the END_DATE parameter is NULL, a repeating window will repeat forever.

WINDOW_PRIORITY   The WINDOW_PRIORITY parameter is relevant only when two windows overlap each other. Because only one window can be in effect at a time, the window priority determines which window will be opened. The valid values are LOW (the default) and HIGH. A high-priority window has precedence.

COMMENTS   The COMMENTS parameter specifies an optional comment about the window.

The following example creates a window that activates the DAY_PLAN resource plan and uses a schedule named WORK_HOURS_SCHEDULE:

```
SQL>  begin
  2  dbms_scheduler.create_window (
  3  window_name => 'WORK_HOURS_WINDOW',
  4  resource_plan => 'DAY_PLAN',
  5  schedule_name => 'WORK_HOURS_SCHEDULE',
  6  duration => INTERVAL '10' HOUR,
  7  window_priority => 'HIGH');
  8  end;
SQL> /


PL/SQL procedure successfully completed.
```

This newly created window will be started based on a schedule named WORK_HOURS_SCHEDULE and will remain in effect for 10 hours. During those 10 hours, the DAY_PLAN resource plan will be in effect. Also, because the priority for this window is set to HIGH, it will take precedence over any overlapping window that has a priority setting of LOW.

Opening and Closing Windows

There are two distinct ways that a window can be opened. The first is based on the window's schedule. The second is by opening it manually by using the DBMS_SCHEDULER.OPEN_WINDOW procedure.

The OPEN_WINDOW procedure opens a window independent of its schedule. The associated resource plan is enabled immediately, and currently executing jobs are subjected to the change in resource plan, just as if the window had opened based on its schedule.

When opening a window manually, you can specify a new duration for the window to remain open; otherwise it will remain open for the duration defined when the window was created.

If the FORCE parameter is set to TRUE in the OPEN_WINDOW procedure, the Scheduler will automatically close any currently open window, even if it has a higher priority. Also, it will not allow any other windows to be opened during the time the manually opened window is open.

The OPEN_WINDOW procedure accepts only three parameters: WINDOW_NAME, DURATION, and FORCE. Here is an example of its usage:

```
SQL>  begin
  2  dbms_scheduler.open_window (
  3  window_name => 'WORK_HOURS_WINDOW',
  4  duration => INTERVAL '20' MINUTE,
  5  force => TRUE);
  6  end;
SQL> /

PL/SQL procedure successfully completed.
```

This example forces the WORK_HOURS_WINDOW to be opened and any current window to close. The new window will remain open for a duration of 20 minutes.

In a similar manner, windows can be manually closed by using the DBMS_SCHEDULER .CLOSE_WINDOW procedure. This procedure accepts the window name as a parameter, as shown here:

```
SQL>  begin
  2  dbms_scheduler.close_window (
  3  window_name => 'WORK_HOURS_WINDOW');
  4  end;
SQL> /

PL/SQL procedure successfully completed.
```

Window Logging

The Oracle Scheduler maintains *window logs* of all window activities. The DBA_SCHEDULER_ WINDOW_LOG view can be used to view log entries for all of the following window activities:

- Creating a new window
- Dropping a window
- Opening a window
- Closing a window
- Overlapping windows
- Disabling a window
- Enabling a window

For example, use the following query to view window log entries:

```
SQL> select log_id, trunc(log_date) log_date,
  window_name, operation
```

```
from dba_scheduler_window_log;

LOG_ID LOG_DATE  WINDOW_NAME          OPERATION
------ --------- -------------------- ---------
   527 25-SEP-04 WEEKEND_WINDOW       OPEN
   544 28-SEP-04 WEEKNIGHT_WINDOW     OPEN
   547 28-SEP-04 WEEKNIGHT_WINDOW     CLOSE
   548 29-SEP-04 WEEKNIGHT_WINDOW     OPEN
   551 29-SEP-04 WEEKNIGHT_WINDOW     CLOSE
   552 30-SEP-04 WEEKNIGHT_WINDOW     OPEN
   559 01-OCT-04 WEEKNIGHT_WINDOW     CLOSE
   560 02-OCT-04 WEEKNIGHT_WINDOW     OPEN
   563 02-OCT-04 WEEKNIGHT_WINDOW     CLOSE
   555 30-SEP-04 WEEKNIGHT_WINDOW     CLOSE
   564 02-OCT-04 WEEKEND_WINDOW       OPEN
```

For each CLOSE operation logged in the DBA_SCHEDULER_WINDOW_LOG view, there will be an associated record in the DBA_SCHEDULER_WINDOW_DETAILS view, as shown here:

```
SQL> select log_id, trunc(log_date) log_date,
  window_name, actual_duration
  from dba_scheduler_window_details;

LOG_ID LOG_DATE  WINDOW_NAME          ACTUAL_DURATION
------- --------- -------------------- ---------------
    547 28-SEP-04 WEEKNIGHT_WINDOW     +000 08:00:00
    551 29-SEP-04 WEEKNIGHT_WINDOW     +000 08:00:00
    559 01-OCT-04 WEEKNIGHT_WINDOW     +000 08:00:00
    563 02-OCT-04 WEEKNIGHT_WINDOW     +000 08:00:00
    555 30-SEP-04 WEEKNIGHT_WINDOW     +000 07:59:58
```

Purging Logs

As with any automatic logging system, window logs must be purged on a regular basis to prevent excessive table growth. Oracle provides an automatic method to purge the log files after a specified number of days.

Scheduler job logs and window logs will be automatically purged based on the setting of the LOG_HISTORY attribute of the Scheduler itself. The value of this parameter determines the number of days that log data should be retained, after which it will be purged. To set this value, use the SET_SCHEDULER_ATTRIBUTE procedure, as in the following example:

```
SQL> begin
  2    DBMS_SCHEDULER.SET_SCHEDULER_ATTRIBUTE(
```

```
  3   'LOG_HISTORY','60');
  4   end;
SQL> /
```

PL/SQL procedure successfully completed.

This example instructs Oracle to automatically purge all records that are over 60 days old.

By default, this procedure sets the history retention period for both Scheduler window logs and Scheduler job logs. To set only one, you may include the WHICH_LOG parameter to specify either WINDOW_LOG or JOB_LOG.

Creating and Using Job Classes

A job class is a container object for the logical grouping of jobs into a larger unit. Classifying jobs in this manner offers several advantages:

- From an administrative perspective, it is easier to manage a small number of job groups than to manage a large number of individual jobs. Certain job characteristics can be assigned at the group level and will be inherited by all jobs within the group. Certain administrative procedures will also operate at the group level, making administrative functions easier.

- Job classes can be assigned to a resource consumer group. This allows you to control resource allocation for all jobs within the group.

- Jobs can be prioritized within the job class. This gives you more control over which jobs should take precedence in case of a conflict. For example, if a conflict occurs, the JOB_ PRIORITY attribute of each job will be evaluated. A job with a value of HIGH takes priority over a job with a value of LOW.

All jobs must belong to exactly one job class. Any job not explicitly assigned to a job class will belong to the DEFAULT_JOB_CLASS class and will inherit the characteristics of that job class. In the following sections, you will learn to create and administer job classes.

Job Class Parameters

Job classes have a specific set of attributes that you can set to define the characteristics of the class. These attributes will be inherited by all jobs assigned to the job class, thereby saving you the work of setting them individually on each job. The available attribute parameters are described here:

JOB_CLASS_NAME   The JOB_CLASS_NAME parameter uniquely identifies the job class in the SYS schema. The name has to be unique in the SYS schema.

RESOURCE_CONSUMER_GROUP   The RESOURCE_CONSUMER_GROUP parameter associates the job group with a specific consumer group. All jobs assigned to the job group will automatically be governed by this consumer group.

SERVICE   The SERVICE parameter specifies the service to which the job class belongs. This means that, in a RAC environment, the jobs in this class will have affinity to the particular service specified. Therefore, they will run only on those database instances that are assigned to the specific service. If this attribute is not set, the default service will be used, meaning that the jobs have no service affinity and can be run by any instance within the cluster. If the SERVICE parameter is specified, the RESOURCE_CONSUMER_GROUP attribute cannot be set. They are mutually exclusive.

LOGGING_LEVEL   The Oracle Scheduler can optionally maintain *job logs* of all job activities. Job logging is determined by the setting of the LOGGING_LEVEL attribute of the job class. The LOGGING_LEVEL parameter specifies how much job information is logged. There are four valid settings for this attribute:

DBMS_SCHEDULER.LOGGING_OFF   No logging will be performed for any jobs in this class.

DBMS_SCHEDULER.LOGGING_RUNS   Detailed information will be written for all runs of each job in the class.

DBMS_SCHEDULER.LOGGING_FULL   Detailed information will be written for all runs of each job in the class, and every operation performed on any job in the class (create, enable, drop, and so on) will be logged.

DBMS_SCHEDULER.LOGGING_FAILED_RUNS   Logs only jobs that failed and the reason for failure. If the job class has a higher logging level the higher level takes precedence.

Note that the valid values for this parameter are all constants defined within the DBMS_SCHEDULER package. Therefore, they must be referenced exactly as shown, with no quotes around them.

LOG_HISTORY   The LOG_HISTORY parameter determines the number of days logged information should be retained. The default value is 30 days. Valid values are 1 to 999. When records have exceeded this limit, the Scheduler will automatically purge them.

COMMENTS   The COMMENTS parameter specifies an optional comment about the job class.

Creating Job Classes

Job classes can be created through the DBMS_SCHEDULER.CREATE_JOB_CLASS procedure, as shown in the following example:

```
SQL> begin
  2     dbms_scheduler.create_job_class(
  3  job_class_name => 'LOW_PRIORITY_CLASS',
  4  resource_consumer_group => 'LOW_GROUP',
```

```
  5  logging_level => DBMS_SCHEDULER.LOGGING_FULL,
  6  log_history => 60,
  7  comments => 'LOW PRIORITY JOB CLASS');
  8 end;
SQL> /

PL/SQL procedure successfully completed.
```

In this example, a job class named LOW_PRIORITY_CLASS was created that will assign all jobs in the group to the LOW_GROUP consumer group.

Dropping Job Classes

Job classes can be dropped by using the DBMS_SCHEDULER.DROP_JOB_CLASS procedure. Dropping a job class that has jobs assigned to it will result in an error. However, it is allowed if the FORCE parameter is set to TRUE. In this case, the job class will be dropped and the jobs assigned to the class will be disabled. Dropping the class has no effect on any currently running instances of member jobs.

Several job classes can also be dropped at the same time by separating the names of the job classes by a comma, as shown in the following example:

```
SQL> begin
  2  dbms_scheduler.drop_job_class(
  3    'LOW_PRIORITY_CLASS, HIGH_PRIORITY_CLASS');
  4  end;
SQL> /

PL/SQL procedure successfully completed.
```

Note that if a list of job classes is used, as in the example in the section "Dropping Job Classes," there is no rollback available. For instance, if the first job class dropped but the second job class failed to drop, the procedure will return an error, but the first job class will not be restored.

Using Advanced Scheduler Concepts to Prioritize Jobs

The Scheduler allows you to prioritize jobs based on your unique business requirements. It gives you control over resource allocation through job classes, as described earlier. It also allows you to change the prioritization based on a schedule.

When working with a job class, you can define a resource consumer group and take advantage of the Database Resource Manager capabilities, as described earlier in this chapter. You can also prioritize jobs within a job class.

Prioritizing Jobs within a Job Class

Within a job class, you can assign priority values from 1 to 5 to individual jobs so that if more than one job within the same class starts at the same time, the job with the highest priority will take precedence over the others. If two jobs have the same priority, the one that had the earlier start date gets the higher priority. Priority rules apply only when comparing jobs within the same class. The default priority for a job is 3; 1 is the highest, and 5 is the lowest.

To change a job priority, use the SET_ATTRIBUTE procedure. For example, here's how to raise the priority of the LNE_JOB1 job to priority 1:

```
BEGIN
DBMS_SCHEDULER.SET_ATTRIBUTE (
    name => 'lne_job1',
    attribute => 'job_priority',
    value => 1);
END;
/
```

> The job_priority attribute is set by default to 3 when you create the job; use the SET_ATTRIBUTE procedure to change the job priority.

Using Scheduler Views

Oracle offers a wide variety of views to access information regarding the Scheduler and its associated objects. These views allow you to see information about currently running jobs and past runs of jobs. Table 12.5 describes the available Scheduler views.

TABLE 12.5   Scheduler Views Available

View	Description
*_SCHEDULER_SCHEDULES	Shows information on all defined schedules.
*_SCHEDULER_PROGRAMS	Shows information on all defined programs.

TABLE 12.5   Scheduler Views Available *(continued)*

View	Description
*_SCHEDULER_PROGRAM_ARGUMENTS	Shows all registered program arguments and the default values if they exist.
*_SCHEDULER_JOBS	Shows all defined jobs, both enabled and disabled.
*_SCHEDULER_GLOBAL_ATTRIBUTE	Shows the current values of all Scheduler attributes.
*_SCHEDULER_JOB_ARGUMENTS	Shows the arguments for all defined jobs.
*_SCHEDULER_JOB_CLASSES	Shows information on all defined job classes.
*_SCHEDULER_WINDOWS	Shows information about all defined windows.
*_SCHEDULER_JOB_RUN_DETAILS	Shows information about all completed (failed or successful) job runs.
*_SCHEDULER_WINDOW_GROUPS	Shows information about all window groups.
*_SCHEDULER_WINGROUP_MEMBERS	Shows the members of all window groups.
*_SCHEDULER_RUNNING_JOBS	Shows the state information on all jobs that are currently being run.

To see information on completed instances of a job, use the code shown here:

```
SQL> select job_name, status, error#
  2  from dba_scheduler_job_run_details
  3   where job_name = 'FAIL_JOB';


JOB_NAME     STATUS          ERROR#
--------     --------------  ------
FAIL_JOB     FAILURE          20000
```

To see the current state of all jobs, use the following code:

```
SQL> select job_name, state
  2  from dba_scheduler_jobs;


JOB_NAME           STATE
-----------------  ---------------
PURGE_LOG          SCHEDULED
GATHER_STATS_JOB   SCHEDULED
```

```
LNE_JOB            SCHEDULED
RAISE_JOB          DISABLED
```

To view windows and their next start dates, the following SQL can be used:

```
SQL> select window_name, next_start_date
  2  from dba_scheduler_windows;

WINDOW_NAME            NEXT_START_DATE
------------------     ------------------------------------
WEEKNIGHT_WINDOW       12-OCT-04 10.00.00.300000 PM -08:00
WEEKEND_WINDOW         16-OCT-04 12.00.00.500000 AM -08:00
```

The DBA_SCHEDULER_JOB_LOG view can be used to view log entries for previously executed jobs, as shown here:

```
SQL> select log_id, trunc(log_date) log_date, owner, job_name, operation from
dba_scheduler_job_log;

LOG_ID LOG_DATE      OWNER JOB_NAME          OPERATION
------ ----------    ----- ----------------- ---------
   522 25-SEP-04     SYS   PURGE_LOG         RUN
   524 25-SEP-04     SYS   ADV_SQL_TUNING    SUCCEEDED
   525 25-SEP-04     SYS   ADV_SQL_TUNING    DROP
   528 25-SEP-04     SYS   GATHER_STATS_JOB  RUN
   484 18-SEP-04     SYS   GATHER_STATS_JOB  RUN
   541 26-SEP-04     SYS   PURGE_LOG         RUN
   543 27-SEP-04     SYS   PURGE_LOG         RUN
   545 28-SEP-04     SYS   GATHER_STATS_JOB  RUN
   546 28-SEP-04     SYS   PURGE_LOG         RUN
   553 30-SEP-04     SYS   GATHER_STATS_JOB  RUN
   622 10-OCT-04     SYS   LNE_JOB           RUN
   549 29-SEP-04     SYS   GATHER_STATS_JOB  RUN
```

Summary

In this chapter, you learned about the new Oracle 11g Scheduler. You learned how it resolves issues such as schedule creep that existed in its predecessor, the DBMS_JOB package.

This chapter also explained the new architecture that underlies the Scheduler. You learned how the job table stores all enabled jobs within the database and how the job-coordinator process queries the job table on a regular basis and stores the job information in a memory cache for faster access. When a job is scheduled to run, the job-coordinator process is automatically started (if it is not already active). It will pass the job information to a job-slave process for execution.

You learned that the job-slave process will gather all the metadata for the job, start a session as the owner of the job, begin a transaction within the session, and then execute the job. When the job completes, the slave commits the transaction and closes the session. The slave then updates the job entry in the job table to show a COMPLETE status. It inserts a new entry into the job log, updates the run count for the job, and then looks for any new work that needs to be done. If none is found, the job-slave process returns to a sleep state.

You also learned that, in a RAC environment, each instance has its own job coordinator, and the job coordinators have the ability to communicate with each other to keep information current. You learned that a RAC environment will still have only one job table that is shared by all the instances. You also learned that jobs can be assigned to a service, as opposed to an instance, ensuring that the job can be run by a different node if an instance is down.

We showed you how, in a Data Guard environment, changes made to the primary are applied to the physical standby. For a logical standby, you have the option to run jobs based on the databases role—either primary or logical standby.

Next, you learned about job objects and how they are created and administered. You saw how the CREATE_JOB procedure is overloaded. You also learned to set job arguments using the SET_JOB_ARGUMENT_VALUE and the SET_JOB_ANYDATA_VALUE procedures as well as how to copy, run, disable, enable, and drop jobs.

We discussed program objects and how they define PL/SQL blocks, stored procedures, or external operating-system executables as well as their arguments and other metadata. You also learned to administer all aspects of program objects.

This chapter also covered schedule objects and how they are created. Schedules specify a start date, an optional end date, and a repeat interval. Together, these elements are used to calculate run dates. You can use the new calendaring syntax to define repeat intervals within the schedules.

You learned about lightweight jobs and the special conditions that may lead you to choose a lightweight job instead of a regular job.

Next you learned about job chains and how to create dependencies between job steps in a chain.

Finally, we discussed windows and how they can be used to switch resource plans at scheduled intervals to control resource allocation for the system. You learned that only one window can be open at any given time and that, when overlapping windows exist, a window with a priority of HIGH will take precedence over a window with a priority of LOW.

Exam Essentials

Know how to simplify management tasks by using the Scheduler. Understand how the Scheduler can be used to automate routine management tasks to run on a repeating basis. Know the types of programs that can be run through the Scheduler (PL/SQL blocks, stored procedures, and external operating-system executables).

Be able to create a job, program, schedule, and window. Know the various CREATE procedures in the DBMS_SCHEDULER package (CREATE_JOB, CREATE_PROGRAM, CREATE_SCHEDULE, and CREATE_WINDOW). Understand the different options that can be used when creating a job (inline definitions versus stored objects). Understand that only a subset of attributes can be defined at creation time. The other attributes can be set by altering the object through the SET_ATTRIBUTE and SET_ATTRIBUTE_NULL procedures.

Know how to create and use job chains. Understand the difference between dependency rules, conditions, and actions. Know how to define chain steps. Know how to create a chain. Know how to add rules to a chain. Know how to enable, start, and stop a chain.

Know how to prioritize jobs. Understand the difference between job class priorities and individual job priorities within a class. Know how to set a job attribute to change the job priority.

Know how to reuse Scheduler components for similar tasks. Understand the difference between inline schedule and program definitions and stored Scheduler object components. Know that a job can reference stored schedule and program objects. Know that a window can reference a stored schedule object. Understand that a job can be reused with different parameters.

Understand how to view information about job executions and job instances. Be aware of the different views available to view Scheduler information. Know that the views use the naming convention of DBA|ALL|USER_SCHEDULER_ as a prefix for all views (for example, DBA_SCHEDULER_JOBS, DBA_SCHEDULER_PROGRAMS, and so on). Know that the DBA_SCHEDULER_JOB_RUN_DETAILS view shows information about job executions and that the DBA_SCHEDULER_RUNNING_JOBS view shows information on jobs that are currently running.

Review Questions

1. When setting arguments for a job, which procedure do you use for types that cannot be implicitly converted to and from a VARCHAR2 datatype?

   A. SET_JOB_ARGUMENT_VALUE

   B. SET_JOB_VALUE_ANYDATA

   C. SET_JOB_ANYDATA_VALUE

   D. SET_SPECIAL_JOB_VALUE

   E. SET_JOB_ANYTYPE_VALUE

2. Which DBMS_SCHEDULER procedures can be used to enable a program? (Choose all that apply.)

   A. ENABLE

   B. ENABLE_PROGRAM

   C. VALIDATE_PROGRAM

   D. SET_ATTRIBUTE

   E. SET_ENABLED

3. Which of the following is not a valid calendaring syntax element?

   A. FREQ

   B. BYHOUR

   C. RUNDATE

   D. INTERVAL

   E. BYMINUTE

4. Which Scheduler view(s) can be queried to see which jobs are currently executing? (Choose all that apply.)

   A. DBA_SCHEDULER_JOB_RUN_DETAILS

   B. DBA_SCHEDULER_RUNNING_JOBS

   C. DBA_SCHEDULER_CURRENT_JOBS

   D. DBA_SCHEDULER_JOBS

   E. DBA_SCHEDULER_EXECUTING_JOBS

5. A schedule defined entirely within the confines of a Scheduler job object is known as a(n) _____.

   A. Fixed schedule

   B. Inline schedule

   C. Stored schedule

   D. Hard-coded schedule

   E. None of the above

6. Which `DBMS_SCHEDULER` procedure(s) can be used to alter an existing job? (Choose all that apply.)

    A. `SET_ATTRIBUTE_NULL`

    B. `ALTER_JOB`

    C. `ALTER_JOB_PARAMETERS`

    D. `ALTER`

    E. `SET_ATTRIBUTE`

7. What is the default value for the `ENABLED` attribute of a job or program when it is created?

    A. `TRUE`

    B. `FALSE`

    C. There is no default. It must be defined at creation time.

    D. `PENDING`

    E. `NULL`

8. To set the history retention period for either window logging or job logging individually, which parameters of the `SET_SCHEDULER_ATTRIBUTE` procedure need to be used? (Choose all that apply.)

    A. `LOG_HISTORY`

    B. `JOB_LOG_RETENTION`

    C. `WINDOW_LOG_RETENTION`

    D. `WHICH_LOG`

    E. `LOG_NAME`

9. Consider the following code snippet:

```
BEGIN
DBMS_SCHEDULER.SET_ATTRIBUTE (
    name => 'lne_job1',
    attribute => 'job_priority',
    value => 1);
END;
/
```

    If this code were executed, which of the following statements would be true?

    A. The priority of the `lne_job1` job would be set to 1.

    B. The `lne_job1` job would be executed synchronously.

    C. The `lne_job1` job would run immediately in the user's current session.

    D. The `lne_job1` job would retain its current priority.

    E. The job will immediately take priority over all running jobs.

10. Which of the following calendaring syntax expressions would evaluate to the last day of every month?

A. FREQ = MONTHLY; BYMONTHDAY = 31

B. FREQ = MONTHLY; BYMONTHDAY = -1

C. FREQ = DAILY; BYDAY = -1

D. FREQ = MONTHLY; BYDAY = 31

E. FREQ = DAILY; BYMONTHDAY = LAST_DAY

11. Which of the following tasks is *not* performed by the job coordinator?

A. Update job log when a job completes

B. Spawn and remove job slaves

C. Write/read job info to/from memory cache

D. Query job table

E. Pass job information to job slaves

12. Which of the following objects can be directly referenced by a window object? (Choose all that apply.)

A. Schedule object

B. Program object

C. Job object

D. Resource plan

E. Resource consumer group

13. Which of the following are valid program types for a lightweight job? (Choose all that apply.)

A. PLSQL_BLOCK

B. EXECUTABLE

C. JAVA_STORED_PROCEDURE

D. STORED_PROCEDURE

E. EXTERNAL

14. Which of the following is not a valid setting for the PROGRAM_TYPE parameter in a program object or the JOB_TYPE parameter in a job object?

A. PLSQL_BLOCK

B. JAVA_STORED_PROCEDURE

C. STORED_PROCEDURE

D. EXECUTABLE

E. None of the above are invalid settings.

15. Which of the following Scheduler elements encourage object reuse? (Choose all that apply.)

    A. Schedule objects

    B. Program arguments

    C. Job classes

    D. Job arguments

    E. All of the above

16. What is the danger associated with stopping a running job by using the STOP_JOB procedure?

    A. The job will need to be reenabled before it will execute again.

    B. The job may hold locks on objects referenced within it.

    C. All jobs within the job group will also be stopped.

    D. The job may leave data in an inconsistent state.

    E. There is no danger in using the STOP_JOB procedure.

17. If a job references a schedule that has been disabled, what will be the result?

    A. The job will be automatically disabled.

    B. The job will never execute.

    C. The job will attempt to execute but will fail.

    D. The job will inherit the DEFAULT_SCHEDULE schedule.

    E. A schedule object cannot be disabled.

18. When a job exceeds the date specified in its END_DATE attribute, which of the following will happen? (Choose all that apply.)

    A. The job will be dropped automatically if the value of the AUTO_DROP attribute is TRUE.

    B. The job will only be disabled if the value of the AUTO_DROP attribute is FALSE.

    C. The STATE attribute of the job will be set to COMPLETED if the value of the AUTO_DROP attribute is FALSE.

    D. All objects referenced by the job will be dropped if the value of the AUTO_DROP attribute is TRUE and the value of the CASCADE attribute is TRUE.

    E. The STATE column of the job table will be set to COMPLETED for the job.

19. Which of the following is true about job chains?

    A. They consist of one or more Scheduler programs.

    B. They are used to implement dependency scheduling.

    C. They are used to implement time-based scheduling.

    D. They are used to implement event-based scheduling.

    E. None of the above.

20. If two windows overlap, which window attribute will determine whether one should be chosen over the other?

A. WINDOW_PRIORITY

B. PRIORITY

C. PRIORITY_LEVEL

D. WINDOW_PRIORITY_LEVEL

E. OVERLAP_RULE

Answers to Review Questions

1. C. The SET_JOB_ANYDATA_VALUE procedure allows you to set job arguments that don't easily convert to and from a string (VARCHAR2) datatype.

2. A, D. Programs (as well as jobs) can be enabled in two ways: by using the ENABLE procedure or by using the SET_ATTRIBUTE procedure to set the ENABLED attribute to TRUE.

3. C. The calendaring syntax does not support an element named RUNDATE. It does not support the concept of specifying a single run date at all. The purpose of the calendaring syntax is to define repeat intervals that will be used to calculate run dates.

4. B, D. The DBA_SCHEDULER_RUNNING_JOBS view shows detailed information about all jobs currently executing. The DBA_SCHEDULER_JOBS view contains the STATE column, which shows a value of RUNNING for an executing job.

5. B. A schedule defined within a job object is known as an inline schedule, whereas an independent schedule object is referred to as a stored schedule. Inline schedules cannot be referenced by other objects.

6. A, E. A job can be altered only by changing the value of one or more of its attributes. This is accomplished by using the SET_ATTRIBUTE and SET_ATTRIBUTE_NULL procedures.

7. B. Jobs and programs are created in a disabled state by default. They must be enabled by setting the ENABLE parameter to TRUE in their respective CREATE statements, or by altering the object after creation.

8. A, D. The LOG_HISTORY parameter defines the retention period for both job logging and window logging by default. However, the WHICH_LOG parameter can be used to specify either JOB_LOG or WINDOW_LOG.

9. A. Executing the SET_ATTRIBUTE procedure with the job_priority attribute changes the priority of a job, with 1 being the highest priority and 5 the lowest. This procedure does not give the job priority over running jobs with the same priority (1).

10. B. The BYMONTHDAY element accepts negative values that represent a specific count of days from the end of the month. Also, the FREQ parameter must be set to MONTHLY because it will execute every month.

11. A. The job coordinator does not update the job log when a job completes. That function is performed by the job slave that has been assigned to the job.

12. A, D. A window does not execute programs or jobs. It specifies a resource plan that will be enabled based on a schedule. Therefore, it can reference both a schedule object and a resource-plan object. And while the resource plan may reference one or more resource consumer groups, the window object does not directly reference them.

13. A, D. PLSQL_BLOCK and STORED_PROCEDURE are the only valid program types that can be used with a lightweight job.

14. B. Java stored procedures cannot be executed by the job Scheduler unless they are called from within a PL/SQL procedure wrapper. This can be done in a stored procedure using PL/SQL's External Procedure feature. Therefore, the job or program type setting would be STORED_PROCEDURE.

15. A, B, D. Schedule objects do not specify any action to be performed; they simply generate execution dates that any job can use. Program and job arguments allow the jobs and programs to be reused by simply changing the arguments that are passed in. Job classes simplify the management of jobs, but they do not specifically encourage job reuse.

16. D. The Scheduler will attempt to wrap the job within a transaction and will execute a rollback if a job is stopped. However, if the job has performed commits, the rollback will roll back only uncommitted changes. This could result in inconsistent data.

17. E. A schedule object does not possess the ENABLED attribute. It is therefore enabled upon creation and can never be disabled.

18. A, B, E. When a job exceeds its end date, it will be dropped only if the AUTO_DROP attribute is set to TRUE. Otherwise, it will be disabled. In either case, the STATE column will be set to COMPLETED in the job table. A job object does not possess a CASCADE attribute or a STATE attribute.

19. B. Job chains are used to implement dependency-based scheduling. A job chain consists of two or more Scheduler programs.

20. A. The WINDOW_PRIORITY attribute can be set to either HIGH or LOW for a window. If two windows overlap and only one of the windows has a priority of HIGH, it will be chosen.

Chapter

13

Implementing Globalization Support

ORACLE DATABASE 11*g*: ADMINISTRATION II EXAM OBJECTIVES COVERED IN THIS CHAPTER:

✓ **Globalization**

  ▪ Customize language-dependent behavior for the database and individual sessions

  ▪ Working with database and NLS character sets

Doing business on a global scale presents a new set of challenges to any company, especially to the DBA. Beyond the obvious issues of language lie a host of less obvious but equally important issues that must be addressed—time-zone differences, mixed currency types, and differing calendars, just to name a few. But Oracle's globalization support features provide the tools needed to meet these challenges.

Globalization support enables you to manage data in multiple languages. It provides the functionality to ensure that native language and locale conventions are followed when dealing with date, time, currency, numeric, and calendar data.

Globalization support also offers datetime datatype options for handling transactions crossing time zones. And it provides a rich set of options for linguistic sorts and searching.

In this chapter, you'll learn what globalization support entails and how it all fits together. You'll see how National Language Support (NLS) parameter settings can change the functionality of many of Oracle's operations. You will learn about datetime datatypes and how they can be used to synchronize data around the globe. You'll also learn about new linguistic sorting and searching options that allow multilingual data to be searched, sorted, and managed simply and efficiently.

Exam objectives are subject to change at any time without prior notice and at Oracle's sole discretion. Please visit Oracle's Training and Certification website (http://www.oracle.com/education/certification/) for the most current exam-objectives listing.

An Overview of Globalization Support

Oracle's globalization support is a collection of features that allow you to manage data in multiple native languages within the same database instance. It also greatly simplifies application development by offering a rich set of globalization functionality to the developer.

Globalization support provides the character sets and datatypes needed to store multilingual data. It ensures that date, time, monetary, numeric, and calendar data will follow any supported *locale* conventions and display properly. It provides utilities and error messages translated to many different languages. It also provides the internal functionality to sort and to query multilingual data using proper linguistic rules.

In the following sections, you will learn about Oracle's globalization support features. You will get an overview of each feature and the functionality that it provides.

You will learn about the architecture upon which globalization support is built. You'll be introduced to the *National Language Support Runtime Library (NLSRTL)* and see how its modular design provides flexibility and saves resources.

You will also learn how applications interact with Oracle from a globalization perspective.

And finally, you will be introduced to *Unicode* and the advantages that it offers in a multilingual environment.

Globalization Support Features

Globalization support provides a rich set of functionality to the Oracle database. But it is important to make two distinctions perfectly clear regarding what globalization support does not do:

- Globalization support does not translate text into different languages.
- Globalization does not control how multilingual text is displayed on client machines.

Globalization support simply provides the infrastructure to allow text to be stored, manipulated, sorted, and searched in many languages using linguistically significant means. It also allows the data to be displayed using the standard conventions for a specific region.

Globalization support includes these features:

Language support Globalization support allows data to be stored, processed, and retrieved in virtually any scripted language. For many of these languages, Oracle provides additional support such as text-sorting conventions, date-formatting conventions (including translated month names), and even error-message and utility-interface translation.

Territory support Cultural conventions often differ between geographical locations. For example, local time format, date format, and numeric and monetary conventions can differ significantly between regions even though they may share a common language. To allow for these differences, the NLS_TERRITORY parameter can be used to define which conventions to follow.

However, these default settings can still be overridden through the use of NLS parameter settings. Overriding the default settings allows finer granularity in defining and customizing display formats to account for special circumstances. For example, it is possible to set the primary currency to the Japanese yen and the secondary currency to the dollar even with the territory defined as India.

Linguistic sorting and searching Globalization support offers culturally accurate case conversion, sorting, and searching for all supported languages. It offers the ability to search and sort based on the rules of language rather than simply on the order in which the characters are encoded in the character set. It also offers *case-insensitive sorts* and searches as well as *accent-insensitive sorts* and searches.

Linguistic sorts are defined separately from the language itself, allowing the ability to share sort definitions between languages. Linguistic sort defaults can also be overridden through the use of NLS parameter settings. This gives you the flexibility to customize your environment as needed.

Character sets and semantics   Oracle supports a vast number of character sets based on national and international standards, including Unicode. Because of the wide variety of *character sets*, users can often find a single set that supports all of the languages they need to support.

Unicode is a universal character set that supports all known written languages. Oracle offers full support of the Unicode 5.0 standard and offers several Unicode encoding options.

Unicode can be defined as the database character set, making it the default datatype for all character columns. If Unicode is not defined as the database character set, it can still be used by defining specific columns as *Unicode datatypes* (in other words, NCHAR, NVARCHAR2, NCLOB).

Many multibyte character sets use variable widths when storing data. This means that, depending on the character being stored, Oracle may use anywhere from 1 to 4 bytes to store it. Therefore, defining column widths in terms of the number of characters, rather than the number of bytes, becomes crucial. *Character semantics* allow character data to be specified in terms of the number of characters regardless of the number of bytes actually required. *Byte semantics*, the default, assume a single-byte character set, where one character always requires 1 byte of storage.

While Unicode may seem like the logical choice for any database, the decision to use it needs to be weighed carefully. There are performance and space-usage penalties associated with using Unicode. If a smaller code set is available that encompasses all of the languages you are likely to ever need, then the overhead of Unicode makes it an illogical choice.

Calendars   Different geographic areas often utilize different calendar systems, which can make international transactions hard to synchronize. Oracle supports seven distinct calendar systems: Gregorian, Japanese Imperial, ROC (Republic of China) Official, Thai Buddha, Persian, English Hijrah, and Arabic Hijrah. Globalization support offers functionality to resolve calendar-system differences.

Locale and calendar customization   Oracle's Locale Builder utility allows customization of globalization definitions, including language, character set, territory, and linguistic sorting. Calendars can also be customized using the NLS Calendar utility. Coverage of Locale Builder and the NLS Calendar utilities fall outside the scope of this book.

Globalization Support Architecture

Globalization support in Oracle 11*g* is implemented through the Oracle National Language Support Runtime Library (NLSRTL). The NLSRTL offers a set of language-independent text and character-processing functions as well as functions for language-convention manipulation. The behavior of these algorithms is determined at runtime (database startup), as the name suggests.

At database startup time, NLSRTL looks for a file named 1x1boot.n1b. This file defines the set of locale definitions available to the database. To determine where to look for this file, NLSRTL will first check the environment for the existence of an ORA_NLS10 variable.

If ORA_NLS10 is defined, it will contain the path to where the 1x1boot.n1b file resides. If the variable is not set, the default location of $ORACLE_HOME/n1s/data will be used instead.

> By default, ORA_NLS10 is not set. It should be set only in a multihomed environment where the locale-specific files are shared.

The 1x1boot.n1b file identifies the set of locales available to the NLSRTL. These locales are defined in a collection of *locale definition files* that reside in the same directory as the 1x1boot.n1b file.

There are four types of locale definition files:

- Language
- Territory
- Character set
- Linguistic sort

Each file contains data relating to only one particular locale type. For each locale type, there can be many different definition files.

This modular design of the locale definition files offers several distinct benefits:

- By using only the set of locales that you need, memory won't be wasted on unnecessary locales.
- Locale definitions can be mixed and matched.
- Locale files can be modified without affecting any other files.
- New locale files can be created without affecting existing files.

All the locale definition files follow the common naming convention:

Code	Position	Meaning
Lx	1–2	The standard prefix for all locale definition files
T	3	Represents the locale type: 0 = language, 1 = territory, 2 = character set, 3 = linguistic sort
Nnnn	4–7	The object ID (in hex)
.n1b	8–11	The standard extension for all locale definition files

For example, the file 1x00001.n1b is the language file for American, as shown in the Locale Builder in Figure 13.1.

FIGURE 13.1 Locale Builder file 1x00001.nlb

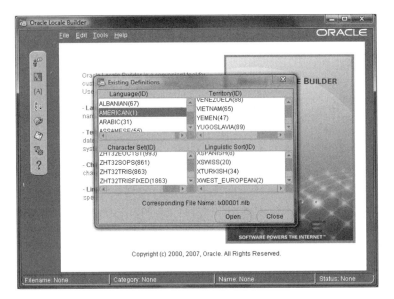

The complete set of locale definition files represents the globalization options available inside the database. Locale definitions can also be added or modified to support new functionality.

Supporting Multilingual Applications

Globalization allows the database to support multitier and client/server applications in any language for which it is configured. Locale-dependent operations are governed by NLS parameters and NLS environment variables set on both the client and server sides.

In the following sections, you will learn how client applications interact with the server from a globalization viewpoint. You will learn the purpose of the character sets defined at database-creation time. You'll learn how data-conversion issues can affect session performance. And finally, you'll learn how clients resolve globalization environment differences when they connect to a server.

Database Character Sets

When a database is created, two session-independent NLS parameters are specified: the database character set and the national character set.

The *database character set* defines the character set that will govern default text storage in the database. This includes all CHAR, VARCHAR2, LONG, and CLOB data as well as all SQL and PL/SQL text.

The *national character set* is an alternate Unicode character set that governs NCHAR, NVARCHAR2, and NCLOB data. You may want to store characters in the database from a character set that is not the database default; for example, the default character set may be US7ASCII, but you may also wish to store Chinese characters in the database. Use the national character set NCHAR, NVARCHAR2, and NCLOB data types to store this non-default character-set data.

Together, these two settings define the available character sets for the database.

Setting the Database Character Set

When you create the database, you specify the database character set thusly using the CHARACTER SET clause, and set the national character set using the NATIONAL CHARACTER SET clause:

```
SQL> CREATE DATABASE LNETEST

...

CHARACTER SET AL32UTF8
NATIONAL CHARACTER SET AL16UTF16

...
```

To identify SQL and PL/SQL source code, the database character set must have either EBCDIC or 7-bit ASCII, depending on the underlying platform, as a subset. Since it is not possible to use a fixed-width multibyte character set as the database character set, you cannot specify AL16UTF16 as the database character set. You can, however, specify AL16UTF16 as the national character set.

Changing the Database Character Set

Once you've created the database, you must re-create it to change the database character sets. The only exception is that if the new character set is a strict superset of all of the schema data, you can use the CSALTER script to change the database character set.

If it is not possible to utilize the CSALTER script, then you can perform a full export of the database, create the new database with the new character set, then import the full database.

Automatic Data Conversion

When a client makes a connection to a database server, the character sets used on both the client and server are compared. If they do not match, Oracle will need to perform automatic data conversion to resolve the difference. There is overhead involved in this conversion process as well as a risk of data loss. Performance will be affected relative to the level of conversion required.

The exception to this rule is when the database character set is a strict *superset* of the client character set. Two things must be true in order to classify a character set as a strict superset of another:

- The superset must contain all of the characters defined in the subset.

- The encoded values of all characters defined in the subset must match their encoded values in the superset.

If Oracle determines that both of these requirements are met, it will not perform automatic data conversion because it is not necessary.

Resolving Client/Server Settings

Any application that connects to the server is considered to be a client, in terms of globalization. Even if the application lives on the same physical machine as the server, it will still be classified as a client. This includes middle-tier application servers. Therefore, from a globalization perspective, all applications are governed by client-side NLS parameters.

When a client application is run, the client NLS environment is initialized from the environment variable settings. All local NLS operations are executed using these settings. *Local NLS operations* are client operations performed independently of any Oracle server session (for example, display formatting in Oracle Developer applications).

When the application completes a connection to the database server, the resulting session is initialized with the NLS environment settings of the server.

However, immediately after the session is established, the client implicitly issues an ALTER SESSION statement to synchronize the session NLS environment to match the client's NLS environment. In fact, the session environment can be modified at any time by using the ALTER SESSION statement, as shown here:

```
SQL*Plus: Release 11.1.0.6.0 - Production on Dim. Oct. 19 20:46:55 2008

Copyright (c) 1982, 2007, Oracle.  All rights reserved.


Connected to:
Oracle Database 11g Enterprise Edition Release 11.1.0.6.0 - Production
With the Partitioning, OLAP, Data Mining and Real Application Testing options

SQL>select sysdate from dual;

SYSDATE
---------
28-AUG-08

SQL> alter session set NLS_LANGUAGE=French;

Session altered.

SQL> select sysdate from dual;

SYSDATE
-----------
28-AOÛT -08
```

```
SQL> alter session set NLS_LANGUAGE=Italian;

Session altered.

SQL> select sysdate from dual;

SYSDATE
---------
28-AGO-08
```

Remember, however, that using ALTER SESSION changes only the session NLS environment. It does not change the client NLS environment.

Using Unicode in a Multilingual Database

Unicode is a universal character set that encompasses all known written languages in the world. Historically, dealing with multiple languages in a database or an application has been a difficult proposition. Existing character sets have always been too limited. Many don't even offer all the characters required for a single language, much less for all languages!

To support a wide variety of languages, it often meant that applications, databases, and programs using different character sets would have to be able to interact and exchange data, all with proper data conversion taking place every step of the way.

To address this problem, Unicode was created with this simple motto:

> Unicode provides a unique number for every character, no matter what the platform, no matter what the program, no matter what the language.
>
> Source: www.unicode.org/standard/WhatIsUnicode.html

Unicode assigns a guaranteed unique value (known as a *code point*) to every character to assure that no conflicts exist. Oracle supports version 5.0 of Unicode and offers the encoding methods listed in Table 13.1.

TABLE 13.1   Oracle-Supported Unicode Encoding Methods

Encoding Method	Description
UTF-8	An 8-bit encoding method that uses 1 to 4 bytes to store characters, as needed. UTF-8 is a strict superset of ASCII, meaning that every character in the ASCII character set is not only represented in the UTF-8 character set, but it also has the same code point value in both character sets. UTF-8 is supported on Unix platforms, HTML, and most Internet browsers.

TABLE 13.1 Oracle-Supported Unicode Encoding Methods *(continued)*

Encoding Method	Description
UCS-2	A fixed-width, 16-bit encoding method, meaning that each character is stored in 2 bytes. Both Microsoft Windows NT and Java support UCS-2 encoding. UCS-2 supports the older Unicode 3 standard; therefore, it does not support supplementary characters.
UTF-16	A strict superset of UCS-2. Offers support of supplementary characters by using two UCS-2 code points for each supplementary character. Newer versions of Windows (2000, XP, Vista) are based on this encoding method.

Unicode can be used in Oracle in several ways:

- It can be defined as the database character set, thereby becoming the default for all SQL CHAR datatypes (CHAR, VARCHAR2, CLOB, and LONG). In this setup, the UTF-8 encoding method will be used.

- It can be used as needed by creating columns using the NCHAR datatypes, also known as Unicode datatypes (NCHAR, NVARCHAR2, and NCLOB). Unicode data can be encoded as either UTF-8 or UTF-16 when used in this scenario.

Using NLS Parameters

Ultimately, Oracle globalization support options are defined by NLS parameter settings. By assigning values to specific NLS parameters, you can control when, where, and how Oracle will utilize globalization support functionality. These settings can be specified in a variety of ways, and their effects may vary accordingly.

On the server side, NLS parameters are read from initialization parameter settings at instance-startup time. The values are stored in the data dictionary, as are the database and national character-set settings.

On the client side, NLS parameters can be defined as environment variables (such as NLS_LANG), or they can be set at the session level by using the ALTER SESSION statement. NLS parameters can also be defined inside SQL function calls with a scope limited to only the current function. Therefore, it is vital to understand the order of precedence that Oracle follows concerning NLS parameter settings.

In the following sections, you'll learn about many of the different NLS parameters, how to set them, and what effect they will have on the system. You'll also learn how Oracle prioritizes NLS parameter settings. Last, you will learn how to use NLS data dictionary and dynamic performance views to access NLS information from the database.

Setting NLS Parameters

Oracle's globalization support is designed to be very simple to use. In many environments, globalization needs can be met by setting a single client-side parameter (NLS_LANG). This is because Oracle automatically derives lower-level specifics from the high-level settings. For instance, if the NLS_TERRITORY parameter is set to AMERICA, Oracle assumes that currency should be displayed as dollars, comma separators should be used, and so on.

However, the granularity provided by Oracle's globalization support allows almost unlimited variations for users with even the most demanding globalization needs.

NLS parameters can be classified into the following categories:

- Language and territory parameters
- Date and time parameters
- Calendar parameters
- Numeric, list, and monetary parameters
- Length semantics

Each category offers one or more individual parameters that can be set to meet your exact globalization needs.

In the following sections, you will learn how to set the NLS_LANG client-side environment variable to specify the NLS environment for your session. You'll also learn about each of the different categories of NLS parameter settings and the different options they offer.

Using the *NLS_LANG* Parameter

NLS_LANG is a client-side environment variable that defines the language, territory, and character set for the client. It is functionally equivalent to setting the NLS_LANGUAGE, NLS_TERRITORY, and NLS_CHARACTERSET parameters individually.

For most clients, the NLS_LANG parameter is all that needs to be set to define the entire globalization environment. This is true because the NLS_LANGUAGE and NLS_TERRITORY settings define the default settings for nearly all other NLS parameters.

The NLS_LANGUAGE parameter, for instance, specifies the default conventions to be used for all of the following globalization elements:

- Language for server messages
- Day and month names and abbreviations
- Symbols to represent a.m., p.m., , AD, and BC
- Sorting sequence for character data
- Affirmative and negative response strings (YES, NO)

The NLS_TERRITORY parameter specifies the default conventions used for these globalization elements:

- Date format
- Decimal character

- Group separator
- Local currency symbol
- ISO currency symbol
- Dual currency symbol
- First day of the week
- Credit/debit symbols
- ISO week flag
- List separator

Therefore, no other NLS parameters need to be set unless the default settings don't meet your needs.

The format for setting the NLS_LANG parameter is as follows:

```
NLS_LANG = language_territory.characterset
```

For example, the following are all valid:

```
NLS_LANG=AMERICAN_AMERICA.US7ASCII
NLS_LANG=JAPANESE_JAPAN.JA16EUC
NLS_LANG=FRENCH_CANADA.WE8ISO8859P1
```

The language element controls the conventions used for Oracle messages, sorting, and day and month names. If language is not set, Oracle will default to AMERICAN. Each language is identified by a unique name, such as FRENCH or GERMAN. Languages also impose a default territory and character set that will be used unless overridden.

The territory element determines the default date, monetary format, and numeric format conventions. If the territory is not defined, the default territory value from the language setting will be used. Territories carry distinct names such as AMERICA, CANADA, and GERMANY.

The character-set element determines the client character set. Normally this would be the Oracle character set that matches the character set of the operating system or terminal. Character sets have unique identifiers such as WE8ISO8859P1, US7ASCII, and JA16EUC.

All NLS_LANG definition components are optional. For example, the following is valid to set the language component independently of the other components:

```
NLS_LANG=FRENCH
```

It is also possible to set the territory and character-set components independently, but the following conventions must be followed:

- Territory must be preceded by an underscore character (_)
- Character set must be preceded by a period (.)

For example, to set the territory to AMERICA, you could use this syntax:

```
NLS_LANG=_AMERICA
```

Oracle Character-Set Naming Convention

The naming convention for Oracle character sets is as follows:

region number_of_bits standard_character_set_name [S][C]

The elements of the naming convention have the following meanings:

- *region* is generally a two-character abbreviation (US, WE, JA).

- *number_of_bits* represents the number of bits used to store one character.

- *standard_character_set_name* represents the common name for the character set. This name can vary in length (ASCII, ISO8859P1, SJIS).

- The optional S and C are used to specify character sets that are exclusive to the server (S) or the client (C) side.

For example, US7ASCII is a 7-bit United States code commonly referred to as ASCII (American Standard Code for Information Interchange).

The Unicode character sets UTF-8 and UTF-E defy Oracle's standard character-set naming convention.

To set the client character set to UTF-8, you could use this syntax:

```
NLS_LANG=.UTF8
```

 Use caution when setting NLS_LANG. It is possible to make combinations that will not function correctly, such as specifying a character set that does not support the specified language.

In the following example, you'll set the NLS_LANG parameter to FRENCH_FRANCE .WE8ISO8859P1 and see how this affects your session. Remember that NLS_LANG is an environment variable setting, so it must be set in the operating system before connecting to Oracle:

```
$ export NLS_LANG=French_France.WE8ISO8859P1
$ sqlplus "/ as sysdba"

SQL*Plus: Release 11.1.0.6.0 - Production on Dim. Oct. 19 20:46:55 2008

Copyright (c) 1982, 2007, Oracle.  All rights reserved.
```

```
Connected to:
Oracle Database 11g Enterprise Edition Release 11.1.0.6.0 - Production
With the Partitioning, OLAP, Data Mining and Real Application Testing options

SQL> select prod_id, time_id,
round(sum(amount_sold),2) amount
from sh.sales
group by prod_id, time_id;

PROD_ID TIME_ID     AMOUNT
---------- -------- ----------
...
        127 19/10/01      87,88
         18 22/12/01    1478,83
         21 29/11/01    1047,02
         22 28/12/01      75,15
         23 22/10/01      21,15
         32 26/10/01      68,94
         45 02/12/01      47,74
        113 13/12/01      23,89
        114 08/12/01      19,05
        121 01/10/01      10,59
        121 20/12/01      32,43
        122 06/11/01      20,86
        128 03/11/01      30,16
        134 23/10/01      43,38

36292 rows selected.
SQL>
```

As you can see in this example, the date and number formats follow the conventions established in the NLS_LANG settings.

Using Language and Territory Parameters

NLS language and territory functionality can also be defined individually using the NLS_LANGUAGE and NLS_TERRITORY parameters.

On the server side, these parameters can be set as initialization parameters. They will then become the default settings for the Oracle instance. For example, the following lines could be inserted into the INIT.ORA file:

```
NLS_LANGUAGE=French
NLS_TERRITORY=France
```

When the database instance is next started, these settings will become the default settings for the instance.

On the client side, these parameters can be set within a session by using the ALTER SESSION statement, as shown here:

```
SQL> alter session set NLS_LANGUAGE=French;

Session altered.

SQL> alter session set NLS_TERRITORY=France;

Session altered.
```

NLS parameters modified using ALTER SESSION have a higher precedence than those set through environment variables such as NLS_LANG. Therefore, they will override the previously set parameter values. This topic will be covered later in this chapter. Of course, the value for NLS_LANGUAGE and NLS_TERRITORY must be legitimate; for example, attempting to set the NLS_TERRITORY to Fredonia will result in an error:

```
SQL> alter session set NLS_TERRITORY=Fredonia;
ERROR:
ORA-12705: Impossible d'acc_der aux fichiers de donn_es
NLS ou l'environnement indiqu_ n'est pas valide
```

And if you don't read French but you wish to know what the error message translates to in American English, simply set your NLS_LANGUAGE to American and then attempt to set the NLS_TERRITORY to Fredonia.

```
SQL> alter session set NLS_LANGUAGE=American;

Session altered.

SQL> alter session set NLS_TERRITORY=Fredonia;
ERROR:
ORA-12705: Cannot access NLS data files or invalid environment specified
```

Using Date and Time Parameters

NLS date and time functionality can also be defined individually using the following NLS parameters:

- NLS_DATE_FORMAT
- NLS_DATE_LANGUAGE
- NLS_TIMESTAMP_FORMAT
- NLS_TIMESTAMP_TZ_FORMAT

All of these parameters can be set within a session by using the ALTER SESSION statement. They can also be defined as initialization parameters and will then become default settings for the entire instance.

NLS_DATE_FORMAT

The NLS_DATE_FORMAT parameter specifies the default format for dates in the current session. It can be defined as any valid date-format mask, such as in this example:

```
SQL> ALTER SESSION SET NLS_DATE_FORMAT = MM/DD/YY;

Session altered.
```

You can even append text literals into the date format, if you wish, by enclosing the literal in double quotes. You must also enclose the entire format string in apostrophes (single quotes), as shown here:

```
SQL> alter session set NLS_DATE_FORMAT ='"Today''s date is "MM/DD/YYYY';

Session altered.

SQL> select sysdate from dual;

SYSDATE
-------------------------
Today's date is 10/19/2008
```

Note that normal quoting rules apply inside the text literal. Therefore, two apostrophes were required to create the string "Today's".

NLS_DATE_LANGUAGE

The NLS_DATE_LANGUAGE parameter governs the language used in the following situations:

- Day and month names and abbreviations displayed by the functions TO_CHAR and TO_DATE
- Day and month names returned by the default date format (NLS_DATE_FORMAT)
- Abbreviations for a.m., p.m., AD, and BC

NLS_DATE_LANGUAGE accepts any valid language as a value and can be set as shown here:

```
SQL> alter session set nls_date_language=Italian;

Session altered.

SQL> select to_char(sysdate,'Day:Dd Month YYYY') from dual;
```

```
TO_CHAR(SYSDATE,'DAY:DDMONT
---------------------------
Domenica :19 Ottobre   2008
```

NLS_TIMESTAMP_FORMAT

The NLS_TIMESTAMP_FORMAT parameter is used to set the default date format for both TIME-STAMP and TIMESTAMP WITH TIME ZONE datatypes. An example is shown here:

```
SQL> alter session set nls_timestamp_format='MM/DD/YYYY HH24:MI:SS.FF';

Session altered.

SQL> select startup_time
from sys.dba_hist_snapshot
where rownum < 3;

STARTUP_TIME
----------------------------------------------------------------------
10/11/2008 11:32:33.000
10/11/2008 11:32:33.000

SQL> select next_run_date
from sys.dba_scheduler_jobs;

NEXT_RUN_DATE
----------------------------------------------------------------------
20/10/08 03:00:00,000000 US/CENTRAL
20/10/08 03:00:00,000000 US/CENTRAL
01/11/08 01:01:01,400000 -05:00
19/10/08 21:26:27,000000 -04:00
19/10/08 20:40:30,000000 -05:00

5 rows selected.
SQL>
```

The TIMESTAMP and TIMESTAMP WITH TIME ZONE datatypes will be covered later in this chapter.

NLS_TIMESTAMP_TZ_FORMAT

Like the NLS_TIMESTAMP_FORMAT parameter, the NLS_TIMESTAMP_TZ_FORMAT parameter is used to set the default date format for TIMESTAMP and TIMESTAMP WITH TIME ZONE datatypes. However, as the name suggests, it adds the option of time-zone formatting, as shown here:

```
SQL> alter session set nls_timestamp_tz_format = 'YYYY/MM/DD HH:MI TZH:TZM';

Session altered.

SQL> select startup_time
from sys.dba_hist_snapshot
where rownum < 3;

STARTUP_TIME
--------------------------------------------------------------------
10/11/2008 11:32:33.000
10/11/2008 11:32:33.000

SQL> select next_run_date
  from sys.dba_scheduler_jobs;

NEXT_RUN_DATE
--------------------------------------------------------------------
2008/10/20 03:00 -05:00
2008/10/20 03:00 -05:00
2008/11/01 01:01 -05:00
2008/10/19 09:26 -04:00
2008/10/19 08:40 -05:00

5 rows selected.
SQL>
```

As you can see in the example, the TZH:TZM element shows the time-zone offset in hours and minutes.

Using Calendar Parameters

Different geographical areas can use different calendaring systems. Oracle 11*g*'s globalization support defines seven distinct calendars, all of which are fully supported:

- Gregorian
- Japanese Imperial
- ROC Official
- Persian

- Thai Buddha
- Arabic Hijrah
- English Hijrah

For each of these calendars, the following information is maintained:

First day of the week   While the United States and many other countries consider Sunday to represent the first day of the week, other countries, such as Germany, consider Monday to be the first day of the week.

First calendar week of the year   Many countries use the week number for things like bookkeeping and scheduling. However, an International Standards Organization (ISO) week can differ from the calendar-week number. (ISO weeks run from Monday through Sunday.) Oracle supports both conventions. Here are the definitions provided by Oracle:

- If January 1 falls on a Friday, Saturday, or Sunday, then the ISO week that includes January 1 is the last week of the previous year because most of the days in the week belong to the previous year.
- If January 1 falls on a Monday, Tuesday, Wednesday, or Thursday, then the ISO week is the first week of the new year because most of the days in the week belong to the new year.

Number of days/months in a year   The number of days and months in a year can differ between calendars, as shown in Table 13.2.

First year of the era   Different regions may also choose a notable year in which to start, much like the Gregorian calendar starts with Anno Domini (Latin for "the year of the Lord"), also known as the Common Era. The Islamic calendar, for example, starts with the year of the Hegria (622 AD, when the prophet Mohammed and his followers migrated from Mecca to Medina). The Japanese Imperial calendar starts from the first year of an Emperor's reign.

The NLS_CALENDAR parameter is used to specify which calendar Oracle should use, as shown here:

```
SQL> alter session set NLS_CALENDAR = 'Persian';
Session altered.

SQL> select sysdate from dual;

SYSDATE
------------------
28 Mehr        1387
```

TABLE 13.2 International Calendar Days/Months in a Year

Calendar	Description
Gregorian	The standard calendar used by most of the world. The Gregorian calendar has 365 days in each year, with 366 days on leap years. The number of days in a month varies. Years are counted from the beginning of the Common Era, or Anno Domini.
Japanese Imperial	Same as Gregorian, but the year starts with the beginning of each Imperial era.
ROC Official	Same as Gregorian, but the year starts with the founding of the Republic of China: Gregorian year 1912 is ROC Official year 1. For example, Gregorian year 2008 is ROC Official year 97.
Persian	The first six months have 31 days each. The next five have 30 days each. The last month has 29 days (30 in a leap year).
Thai Buddha	Same as Gregorian, but the year begins with BE (Buddhist Era), which starts with the death of Gautama Buddha; for example, Gregorian year 2008 is Thai Buddha year 2551, or Gregorian plus 543 years.
Arabic Hijrah	Has 12 months, with 354 or 355 days.
English Hijrah	Has 12 months, with 354 or 355 days.

Using Numeric, List, and Monetary Parameters

Number-formatting conventions define how Oracle should display large numbers and numeric lists.

In the United States, for example, the following convention is followed:

1,234,567.89

Germany, on the other hand, uses a convention that is diametrically opposite:

1.234.567,89

In the following sections, you'll learn to use the various numeric, list, and monetary NLS parameters.

NLS_NUMERIC_CHARACTERS

The NLS_NUMERIC_CHARACTERS parameter defines the characters that represent the decimal and group separator (for example, thousands, millions, and so on) elements in the number-format mask. These elements are represented by the letters *D* and *G*, respectively, in the number-format mask. Any single-byte character can be assigned, with the following exceptions:

- The decimal character and the group separator cannot be the same character.
- They cannot be numeric.
- They cannot have mathematical significance (+, −, <, >).

When this parameter is set, the decimal character comes before the group separator, as shown here:

```
SQL> alter session set NLS_NUMERIC_CHARACTERS=",.";

Session altered.

SQL> select cust_id, to_char(sum(amount_sold), '9G999G999D99') big_sales
from sh.sales
group by cust_id
having sum(amount_sold) > 30000;
CUST_ID    BIG_SALES
---------- -------------
...
      6960    33.407,59
      7680    33.528,24
      3080    43.395,67
     12600    49.980,28
850 rows selected.
SQL>
```

As you can see, the decimal character is now represented by a comma. The group separator, on the other hand, is now represented by a period.

NLS_LIST_SEPARATOR

The NLS_LIST_SEPARATOR parameter specifies the character used to separate values in a list of values. The following restrictions apply to the NLS_LIST_SEPARATOR parameter:

- It cannot be numeric.
- It cannot be the same character as the numeric or monetary decimal character.
- It cannot have mathematical significance (+, −, <, >).

 The NLS_LIST_SEPARATOR parameter is strictly a client-side setting. It has no meaning on the server. Therefore, it is set through a client-side environment variable but does not execute an implicit ALTER SESSION when a server connection is established.

NLS_CURRENCY

The NLS_CURRENCY parameter defines the currency symbol that will be displayed by the element *L* in the number-format mask, as shown here:

```
SQL> alter session set NLS_CURRENCY = "£";

Session altered.

SQL> select to_char(123.45,'L9G999G999D99') amount
from dual;

AMOUNT
----------------------
                £123.45
```

The NLS_CURRENCY parameter is not limited to a single character. It can be set to a string as well:

```
SQL> alter session set NLS_CURRENCY = " USD";

Session altered.

SQL>  select to_char(123.45,'9G999G999D99L') amount
  2    from dual;

AMOUNT
----------------------
          123.45 USD
```

Notice in the example that a space is embedded at the beginning of the string. Without the space, the output would appear as shown here:

```
AMOUNT
----------------------
          123.45USD
```

NLS_ISO_CURRENCY

The NLS_ISO_CURRENCY parameter is used to prevent ambiguity in the currency symbol. For example, the dollar sign ($) can be used for both Australian and American dollars. NLS_ISO_CURRENCY uses a unique text string in place of the currency sign. Several common examples are shown here:

USD: United States

AUD: Australia

EEK: Estonia

EUR: Germany

GBP: United Kingdom

The NLS_ISO_CURRENCY parameter defines the currency symbol that will be displayed by the C element of the number-format mask. It can be modified using the ALTER SESSION statement, but instead of a text string, it requires a valid territory name, as follows:

```
SQL>  alter session set NLS_ISO_CURRENCY=France;

Session altered.

SQL> select to_char(123.45,'9G999G999D99C') amount
  2  from dual;

AMOUNT
-------------------
          123.45EUR
```

Using the *NLS_LENGTH_SEMANTICS* Parameter

Single-byte character sets always use one byte to store one character. This makes storage calculation a breeze. But when you're using a multibyte character set, such as Unicode, a single character may use several bytes of storage. Column sizing becomes much more difficult in this situation.

Length semantics, originally introduced in Oracle9*i*, make it possible to size columns using either bytes or characters. The method of calculating the length of character strings in bytes is known as byte semantics. Calculating the length in characters is referred to as character semantics.

The NLS_LENGTH_SEMANTICS parameter defines the default method of length semantics to either BYTE (the default) or CHAR. An example is shown here:

```
SQL> alter system set NLS_LENGTH_SEMANTICS = CHAR;

System altered.
```

Consider the following example:

```
SQL> create table test_table (
Last_name VARCHAR2(25));

Table created.
```

When length semantics are set to CHAR, the LAST_NAME column in this table will hold 25 characters, no matter how many actual bytes of storage are required.

When length semantics are set to BYTE, the LAST_NAME column will allocate 25 bytes of storage. If the character set requires 3 bytes to store a single character (or symbol), only 8 characters can be stored.

The default setting can be overridden by declaring the length semantics directly in the CREATE TABLE statement. For example, when you're defining a character column, character semantics can be forced using the following syntax:

```
SQL> create table test_table (
Last_name VARCHAR2(25 CHAR));

Table created.
```

This example forces the use of character semantics, regardless of the setting of the NLS_LENGTH_SEMANTICS parameter.

There are a few exceptions to consider when dealing with length semantics:

- NCHAR, NVARCHAR, CLOB, and NCLOB datatypes are not affected by the NLS_LENGTH_SEMANTICS parameter value. These are datatypes designed specifically for multi-byte character data; therefore they will always use character semantics.

- Tables in the SYS and SYSTEM tablespaces are not governed by the NLS_LENGTH_SEMANTICS parameter. All data dictionary tables always use byte semantics.

Prioritizing NLS Parameters

Oracle databases often represent only one tier in a multitier environment. For instance, let's assume that Arren is a user in France. He uses a custom, client-side application that connects to an application server in Italy. The application server connects to a transaction-processing gateway in Sweden. The transaction-processing gateway connects to the Oracle database in the United States.

Each of these machines may have NLS settings appropriate for their respective locale, but none match the settings of the database server. How does the database server determine the NLS settings to honor?

There are several different ways in which NLS parameters can be specified. Therefore, when conflicting settings are issued, Oracle needs to have a method of prioritizing to determine which setting will ultimately be used.

NLS parameters can be defined using any of the following methods:

- Setting server-initialization parameters
- Setting client-environment variables
- Using the ALTER SESSION statement
- By executing SQL functions
- As default values

In the following sections, you will learn about each of the methods of setting NLS parameter values as well as how Oracle chooses to prioritize them.

Setting Server-Initialization Parameters

NLS settings can be defined as initialization parameters on the server. Initialization parameters are loaded at instance-startup time, as in this example:

```
NLS_LANGUAGE=FRENCH
```

The effect of initialization-parameter settings will be seen only on the server. They have no effect on the client side. They will, however, govern sessions created by the client to the server, unless the client NLS environment overrides them.

Setting Client Environment Variables

Environment variables on the client side will govern local client-side NLS operations (operations that don't involve the database). They will also override server-side NLS settings for sessions created from the client.

In the following example, the environment variable NLS_LANGUAGE is set to French before a session is opened. Note that in a Windows environment, the environment variable could be set either using the set command or in the Environment tab in the System Properties window.

```
$ export NLS_LANGUAGE=French

$ sqlplus "/ as sysdba"

SQL*Plus: Release 11.1.0.6.0 - Production on Dim. Oct. 19 21:22:15 2008

Copyright (c) 1982, 2007, Oracle.  All rights reserved.


Connected to:
Oracle Database 11g Enterprise Edition Release 11.1.0.6.0 - Production
With the Partitioning, OLAP, Data Mining and Real Application Testing options
SQL> select to_char(sysdate, 'Mon') from dual;
TO_CH
-----
Oct.
```

When the client-side environment variable NLS_LANG was set, the server's NLS settings were overridden for the session. The client program accomplishes this by issuing an implicit ALTER SESSION statement when a new session is opened.

Using the *ALTER SESSION* Statement

Setting NLS parameters using the ALTER SESSION statement also overrides the server-side NLS settings for the current session, as in this example:

```
SQL> ALTER SESSION set NLS_SORT = FRENCH;

Session altered.
```

Using ALTER SESSION also overrides any previous ALTER SESSION settings. Therefore, an explicit ALTER SESSION statement overrides settings from the client environment variables (which perform an implicit ALTER SESSION call).

Setting NLS Parameters in SQL Functions

NLS parameters can also be set inside certain SQL functions. Inline NLS parameter settings have the highest priority and will override any other NLS settings. However, their scope is limited to the immediate SQL function, as shown here:

```
SQL> select to_char(sysdate, 'DD/MON/YYYY','nls_date_language=Italian')
from dual;
TO_CHAR(SYS
-----------
19/OTT/2008


SQL> select to_char(sysdate, 'DD/MON/YYYY') from dual;

TO_CHAR(SYSDA
-------------
19/OCT./2008
```

As you can see in this example, the inline NLS parameter setting affected only the function in which it was called. It had no effect on the subsequent statement.

Only specific SQL functions will accept inline NLS parameter settings.

Prioritization Summary

As you learned in the preceding sections, there are five distinct methods in which NLS parameters can be specified. Oracle prioritizes these methods to ensure that conflicting settings can be resolved. Table 13.3 summarizes these methods for NLS parameter prioritization as well as the scope for each method.

TABLE 13.3   NLS Parameter–Setting Precedence

Method	Priority	Scope
Set in SQL functions	1	Current SQL function
Explicit ALTER SESSION statement	2	Current session
Client environment variable (implicit ALTER SESSION statement)	3	Current session
Set by server-initialization parameter	4	Instance
Default	5	Instance

Using NLS Views

Information relating to Oracle NLS settings is stored in the data dictionary and inside fixed tables in memory. This information consists of NLS settings for the session, instance, and database. You can also view a list of the valid values that may be specified when setting NLS parameters.

The following views can be queried to find NLS information from the data dictionary and from dynamic performance tables:

- NLS_SESSION_PARAMETERS
- NLS_INSTANCE_PARAMETERS
- NLS_DATABASE_PARAMETERS
- V$NLS_VALID_VALUES

We will look at each of these views in the following sections.

NLS_SESSION_PARAMETERS

The NLS_SESSION_PARAMETERS view offers an insight into the current NLS settings for your session. Here is an example, continuing with the environment and session NLS parameters set earlier:

```
SQL> select * from nls_session_parameters;

PARAMETER                       VALUE
------------------------------- ---------------------------
NLS_LANGUAGE                    FRENCH
NLS_TERRITORY                   FRANCE
```

```
NLS_CURRENCY
NLS_ISO_CURRENCY                 FRANCE
NLS_NUMERIC_CHARACTERS           ,
NLS_CALENDAR                     GREGORIAN
NLS_DATE_FORMAT                  DD/MM/RR
NLS_DATE_LANGUAGE                FRENCH
NLS_SORT                         FRENCH
NLS_TIME_FORMAT                  HH24:MI:SSXFF
NLS_TIMESTAMP_FORMAT             DD/MM/RR HH24:MI:SSXFF
NLS_TIME_TZ_FORMAT               HH24:MI:SSXFF TZR
NLS_TIMESTAMP_TZ_FORMAT          DD/MM/RR HH24:MI:SSXFF TZR
NLS_DUAL_CURRENCY
NLS_COMP                         BINARY
NLS_LENGTH_SEMANTICS             BYTE
NLS_NCHAR_CONV_EXCP              FALSE

17 rows selected.
```

You will notice that the NLS_SESSION_PARAMETERS view is restricted to show only the current session and nothing more. You may also see settings here that you don't remember specifying. If so, the values represent either the default setting or the value derived from a higher-level NLS parameter. For example, if NLS_TERRITORY is set to AMERICA, the NLS_CURRENCY parameter will automatically be set to use dollars.

NLS_INSTANCE_PARAMETERS

The NLS_INSTANCE_PARAMETERS view returns NLS settings for the entire instance rather than for a single session. These are settings that have been set explicitly through initialization parameters or ALTER SYSTEM statements. Here is an example:

```
SQL> select * from nls_instance_parameters;

PARAMETER                        VALUE
-----------------------------    --------------
NLS_LANGUAGE                     AMERICAN
NLS_TERRITORY                    AMERICA
NLS_SORT
NLS_DATE_LANGUAGE
NLS_DATE_FORMAT
NLS_CURRENCY
NLS_NUMERIC_CHARACTERS
NLS_ISO_CURRENCY
NLS_CALENDAR
```

```
NLS_TIME_FORMAT
NLS_TIMESTAMP_FORMAT
NLS_TIME_TZ_FORMAT
NLS_TIMESTAMP_TZ_FORMAT
NLS_DUAL_CURRENCY
NLS_COMP                    BINARY
NLS_LENGTH_SEMANTICS        BYTE
NLS_NCHAR_CONV_EXCP         FALSE

17 rows selected.
```

The results from the NLS_INSTANCE_PARAMETERS view show that many parameters have not been explicitly set. Instead, they derive their value from higher-level parameters. For example, NLS_SORT derives its value from NLS_LANGUAGE, while the currency-, date-, and time-related parameters are derived from NLS_TERRITORY.

NLS_DATABASE_PARAMETERS

The NLS_DATABASE_PARAMETERS view shows NLS settings for the database itself. These represent the default values that will govern the instance, unless they are overridden by initialization parameter settings.

An example is shown here:

```
SQL> select * from nls_database_parameters;
```

PARAMETER	VALUE
NLS_LANGUAGE	AMERICAN
NLS_TERRITORY	AMERICA
NLS_CURRENCY	$
NLS_ISO_CURRENCY	AMERICA
NLS_NUMERIC_CHARACTERS	.,
NLS_CHARACTERSET	WE8MSWIN1252
NLS_CALENDAR	GREGORIAN
NLS_DATE_FORMAT	DD-MON-RR
NLS_DATE_LANGUAGE	AMERICAN
NLS_SORT	BINARY
NLS_TIME_FORMAT	HH.MI.SSXFF AM
NLS_TIMESTAMP_FORMAT	DD-MON-RR HH.MI.SSXFF AM
NLS_TIME_TZ_FORMAT	HH.MI.SSXFF AM TZR
NLS_TIMESTAMP_TZ_FORMAT	DD-MON-RR HH.MI.SSXFF AM TZR
NLS_DUAL_CURRENCY	$
NLS_COMP	BINARY

```
NLS_LENGTH_SEMANTICS              BYTE
NLS_NCHAR_CONV_EXCP               FALSE
NLS_NCHAR_CHARACTERSET            AL16UTF16
NLS_RDBMS_VERSION                 11.1.0.6.0

20 rows selected.
```

The values shown in the NLS_DATABASE_PARMETERS view are set at database-creation time and based on the parameters used in the CREATE DATABASE statement.

V$NLS_VALID_VALUES

The V$NLS_VALID_VALUES dynamic performance view lists all valid values for each of the following NLS parameters: NLS_LANGUAGE, NLS_SORT, NLS_TERRITORY, and NLS_CHARACTERSET.

The following example shows a truncated listing:

```
SQL>  select *
  from v$nls_valid_values
  where value like '%GER%';


PARAMETER        VALUE             ISDEP
---------------  ---------------   -----

LANGUAGE         GERMAN            FALSE
LANGUAGE         GERMAN DIN        FALSE
TERRITORY        GERMANY           FALSE
TERRITORY        ALGERIA           FALSE
SORT             GERMAN            FALSE
SORT             XGERMAN           FALSE
SORT             GERMAN_DIN        FALSE
SORT             XGERMAN_DIN       FALSE

8 rows selected.
SQL>
```

Using Datetime Datatypes

A challenge in managing data in a global environment is synchronizing transactions that occur across time zones. Oracle's globalization support offers special datatypes and functionality to manage dates and times across differing time zones.

In the following sections, you'll learn about the Oracle datatypes that store date and time information. The data stored using these datatypes are often called datetimes, and you'll learn about the following:

- DATE
- TIMESTAMP
- TIMESTAMP WITH TIME ZONE
- TIMESTAMP WITH LOCAL TIME ZONE

You'll also be introduced to several datetime SQL functions. Last, time-zone parameters and files will be covered.

Using the DATE Datatype

The DATE datatype is used to store date information as well as time information in the database. In fact, every date stored as a DATE datatype will have an accompanying time, even if no time was specified when the date was stored. See Exercise 13.1, "Time Elements in DATE Datatypes," for further information on time elements.

To define a column using the DATE datatype, use the DATE keyword as shown here:

```
SQL> create table birthdates (
  client_id NUMBER,
  birthdate DATE);

Table created.
```

Oracle dates consist of seven parts: century, year, month, day, hours, minutes, and seconds (elapsed since midnight). In fact, they are stored internally in the database as seven separate one-byte elements.

To demonstrate, insert a row into the BIRTHDATES table that was created earlier:

```
SQL> insert into birthdates
  values(1, TO_DATE('01-DEC-68'));

1 row created.

SQL> commit;

Commit complete.
```

Next, select the date from the table using the following TO_CHAR formatting option:

```
SQL> select to_char(birthdate,'YYYY-MM-DD:HH24:MI:SS')
from birthdates;
```

```
TO_CHAR(BIRTHDATE,'
------------------
1968-12-01:00:00:00
```

You can see the elements displayed clearly when using this formatting option. However, that doesn't tell you anything about how the data is stored internally. To see that, use the DUMP function, as shown here:

```
SQL> select dump(birthdate)
  from birthdates;


DUMP(BIRTHDATE)
------------------------------------------------------
Typ=12 Len=7: 119,168,12,1,1,1,1
```

The DUMP function shows the datatype, the length (number of bytes), and the actual byte values for a particular element. So, the example shows that the BIRTHDATE element is stored internally as a DATE datatype (typ=12). It occupies 7 bytes (Len=7) of storage, and the values stored in those bytes are 119, 168, 12, 1, 1, 1, and 1. The century is recorded in the first byte as 100 + the century. The year is recorded in the second byte as 100 + the year. The month and day of the month are stored in subsequent bytes. The hour, minute, and second are each incremented by 1.

Oracle stores the century and the year elements using excess-100 notation, which means that it adds 100 to the number before storing it. Also, the hours, minutes, and seconds elements are stored using excess-1 notation. As you probably guessed, that means that it adds 1 to each number before storing it.

Therefore, if the stored values were converted to standard decimal notation, this is what we would see:

```
DUMP(BIRTHDATE)
------------------------------------------------------
Typ=12 Len=7: 19,68,12,1,1,1,1
```

Now, you can see that the stored values do indeed match the original date, as shown here:

```
SQL> select to_char(birthdate,'YYYY-MM-DD:HH24:MI:SS')
  from birthdates;


TO_CHAR(BIRTHDATE,'
------------------
1968-12-01:00:00:00
```

By better understanding how the data is stored internally, you can think of dates as collections of individual elements that can be accessed together or individually. In Exercise 13.1, we will practice storing date and time values in columns with different data types, then query and compare the results.

EXERCISE 13.1

Time Elements in DATE Datatypes

DATE datatypes always store both a date and a time. If no time is specified when storing a date, Oracle will use a default time of midnight. This can be problematic if you're not careful, as this exercise will demonstrate.

1. First, confirm the date by selecting SYSDATE from dual:

   ```
   SQL> select sysdate from dual;


   SYSDATE
   ---------
   19-OCT-08
   ```

2. Create a table with a VARCHAR2 column to contain a date string and a DATE column:

   ```
   SQL> create table conv_dates (datestring varchar2(15),
   converted_date date);
   Table created.
   ```

3. Insert the current date into a table column defined as a datatype of DATE:

   ```
   SQL> insert into conv_dates
     values ('10-19-2008', to_date('10-19-2008','MM-DD-YYYY'));


   1 row created.


   SQL> commit;


   Commit complete.
   ```

4. Execute the following SQL:

   ```
   SQL> select * from conv_dates where converted_date = sysdate;


   no rows selected
   ```

Even though the two dates appear identical, the query fails to return any matching rows. The following queries will show you the reason:

```
SQL> select
 to_char(converted_date, 'MM-DD-YYYY HH24:MI')
 from conv_dates;
```

```
TO_CHAR(CONVERTE
----------------
10-19-2008 00:00
12-01-1968 00:00

SQL> select
  to_char(sysdate,'MM-DD-YYYY HH24:MI')
  from dual;

TO_CHAR(SYSDATE,
----------------
10-19-2008 22:22
```

Because no time element was defined when you inserted the rows into the CONV_DATES table, Oracle defaulted the time to midnight. SYSDATE, on the other hand, returns the current date and the current time. Therefore, unless you happen to run the query at exactly midnight, the query returns no rows.

To resolve this problem, you can use the TRUNC function, as shown here:

```
SQL> select * from conv_dates
  where trunc(converted_date) = trunc(sysdate);

DATESTRING      CONVERTED_
--------------- ----------
10-19-2008      19/10/08
```

The TRUNC function removes the time element from the date element in a DATE value. With the time element gone, the query returns one row, as expected.

When entering date information into a DATE datatype, you can specify it in several ways:

Literal The date can be entered as a literal, which matches the NLS_DATE_FORMAT format. For example, if NLS_DATE_FORMAT is defined as 'MM-DD-YYYY', then a literal of '12-21-2000' would be acceptable, as shown in this example:

```
SQL> alter session set NLS_DATE_FORMAT = "MM-DD-YYYY";

Session altered.
```

```
SQL> insert into birthdates
values(2, '12-21-2000');

1 row created.
```

Note that in this example, because no time portion was specified, Oracle will set the time elements to represent midnight.

ANSI date literal   An American National Standards Institute (ANSI) date literal contains no time element. It must be formatted exactly as shown here:

```
DATE 'YYYY-MM-DD'
```

Dates can be entered using the ANSI date-literal format at any time, regardless of the NLS_ DATE_FORMAT setting. Here's an example:

```
SQL> insert into birthdates
  2  values(3, DATE '1969-08-23');

1 row created.
```

TO_DATE function   Dates can also be entered by using the **TO_DATE** function. This function converts text strings to DATE types based on the format specified. An example is shown here:

```
SQL> insert into birthdates
     values(4, to_date('04-19-1977 13:45', 'MM-DD-YYYY HH24:MI');
```

This example specifies not only the date, but also the hours and minutes elements of the time.

The TO_DATE function can also be handy for converting dates that have been stored as character types. Consider the following examples using the CONV_DATES table created earlier in this section. This table will hold a string of 15 characters and a date. Now, a string representation of two dates will be inserted in the table. Note that they are being stored as VARCHAR2 character data, not as dates:

```
SQL> insert into conv_dates (datestring)
     values ('12-01-1968');

1 row created.

SQL> insert into conv_dates (datestring)
     values ('04-09-1965');

1 row created.
```

```
SQL> commit;

Commit complete.
```

Next, the strings will be converted and stored as dates by using the TO_DATE function:

```
SQL> update conv_dates
  set converted_date =
  to_date(datestring,'MM-DD-YYYY');

2 rows updated.

SQL> commit;

Commit complete.
```

Now both will be selected, as shown here:

```
SQL> select * from conv_dates;

DATESTRING      CONVERTED_D
--------------- -----------
12-01-1968      01-DEC-1968
04-09-1965      09-APR-1965
```

As you can see in this example, the TO_DATE function converted the dates stored as VARCHAR2 data in the DATESTRING column into the DATE datatype format, which was subsequently stored in the CONVERTED_DATE column.

Using the TIMESTAMP Datatype

The TIMESTAMP datatype offers all the date and time elements found in the DATE datatype in addition to the extended functionality of storing fractional seconds.

By default, the TIMESTAMP datatype stores fractional seconds to six digits of precision. This can be changed, however, by specifying a number from 0 and 9 in parentheses after the TIMESTAMP keyword. This number determines the digits of precision for the fractional seconds, as shown here:

```
SQL> create table test_stamp (stamp timestamp(2));

Table created.
```

```
SQL> insert into test_stamp
select to_timestamp('19-OCT-2008 17:54.38.92',
'DD-MON-YYYY HH24:MI:SS:FF')
from dual;

1 row created.

SQL> commit;

Commit complete.

SQL> select * from test_stamp;

STAMP
------------------------------------
19-OCT-08 05.54.38.92 PM
```

As you can see, the timestamp was entered using the TO_TIMESTAMP function (which is similar to the TO_DATE function). Notice that fractional seconds can be specified by using the FF element in the date mask.

The TIMESTAMP datatype should be used when locale information (time zone) is not required but fractional-second granularity is. For example, application event logging is a common use of the TIMESTAMP datatype.

Using the TIMESTAMP WITH TIME ZONE Datatype

The TIMESTAMP WITH TIME ZONE datatype extends the functionality of the TIMESTAMP datatype by including time-zone information. The time-zone data is stored as an offset (hours and minutes) between the local time and the UTC (Coordinated Universal Time, formerly known as Greenwich mean time). It can be displayed either in this form or in the form of a region name.

Like the TIMESTAMP datatype, the TIMESTAMP WITH TIME ZONE datatype stores fractional seconds to six digits of precision. This can be changed by specifying a number from 0 and 9 in parentheses between the TIMESTAMP keyword and the WITH TIME ZONE keywords. This number determines the digits of precision for the fractional seconds, as in this example:

```
SQL> create table stamp_tz (stamp_tz TIMESTAMP(4) WITH TIME ZONE);
Table created
```

The TIMESTAMP WITH TIME ZONE is recommended when local information and precise time transactions across time zones need to be synchronized. For example, a bank with branches in different time zones needs to post transactions in real time, regardless of location.

Using the TIMESTAMP WITH LOCAL TIME ZONE Datatype

The TIMESTAMP WITH TIME ZONE datatype doesn't actually store time-zone information at all. Instead, when a record is inserted into a column defined with a datatype of TIMESTAMP WITH LOCAL TIME ZONE, the following happens:

- If the incoming data has no time-zone element, it is assumed to be local time and is stored as is.

- If the incoming data has a time-zone element but the time zone matches the local time zone, the time-zone element is dropped and the data is stored.

- If the incoming data has a time-zone element and the time zone does not match the local time zone, the timestamp is adjusted to local time. The data is then stored without a time-zone element.

Using this method synchronizes all time elements to the local time, allowing a company that spans multiple time zones to see data in real time relative to the local time zone. One way to utilize this datatype is to use the supplied CURRENT_TIMESTAMP function, which returns the current date and time in the session time zone, in a value of datatype TIMESTAMP WITH TIME ZONE.

 Real World Scenario

Using the TIMESTAMP WITH LOCAL TIME ZONE Datatype

Suppose your company is headquartered in London and you have a branch office in New York. Transactions from the branch office need to be stored in your London database and synchronized to London time.

The time-zone information for London is as follows:

Element	Value
Standard time zone	No UTC offset
Daylight Savings Time	+1 hour
Current time-zone offset	UTC +1 hour
Time-zone abbreviation	BST (British summer time)
Current time	Friday, September 3, 2008, at 1:15:14 p.m. BST

The time-zone information for New York is as follows:

Element	Value
Standard time zone	UTC –5 hours
Daylight Savings Time	+1 hour
Current time-zone offset	UTC –4 hours
Time-zone abbreviation	EDT (eastern daylight time)
Current time	Friday, September 3, 2008, at 8:15:14 a.m. EDT

As you can see, London is currently one hour ahead of UTC, whereas New York is four hours behind. Therefore, London's time is five hours ahead of New York's.

Now, suppose a transaction comes in from your New York branch to your London office. The timestamp data will be stored in a column defined with the TIMESTAMP WITH LOCAL TIME ZONE datatype. Before storing the data, Oracle synchronizes the time by adding five hours to the timestamp value and drops the time-zone element.

In Exercise 13.2, you'll see the functionality of the TIMESTAMP WITH LOCAL TIME ZONE datatype.

EXERCISE 13.2

Using TIMESTAMP WITH LOCAL TIME ZONE

To demonstrate the functionality of the TIMESTAMP WITH LOCAL TIME ZONE datatype, perform the following steps:

1. Create table `timezone_test` with two columns: x as TIMESTAMP and y as TIMESTAMP WITH LOCAL TIME ZONE. Set your server time zone to UTC –5:

    ```
    SQL> create table timezone_test (x timestamp,
    y timestamp with local time zone);
    Table created.
    ```

2. Alter the session time zone to 5 hours behind UTC, and then insert sysdate into both columns in the `timezone_test` table.

    ```
    SQL> ALTER SESSION SET TIME_ZONE = '-5:00';
    SQL> insert into timezone_test values (sysdate, sysdate);
    1 row created.
    ```

3. Insert the client time into both columns using the `current_timestamp` function, and query the results:

    ```
    SQL> insert into timezone_test values (current_timestamp,
    current_timestamp);
    1 row created.
    SQL> select * from timezone_test;
    X                            Y
    ---------------------------- ----------------------------
    11-NOV-08 07.25.31.000000 PM   11-NOV-08 07.25.31.000000 PM
    11-NOV-08 07.25.36.897000 PM   11-NOV-08 07.25.36.897000 PM
    SQL>
    ```

4. Modify your local time zone to UTC –7, and repeat step 3:

    ```
    SQL> ALTER SESSION SET TIME_ZONE = '-7:00';
    SQL> insert into timezone_test values (current_timestamp,
    current_timestamp);
    1 row created.
    SQL> select * from timezone_test;
    X                            Y
    ---------------------------- ----------------------------
    11-NOV-08 07.25.31.000000 PM   11-NOV-08 05.25.31.000000 PM
    11-NOV-08 07.25.36.897000 PM   11-NOV-08 05.25.36.897000 PM
    11-NOV-08 05.31.35.104000 PM   11-NOV-08 05.31.35.104000 PM
    ```

5. Modify your local time zone to UTC –5, and query the `timezone_test` table:

    ```
    SQL> ALTER SESSION SET TIME_ZONE = '-5:00';
    SQL> select * from timezone_test;
    X                            Y
    ---------------------------- ----------------------------
    11-NOV-08 07.25.31.000000 PM   11-NOV-08 07.25.31.000000 PM
    11-NOV-08 07.25.36.897000 PM   11-NOV-08 07.25.36.897000 PM
    11-NOV-08 05.31.35.104000 PM   11-NOV-08 07.31.35.104000 PM
    ```

    Note that column y, the TIMESTAMP WITH TIMEZONE column, shows the corrected time based on the local time zone because the time-zone data was retained. Note that column x does not retain the time-zone data and is not corrected if the time zone changes.

Using Linguistic Sorts and Searches

Different languages follow different rules when it comes to sorting text. Unfortunately, that means that there is no "one-size-fits-all" algorithm that can be used. Instead, Oracle's global support functionality allows not only binary sorting methods but also linguistic sorting and searching methodologies to provide the flexibility to support the needs of many languages.

In the following sections, you will learn the methods that Oracle uses when it performs text-sorting operations. You will also learn about the different NLS parameters that impact linguistic sorting and searching. Next, you will learn about the different types of linguistic sorts supported by Oracle. Last, you will learn about linguistic text searches.

An Overview of Text Sorting

There are many ways in which text sorting can be accomplished. Sort order can be case sensitive or case can be ignored. *Diacritics* (accent marks) can be considered or ignored. Sorting can be done phonetically or based on the appearance of the character.

Some languages even consider groupings of characters to have a specific sort order. For example, traditional Spanish treats *ch* as a character that sorts after the letter *C*. Therefore, when sorting the words *cat*, *dog*, *cow*, and *chinchilla*, the correct sort sequence would be *cat*, *cow*, *chinchilla*, and *dog*.

To support these different sorting methods, Oracle offers two basic categories of sorting: binary and linguistic.

Binary Sorts

Binary sorts are the fastest and most efficient sorting method offered by Oracle. However, they are also the most limited. Binary sorts perform a numeric sort based on the encoded value (in the character set) for each character. As long as the character set encodes all of the characters in the proper sort order, this method works very well. The performance is also exceptional.

For example, in the US7ASCII character set, alphabetical characters are encoded as shown in Table 13.4. Note that this is just a subset of the character set.

TABLE 13.4 US7ASCII Alphabetical Characters

Char	Value	Char	Value	Char	Value	Char	Value
A	65	N	78	a	97	n	110
B	66	O	79	b	98	o	111
C	67	P	80	c	99	p	112

TABLE 13.4 US7ASCII Alphabetical Characters *(continued)*

Char	Value	Char	Value	Char	Value	Char	Value
D	68	Q	81	d	100	q	113
E	69	R	82	e	101	r	114
F	70	S	83	f	102	s	115
G	71	T	84	g	103	t	116
H	72	U	85	h	104	u	117
I	73	V	86	i	105	v	118
J	74	W	87	j	106	w	119
K	75	X	88	k	107	x	120
L	76	Y	89	l	108	y	121
M	77	Z	90	m	109	z	122

Because the encoded values ascend in correlation with the characters, a binary sort will always perform a proper alphabetical sort. In addition, uppercase characters will always sort higher than lowercase characters.

However, different languages may share the same alphabet (and therefore, the same character set) yet utilize a sort order that deviates from the encoding order of the character set. In this situation, binary sorting will fail to produce an acceptable result.

Binary sorting is Oracle's default sorting method.

Linguistic Sorts

Linguistic sorts, unlike binary sorts, operate independently of the underlying encoded values. Instead, they allow character data to be sorted based on the rules of specific languages. Linguistic sorts offer the flexibility to deal with the caveats imposed by different languages.

Oracle provides a rich set of linguistic sort definitions that cover most of the languages of the world. However, it also provides the ability to define new definitions or to modify existing definitions. The Oracle Locale Builder, a graphical tool that ships with Oracle 11g, can be used to view, create, and modify sort definitions and other locale definitions. However, as mentioned earlier, Locale Builder is not covered in this book.

Linguistic sorts are defined using a variety of rules that govern the sorting process. The following elements are available and can be used to create a comprehensive linguistic sort:

Base letters   Base letters are the individual letters upon which other characters are based. The derived characters would map back to the base letter to determine the sorting value. For example, the character *A* is a base letter, while *À*, *Á*, *Ā*, *Ä*, *a*, *à*, *á*, and *ä* would all map to *A* as a base letter.

Ignorable characters   Ignorable characters, just as the name implies, can be defined as having no effect on sort order. Diacritics, such as the umlaut, can be classified as ignorable, as can certain punctuation characters, such as the hyphen. Therefore, a word such as *e-mail* would be sorted the same as *email*.

Contracting characters   Contracting characters represent two or more characters that are treated linguistically as a single character. An example—the traditional Spanish *ch* string—was explained earlier in this section. Contracting characters require flexibility in the sorting algorithm to read ahead to the next character to determine if a contracting character has been found.

Expanding characters   With some locales, repeating or commonly occurring strings of characters are compressed into a single character for brevity's sake. However, the character needs to sort as if all characters are present. These are referred to as expanding characters.

For example, the *ö* character should be treated as the string *oe* for sorting purposes.

Context-sensitive characters   With certain languages, characters are sorted differently based upon their relationship to other characters. These are generally characters that modify the preceding character. For example, a Japanese length mark is sorted according to the vowel that precedes it.

Canonical equivalence   When a Unicode character set is used, the character *ö* and the string *o¨* can be considered equal from a sorting perspective. This is because the code points of the two-character string match the code point of the individual character. The two are said to have canonical equivalence.

In situations of canonical equivalence, the value of the `CANONICAL_EQUIVALENCE` linguistic flag (with a value of `TRUE` or `FALSE`) determines whether the rules of canonical equivalence should be followed.

Reverse secondary sorting   In some languages, strings containing diacritics will be sorted from left to right on the base characters and then from right to left on the diacritics. This is referred to as reverse secondary sorting. For example, resumé would sort before résume because of the position of the diacritic from left to right.

The `REVERSE_SECONDARY=TRUE` linguistic flag enables this functionality.

Character rearrangement   In certain languages (notably Thai and Laotian dialects), sorting rules declare that certain characters should switch places with the following character before sorting. This generally happens when a consonant is preceded by a vowel sound. In this case, the consonant is given priority, forcing the characters to be switched before the sort begins.

The SWAP_WITH_NEXT linguistic flag can determine whether character rearrangement will occur within a sort definition.

 Don't confuse linguistic flags with Oracle parameter settings. Linguistic flags are defined for specific sort-order definitions when they are created.

These different sorting methods represent the toolset available to sort and search text. Different languages may use one or more of the linguistic methods listed here. But as long as the rules of a language can be described using these methods, Oracle is able to perform linguistic sorts, either through an existing sort definition or through a custom sort definition.

Using Linguistic Sort Parameters

Linguistic sorts are generally applicable to a specific language or to a specific character set. And, as mentioned previously, there are many predefined linguistic sort definitions that may be utilized. Therefore, it is unlikely that you would ever need to define your own.

You can instruct Oracle to utilize specific linguistic sorts by setting the appropriate NLS sort parameters. In this section, you will learn about the NLS_SORT and NLS_COMP parameters and how they affect linguistic sorting operations.

NLS_SORT

The NLS_SORT parameter defines which type of sorting—binary or linguistic—should be performed for SQL sort operations. By default, the value for NLS_SORT is the default sort method defined for the language identified in the NLS_LANGUAGE parameter. For example, if the NLS_LANGUAGE parameter is set to AMERICAN, the default value for the NLS_SORT parameter will be BINARY.

To instruct Oracle to use linguistic sorting, this parameter can be set to the name of any valid linguistic sort definition, as shown here:

```
SQL> alter session set NLS_SORT = German;
Session altered.
```

A list of valid sort definition names is shown here. You could also query the V$NLS_VALID_VALUES view (as shown earlier in this chapter).

ARABIC	GERMAN	SWISS
ARABIC_ABJ_MATCH	GERMAN_DIN	TCHINESE_RADICAL_M
ARABIC_ABJ_SORT	GREEK	TCHINESE_STROKE_M
ARABIC_MATCH	HEBREW	THAI_DICTIONARY
ASCII7	HKSCS	THAI_M

AZERBAIJANI	HUNGARIAN	THAI_TELEPHONE
BENGALI	ICELANDIC	TURKISH
BIG5	INDONESIAN	UKRAINIAN
BINARY	ITALIAN	UNICODE_BINARY
BULGARIAN	JAPANESE	VIETNAMESE
CANADIAN FRENCH	JAPANESE_M	WEST_EUROPEAN
CANADIAN_M	KOREAN_M	XAZERBAIJANI
CATALAN	LATIN	XCATALAN
CROATIAN	LATVIAN	XCROATIAN
CZECH	LITHUANIAN	XCZECH
CZECH_PUNCTUATION	MALAY	XCZECH_PUNCTUATION
DANISH	NORWEGIAN	XDANISH
DANISH_M	POLISH	XDUTCH
DUTCH	PUNCTUATION	XFRENCH
EBCDIC	ROMANIAN	XGERMAN
EEC_EURO	RUSSIAN	XGERMAN_DIN
EEC_EUROPA3	SCHINESE_PINYIN_M	XHUNGARIAN
ESTONIAN	SCHINESE_RADICAL_M	XPUNCTUATION
FINNISH	SCHINESE_STROKE_M	XSLOVAK
FRENCH	SLOVAK	XSLOVENIAN
FRENCH_M	SLOVENIAN	XSPANISH
GBK	SPANISH	XSWISS
GENERIC_BASELETTER	SPANISH_M	XTURKISH
GENERIC_M	SWEDISH	XWEST_EUROPEAN

By using the NLS_SORT parameter, you can make the following changes to Oracle's default functionality:

- Set the default sort method for all ORDER BY operations.
- Set the default sort value for the NLSSORT function.

It is important to note that not all SQL functionality supports linguistic sorting. Certain functions support only binary sorts. However, most of the commonly used methods are supported. Also, all NLS-specific SQL functions (for example, NLSSORT) will support linguistic sorts.

The methods listed here support linguistic sorting:

- ORDER BY
- BETWEEN
- CASE WHEN
- HAVING
- IN/OUT
- START WITH
- WHERE

By default, all of these operations will perform binary sorts. When you set the NLS_SORT parameter, SQL statements using the WHERE operation will perform linguistic sorts by default.

The following example demonstrates the use of the NLS_SORT parameter. Initially, you can see that your session has no value set for NLS_SORT. Therefore, it will inherit the default setting from the NLS_LANGUAGE parameter (BINARY).

```
SQL> show parameters NLS_LANGUAGE

NAME                                 TYPE        VALUE
------------------------------------ ----------- ----------
nls_language                         string      AMERICAN

SQL> show parameters NLS_SORT

NAME                                 TYPE        VALUE
------------------------------------ ----------- ----------
nls_sort                             string
```

As you learned earlier, the default sort for the language AMERICAN is BINARY. The default setting for NLS_COMP is BINARY as well. Therefore, you can expect that, by default, Oracle will perform a binary sort unless otherwise specified, as shown here:

```
SQL> select * from sort_test
  order by name;

NAME
-------------------------------
Finsteraarhornhutte
Grünhornlücke
einschließlich
```

```
finsteraarhornhütte
grünhornlücke
```

```
5 rows selected.
```

As expected, Oracle sorted the rows based on the encoded value of the characters in the US7ASCII character set. Therefore, all uppercase characters sort before lowercase characters.

Because the words in this table are of German origin, it is logical that you might want to sort them using a German sorting method. To change the sorting method for a GROUP BY clause, the NLS_SORT parameter can be set as shown here:

```
SQL> alter session set NLS_SORT=German_din;
```

```
Session altered.
```

```
SQL> select * from sort_test
  order by name;
```

```
NAME
-------------------------------------------
einschließlich
Finsteraarhornhutte
finsteraarhornhütte
Grünhornlücke
grünhornlücke
```

```
5 rows selected.
```

As you can see, setting the NLS_SORT parameter changed the default sorting method to a linguistic sort instead of a binary sort.

In the next step, another query is executed, this time using a WHERE condition rather than an ORDER BY clause:

```
SQL> select * from sort_test
  2  where name > 'einschließlich';
```

```
NAME
--------------------------------------
finsteraarhornhütte
grünhornlücke
```

```
2 rows selected.
```

The result of this query might not be what you expect. Instead of the expected four rows (which a linguistic sort would have returned), only two rows are returned, indicating that a binary sort took place instead.

Remember, the NLS_SORT parameter overrides the default sorting method for ORDER BY operations and for the NLSSORT function, but it has no effect on other sort operations, such as WHERE conditions. Therefore, this query ignored the parameter entirely.

To perform a linguistic sort, you call the NLSSORT function. Normally, the function would be called like this:

```
SQL> select * from sort_test
  where nlssort(name, 'NLS_SORT=German_din') >
  nlssort('einschließlich','NLS_SORT=German_din');


NAME
--------------------------------------------------
Finsteraarhornhutte
finsteraarhornhütte
Grünhornlücke
grünhornlücke


4 rows selected.
```

However, because the NLS_SORT parameter defines the default sort for the NLSSORT function, specifying the sort inside the function is unnecessary. The following method works as well:

```
SQL> select * from sort_test
  where nlssort(name) > nlssort('einschließlich');

NAME
--------------------------------------------------
Finsteraarhornhutte
finsteraarhornhütte
Grünhornlücke
grünhornlücke


4 rows selected.
```

As you can see, in both queries the sort was performed linguistically and returned the expected rows.

The NLS_SORT parameter is very limited in relation to linguistic sorting. The NLS_COMP parameter, on the other hand, makes linguistic sorting much easier.

NLS_COMP

The NLS_COMP parameter works in conjunction with the NLS_SORT parameter to make linguistic sorts easier to use. When the NLS_COMP parameter is set to a value of ANSI, all of the following SQL operations will default to linguistic sorting (using the language specified in NLS_SORT parameter):

- ORDER BY
- BETWEEN
- CASE WHEN
- HAVING
- IN/OUT
- START WITH
- WHERE

Setting the NLS_COMP parameter makes it unnecessary to call the NLSSORT function when using these sort operations. As you can guess, this makes linguistic sorting much easier to perform.

The NLS_COMP parameter can be set to either BINARY (the default) or ANSI.

The following example shows the usage of the NLS_COMP parameter:

```
SQL> alter session set NLS_SORT=German_din;

Session altered.

SQL> alter session set NLS_COMP=ANSI;

Session altered.

SQL> select * from sort_test
  2  where name > 'einschließlich';

NAME
-----------------------------------------
Finsteraarhornhutte
finsteraarhornhütte
Grünhornlücke
grünhornlücke

4 rows selected.
```

As you can see, the query performed the linguistic sort and returned the expected results, even without using the NLSSORT function.

If the NLS_COMP parameter is set back to BINARY, binary sorting occurs once again:

```
SQL> alter session set NLS_COMP=BINARY;

Session altered.

SQL> select * from sort_test
  2  where name > 'einschließlich';

NAME
-------------------------------------------
finsteraarhornhütte
grünhornlücke

2 rows selected.
```

Linguistic Sort Types

When performing linguistic sorts, Oracle uses different methodologies, depending upon the number of languages involved in the sort. If character data in only one language is being sorted, this is classified as a monolingual linguistic sort. If more than one language is involved in the sort, it is classified as a multilingual linguistic sort.

In the following sections, you will learn the methodology that Oracle implements in performing both monolingual and multilingual linguistic sorts. You will also learn about accent-insensitive and case-insensitive linguistic sorts.

Monolingual Linguistic Sorts

When dealing with only a single language inside a sort, Oracle performs a two-step process to compare character strings. First, the major value of the strings is compared. Next, if necessary, the minor value of the strings is compared.

Major and minor values are sort values assigned to letters in the character set. A base letter and those derived from it will generally share a common major value, but they will have different minor values based on the desired sort order.

Here's an example:

Letter	Major Value	Minor Value
A	30	10
A	30	20
Ä	30	30
Ä	30	40
B	40	10

The example shows that all four variations of the letter *A* have identical major values, but differing minor values. When two letters share a major value, the minor value will determine the sort order.

The major-value numbers are assigned to a *Unicode code point* (a 16-bit binary value that defines a character in a Unicode character set).

Multilingual Linguistic Sorts

Multilingual sorts offer the ability to sort mixed languges within the same sort. For example, if you have a table that stores names in both English and Spanish, a multilingual sort should be used.

Multilingual sorts perform three levels of evaluation: primary, secondary, and tertiary.

Primary sorts assign a primary sort value based on the base letter of each character (diacritics and case are ignored). If a character is defined as ignorable, it is assigned a primary value of zero.

Secondary-level sorts consider diacritics to differentiate accented letters from base letters in assigning a secondary sort level. For example, *A* and *ä* share the same base letter, so they have the same primary sort level but they will have different secondary levels.

Tertiary-level sorts consider character case to differentiate uppercase and lowercase letters. Tertiary sorts also handle special characters such as *, +, and -.

Consider the following words:

Fahrvergnügen

Fahrvergnugen

farhrvergnugen

fahrvergnügen

Because all of these words share the same base letters in the same order, all of them would be considered equivalent at the primary sort level. After a secondary-level sort, they would be ordered similarly to the following list:

Fahrvergnugen

farhrvergnugen

Fahrvergnügen

fahrvergnügen

The secondary-level sort is concerned only with diacritics, so it will sort characters without diacritics above those with diacritics. After that, the words are displayed in their primary sort order. Because the words in this example have identical primary sort orders, there is no guarantee which word will appear before the other. The only guarantee is that those with diacritics will sort after those without.

After the tertiary-level sort is performed, the list should look exactly like this:

farhrvergnugen

Fahrvergnugen

fahrvergnügen

Fahrvergnügen

The tertiary-level sort applies the case rule to the data, forcing lowercase letters to sort before uppercase letters. This is the final result of the sort after applying all three multilingual sorting levels.

In keeping with the ISO 14651 standard for multilingual sorting, Oracle appends an _M to the sort name to identify it as multilingual. For example, FRENCH_M identifies a French multilingual sort, whereas FRENCH identifies a French monolingual sort. Table 13.5 shows the multilingual sorts predefined in Oracle 11*g*.

TABLE 13.5   Multilingual Sorts Available in Oracle 11g

Multilingual Sort Name	Description
CANADIAN_M	Canadian French
DANISH_M	Danish
FRENCH_M	French
GENERIC_M	Generic based on ISO 14651
JAPANESE_M	Japanese
KOREAN_M	Korean
SPANISH_M	Traditional Spanish
THAI_M	Thai
SCHINESE_RADICAL_M	Simplified Chinese
SCHINESE_STROKE_M	Simplified Chinese
SCHINESE_PINYIN_M	Simplified Chinese
TCHINESE_RADICAL_M	Traditional Chinese
TCHINESE_STROKE_M	Traditional Chinese

Case-Insensitive and Accent-Insensitive Linguistic Sorts

Oracle, by default, will always consider both the case of the characters and any diacritics when performing sort operations. As you've seen in previous examples, linguistic sorts have rules to govern precedence between uppercase and lowercase words, as well as those words containing diacritics.

However, you may wish to override this functionality from time to time and choose to ignore case and/or diacritics. Oracle 11*g* offers case-insensitive and accent-insensitive sorting options to allow for these cases.

To specify case-insensitive or accent-insensitive sorts, the NLS_SORT parameter is used, but with the following changes:

- For a case-insensitive linguistic sort, append the string _CI to the sort name.
- For an accent-insensitive linguistic sort, append the string _AI to the sort name.

 Accent-insensitive sorts are also case insensitive by default.

For example, to specify a French, multilingual, accent-insensitive sort, use the following:

NLS_SORT = French_M_AI

Here is how to specify a German, monolingual, case-insensitive sort:

NLS_SORT = German_CI

Case-Insensitive and Accent-Insensitive Binary Sorts

Binary sorts can also be designated as case insensitive or accent insensitive. The NLS_SORT parameter can be set to BINARY_CI or BINARY_AI. Table 13.6 shows how the sort will be affected by these settings.

TABLE 13.6   Binary Case and Accent-Insensitive Sort Options

Sort Name	Sort Type	Case Insensitive?	Accent Insensitive?
BINARY_CI	Binary	Yes	No
BINARY_AI	Binary	Yes	Yes

As you can see, using the BINARY_AI sort will result in both an accent-insensitive and case-insensitive sort.

Searching Linguistic Strings

Linguistic searches are closely related to linguistic sorts and are directly affected by the NLS_SORT setting. To accomplish linguistically meaningful searches, Oracle must apply the same rules it applies for linguistic sorts.

Earlier in this section, you saw several examples of linguistic string searching, including the following:

```
SQL> select * from sort_test
  2  where name > 'einschließlich';


NAME
-----------------------------------------
Finsteraarhornhutte
finsteraarhornhütte
Grünhornlücke
grünhornlücke


4 rows selected.
```

When you set the NLS_COMP parameter to ANSI and the NLS_SORT parameter to the desired sort language, the WHERE operator (as well as several others) will perform linguistic searching by default.

And, just as you did with sorts, if the NLS_SORT is set to ignore case or accents, linguistic searches will follow suit, as in this example:

```
SQL> alter session set NLS_COMP=ANSI;


Session altered.
SQL> alter session set NLS_SORT=German_din_ci;


Session altered.


SQL> select * from sort_test
  2  where name = 'Grünhornlücke';


NAME
-----------------------------------------
Grünhornlücke
grünhornlücke
```

As you can see, the search ignored the case and returned both rows that matched. This is the expected functionality of the case-insensitive search.

In the next example, the NLS_SORT parameter will be set to define an accent-insensitive search:

```
SQL> alter session set NLS_SORT=German_din_ai;


Session altered.
```

```
SQL> select * from sort_test
  where name = 'Finsteraarhornhutte';

NAME
------------------------------------------------
Finsteraarhornhutte
finsteraarhornhütte
```

When the `NLS_SORT` parameter defined an accent-insensitive search, both accents and case were ignored. This is the expected functionality for accent-insensitive searches.

Summary

In this chapter, you learned about Oracle's global support functionality and how it simplifies the issues related to multilingual databases. You learned about the internal architecture that makes globalization support possible. You saw how the NLS Runtime Library (NLSRTL) integrates with the Oracle locale definition files to provide functionality. You also learned that the modular nature of the locale definition files provides great flexibility while reducing memory usage.

You learned about the main components of globalization support: language, territory, character set, and linguistic sorts. You saw how these four components provide default settings for all the other NLS options. You then learned that those default settings can be overridden with a variety of methods.

We introduced you to the many character sets that Oracle supports, including the important Unicode character set. You saw how the Unicode character set can support all known written languages in the world.

You also learned about using NLS parameters to modify your globalization environment as needed. You learned about the different categories of NLS parameters, including language and territory parameters, date and time parameters, linguistic sort parameters, calendar parameters, and more.

This chapter introduced you to the datetime datatypes and explained how the TIMESTAMP WITH TIME ZONE and TIMESTAMP WITH LOCAL TIME ZONE datatypes can be used to synchronize transactions occurring across time zones.

Last, you learned about linguistic sorting and searching and how globalization support allows culturally appropriate sorting and searching. You also learned about monolingual and multilingual sorts and how each evaluates text strings when performing a sort operation. You learned that multilingual sorts can be identified by the _M appended to the sort definition name.

You learned how, in conjunction with linguistic sorting and searching, you can perform case-insensitive and accent-insensitive operations by appending _CI or _AI to the end of the `NLS_SORT` parameter value.

Exam Essentials

Be able to customize language-dependent behavior for the database and individual sessions.   Be aware of the different NLS parameters and the different ways that they can be set (initialization parameters, environment variables, the ALTER SESSION statement). Know the order of precedence for NLS parameter settings. Know which parameters apply only to the client or the server.

Know how to specify different linguistic sorts for queries.   Understand the mechanisms for producing linguistic sorts versus binary sorts. Know how to specify both case-insensitive and accent-insensitive linguistic sorts. Know how to differentiate between multilingual and monolingual sort definitions.

Understand how to use datetime datatypes.   Understand the purpose of datetime datatypes. Know the different datetimes covered in this chapter: DATE, TIMESTAMP, TIMESTAMP WITH TIME ZONE, and TIMESTAMP WITH LOCAL TIME ZONE. Understand the differences between the various datetime datatypes and how they relate to globalization.

Know how to query data using case-insensitive and accent-insensitive searches.   Know the syntax for specifying case-insensitive and accent-insensitive operations. Understand which SQL operations support linguistic operations. Know which NLS parameters control case-insensitive and accent-insensitive searching.

Understand how to obtain globalization support configuration information.   Know the views available to see globalization information: NLS_SESSION_PARAMETERS, NLS_INSTANCE_ PARAMETERS, NLS_DATABASE_PARAMETERS, and V$NLS_VALID_VALUES. Understand the information returned by each of these views.

Understand globalization support architecture.   Know the purpose of the NLSRTL. Understand the location, purpose, and file-naming conventions of locale definition files. Know the four types of locale definition files: language, territory, character set, and linguistic sort.

Review Questions

1. Globalization support is implemented through the text- and character-processing functions provided by which Oracle feature?

    A. RSTLNE

    B. NLSRTL

    C. LISTENER

    D. NLSSORT

    E. Linguistic sorts

2. What elements of globalization can be explicitly defined using the NLS_LANG environment variable? (Choose all that apply.)

    A. NLS_LANGUAGE

    B. NLS_SORT

    C. NLS_CALENDAR

    D. NLS_CHARACTERSET

    E. NLS_TERRITORY

3. Given two different character sets (*A* and *B*), which of the following must be true for *A* to be considered a strict superset of *B*? (Choose all that apply.)

    A. *A* must contain all of the characters defined in *B*.

    B. *A* must be Unicode.

    C. The encoded values in *A* must match the encoded values in *B* for all characters defined in *B*.

    D. *A* must be a multibyte character set.

    E. The encoded values in *A* must match the encoded values in *B* for all numeric and alphabetic characters in *B*.

4. The NLS_SORT parameter sets the default sort method for which of the following operations? (Choose all that apply.)

    A. WHERE clause

    B. ORDER BY clause

    C. BETWEEN clause

    D. NLSSORT function

    E. NLS_SORT function

5. Which view shows all valid values for the NLS_LANGUAGE, NLS_SORT, NLS_TERRITORY, and NLS_CHARACTERSET parameters?

    A. V$VALID_NLS_VALUES

    B. NLS_VALID_VALUES

    C. NLS_VALUE_OPTIONS

    D. V$NLS_VALUE_OPTIONS

    E. V$NLS_VALID_VALUES

6. Which of the following datatypes store time-zone information in the database?

A. TIMESTAMP

B. DATE

C. TIMESTAMP WITH TIME ZONE

D. TIMESTAMP WITH LOCAL TIME ZONE

E. DATETIME

7. Which of the following are valid settings for the NLS_COMP parameter? (Choose all that apply.)

A. ASCII

B. ANSI

C. BINARY

D. MONOLINGUAL

E. MULTILINGUAL

8. NLS parameters can be set using the five methods listed. Put the methods in order from highest to lowest according to Oracle's order of precedence:

a. Default setting

b. Client environment variable

c. Explicit ALTER SESSION statement

d. Inside SQL function

e. Server initialization parameter

A. b, d, e, a, c

B. e, a, b, c, d

C. d, c, b, e, a

D. a, b, d, c, e

E. d, c, b, a, e

9. What can you determine about the following linguistic sorts based only on their names?

1. GERMAN

2. FRENCH_M

A. 1 is a monolingual sort.

B. 2 is a monolingual sort.

C. 1 is case insensitive.

D. Both 1 and 2 are case insensitive.

E. Case sensitivity is unknown.

10. In a database with the database character set of US7ASCII and a national character set of UTF-8, which datatypes would be capable of storing Unicode data by default?

   A. VARCHAR2

   B. CHAR

   C. NVARCHAR2

   D. CLOB

   E. LONG

11. Automatic data conversion will occur if which of the following happens?

   A. The client and server have different NLS_LANGUAGE settings.

   B. The client and server character sets are not the same, and the database character set is not a strict superset of the client character set.

   C. The client and server are in different time zones.

   D. The client requests automatic data conversion.

   E. The AUTO_CONVERT initialization parameter is set to TRUE.

12. Which of the following NLS_SORT parameter values would result in case-insensitive and accent-insensitive binary sorts?

   A. NLS_SORT = BINARY

   B. NLS_SORT = BINARY_AI

   C. NLS_SORT = BINARY_CI

   D. NLS_SORT = BINARY_AI_CI

   E. Binary sorts are case insensitive and accent insensitive by default.

13. Which NLS parameter can be used to change the default Oracle sort method from binary to linguistic for the SQL SELECT statement?

   A. NLS_LANG

   B. NLS_SORT

   C. NLS_COMP

   D. NLS_SORT

   E. None of the above

14. Which of the following would be affected by setting NLS_LENGTH_SEMANTICS=CHAR?

   A. All objects in the database

   B. Tables owned by SYS and SYSTEM

   C. Data dictionary tables

   D. NCHAR columns

   E. CHAR columns

15. Which is not a valid locale definition file type?

   A. Language

   B. Linguistic sort

   C. Calendar

   D. Territory

   E. Character set

16. How many different calendars does Oracle 11*g* support?

   A. 22

   B. 7

   C. 6

   D. 15

   E. 2

17. Which NLS parameter directly governs linguistic searches?

   A. NLS_SEARCH_L

   B. NLS_SORT

   C. NLS_SEARCH

   D. NLS_SORT_L

   E. None of the above

18. True or false? Case-insensitive sorts are always accent insensitive by default.

   A. True

   B. False

19. What is the name of the file that identifies the set of available locale definitions?

   A. locale.def

   B. lxdef.ora

   C. lx1boot.nlb

   D. lx1boot.ora

   E. lang.def

20. Which of the following is not a valid linguistic sort element?

   A. Accent expansion

   B. Canonical equivalence

   C. Reverse secondary sorting

   D. Ignorable characters

   E. Character rearrangement

Answers to Review Questions

1. B. The NLS Runtime Library (NLSRTL) provides the language-independent text- and character-processing functionality for Oracle.

2. A, D, E. The client-side NLS_LANG parameter can define language, territory, and character set all at once. Though the value for NLS_SORT is derived from the NLS_LANGUAGE parameter setting, it is not *explicitly* set by NLS_LANG. NLS_CALENDAR is not affected by the setting of NLS_LANG.

3. A, C. A strict superset must contain all characters found in the other character set and have matching encoded values for those characters.

4. A, D. The NLS_SORT parameter defines the default sort method (binary or linguistic) for both SQL WHERE clause operations and NLSSORT function operations. The default sort method for ORDER BY and BETWEEN (and all other SQL operations that support linguistic sorts) is defined by the NLS_COMP parameter. NLS_SORT is an invalid function name.

5. E. The V$NLS_VALID_VALUES view shows the names of all language, territory, sort, and character-set definitions that are available in the database.

6. C. Only the TIMESTAMP WITH TIME ZONE datatype actually stores time-zone information in the database. The TIMESTAMP WITH LOCAL TIME ZONE datatype converts the timestamp to local time and drops the time-zone information before storing it in the database. DATE and TIMESTAMP datatypes do not deal with time-zone information at all. DATETIME is not a valid datatype.

7. B, C. The NLS_COMP parameter can be set to BINARY or ANSI. This parameter determines the default sort type for certain SQL functions. (A setting of ANSI specifies that linguistic sorts should be used.)

8. C. NLS settings embedded in a SQL function have the highest precedence, followed by explicit ALTER SESSION statements, client environment variables (which execute an implicit ALTER SESSION statement), server-initialization parameters, and finally default settings.

9. A. A is the only true statement. An _M appended to the end of a sort name denotes a multilingual sort. Its absence denotes a monolingual sort. Case-sensitive and accent-insensitive sorts have _CI or _AI appended to the name. Its absence denotes case sensitivity and accent sensitivity.

10. C. NLS datatypes (NCHAR, NVARCHAR, and NCLOB) store data using the character set defined as the national character set by default. Because the national character set is UTF-8 (a Unicode character set), data stored in these datatypes will be Unicode data by default. All other datatypes use the character set defined as the database character set. Because US7ASCII is not a Unicode character set, it does not store Unicode data by default.

11. B. Automatic data conversion occurs when data is moved between character sets. However, if the server character set is a strict superset of the client character set, no conversion is necessary.

12. B. The _AI suffix implies that an accent-insensitive sort will be performed. Accent-insensitive sorts are also case insensitive by default. The _CI suffix implies that a case-insensitive sort will be performed, but it will not be accent insensitive. Specifying both suffixes (_AI_CI) is illegal.

13. E. The SQL SELECT statement does not invoke a sort.

14. E. Only option E is correct. Tables owned by the SYS and SYSTEM users are not affected by default-length semantics. Data dictionary tables always use byte semantics, and NCHAR columns always use character semantics. Therefore, neither is affected by the setting of the NLS_LENGTH_SEMANTICS parameter.

15. C. Calendar definitions are not stored as locale definition files. Only languages, linguistic sorts, territories, and character set definitions are stored as locale definition files.

16. B. Oracle supports seven distinct calendars: Gregorian, Japanese Imperial, ROC Official, Persian, Thai Buddha, Arabic Hijrah, and English Hijrah.

17. B. Linguistic searches are closely related to linguistic sorts and are governed by the NLS_SORT parameter.

18. B. Accent-insensitive sorts are always case insensitive, not the other way around.

19. C. The lx1boot.nlb file identifies the available locale definitions to the NLSRTL.

20. A. Linguistic sort elements define the rules for linguistic sorting. There is no linguistic sort element named "accent expansion." The other choices are all valid rules.

Appendix

A

Lab Exercises

This appendix contains lab exercises for each chapter so that you can practice your skills before the exam.

Lab 1.1: Creating an ASM Instance

This lab was created using Windows XP. However, it should also work using Unix (and in fact was tested using Linux). We have taken certain liberties in this lab to make the use of Automatic Storage Management (ASM) as easy as possible. We will note them as the lab proceeds. Where there is a difference between the use of Windows and Unix, we will note that difference and provide some guidance. The RMAN labs will be using ASM as the flash recovery area (FRA), so this lab and Lab 1.2 will be prerequisites to future labs.

To create your ASM instance, do the following:

1. Start the Oracle Database Configuration Assistant (DBCA). You should be familiar with this tool as it was covered as a part of your OCA studies.

2. Click though the Welcome page and select Configure Automatic Storage Management from the DBCA Operations page.

3. A window appears indicating that you need to install Oracle Cluster Synchronization Service (CSS) and that it needs to be running. The window will instruct you on how to install this service (running `localconfig reset`). Open a command-line window and run the command to configure CSS. Here is an example of the output from this command after a successful execution:

```
C:\>c:\oracle\product\11.1.0\db_1\bin\localconfig reset
Step 1:  stopping local CSS stack
Step 2:  deleting OCR repository
Step 3:  creating new OCR repository
Successfully accumulated necessary OCR keys.
Creating OCR keys for user 'robert', privgrp ''..
Operation successful.
Step 4:  creating new CSS service
successfully created local CSS service
successfully reset location of CSS setup
```

After configuring CSS, click OK in the DBCA pop-up window and then Next on the DBCA Operations page to continue.

4. You will be prompted for the SYS password in the DBCA. Enter the password you want to use for SYS. Click Next.

5. A pop-up window appears indicating that DBCA will create the ASM instance. Click OK to create the instance.

6. The DBCA ASM Disk Groups page appears. We will add disk groups to our ASM instance in the next lab, so simply click Finish to complete the ASM instance creation. A pop-up window appears asking if you want to perform another operation. Click the No button to exit DBCA.

7. Check to see whether you can connect to your ASM instance. In Windows, from a command line set your ORACLE_SID=+ASM and connect to the ASM instance, as shown here:

```
C:\Documents and Settings\Robert>sqlplus sys as sysasm
SQL*Plus: Release 11.1.0.6.0 - Production on Sun Aug 10 13:21:17 2008
Copyright (c) 1982, 2007, Oracle.  All rights reserved.
Enter password:
Connected to:
Oracle Database 11g Enterprise Edition Release 11.1.0.6.0 - Production
With the Partitioning, OLAP, Data Mining
and Real Application Testing options
SQL>
```

8. Shut down and then start up your ASM service with the shutdown command:

```
C:\Documents and Settings\Robert>sqlplus sys as sysasm
SQL*Plus: Release 11.1.0.6.0 - Production on Sun Aug 10 18:37:11 2008
Copyright (c) 1982, 2007, Oracle.  All rights reserved.
Enter password:
Connected to:
Oracle Database 11g Enterprise Edition Release 11.1.0.6.0 - Production
With the Partitioning, OLAP, Data Mining
and Real Application Testing options
SQL> shutdown immediate
ORA-15100: invalid or missing diskgroup name
ASM instance shutdown
SQL> startup
ASM instance started
Total System Global Area  535662592 bytes
Fixed Size                  1334380 bytes
Variable Size             509162388 bytes
ASM Cache                  25165824 bytes
ORA-15110: no diskgroups mounted
```

Lab 1.2: Creating ASM Disk Groups

In this lab, you will create two ASM disk groups that you will be able to use. Because of the wide variety of ways that disks might be presented, we will use a rather simplified way of creating ASM disk groups. While Oracle/ASM does not directly support creation of ASM disk groups on existing file systems, we can use a hidden parameter and some simple OS magic to get it to do so.

The method we will use in this lab is not supported by Oracle, so you should not use it in any kind of production install. Rather, refer to the Oracle documentation for the appropriate way of creating disk groups based on the disk setup that you have and your operating system. Don't worry if this method is not directly supported by Oracle from the point of view of the OCP exam. You will not be tested on using tools such as asmtool or asmtoolg (which you might use in an actual install) in your OCP exam.

This lab is still important, though. It will give you your first experiences managing an ASM instance. You will use ASM commands and query ASM views. As a result, the material within the lab itself is fully relevant to the OCP exam.

1. Ensure that your ASM service is running (on Windows) by running net start and look for the Oracle service called OracleASMService+ASM. If you are running Unix, from the command line use the ps command (ps -ef|grep +ASM) to determine if ASM is running. If ASM is not running, start up the ASM instance as shown in Lab 1.1, step 7.

2. If ASM is running, set the following parameter so that you can create disk groups. Note that the parameter we are setting called _ASM_ALLOW_ONLY_RAW_DISKS is not supported by Oracle. We are only using is in this lab to provide a consistent way of creating a disk group that can be used on all operating systems. Never do this in an actual production database.

    ```
    Alter system set "_asm_allow_only_raw_disks"=false scope=spfile;
    ```

3. Restart your Oracle ASM instance so the parameter change will take effect:

    ```
    SQL> startup force
    ASM instance started
    Total System Global Area   535662592 bytes
    Fixed Size                   1334380 bytes
    Variable Size              509162388 bytes
    ASM Cache                   25165824 bytes
    ORA-15110: no diskgroups mounted
    ```

4. Create a directory to hold the files you will be creating for ASM.

    ```
    Mkdir c:\oracle\oradata\asmfiles
    ```

5. You now need to create three files that can attach to your ASM instance. These three files will simulate three disk devices that might appear if you had added a disk to your system. To create these files, you will need to use the Perl interpreter that comes with Oracle.

6. CD to your ORACLE_HOME directory where your Oracle software is installed.

7. Continue to the directory where perl.exe is located. This is typically ORACLE_HOME\perl\5.8.3\bin\MSWin32-x86-multi-thread in a Windows environment. You can quickly find the correct home on your operating system by using the dir command or the ls command and recursively finding perl.exe, as shown in this example:

```
C:\oracle\product\11.1.0\db_1>dir perl.exe /s
 Volume in drive C has no label.
 Volume Serial Number is 08DE-E1AB
 Directory of C:\oracle\product\11.1.0\db_1\perl\5.8.3\
bin\MSWin32-x86-multi-thread
11/15/2004  12:35 PM                16,384 perl.exe
               1 File(s)            16,384 bytes
```

8. Having found the perl.exe executable, you will need to run the following code through the interpreter three times, one time for each of the ASM files you will be using. Each ASM file in this example will be 1GB in size. Here is the code that you will execute:

```
my $s='0' x 2**20;
open(DF1,">C:/oracle/oradata/asm_disk/_file_disk1") ||
die "Cannot create file - $!\n";
open(DF2,">C:/oracle/oradata/asm_disk/_file_disk2") ||
die "Cannot create file - $!\n";
open(DF3,">C:/oracle/oradata/asm_disk/_file_disk3") ||
die "Cannot create file - $!\n";
for (my $i=1; $i<1000; $i++) {
  print DF1 $s;
  print DF2 $s;
  print DF3 $s;
}
exit
```

9. Save this code to a file called create_files.pl and execute this file with Perl, as shown here:

```
Perl create_files.pl
```

Having executed this Perl program, you have in essence created three virtual disks. At least, that's what they will look like to ASM.

10. Having created your three "disks," you are ready to create disk groups and associate them with your files. ASM will need to know where to find the files. You set the parameter ASM_DISKSTRING to indicate to ASM where it will find files associated with ASM. Here you set ASM_DISKSTRING to the appropriate location:

```
SQL>Alter system set ASM_DISKSTRING='c:\oracle\oradata\asmfiles\_file*';
```

11. Having set the ASM_DISKSTRING parameter, you should now be able to see the "fake" disk devices you just created by querying the V$ASM_DISK view, as shown in this example:

```
SQL> SELECT group_number "GROUP", disk_number "DISK", mount_status,
  2  header_status, state, path
  3  FROM   v$asm_disk;
GROUP DISK MOUNT_S HEADER_STATU STATE    PATH
----- ---- ------- ------------ -------- ---------------------------------
0        0 CLOSED  CANDIDATE    NORMAL   C:\ORACLE\ORADATA\ASMFILES\_FILE_DISK1
0        2 CLOSED  CANDIDATE    NORMAL   C:\ORACLE\ORADATA\ASMFILES\_FILE_DISK3
0        1 CLOSED  CANDIDATE    NORMAL   C:\ORACLE\ORADATA\ASMFILES\_FILE_DISK2
```

12. You can now create ASM disk groups. Notice that each disk group is listed as a CANDIDATE disk. This does not mean it's running for office, but rather that it can be used in the creation of a disk group. Let's create our first disk group!

You will use the `create diskgroup` command from SQL*Plus to create two disk groups. You will call them dgroup1 and dgroup2. Dgroup1 will use two of the "disks." They will be mirrored copies of each other, providing redundancy. Dgroup2 will use external redundancy and just use one of the "disks." Here are the `create diskgroup` commands:

```
CREATE DISKGROUP dgroup1 NORMAL REDUNDANCY
failgroup diskcontrol1 DISK
'C:\ORACLE\ORADATA\ASMFILES\_FILE_DISK1' NAME file_disk1
failgroup diskcontrol2 DISK
'C:\ORACLE\ORADATA\ASMFILES\_FILE_DISK2' NAME file_disk2;
CREATE DISKGROUP dgroup2 EXTERNAL REDUNDANCY
DISK 'C:\ORACLE\ORADATA\ASMFILES\_FILE_DISK3' NAME file_disk3;
```

13. You should now be able to see the disk groups that you just created by querying the V$ASM_DISKGROUP view, as shown here.

```
SQL> select group_number, name from v$ASM_DISKGROUP;
GROUP_NUMBER NAME
------------ ------------------------------
           1 DGROUP1
           2 DGROUP2
```

14. Use show parameter to display the ASM_DISKGROUPS parameter to see that it has been updated with the new disk groups.

```
SQL> show parameter asm_diskgroups
NAME                                 TYPE        VALUE
------------------------------------ ----------- -----------------
asm_diskgroups                       string      DGROUP1, DGROUP2
```

In the next lab, you will actually create tablespaces using these disk groups!

Lab 1.3: Using ASM Disk Groups from a Database

This lab will walk you through the creation of a tablespace using ASM. This lab assumes you have a database called ORCL created, and that your ASM instance is up and running.

1. Make sure your ASM instance is up and running. Log into the ASM instance and ensure that its status is STARTED.

```
C:\set ORACLE_SID=+ASM
C:\>sqlplus sys as sysasm
SQL*Plus: Release 11.1.0.6.0 - Production on Mon Aug 11 20:43:28 2008
Copyright (c) 1982, 2007, Oracle.  All rights reserved.
Enter password:
Connected to:
Oracle Database 11g Enterprise Edition Release 11.1.0.6.0 - Production
With the Partitioning, OLAP, Data Mining
and Real Application Testing options
SQL> select status from v$instance;
STATUS
------------
STARTED
```

2. Using the V$ASM_DISKGROUP view, make sure you have sufficient space in your disk groups and that they are mounted.

```
SQL> select name, state, free_mb, total_mb
  2  from v$asm_diskgroup;
NAME                          STATE        FREE_MB    TOTAL_MB
----------------------------- ----------- ---------- ----------
DGROUP1                       MOUNTED         1896       1998
DGROUP2                       MOUNTED          949        999
```

3. Log into the ORCL database.

```
C:\>set oracle_sid=orcl
C:\>sqlplus sys as sysdba
SQL*Plus: Release 11.1.0.6.0 - Production on Mon Aug 11 20:50:06 2008
Copyright (c) 1982, 2007, Oracle.  All rights reserved.
Enter password:
Connected to:
Oracle Database 11g Enterprise Edition Release 11.1.0.6.0 - Production
With the Partitioning, OLAP, Data Mining
and Real Application Testing options
```

4. Create the first tablespace called ASM_TBS_ONE. We will use the ASM disk group
   DGROUP1 to store the underlying database datafile.

```
SQL> Create tablespace ASM_TBS_ONE Datafile '+DGROUP1' size 200m;
Tablespace created.
```

5. Once the tablespace is created, look at the filename information in DBA_DATA_FILES.

```
SQL> select file_name from dba_data_files
where tablespace_name='ASM_TBS_ONE';
FILE_NAME
-------------------------------------------------------------------------
+DGROUP1/orcl/datafile/asm_tbs_one.256.662503917
```

Note the file-naming convention. When you used just the DGROUP1 in the CREATE
TABLESPACE command, Oracle created a default directory structure and also a
default file-naming convention.

6. Create the second tablespace ASM_TBS_TWO in DGROUP2. This time we will use our
   own directory structure and file-naming convention.

```
SQL> Create tablespace ASM_TBS_TWO
  2  Datafile '+DGROUP2/oradata/orcl/dbf/asm_tbs_two.dbf' size 200m;
Create tablespace ASM_TBS_TWO
*
ERROR at line 1:
ORA-01119: error in creating database file
'+DGROUP2/oradata/orcl/dbf/asm_tbs_two.dbf'
ORA-17502: ksfdcre:4 Failed to create file
+DGROUP2/oradata/orcl/dbf/asm_tbs_two.dbf
ORA-15173: entry 'oradata' does not exist in directory '/'
```

The error occurred because we did not create the underlying directory structure. We will need to do this from the ASM instance.

7. Connect to the ASM instance.

```
C:\set ORACLE_SID=+ASM
C:\>sqlplus sys as sysasm
SQL*Plus: Release 11.1.0.6.0 - Production on Mon Aug 11 20:43:28 2008
Copyright (c) 1982, 2007, Oracle.  All rights reserved.
Enter password:
Connected to:
Oracle Database 11g Enterprise Edition Release 11.1.0.6.0 - Production
With the Partitioning, OLAP, Data Mining
and Real Application Testing options
```

8. Using the ALTER DISKGROUP command, create the directory structure in DGROUP2.

```
SQL> Alter diskgroup dgroup2
  2  Add directory '+DGROUP2/oradata';
Diskgroup altered.
SQL> Alter diskgroup dgroup2
  2  Add directory '+DGROUP2/oradata/orcl';
Diskgroup altered.
SQL> Alter diskgroup dgroup2
  2  Add directory '+DGROUP2/oradata/orcl/dbf';
Diskgroup altered.
```

9. Now log into the ORCL database and try again.

```
C:\>set oracle_sid=orcl
C:\>sqlplus sys as sysdba
SQL*Plus: Release 11.1.0.6.0 - Production on Mon Aug 11 20:50:06 2008
Copyright (c) 1982, 2007, Oracle.  All rights reserved.
Enter password:
Connected to:
Oracle Database 11g Enterprise Edition Release 11.1.0.6.0 - Production
With the Partitioning, OLAP, Data Mining
and Real Application Testing options
Create tablespace ASM_TBS_TWO
Datafile '+DGROUP2/oradata/orcl/dbf/asm_tbs_two.dbf' size 200m;
```

Lab 2.1: Executing a Manual Offline (Cold) Backup

In this lab, you will perform an offline backup. This lab will work if your database is in NOARCHIVELOG or ARCHIVELOG mode. In the Chapter 3 lab exercises, you will use the backup created in this lab to restore your database.

 This exercise assumes that you do not have any tablespaces using space in an ASM instance. Though offline backups are possible with ASM, we strongly advise that you use RMAN to perform your backups. The OCP exam will not test your knowledge of manual backups of databases using ASM.

1. Create a directory to copy your backup-related files to. In this example, we will be using c:\oracle\orabackup\orcl\cold.

    ```
    C:\>mkdir oracle
    C:\>cd oracle
    C:\oracle>mkdir orabackup
    C:\oracle>cd orabackup
    C:\oracle\orabackup>mkdir orcl
    C:\oracle\orabackup>cd orcl
    C:\oracle\orabackup\orcl>mkdir cold
    ```

2. Log into your database using SQL*Plus.

    ```
    C:\oracle\orabackup\orcl>sqlplus sys as sysdba
    SQL*Plus: Release 11.1.0.6.0 - Production on Thu Aug 14 18:57:13 2008
    Copyright (c) 1982, 2007, Oracle.  All rights reserved.
    Enter password:
    Connected to:
    Oracle Database 11g Enterprise Edition Release 11.1.0.6.0 - Production
    With the Partitioning, OLAP, Data Mining
    and Real Application Testing options
    SQL>
    ```

3. Using the DBA_DATA_FILES view, determine the datafiles that you will need to back up.

    ```
    SQL> select tablespace_name, file_name from dba_data_files;
    TABLESPACE_NAME FILE_NAME
    --------------- ---------------------------------------
    USERS           C:\ORACLE\ORADATA\ORCL\USERS01.DBF
    UNDOTBS1        C:\ORACLE\ORADATA\ORCL\UNDOTBS01.DBF
    ```

SYSAUX	C:\ORACLE\ORADATA\ORCL\SYSAUX01.DBF
SYSTEM	C:\ORACLE\ORADATA\ORCL\SYSTEM01.DBF

Note, for the purpose of this lab, that all of our datafiles, control files, and online redo logs are in the same directory. Also note that the number of files in your database may be different than those shown in this lab.

4. Using the V$LOGFILE view, determine the online redo logs that will require a backup.

```
SQL> select member from v$logfile;
MEMBER
---------------------------------
C:\ORACLE\ORADATA\ORCL\REDO03.LOG
C:\ORACLE\ORADATA\ORCL\REDO02.LOG
C:\ORACLE\ORADATA\ORCL\REDO01.LOG
```

Again, the number of online redo logs in your database may be different than the number in this lab.

5. Using the V$CONTROLFILE view, determine the location of the database control files that will be backed up.

```
SQL> select name from v$controlfile;
NAME
-----------------------------------
C:\ORACLE\ORADATA\ORCL\CONTROL01.CTL
C:\ORACLE\ORADATA\ORCL\CONTROL02.CTL
C:\ORACLE\ORADATA\ORCL\CONTROL03.CTL
```

6. From the SQL*Plus prompt, shut down the database with the shutdown immediate command.

```
SQL> shutdown immediate
Database closed.
Database dismounted.
ORACLE instance shut down.
```

7. Once the database is shut down, exit SQL*Plus.

```
SQL>exit
C:\oracle\orabackup\orcl>
```

8. Using the OS Copy command, copy the database datafiles, control files, and online redo logs to the backup directory created in step 1. In our example, they are all in the same directory, so this is easy to do.

```
        C:\oracle\orabackup\orcl>Copy c:\oracle\oradata\orcl\*.*
        c:\oracle\orabackup\orcl\cold
c:\oracle\oradata\orcl\CONTROL01.CTL
c:\oracle\oradata\orcl\CONTROL02.CTL
c:\oracle\oradata\orcl\CONTROL03.CTL
c:\oracle\oradata\orcl\RED001.LOG
c:\oracle\oradata\orcl\RED002.LOG
c:\oracle\oradata\orcl\RED003.LOG
c:\oracle\oradata\orcl\SYSAUX01.DBF
c:\oracle\oradata\orcl\SYSTEM01.DBF
c:\oracle\oradata\orcl\TEMP01.DBF
c:\oracle\oradata\orcl\UNDOTBS01.DBF
c:\oracle\oradata\orcl\USERS01.DBF
        11 file(s) copied.
```

You will notice that we backed up a file called TEMP01.DBF that didn't show up in the list of files. This is the tempfile associated with the temporary tablespace. Technically, we didn't need to back this file up because when we do a restore, we just re-create it.

9. Start SQL*Plus connecting as sys as sysdba. Restart the database with the startup command. You have completed your backup.

```
C:\oracle\orabackup\orcl>sqlplus sys as sysdba
SQL*Plus: Release 11.1.0.6.0 - Production on Thu Aug 14 19:31:56 2008
Copyright (c) 1982, 2007, Oracle.  All rights reserved.
Enter password:
Connected to an idle instance.
SQL> startup
ORACLE instance started.
Total System Global Area  397557760 bytes
Fixed Size                  1333452 bytes
Variable Size             268437300 bytes
Database Buffers          121634816 bytes
Redo Buffers                6152192 bytes
Database mounted.
Database opened.
```

Lab 2.2: Putting the Database in ARCHIVELOG Mode

In this exercise, you will configure the database for ARCHIVELOG mode. You will then actually put the database in ARCHIVELOG mode.

1. Create a directory called `c:\oracle\arch\arch`.

    ```
    C:\>mkdir oracle
    C:\>cd oracle
    C:\oracle>mkdir arch
    C:\oracle>cd arch
    C:\oracle\arch>mkdir orcl
    C:\oracle\arch>cd orcl
    C:\oracle\arch\orcl>
    ```

2. Log into your database using SQL*Plus. Check the log mode the database is in by querying the `LOG_MODE` column in `V$DATABASE`.

    ```
    C:\oracle\orabackup\orcl>sqlplus sys as sysdba
    SQL*Plus: Release 11.1.0.6.0 - Production on Thu Aug 14 19:37:19 2008
    Copyright (c) 1982, 2007, Oracle.  All rights reserved.
    Enter password:
    Connected to:
    Oracle Database 11g Enterprise Edition Release 11.1.0.6.0 - Production
    With the Partitioning, OLAP, Data Mining
    and Real Application Testing options
    SQL> select log_mode from v$database;
    LOG_MODE
    ------------

    NOARCHIVELOG
    ```

3. Using the `alter system` command, set the `LOG_ARCHIVE_DEST_1` parameter to point to the new directory you created in step 1.

    ```
    SQL> Alter system set log_archive_dest_1='location=c:\oracle\arch\orcl';
    System altered.
    ```

4. Shut down the database using the `shutdown immediate` command.

    ```
    SQL> shutdown immediate
    Database closed.
    ```

```
Database dismounted.
ORACLE instance shut down.
```

5. Put the database in MOUNT mode with the startup mount command. Confirm that
   the database is in MOUNT mode by querying the OPEN_MODE column in V$DATABASE.

```
SQL> startup mount
ORACLE instance started.
Total System Global Area  397557760 bytes
Fixed Size                  1333452 bytes
Variable Size             272631604 bytes
Database Buffers          117440512 bytes
Redo Buffers                6152192 bytes
Database mounted.
SQL> select open_mode from v$database;
OPEN_MODE
----------
MOUNTED
```

6. Now put the database in ARCHIVELOG mode using the alter database archivelog
   command.

```
SQL> alter database archivelog;
Database altered.
```

7. Open the database with the alter database open command. Check the LOG_MODE parameter of the V$DATABASE view to ensure that the database is in ARCHIVELOG mode.

```
SQL> alter database open;
Database altered.
SQL> select log_mode from v$database;
LOG_MODE
------------
ARCHIVELOG
```

8. To ensure that the database is configured correctly, force a log switch.

```
SQL> Alter system switch logfile;
System altered.
```

9. Now check the directory c:\oracle\arch\orcl to ensure that the archived redo logs
   are being created correctly.

```
SQL> Host dir c:\oracle\arch\orcl
 Volume in drive C has no label.
```

```
Volume Serial Number is 08DE-E1AB
 Directory of c:\oracle\arch\orcl
08/14/2008  07:48 PM    <DIR>          .
08/14/2008  07:48 PM    <DIR>          ..
08/14/2008  07:48 PM            1,024 ARC00003_0662757171.001
              1 File(s)        1,024 bytes
              2 Dir(s)  12,981,006,336 bytes free
```

Lab 2.3: Executing a Manual Online (Hot) Backup

In this lab, you will perform an online/hot backup of your database, with the database still running.

1. Create a directory for the backups. In this lab, we use c:\oracle\orabackup\orcl\hot. We assume that the directory structure c:\oracle\orabackup\orcl is already created from the work you did in Lab 2.1.

    ```
    C:\>cd oracle\orabackup\orcl
    C:\oracle\orabackup\orcl> mkdir hot
    ```

2. Log into your database using SQL*Plus. Check the log mode the database is in by querying the LOG_MODE column in V$DATABASE. It should be in ARCHIVELOG mode.

    ```
    C:\oracle\orabackup\orcl>sqlplus sys as sysdba
    SQL*Plus: Release 11.1.0.6.0 - Production on Thu Aug 14 19:37:19 2008
    Copyright (c) 1982, 2007, Oracle.  All rights reserved.
    Enter password:
    Connected to:
    Oracle Database 11g Enterprise Edition Release 11.1.0.6.0 - Production
    With the Partitioning, OLAP, Data Mining
    and Real Application Testing options
    SQL> select log_mode from v$database;
    LOG_MODE
    ------------
    ARCHIVELOG
    ```

3. Using the DBA_DATA_FILES view, determine the datafiles that you will need to back up.

    ```
    SQL> select tablespace_name, file_name from dba_data_files;
    ```

```
TABLESPACE_NAME FILE_NAME
--------------- ----------------------------------------
USERS           C:\ORACLE\ORADATA\ORCL\USERS01.DBF
UNDOTBS1        C:\ORACLE\ORADATA\ORCL\UNDOTBS01.DBF
SYSAUX          C:\ORACLE\ORADATA\ORCL\SYSAUX01.DBF
SYSTEM          C:\ORACLE\ORADATA\ORCL\SYSTEM01.DBF
```

4. Using the V$LOG view, determine which sequence is the current online redo log sequence. You must ensure that you have this log sequence and all logs generated during the backup in order to be able to restore the backup.

```
SQL> select group#, sequence#, status from v$log;
   GROUP#   SEQUENCE# STATUS
---------- ---------- ----------------
        1           4 CURRENT
        2           2 INACTIVE
        3           3 INACTIVE
```

5. Put the database in hot backup mode with the `alter database begin backup` command.

```
SQL> alter database begin backup;
Database altered.
```

6. Copy all database datafiles (in our case, they all have an extension of .dbf) to the backup directory created in step 1.

```
SQL>host C:\oracle\orabackup\orcl>>Copy c:\oracle\oradata\orcl\*.dbf
 c:\oracle\orabackup\orcl\hot\*.*

c:\oracle\oradata\orcl\SYSAUX01.DBF
c:\oracle\oradata\orcl\SYSTEM01.DBF
c:\oracle\oradata\orcl\TEMP01.DBF
c:\oracle\oradata\orcl\UNDOTBS01.DBF
c:\oracle\oradata\orcl\USERS01.DBF
        5 file(s) copied.
```

7. Using the V$LOG view, determine which sequence is the current online redo log sequence. You must ensure that you have this log sequence and all logs generated during the backup in order to be able to restore the backup. In our case, we need log sequences starting with 4 (the sequence when we started our backup) and continuing through log sequence 7.

```
SQL> select group#, sequence#, status from v$log;

   GROUP#   SEQUENCE# STATUS
```

```
---------- ---------- ----------------
        1          7 CURRENT
        2          5 INACTIVE
        3          6 INACTIVE
```

8. Take the database out of hot backup mode with the `alter database end backup` command.

```
SQL> alter database end backup;
Database altered.
```

9. Use the `alter system switch logfile` command to force a switch from log sequence 7.

```
SQL> alter system switch logfile;
```

 There may be times when you will need to use the `alter system archive log all;` command to get the latest archived redo-log files archived in a timely manner.

10. Check the archive-log directory to make sure log-file sequences 4 through 7 have been created. Note that we also checked the `LOG_ARCHIVE_FORMAT` parameter value. This is so we can know in the filename of the archived redo logs where the sequence number is.

```
SQL> show parameter log_archive_format
NAME                                 TYPE        VALUE
------------------------------------ ----------- -----------
log_archive_format                   string      ARC%S_%R.%T
SQL> show parameter log_archive_dest_1
NAME                                 TYPE      VALUE
------------------------------------ -------- ------------------------
log_archive_dest_1                   string    location=c:\oracle\arch\orcl
log_archive_dest_10                  string

SQL> host dir c:\oracle\arch\orcl
 Volume in drive C has no label.
 Volume Serial Number is 08DE-E1AB
 Directory of c:\oracle\arch\orcl
08/16/2008  05:25 PM    <DIR>          .
08/16/2008  05:25 PM    <DIR>          ..
08/14/2008  07:48 PM             1,024 ARC00003_0662757171.001
08/15/2008  05:01 AM        49,038,848 ARC00004_0662757171.001
08/15/2008  10:12 PM        48,250,880 ARC00005_0662757171.001
08/16/2008  09:00 AM        48,244,736 ARC00006_0662757171.001
08/16/2008  05:25 PM        34,351,104 ARC00007_0662757171.001
```

```
    5 File(s)    179,886,592 bytes
    2 Dir(s)   9,701,888,000 bytes free
```

Note in this output that the filename convention has the sequence number of the archived redo log right after the ARC value. Thus we have ARC00003 for log sequence 3, ARC00004 for log sequence 4, and so on. In the preceding output, we appear to have all log sequences that are required to recover this backup.

11. Copy the archived redo logs to the backup location.

```
SQL> Host copy c:\oracle\arch\orcl\arc*.* c:\oracle\orabackup\orcl\hot\*.*
c:\oracle\arch\orcl\ARC00003_0662757171.001
c:\oracle\arch\orcl\ARC00004_0662757171.001
c:\oracle\arch\orcl\ARC00005_0662757171.001
c:\oracle\arch\orcl\ARC00006_0662757171.001
c:\oracle\arch\orcl\ARC00007_0662757171.001
        5 file(s) copied.
```

12. Check the backup directory to ensure that all the files needed are in place.

```
SQL> Host dir c:\oracle\orabackup\orcl\hot\*.*
 Volume in drive C has no label.
 Volume Serial Number is 08DE-E1AB
 Directory of c:\oracle\orabackup\orcl\hot
08/16/2008  05:36 PM    <DIR>          .
08/16/2008  05:36 PM    <DIR>          ..
08/14/2008  07:48 PM             1,024 ARC00003_0662757171.001
08/15/2008  05:01 AM        49,038,848 ARC00004_0662757171.001
08/15/2008  10:12 PM        48,250,880 ARC00005_0662757171.001
08/16/2008  09:00 AM        48,244,736 ARC00006_0662757171.001
08/16/2008  05:25 PM        34,351,104 ARC00007_0662757171.001
08/15/2008  05:40 PM       594,485,248 SYSAUX01.DBF
08/15/2008  05:40 PM       723,525,632 SYSTEM01.DBF
08/14/2008  10:03 PM        20,979,712 TEMP01.DBF
08/15/2008  05:40 PM        26,222,592 UNDOTBS01.DBF
08/15/2008  05:40 PM         5,251,072 USERS01.DBF
              10 File(s)  1,550,350,848 bytes
               2 Dir(s)  9,521,692,672 bytes free
```

Here is a checklist:

- Datafiles: Check
- Redo log sequences 4 through 7: Check

13. This is an optional step. Now that we know our archived redo logs were copied successfully, we can remove them from the archive-log directory if we want.

```
SQL> Host del c:\oracle\arch\orcl\ARC00003_0662757171.001
SQL> Host del c:\oracle\arch\orcl\ARC00004_0662757171.001
SQL> Host del c:\oracle\arch\orcl\ARC00005_0662757171.001
SQL> Host del c:\oracle\arch\orcl\ARC00006_0662757171.001
SQL> Host del c:\oracle\arch\orcl\ARC00007_0662757171.001
```

This completes your online backup. You will use this backup to recover your database
in a Chapter 3 lab.

In the Chapter 3 labs, we will be doing full database recoveries. This will
require all of the archived redo logs generated by the database, including
those created after this backup. Make sure you do not delete any archived
redo logs that are not backed up. If you want to back up later archived redo
logs, simply repeat step 8 of Lab 2.3 as often as needed.

Lab 3.1: Executing a Time-Based Point-in-Time Recovery

In this exercise, you will do a point-in-time recovery by restoring the database to a given
point in time.

1. Back up the database. Details on how to do a full online database backup are found in
Chapter 2. In summary, follow these steps:

   a. Put the database in hot backup mode.

   b. Copy all database datafiles to a backup location.

   c. Take the database out of hot backup mode.

   d. Force a log switch. Back up the archived redo logs.

Here is an example of a backup:

```
[oracle@localhost orcl]$ sqlplus "/ as sysdba"
SQL*Plus: Release 11.1.0.6.0 - Production on Sun Aug 17 15:35:48 2008
Copyright (c) 1982, 2007, Oracle.  All rights reserved.
Connected to:
Oracle Database 11g Enterprise Edition Release 11.1.0.6.0 - Production
With the Partitioning, OLAP, Data Mining
```

```
and Real Application Testing options
SQL> alter database begin backup;
Database altered.
SQL> host cp /oracle01/oradata/orcl/*.dbf /oracle01/backup/orcl
SQL> alter database end backup;
Database altered.
SQL> alter system switch logfile;
System altered.
SQL> host cp /oracle01/backup/arch/* /oracle01/backup/orcl/*
SQL> alter database backup controlfile to trace;
Database altered.
SQL> alter database backup controlfile to
 '/oracle01/oradata/orcl/control1.bak';
Database altered.
```

2. Next, log into the database as scott/tiger and create a new table. Insert two records into the new table and commit the insert.

```
SQL> connect scott/tiger
Connected.
SQL> create table time_table (col_one date);
Table created.
SQL> insert into time_table values (sysdate);
1 row created.
SQL> insert into time_table values (sysdate);
1 row created.
SQL> commit;
Commit complete.
SQL> alter session set nls_date_format='mm/dd/yyyy hh24:mi:ss';
Session altered.
SQL> select * from time_table;
COL_ONE
-------------------
08/17/2008 22:03:59
08/17/2008 22:03:59
```

3. Wait a minute or so (however long you like) and add two more records. Commit the inserts.

```
SQL> insert into time_table values (sysdate);
1 row created.
SQL> insert into time_table values (sysdate);
```

```
1 row created.
SQL> commit;
Commit complete.
SQL> select * from time_table;
COL_ONE
------------------
08/17/2008 22:03:59
08/17/2008 22:03:59
08/17/2008 22:04:45
08/17/2008 22:04:45
```

4. Shut down the database.

```
SQL> connect sys as sysdba
Enter password:
Connected.
SQL> shutdown immediate
Database closed.
Database dismounted.
ORACLE instance shut down.
```

5. Once you are sure the database is down, restore the database datafiles from their backup location to the location where the database files belong.

```
[oracle@localhost orcl]$ pwd
/oracle01/backup/orcl
[oracle@localhost orcl]$ cp *.dbf /oracle01/oradata/orcl/*
```

6. Mount the database.

```
[oracle@localhost orcl]$ sqlplus "/ as sysdba"
SQL*Plus: Release 11.1.0.6.0 - Production on Sun Aug 17 17:53:14 2008
Copyright (c) 1982, 2007, Oracle.  All rights reserved.
Connected to an idle instance.
SQL> startup mount
ORACLE instance started.
Total System Global Area  167395328 bytes
Fixed Size                  1298612 bytes
Variable Size             142610252 bytes
Database Buffers           20971520 bytes
Redo Buffers                2514944 bytes
Database mounted.
```

7. Recover the database using the `recover database until time` command. Use a time that is after the time listed in the second insert in the TIME_TABLE (22:03:59 in our example). In this case, we will recover to 22:04:00. Enter **AUTO** if prompted for an archived redo log to apply.

```
SQL> recover database until time '2008-08-17:22:04:00';
Media recovery complete.
```

8. Open the database with the `alter database open resetlogs` command. Note that once you have done this, you will not be able to recover any data that was entered after the point of the recovery.

```
SQL> alter database open resetlogs;
Database altered.
```

9. Log into the scott schema. Do a `select * from test_table`. You should have only two records in the table.

```
SQL> Connect scott/tiger
Connected.
SQL> select * from time_table;
COL_ONE
-------------------
08/17/2008 22:03:59
08/17/2008 22:03:59
```

Lab 3.2: Recovering from Control-File Loss with a Backup Control File

In this lab we will be recovering a database that has experienced the complete loss of its control files. We will be using a backup control file to perform the recovery.

1. Back up the database. Details on how to do a full online database backup are found in Chapter 2. In summary, follow these steps:

   a. Put the database in hot backup mode.

   b. Copy all database datafiles to a backup location.

   c. Take the database out of hot backup mode.

   d. Force a log switch. Back up the archived redo logs.

Here is an example of a backup:

```
[oracle@localhost orcl]$ sqlplus "/ as sysdba"
SQL*Plus: Release 11.1.0.6.0 - Production on Sun Aug 17 15:35:48 2008
Copyright (c) 1982, 2007, Oracle.  All rights reserved.
Connected to:
Oracle Database 11g Enterprise Edition Release 11.1.0.6.0 - Production
With the Partitioning, OLAP, Data Mining
and Real Application Testing options
SQL> alter database begin backup;
Database altered.
SQL> host cp /oracle01/oradata/orcl/*.dbf /oracle01/backup/orcl
SQL> alter database end backup;
Database altered.
SQL> alter system switch logfile;
System altered.
SQL> host cp /oracle01/backup/arch/* /oracle01/backup/orcl/*
SQL> alter database backup controlfile to trace;
Database altered.
SQL> alter database backup controlfile to
  '/oracle01/oradata/orcl/control1.bak';
Database altered.
```

2. Find the location of the control files.

```
SQL> select name from v$controlfile;
NAME
--------------------------------------------------------------------------
/oracle01/oradata/orcl/control01.ctl
/oracle01/oradata/orcl/control02.ctl
/oracle01/oradata/orcl/control03.ctl
```

3. Shut down the database.

```
SQL> connect sys as sysdba
Enter password:
Connected.
SQL> shutdown immediate
Database closed.
Database dismounted.
ORACLE instance shut down.
```

4. Remove all control files.

```
SQL> host rm /oracle01/oradata/orcl/control01.ctl
SQL> host rm /oracle01/oradata/orcl/control02.ctl
SQL> host rm /oracle01/oradata/orcl/control03.ctl
```

5. Start up the database. Notice the error resulting from loss of all control files.

```
SQL> startup
ORACLE instance started.
Total System Global Area  159027200 bytes
Fixed Size                  1298556 bytes
Variable Size             134221700 bytes
Database Buffers           20971520 bytes
Redo Buffers                2535424 bytes
ORA-00205: error in identifying control file, check alert log for more info
```

6. Copy the backup control file into place.

```
SQL>Host cp /oracle01/backup/orcl/control.bak
/oracle01/oradata/orcl/control01.ctl
SQL>Host cp /oracle01/backup/orcl/control.bak
/oracle01/oradata/orcl/control02.ctl
SQL>Host cp /oracle01/backup/orcl/control.bak
/oracle01/oradata/orcl/control03.ctl
```

7. Mount the database with the `alter database mount` command.

```
SQL> alter database mount;
Database altered.
```

8. Recover the database by issuing the `recover database using backup controlfile` command. Since you have all the online redo logs, you can do a complete recovery. If prompted to recover using archived redo logs, enter **AUTO**.

```
SQL> recover database using backup controlfile;
ORA-00279: change 5026597 generated at 08/19/2008 16:23:33
needed for thread 1
ORA-00289: suggestion :
/oracle01/flash_recovery_area/ORCL/archivelog/2008_08_19/o1_mf_1_10_%u_.arc
ORA-00280: change 5026597 for thread 1 is in sequence #10
Specify log: {<RET>=suggested | filename | AUTO | CANCEL}
auto
ORA-00308: cannot open archived log
```

```
'/oracle01/flash_recovery_area/ORCL/archivelog/2008_08_19
/o1_mf_1_10_%u_.arc'
ORA-27037: unable to obtain file status
Linux Error: 2: No such file or directory
Additional information: 3
ORA-00308: cannot open archived log
'/oracle01/flash_recovery_area/ORCL/archivelog/2008_08_19
/o1_mf_1_10_%u_.arc'
ORA-27037: unable to obtain file status
Linux Error: 2: No such file or directory
Additional information: 3
```

9. (This step is not required if step 8 completed with a message that said media recovery successful.) If you get the error message we got above (you may not), determine which online redo log contains the sequence number needing to be restored by querying V$LOG and V$LOGFILE as shown here.

```
SQL> select a.group#, a.member, b.sequence#
  2  from v$logfile a, v$log b
  3* where a.group#=b.group#;
    GROUP# MEMBER                                    SEQUENCE#
---------- -------------------------------------- ----------
         1 /oracle01/oradata/orcl/redo01.log             10
         1 /oracle01/oradata/orcl/redo01a.log            10
         2 /oracle01/oradata/orcl/redo02a.log             8
         2 /oracle01/oradata/orcl/redo02.log              8
         3 /oracle01/oradata/orcl/redo03a.log             9
         3 /oracle01/oradata/orcl/redo03.log              9
```

In this case, the online redo-log file /oracle01/oradata/orcl/redo01.log contains sequence 10, which we need to restore. Start recovery again, and apply the online redo-log file as shown here.

```
SQL> recover database using backup controlfile;
ORA-00279: change 5026597 generated at 08/19/2008 16:23:33
needed for thread 1
ORA-00289: suggestion :
/oracle01/flash_recovery_area/ORCL/archivelog/2008_08_19/o1_mf_1_10_%u_.arc
ORA-00280: change 5026597 for thread 1 is in sequence #10
Specify log: {<RET>=suggested | filename | AUTO | CANCEL}
/oracle01/oradata/orcl/redo01.log
Log applied.
Media recovery complete.
```

10. Open the database with the `alter database open resetlogs` command. Since you are using a backup control file, you must use the `resetlogs` command.

```
SQL> alter database open resetlogs;
Database altered.
```

Lab 3.3: Recovering from Loss of the Current Online Redo Log

In this lab we will be recovering from the loss of the current online redo log. This is perhaps one of the worst-case situations that you would face as an Oracle DBA!

1. Back up the database. Details on how to do a full online database backup are found in Chapter 2. In summary, follow these steps:

    a. Put the database in hot backup mode.

    b. Copy all database datafiles to a backup location.

    c. Take the database out of hot backup mode.

    d. Force a log switch. Back up the archived redo logs.

    Here is an example of a backup:

```
[oracle@localhost orcl]$ sqlplus "/ as sysdba"
SQL*Plus: Release 11.1.0.6.0 - Production on Sun Aug 17 15:35:48 2008
Copyright (c) 1982, 2007, Oracle.  All rights reserved.
Connected to:
Oracle Database 11g Enterprise Edition Release 11.1.0.6.0 - Production
With the Partitioning, OLAP, Data Mining
and Real Application Testing options
SQL> alter database begin backup;
Database altered.
SQL> host cp /oracle01/oradata/orcl/*.dbf /oracle01/backup/orcl
SQL> alter database end backup;
Database altered.
SQL> alter system switch logfile;
System altered.
SQL> host cp /oracle01/backup/arch/* /oracle01/backup/orcl/*
SQL> alter database backup controlfile to trace;
Database altered.
SQL> alter database backup controlfile to
  '/oracle01/oradata/orcl/control1.bak';
Database altered.
```

2. Determine the location of the online redo logs by querying the MEMBER column of the V$LOGFILE view.

```
SQL> select member from v$logfile;
MEMBER
----------------------------------------------------------------------
/oracle01/oradata/orcl/redo03.log
/oracle01/oradata/orcl/redo02.log
/oracle01/oradata/orcl/redo01.log
/oracle01/oradata/orcl/redo01a.log
/oracle01/oradata/orcl/redo02a.log
/oracle01/oradata/orcl/redo03a.log
```

3. While the database is still running, remove all of the online redo logs.
```
SQL> host rm /oracle01/oradata/orcl/redo03.log
SQL> host rm /oracle01/oradata/orcl/redo02.log
SQL> host rm /oracle01/oradata/orcl/redo01.log
SQL> host rm /oracle01/oradata/orcl/redo01a.log
SQL> host rm /oracle01/oradata/orcl/redo02a.log
SQL> host rm /oracle01/oradata/orcl/redo03a.log
```

Note that this lab is set up to demonstrate recovering a database from an actual crash as a result of the loss of the online redo logs. If the database has not actually crashed, you would issue an alter database checkpoint command and then try an alter database clear logfile command to try to save the database from crashing.

4. If the database is still running, simulate a crash using the shutdown abort command.

```
SQL> shutdown abort
ORACLE instance shut down.
```

5. Start up the database to see the error you will receive.

```
SQL> startup
ORACLE instance started.
Total System Global Area  159027200 bytes
Fixed Size                  1298556 bytes
Variable Size             134221700 bytes
Database Buffers           20971520 bytes
Redo Buffers                2535424 bytes
Database mounted.
ORA-00313: open failed for members of log group 1 of thread 1
```

```
ORA-00312: online log 1 thread 1: '/oracle01/oradata/orcl/redo01a.log'
ORA-27037: unable to obtain file status
Linux Error: 2: No such file or directory
Additional information: 3
ORA-00312: online log 1 thread 1: '/oracle01/oradata/orcl/redo01.log'
ORA-27037: unable to obtain file status
Linux Error: 2: No such file or directory
Additional information: 3
```

6. Restore the database from the backup taken in step 1.

```
[oracle@localhost orcl]$ cp /oracle01/backup/orcl/*.gz . &
```

7. Mount the database using the startup mount command.

```
[oracle@localhost orcl]$ sqlplus / as sysdba
SQL*Plus: Release 11.1.0.6.0 - Production on Sun Aug 17 16:26:56 2008
Copyright (c) 1982, 2007, Oracle.  All rights reserved.
Connected to an idle instance.
SQL> startup mount
ORACLE instance started.
Total System Global Area  167395328 bytes
Fixed Size                  1298612 bytes
Variable Size             142610252 bytes
Database Buffers           20971520 bytes
Redo Buffers                2514944 bytes
Database mounted.
```

8. Using the V$ARCHIVED_LOG, determine the last log sequence number archived.

```
SQL> select max(sequence#) from v$archived_log
  2 where resetlogs_change#=
  3 (select max(resetlogs_change#) from v$archived_log);
MAX(SEQUENCE#)
--------------
            9
```

9. Recover the database using the recover database until cancel command. Use the last archived redo log sequence number found in step 8 as the sequence to recover to. Once you reach that sequence number, cancel the recovery.

```
SQL> recover database using backup controlfile until cancel;
SQL> recover database until cancel using backup controlfile;
ORA-00279: change 5026562 generated at 08/19/2008 16:23:14
```

```
needed for thread 1
ORA-00289: suggestion :
/oracle01/flash_recovery_area/ORCL/archivelog/2008_08_19/
o1_mf_1_9_4bpm2cgp_.arcORA-00280: change 5026562
for thread 1 is in sequence #9
Specify log: {<RET>=suggested | filename | AUTO | CANCEL}
ORA-00279: change 5026597 generated at 08/19/2008 16:23:33
needed for thread 1
ORA-00289: suggestion :
/oracle01/flash_recovery_area/ORCL/archivelog/2008_08_19/
o1_mf_1_10_4bpm2bt3_.arc
ORA-00280: change 5026597 for thread 1 is in sequence #10
ORA-00278: log file
'/oracle01/flash_recovery_area/ORCL/archivelog/2008_08_19/
o1_mf_1_9_4bpm2cgp_.arc' no longer needed for this recovery
Specify log: {<RET>=suggested | filename | AUTO | CANCEL}
cancel
Media recovery cancelled.
```

10. Open the database with the `alter database open resetlogs` command. Your recovery is complete.

```
SQL> alter database open resetlogs;
Database altered.
```

Lab 4.1: Creating an RMAN Offline Backup

In this lab, you will be creating an RMAN offline backup. You can back up databases in NOARCHIVELOG or ARCHIVELOG mode with offline backups.

1. Start RMAN.

```
C:\>rman target=/
Recovery Manager: Release 11.1.0.6.0 - Production on
Thu Sep 11 18:58:55 2008
Copyright (c) 1982, 2007, Oracle.  All rights reserved.
connected to target database: ORCL (DBID=1190537904)
```

2. Shut down the database from RMAN using the RMAN `shutdown immediate` command. Then start the database in MOUNT mode with the RMAN `startup mount` command.

```
RMAN> shutdown immediate
using target database control file instead of recovery catalog
database closed
database dismounted
Oracle instance shut down
RMAN> startup mount
connected to target database (not started)
Oracle instance started
database mounted
Total System Global Area    397557760 bytes
Fixed Size                    1333452 bytes
Variable Size               281020212 bytes
Database Buffers            109051904 bytes
Redo Buffers                  6152192 bytes
```

3. Back up the database using the `backup` command. In this case, we are not going to back up the database archived redo logs if the database is in ARCHIVELOG mode. Since it was shut down in a consistent manner, we don't need to back up any archived redo logs to restore this backup.

```
RMAN> Backup database;
Starting backup at 11-SEP-08
allocated channel: ORA_DISK_1
channel ORA_DISK_1: SID=155 device type=DISK
channel ORA_DISK_1: starting compressed full datafile backup set
channel ORA_DISK_1: specifying datafile(s) in backup set
input datafile file number=00002 name=C:\ORACLE\ORADATA\ORCL\SYSAUX01.DBF
input datafile file number=00001 name=C:\ORACLE\ORADATA\ORCL\SYSTEM01.DBF
input datafile file number=00005 name=C:\ORACLE\ORADATA\ORCL\UNDOTBS02.DBF
input datafile file number=00004 name=C:\ORACLE\ORADATA\ORCL\USERS01.DBF
channel ORA_DISK_1: starting piece 1 at 11-SEP-08
channel ORA_DISK_1: finished piece 1 at 11-SEP-08
piece handle=C:\ORACLE\FLASH_RECOVERY_AREA\ORCL
\BACKUPSET\2008_09_11\O1_MF_NNNDF_TAG20080911T204331_4DMOTSN1_.BKP
tag=TAG20080911T204331 comment=NONE
channel ORA_DISK_1: backup set complete, elapsed time: 00:05:26
Finished backup at 11-SEP-08
Starting Control File and SPFILE Autobackup at 11-SEP-08
```

```
piece handle=C:\ORACLE\FLASH_RECOVERY_AREA\ORCL
\AUTOBACKUP\2008_09_11\O1_MF_S_665181628_4DMP5C9P_.BKP comment=NONE
Finished Control File and SPFILE Autobackup at 11-SEP-08
```

4. Restart the database with the RMAN command `alter database open`.

```
RMAN> Alter database open;
database opened
```

Lab 4.2: Creating an RMAN Incremental Backup

In this lab, we will be creating an incremental backup. We will also be looking at the size of the resulting backup sets to compare the backup set sizes and the impacts of the level-0 and level-1 incremental backups.

1. Log into the database using SQL*Plus.

```
C:\oracle\admin\ORCL\wallet>set oracle_sid=orcl
C:\oracle\admin\ORCL\wallet>sqlplus "/ as sysdba"
SQL*Plus: Release 11.1.0.6.0 - Production on Thu Sep 11 18:56:27 2008
Copyright (c) 1982, 2007, Oracle.  All rights reserved.
Connected to:
Oracle Database 11g Enterprise Edition Release 11.1.0.6.0 - Production
With the Partitioning, OLAP, Data Mining
and Real Application Testing options
SQL>
```

2. Query the LOG_MODE column of the V$DATABASE view to confirm that the database is in ARCHIVELOG mode. If the database is not in ARCHIVELOG mode, refer to Chapter 2 for information on how to put the database in ARCHIVELOG mode.

```
SQL> Select log_mode from v$database;
LOG_MODE
------------
ARCHIVELOG
```

3. Exit SQL*Plus and start RMAN.

```
SQL> exit
Disconnected from Oracle Database 11g Enterprise Edition
```

```
Release 11.1.0.6.0 - Production
With the Partitioning, OLAP, Data Mining
and Real Application Testing options
C:\oracle\admin\ORCL\wallet>rman target=/
Recovery Manager: Release 11.1.0.6.0 - Production
on Thu Sep 11 18:58:55 2008
Copyright (c) 1982, 2007, Oracle.  All rights reserved.
connected to target database: ORCL (DBID=1190537904)
```

4. Execute the RMAN backup using the backup database command. Include the
incremental level 0 option. You will back up the archived redo logs at the same
time with the plus archivelog option. Remove the archived redo logs after they are
backed up using the delete input option.

```
RMAN> Backup incremental level 0 database plus archivelog delete input;
```

5. Exit RMAN and log into SQL*Plus.

6. Query the V$BACKUP_DATAFILE and V$BACKUP_SET views to determine the size of the
backup image (found in the BLOCKS column).

```
SQL> select a.set_count, a.start_time, a.completion_time, sum(b.blocks)
  2  from v$backup_set a, v$backup_datafile b
  3  where a.set_count=b.set_count
  4  and to_char(a.start_time, 'mm/dd/yyyy hh24:mi:ss')=
  5  (select to_char(max(start_time), 'mm/dd/yyyy hh24:mi:ss')
  6   from v$backup_set
  7   where incremental_level=0)
  8  group by a.set_count, a.start_time, a.completion_time ;
 SET_COUNT START_TIM COMPLETIO SUM(B.BLOCKS)
---------- --------- --------- -------------
       155 11-SEP-08 11-SEP-08        144318
```

7. Exit RMAN. Sign into the database using SQL*Plus. Add a table to the scott (or any
other) schema. Insert and commit records into that table.

```
RMAN> Exit
Recovery Manager complete.
C:\Documents and Settings\Robert>Sqlplus scott/tiger
SQL*Plus: Release 11.1.0.6.0 - Production on
Thu Sep 11 20:37:39 2008
Copyright (c) 1982, 2007, Oracle.  All rights reserved.
Connected to:
Oracle Database 11g Enterprise Edition
Release 11.1.0.6.0 - Production
```

```
With the Partitioning, OLAP, Data Mining and Real Application
Testing options
SQL> Create table my_new_table (id number);
Table created.
SQL> Insert into my_new_table values (1);
1 row created.
SQL> Commit;
Commit complete.
SQL> Exit
```

8. Sign into RMAN. Perform a level-1 incremental backup.

```
RMAN> Backup incremental level 1 database plus archivelog delete input;
```

9. Query the V$BACKUP_DATAFILE and V$BACKUP_SET views again to determine the size of the backup image (found in the BLOCKS column). Since we are not doing an outer join here, the query will not return any rows until the backup in step 8 has completed. Note that the level-1 incremental backup is much smaller in the output than that in step 6.

```
SQL> select a.set_count, a.start_time, a.completion_time, sum(b.blocks)
  2  from v$backup_set a, v$backup_datafile b
  3  where a.set_count=b.set_count
  4  and to_char(a.start_time, 'mm/dd/yyyy hh24:mi:ss')=
  5  (select to_char(max(start_time), 'mm/dd/yyyy hh24:mi:ss')
  6   from v$backup_set
  7   where incremental_level=1)
  8   group by a.set_count, a.start_time, a.completion_time ;
 SET_COUNT START_TIM COMPLETIO SUM(B.BLOCKS)
---------- --------- --------- -------------
       159 11-SEP-08 11-SEP-08            45
```

Lab 4.3: Creating an Image-Copy Backup

In this lab, you will create an image-copy backup of your database. We assume your database is in ARCHIVELOG mode for this backup.

1. Log into the database using SQL*Plus.

```
C:\oracle\admin\ORCL\wallet>set oracle_sid=orcl
C:\oracle\admin\ORCL\wallet>sqlplus "/ as sysdba"
SQL*Plus: Release 11.1.0.6.0 - Production on Thu Sep 11 18:56:27 2008
Copyright (c) 1982, 2007, Oracle.  All rights reserved.
```

Connected to:
Oracle Database 11*g* Enterprise Edition Release 11.1.0.6.0 - Production
With the Partitioning, OLAP, Data Mining
and Real Application Testing options
SQL>

2. Using the backup as copy command, create an image copy of the database.

```
RMAN> Backup as copy database;
Starting backup at 11-SEP-08
using channel ORA_DISK_1
channel ORA_DISK_1: starting datafile copy
input datafile file number=00002 name=C:\ORACLE\ORADATA\ORCL\SYSAUX01.DBF
output file name=C:\ORACLE\FLASH_RECOVERY_AREA\ORCL
\DATAFILE\O1_MF_SYSAUX_4DMQJBMK_.DBF tag=TAG20080911T211158
RECID=23 STAMP=665183712
channel ORA_DISK_1: datafile copy complete, elapsed time: 00:03:16
channel ORA_DISK_1: starting datafile copy
input datafile file number=00001 name=C:\ORACLE\ORADATA\ORCL\SYSTEM01.DBF
output file name=C:\ORACLE\FLASH_RECOVERY_AREA\ORCL
\DATAFILE\O1_MF_SYSTEM_4DMQPMC7_.DBF tag=TAG20080911T211158
RECID=24 STAMP=665184016
channel ORA_DISK_1: datafile copy complete, elapsed time: 00:04:56
channel ORA_DISK_1: starting datafile copy
input datafile file number=00005 name=C:\ORACLE\ORADATA\ORCL\UNDOTBS02.DBF
output file name=C:\ORACLE\FLASH_RECOVERY_AREA\ORCL
\DATAFILE\O1_MF_UNDOTBS2_4DMRO3BY_.DBF tag=TAG20080911T211158
RECID=25 STAMP=665184046
channel ORA_DISK_1: datafile copy complete, elapsed time: 00:00:15
channel ORA_DISK_1: starting datafile copy
input datafile file number=00004 name=C:\ORACLE\ORADATA\ORCL\USERS01.DBF
output file name=C:\ORACLE\FLASH_RECOVERY_AREA\ORCL
\DATAFILE\O1_MF_USERS_4DMROS6S_.DBF tag=TAG20080911T211158
RECID=26 STAMP=665184058
channel ORA_DISK_1: datafile copy complete, elapsed time: 00:00:03
Finished backup at 11-SEP-08
Starting Control File and SPFILE Autobackup at 11-SEP-08
piece handle=C:\ORACLE\FLASH_RECOVERY_AREA\ORCL
\AUTOBACKUP\2008_09_11\O1_MF_S_665184060_4DMR163F_.BKP comment=NONE
Finished Control File and SPFILE Autobackup at 11-SEP-083.
```

Lab 5.1: Implementing RVPC

In this lab, you will implement RMAN virtual private catalog (RVPC) in the recovery catalog.

1. First you need to create the RVPC database account. Log into the recovery-catalog database as a privileged user (for example, SYS) and issue the `create user` command.

    ```
    C:\Documents and Settings\Robert>sqlplus rcat_user/rcat_user@rcat
    SQL*Plus: Release 11.1.0.6.0 - Production on Tue Sep 16 20:33:07 2008
    Copyright (c) 1982, 2007, Oracle.  All rights reserved.
    Connected to:
    Oracle Database 11g Enterprise Edition Release 11.1.0.6.0 - Production
    With the Partitioning, OLAP, Data Mining
    and Real Application Testing options
    SQL> create user rcat_001 identified by rcat_001
      2  default tablespace rcat_data
      3  quota unlimited on rcat_data;
    User created.
    ```

2. Grant the `recovery_catalog_owner` privilege to the new user. Here is an example of this operation:

    ```
    SQL> grant recovery_catalog_owner to rcat_001;
    Grant succeeded.
    ```

3. Create the virtual catalog. To do this, you log into RMAN and use the `create virtual catalog` command, as shown in this example:

    ```
    C:\Documents and Settings\Robert>rman catalog=rcat_001/rcat_001@rcat
    Recovery Manager: Release 11.1.0.6.0 - Production
    on Tue Sep 16 20:30:04 2008
    Copyright (c) 1982, 2007, Oracle.  All rights reserved.
    connected to recovery catalog database
    RMAN> Create virtual catalog;
    found eligible base catalog owned by RCAT_USER
    created virtual catalog against base catalog owned by RCAT_USER
    ```

4. Now that you have created the RVPC account, you need to indicate to the recovery-catalog database which databases this account will have access too. Log into RMAN

and connect to the recovery catalog. Use the grant command and register the ORCL database to rcat_001.

```
C:\Documents and Settings\Robert>rman catalog=rcat_user/rcat_user@rcat
Recovery Manager: Release 11.1.0.6.0 - Production
on Tue Sep 16 20:25:32 2008
Copyright (c) 1982, 2007, Oracle.  All rights reserved.
connected to recovery catalog database
RMAN> grant catalog for database orcl to rcat_001;
Grant succeeded.
```

5. Query the RC_DATABASE view and see that only the ORCL database can be seen in the RVPC.

```
C:\Documents and Settings\Robert>sqlplus rcat_001/rcat_001@rcat
SQL*Plus: Release 11.1.0.6.0 - Production on Tue Sep 16 20:33:07 2008
Copyright (c) 1982, 2007, Oracle.  All rights reserved.
Connected to:
Oracle Database 11g Enterprise Edition Release 11.1.0.6.0 - Production
With the Partitioning, OLAP, Data Mining and Real Application
Testing options
SQL> Select name from rc_database;
NAME
--------
ORCL
```

Lab 6.1: Restoring a Datafile Online

In this activity, we will restore a datafile while the rest of the database is online. This activity builds on the backup done in Exercise 4.2 in Chapter 4. You should have completed Exercise 4.2 prior to executing this activity. Please note that the output you experience from this exercise will probably differ from the output shown here.

1. Log into the database as SYS using SQL*Plus.

```
C:\oracle>set oracle_sid=orcl
C:\oracle>sqlplus sys as sysdba
SQL*Plus: Release 11.1.0.6.0 - Production on Fri Oct 3 00:31:07 2008
Copyright (c) 1982, 2007, Oracle.  All rights reserved.
Enter password:
Connected to:
```

```
Oracle Database 11g Enterprise Edition Release 11.1.0.6.0 - Production
With the Partitioning, OLAP, Data Mining
and Real Application Testing options
SQL>
```

2. Determine the location of the database datafiles and their associated FILE_ID's.

```
SQL> select file_id, file_name from dba_data_files;
FILE_ID FILE_NAME
------- ----------------------------------------------------------------
      4
C:\ORACLE\FLASH_RECOVERY_AREA\ORCL\DATAFILE\O1_MF_USERS_4G2Q1YTC_.DBF
        3 C:\ORACLE\ORADATA\ORCL\UNDOTBS01.DBF
        2 C:\ORACLE\ORADATA\ORCL\SYSAUX01.DBF
        1 C:\ORACLE\ORADATA\ORCL\SYSTEM01.DBF
```

3. Shut down the database.

```
SQL> shutdown abort
ORACLE instance shut down.
```

4. Exit SQL*Plus.

```
SQL> quit
Disconnected from Oracle Database 11g Enterprise Edition
Release 11.1.0.6.0 - Production
With the Partitioning, OLAP, Data Mining
and Real Application Testing options
C:\oracle>
```

5. From the operating prompt, delete one of the database datafiles listed in step 3. Make sure, before you delete the file, that you note its datafile number, the filename, and the location. In our example, we will delete datafile 4, which is the datafile associated with the USERS tablespace.

```
C:\oracle>Del
C:\ORACLE\FLASH_RECOVERY_AREA\ORCL\DATAFILE\O1_MF_USERS_4G2Q1YTC_.DBF
```

6. Log into the database as SYS using SQL*Plus.

```
C:\oracle>sqlplus sys as sysdba
SQL*Plus: Release 11.1.0.6.0 - Production on Fri Oct 3 00:35:25 2008
Copyright (c) 1982, 2007, Oracle.  All rights reserved.
Enter password:
Connected to an idle instance.
```

7. Start the database. Notice the error that you receive.

```
SQL> startup
ORACLE instance started.
Total System Global Area  364081152 bytes
Fixed Size                  1333228 bytes
Variable Size             264243220 bytes
Database Buffers           92274688 bytes
Redo Buffers                6230016 bytes
Database mounted.
ORA-01157: cannot identify/lock data file 4 - see DBWR trace file
ORA-01110: data file 4:
'C:\ORACLE\FLASH_RECOVERY_AREA\ORCL\DATAFILE\O1_MF_USERS_4G2Q1YTC_.DBF'
```

8. Use the `alter database datafile offline` command to take datafile 4 offline.

```
SQL> Alter database datafile 4 offline;
Database altered.
```

9. Open the database with the `alter database open` command. Exit SQL*Plus after the database has opened.

```
SQL> Alter database datafile 4 offline;
Database altered.
SQL> alter database open;
Database altered.
SQL> exit
Disconnected from Oracle Database 11g Enterprise Edition
Release 11.1.0.6.0 - Production
With the Partitioning, OLAP, Data Mining
and Real Application Testing options
```

10. Start RMAN. We will assume you are not using a recovery catalog during this exercise.

```
C:\oracle>rman target=/
Recovery Manager: Release 11.1.0.6.0 - Production
on Fri Oct 3 00:37:44 2008
Copyright (c) 1982, 2007, Oracle.  All rights reserved.
connected to target database (not started)
```

11. Restore database datafile 4 with the `restore datafile` command.

```
RMAN> restore datafile 4;
Starting restore at 10/03/2008 02:16:38
```

```
using target database control file instead of recovery catalog
allocated channel: ORA_DISK_1
channel ORA_DISK_1: SID=133 device type=DISK
channel ORA_DISK_1: starting datafile backup set restore
channel ORA_DISK_1: specifying datafile(s) to restore from backup set
channel ORA_DISK_1: restoring datafile 00004 to
C:\ORACLE\FLASH_RECOVERY_AREA\ORCL\DATAFILE\O1_MF_USERS_4G2Q1YTC_.DBF
channel ORA_DISK_1: reading from backup piece
 C:\ORACLE\FLASH_RECOVERY_AREA\ORCL\BACKUPSET\2008_10_03
\O1_MF_NNNDF_TAG20081003T001928_4GCGCQQ4_.BKP
channel ORA_DISK_1: piece
handle=C:\ORACLE\FLASH_RECOVERY_AREA\ORCL\BACKUPSET\2008_10_03
\O1_MF_NNNDF_TAG20081003T001928_4GCGCQQ4_.BKP tag=TAG20081003T001928
channel ORA_DISK_1: restored backup piece 1
channel ORA_DISK_1: restore complete, elapsed time: 00:00:03
Finished restore at 10/03/2008 02:16:42
```

12. Recover datafile 4 with the `recover datafile` command.

```
RMAN> recover datafile 4;
Starting recover at 10/03/2008 02:17:53
using channel ORA_DISK_1
starting media recovery
archived log for thread 1 with sequence 3 is already on disk as file
C:\ORACLE\PRODUCT\11.1.0\DB_1\RDBMS\ARC00003_0667012858.001
archived log for thread 1 with sequence 4 is already on disk as file
 C:\ORACLE\FLASH_RECOVERY_AREA\ORCL\ARCHIVELOG\2008_10_03
\O1_MF_1_4_4GCMC8GV_.ARC
archived log for thread 1 with sequence 1 is already on disk as file
C:\ORACLE\FLASH_RECOVERY_AREA\ORCL\ARCHIVELOG\2008_10_03
\O1_MF_1_1_4GCO4G15_.ARC
archived log file
name=C:\ORACLE\PRODUCT\11.1.0\DB_1\RDBMS\ARC00003_0667012858.001
thread=1 sequence=3
archived log file
name=C:\ORACLE\FLASH_RECOVERY_AREA\ORCL\ARCHIVELOG\2008_10_03
\O1_MF_1_4_4GCMC8GV_.ARC thread=1 sequence=4
media recovery complete, elapsed time: 00:00:01
Finished recover at 10/03/2008 02:17:55
```

13. Bring the datafile online using the RMAN `sql` command calling the SQL statement `alter database datafile online`.

```
RMAN> sql 'alter database datafile 4 online';
sql statement: alter database datafile 4 online
```

The datafile has been restored online and the lab is complete.

Lab 6.2: Performing a Change-Based Recovery with RMAN

In this activity, you will restore the database to a specific SCN, or system change number. This activity builds on the backup done in Exercise 4.2 in Chapter 4. You should have completed Exercise 4.2 prior to executing this activity. Please note that the output you experience from this exercise will probably differ from the output shown here.

1. Start SQL*Plus.

```
C:\oracle>sqlplus sys as sysdba
SQL*Plus: Release 11.1.0.6.0 - Production on Fri Oct 3 00:35:25 2008
Copyright (c) 1982, 2007, Oracle.  All rights reserved.
Enter password:
```

2. The database should already be started. If not, start it with the `startup` command. To determine the current SCN, issue the following query:

```
SQL> select current_scn from v$database;
CURRENT_SCN
-----------
    1095172
```

This is the SCN that we will recover to. Your SCN is likely to be very different.

3. Start RMAN. We will assume you are not using a recovery catalog during this exercise.

```
C:\oracle>rman target=/
Recovery Manager: Release 11.1.0.6.0 - Production on Fri Oct 3 00:37:44 2008
Copyright (c) 1982, 2007, Oracle.  All rights reserved.
```

4. To prepare for the restore, put the database in MOUNT mode with the `startup force mount` RMAN command.

```
RMAN> startup force mount
Oracle instance started
```

```
database mounted
Total System Global Area    364081152 bytes
Fixed Size                    1333228 bytes
Variable Size              289409044 bytes
Database Buffers            67108864 bytes
Redo Buffers                6230016 bytes
```

5. Issue the `restore database until scn` command to restore the database to the SCN identified in step 3. In our case, the command will be `restore database until scn 1095172`; your command will have a different change number.

```
RMAN> restore database until scn 1095172;
Starting restore at 10/03/2008 11:48:17
using target database control file instead of recovery catalog
allocated channel: ORA_DISK_1
channel ORA_DISK_1: SID=155 device type=DISK
channel ORA_DISK_1: starting datafile backup set restore
channel ORA_DISK_1: specifying datafile(s) to restore from backup set
channel ORA_DISK_1: restoring datafile 00001 to
C:\ORACLE\ORADATA\ORCL\SYSTEM01.DBF
channel ORA_DISK_1: restoring datafile 00002 to
C:\ORACLE\ORADATA\ORCL\SYSAUX01.DBF
channel ORA_DISK_1: restoring datafile 00003 to
C:\ORACLE\ORADATA\ORCL\UNDOTBS01.DBF
channel ORA_DISK_1: restoring datafile 00004 to
C:\ORACLE\FLASH_RECOVERY_AREA\ORCL\DATAFILE\O1_MF_USERS_4G2Q1YTC_.DBF
channel ORA_DISK_1: reading from backup piece
C:\ORACLE\FLASH_RECOVERY_AREA\ORCL\BACKUPSET\2008_10_03
\O1_MF_NNNDF_TAG20081003T001928_4GCGCQQ4_.BKP
channel ORA_DISK_1:
piece handle=C:\ORACLE\FLASH_RECOVERY_AREA\ORCL\BACKUPSET\2008_10_03
\O1_MF_NNNDF_TAG20081003T001928_4GCGCQQ4_.BKP tag=TAG20081003T001928
channel ORA_DISK_1: restored backup piece 1
channel ORA_DISK_1: restore complete, elapsed time: 00:07:25
Finished restore at 10/03/2008 11:55:44
```

6. Recover the database with the `recover database until scn` command. Our command would be `recover database until scn 1095172`; your command will have a different date and time.

```
RMAN> recover database until scn 1095172;
Starting recover at 10/03/2008 11:57:24
```

```
using channel ORA_DISK_1
starting media recovery
archived log for thread 1 with sequence 3 is already on disk as file
C:\ORACLE\PRODUCT\11.1.0\DB_1\RDBMS\ARC00003_0667012858.001
archived log for thread 1 with sequence 4 is already on disk as file
C:\ORACLE\FLASH_RECOVERY_AREA\ORCL\ARCHIVELOG\2008_10_03
\O1_MF_1_4_4GCMC8GV_.ARC
archived log for thread 1 with sequence 1 is already on disk as file
C:\ORACLE\FLASH_RECOVERY_AREA\ORCL\ARCHIVELOG\2008_10_03
\O1_MF_1_1_4GCO4G15_.ARC
archived log file
name=C:\ORACLE\PRODUCT\11.1.0\DB_1\RDBMS\ARC00003_0667012858.001
thread=1 sequence=3
archived log file
name=C:\ORACLE\FLASH_RECOVERY_AREA\ORCL\ARCHIVELOG\2008_10_03
\O1_MF_1_4_4GCMC8GV_.ARC thread=1 sequence=4
media recovery complete, elapsed time: 00:00:28
Finished recover at 10/03/2008 11:57:54
```

7. Open the database with the `alter database open resetlogs` command.

```
RMAN> alter database open resetlogs;
database opened
```

The database is open. This concludes the exercise.

Lab 6.3: Restoring a Control File from an Autobackup

In this activity, we will simulate loss of a control file and subsequent recovery. This activity builds on the backup done in Exercise 4.2. We assume that you have configured control-file autobackups as done in Exercise 4.1. You should have completed Exercises 4.1 and 4.2 prior to executing this activity. Please note that the output you experience from this exercise will probably differ from the output shown here.

1. Start SQL*Plus.

```
C:\oracle>sqlplus sys as sysdba
SQL*Plus: Release 11.1.0.6.0 - Production on Fri Oct 3 00:35:25 2008
Copyright (c) 1982, 2007, Oracle.  All rights reserved.
Enter password:
```

2. The database should be started. If not, start the database with the `startup force` command. From the SQL*Plus prompt, determine the current location of the database control files by issuing the query `select name from v$controlfile;`.

```
SQL> select name from v$controlfile;
NAME
-----------------------------------
C:\ORACLE\ORADATA\ORCL\CONTROL01.CTL
C:\ORACLE\ORADATA\ORCL\CONTROL02.CTL
C:\ORACLE\ORADATA\ORCL\CONTROL03.CTL
```

3. Shut down the database and exit SQL*Plus.

```
SQL> shutdown immediate
Database closed.
Database dismounted.
ORACLE instance shut down.
SQL> exit
Disconnected from Oracle Database 11g Enterprise Edition Release
11.1.0.6.0 - Production
With the Partitioning, OLAP, Data Mining
and Real Application Testing options
```

4. From the OS, remove all of the database control files.

```
C:\oracle>del C:\ORACLE\ORADATA\ORCL\CONTROL01.CTL
C:\oracle>del C:\ORACLE\ORADATA\ORCL\CONTROL02.CTL
C:\oracle>del C:\ORACLE\ORADATA\ORCL\CONTROL03.CTL
```

5. Start RMAN.

```
C:\oracle>rman target=/
Recovery Manager: Release 11.1.0.6.0 - Production
on Fri Oct 3 00:37:44 2008
Copyright (c) 1982, 2007, Oracle.  All rights reserved.
connected to target database (not started)
```

6. Try to start up the database. What error do you get?

```
RMAN> startup
Oracle instance started
RMAN-00571: ============================================================
RMAN-00569: =============== ERROR MESSAGE STACK FOLLOWS ===============
RMAN-00571: ============================================================
```

```
RMAN-03002: failure of startup command at 10/03/2008 12:09:57
ORA-00205: error in identifying control file, check alert log for more info
```

7. Issue the restore controlfile from autobackup command from RMAN to restore the control files.

```
RMAN> restore controlfile from autobackup;
Starting restore at 10/03/2008 12:10:24
using target database control file instead of recovery catalog
allocated channel: ORA_DISK_1
channel ORA_DISK_1: SID=155 device type=DISK
recovery area destination: c:\oracle\flash_recovery_area
database name (or database unique name) used for search: ORCL
channel ORA_DISK_1: AUTOBACKUP
C:\ORACLE\FLASH_RECOVERY_AREA\ORCL\AUTOBACKUP\2008_09_28
\O1_MF_S_666651824_4G0KDSG5_.BKP found in the recovery area
AUTOBACKUP search with format "%F" not attempted because DBID was not set
channel ORA_DISK_1: restoring control file from AUTOBACKUP
C:\ORACLE\FLASH_RECOVERY_AREA\ORCL\AUTOBACKUP\2008_09_28
\O1_MF_S_666651824_4G0KDSG5_.BKP
channel ORA_DISK_1: control file restore from AUTOBACKUP complete
output file name=C:\ORACLE\ORADATA\ORCL\CONTROL01.CTL
output file name=C:\ORACLE\ORADATA\ORCL\CONTROL02.CTL
output file name=C:\ORACLE\ORADATA\ORCL\CONTROL03.CTL
Finished restore at 10/03/2008 12:10:33
```

8. Mount the database.

```
RMAN> alter database mount;
database mounted
released channel: ORA_DISK_1
```

9. Recover the database with the recover database command.

```
RMAN> recover database;
Starting recover at 10/03/2008 14:03:49
Starting implicit crosscheck backup at 10/03/2008 14:03:49
allocated channel: ORA_DISK_1
channel ORA_DISK_1: SID=150 device type=DISK
Crosschecked 3 objects
Finished implicit crosscheck backup at 10/03/2008 14:03:54
Starting implicit crosscheck copy at 10/03/2008 14:03:54
using channel ORA_DISK_1
Finished implicit crosscheck copy at 10/03/2008 14:03:54
```

```
searching for all files in the recovery area
cataloging files...
cataloging done
List of Cataloged Files
=======================
File Name: C:\ORACLE\FLASH_RECOVERY_AREA\ORCL\AUTOBACKUP\2008_10_03
\01_MF_S_667144857_4GDYJ29H_.BKP
using channel ORA_DISK_1
starting media recovery
archived log for thread 1 with sequence 4 is already on disk as file
C:\ORACLE\ORADATA\ORCL\RED001.LOG
archived log file
name=C:\ORACLE\ORADATA\ORCL\RED001.LOG thread=1 sequence=4
media recovery complete, elapsed time: 00:00:00
Finished recover at 10/03/2008 14:03:59
```

10. Open the database with the `alter database open resetlogs` command.

```
RMAN> alter database open resetlogs;
database opened
```

The database is open. This concludes the exercise.

Lab 7.1: Monitoring RMAN Backups

In this exercise, we will monitor the progress of RMAN backups. We will also experiment with the duration command.

1. Log into RMAN, connecting to your recovery catalog.

```
C:\Documents and Settings\Robert>set oracle_sid=orcl
C:\Documents and Settings\Robert>rman target=/
catalog=rcat_user/rcat_user@rcat
Recovery Manager: Release 11.1.0.6.0 - Production
on Sun Oct 19 14:51:06 2008
Copyright (c) 1982, 2007, Oracle.  All rights reserved.
connected to target database: ORCL (DBID=1195614221)
connected to recovery catalog database
```

2. From another command-line window, log into SQL*Plus.

```
C:\Documents and Settings\Robert>set oracle_sid=orcl
C:\Documents and Settings\Robert>sqlplus / as sysdba
```

```
SQL*Plus: Release 11.1.0.6.0 - Production on Sun Oct 19 22:07:29 2008
Copyright (c) 1982, 2007, Oracle.  All rights reserved.
Connected to:
Oracle Database 11g Enterprise Edition Release 11.1.0.6.0 - Production
With the Partitioning, OLAP, Data Mining
and Real Application Testing options
SQL>
```

3. From the RMAN session, start an RMAN backup. We assume you have configured RMAN for backups as discussed in Chapter 2.

```
RMAN> Backup as compressed backupset database plus archivelog delete input;
```

4. While the RMAN backup is running, change to the SQL*Plus session and query the V$SESSION_LONGOPS view, as shown here.

```
SQL> Select sid, serial#, opname, time_remaining
  2  From v$session_longops
  3  Where sid in (select sid from v$session
  4                       Where program like '%rman%')
  5 And time_remaining > 0;
       SID    SERIAL# OPNAME                         TIME_REMAINING
---------- ---------- ------------------------------ --------------
       133         14 RMAN: aggregate input                      87
       126         33 RMAN: full datafile backup                179
```

5. Rerun the query listed in step 4, monitoring the TIME_REMAINING column. This will give you an idea of how long the backup will take.

6. When the backup completes, note how long it took to run. Ours took 4 minutes and 55 seconds, as shown here.

```
channel ORA_DISK_1: backup set complete, elapsed time: 00:04:55
Finished backup at 19-OCT-08
```

7. Once the RMAN backup is complete, run a second RMAN backup using the duration command with the minimize load database option as shown here.

```
RMAN> Backup as compressed backupset duration 1:00 minimize load database;
```

8. Monitor the backup with the V$SESSION_LONGOPS view again. How has the TIME_ REMAINING column changed since you used the duration command? Here is what we saw when we queried the view. Note that TIME_REMAINING is now much higher.

```
SQL> Select sid, serial#, opname, time_remaining
  2  From v$session_longops
```

```
 3  Where sid in (select sid from v$session
 4                           Where program like '%rman%')
 5 And time_remaining > 0;
     SID    SERIAL# OPNAME                            TIME_REMAINING
---------- ---------- ------------------------------ --------------
       126         33 RMAN: full datafile backup                3130
```

9. When the backup ends, note how the runtime has changed.

Lab 7.2: One of My Backups Is Missing!

Sometimes it happens—the unexpected. This lab is about one of those cases.

1. Log into RMAN, connecting to your recovery catalog.

```
C:\Documents and Settings\Robert>set oracle_sid=orcl
C:\Documents and Settings\Robert>rman target=/
catalog=rcat_user/rcat_user@rcat
Recovery Manager: Release 11.1.0.6.0 - Production
on Sun Oct 19 14:51:06 2008
Copyright (c) 1982, 2007, Oracle.  All rights reserved.
connected to target database: ORCL (DBID=1195614221)
connected to recovery catalog database
```

2. List all of the archived redo logs currently in the control file. Note that these are not backups of the archived redo logs, but the actual archived redo logs themselves.

```
RMAN> list archivelog all;
List of Archived Log Copies for database with db_unique_name ORCL
=====================================================================
Key     Thrd Seq    S Low Time
------- ---- ------- - ---------
1773    1    23      A 18-OCT-08
        Name: C:\ORACLE\PRODUCT\11.1.0\DB_1\RDBMS\ARC00023_0667833490.001
1779    1    24      A 19-OCT-08
        Name: C:\ORACLE\PRODUCT\11.1.0\DB_1\RDBMS\ARC00024_0667833490.001
1787    1    25      A 19-OCT-08
        Name: C:\ORACLE\PRODUCT\11.1.0\DB_1\RDBMS\ARC00025_0667833490.001
```

3. Next, remove the last archived redo log listed.

```
RMAN> Host 'del C:\ORACLE\PRODUCT\11.1.0\DB_1\RDBMS\
ARC00025_0667833490.001';
host command complete
```

4. Now try to execute a backup.

```
RMAN> Backup as compressed backupset database plus archivelog delete input;
Starting backup at 20-OCT-08
current log archived
using channel ORA_DISK_1
RMAN-00571: ===========================================================
RMAN-00569: =============== ERROR MESSAGE STACK FOLLOWS ===============
RMAN-00571: ===========================================================
RMAN-03002: failure of backup plus archivelog command
at 10/20/2008 00:34:26
RMAN-06059: expected archived log not found, lost
of archived log compromises
recoverability
ORA-19625: error identifying file
C:\ORACLE\PRODUCT\11.1.0\DB_1\RDBMS\ARC00025_0667833490.001
ORA-27041: unable to open file
OSD-04002: unable to open file
O/S-Error: (OS 2) The system cannot find the file specified.
```

5. Notice that the backup failed because of the missing archived redo log. Run the command crosscheck archivelog all to mark the archived redo log as expired. This will allow you to rerun the backup.

```
RMAN> Crosscheck archivelog all;
released channel: ORA_DISK_1
allocated channel: ORA_DISK_1
channel ORA_DISK_1: SID=126 device type=DISK
validation succeeded for archived log
archived log file name=C:\ORACLE\PRODUCT\11.1.0\DB_1\RDBMS\
ARC00023_0667833490.001 RECID=43 STAMP=668556384
validation succeeded for archived log
archived log file name=C:\ORACLE\PRODUCT\11.1.0\DB_1\RDBMS\
ARC00024_0667833490.001 RECID=45 STAMP=668556995
validation failed for archived log
archived log file name=C:\ORACLE\PRODUCT\11.1.0\DB_1\RDBMS\
ARC00025_0667833490.001 RECID=47 STAMP=668557334
```

```
validation succeeded for archived log
archived log file
name=C:\ORACLE\FLASH_RECOVERY_AREA\ORCL\ARCHIVELOG\2008_10_20\
01_MF_1_26_4HR9MCQX_.ARC RECID=50 STAMP=668565264
validation succeeded for archived log
archived log file name=C:\ORACLE\PRODUCT\11.1.0\DB_1\RDBMS\
ARC00026_0667833490.001 RECID=49 STAMP=668565264
Crosschecked 5 objects
```

6. Run the `list archivelog all` command. Notice that the status column (so clearly named S) is now X (expired) instead of A (available):

```
RMAN> list archivelog all;
List of Archived Log Copies for database with db_unique_name ORCL
=====================================================================
Key      Thrd Seq      S Low Time
-------  ---- -------  - ---------
1773     1    23       A 18-OCT-08
         Name: C:\ORACLE\PRODUCT\11.1.0\DB_1\RDBMS\ARC00023_0667833490.001
1779     1    24       A 19-OCT-08
         Name: C:\ORACLE\PRODUCT\11.1.0\DB_1\RDBMS\ARC00024_0667833490.001
1787     1    25       X 19-OCT-08
         Name: C:\ORACLE\PRODUCT\11.1.0\DB_1\RDBMS\ARC00025_0667833490.001
1898     1    26       A 19-OCT-08
         Name: C:\ORACLE\FLASH_RECOVERY_AREA\ORCL\ARCHIVELOG\2008_10_20\
01_MF_1_26_4HR9MCQX_.ARC
1897     1    26       A 19-OCT-08
         Name: C:\ORACLE\PRODUCT\11.1.0\DB_1\RDBMS\ARC00026_0667833490.001
```

Lab 8.1: Duplicating a Database Using Active Database Duplication

In this exercise, we will use backup-based duplication to create a database on the same system that the target database resides on. For this exercise, your database should be running in ARCHIVELOG mode and all networking to the target database should already be configured.

1. If you are running in Windows, create the service for the new database with `oradim`. In this example, we are creating a new database instance called `neworcl`.

```
C:\>oradim -new -sid neworcl
Instance created.
```

If there are any other OS-specific operations required to create a database instance, complete those now.

2. Create the password file for the `neworcl` instance.

```
C:\>orapwd file=c:\oracle\product\11.1.0\db_1\database\pwdneworcl.ora
Enter password for SYS:
```

3. Create a temporary pfile for the `neworcl` auxiliary instance using your editor of choice. The pfile should be contained in the `ORACLE_HOME\database` directory of the auxiliary instance and should be named `initneworcl.ora`. The pfile should have these parameters in it:

```
db_name=neworcl
memory_target=300m
control_files='c:\oracle\oradata\neworcl\control01.ctl',
'c:\oracle\oradata\neworcl\control02.ctl'
```

We will do the actual file-location conversions during the duplication.

4. Create the directory c:\oracle\oradata\neworcl

```
mkdir c:\oracle\oradata\neworcl
```

5. `Startup nomount` the auxiliary instance.

```
C:\oracle\product\11.1.0\db_1\database>set oracle_sid=neworcl
C:\oracle\product\11.1.0\db_1\database>sqlplus "/ as sysdba"
SQL*Plus: Release 11.1.0.6.0 - Production on Sat Oct 4 23:09:52 2008
Copyright (c) 1982, 2007, Oracle.  All rights reserved.
Connected to an idle instance.
SQL> startup nomount
ORACLE instance started.
Total System Global Area   313860096 bytes
Fixed Size                   1332892 bytes
Variable Size              192940388 bytes
Database Buffers           113246208 bytes
Redo Buffers                 6340608 bytes
```

6. Configure service name resolution for your new auxiliary database. The method of this configuration will vary based on your site. In our case, we created an entry in the `tnsnames.ora` file on our server that looked like this:

```
NEWORCL =
  (DESCRIPTION =
    (ADDRESS = (PROTOCOL = TCP)(HOST = 192.168.2.2)(PORT = 1521))
    (CONNECT_DATA =
```

```
   (SERVER = DEDICATED)
   (SERVICE_NAME = neworcl)
 ) )
```

7. Now you will need to hard-code the instance name into the listener.ora file until the duplication of the database has been completed. You will get network errors if you do not hard-code the auxiliary instance in the listener.ora file. Here's an example of the entry in our listener.ora:

```
SID_LIST_LISTENER =
  (SID_LIST =
    (SID_DESC =
       (ORACLE_HOME=C:\oracle\product\11.1.0\db_1\NETWORK\ADMIN)
       (SID_NAME=neworcl)
    ) )
LISTENER =
  (DESCRIPTION_LIST =
    (DESCRIPTION =
      (ADDRESS = (PROTOCOL = TCP)(HOST = 192.168.2.2)(PORT = 1521))
      (ADDRESS = (PROTOCOL = IPC)(KEY = EXTPROC1521))
    ) )
```

8. Test the network connectivity to the auxiliary instance.

```
C:\oracle\product\11.1.0\db_1\database>sqlplus sys/robert@neworcl as sysdba
SQL*Plus: Release 11.1.0.6.0 - Production on Sat Oct 4 23:17:50 2008
Copyright (c) 1982, 2007, Oracle.  All rights reserved.
Connected to:
Oracle Database 11g Enterprise Edition Release 11.1.0.6.0 - Production
With the Partitioning, OLAP, Data Mining
and Real Application Testing options
SQL> select instance_name from v$instance;
INSTANCE_NAME
----------------
neworcl
```

If the connection fails, review the network configuration and ensure that the new auxiliary instance is running.

9. Start RMAN and connect to the target and the auxiliary databases.

```
C:\oracle\product\11.1.0\db_1\database>Set oracle_sid=orcl
C:\oracle\product\11.1.0\db_1\database>Rman target=sys/robert
```

```
auxiliary=sys/Robert@neworcl
Recovery Manager: Release 11.1.0.6.0 - Production
on Sat Oct 4 23:19:55 2008
Copyright (c) 1982, 2007, Oracle.  All rights reserved.
connected to target database: ORCL (DBID=1194923408)
connected to auxiliary database: NEWORCL (not mounted)
```

10. We are now ready to start the database duplication. Issue the `duplicate database` command, as shown here:

```
duplicate target database to neworcl from active database
nofilenamecheck
spfile set control_files 'c:\oracle\oradata\neworcl\control01.ctl',
'c:\oracle\oradata\neworcl\control02.ctl'
set db_file_name_convert
 'c:\oracle\oradata\orcl','c:\oracle\oradata\neworcl'
set log_file_name_convert 'c:\oracle\oradata\orcl','c:\oracle\oradata\
neworcl';
```

This command does the following:

- It starts the duplication process. We are using active database duplication, so no database backup is required.

- The `SPFILE` parameter will result in the target database spfile being copied over to the duplicate database. The duplicate database will use this spfile.

- The `set` commands (`set control_files`, `set db_file_name_convert`, and `set log_file_name_convert`) modify or add parameters to the spfile being copied to the duplicate database.

This `duplicate` command will result in a great deal of output, which we have decided not to include here as it seems a great waste of a perfectly good tree. Here is the output that you hopefully will see at the end of the database duplication:

```
database opened
Finished Duplicate Db at 04-OCT-08
```

There are several bugs in 11.1.0.6 that may cause a failure of active database duplications. We experienced one or two of these when writing this book. This exercise should work well on a new database that has just been created or a database with the latest patch sets installed.

11. Connect to the duplicated database to verify it is open.

```
C:\oracle\product\11.1.0\db_1\database>set oracle_sid=neworcl
C:\oracle\product\11.1.0\db_1\database>sqlplus sys/Robert as sysdba
```

```
SQL*Plus: Release 11.1.0.6.0 - Production on Sun Oct 5 00:04:02 2008
Copyright (c) 1982, 2007, Oracle.  All rights reserved.
Connected to:
Oracle Database 11g Enterprise Edition Release 11.1.0.6.0 - Production
With the Partitioning, OLAP, Data Mining
and Real Application Testing options
SQL> select name, open_mode from v$database;
NAME      OPEN_MODE
--------- ----------
AUXDB     READ WRITE
```

Lab 8.2: Duplicating a Database Using Backup-Based Duplication to a Different Point in Time

In this exercise, you will use backup-based duplication to create a database on the same system that the target database resides on. For this exercise, your database should be running in ARCHIVELOG mode and all networking to the target database should already be configured.

1. Back up your database as shown in Exercise 4.2.

2. Start RMAN and confirm that you have a valid backup with the `list backup of database summary` command and the `restore database validate` command. Note that your output will likely look very different from ours.

```
C:\Documents and Settings\Robert>rman target=/
Recovery Manager: Release 11.1.0.6.0 - Production
on Sat Oct 4 22:56:10 2008
Copyright (c) 1982, 2007, Oracle.  All rights reserved.
connected to target database: ORCL (DBID=1194923408)
RMAN> list backup of database summary;
using target database control file instead of recovery catalog
List of Backups
===============
Key     TY LV S Device Type Completion Time #Pieces #Copies Compressed Tag
------- -- -- - ----------- --------------- ------- ------- ---------- ---
2       B  F  A DISK        03-OCT-08       1       1       YES
TAG20081003T135426
RMAN> restore database validate;
```

```
Starting restore at 04-OCT-08
allocated channel: ORA_DISK_1
channel ORA_DISK_1: SID=127 device type=DISK
channel ORA_DISK_1: starting validation of datafile backup set
channel ORA_DISK_1: reading from backup piece
C:\ORACLE\FLASH_RECOVERY_AREA\ORCL\BACKUPSET\2008_10_03
\O1_MF_NNNDF_TAG20081003T135426_4GDY3S9H_.BKP
channel ORA_DISK_1: piece
handle=C:\ORACLE\FLASH_RECOVERY_AREA\ORCL\BACKUPSET\2008_10_03
\O1_MF_NNNDF_TAG20081003T135426_4GDY3S9H_.BKP tag=TAG20081003T135426
channel ORA_DISK_1: restored backup piece 1
channel ORA_DISK_1: validation complete, elapsed time: 00:01:36
Finished restore at 04-OCT-08
C:\Documents and Settings\Robert>set oracle_sid=orcl
```

3. If you are running in Windows, create the service for the new database with `oradim`. In this example, we are creating a new database instance called `neworcl`.

    ```
    C:\>oradim -new -sid neworcl
    Instance created.
    ```

    If there are any other OS-specific operations required to create a database instance, complete those now.

4. Create the password file for the `neworcl` instance.

    ```
    C:\>orapwd file=c:\oracle\product\11.1.0\db_1\database\pwdneworcl.ora
    Enter password for SYS:
    ```

5. Create a temporary pfile for the `neworcl` auxiliary instance using your editor of choice. The pfile should be contained in the `ORACLE_HOME\database` directory of the auxiliary instance and should be named `initneworcl.ora`. The pfile should have these parameters in it:

    ```
    db_name=neworcl
    memory_target=300m
    control_files='c:\oracle\oradata\neworcl\control01.ctl',
    'c:\oracle\oradata\neworcl\control02.ctl'
    ```

    We will do the actual file-location conversions during the duplication.

6. Create the directory `c:\oracle\oradata\neworcl`.

    ```
    mkdir c:\oracle\oradata\neworcl
    ```

7. Start up the auxiliary instance.

```
C:\oracle\product\11.1.0\db_1\database>set oracle_sid=neworcl
C:\oracle\product\11.1.0\db_1\database>sqlplus "/ as sysdba"
SQL*Plus: Release 11.1.0.6.0 - Production on Sat Oct 4 23:09:52 2008
Copyright (c) 1982, 2007, Oracle.  All rights reserved.
Connected to an idle instance.
SQL> startup nomount
ORACLE instance started.
Total System Global Area  313860096 bytes
Fixed Size                  1332892 bytes
Variable Size             192940388 bytes
Database Buffers          113246208 bytes
Redo Buffers                6340608 bytes
```

8. Configure service name resolution for your new auxiliary database. The method of this configuration will vary based on your site. In our case, we created an entry in the tnsnames.ora file on our server that looked like this:

```
NEWORCL =
  (DESCRIPTION =
    (ADDRESS = (PROTOCOL = TCP)(HOST = 192.168.2.2)(PORT = 1521))
    (CONNECT_DATA =
      (SERVER = DEDICATED)
      (SERVICE_NAME = neworcl)
    )  )
```

9. Now you will need to hard-code the instance name into the listener.ora file until the duplication of the database has been completed. You will get network errors if you do not hard-code the auxiliary instance in the listener.ora file. Here's an example of the entry in our listener.ora:

```
SID_LIST_LISTENER =
  (SID_LIST =
    (SID_DESC =
      (ORACLE_HOME=C:\oracle\product\11.1.0\db_1\NETWORK\ADMIN)
      (SID_NAME=neworcl)
    )  )
LISTENER =
  (DESCRIPTION_LIST =
    (DESCRIPTION =
      (ADDRESS = (PROTOCOL = TCP)(HOST = 192.168.2.2)(PORT = 1521))
      (ADDRESS = (PROTOCOL = IPC)(KEY = EXTPROC1521))
    )  )
```

10. Test the network connectivity to the auxiliary instance.

```
C:\oracle\product\11.1.0\db_1\database>sqlplus sys/robert@neworcl as sysdba
SQL*Plus: Release 11.1.0.6.0 - Production on Sat Oct 4 23:17:50 2008
Copyright (c) 1982, 2007, Oracle.  All rights reserved.
Connected to:
Oracle Database 11g Enterprise Edition Release 11.1.0.6.0 - Production
With the Partitioning, OLAP, Data Mining
and Real Application Testing options
SQL> select instance_name from v$instance;
INSTANCE_NAME
----------------
neworcl
```

If the connection fails, review the network configuration and ensure that the new auxiliary instance is running.

11. Connect to the ORCL database using the scott account.

```
C:\Documents and Settings\Robert>sqlplus scott/tiger
SQL*Plus: Release 11.1.0.6.0 - Production on Sat Oct 11 14:43:14 2008
Copyright (c) 1982, 2007, Oracle.  All rights reserved.
Connected to:
Oracle Database 11g Enterprise Edition Release 11.1.0.6.0 - Production
With the Partitioning, OLAP, Data Mining
and Real Application Testing options
SQL>
```

If you are using a new database, you may need to unlock the scott account.

```
SQL> alter user scott account unlock;
User altered.
SQL> alter user scott identified by tiger;
User altered.
```

12. In the scott schema, create a table called DUPE_TABLE.

```
SQL> create table dupe_table(id number, the_date date);
Table created.
```

13. Insert a record in the DUPE_TABLE table and commit.

```
SQL> Insert into dupe_table values (1, sysdate);
1 row created.
SQL> commit;
Commit complete.
```

14. Wait for a minute or so. Insert a second record in the DUPE_TABLE table and commit.

```
SQL> Insert into dupe_table values (1, sysdate);
1 row created.
SQL> commit;
Commit complete.
```

15. Select from the DUPE_TABLE table.

```
SQL> select * from dupe_table;
        ID THE_DATE
---------- --------------------
         1 10/11/2008 14:46:14
         1 10/11/2008 14:48:25
```

16. Connect as sys and force a log switch. This is because database duplications from backup will use only archived redo logs to recover a database. Online redo logs are not used. This is not true with active database duplications.

```
SQL> connect sys/robert as sysdba
Connected.
SQL> alter system switch logfile;
System altered.
```

17. Start RMAN and connect to the target and the auxiliary databases.

```
C:\oracle\product\11.1.0\db_1\database>Set oracle_sid=orcl
C:\oracle\product\11.1.0\db_1\database>Rman target=/
auxiliary=sys/Robert@neworcl
Recovery Manager: Release 11.1.0.6.0 - Production
on Sat Oct 4 23:19:55 2008
Copyright (c) 1982, 2007, Oracle.  All rights reserved.
connected to target database: ORCL (DBID=1194923408)
connected to auxiliary database: NEWORCL (not mounted)
```

18. We are now ready to start the database duplication. Issue the duplicate database command, recovering the database to a time in between the two insert records. We recommend you recover to about 5 seconds before the second record, as shown here:

```
duplicate target database to neworcl
until time "to_date('10/11/2008 14:48:20','mm/dd/yyyy hh24:mi:ss')"
nofilenamecheck
spfile set control_files=
'c:\oracle\oradata\neworcl\control01.ctl',
```

```
'c:\oracle\oradata\neworcl\control02.ctl'
set db_file_name_convert
'c:\oracle\oradata\orcl','c:\oracle\oradata\neworcl'
set log_file_name_convert
'c:\oracle\oradata\orcl','c:\oracle\oradata\neworcl';
```

This command does the following:

- It starts the duplication process.

- It starts the duplication process restoring the database to the specific point in time using backups of the database and archived redo logs. The restore will be to the point in time listed in the until time clause.

- The SPFILE parameter will result in the target database spfile being copied over to the duplicate database. The duplicate database will use this spfile.

- The set commands (set control_files, set db_file_name_convert, and set log_file_name_convert) modify or add parameters to the spfile being copied to the duplicate database.

This duplicate command will result in a great deal of output, which we have decided not to include here as it seems a great waste of a perfectly good tree. Here is the output that you hopefully will see at the end of the database duplication:

```
database opened
Finished Duplicate Db at 04-OCT-08
```

19. Connect to the duplicated database to verify that it is open.

```
C:\oracle\product\11.1.0\db_1\database>set oracle_sid=neworcl
C:\oracle\product\11.1.0\db_1\database>sqlplus sys/Robert as sysdba
SQL*Plus: Release 11.1.0.6.0 - Production on Sun Oct 5 00:04:02 2008
Copyright (c) 1982, 2007, Oracle.  All rights reserved.
Connected to:
Oracle Database 11g Enterprise Edition Release 11.1.0.6.0 - Production
With the Partitioning, OLAP, Data Mining
and Real Application Testing options
SQL> select name, open_mode from v$database;
NAME      OPEN_MODE
--------- ----------
AUXDB     READ WRITE
```

20. Connect to the scott schema. Query the DUPE_TABLE and ensure that only one record now exists.

```
SQL> connect scott/tiger
Connected.
```

```
SQL> select * from dupe_table;
        ID THE_DATE
---------- ---------
         1 11-OCT-08
```

If you want to run this exercise again after the first successful run, you will need to perform these steps:

1. Shut down the auxiliary instance (now it's a new database!).

2. Remove the spfile assigned to the auxiliary instance.

3. Mount the auxiliary instance with the `Startup nomount` command.

Lab 9.1: Using the Recycle Bin

This lab was created using Windows XP. However, it should also work using Unix (and in fact was tested using Linux). This lab shows you how to set up the Recycle Bin and use it to restore a dropped table. The overall steps are as follows: create a table, insert data into the table, enable the Recycle Bin, drop the table, restore the table from the Recycle Bin, and query the table to verify the contents.

1. Create the table.

```
SQL> create table recycle_test (x number, y varchar2(10));
Table created.
SQL>
```

2. Next, we'll add some rows and commit the transaction.

```
SQL>
insert into recycle_test values (1, 'row 1');
insert into recycle_test values (2, 'row 2');
insert into recycle_test values (3, 'row 3');
insert into recycle_test values (4, 'row 4');
insert into recycle_test values (5, 'row 5');
Commit;
SQL>
```

3. Then, enable the Recycle Bin for the session.

```
SQL> ALTER SESSION SET recyclebin = ON;
Session altered.
```

4.   Now drop the table.

```
SQL> drop table recycle_test;
Table dropped.
```

5.   Restore the table from the Recycle Bin.

```
SQL> flashback table recycle_test to before drop;
Flashback complete.
```

6.   Finally, query the table and verify the contents.

```
SQL> select * from recycle_test;

        X Y
---------- ----------
        1 row 1
        2 row 2
        3 row 3
        4 row 4
        5 row 5
```

Lab 9.2: Performing a More Complex Flashback Query Analysis

This lab shows you how to perform a more complex analysis using the Flashback Query feature. We'll create and populate a table, then step through adding rows and querying the table at various points in time to demonstrate the feature.

1.   Create the table.

```
SQL> create table flashback_query_test
         (x number,
          y varchar2(10),
          z date
         );
Table created.
```

2.   Now insert five rows of data and commit.

```
SQL>
insert into flashback_query_test values (1, 'row 1', sysdate);
```

```
insert into flashback_query_test values (2, 'row 2', sysdate);
insert into flashback_query_test values (3, 'row 3', sysdate);
insert into flashback_query_test values (4, 'row 4', sysdate);
insert into flashback_query_test values (5, 'row 5', sysdate);
commit;
Commit complete.
```

3. Now query the table to view the results.

```
SQL> alter session set nls_date_format = 'dd-mon-yy hh24:mi:ss';

Session altered.

SQL> select * from flashback_query_test;
         X Y           Z
---------- ---------- --------------------
         1 row 1      21-nov-2008 13:48:51
         2 row 2      21-nov-2008 13:48:51
         3 row 3      21-nov-2008 13:48:51
         4 row 4      21-nov-2008 13:48:51
         5 row 5      21-nov-2008 13:48:51
SQL>
```

4. Query the table, specifying a timestamp after the table was created but prior to inserting the first five rows:

```
SQL> select * from flashback_query_test
     as of timestamp(to_timestamp(
     '21-nov-2008 13:48:50','DD-MON-YYYY HH24:MI:SS'));

no rows selected

SQL>
```

5. Now insert five more rows, wait five minutes, then insert five more rows, then commit. The results should look similar to this:

```
insert into flashback_query_test values (6, 'row 6', sysdate);
insert into flashback_query_test values (7, 'row 7', sysdate);
insert into flashback_query_test values (8, 'row 8', sysdate);
insert into flashback_query_test values (9, 'row 9', sysdate);
insert into flashback_query_test values (10, 'row 10', sysdate);
commit;
```

Wait here five minutes.

```
insert into flashback_query_test values (11, 'row 11', sysdate);
insert into flashback_query_test values (12, 'row 12', sysdate);
insert into flashback_query_test values (13, 'row 13', sysdate);
insert into flashback_query_test values (14, 'row 14', sysdate);
insert into flashback_query_test values (15, 'row 15', sysdate);
commit;
```

```
SQL> select * from flashback_query_test;
         X Y              Z
---------- ---------- --------------------
         1 row 1       21-nov-2008 13:48:51
         2 row 2       21-nov-2008 13:48:51
         3 row 3       21-nov-2008 13:48:51
         4 row 4       21-nov-2008 13:48:51
         5 row 5       21-nov-2008 13:48:51
         6 row 6       21-nov-2008 13:50:00
         7 row 7       21-nov-2008 13:50:00
         8 row 8       21-nov-2008 13:50:00
         9 row 9       21-nov-2008 13:50:00
        10 row 10      21-nov-2008 13:50:00
        11 row 11      21-nov-2008 13:55:00
        12 row 12      21-nov-2008 13:55:00
        13 row 13      21-nov-2008 13:55:00
        14 row 14      21-nov-2008 13:55:00
        15 row 15      21-nov-2008 13:55:00

15 rows selected.

SQL>
```

6. Now that you have different discrete insert times, you can run queries that show the state of the table at various points in time. Run an AS OF query that will show only rows 1 through 10, based on the timestamp that was inserted.

```
SQL> select * from flashback_query_test
     as of timestamp(to_timestamp(
     '21-nov-2008 13:51:00','DD-MON-YYYY HH24:MI:SS'));

         X Y              Z
---------- ---------- --------------------
         1 row 1       21-nov-2008 13:48:51
```

```
 2  row 2        21-nov-2008 13:48:51
 3  row 3        21-nov-2008 13:48:51
 4  row 4        21-nov-2008 13:48:51
 5  row 5        21-nov-2008 13:48:51
 6  row 6        21-nov-2008 13:50:00
 7  row 7        21-nov-2008 13:50:00
 8  row 8        21-nov-2008 13:50:00
 9  row 9        21-nov-2008 13:50:00
10  row 10       21-nov-2008 13:50:00
```

```
10 rows selected.
```

```
SQL>
```

7. Now insert five more rows, but don't commit. Run a query showing the new rows in the table, and then an AS OF query with a timestamp following the insert that shows that the data is not committed and not available for Flashback Query.

```
SQL>
insert into flashback_query_test values (16, 'row 16', sysdate);
insert into flashback_query_test values (17, 'row 17', sysdate);
insert into flashback_query_test values (18, 'row 18', sysdate);
insert into flashback_query_test values (19, 'row 19', sysdate);
insert into flashback_query_test values (20, 'row 20', sysdate);
```

```
SQL> select * from flashback_query_test;
```

```
     X Y           Z
---------- ---------- --------------------
     1  row 1        21-nov-2008 13:48:51
     2  row 2        21-nov-2008 13:48:51
     3  row 3        21-nov-2008 13:48:51
     4  row 4        21-nov-2008 13:48:51
     5  row 5        21-nov-2008 13:48:51
     6  row 6        21-nov-2008 13:50:00
     7  row 7        21-nov-2008 13:50:00
     8  row 8        21-nov-2008 13:50:00
     9  row 9        21-nov-2008 13:50:00
    10  row 10       21-nov-2008 13:50:00
    11  row 11       21-nov-2008 13:55:00
    12  row 12       21-nov-2008 13:55:00
```

```
        13 row 13      21-nov-2008 13:55:00
        14 row 14      21-nov-2008 13:55:00
        15 row 15      21-nov-2008 13:55:00
        16 row 16      21-nov-2008 14:00:00
        17 row 17      21-nov-2008 14:00:00
        18 row 18      21-nov-2008 14:00:00
        19 row 19      21-nov-2008 14:00:00
        20 row 20      21-nov-2008 14:00:00

20 rows selected.

SQL>
SQL> select * from flashback_query_test
        as of timestamp(to_timestamp(
        '21-nov-2008 14:05:00','DD-MON-YYYY HH24:MI:SS'));

         X Y          Z
---------- ---------- --------------------
         1 row 1      21-nov-2008 13:48:51
         2 row 2      21-nov-2008 13:48:51
         3 row 3      21-nov-2008 13:48:51
         4 row 4      21-nov-2008 13:48:51
         5 row 5      21-nov-2008 13:48:51
         6 row 6      21-nov-2008 13:50:00
         7 row 7      21-nov-2008 13:50:00
         8 row 8      21-nov-2008 13:50:00
         9 row 9      21-nov-2008 13:50:00
        10 row 10     21-nov-2008 13:50:00
        11 row 11     21-nov-2008 13:55:00
        12 row 12     21-nov-2008 13:55:00
        13 row 13     21-nov-2008 13:55:00
        14 row 14     21-nov-2008 13:55:00
        15 row 15     21-nov-2008 13:55:00

15 rows selected.

SQL>
```

8. Commit and then requery, noting that the AS OF timestamp must be after the commit for you to see the committed data using Flashback Query.

```
SQL> commit;
SQL> select sysdate from dual;
SYSDATE
--------------------
21-nov-2008 14:21:41

SQL> select * from flashback_query_test
        as of timestamp(to_timestamp(
     '21-nov-2008 14:21:41','DD-MON-YYYY HH24:MI:SS'));

         X Y            Z
---------- ---------- --------------------
         1 row 1       21-nov-2008 13:48:51
         2 row 2       21-nov-2008 13:48:51
         3 row 3       21-nov-2008 13:48:51
         4 row 4       21-nov-2008 13:48:51
         5 row 5       21-nov-2008 13:48:51
         6 row 6       21-nov-2008 13:50:00
         7 row 7       21-nov-2008 13:50:00
         8 row 8       21-nov-2008 13:50:00
         9 row 9       21-nov-2008 13:50:00
        10 row 10      21-nov-2008 13:50:00
        11 row 11      21-nov-2008 13:55:00
        12 row 12      21-nov-2008 13:55:00
        13 row 13      21-nov-2008 13:55:00
        14 row 14      21-nov-2008 13:55:00
        15 row 15      21-nov-2008 13:55:00
        16 row 16      21-nov-2008 14:00:00
        17 row 17      21-nov-2008 14:00:00
        18 row 18      21-nov-2008 14:00:00
        19 row 19      21-nov-2008 14:00:00
        20 row 20      21-nov-2008 14:00:00

20 rows selected.
SQL>
```

Lab 9.3: Using Flashback Data Archive

In this lab you'll exercise the Flashback Data Archive feature. You'll create an archive table for a populated base table and observe the audit migrations to the archive table, then observe purging from the archive table.

1. Create the flashback data archive.

```
SQL>create flashback archive default default_flash_archive
tablespace user_data quota 10m retention 1 day;
```

2. Now we'll use the previously created `flashback_query_test` table as the base table for the archive.

```
SQL> alter table flashback_query_test flashback
 archive default_flash_archive;
Table altered.
```

3. Now we'll manipulate the data and observe the flashback data archive.

```
SQL> select sysdate from dual;

SYSDATE
--------------------
21-nov-2008 15:58:44

SQL> delete from flashback_query_test where x > 15;

5 rows deleted.

SQL> commit;

Commit complete.

SQL> select * from flashback_query_test;

        X Y          Z
---------- ---------- --------------------
        1 row 1      21-nov-2008 13:48:51
        2 row 2      21-nov-2008 13:48:51
        3 row 3      21-nov-2008 13:48:51
        4 row 4      21-nov-2008 13:48:51
        5 row 5      21-nov-2008 13:48:51
```

```
 6  row 6       21-nov-2008 13:50:00
 7  row 7       21-nov-2008 13:50:00
 8  row 8       21-nov-2008 13:50:00
 9  row 9       21-nov-2008 13:50:00
10  row 10      21-nov-2008 13:50:00
11  row 11      21-nov-2008 13:55:00
12  row 12      21-nov-2008 13:55:00
13  row 13      21-nov-2008 13:55:00
14  row 14      21-nov-2008 13:55:00
15  row 15      21-nov-2008 13:55:00
```

15 rows selected.

4. Query the base table using the AS OF clause, specifying a timestamp prior to the delete timestamp. You'll observe that all the rows are returned.

```
SQL> select * from flashback_query_test
as of timestamp(to_timestamp('21-nov-2008 15:58:00',
'DD-MON-YYYY HH24:MI:SS'));

         X  Y          Z
---------- ---------- --------------------
        16  row 16     21-nov-2008 15:08:54
        17  row 17     21-nov-2008 15:08:54
        18  row 18     21-nov-2008 15:08:54
        19  row 19     21-nov-2008 15:08:54
        20  row 20     21-nov-2008 15:08:54
         2  row 2      21-nov-2008 13:48:51
         4  row 4      21-nov-2008 13:48:51
        14  row 14     21-nov-2008 13:55:00
         1  row 1      21-nov-2008 13:48:51
         7  row 7      21-nov-2008 13:50:00
        13  row 13     21-nov-2008 13:55:00
        15  row 15     21-nov-2008 13:55:00
         3  row 3      21-nov-2008 13:48:51
         8  row 8      21-nov-2008 13:50:00
         6  row 6      21-nov-2008 13:50:00
         9  row 9      21-nov-2008 13:50:00
        10  row 10     21-nov-2008 13:50:00
         5  row 5      21-nov-2008 13:48:51
        11  row 11     21-nov-2008 13:55:00
```

```
   12 row 12      21-nov-2008 13:55:00
```

20 rows selected.

5. Verify the timestamp for the delete.

```
SQL> select * from flashback_query_test
as of timestamp(to_timestamp('21-nov-2008 16:00:00',
'DD-MON-YYYY HH24:MI:SS'));
```

```
         X Y              Z
---------- ----------     --------------------
         2 row 2         21-nov-2008 13:48:51
         4 row 4         21-nov-2008 13:48:51
        14 row 14        21-nov-2008 13:55:00
         1 row 1         21-nov-2008 13:48:51
         7 row 7         21-nov-2008 13:50:00
        13 row 13        21-nov-2008 13:55:00
        15 row 15        21-nov-2008 13:55:00
         3 row 3         21-nov-2008 13:48:51
         8 row 8         21-nov-2008 13:50:00
         6 row 6         21-nov-2008 13:50:00
         9 row 9         21-nov-2008 13:50:00
        10 row 10        21-nov-2008 13:50:00
         5 row 5         21-nov-2008 13:48:51
        11 row 11        21-nov-2008 13:55:00
        12 row 12        21-nov-2008 13:55:00
```

15 rows selected.

6. Now run the query again as many times as you like prior to the end of the 10-day retention period, and you should see the following results:

```
SQL> select * from flashback_query_test
as of timestamp(to_timestamp('21-nov-2008 15:58:00',
'DD-MON-YYYY HH24:MI:SS'));
```

```
         X Y              Z
---------- ----------     --------------------
        16 row 16        21-nov-2008 15:08:54
        17 row 17        21-nov-2008 15:08:54
        18 row 18        21-nov-2008 15:08:54
```

```
19  row 19      21-nov-2008 15:08:54
20  row 20      21-nov-2008 15:08:54
 2  row 2       21-nov-2008 13:48:51
 4  row 4       21-nov-2008 13:48:51
14  row 14      21-nov-2008 13:55:00
 1  row 1       21-nov-2008 13:48:51
 7  row 7       21-nov-2008 13:50:00
13  row 13      21-nov-2008 13:55:00
15  row 15      21-nov-2008 13:55:00
 3  row 3       21-nov-2008 13:48:51
 8  row 8       21-nov-2008 13:50:00
 6  row 6       21-nov-2008 13:50:00
 9  row 9       21-nov-2008 13:50:00
10  row 10      21-nov-2008 13:50:00
 5  row 5       21-nov-2008 13:48:51
11  row 11      21-nov-2008 13:55:00
12  row 12      21-nov-2008 13:55:00

20 rows selected.
SQL>
```

Just to verify that you are using the flasback data archive and not undo, you can shut down and start up the database to clear the undo tablespace, and you will still see the query results demonstrated in this section.

Lab 10.1: Using Support Workbench to Report a Problem to Oracle Support

This lab was created using Oracle Enterprise Manager (OEM) running on Windows XP. However, it should also work using Unix.

This lab shows you the basic steps to follow to use the Oracle Support Workbench to open a support ticket with Oracle. Using the OEM user interface, the directions will be presented to you on each page, so you should have no problem opening the support ticket—that is, if you have an Oracle support agreement. If you have an Oracle support agreement, perform the following steps to completion. If you don't have an Oracle support agreement, follow until step 5.

1. Open Support Workbench.
2. View your alerts and select a critical error alert.
3. View the problem details.
4. Gather any additional diagnostic information.

5. Create a service request.

6. Package and upload the data to Oracle Support.

7. Track the service request and implement any recommended changes.

8. Close the incident.

Lab 10.2: Performing Block Media Recovery

In this lab, you will perform block media recovery of a corrupt data file. This lab was created on Windows XP and uses a tool specifically for Windows. However, it should also work using Unix, using Unix-specific commands.

These are the basic prerequisites and steps for this exercise:

1. Make sure you have a hex editor.

2. Ensure that the database is in ARCHIVELOG mode.

3. Create a new tablespace called USER_DATA.

4. Create a new table in the USER_DATA tablespace.

5. Take a hot full backup of the database.

6. Use the hex editor to corrupt the datafile for the USER_DATA tablespace.

7. Run the dbv command and the SQL queries to identify the corrupt blocks.

8. Perform the block media recovery.

9. Validate the results.

Here are the specific steps:

1. If using Windows, download and install a hex editor.

2. Make sure the database is in ARCHIVELOG mode.

```
SQL> show parameter log_archive_start
NAME                                 TYPE         VALUE
------------------------------------ -----------  -----------
log_archive_start                    boolean      FALSE

SQL> shutdown immediate;
Database closed.
Database dismounted.
ORACLE instance shut down.
SQL> exit

sqlplus sys/orcl as sysdba
```

```
SQL*Plus: Release 11.1.0.6.0 - Production on Sat Nov 22 17:55:34 2008

Copyright (c) 1982, 2007, Oracle.  All rights reserved.

Connected to an idle instance.

SQL> startup mount
ORACLE instance started.

Total System Global Area  732352512 bytes
Fixed Size                  1335696 bytes
Variable Size             444599920 bytes
Database Buffers          281018368 bytes
Redo Buffers                5398528 bytes
Database mounted.
SQL> alter database archivelog;

Database altered.

SQL> archive log start;
Statement processed.
SQL> alter database open;

Database altered.

SQL>
```

3. Create a new tablespace called USER_DATA.

```
SQL> create tablespace user_data datafile
'c:\oracle\oradata\orcl\user_data01.dbf' size 10 m;

Tablespace created.
SQL>
```

4. Create a new table in the USER_DATA tablespace.

```
SQL> create table block_corruption_test
tablespace user_data
as select * from flashback_query_test;

Table created.
SQL>
```

5. Take a hot full RMAN backup of the database.

```
rman target=sys/orcl

Recovery Manager: Release 11.1.0.6.0 - Production on
 Sat Nov 22 18:17:45 2008

Copyright (c) 1982, 2007, Oracle.  All rights reserved.

connected to target database: ORCL (DBID=1190467526)

RMAN> backup database plus archivelog;
Starting backup at 22-NOV-08
current log archived
allocated channel: ORA_DISK_1
channel ORA_DISK_1: SID=130 device type=DISK
channel ORA_DISK_1: starting archived log backup set
channel ORA_DISK_1: specifying archived log(s) in backup set
input archived log thread=1 sequence=210 RECID=184 STAMP=670763775
input archived log thread=1 sequence=211 RECID=185 STAMP=670765527
input archived log thread=1 sequence=212 RECID=186 STAMP=670847849
input archived log thread=1 sequence=213 RECID=187 STAMP=671056681
input archived log thread=1 sequence=214 RECID=188 STAMP=671313636
input archived log thread=1 sequence=215 RECID=189 STAMP=671387999
input archived log thread=1 sequence=216 RECID=190 STAMP=671459676
input archived log thread=1 sequence=217 RECID=191 STAMP=671461419
input archived log thread=1 sequence=218 RECID=192 STAMP=671481182
input archived log thread=1 sequence=219 RECID=194 STAMP=671481209
channel ORA_DISK_1: starting piece 1 at 22-NOV-08
channel ORA_DISK_1: finished piece 1 at 22-NOV-08
piece handle=C:\TEMP\ORABACKUP\41K0BVRH_1_1
tag=TAG20081122T183330 comment=NONE
channel ORA_DISK_1: backup set complete, elapsed time: 00:03:46
Finished backup at 22-NOV-08

Starting backup at 22-NOV-08
using channel ORA_DISK_1
channel ORA_DISK_1: starting full datafile backup set
channel ORA_DISK_1: specifying datafile(s) in backup set
```

```
input datafile file number=00001 name=C:\ORACLE\ORADATA\ORCL\SYSTEM01.DBF
input datafile file number=00002 name=C:\ORACLE\ORADATA\ORCL\SYSAUX01.DBF
input datafile file number=00003 name=C:\ORACLE\ORADATA\ORCL\UNDOTBS01.DBF
input datafile file number=00005 name=C:\ORACLE\ORADATA\ORCL\EXAMPLE01.DBF
input datafile file number=00006
name=C:\ORACLE\ORADATA\ORCL\USER_DATA01.DBF
input datafile file number=00004 name=C:\ORACLE\ORADATA\ORCL\USERS01.DBF
channel ORA_DISK_1: starting piece 1 at 22-NOV-08
channel ORA_DISK_1: finished piece 1 at 22-NOV-08
piece handle=C:\TEMP\ORABACKUP\42K0C03A_1_1
 tag=TAG20081122T184601 comment=NONE
channel ORA_DISK_1: backup set complete, elapsed time: 00:02:26
channel ORA_DISK_1: starting full datafile backup set
channel ORA_DISK_1: specifying datafile(s) in backup set
including current control file in backup set
including current SPFILE in backup set
channel ORA_DISK_1: starting piece 1 at 22-NOV-08
channel ORA_DISK_1: finished piece 1 at 22-NOV-08
piece handle=C:\TEMP\ORABACKUP\43K0C08F_1_1
 tag=TAG20081122T184601 comment=NONE
channel ORA_DISK_1: backup set complete, elapsed time: 00:00:02
Finished backup at 22-NOV-08

Starting backup at 22-NOV-08
current log archived
using channel ORA_DISK_1
channel ORA_DISK_1: starting archived log backup set
channel ORA_DISK_1: specifying archived log(s) in backup set
input archived log thread=1 sequence=220 RECID=195 STAMP=671482150
channel ORA_DISK_1: starting piece 1 at 22-NOV-08
channel ORA_DISK_1: finished piece 1 at 22-NOV-08
piece handle=C:\TEMP\ORABACKUP\44K0C097_1_1
 tag=TAG20081122T184910 comment=NONE
channel ORA_DISK_1: backup set complete, elapsed time: 00:00:01
Finished backup at 22-NOV-08

RMAN>
```

In Step 6 you will use a hex editor to corrupt a datafile. You will lose data, so complete Step 6 only in an isolated testing environment!

6. Use the hex editor to corrupt the datafile for the USER_DATA tablespace. First issue the SQL command to make the USER_DATA tablespace offline, then use the hex editor to search for a text string found in the target table (for example, row 1), and then replace the data with zeroes. Save the file, exit, then issue the command to make the tablespace online.

```
SQL> alter tablespace user_data offline;

Tablespace altered.

SQL>
```

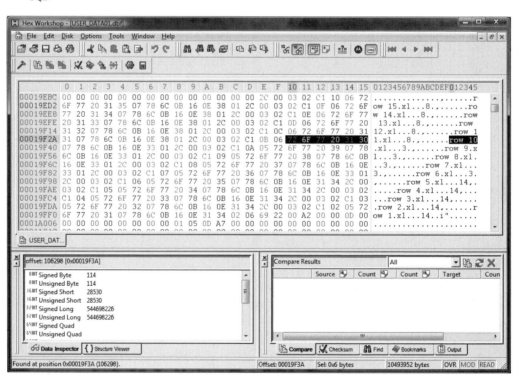

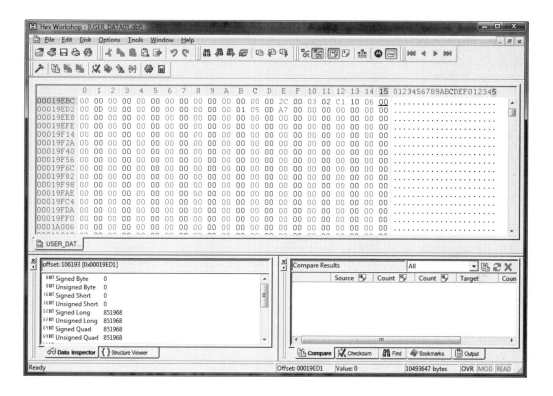

```
SQL> alter tablespace user_data online;

Tablespace altered.

SQL>
```

7. Run the dbv command and the SQL queries to identify the corrupt blocks.

```
c:\dbv file=c:\oracle\oradata\orcl\user_data01.dbf
DBVERIFY: Release 11.1.0.6.0 - Production on Sat Nov 22 19:27:57 2008

Copyright (c) 1982, 2007, Oracle.  All rights reserved.

DBVERIFY - Verification starting : FILE =
 c:\oracle\oradata\orcl\user_data01.dbf

Page 12 is influx - most likely media corrupt
Corrupt block relative dba: 0x0180000c (file 6, block 12)
Fractured block found during dbv:
```

```
Data in bad block:
 type: 6 format: 2 rdba: 0x0180000c
 last change scn: 0x0000.00622269 seq: 0x2 flg: 0x04
 spare1: 0x0 spare2: 0x0 spare3: 0x0
 consistency value in tail: 0x00000000
 check value in block header: 0xc476
 computed block checksum: 0xdd1e



DBVERIFY - Verification complete

Total Pages Examined        : 1280
Total Pages Processed (Data) : 0
Total Pages Failing   (Data) : 0
Total Pages Processed (Index): 0
Total Pages Failing   (Index): 0
Total Pages Processed (Other): 11
Total Pages Processed (Seg)  : 0
Total Pages Failing   (Seg)  : 0
Total Pages Empty           : 1268
Total Pages Marked Corrupt  : 1
Total Pages Influx          : 1
Total Pages Encrypted       : 0
Highest block SCN           : 6431341 (0.6431341)



SQL> select * from block_corruption_test;
select * from block_corruption_test
            *
ERROR at line 1:
ORA-01578: ORACLE data block corrupted (file # 6, block # 12)
ORA-01110: data file 6: 'C:\ORACLE\ORADATA\ORCL\USER_DATA01.DBF'


SQL>
SQL> select file#, block#, blocks, corruption_type "TYPE"
```

```
from v$database_block_corruption;

    FILE#      BLOCK#     BLOCKS TYPE
---------- ---------- ---------- ---------
        6         12          1 FRACTURED

SQL>
```

8. Perform the block media recovery using RMAN. Either recover the specific block or recover all the blocks in the corruption list.

```
RMAN> recover datafile 6 block 12;

RMAN> recover corruption list;
C:\rman target=sys/orcl

Recovery Manager: Release 11.1.0.6.0 - Production on
 Sat Nov 22 19:37:52 2008

Copyright (c) 1982, 2007, Oracle.  All rights reserved.

connected to target database: ORCL (DBID=1190467526)

RMAN> recover datafile 6 block 12;

Starting recover at 22-NOV-08
using target database control file instead of recovery catalog
allocated channel: ORA_DISK_1
channel ORA_DISK_1: SID=138 device type=DISK

channel ORA_DISK_1: restoring block(s)
channel ORA_DISK_1: specifying block(s) to restore from backup set
restoring blocks of datafile 00006
channel ORA_DISK_1: reading from backup piece
 C:\TEMP\ORABACKUP\42K0C03A_1_1
channel ORA_DISK_1: piece handle=C:\TEMP\ORABACKUP\42K0C03A_1_1
 tag=TAG20081122T
184601
channel ORA_DISK_1: restored block(s) from backup piece 1
channel ORA_DISK_1: block restore complete, elapsed time: 00:00:01
```

```
starting media recovery
media recovery complete, elapsed time: 00:00:03

Finished recover at 22-NOV-08

RMAN>
```

9. Validate the results.

```
SQL>select file#, block#, blocks, corruption_type "TYPE"
from v$database_block_corruption;

no rows selected

SQL> select * from block_corruption_test;

         X Y             Z
---------- ---------- ---------
         1 row 1       22-NOV-08
         2 row 2       22-NOV-08
         3 row 3       22-NOV-08
         4 row 4       22-NOV-08
         5 row 5       22-NOV-08
         6 row 6       22-NOV-08
         7 row 7       22-NOV-08
         8 row 8       22-NOV-08
         9 row 9       22-NOV-08
        10 row 10      22-NOV-08
        11 row 11      22-NOV-08
        12 row 12      22-NOV-08
        13 row 13      22-NOV-08
        14 row 14      22-NOV-08
        15 row 15      22-NOV-08

15 rows selected.

SQL>
```

Lab 11.1: Exporting a Transportable Tablespace

This lab was created using Windows XP. However, it should also work using Unix (and in fact was tested using Linux). In this lab, you'll export a transportable tablespace set.

1. Query the v$transportable_platform view to determine which destination platforms are compatible with the source database platform.

```
SQL> select * from v$transportable_platform;
PLATFORM_ID PLATFORM_NAME                            ENDIAN_FORMAT
----------- ---------------------------------------- --------------
          1 Solaris[tm] OE (32-bit)                  Big
          2 Solaris[tm] OE (64-bit)                  Big
          7 Microsoft Windows IA (32-bit)            Little
         10 Linux IA (32-bit)                        Little
          6 AIX-Based Systems (64-bit)               Big
          3 HP-UX (64-bit)                           Big
          5 HP Tru64 UNIX                            Little
          4 HP-UX IA (64-bit)                        Big
         11 Linux IA (64-bit)                        Little
         15 HP Open VMS                              Little
          8 Microsoft Windows IA (64-bit)            Little
          9 IBM zSeries Based Linux                  Big
         13 Linux 64-bit for AMD                     Little
         16 Apple Mac OS                             Big
         12 Microsoft Windows 64-bit for AMD         Little
         17 Solaris Operating System (x86)           Little
         18 IBM Power Based Linux                    Big
         19 HP IA Open VMS                           Little
         20 Solaris Operating System (AMD64)         Little
19 rows selected.
SQL>
```

2. After you have identified the names of the tablespaces you want to transport, execute the DBMS_TTS.TRANSPORT_SET_CHECK procedure. Next, query the TRANSPORT_SET_VIOLATIONS view.

```
SQL> SET SERVEROUTPUT ON
SQL> exec dbms_tts.transport_set_check ('USER_DATA');
PL/SQL procedure successfully completed.
```

```
SQL> SELECT * FROM TRANSPORT_SET_VIOLATIONS;
SQL>
```

3. To generate the transportable tablespace set, you'll need to place the tablespaces in read-only mode.

```
SQL>alter tablespace user_data read only;
Tablespace altered.
```

4. Exit to the host prompt and execute the data pump export utility to export the metadata.

```
SQL>host
C:\>expdp dumpfile=expdat.dmp DIRECTORY=exp_dir
 TRANSPORT_TABLESPACES= user_data


Export: Release 11.1.0.6.0 - Production on Sunday, 28
 September, 2008 14:40:19


Copyright (c) 2003, 2007, Oracle.  All rights reserved.


Username: sys as sysdba
Password:


Connected to: Oracle Database 11g Enterprise Edition
 Release 11.1.0.6.0 - Produc
tion
With the Partitioning, OLAP, Data Mining and Real
 Application Testing options
Starting "SYS"."SYS_EXPORT_TRANSPORTABLE_01":
  sys/******** AS SYSDBA dumpfile=e
xpdat.dmp DIRECTORY=EXP_DIR TRANSPORT_TABLESPACES= user_data
Processing object type TRANSPORTABLE_EXPORT/PLUGTS_BLK
Processing object type TRANSPORTABLE_EXPORT/TABLE
Processing object type TRANSPORTABLE_EXPORT/INDEX
Processing object type TRANSPORTABLE_EXPORT/CONSTRAINT/CONSTRAINT
Processing object type TRANSPORTABLE_EXPORT/INDEX_STATISTICS
Processing object type TRANSPORTABLE_EXPORT/TABLE_STATISTICS
Processing object type TRANSPORTABLE_EXPORT/POST_INSTANCE/PLUGTS_BLK
Master table "SYS"."SYS_EXPORT_TRANSPORTABLE_01"
 successfully loaded/unloaded
**************************
Dump file set for SYS.SYS_EXPORT_TRANSPORTABLE_01 is:
```

```
   C:\TEMP\EXPDAT.DMP
************************
Datafiles required for transportable tablespace USER_DATA:
   C:\ORACLE\ORADATA\ORCL\USER_DATA01.DBF
Job "SYS"."SYS_EXPORT_TRANSPORTABLE_01" successfully completed at 14:41:47
```

5. Now copy the tablespace database files to the staging area, either local or remote. Once the copy is complete, return to SQL*Plus and place the tablespaces in read-write mode:

```
SQL>alter tablespace user_data read write;
Tablespace altered.
SQL>
```

Lab 11.2: Testing Resumable Space Allocation

In this lab, you will perform a more detailed resumable-space-allocation exercise. You will create a table, start an insert operation that will create a resumable condition, monitor the table's space utilization, and then remedy the condition.

1. Shrink the existing USER_DATA tablespace and create a table with minimal storage values.

```
SQL> alter database datafile
'c:\oracle\oradata\orcl\user_data01.dbf'
resize 10 m;

Database altered.

SQL> create table scott.resumable_test
(x number, y varchar2(10))
storage (initial 1k maxextents 1)
tablespace user_data;

Table created.
```

2. Start an insert operation.

```
SQL> insert into resumable_test values (1, 'testtest');
SQL> insert into resumable values (1, 'testtest');
1 row created.
SQL> insert into resumable select * from resumable;
1 row created.
```

```
SQL> /
2 rows created.
SQL> /
4 rows created.
SQL> /
8 rows created.
SQL> /
16 rows created.
SQL> /
32 rows created.
SQL> /
64 rows created.
SQL> /
128 rows created.
SQL> /
256 rows created.
SQL> /
512 rows created.
SQL> /
1024 rows created.
SQL> /
2048 rows created.
SQL> /
4096 rows created.
SQL> /
8192 rows created.
SQL> /
16384 rows created.
SQL> /
32768 rows created.
SQL> /
65536 rows created.
SQL> /
131072 rows created.
SQL> /
```

The session should hang at this point.

3. Monitor the operation from another SQL*Plus session:

```
SQL> select session_id, sql_text, error_msg from dba_resumable;
```

```
SESSION_ID
----------

SQL_TEXT
-------------------------

ERROR_MSG
-------------------------

       125
insert into resumable select * from resumable
ORA-01653: unable to extend table
 SCOTT.RESUMABLE_TEST by 128 in tablespace
USER_DATA

SQL>
```

4. Remedy the resumable condition.

```
SQL> alter database datafile
'c:\oracle\oradata\orcl\user_data01.dbf'
resize 100 m;
```

5. Verify the resumable condition.

```
SQL> select session_id, sql_text, error_msg from dba_resumable;
no rows selected
SQL>
```

Lab 11.3: Manually Configuring the SGA

In this lab, you will modify initialization parameters and configure the SGA. You will start with an instance that uses Automatic Memory Management, then you'll step through modifying the parameters to utilize Automatic Shared Memory Management, and finally you'll manually configure each of the SGA components. This is the basic procedure:

Here's an example:

1. Configure the instance for Automatic Memory Management.

```
SQL> show parameter memory
```

```
NAME                                 TYPE          VALUE
------------------------------------ ------------- -----
hi_shared_memory_address             integer       0
memory_max_target                    big integer   1000M
memory_target                        big integer   0
shared_memory_address                integer       0
SQL>
SQL>alter system set memory_target=1000m scope=both;

System altered.

SQL>show parameter memory

NAME                                 TYPE          VALUE
------------------------------------ ------------- -----
hi_shared_memory_address             integer       0
memory_max_target                    big integer   1000M
memory_target                        big integer   1000M
shared_memory_address                integer       0
SQL>
```

Since both memory_target and memory_max_target are set to a nonzero value, the instance is running in Automatic Memory Management mode.

2. Modify the configuration to use Automatic Shared Memory Management.

```
SQL> show parameter sga

NAME                                 TYPE          VALUE
------------------------------------ ------------- -----
lock_sga                             boolean       FALSE
pre_page_sga                         boolean       FALSE
sga_max_size                         big integer   700M
sga_target                           big integer   0
SQL>
SQL>alter system set sga_target=700m scope=both;

System altered.
SQL>alter system set memory_target=0 scope=both;
```

System altered.

SQL>

Since SGA_TARGET and SGA_MAX_SIZE are set to a nonzero value and MEMORY_TARGET is set to zero, you're now running the instance in Automatic Shared Memory Management mode.

3. Manually configure each of the SGA components.

```
SQL> show parameter pool

NAME                                 TYPE          VALUE
------------------------------------ -----------   --------
_shared_io_pool_size                 big integer   0
buffer_pool_keep                     string
buffer_pool_recycle                  string
global_context_pool_size             string
java_pool_size                       big integer   12M
large_pool_size                      big integer   0
olap_page_pool_size                  big integer   0
shared_pool_reserved_size            big integer   14050918
shared_pool_size                     big integer   0
streams_pool_size                    big integer   32M
SQL>
SQL>alter system set large_pool_size=4m scope=both;
SQL>alter system set shared_pool_size=268m scope=both;
SQL>alter system set sga_target=0 scope=both;
```

By setting the value of SGA_TARGET to zero, you effectively begin managing the SGA manually. You'll need to set the individual pool sizes to nonzero values, as shown earlier.

Lab 12.1: Creating a Local External Job

This lab was created using Windows XP. However, it should also work using Unix (and in fact was tested using Linux).

This lab shows you how to create a local external job that is also a detached job. A detached job starts another process and then exits. Use a detached job when it is impractical or impossible to wait for the job to complete. A detached job must point to a program that has its detached attribute set to TRUE. These are the overall steps: create the external shell script that invokes an RMAN script, create the RMAN script that performs an archive log backup, and create the job and use a detached local external program.

1. Create the shell script that executes the RMAN script.

```
$ORACLE_HOME/scripts/archivelogbackup.sh
#!/bin/sh
export ORACLE_HOME=/ora01/oracle/product/11.1.0
export ORACLE_SID=orcl
export LD_LIBRARY_PATH=$LD_LIBRARY_PATH:$ORACLE_HOME/lib
$ORACLE_HOME/bin/rman TARGET / @$ORACLE_HOME/scripts/archivelogbackup.rman
trace /ora01/oracle/orcl/backup/logs/archivelogbackup.out &
exit 0
```

2. Next, create the RMAN script that runs the archive log backup.

```
$ORACLE_HOME/scripts/archivelogbackup.rman
run {
BACKUP DEVICE TYPE sbt
ARCHIVELOG LIKE '/oraarc01/orcl%arc%'
DELETE ALL INPUT;
# Let the scheduler know that the detached job completed
sql " BEGIN DBMS_SCHEDULER.END_DETACHED_JOB_RUN(''sys.archivelog_backup'',
0,null); END; ";
}
```

3. Finally, return to SQL*Plus and execute the following PL/SQL block. Note that the ? embedded in the program_action field is a shortcut value for ORACLE_HOME:

```
BEGIN
DBMS_SCHEDULER.CREATE_PROGRAM(
    program_name => 'sys.archivelog_backup',
    program_type => 'executable',
    program_action => '?/scripts/archivelogbackup.sh',
    enabled => TRUE);
DBMS_SCHEDULER.SET_ATTRIBUTE('sys.archivelog_backup', 'detached', TRUE);
DBMS_SCHEDULER.CREATE_JOB(
    job_name => 'sys.archivelog_backup',
    program_name => 'sys.archivelog_backup',
```

```
    repeat_interval => 'FREQ=HOURLY;INTERVAL=4');
DBMS_SCHEDULER.ENABLE('sys.archivelog_backup');
END;
/
```

Lab 12.2: Creating a Job Window

This lab shows you how to create and use a job window in the Scheduler. Here are the steps:

1. Create a simple resource plan.
2. Create a job schedule.
3. Create a job window to utilize the resource plan.
4. Open the job window explicitly.
5. Close the job window explicitly.

Here's a specific example:

1. Create a simple resource plan.

```
SQL>begin
    dbms_resource_manager.create_simple_plan(simple_plan => 'LNE_PLAN1',
    consumer_group1 => 'LNEGROUP1', group1_percent => 80,
    consumer_group2 => 'LNEROUP2', group2_percent => 20);
end;
/
PL/SQL procedure successfully completed.

SQL>
```

2. Create a job schedule.

```
SQL>begin
  dbms_scheduler.create_schedule(
  schedule_name => 'NIGHTLY_BATCH_SCHEDULE',
  start_date => SYSTIMESTAMP,
  repeat_interval => 'FREQ=DAILY; BYHOUR=20',
  comments => 'Runs nightly at 9:00 PM');
  end;
 /
```

```
PL/SQL procedure successfully completed.

SQL>
```

3. Create a job window to utilize the resource plan.

```
SQL>begin
    dbms_scheduler.create_window (
    window_name => 'NIGHTLY_BATCH_WINDOW',
    resource_plan => 'LNE_PLAN1',
    schedule_name => 'NIGHTLY_BATCH_SCHEDULE',
    duration => INTERVAL '10' HOUR,
    window_priority => 'HIGH');
    end;
/
PL/SQL procedure successfully completed.

SQL>
```

4. Open the job window explicitly for a 10-hour duration.

```
SQL>begin
    dbms_scheduler.open_window (
    window_name => 'NIGHTLY_BATCH_WINDOW',
    duration => INTERVAL '600' MINUTE,
    force => TRUE);
    end;
SQL> /

PL/SQL procedure successfully completed.
```

5. Close the job window explicitly.

```
SQL> begin
    dbms_scheduler.close_window (
    window_name => 'NIGHTLY_BATCH_WINDOW');
    end;
SQL> /

PL/SQL procedure successfully completed.
```

Lab 13.1: Using the Locale Builder to Create a New Linguistic Sort

This lab was created using Windows XP. However, it should also work using Unix (and in fact was tested using Linux).

This lab shows you how to use the Oracle Locale Builder to create a new linguistic sort.

1. Open Oracle Locale Builder.

2. Choose to create a new file, and then choose Linguistic Sort.

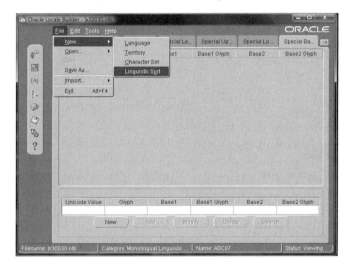

3. Select Monolingual Linguistic Sort.

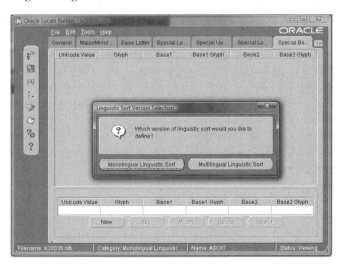

4. Click the Show Existing Definitions button.

5. Choose ASCII7 as the character set/collation name, and then click Open.

6. Change the collation name to your choice, and change the collation ID to a number between 1000 and 2000.

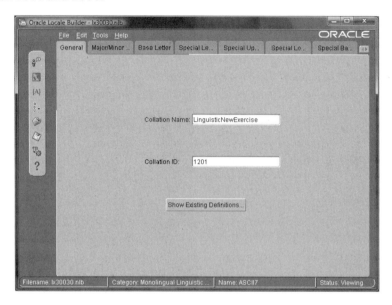

7. Modify a few of the special letters by choosing the Unicode value or copying the glyph.

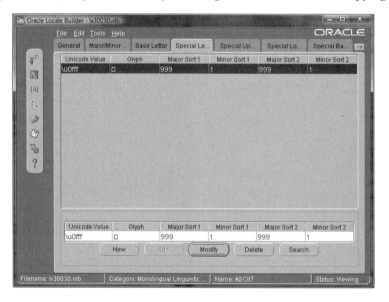

8. Save the file with a new unique name.

Lab 13.2: Setting NLS Parameters

In this lab, you will practice setting NLS parameters for the instance and for the session and observe how parameters are prioritized. Here are the general steps:

1. Show and modify instance NLS parameters.

2. Modify and observe the effects of setting session NLS variables.

3. Demonstrate NLS-parameter priorities.

   Here's an example:

1. Show and modify instance NLS parameters.

```
SQL> show parameter nls
```

NAME	TYPE	VALUE
nls_calendar	string	
nls_comp	string	BINARY
nls_currency	string	
nls_date_format	string	
nls_date_language	string	
nls_dual_currency	string	
nls_iso_currency	string	
nls_language	string	AMERICAN
nls_length_semantics	string	BYTE
nls_nchar_conv_excp	string	FALSE
nls_numeric_characters	string	
nls_sort	string	
nls_territory	string	AMERICA
nls_time_format	string	
nls_time_tz_format	string	
nls_timestamp_format	string	
nls_timestamp_tz_format	string	

```
SQL>
```

Only `nls_nchar_conv_excp` and `nls_lenght_semantics` are dynamically system modifiable or instance modifiable. You can, however, modify the parameter with `scope=spfile` and restart the instance to take effect.

```
SQL> alter system set nls_date_format='dd-mon-yyyy hh24:mi:ss'
  scope=spfile;
/
```

```
System altered.
SQL> shutdown immediate;
Database closed.
Database dismounted.
ORACLE instance shut down.

SQL> startup
ORACLE instance started.

Total System Global Area  732352512 bytes
Fixed Size                  1335696 bytes
Variable Size             444599920 bytes
Database Buffers          281018368 bytes
Redo Buffers                5398528 bytes
Database mounted.
Database opened.
SQL> show parameter nls

NAME                                TYPE        VALUE
----------------------------------- ----------- ----
------------------------
nls_calendar                        string
nls_comp                            string      BINARY
nls_currency                        string
nls_date_format                     string      dd-mon-yyyy hh24:mi:ss
nls_date_language                   string
nls_dual_currency                   string
nls_iso_currency                    string
nls_language                        string      AMERICAN
nls_length_semantics                string      BYTE
nls_nchar_conv_excp                 string      FALSE
nls_numeric_characters              string
nls_sort                            string
nls_territory                       string      AMERICA
nls_time_format                     string
nls_time_tz_format                  string
nls_timestamp_format                string
nls_timestamp_tz_format             string
SQL>
```

You can also observe the system NLS parameters by querying the NLS_INSTANCE_
PARAMETERS view.

2. Modify and observe the effects of setting session NLS variables. Query the NLS_SESSION_ PARAMETERS view to see your session parameter settings.

```
SQL> select * from nls_session_parameters
SQL> /

PARAMETER                    VALUE
---------------------------- ----------------------------
NLS_LANGUAGE                 AMERICAN
NLS_TERRITORY                AMERICA
NLS_CURRENCY                 $
NLS_ISO_CURRENCY             AMERICA
NLS_NUMERIC_CHARACTERS       .,
NLS_CALENDAR                 GREGORIAN
NLS_DATE_FORMAT              DD-MON-RR
NLS_DATE_LANGUAGE            AMERICAN
NLS_SORT                     BINARY
NLS_TIME_FORMAT              HH.MI.SSXFF AM
NLS_TIMESTAMP_FORMAT         DD-MON-RR HH.MI.SSXFF AM
NLS_TIME_TZ_FORMAT           HH.MI.SSXFF AM TZR
NLS_TIMESTAMP_TZ_FORMAT      DD-MON-RR HH.MI.SSXFF AM TZR
NLS_DUAL_CURRENCY            $
NLS_COMP                     BINARY
NLS_LENGTH_SEMANTICS         BYTE
NLS_NCHAR_CONV_EXCP          FALSE

17 rows selected.

SQL> select sysdate from dual;

SYSDATE
---------
23-NOV-08

SQL>
```

Modify the session NLS_DATE_FORMAT, and query.

```
SQL> alter session set nls_date_format='dd-mon-yyyy hh24:mi:ss';
Session altered.
```

```
SQL> select * from nls_session_parameters;

PARAMETER                      VALUE
------------------------------ ----------------------------
NLS_LANGUAGE                   AMERICAN
NLS_TERRITORY                  AMERICA
NLS_CURRENCY                   $
NLS_ISO_CURRENCY               AMERICA
NLS_NUMERIC_CHARACTERS         .,
NLS_CALENDAR                   GREGORIAN
NLS_DATE_FORMAT                dd-mon-yyyy hh24:mi:ss
NLS_DATE_LANGUAGE              AMERICAN
NLS_SORT                       BINARY
NLS_TIME_FORMAT                HH.MI.SSXFF AM
NLS_TIMESTAMP_FORMAT           DD-MON-RR HH.MI.SSXFF AM
NLS_TIME_TZ_FORMAT             HH.MI.SSXFF AM TZR
NLS_TIMESTAMP_TZ_FORMAT        DD-MON-RR HH.MI.SSXFF AM TZR
NLS_DUAL_CURRENCY              $
NLS_COMP                       BINARY
NLS_LENGTH_SEMANTICS           BYTE
NLS_NCHAR_CONV_EXCP            FALSE

17 rows selected.

SQL> select sysdate from dual;

SYSDATE
-------------------
23-nov-2008 00:11:38

SQL>
```

3. Demonstrate NLS-parameter priorities. Modify the session NLS_LANGUAGE, and query.

```
SQL> alter session set nls_language='GERMAN';

Session altered.

SQL> select * from nls_session_parameters;
```

```
PARAMETER                    VALUE
---------------------------- ----------------------------
NLS_LANGUAGE                 GERMAN
NLS_TERRITORY                AMERICA
NLS_CURRENCY                 $
NLS_ISO_CURRENCY             AMERICA
NLS_NUMERIC_CHARACTERS       .,
NLS_CALENDAR                 GREGORIAN
NLS_DATE_FORMAT              dd-mon-yyyy hh24:mi:ss
NLS_DATE_LANGUAGE            GERMAN
NLS_SORT                     GERMAN
NLS_TIME_FORMAT              HH.MI.SSXFF AM
NLS_TIMESTAMP_FORMAT         DD-MON-RR HH.MI.SSXFF AM
NLS_TIME_TZ_FORMAT           HH.MI.SSXFF AM TZR
NLS_TIMESTAMP_TZ_FORMAT      DD-MON-RR HH.MI.SSXFF AM TZR
NLS_DUAL_CURRENCY            $
NLS_COMP                     BINARY
NLS_LENGTH_SEMANTICS         BYTE
NLS_NCHAR_CONV_EXCP          FALSE

17 rows selected.

SQL>
```

Notice that when you set the NLS_LANGUAGE, the NLS_DATE_LANGUAGE and NLS_SORT also changed but the NLS_TERRITORY and NLS_ISO_CURRENCY did not. Now change the NLS_LANGUAGE back and observe.

```
SQL> alter session set nls_language='AMERICAN';

Session altered.

SQL> select * from nls_session_parameters;

PARAMETER                    VALUE
---------------------------- ----------------------------
NLS_LANGUAGE                 AMERICAN
NLS_TERRITORY                AMERICA
NLS_CURRENCY                 $
NLS_ISO_CURRENCY             AMERICA
```

```
NLS_NUMERIC_CHARACTERS          .,
NLS_CALENDAR                    GREGORIAN
NLS_DATE_FORMAT                 dd-mon-yyyy hh24:mi:ss
NLS_DATE_LANGUAGE               AMERICAN
NLS_SORT                        BINARY
NLS_TIME_FORMAT                 HH.MI.SSXFF AM
NLS_TIMESTAMP_FORMAT            DD-MON-RR HH.MI.SSXFF AM
NLS_TIME_TZ_FORMAT              HH.MI.SSXFF AM TZR
NLS_TIMESTAMP_TZ_FORMAT         DD-MON-RR HH.MI.SSXFF AM TZR
NLS_DUAL_CURRENCY               $
NLS_COMP                        BINARY
NLS_LENGTH_SEMANTICS            BYTE
NLS_NCHAR_CONV_EXCP             FALSE

17 rows selected.

SQL>
```

Note the NLS_LANGUAGE sets a default for NLS_DATE_LANGUAGE and NLS_SORT; however, you can modify NLS_DATE_LANGUAGE and NLS_SORT independently.

```
SQL> alter session set nls_sort='GERMAN';

Session altered.

SQL> select * from nls_session_parameters;

PARAMETER                       VALUE
------------------------------  ----------------------------
NLS_LANGUAGE                    AMERICAN
NLS_TERRITORY                   AMERICA
NLS_CURRENCY                    $
NLS_ISO_CURRENCY                AMERICA
NLS_NUMERIC_CHARACTERS          .,
NLS_CALENDAR                    GREGORIAN
NLS_DATE_FORMAT                 dd-mon-yyyy hh24:mi:ss
NLS_DATE_LANGUAGE               AMERICAN
NLS_SORT                        GERMAN
NLS_TIME_FORMAT                 HH.MI.SSXFF AM
NLS_TIMESTAMP_FORMAT            DD-MON-RR HH.MI.SSXFF AM
NLS_TIME_TZ_FORMAT              HH.MI.SSXFF AM TZR
```

```
NLS_TIMESTAMP_TZ_FORMAT        DD-MON-RR HH.MI.SSXFF AM TZR
NLS_DUAL_CURRENCY              $
NLS_COMP                       BINARY
NLS_LENGTH_SEMANTICS           BYTE
NLS_NCHAR_CONV_EXCP            FALSE

17 rows selected.

SQL>
```

If I now set the NLS_LANGUAGE to American, it will overlay the NLS_SORT value with BINARY:

```
SQL> alter session set nls_language='AMERICAN';

Session altered.

SQL> select * from nls_session_parameters;

PARAMETER                      VALUE
------------------------------ ----------------------------

NLS_LANGUAGE                   AMERICAN
NLS_TERRITORY                  AMERICA
NLS_CURRENCY                   $
NLS_ISO_CURRENCY               AMERICA
NLS_NUMERIC_CHARACTERS         .,
NLS_CALENDAR                   GREGORIAN
NLS_DATE_FORMAT                dd-mon-yyyy hh24:mi:ss
NLS_DATE_LANGUAGE              AMERICAN
NLS_SORT                       BINARY
NLS_TIME_FORMAT                HH.MI.SSXFF AM
NLS_TIMESTAMP_FORMAT           DD-MON-RR HH.MI.SSXFF AM
NLS_TIME_TZ_FORMAT             HH.MI.SSXFF AM TZR
NLS_TIMESTAMP_TZ_FORMAT        DD-MON-RR HH.MI.SSXFF AM TZR
NLS_DUAL_CURRENCY              $
NLS_COMP                       BINARY
NLS_LENGTH_SEMANTICS           BYTE
NLS_NCHAR_CONV_EXCP            FALSE

17 rows selected.

SQL>
```

Lab 13.3: Performing Linguistic Sorts

In this exercise, you will create a table and populate it with values that are easily sorted. You will then modify the NLS parameters that affect linguistic sorts and query the table, observing how the NLS-parameter settings modify the sort results. Here are the steps:

1. Create a table for linguistic sorts, and populate it.
2. Verify your session NLS parameters.
3. Query the sort table.
4. Modify the sort parameter.
5. Query the table and observe the differences in the sort results.

Here's an example:

1. Create a table for linguistic sorts, and populate it.

```
SQL> create table linguistic_sort_test (x number, y varchar2(1));

Table created.

SQL>

insert into linguistic_sort_test values (1,'A');
insert into linguistic_sort_test values (2,'B');
insert into linguistic_sort_test values (3,'C');
insert into linguistic_sort_test values (4,'D');
insert into linguistic_sort_test values (5,'E');
insert into linguistic_sort_test values (6,'F');
insert into linguistic_sort_test values (7,'G');
insert into linguistic_sort_test values (8,'H');
insert into linguistic_sort_test values (9,'I');
insert into linguistic_sort_test values (10,'J');
insert into linguistic_sort_test values (11,'a');
insert into linguistic_sort_test values (12,'b');
insert into linguistic_sort_test values (13,'c');
insert into linguistic_sort_test values (14,'d');
insert into linguistic_sort_test values (15,'e');
insert into linguistic_sort_test values (16,'f');
insert into linguistic_sort_test values (17,'g');
insert into linguistic_sort_test values (18,'h');
insert into linguistic_sort_test values (19,'i');
insert into linguistic_sort_test values (20,'j');
commit;
```

2.   Verify your session NLS parameters.

```
SQL> select * from nls_session_parameters;
```

PARAMETER	VALUE
NLS_LANGUAGE	AMERICAN
NLS_TERRITORY	AMERICA
NLS_CURRENCY	$
NLS_ISO_CURRENCY	AMERICA
NLS_NUMERIC_CHARACTERS	.,
NLS_CALENDAR	GREGORIAN
NLS_DATE_FORMAT	dd-mon-yyyy hh24:mi:ss
NLS_DATE_LANGUAGE	AMERICAN
NLS_SORT	BINARY
NLS_TIME_FORMAT	HH.MI.SSXFF AM
NLS_TIMESTAMP_FORMAT	DD-MON-RR HH.MI.SSXFF AM
NLS_TIME_TZ_FORMAT	HH.MI.SSXFF AM TZR
NLS_TIMESTAMP_TZ_FORMAT	DD-MON-RR HH.MI.SSXFF AM TZR
NLS_DUAL_CURRENCY	$
NLS_COMP	BINARY
NLS_LENGTH_SEMANTICS	BYTE
NLS_NCHAR_CONV_EXCP	FALSE

```
17 rows selected.

SQL>
```

3.   Query the sort table. Order by the numeric value as a baseline or control query, and then order by the character column using the default BINARY sort.

```
SQL> select * from linguistic_sort_test order by x;

         X Y
---------- -
         1 A
         2 B
         3 C
         4 D
         5 E
         6 F
         7 G
```

```
        8 H
        9 I
       10 J
       11 a
       12 b
       13 c
       14 d
       15 e
       16 f
       17 g
       18 h
       19 i
       20 j

20 rows selected.

SQL>


SQL> select * from linguistic_sort_test order by y;

        X Y
---------- -
        1 A
        2 B
        3 C
        4 D
        5 E
        6 F
        7 G
        8 H
        9 I
       10 J
       11 a
       12 b
       13 c
       14 d
       15 e
       16 f
       17 g
```

```
        18 h
        19 i
        20 j

20 rows selected.
```

4. Modify the sort parameter. The default was BINARY; we'll modify it to EBCDIC to demonstrate the simple difference.

```
SQL>
SQL> alter session set nls_sort='EBCDIC';

Session altered.
```

5. Query the table and observe the differences in the sort results from the previous query.

```
SQL> select * from linguistic_sort_test order by y;

         X Y
---------- -
        11 a
        12 b
        13 c
        14 d
        15 e
        16 f
        17 g
        18 h
        19 i
        20 j
         1 A
         2 B
         3 C
         4 D
         5 E
         6 F
         7 G
         8 H
         9 I
        10 J

20 rows selected.
```

Notice that the EBCDIC sort placed the lowercase letters at the beginning of the sort because they have a lower EBCDIC value than their uppercase counterparts.

If we now set the NLS_SORT value to ASCII7, you'll see the same results as BINARY for this simple sort.

```
SQL> alter session set nls_sort='ASCII7';

Session altered.

SQL> select * from linguistic_sort_test order by y;

         X Y
---------- -
         1 A
         2 B
         3 C
         4 D
         5 E
         6 F
         7 G
         8 H
         9 I
        10 J
        11 a
        12 b
        13 c
        14 d
        15 e
        16 f
        17 g
        18 h
        19 i
        20 j

20 rows selected.
```

Now if you set the NLS_SORT to CROATIAN, you'll see something really interesting.

```
SQL> alter session set nls_sort='CROATIAN';
```

Session altered.

```
SQL> select * from linguistic_sort_test order by y;

         X Y
---------- -
         1 A
        11 a
         2 B
        12 b
         3 C
        13 c
         4 D
        14 d
         5 E
        15 e
         6 F
        16 f
         7 G
        17 g
         8 H
        18 h
         9 I
        19 i
        10 J
        20 j

20 rows selected.

SQL>
```

And when you set NLS_SORT to THAI_M, you'll see the opposite pattern from the one for CROATIAN.

```
SQL> alter session set nls_sort='THAI_M';

Session altered.

SQL> select * from linguistic_sort_test order by y;
```

```
        X Y
---------- -
       11 a
        1 A
       12 b
        2 B
       13 c
        3 C
       14 d
        4 D
       15 e
        5 E
       16 f
        6 F
       17 g
        7 G
       18 h
        8 H
       19 i
        9 I
       20 j
       10 J
```

20 rows selected.

SQL>

Remember that setting NLS_LANGUAGE will override the NLS_SORT setting, but NLS_SORT can be set to whatever valid setting you choose following a change to NLS_LANGUAGE.

Appendix
B

About the Companion CD

IN THIS APPENDIX:

- ✓ What you'll find on the CD
- ✓ System requirements
- ✓ Using the CD
- ✓ Troubleshooting

What You'll Find on the CD

The following sections are arranged by category and summarize the software and other goodies you'll find on the CD. If you need help with installing the items provided on the CD, refer to the installation instructions in the "Using the CD" section of this appendix.

Some programs on the CD might fall into one of these categories:

Shareware programs are fully functional, free, trial versions of copyrighted programs. If you like particular programs, register with their authors for a nominal fee and receive licenses, enhanced versions, and technical support.

Freeware programs are free, copyrighted games, applications, and utilities. You can copy them to as many computers as you like—for free—but they offer no technical support.

GNU software is governed by its own license, which is included inside the folder of the GNU software. There are no restrictions on distribution of GNU software. See the GNU license at the root of the CD for more details.

Trial, *demo*, or *evaluation* versions of software are usually limited either by time or by functionality (such as not letting you save a project after you create it).

Sybex Test Engine

For Windows

The CD contains the Sybex test engine, which includes all of the assessment test and chapter review questions in electronic format, as well as two bonus exams located only on the CD.

PDF of the Book

For Windows

We have included an electronic version of the text in .pdf format. You can view the electronic version of the book with Adobe Reader.

Adobe Reader

For Windows

We've also included a copy of Adobe Reader so you can view PDF files that accompany the book's content. For more information on Adobe Reader or to check for a newer version, visit Adobe's website at www.adobe.com/products/reader/.

Electronic Flashcards

For PC, Pocket PC, and Palm

These handy electronic flashcards are just what they sound like. One side contains a question or fill-in-the-blank question, and the other side shows the answer.

System Requirements

Make sure your computer meets the minimum system requirements shown in the following list. If your computer doesn't match up to most of these requirements, you may have problems using the software and files on the companion CD. For the latest and greatest information, please refer to the ReadMe file located at the root of the CD-ROM.

- A PC running Microsoft Windows 98, Windows 2000, Windows NT4 (with SP4 or later), Windows Me, Windows XP, or Windows Vista

- An Internet connection

- A CD-ROM drive

Using the CD

To install the items from the CD to your hard drive, follow these steps:

1. Insert the CD into your computer's CD-ROM drive. The license agreement appears.

Windows users: The interface won't launch if you have autorun disabled. In that case, click Start ➢ Run (for Windows Vista, Start ➢ All Programs ➢ Accessories ➢ Run). In the dialog box that appears, type **D:\Start.exe**. (Replace *D* with the proper letter if your CD drive uses a different letter. If you don't know the letter, see how your CD drive is listed under My Computer.) Click OK.

2. Read the license agreement, and then click the Accept button if you want to use the CD.

The CD interface appears. The interface allows you to access the content with just one or two clicks.

Troubleshooting

Wiley has attempted to provide programs that work on most computers with the minimum system requirements. Alas, your computer may differ, and some programs may not work properly for some reason.

The two likeliest problems are that you don't have enough memory (RAM) for the programs you want to use or you have other programs running that are affecting installation or running of a program. If you get an error message such as "Not enough memory" or "Setup cannot continue," try one or more of the following suggestions and then try using the software again:

Turn off any antivirus software running on your computer.   Installation programs sometimes mimic virus activity and may make your computer incorrectly believe that it's being infected by a virus.

Close all running programs.   The more programs you have running, the less memory is available to other programs. Installation programs typically update files and programs; so if you keep other programs running, installation may not work properly.

Have your local computer store add more RAM to your computer.   This is, admittedly, a drastic and somewhat expensive step. However, adding more memory can really help the speed of your computer and allow more programs to run at the same time.

Customer Care

If you have trouble with the book's companion CD-ROM, please call the Wiley Product Technical Support phone number at (800) 762-2974. Outside the United States, call +1(317) 572-3994. You can also contact Wiley Product Technical Support at http:// sybex.custhelp.com. John Wiley & Sons will provide technical support only for installation and other general quality-control items. For technical support on the applications themselves, consult the program's vendor or author.

To place additional orders or to request information about other Wiley products, please call (877) 762-2974.

Glossary

A

active database duplication   Active database duplication is an RMAN duplication process that occurs over the network and does not use RMAN backups as the source of the duplication.

active online redo log group   This is an online redo log that is not currently in use by the database but has not been archived.

archived redo logs   Copies of the online redo logs. Critical to database recovery when the database is in ARCHIVELOG mode.

ARCHIVELOG mode   When in ARCHIVELOG mode, the database will generate archived redo logs and, by applying those files and the online redo logs, can be recovered to any point other than the point of the last backup.

archiver process (ARCH)   The process responsible for copying an online redo log to an archived redo log after a log switch has completed.

ASM   See Automatic Storage Management.

ASM fast disk resync   Method of quickly recovering from hardware failures that impact disk availability but do not corrupt the data on the disk itself.

ASM instance   Running Oracle instance specific to ASM functionality.

ASM preferred mirror read   When one set of disks is local and the other remote, this allows you to indicate to ASM that it should read from a specific failure group set of disks (typically the local set).

ASM redundancy   Method of protecting data on ASM disks by mirroring the data on one or more ASM failure groups.

ASM_DISKSTRING   Parameter that indicates to the Oracle ASM instance where to look for ASM disks upon instance startup.

ASMCMD   Command-line tool used to manage ASM instances.

automated channel failover   The ability of other channels to automatically restart failed RMAN activities from a channel that has failed.

Automatic Diagnostic Repository (ADR)   File-based repository for database diagnostic data.

automatic instance   Temporary instance created automatically when performing RMAN tablespace point-in-time recovery.

Automatic Memory Management   Default memory-management model in Oracle 11*g*; when you set a nonzero value for MEMORY_TARGET and MEMORY_MAX_TARGET, Oracle will manage SGA and PGA memory pools, caches, and work-area sizes dynamically.

Automatic PGA Memory Management   When you set the value of MEMORY_TARGET and MAX_MEMORY_TARGET to zero and set a nonzero value for PGA_AGGREGATE_TARGET, Oracle will manage PGA memory components automatically, resizing as needed within the value specified.

Automatic Shared Memory Management   When you set the value of MEMORY_TARGET and MAX_MEMORY_TARGET to zero and set a nonzero value for SGA_MAX_SIZE and SGA_TARGET, Oracle will manage SGA memory components automatically, resizing as needed within the value specified.

Automatic Storage Management   An Oracle native file system management system that provides a volume manager, fault tolerance, and load balancing of disks assigned to Oracle databases. Both stand-alone and clustered databases are supported.

Automatic Undo Management (AUM)   Oracle functionality that simplifies management of undo tablespaces. AUM works to meet undo retention goals while ensuring that adequate space is available for new transactions.

auxiliary instance   Instance manually created when database duplication is performed or automatically created during tablespace point-in-time recovery. This instance is used as the destination database and will become the duplicated database during a database duplication, or is temporarily used during a tablespace point-in-time recovery.

auxiliary set   The set of database datafiles required to create the automatic instance during a tablespace point-in-time recovery.

B

backup-based database duplication   Database duplication dependent on the presence of RMAN backups and archived redo logs.

backup optimization   When enabled, will prevent unnecessary backups of read-only database datafiles.

backup set   A logical entity representing a single backup of specific database tablespace datafiles. Individual database datafiles are always contained within a single RMAN backup set. A backup set comprises one or more physical files called backup-set pieces.

backup-set compression   Zip-like compression of RMAN backup sets used to reduce the size of the RMAN backup-set pieces, and thus the entire backup.

backup-set piece   Default physical file used by RMAN to back up a database. Backup-set pieces are physical files. Many backup-set pieces may belong to one logical structure called a backup set.

binary sorting   Ordering character strings based on their binary coded values.

block-change tracking file   Physical file used to track changed blocks. Level-1 incremental backups use these files to improve performance of incremental backups by avoiding unnecessary datafile IO.

block media recovery   A technique for restoring and recovering individual data blocks that have been identified as corrupt while all database files remain online and available.

byte semantics   Assumes a single-byte character set, where one character always requires one byte of storage; treatment of strings as a sequence of bytes.

C

chain   Two or more Scheduler programs that are linked together to meet an objective, where the outcome of one job determines the next steps in the chain.

change-based recovery   Recovery of the database based on a specific system change number (SCN).

channel   A connection from the database server to the backup destination (disk or MML layer). Each RMAN backup or recovery has at least one channel allocated. Multiple channels provide for parallel backup and recovery in RMAN.

character semantics   Allows character data to be specified in terms of the number of characters regardless of the number of bytes required.

character set   A collection of elements that represent textual information for a specific language or group of languages.

complete database recovery   Recovering the database to the point of failure by applying all archived redo logs and all redo in the online redo logs.

complete recovery   A recovery of the database to the point of the last completed transaction. This kind of recovery involves no data loss. Complete recovery is synonymous with point-of-failure recovery.

consistent shutdown   A shutdown of the database that leaves the datafiles in a consistent state.

control file   A critical database file that contains metadata related to the database, such as the location of the database datafiles, redo logs, and archived redo logs.

control-file autobackups   An RMAN feature providing automatic backup and restore of the database control files and spfiles. Also provides for easy recovery of these database-related files.

convert   The RMAN command that allows the DBA to transport databases and tablespaces from one platform to another where the source and destination platforms have different endianness.

corrupt block   An Oracle block that is not in a recognized Oracle format or whose contents are not internally consistent. Corruption is usually caused by hardware or operating-system problems. In Oracle, block corruption is classified as either logical, caused by an Oracle internal error, or physically corrupt media, meaning the block format is not correct.

crash or instance recovery   A recovery from a database that has been shut down in an inconsistent manner. This kind of recovery does not require user intervention because the Oracle database uses the online redo logs to bring the database to a consistent state.

cumulative incremental backup   An incremental backup that contains all database data blocks changed since the last level 0 backup.

current online redo log group   The online redo log group that is currently in use by the database.

D

datafile recoveries   The recovery of specific database datafiles instead of the entire database or a specific tablespace.

database   A collection of datafiles that is used to store data.

database character set   The character set that will govern default text storage in the database.

database control file   The file that contains configuration information on the database associated with the control file, such as the location of datafiles, redo logs, and RMAN-related information.

database datafiles   The physical media used to store database data. Tablespaces are assigned to one or more database datafiles.

database duplication   The process of creating one database from another.

database incarnation   Indicates the logical life of a given database. The first incarnation begins at the creation of a database and ends at the point the `resetlogs` command is used when creating a database.

database parameter file (pfile)   A text-based file that contains database-related parameters and their settings.

Database Replay   An Oracle feature that allows the capture of a workload and replay on a similar database in a test environment.

Database Resource Manager   The Oracle feature that allows the DBA to manage resource allocation by creating directives, plans, and groups.

database writer process (DBWR)   The process responsible for writing database changes to the database datafiles.

DBID   Stands for database ID. This number uniquely identifies an Oracle database.

dependency scheduling   Scheduling jobs based on the outcomes of previous jobs. In the Oracle Scheduler, job chains are used to implement dependency-based scheduling.

destination host   The host that is the destination of a duplicate operation.

differential incremental backup   An incremental backup that contains all database data blocks changed since the last level-1 differential incremental backup.

disk group   Equivalent to a logical volume in ASM. Individual LUNs (disks) are assigned to disk groups. Fault tolerance is supported at the disk-group level through mirroring.

disk-group attributes   Attributes assigned individually to specific disk groups, such as disk repair time.

duplexing   A method of creating more than one copy of a database backup during the backup.

dynamic performance data dictionary views   Views that provide near-real-time information on the database, including metadata about database structures. Much of the data in dynamic performance views comes from the database control file.

E

endianness   Or endian format. The byte order used by a particular hardware platform. When the sequence of bytes with increasing significance is stored with increasing memory addresses, this is referred to as little endian. If the most significant byte is stored first, this is referred to as big endian. When bytes are exchanged between platforms with different endianness, a conversion process must occur before the bytes will make sense to the destination computer.

event-based scheduling   The concept of executing a job based on an event that signals the Scheduler, regardless of time or dependencies.

F

failure groups (or FAILGROUPS)   Failure groups provide for data redundancy in an ASM disk group. Each failure group is assigned one or more disks. Data in one failure group is redundantly copied to the other failure groups in the disk group.

flash recovery area (FRA)   File system dedicated to back-up and recovery purposes. Can contain many recovery-related components, such as backup set pieces, archived redo logs, and copies of the database control files.

Flashback Data Archive   An Oracle feature that allows one to archive all DML changes to a table and retain those changes for a specified retention period. The archive is queryable; the retention period is automatically enforced.

Flashback Database   An Oracle feature that allows a point-in-time logical recovery of the entire database to a timestamp, SCN, or named recovery point. Flashback Database uses flashback logs stored in the flash recovery area. It can't be used for media recovery.

Flashback Drop   An Oracle feature that allows dropped objects to be recovered from the Recycle Bin instead of requiring an expensive incomplete recovery process to be performed.

Flashback Table   An Oracle feature that allows tables (and their dependent objects) to be recovered to an earlier point in time while the tablespace remains online and without the overhead of an incomplete recovery.

Flashback Transaction Query   An Oracle feature that allows users to identify changes made to tables at a transactional level.

Flashback Versions Query   A feature that allows users to view all versions of data that have existed over a period of time for a specific table.

I

image copies   Exact byte-for-byte copies of database datafiles backed up by RMAN. Image copies are made with the backup as copy command. Can be used for quick database restores.

inactive online redo log group   One of the online redo log groups of the database that is not in use and has been archived.

incident   In Oracle 11g, a single occurrence of a problem.

Incident Packaging Service (IPS)   Enables you to automatically gather the diagnostic data pertaining to a critical error into a zip file for transmission to Oracle Support.

incomplete recovery   Also called point-in-time recovery. Recovery of the database to a earlier point in time, SCN, or log sequence number than the current ones.

inconsistent shutdown   A shutdown of the database that leaves the datafiles in an inconsistent state. An inconsistent shutdown of the database will definitely result in an instance recovery. In some cases, an inconsistent shutdown (due to loss of a datafile, for example) could lead to media recovery.

incremental database backups   Backups of an Oracle database by RMAN. Includes a level-0 backup, which is a full backup of the database, and a level-1 backup, which incrementally backs up only changed database blocks.

incrementally updated backups   Combination of a backup image copy and incremental backups that allow for very fast recovery of the Oracle database.

instance   Collection of database processes and memory.

J

job   An instruction to the Scheduler to execute a specific program at a specific time on a specific date, for example.

job class   A logical way of grouping jobs that have similar business or performance attributes.

job coordinator   The Oracle background process that is responsible for ensuring that jobs are run on schedule.

job table   The master table in the Oracle database that contains the information for all enabled jobs in the database.

L

length semantics   Determines how you treat the length of a character string. The length can be treated as a sequence of characters or bytes.

level-0 incremental backup   Essentially, a full backup of the Oracle database. A level-0 incremental backup is required to be able to perform subsequent level-1 incremental backups. Whole-database backups are not the same as incremental level-0 backups.

level-1 incremental backup   Backups of changed blocks in Oracle databases. Can be based on either a differential backup strategy or a cumulative incremental strategy.

log sequenced–based recovery   Recovery of the database based on a specific log sequence number.

log sequence number point-in-time recovery   A method of incomplete recovery used to restore the database to a specific log sequence number.

log writer process (LGWR)   The process responsible for writing redo data from the redo log buffer in the SGA to the online redo logs of the database.

logical corruption   Data inconsistencies caused by user error (where a user can be a user, developer, DBA, or program that modifies data in the database).

M

Media Management Library (MML)   An Oracle-created API that allows media-product vendors to write interfaces into RMAN. RMAN channels that are allocated to SBT instead of disk will be directed to the MML layer. This layer must first be configured according to vendor instructions.

media recovery   Recovery of the database, typically by means of database backups, that requires DBA intervention.

MOUNT mode   One of three modes that the database can be in. When the database is open in MOUNT mode, it has read the database control file but not yet opened the database datafiles.

multibyte character   A character whose character code consists of two or more bytes under a certain encoding scheme.

multiplexing   The ability to create more than one copy of a database backup to a different location (but on the same type of media). It is essentially making parallel copies of the backup.

multiselection backups   Multiselection backups provide the ability to chunk up large database datafiles into individual backup channels. This allows for parallelization of backups of individual datafiles.

N

national character set   An character set that is an alternative to the database character set that governs NCHAR, NVARCHAR2, and NCLOB data.

National Language Support (NLS)   Allows users to interact with the database in their native language.

NOARCHIVELOG mode   When in NOARCHIVELOG mode, the database will not generate archived redo logs and can not be recovered to any point other than the point of the last backup.

O

online datafile recovery   Recovery of a database datafile while the database is open.

online redo logs   Persistent mechanism that stores redo copied from the redo-log buffer by the LGWR process.

online tablespace recovery   Recovery of all tablespace datafiles while the database is open.

Oracle data dictionary   Views in the database that provide metadata information about the database, including database configuration, objects, users, and other information.

Oracle Database Configuration Assistant (DBCA)   Oracle graphical interface used to create both ASM instances and Oracle databases.

orapwd   The program that creates the Oracle database password file.

P

parameter file   A file that defines global database settings such as memory allocations. Can be either a pfile, which is text-based, or an spfile, which is managed by the Oracle server.

point-in-time recovery   Recovery of the database based on a specific point in time. Also called incomplete recovery. Recovery of the database to an earlier point in time, SCN, or log sequence number than the current ones.

point-of-failure recovery   This is a recovery of the database to the point of the last completed transaction. This kind of recovery involves no data loss. Point-of-failure recovery is synonymous with complete recovery.

problem   In Oracle 11g, a critical error in the database.

program   Defines the action that will occur when a job runs.

R

recover command   RMAN command used to recover a database, tablespace, or datafile. Causes the application of incremental backups and archived redo logs to complete the database recovery.

recovery catalog   The recovery catalog is an optional database schema that maintains a record of all RMAN backup operations.

recovery catalog stored scripts   These are scripts stored in the recovery catalog. These scripts can be called by RMAN for backup, recovery, or reporting purposes.

recovery catalog views   Views that can be queried by the DBA to look at RMAN-related metadata in the recovery catalog.

recovery set   Set of tablespaces to be recovered during tablespace point-in-time recovery.

Recycle Bin   A logical container that stores objects dropped from the database. The Recycle Bin (in conjunction with the Flashback Drop feature) offers users a simple method of querying and recovering objects that may have been dropped by accident.

redo-log buffer   The memory area in the SGA to which redo is initially written.

redo log sequence number   A unique number assigned to each online redo log to define the order in which it was written to.

redo logfile group   A set of one or more online redo logs. Each redo logfile group is written to one at a time and may have one or more copies of the redo log called members.

Redo logfile member   One or more files in a redo logfile group. These files are written to in parallel and are used to protect each online redo log from failure.

resource consumer group   A logical grouping of users based on resource-consumption requirements and business needs.

resource plan   A group of resource-plan directives that specify how resources should be distributed among the consumer groups.

resource-plan directive   Defines resource allocation rules and connects resource plans to consumer groups.

restore command   RMAN command used to restore the database from a previous RMAN backup. This command will cause RMAN to restore datafiles from backup-set pieces or image copies.

resumable space allocation   The Oracle feature that enables transactions to suspend and wait for a space condition to be resolved within a specified time without aborting the transaction. When the space condition is resolved, the transaction will resume.

RETENTION GUARANTEE   An option that, when enabled, will guarantee that unexpired undo records will never be removed from the undo tablespace. They will be maintained until they expire (at the end of the retention period), even at the expense of new transactions failing because of lack of undo space.

retention policies   Retention policies determine how long database backups will be considered valid in RMAN. After the retention period expires, backups will be marked as obsolete and be eligible for removal.

RMAN   Oracle's provided backup and recovery tool.

RMAN backup-format specification   The backup-format specification is used to indicate the file-naming convention to be used when creating an RMAN backup-set piece.

RMAN command-line interface (RCLI)   Used to access RMAN and perform RMAN-related activities.

RMAN persistent configuration settings   Provide the ability to configure backup- and recovery-related settings that become the default value for RMAN backup and recovery operations.

RMAN virtual private catalog   An optional feature of the RMAN recovery catalog that provides the ability to limit access to records in the recovery catalog to specific sets of users.

run block   A block of RMAN commands that starts with a run command. The commands are enclosed in braces.

S

schedule   A schedule contains a start date, an optional end date, and a repeat interval.

SBT   Device designation that indicates the backup, restore or maintenance operation will use the MML layer instead of a disk device.

SCN-based point-in-time recovery   A method of recovery that restores the database to a specific point in time based on a database SCN.

Segment Shrink   An online Segment Shrink operation reduces the size of a segment by moving rows and consolidating the space used, eliminating unused space above and below the high-water mark.

service request   A request to Oracle Support to assist with a technical problem.

snapshot control file   A consistent copy of the control file created at the beginning of an RMAN backup operation.

source host   The database host machine where the target database is located.

space pressure   A situation that occurs when Oracle cannot allocate any further extents in a tablespace without extending the tablespace. When this situation occurs, Oracle will purge objects from the Recycle Bin rather than extend the tablespace.

SQL Access Advisor   The SQL advisor that analyzes the schema design for a workload and recommends indexes, partitions, and materialized views to improve performance.

SQL Tuning Advisor   One of the SQL advisors; it takes one or more SQL statements as input and produces tuning advice.

SQL tuning set (STS)   A database object that stores a set of SQL statements along with their execution context and statistics.

static data dictionary views   Data dictionary views that provide metadata information on various database structures such as tables, indexes, and other database objects.

substitution variables   Variables used in place of literal values. Each time you execute code with the substitution variable, you can indicate the value of that variable or RMAN will prompt you for the value of that variable when you run the code.

Support Workbench   An environment within Oracle Enterprise Manager that provides a workflow for investigating, diagnosing, reporting, submitting service requests to Oracle Support, and resolving problems.

suspended transaction   A transaction that has encountered a space condition and is waiting for the space condition to be resolved. The transaction will abort if the suspend condition is not resolved within the time-out.

system change number (SCN)   An internal counter that is used to maintain the order and dependency of transactions within a given database.

T

tablespace   A logical storage area that is assigned to one or more database datafiles. Oracle objects (such as tables) are assigned to a tablespace when they are created.

tablespace point-in-time recovery   The process of recovering one or more tablespaces in a database to a previous point in time.

tablespace recoveries   See online tablespace recovery.

tag   A specific name given to an RMAN backup. It can be referenced during subsequent RMAN operations such as recoveries.

time-based point-in-time recovery   A method of recovery that restores the database to a specific point in time based on a time defined in the `restore` and `recover` commands.

transportable database   In Oracle 11g, the feature that allows the DBA to copy an entire database from one platform to another.

transportable tablespace set   The datafiles associated with a group of tablespaces along with the exported metadata that encapsulates the self-contained set of objects that are to be transported.

U

undo record   A row stored in the undo tablespace that contains the data necessary to undo a transaction (or a piece of a transaction).

UNDO_RETENTION   An Oracle parameter that governs the length of time that undo records will be retained in the undo tablespace after their associated transaction has completed.

Unicode   The universal character set that supports all known written languages.

W

white-space compression   RMAN's default behavior, attempting to reduce the size of backup sets by not including blocks that are unused in the backup.

whole-database backup   A complete backup of an Oracle database using the `backup` command.

window   A recurring block of time during which a specific resource plan should be enabled to govern resource allocation for the database.

window group   A logical method of grouping windows to simplify management by allowing them to be managed as one object.

Index

Note to the reader: Throughout this index **boldfaced** page numbers indicate primary discussions of a topic. *Italicized* page numbers indicate illustrations.

E

W

Wiley Publishing, Inc.
End-User License Agreement

The Best OCP: Oracle Database 11*g* Book/CD Package on the Market!

Get ready for your Oracle Certified Professional for Oracle Database 11g certification and the Oracle Database 11g: Administration II (1Z0-053) exam with the most comprehensive and challenging sample tests anywhere!

The Sybex Test Engine features:

- All the review questions, as covered in each chapter of the book.
- Challenging questions representative of those you'll find on the real exam.
- Two full-length bonus exams available only on the CD.
- An Assessment Test to narrow your focus to certain objective groups.

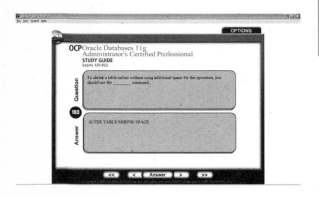

Use the Electronic Flashcards for PCs or Palm devices to jog your memory and prep last-minute for the exam!

- Reinforce your understanding of key concepts with these hardcore flashcard-style questions.
- Download the Flashcards to your Palm device and go on the road. Now you can study for the Oracle Database 11*g*: Administration II (1Z0-053) exams anytime, anywhere.

Search through the complete book in PDF!

- Access the entire *OCP: Oracle Database 11g Administrator Certified Professional Study Guide* complete with figures and tables, in electronic format.
- Search the *OCP: Oracle Database 11g Administrator Certified Professional Study Guide* chapters to find information on any topic in seconds.

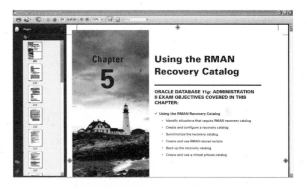